ANTHONY REID
and
THE STUDY OF THE
SOUTHEAST ASIAN PAST

The **Nalanda-Sriwijaya Series**, established under the publishing program of the Institute of Southeast Asian Studies, Singapore, has been created as a publications avenue for the Nalanda-Sriwijaya Centre. The Centre focuses on the ways in which Asian polities and societies have interacted over time. To this end, the series invites submissions which engage with Asian historical connectivities. Such works might examine political relations between states; the trading, financial and other networks which connected regions; cultural, linguistic and intellectual interactions between societies; or religious links across and between large parts of Asia.

The **Institute of Southeast Asian Studies (ISEAS)** was established as an autonomous organization in 1968. It is a regional centre dedicated to the study of socio-political, security and economic trends and developments in Southeast Asia and its wider geostrategic and economic environment. The Institute's research programmes are the Regional Economic Studies (RES, including ASEAN and APEC), Regional Strategic and Political Studies (RSPS), and Regional Social and Cultural Studies (RSCS).

ISEAS Publishing, an established academic press, has issued more than 2,000 books and journals. It is the largest scholarly publisher of research about Southeast Asia from within the region. ISEAS Publishing works with many other academic and trade publishers and distributors to disseminate important research and analyses from and about Southeast Asia to the rest of the world.

ANTHONY REID
and
THE STUDY OF THE SOUTHEAST ASIAN PAST

EDITED BY GEOFF WADE AND LI TANA

INSTITUTE OF SOUTHEAST ASIAN STUDIES
Singapore

First published in Singapore in 2012 by
ISEAS Publishing
Institute of Southeast Asian Studies
30 Heng Mui Keng Terrace
Pasir Panjang
Singapore 119614

E-mail: publish@iseas.edu.sg
Website: <http://bookshop.iseas.edu.sg>

All rights reserved. No part of this publication may be reproduced, stored in a retrieval system, or transmitted in any form or by any means, electronic, mechanical, photocopying, recording or otherwise, without the prior permission of the Institute of Southeast Asian Studies.

© 2012 Institute of Southeast Asian Studies, Singapore

The responsibility for facts and opinions in this publication rests exclusively with the authors and their interpretations do not necessarily reflect the views or the policy of the publisher or its supporters.

ISEAS Library Cataloguing-in-Publication Data

Anthony Reid and the study of the Southeast Asian past / edited by Geoff Wade and Li Tana.
1. Reid, Anthony, 1939–
2. Southeast Asia—Historiography.
3. Southeast Asia—History.
I. Wade, Geoff.
II. Li, Tana, 1959–
III. Reid, Anthony, 1939–
DS524.4 A62   2012

ISBN 978-981-4311-96-0 (soft cover)
ISBN 978-981-4311-97-7 (e-book, PDF)

Cover design by Rinkoo Bhowmik
Cover photograph by Chandan Dubey: Tapestry in cotton and hemp.

Typeset by Superskill Graphics Pte Ltd
Printed in Singapore by Mainland Press Pte Ltd

CONTENTS

Acknowledgements   ix

The Contributors   xi

PART I   Introduction

1. Anthony Reid: Through Time and Space   3
   Geoff Wade and Li Tana

PART II   The Scholarship of Anthony Reid

2. The Past as Threat, the Past as Promise: The Historical Writing of Anthony Reid   31
   Robert Cribb

PART III   Southeast Asia in the World

3. Southeast Asia and Eurasia during a Thousand Years   47
   Victor Lieberman

4. A Two-Ocean Mediterranean   69
   Wang Gungwu

5. The Concepts of Space and Time in the Southeast Asian Archipelago   85
   Denys Lombard (Translated by Helen Reid)

6. Dominion over Palm and Pine:
   Early Indonesia's Maritime Reach   101
   Ann Kumar

PART IV Early Modern Southeast Asia

7. Southeast Asian Islam and Southern China in the
   Fourteenth Century   125
   Geoff Wade

8. *Lancaran, Ghurab* and *Ghali*: Mediterranean Impact on
   War Vessels in Early Modern Southeast Asia   146
   Pierre-Yves Manguin

9. Weather, History and Empire: The Typhoon Factor and the
   Manila Galleon Trade, 1565–1815   183
   James Francis Warren

10. Interracial Marriages and the Overseas Family:
    The Case of the Portuguese Topasses in Timor   221
    Barbara Watson Andaya and Leonard Y. Andaya

11. A Note on the *Čhām* Diaspora in the Ayutthayan Kingdom   241
    Ishii Yoneo

12. Tongking in the Age of Commerce   246
    Li Tana

PART V Modern Southeast Asia

13. Hadhrami Projections of Southeast Asian Identity   271
    Jeyamalar Kathirithamby-Wells

14. Absent at the Creation: Islamism's Belated,
    Troubled Engagement with Early Indonesian Nationalism   303
    Robert Elson

15. Chinese Shrines Contested: Power and Politics in Chinese
    Communities in Bangkok in the Early Twentieth Century   336
    Koizumi Junko

Appendix

16. Anthony Reid: A Bibliography   357

Index   385

ACKNOWLEDGEMENTS

The editors would like to thank the following for their assistance in facilitating the production of this volume:

Ambassador K. Kesavapany, Professor Tansen Sen, Mrs Helen Reid, Ms Triena Ong, Mr Mark Iñigo M. Tallara, Ms Rahilah Yusuf, Ms Rinkoo Bhowmik, Ms Lucy Liu, Dr Christian Lammerts, Professor Koizumi Junko and Ms Fujita Kayoko.

THE CONTRIBUTORS

Barbara Watson Andaya (Ph.D., Cornell University) is Professor of Asian Studies at the University of Hawai'i at Mānoa. Although her specific area of expertise is the western Malay-Indonesia archipelago, her teaching and research interests extend across all Southeast Asia. Her most recent book is *The Flaming Womb: Repositioning Women in Southeast Asian History, 1500–1800* (2006). Her current project is a history of the localization of Christianity in Southeast Asia, 1511–1900.

Leonard Y. Andaya received his B.A. in History from Yale University, and an M.A. and Ph.D. in Southeast Asian history at Cornell University. He has held positions at the University of Malaya, the Australian National University, the University of Auckland, and the University of Hawai'i, where he has been professor of Southeast Asian history since 1993. His area of specialization is early modern Southeast Asia, particularly Malaysia and Indonesia.

Robert Cribb is Professor in the College of Asia and the Pacific at the Australian National University. His research has focussed on Indonesian history, including the role of the criminal underworld in Indonesia's national struggle, the mass killing of communists in 1965–66, the nature of colonial law and the politics of nature conservation. He has also written a number of general works on Indonesian history including, most recently, a *Digital Atlas of Indonesian History* (2010).

R.E. Elson is Emeritus Professor of Southeast Asian History, the University of Queensland, Brisbane, Australia. His research focuses on the modern and contemporary history of Southeast Asia, especially Indonesia. His current research projects include Islamism and secularism in modern Indonesian history and the history of maritime territoriality in the Indonesian seas. He is author of five books and numerous articles and chapters on the modern history of Indonesia and, more broadly, of Southeast Asia. He has served as President of the Asian Studies Association of Australia and as chair of the Australian Research Council's Expert Advisory Committee for the Humanities and Creative Arts. He was elected as a Fellow of the Australian Academy of the Humanities in 1995. His most recent book is *The Idea of Indonesia: A History* (2008).

Ishii Yoneo (1929–2010) was one of Japan's most respected scholars of Thailand and Southeast Asia. After a stint in the Foreign Ministry, Ishii-sensei returned to academe and was one of the founding members of the Center for Southeast Asian Studies at Kyoto University in 1965, later assuming the directorship (1985–90). He subsequently moved to Sophia University in 1990, where he taught and researched for seven years, including two years as director of the Institute of Asian Cultures. In 1997, he retired from Sophia and became the Rector of Kanda University of International Studies, a position he retained until 2004. He published profusely and also worked for the development of digital archives on Japan-Asia relations when serving as the director of the Japan Center for Asian Historical Records (JACAR), National Archives of Japan, from 2001 until he passed away.

Jeyamalar Kathirithamby-Wells formerly held the Chair of Asian History at the University of Malaya, Kuala Lumpur. Currently resident in the UK, she researches and teaches in Cambridge. She has worked extensively on Southeast Asia during the early modern period and, in recent years, has expanded her research interests to include environmental and conservation history. Apart from publishing numerous articles and monographs, she contributed to the *Cambridge History of Southeast Asia* (1992), edited with John Villers *The Southeast Asian Port and Polity* (1990) and more recently authored *Nature and Nation: Forests and Development in Peninsular Malaysia* (2005).

Koizumi Junko is Professor in the Center for Southeast Asian Studies, Kyoto University. She is a historian working on Thai history and historiography focused on the Early Bangkok period. Her recent English publications include "Between Tribute and Treaty: Sino-Siamese relations from the late nineteenth century to the early twentieth century," in Anthony Reid and Zheng Yangwen (ed.), *Negotiating Asymmetry: China's Place in Asia* (2009).

Ann Kumar is a Visiting Fellow, School of Culture, History & Language, College of Asia and the Pacific at the Australian National University where she long served as a lecturer. Her interests include the nation-state in contemporary Southeast Asia; Indonesian politics; Indonesian Islam; Indonesia's Writing Traditions; and early relations between Java and Japan. Her publications include *Illuminations: The Writing Traditions of Indonesia: Featuring Manuscripts from the National Library of Indonesia* (1996) and *Globalizing the Prehistory of Japan: Language, Genes and Civilization* (2009).

Li Tana is a Senior Fellow in Pacific and Asian History, School of Culture, History and Language, College of Asia and the Pacific, Australian National University. Her works include *Nguyen Cochinchina* (SEAP, Cornell, 1998) and *Water Frontier* (2004, co-ed. with Nola Cooke). She researches the maritime history of Vietnam and the history of overseas Chinese.

Denys Lombard (1938–1998) was educated at the Sorbonne, the École Pratique des Hautes Études and the École des Languages Orientale and was one of France's foremost Asianists. In 1993, he assumed the directorship of the École Français d'Extrême-Orient, a position he retained until his death. He was involved in researches on Southeast Asia, Overseas Chinese, the Arab world and the history of maritime Asia. Key works include *Le sultanat d'Atjeh* (1967); *Le carrefour javanais. Essai d'histoire globale* (1990), and with Claudine Salmon, *Les Chinois de Jakarta, temples et vie collective* (1980). He was instrumental in the establishment of the journal *Archipel*.

Pierre-Yves Manguin is a professor at the Ecole française d'Extrême-Orient (EFEO, French School of Asian Studies), and teaches at the Ecole des Hautes Etudes en Sciences Sociales (EHESS, Paris). His research focuses on history and archaeology of the coastal states and trade networks of Southeast Asia. He has led archaeological work in Indonesia and Vietnam and published on themes related to maritime history and archaeology of Southeast Asia, the Indian Ocean and South China Sea, and on the archaeology of Funan (Vietnam), Srivijaya (South Sumatra), and Tarumanagara (West Java).

Helen Reid graduated with a B.A. from Auckland in 1959, and a Ph.D. in French literature from the ANU in 1980. Initially she taught French and English in France, Germany, Malaysia, Indonesia and Australia. More recently she was Policy Officer for Languages Other Than English in the ACT Teaching Service, then Language Specialist in the Australian Foreign Service, and most recently a Visiting Professor in the Language Resource Program at the University of California, Los Angeles.

Victor Lieberman, a specialist in precolonial Burma and a comparativist interested in global patterns, is the Marvin B. Becker Collegiate Professor of History and Professor of Southeast Asian History at the University of Michigan. His most recent work is a two-volume study *Strange Parallels: Southeast Asia in Global Context, c. 800–1830. Volume 1: Integration on the Mainland*, which won the 2004 World History Association Book Prize; and *Volume 2: Mainland Mirrors: Europe, Japan, China, South Asia, and the Islands*, which appeared in 2009.

Geoff Wade is a historian with interests in Sino-Southeast Asian historical interactions and comparative historiography. Currently a Senior Research Fellow in the Nalanda-Sriwijaya Centre, Institute of Southeast Asian Studies, Singapore, he was formerly engaged with the Southeast Asia-China Interactions cluster of the Asia Research Institute, National University of Singapore (2002–09) and, before that, with the China-ASEAN Project at the Centre of Asian Studies, University of Hong Kong (1996–2002). His online database *Southeast Asia in the Ming Shi-lu: An Open Access Resource* (<http://epress.nus.edu.sg/msl/>) provides in English translation 3,000+ references to Southeast Asia as extracted from the Ming imperial annals, while his most recent edited work *China and Southeast Asia* (2009) comprises a 6-volume survey of seminal works on Southeast Asia-China interactions over time.

Wang Gungwu obtained his B.A. (Hons.) and M.A. from the University of Malaya in Singapore and his Ph.D. from the University of London (1957). He is University Professor of the National University of Singapore, Emeritus Professor of the Australian National University, Fellow and former President of the Australian Academy of the Humanities; Foreign Honorary Member of the American Academy of Arts and Science; and Chairman of the East Asian Institute, the Institute of Southeast Asian Studies and the Lee Kuan Yew School of Public Policy in Singapore. From 1986 to 1995, he was Vice-Chancellor of the University of Hong Kong.

James Francis Warren is Professor of Southeast Asian Modern History at Murdoch University in Western Australia. He has held several visiting professorships in Japan and Singapore and is the author of several influential books, including his ground breaking first volume, *The Sulu Zone 1768–1898, The Dynamics of External Trade, Slavery and Ethnicity in the Transformation of a Southeast Asian Maritime State*. He is currently working on a history of the impact of the typhoon on the Philippines. In 2003 he was awarded the Centenary Medal of Australia for service to Australian society and the Humanities in the study of Ethnohistory.

PART I
Introduction

1

ANTHONY REID: THROUGH TIME AND SPACE

Geoff Wade and Li Tana

Anthony John Stanhope Reid — a name not familiar to any but close family — is more widely recognized by the abbreviated version, Anthony Reid, or simply as Tony. Under these various names he is known as a husband, father, grandfather, Catholic, intellectual, New Zealander, Australian, tennis-player, Canberra denizen, Aceh scholar, institute founder, author, mentor and friend, but more broadly as an eminent historian of the area we today term Southeast Asia. It is to this aspect of Tony Reid that the present volume is dedicated. While in the following chapter Robert Cribb more directly engages with the intellectual strands of Tony's life, this Introductory piece will attempt to introduce the journeys which Tony and his family have made through time and space.

To have been born into the family of a senior civil servant in New Zealand in the middle of 1939 was probably not the worst way to come into the world, although the timing could have been better. Young Reid did not know this at the time, but war clouds were gathering in Europe and the Dominion of New Zealand (which had rashly decided against joining the Federation of Australia at its establishment in 1901) was preparing itself to assist Britain in her hour of need. The beginnings of a Pacific War in 1941 and the fall of Singapore early in the following year brought much closer threats to the New Zealand realm and a growing recognition that Mother Britain might not always be there to protect its people. It was thus that the need for a more overt foreign policy and a national diplomatic service asserted itself in New

Zealand and, as eyes turned across the Pacific seeking new defenders, Reid Senior[1] was in 1943 sent to help set up the first New Zealand mission in Washington. It was only in the following year that trans-Pacific Ocean travel was considered sufficiently safe to allow the Reid children to join their parents in the United States' capital. Thus began Tony Reid's experience with travel beyond the land of his birth and his engagement with worlds beyond those with which he was familiar.

Four years of schooling in the United States and later visits from New Zealand to Jakarta subsequent to his father's appointment as the United Nations representative in Indonesia[2] seem to have induced little other than feelings of trauma and displacement in the young Reid.

Apparently, neither an interest in the study of history nor an enthusiastic engagement with Asia marked the early years of Anthony Reid. He did not even study history at school, but began to be interested in the subject when attending Victoria University of Wellington where he was to obtain his Bachelor degree in Economics and History (1960) and subsequently a Masters in History (1961). It was during these years that Emily Sadka[3] taught an undergraduate class in Southeast Asian history which was extremely innovative for 1958 in New Zealand[4] and undoubtedly played some role in the future course of Tony Reid's life.

Tony suggests that his fascination with history (and possibly even with history in a maritime realm) was further stimulated during his University years, when his parents, again overseas, arranged for him to stay with John Beaglehole,[5] the biographer of Captain James Cook, and at that time one of New Zealand's few globally prominent historians. It was also at this time that he began to publish. His first article, which engaged with the nexus of church and state in New Zealand during the Great Depression (the subject of his Masters thesis), appeared in a student journal,[6] and reflected aspects both of Tony's engagement with the Student Christian Movement at university and of the Methodism which so marked much of Reid family life. The issue over which he wrestled at the time — 'How is one to improve the world?' — is a question which has stayed with this historian throughout his life.

It was during these years of intellectual exploration and development that he was to meet his future soulmate Helen Gray, during a New Zealand inter-university summer camp at Curious Cove in the Marlborough Sounds. They were brought together by basketball but differed in their respective religions, Helen being from a staunch Auckland Catholic background. But there was no time then for serious romance. They were young and they had things to do. New Zealand is small, and New Zealand in the early 1960s was perhaps not the most exciting place for young men or women seeking to find their way in the world. Reflecting later on these early experiences, Tony was to aver: "Growing up in New Zealand definitely contributed to my interest in the rest of the world. It bred a kind of internationalism; since the centre of the world was so clearly not New Zealand, it had to be somewhere else."[7] What was someone to do if he had just completed a Masters in History and he wanted to change the world?

Tony Reid wanted to get away from New Zealand, to pursue a Ph.D. on some aspect of Indonesia or to join the Foreign Office and be posted to some foreign clime. Asia and an awareness of cultural difference had by this time intruded themselves into Reid's life through his visits to Indonesia in the early 1950s and to Japan in 1957 when his father served as New Zealand Ambassador to that country, as well as through his studies at Victoria University and his links with the Colombo Plan scholars who were coming from Southeast and South Asia to study in New Zealand in the 1950s.[8] Through organizing programmes for the new Colombo Plan arrivals at Victoria University in the late 1950s, Tony came into contact with a range of these students and became more familiar with the issues which these new countries of Asia faced. He recalls today that "Southeast Asia was the challenge — whether thinking of poverty and development, of politics, or of cultural otherness. It was there and it was exciting. It has become less obvious now, but for my 1950s generation there was a real movement, a reformist challenge to 'do something'."[9]

Whatever the "something" Reid was destined to do, it would probably need some further preparation. Thus he set about applying for scholarships, firstly the prestigious Rhodes scholarship[10] which required a personal interview with the Governor-General, the vice-regal representative in New Zealand. Tony's failure to secure a Rhodes scholarship obviously still rankles and he assigns the reason for this to his preference at the time for basketball over the "manly sport" of rugby.[11] But he must have impressed someone during the selection process as he was soon offered the lesser prize of an Orford studentship[12] to King's College, Cambridge. It was thus in 1961 that young New Zealander Tony Reid upped stumps and removed to the august University of Cambridge.

He was however not quite ready for the efforts of the historians at Kings to urge this young man, who had already attained his masters degree in New Zealand, to start his undergraduate studies anew under the university's Tripos system. Eventually Reid's studied tenaciousness was to win out and he was accepted as a postgraduate student, a rare species in Cambridge at the time. The selection of a supervisor was to be the next obstacle to be tackled and the closest the university could come to someone who could supervise a doctoral thesis on Indonesia was Victor Purcell, a specialist in the Chinese of Southeast Asia who had served as a Malayan colonial public servant prior to taking up his post in Cambridge in 1949.[13] As Tony noted "I wasn't at all interested in the Chinese at that stage, nor he much in Indonesia,"[14] but at least a nominal mentor-student relationship was to last throughout his doctoral studies. A relationship which was to engage him for much longer in his life, however, was that with Helen Gray, who had, like many Antipodean graduates at the time, travelled to London in order to explore the Continent. It was only after a bit of scootering through Europe and some time spent teaching English in London and Paris that she and Tony became engaged. Helen then found a job teaching English in Aachen while Tony worked across the Dutch border in the colonial archives near Arnhem. They were married in 1963, at the beginning of Tony's third year at Cambridge.

The subject chosen for his doctorate — the political history of Aceh — might have, as he claims, been an "arbitrary" choice, but the results of that choice have followed him ever since. The engagement of Purcell with his own endeavours saw Tony spending much time in London with historians at the School of Oriental and African Studies, including Jeremy Cowan.[15] Extending beyond Cowan's advice to study the area around Medan in Sumatra, Reid was drawn to the immense paper trail for Aceh which existed in the archives. He thus began to investigate the process by which in the late nineteenth century the independent states of North Sumatra, notably Aceh, were absorbed into Netherlands India through a succession of wars in a global context of competition between the Dutch, the British and, to some degree, the Turks. After four years of study, in January 1965, the thesis was submitted. Described today by the author as "a fairly conventional diplomatic thesis, with some interesting data but no ambitious new paradigm or anything of the sort," it was to be published four years later, when the Reids were based in Kuala Lumpur, as *The Contest for North Sumatra: Atjeh, the Netherlands and Britain 1858–1898*.[16] But the book, well ahead of its time in terms of trying to understand the roots of the Aceh problems, was to find avid readers, especially among those most intimately engaged with the north of Sumatra. When, in the 1970s, Tony received a letter from Hasan Tiro,[17] who was then leading a guerrilla war for Aceh independence, noting that his book had inspired his fighters in the jungle, he was less than complimentary. "I was incredulous and frankly appalled. I told nobody at the time. It seemed inconceivable that this pedestrian dissertation written entirely in Europe, with scarcely any knowledge of modern Aceh (I was able to visit Aceh only once between thesis and book because of *konfrontasi*), could have had such an effect."[18]

But the doctorate was finished and life awaited. Job applications were dispersed widely and then Tony and Helen did what many young Antipodean travellers in Europe felt was almost *de rigueur*, buying a Volkswagen van, which doubled as transport and hotel, and began travelling back across the Eurasian continent. In the mid-1960s, the areas across the Middle East which today have become no-go zones for travellers were still open for intrepid tourists and the Reids were certainly that. First they travelled through Yugoslavia and Greece before crossing into Turkey where a telegram awaited the young travellers. It was a piece of paper which was to forever change the lives of both Tony and Helen, offering as it did a position teaching history at the University of Malaya. It was a godsend in a way, in that it would allow Tony to live just across the Straits from the island he had spent years studying, an island closed to him at this time through the tensions of *konfrontasi*. Time was thus tight but the Reids still managed to fit in Jerusalem, Damascus, Baghdad and Isfahan before travelling into India and across the subcontinent to Madras where their trusty vehicle was loaded on the docks in Madras to be shipped across the Bay of Bengal to Malaysia. The Reids travelled by the same ship, ending their Eurasian travels with both a lifetime of memories and hepatitis.

When Dr Reid took up his first teaching position in the History Department of the University of Malaya, Malaysia was but 2 years old, and within a few months (in August 1965 in fact) Singapore was to leave the Federation and start life as an independent state. We have it on good authority that Singapore's departure from Malaysia was likely unrelated to the arrival of the Reids in Kuala Lumpur. But, what a History Department it was for Tony, the budding Southeast Asianist, in which to begin his career. Heading the department was Wang Gungwu,[19] while other staff members included the Indonesianist Jan Pluvier,[20] Jeya Kathirithamby,[21] as well as David Bassett,[22] Khoo Kay Kim,[23] Bill Roff,[24] and Tony Short.[25] David Wyatt[26] and Gerald Maryanov[27] also visited as Fulbright scholars.

Tasked with teaching the history of Early Modern Southeast Asia, a topic he admits to having known little about at the time, Tony obviously found the subject of some interest and it was this course which laid the seeds for much of his later scholarship. In his efforts to understand the contemporary shape of Southeast Asia, Tony also began to travel in the region. From late 1966 he was able to visit Sumatra and was struck by the contrasts between the societies of Sumatra and of the peninsula, bringing home to him the essential transformational role of revolution in eliminating *ancien regimes* and inducing him to study "the 'social revolution' of Aceh and

East Sumatra, which overthrew the old order of sultans, rajas and ulèëbalangs in a few violent months of 1945–46."[28] The book which emerged from his interviews of many revolutionaries, administrators and surviving aristocrats was published a decade later in 1979.[29]

While the years in Kuala Lumpur engendered in the Reids an abiding affection for Malaysia and brought a daughter and son into their lives, the political events which occurred during this period also obviously bequeathed their scars. Witnessing from across the water the terrible events of 1965–66 in Indonesia[30] and, at first hand, the dark days that followed 13 May 1969 in Malaysia,[31] this family had new perspectives brought to their lives.[32] With the institution of the New Economic Policy in 1969, reforms were also being introduced into Malaysia, with the promotion of national education and new affirmative action policies. Education in the Malay language by Malay staff thus became a key agenda and the consequent changes in Malaysian tertiary education began just as Tony was offered a new position, to the south of Malaysia, in the growing Australian National University in Canberra.

Thus it happened that after five academic years in Malaysia, the Reids shifted camp to the quiet suburbs of Australia's national capital. At the Research School of Pacific and Asian Studies, the premier centre of Asian studies in Australia at the time, Tony took up a rare position, an essentially research appointment. Wang Gungwu, his former colleague in Kuala Lumpur, was already well-ensconced in the Research School by the time Tony arrived[33] and the range of other scholars who passed through (and often long remained) in the Coombs Building during these years in the 1970s and 1980s is legion. It was a golden age in Australia's Southeast Asian studies, as well as Chinese studies, and it was in this environment that Tony started to more fully develop his ideas on the early modern period in Southeast Asian history. "I started rather cautiously proposing a few ideas, about what at one stage I called 'the origins of poverty in Southeast Asia,'[34] and was able to do some serious research on it during a sabbatical in Europe in 1978. The problem of slavery arose in that early stage of trying to understand the pre-colonial social systems. How should one render a concept that appeared so frequently in the sources, but remains controversial and unhelpfully pejorative in contemporary culture? I convinced myself, though not all of my collaborators in the project, that slavery was a critical institution in Southeast Asian history, precisely as a point of interaction between cultures, and between the state and non-state domains."[35] These ideas came together in the early 1980s with an edited volume on slavery and bondage in Southeast Asia.[36]

Reid was also to engage himself in many of the joint projects which brought scholars of various fields at the ANU into conversations with each other.

With David Marr,[37] he edited a volume on Southeast Asian historiography,[38] while the two men also developed a long-lasting friendship and tennis affiliation. The *Perceptions of the Past in Southeast Asia* volume was of particular interest, beyond its innate intellectual contribution, in that it was published by Heinemann for the Asian Studies Association of Australia (ASAA), a nascent organization which Tony had been a key figure in establishing. He had been appointed as convenor of a working committee when a provisional ASAA was established at the ANZAAS Conference in 1975. A formal executive was elected in 1976, and Tony was asked to continue the ASAA Newsletter which he had been editing since 1975. He convinced the ASAA executive of the need for a Publications Officer, a position Professor Reid was quickly placed into, and it was in this post with the assistance of Robin Jeffrey that he expanded the Newsletter into the *ASAA Review*.[39] At the same time, he developed a publication series intended to bring the work of Australian Asianists to the world.[40] In the early 1980s the Reid family sojourned in Sulawesi, Indonesia where Tony taught for the period 1980–81 before returning to ANU.[41]

The 1980s saw within the Research School of Pacific and Asian Studies at ANU the development of innovative research in a wide range of spheres. These were indeed years of vibrance. As one example, forty historians of earlier Southeast Asia gathered at RSPAS in May 1984 to discuss Southeast Asian history from the ninth to fourteenth centuries, with the conference giving rise to a seminal collection of studies.[42] The anthropologists were also active, bringing the International Conference on Thai Studies to Canberra in 1987, which in a way sparked the creation of the Thai-Yunnan Project, led by Gehan Wijeyewardene,[43] and the *Thai-Yunnan Newsletter*[44] which examined the changing relations across the China-Southeast Asia interface.

Meanwhile, it was the origins of poverty in Southeast Asia which continued to engage Reid,[45] and after the publication of the 'Bondage' book, his research began to broaden on the basis of his earlier teaching of Early Modern Southeast Asian history, into an exploration of the entire social context of what he was to call the 'Age of Commerce' in Southeast Asia. The major fruits of this research first appeared in 1988 with the first volume of the set.[46] The second was to follow five years later.[47] These volumes were to help disseminate the name of Anthony Reid throughout the world.

This huge-scale project grew partly out of his slavery and bondage study and partly out of an interest in the Southeast Asian predilection for investing in people rather than in institutions, together with the apparent difficulties of conserving capital in the region. In the creation of the Age of Commerce volumes, intellectual debts were acknowledged to Fernand Braudel. Tony admitted that "Having discovered *La Méditerranée*[48] some distance into the project I was greatly relieved to find that someone much wiser than I had managed to write inspiring early modern history around a maritime unit. I could not have had the courage to be so ambitious without that important precedent."[49] He also found inspiration in other members of the *Annales* school, notably Emmanuel Le Roy Ladurie.[50] Further scholars whom he cites as being key influences include Geoffrey Parker,[51] Charles Tilley[52] and the anthropologist Jack Goody.[53]

The reactions to this new paradigm in Southeast Asian history were diverse. However, it was generally accepted that it would change the terms of regional enquiry. There were plaudits for extending the scope of Southeast Asian history beyond the confines of the palaces and *keratons* to the lives of the farmer and the petty trader and for bringing a regional coherence to the previously disparate and dispersed studies of early modern Southeast Asia. One major criticism was that the books drew broad conclusions about Southeast Asia mainly on the basis of the experiences of the island world.[54]

An element of the books which drew unexpected criticism was the quantitative element which Reid introduced to his construction of the Southeast Asian past. It was this inclination to look for numbers, often incomplete and sometimes conjectural, in the Southeast Asian past that had seen Tony begin to develop a focus on the economic history of Southeast Asia at the Research School of Pacific and Asian Studies in the late 1980s. Linked by the *ECHOSEA Newsletter*, 200 scholars around the globe joined the project's network,[55] and August 1989 saw 50 scholars converge on Canberra for a workshop to explore the possibilities of writing an economic history of Southeast Asia, with individual country volumes as well as theme-based overviews being planned, all under the generous funding of the Henry Luce Foundation. While the overall economic history never came to be, under the guidance of Tony Reid as convenor, the project did produce a range of books, some jointly published with KITLV in the Netherlands and with the Institute of Southeast Asian Studies in Singapore, which have remained useful references.[56]

It was a dynamic time for Tony (who had been named as Professor of Southeast Asian History in 1989), for the Research School and for the many scholars who engaged in various ways with the ECHOSEA project. Reflecting one of his increasing preoccupations, the project Newsletter of April 1992 noted that: "Anthony Reid will lead an international group of scholars looking comparatively at the states of Southeast Asia and Korea during their 'last stand' before high colonialism overtook them." This project, funded by the Toyota Foundation, was to give rise to a conference and the celebrated volume known widely as "*The Last Stand.*"[57]

A tragedy occurred during the early years of the ECHOSEA Project when one of its most promising contributors, Jennifer Cushman,[58] died unexpectedly. She had graduated from the Southeast Asia Programme of Cornell University in 1975 with a doctoral dissertation on the Chinese junk trade to Siam, and had then taken up a post in Australia at the Far Eastern History Department of ANU. Here she had become heavily involved in the various projects engaging with the Chinese in Southeast Asia, and her death left a vacuum in this field, a space which Tony worked hard to fill. He established a memorial fund in her name and organized a special series of ten commemorative lectures, which were revised and published in her honour.[59] Together with Craig Reynolds,[60] Tony also established, through the Cushman memorial fund, a Centre for the Study of the Chinese Southern Diaspora — a category which includes the Chinese communities in Southeast Asia as well as New Guinea, Australia, New Zealand, and the Pacific islands.[61]

Engagement with studies of Chinese people in Southeast Asia was, however, not really a new endeavour for Reid. He had, it will be recalled, studied at Cambridge under Victor Purcell, a man who had gained fame through his studies of the Chinese in Southeast Asia, and in a commemorative article for Purcell in the early 1970s, Tony had examined the migration of Chinese into North Sumatra.[62] He also subsequently wrote on Chinese shipping to Java[63] and in Southeast Asia more generally,[64] and on Chinese involvement in revenue farming.[65] His *magnum opus* also engaged greatly with the role of China and Chinese during the Southeast Asian Age of Commerce.

But Tony was to push the envelope a bit further than most in this area. Having observed the activities of Chinese businesses and economic activity throughout Southeast Asia, he felt that there was potential for comparing the experiences of the Chinese in this region with the Jews of Europe.[66] "Southeast Asianists and especially Southeast Asians steered well clear of it, and this itself began to seem a problem to me," he recalled recently.[67] His Chinese Southeast Asian friends did not like the idea at all. However he found a suitable Europeanist collaborator in Daniel Chirot,[68] and the two scholars organized a large meeting in San Diego in 1994 to conduct the comparative workshop. Papers from the conference were published in a jointly-edited volume.[69] Tony concludes in retrospect: "It was an interesting episode, from which both sides learned a lot. While it remains true that the two communities have almost nothing in common *per se*, there are certain historical situations when entrepreneurial minorities become particularly endangered. Perhaps in both cases the gap between ruler and ruled was filled by an entrepreneurial minority. In the end, we took care to keep the book on a very analytic level."[70]

During his writing, administering and teaching at ANU, Tony was also able to supervise some 25 doctoral students, researching topics stretching geographically from southern China to Indonesia and on topics ranging over the last 500 years. Many of these students have themselves gone on to become prominent scholars in Southeast Asian history. Such graduate supervision was to continue at both UCLA and NUS.[71]

Towards the end of the century Tony was persuaded to take up a position in the University of California, Los Angeles, to establish a Centre for Southeast Asian Studies. The almost unbelievable news that Tony Reid was going to leave ANU filtered around the world long before the event occurred. In 1999 Helen and Tony set off to start a new life in Los Angeles, a city somewhat different to Canberra. Their son Daniel had a few years earlier taken up an editing job in Hollywood and thus they already had family in the City of Angels. The task of establishing the new Centre at UCLA, which grew out of a renewed interest in the region throughout the United States, was realized very quickly and the Centre's continuing success is reflected on its website.[72]

It was at this juncture that Professor Wang Gungwu contacted Tony. Then director of the East Asian Institute within the National University of Singapore, Professor Wang had been tasked by the University to recommend someone to direct a new institute being established within that University — the Asia Research Institute (ARI). Tony was apparently very willing to take up this post, which allowed him once again to work in Southeast Asia, with Southeast Asians, on Southeast Asia. ARI was vibrant from its earliest years. Tony utilized his broad connections and his own perceptions of the key issues facing Asia to create within the Institute a range of research foci, many of which are still in place. Scholars from around the world, but particularly from Asia, were brought to Singapore to both learn and to teach, and the enthusiasm created by the various research projects, and numerous workshops and conferences resulted in Singapore receiving global recognition for this new humanities and social sciences research institute. The Institute remains today a major fixture in the Singapore academic scene.[73]

Back in Southeast Asia, after the first few hectic years which were dedicated to establishing the new body, Tony was able to re-engage with some of what might be called his continuing themes. His earlier focus on Aceh history found new outlets through both his physical proximity to the area and the political developments which were occurring in Aceh in the first half of the 2000s.[74] The horrors of the 2004 tsunami brought global attention to this area and were also an impetus for the discussions and eventual peace agreement between the Indonesian Government and the Free Aceh Movement in August 2005.

It was only after the signing of this agreement that Tony felt able to travel to Sweden to meet with Hasan di Tiro, the Acehnese independence leader who had written to him 30 years earlier, as well as with Malik Mahmud, another GAM leader in exile. Subsequently, Tony developed a wide range of Aceh studies within ARI and was also a catalyst in the establishment of the International Centre for Aceh and Indian Ocean Studies on the campus of Syiah Kuala University in Banda Aceh.[75]

Another sphere which Tony actively developed during his years at ARI was the field of Southeast Asia-China interactions. This "cluster," as it was called, drew on his earlier researches of Sino-Southeast Asian economic relations and expanded into a wide range of conferences and publications which extended from studies of "Offshore Asia" to regional archaeology and from *I La Galigo* to the Cold War in Southeast Asia. The enthusiasm which Tony injected into these new projects was unabated by his administrative tasks, and the range of scholars who passed through the cluster gives some idea of its vibrance and diversity.[76] These intra-Asian interaction initiatives were to eventually give rise to the Nalanda-Sriwijaya Centre,[77] now located in the Institute of Southeast Asian Studies in Singapore, and were also influential in developing global study of long-term interactions among various parts of Asia.

Reid was also able to return to some of his enduring academic preoccupations while in Singapore. Fascination with revolution and nationalism was manifested in his *Imperial Alchemy* (2009), which underlined the enormous importance of revolution in Southeast Asia. He saw the revolutionary break with past legal and customary constraints in favour of the sacralization of a revolutionary moment as having results even more decisive in Asia than in Europe. "Indonesia's unification as a centralized nation-state (not to mention China's) would have been impossible without it."[78] Tony's long engagement with the study of Islam in Southeast Asia was also pursued to a zenith, through his joint editorship of Volume Three of the *New Cambridge History of Islam*, published in 2010.[79]

The academic excellence of Anthony Reid has not gone unnoticed by the global academic community over the years. In 2010 his alma mater ('Vic') in Wellington awarded Tony an honorary doctorate, while the Association of Asian Studies in the United States conferred upon him a 'Distinguished Contribution to Asian Studies' award at its conference in Philadelphia. Earlier accolades included being elected as a corresponding fellow at the British Academy (2008), a corresponding member of the Royal Historical Society (1997) and a Fellow of the Australian Academy of the Humanities (1987). For his scholarship on Asia, he was the recipient of the Academic Prize of the 13th Fukuoka Asian Culture Prizes (2002), while for his stalwart contributions to the Asian Studies Association of Australia, he was elected its first Life Member (2003).

But for Tony Reid, kudos could be awarded as much to Helen as to himself as she has long been his "muse, mentor and guide" in many spheres of life. A scholar of French literature, Helen Reid has been intimately engaged in every one of the events, processes and publications detailed above. She has also contributed to this volume through her translation of Denys Lombard's article "Les concepts d'espace et de temps dans l'archipel insulindien."

The Reids left Singapore and their many friends in the Republic in 2009 to return to Canberra where Tony is now ensconced in the Department of Political & Social Change within the College of Asia and the Pacific (the newest manifestation of the former Research School of Pacific and Asian Studies) at ANU. Retirement has indeed allowed Tony and Helen more time to enjoy the pleasures of family. Now doting grandparents twice over, the Reids' frequent visits to Britain where their daughter Kate, son-in-law Curt and grandchildren Reid (sic!) and Ainslie live,[80] seem to invigorate them even more than an evening of tennis. Their son Daniel maintains the family flag in Los Angeles and other relatives are spread through the Antipodes. Travel remains an essential and pleasant task both for academic and family purposes.

As academic administrative tasks have now been firmly bid farewell, Tony Reid can devote himself more fully to research. While he complains that as one enters the "serene seventies" one seems to be asked to reminisce as much as to create, he already has three new books in process with creative energies seemingly more charged than diminished. Today, as the contributors to this volume jointly celebrate Anthony Reid's role to date in the field of Southeast Asian history through their essays which engage with one or another aspect of Tony's oeuvre, we all anxiously await to read what he produces in the years to come.

Notes

1. John Stanhope Reid, father of Anthony Reid, graduated with an LLB at Victoria University College in 1924 and later served in the New Zealand Foreign Service.
2. Reid Senior was appointed as Representative of the United Nations in Jakarta in 1952, serving the offices of the World Health Organization and the Food and Agriculture Organization.
3. Emily Sadka, a graduate of Raffles Girls School in Singapore, taught briefly at Victoria University before proceeding to Canberra as one of the earliest doctoral candidates at the Australian National University, completing her doctorate in

1966. Her revised thesis was later to be published as *The Protected Malay States, 1874–1895* (Kuala Lumpur: University of Malaya Press, 1968). She died of illness in July 1968.
4. That said, it is remarkable the degree to which the Victoria University of Wellington produced scholars who were to make such major marks in Southeast Asian studies globally. In the late 1940s, there was Harry Benda who went on to a pioneering chair at Yale, and later the geographer Terry McGee who proceeded to a career at the University of British Columbia, William Roff who went to Columbia, Margaret Clark who taught at Victoria, Anne Booth who made a career at the School of Oriental and African Studies at the University of London, and of course Anthony Reid himself.
5. John Cawte Beaglehole (1901–71). Born in Wellington, he graduated in history from Victoria University College in 1924. He received a PhD at the London School of Economics and returned to New Zealand in 1930, where he held temporary lecturing positions with the Workers' Educational Association and at Auckland University College (now the University of Auckland). He was appointed lecturer in history at Victoria in 1936, then senior research fellow in colonial history in 1948 and Professor in 1963. He retired in 1966. Beaglehole's life is detailed in Tim Beaglehole, *A Life of J.C. Beaglehole: New Zealand Scholar* (Wellington: Victoria University Press, 2006). Among his best-known publications are: *The Exploration of the Pacific* (London: A. and C. Black, 1934); and *The Journals of Captain James Cook on his Voyages of Discovery* (Cambridge: Hakluyt Society, 1955). A full bibliography of his writings is available in Margery Walton et al, *John Cawte Beaglehole: A Bibliography* (Wellington: Alexander Turnbull Library, 1972).
6. Anthony Reid, "Church & State in New Zealand", *Student* (Wellington, c. Aug. 1961).
7. Leonard Blussé and Carolien Stolte, "Studying Southeast Asia in and for Southeast Asia. An Interview with Anthony Reid", *Itinerario* 34, no. 2 (2010): 7–18. See p. 7.
8. The Colombo Plan was initially a Cold War anti-Communist programme which grew out of a British Commonwealth Conference of Foreign Ministers held in Colombo in January 1950. Initially entitled the 'Colombo Plan for Cooperative Economic Development in South and Southeast Asia' and criticised by some for failing to address political concerns in these countries and territories, it funded both development infrastructure projects in these countries and provided education for a considerable number of their students to study and train in Australia, Canada, New Zealand, Pakistan, and the UK.
9. Blussé and Stolte, "Studying Southeast Asia in and for Southeast Asia", p. 10.
10. The Rhodes Scholarships are prestigious international scholarships offered for postgraduate study at the University of Oxford. They are named for and funded through the estate of Cecil Rhodes, British businessman in Africa, founder of De Beers and erstwhile prime minister of the Cape Colony.

11. Blussé and Stolte, "Studying Southeast Asia in and for Southeast Asia", p. 10.
12. The 'Orford Studentship' was a scholarship to King's College named in honour of J.R. Orford and open to students of New Zealand universities. Joseph Robinson Orford (1863–1924) was a celebrated graduate of King's College who, after migrating to New Zealand in 1894, established and became the headmaster of the Waihi School in Winchester.
13. Victor William Williams Saunders Purcell (1896–1965), served in the British Army during World War I and subsequently joined the Malayan Civil Service where he acquired skills in the Chinese language. Following World War II he served as a United Nations adviser before being appointed as lecturer in Far Eastern History at Cambridge University. His earlier life is detailed in *The Memoirs of a Malayan Official* (London: Cassell, 1965), while his most famous works include *The Chinese in Malaya* (London: Oxford University Press, 1948) and *The Chinese in Southeast Asia* (London: Oxford University Press, 1951). He was also known for polemical works such as *Malaya: Communist or Free* (Stanford: Stanford University Press, 1954).
14. Blussé and Stolte, "Studying Southeast Asia in and for Southeast Asia", p. 10.
15. Charles Donald (Jeremy) Cowan. A prominent British historian of Southeast Asia. After teaching at the University of Malaya in Singapore, Cowan returned to Britain and served at SOAS as both Lecturer in the History of Southeast Asia and later Professor of Oriental History. From 1976–89, he was director of SOAS. Together with Charles Fisher, Stuart Simmonds, Maurice Freedman and David Bassett, Cowan was one of the founders of the Association of South-East Asian Studies of the United Kingdom His major works include: *Nineteenth Century Malaya: the origins of British Political Control* (London: Oxford University Press, 1961); *The Economic Development of Southeast Asia: studies in economic history and political economy* (London: Allen & Unwin, 1964); *The Economic Development of China and Japan: studies in economic history and political economy* (London: Allen & Unwin, 1964); and *Sir Frank Swettenham's Malayan journals, 1874–1876* (Kuala Lumpur: Oxford University Press, 1975).
16. Anthony Reid, *The Contest for North Sumatra: Atjeh, the Netherlands and Britain 1858–1898* (Kuala Lumpur and Singapore: Oxford University Press/University of Malaya Press, 1969).
17. Tengku Hasan Muhammad di Tiro (1925–2010) was the founder of the Gerakan Aceh Merdeka (Free Aceh Movement). A grandson of Tengku Cik di Tiro, who had been killed fighting the Dutch in 1891, Hasan Tiro founded GAM in 1976 and led a guerilla force seeking a separate political status for Aceh. After being wounded he fled the country and settled in Sweden from 1980, remaining a leader in exile until he returned to Aceh in 2008. GAM formally abandoned its independence goals following a peace agreement reached in Helsinki in 2005.
18. Blussé and Stolte, "Studying Southeast Asia in and for Southeast Asia", p. 12.
19. A historian of China, Southeast Asia and the Chinese Overseas, Wang Gungwu had studied at the University of Malaya in 1949 and then at the University

of London before returning to teach at the University of Malaya in 1957. He moved to the Kuala Lumpur campus in 1959 and was appointed as Professor of History at that University in 1966. Some further details of the life of Wang Gungwu as well as a comprehensive bibliography of his works are available in *Wang Gungwu, Junzi. Scholar-Gentleman in Conversation with Asad-ul Iqbal Latif* (Singapore: ISEAS, 2010).

20. Jan M. Pluvier was later to return to the Netherlands and take up a post at the University of Amsterdam where he remained until retirement. His works include: *Confrontations: A Study in Indonesian Politics* (London: Oxford University Press, 1965); *A Handbook and Chart of Southeast Asian History* (London: Oxford University Press, 1967); *Southeast Asia from Colonialism to Independence* (London: Oxford University Press, 1974) and *Historical Atlas of Southeast Asia* (Leiden: Brill, 1995).

21. Jeyamalar Kathirithamby (later Kathirithamby-Wells) was born in Kuala Lumpur, and obtained her doctorate from the University of London. She taught in the History Department of University Malaya and subsequently with the Centre of South Asian Studies, University of Cambridge. Her works include: *The British West Sumatran Presidency, 1760–1785: Problems of Early Colonial Enterprise* (Kuala Lumpur, University of Malaya Press, 1977); (ed. with John Villiers), *The Southeast Asian Port and Polity: Rise and Demise* (Singapore: Singapore University Press, 1990); and *Nature and Nation: Forests and Development in Peninsular Malaysia*, (Copenhagen: NIAS Press: 2005).

22. David Bassett moved from Kuala Lumpur in 1968 to the University of Hull. He later authored *British Trade and Policy in Indonesia and Malaysia in the Late Eighteenth Century* (Zug: Inter Documentation Company, 1971); *Britain and Southeast Asia* (Hull: University of Hull, 1980); and *The British in Southeast Asia during the Seventeenth and Eighteenth Centuries* (Hull: University of Hull, 1990).

23. Khoo Kay Kim obtained his bachelor, masters and doctoral degrees from the University of Malaya and remained with the History Department of the University throughout his career. Publications include *The Western Malay States, 1850–1873: The Effects of Commercial Development on Malay Politics* (Kuala Lumpur and New York: Oxford University Press, 1972); and *Sabah: History and Society* (Kuala Lumpur: Malaysian Historical Society, 1981).

24. A scholar of the social and intellectual history of Islam in Southeast Asia, William R. Roff was a fellow graduate of Tony's from Victoria University before proceeding to pursue doctoral studies at ANU. During his time in Kuala Lumpur, his doctoral thesis was published as *The Origins of Malay Nationalism* (New Haven: Yale University Press, 1967). In 1969, he moved to take up a position at Columbia University and he subsequently edited *Kelantan: Religion, Society and Politics in a Malay State* (Kuala Lumpur: Oxford University Press, 1974). Today he is attached to Edinburgh University.

25. Anthony Short became a historian of the Malayan Emergency and guerila

warfare, with works including *The Communist Insurrection in Malaya 1948–1960* (London: Muller, 1975), and *The Origins of the Vietnam War* (London: Longman, 1989).

26. A historian of Thailand, David Wyatt (1937–2006) spent a semester on a Fulbright Scholarship at the University of Malaya in 1967. From 1969 until his death he taught at Cornell University. His works include *The Politics of Reform in Thailand* (New Haven: Yale University Press, 1969); *Hikayat Patani: The Story of Patani* (with H. Teeuw), 2 vols. (The Hague: Martinus Nijhoff, 1970), *Thailand: A Short History* (New Haven: Yale University Press, 1984), and *The Chiang Mai Chronicle* (with Aroonrut Wichienkeeo) (Chiang Mai: Silkworm Press, 1995).

27. Gerald Seymour Maryanov is a political scientist, with works including *Decentralization in Indonesia as a Political Problem* (Ithaca: Cornell University, 1958) and *Conflict and Political Development in Southeast Asia* (Athens: Ohio University Centre for International Studies, 1969).

28. Blussé and Stolte, "Studying Southeast Asia in and for Southeast Asia", p. 13.

29. *The Blood of the People: Revolution and the End of Traditional Rule in Northern Sumatra* (Kuala Lumpur: OUP, 1979 (Indonesian translation as *Perjuangan Rakyat*, Sinar Harapan, 1986).

30. The killings throughout Indonesia which followed the murder of six generals on the night of 30 September 1965 and the context which gave rise to these occurrences are fully detailed in John Roosa's *Pretext for Mass Murder: The September 30th Movement & Suharto's Coup d'État in Indonesia* (Madison: University of Wisconsin Press, 2007).

31. The events which occurred in Malaysia on 13 May 1969 and in the following weeks are highly contested in Malaysian historiography. The events derived from the results of the Malaysian general election on 10 May 1969 when the opposition DAP made huge gains. Violence between Malay and Chinese groups subsequently ensued, providing the pretext for the declaration of a state of national emergency, the suspension of Parliament and the creation of a Malay-dominated National Operations Council which governed the country until 1971.

32. See Anthony Reid, "The Kuala Lumpur Riots and the Malaysian Political System", *Australian Outlook* 23, no. 3 (1970): 258–78.

33. Wang Gungwu went on to head the Research School of Pacific and Asian Studies from 1975 to 1980.

34. "Trade and the Problem of Royal Power in Aceh, c.1550–1700", in *Pre-Colonial State Systems in Southeast Asia: the Malay Peninsula, Sumatra, Bali-Lombok, South Celebes*, edited by Anthony Reid and Lance Castles, (Kuala Lumpur: MBRAS, 1975), pp. 45–55. A special lecture on The Origins of Poverty in Southeast Asia, at the Third New Zealand Conference of Asian Studies, Auckland, 1979, was later published as "The Origins of Poverty in Indonesia", in *Indonesia-Australian Perspectives,* ed. J.J. Fox, J.A.C. Mackie & Peter McCawley. (Canberra: RSPacS, ANU, 1981): pp. 441–54.

35. Blussé and Stolte, "Studying Southeast Asia in and for Southeast Asia", p. 15.
36 Anthony Reid ed., *Slavery, Bondage and Dependency in Southeast Asia* (St Lucia: Queensland University Press, 1983).
37. David G. Marr is a scholar of Vietnamese history who served from 1975 in the RSPAS at ANU, a post from which he has now retired. He had earlier served as editor of *Vietnam Today*; had directed the Indochina Resource Centre (Washington and Berkeley); and taught at Cornell University and the University of California. Major works include *Vietnamese Anticolonialism, 1885–1925* (Berkeley: UC Press, 1971); *Vietnamese Tradition on Trial 1920–1945* (Berkeley: UC Press, 1981); and *Vietnam 1945: the Quest for Power* (Berkeley: UC Press, 1995).
38. Anthony Reid and David Marr (eds.), *Perceptions of the Past in Southeast Asia* (Singapore: Heinemann for ASAA 1979).
39. A political scientist, Robin Jeffrey was a Research Fellow at the ANU from 1973 to 1978 before taking up a post at Latrobe University (1979–2005). He then returned to ANU and served as Director of the RSPAS (2005–08). Key works include: *The Decline of Nayar Dominance: Society and Politics in Travancore, 1847–1908* (London: Chatto & Windus, 1976); *Politics, Women and Well-Being: How Kerala Became 'a Model'* (London: Macmillan and New Delhi: Oxford University, 1992); and *India's Newspaper Revolution: Capitalism, Politics and the Indian-Language Press, 1977–97* (London: C. Hurst, 2000).
40. The series was published first with Heinemann (1977–81), and later with Oxford University Press (East Asia) (1981–86). See <http://asaa.asn.au/publications/seapshistory.php>. Details of the books published by ASAA can be found at <http://asaa.asn.au/publications/books.php>.
41. In Sulawesi, Tony was engaged with the Social Science Research Training Centre, Ujung Pandang. The Reid family experiences of this period were later used to compile a guide book, Helen Reid & Anthony Reid, *South Sulawesi* (Berkeley: Periplus Editions, 1988).
42. David G. Marr and A.C. Milner (eds.), *Southeast Asia in the 9th to 14th Centuries* (Canberra and Singapore: RSPAS and ISEAS, 1986).
43. A prominent anthropologist of Thailand and Tai societies, Gehan Wijeyewardene's (1932–2000) key works include *Place and Emotion in Northern Thai Ritual Behaviour* (Bangkok: Pandora, 1986); (ed. with E.C. Chapman), *Patterns and Illusions: Thai History and Thought* (Canberra: RSPAS, 2000); and (ed.) *Ethnic Groups across National Borders in Mainland Southeast Asia* (Singapore: ISEAS, 1990). Further details of his scholarly and personal background can be found in Ananda Rajah, "Gehan Wijeyewardene (1932–2000)", *The Asia Pacific Journal of Anthropology* 2, no. 1 (May 2001): 89–108.
44. Further details of the Thai-Yunnan Project and an archive of the *Thai-Yunnan Newsletter* can be found here <http://rspas.anu.edu.au/anthropology/thai-yunnan.php#addition>.
45. Tony suggests that this continuing concern likely indicated that the "Methodist

social conscience hadn't quite deserted the Catholic adult." See Blussé and Stolte, "Studying Southeast Asia in and for Southeast Asia", p. 14.
46. *Southeast Asia in the Age of Commerce, 1450–1680*. Vol. I: *The Lands below the Winds* (New Haven: Yale University Press, 1988).
47. *Southeast Asia in the Age of Commerce, 1450–1680*. Vol. II: *Expansion and Crisis* (New Haven: Yale University Press, 1993).
48. Fernand Braudel, *La Méditerranée et le monde méditerranéen à l'époque de Philippe II* (Paris, A. Colin, 1949). Fernand Braudel (1902–85) was a leader of the French *Annales* school of historiography, one of the key streams in international history-writing post-1950. Following *La Méditerranée*, in which he stressed the regional and *longue durée* aspects of history, Braudel produced a magisterial 3-volume work entitled *Civilisation Matérielle, Economie et Capitalisme, XVe–XVIIIe* (Paris: A. Colin, 1979) which examined the overall history of the preindustrial modern world.
49. See Blussé and Stolte, "Studying Southeast Asia in and for Southeast Asia", p. 15.
50. Emmanuel Le Roy Ladurie (1929–) is a historian of both the microhistory and macrohistory of France. His famous *Les paysans de Languedoc* (Paris: S.E.V.P.E.N., 1966) brings together a huge range of quantitative information, such as wage, tax, rent and profit records in combination with a sophisticated theoretical framework to examine the French peasantry over several centuries. His most famous work *Montaillou, village occitan de 1294 à 1324* (Paris: Gallimard, 1975) provides a richly detailed study of the social milieu of a French village during the 14th century based on the records of the regional Inquisitor.
51. Noel Geoffrey Parker (1943–) is a prominent military historian of Europe over the 16th–18th centuries. Key works include: *The Thirty Years' War* (London: Routledge and Kegan Paul, 1984); and *The Military Revolution: Military Innovation and the Rise of the West, 1500–1800* (Cambridge: Cambridge University Press, 1988). His influence on the military revolution section of Reid's *Age of Commerce* is evident.
52. Charles Tilley (1929-2008) was a sociologist, historian and political scientist influential in the emergence of the field of historical sociology and the use of quantitative methods in historical enquiry. Most famous of his works include: *Coercion, Capital, and European States, AD 990–1990* (Cambridge, Mass: B. Blackwelll, 1990) and, more recently, *Social Movements, 1768–2004* (Boulder: Paradigm, 2004); and *Contention & Democracy in Europe, 1650–2000* (Cambridge: Cambridge University Press, 2004).
53. John (Jack) Rankine Goody (1919–) is a British anthropologist who taught social anthropology at Cambridge 1954–1984. In his work, he stressed the role of literacy as well as economic surplus and the urbanization and bureaucratic structures which derived therefrom, in social structures and social change. Key works include: *The Domestication of the Savage Mind* (Cambridge: Cambridge University Press, 1977); *The Logic of Writing and the Organization*

of Society (Cambridge: Cambridge University Press, 1986); and *The East in the West* (Cambridge, Cambridge University Press, 1986).

54. For an example of such critiques, see Victor Lieberman, "An Age of Commerce in Southeast Asia? Problems of Regional Coherence — A Review Article", *The Journal of Asian Studies* 54, no. 3 (Aug. 1995): 796–807.
55. A listing of the participating scholars in the ECHOSEA network can be found here <http://150.203.231.80/coombspapers/coombsarchives/southeast-asia-economic-history/echosea-newsltr-3.txt>.
56. Including: Jennifer Brewster and Anne Booth (comp.*)*, *Bibliography of statistical sources on Southeast Asia, c. 1750–1990* (Canberra: RSPAS, ANU, 1990); M.R. Fernando and David Bulbeck (eds.), *Chinese economic activity in Netherlands India: Selected Translations from the Dutch* (Singapore: Institute of Southeast Asian Studies, 1992); Li Tana and Anthony Reid (eds.), *Southern Vietnam under the Nguyen: Documents on the Economic History of Cochinchina (Dang Trong) 1602–1777* (Canberra and Singapore: RSPAS and Institute of Southeast Asian Studies, 1993); David Bulbeck, Anthony Reid, Lay Cheng Tan and Yiqi Wu (comp.), *Southeast Asian Exports since the 14th Century: Cloves, Pepper, Coffee and Sugar* (Leiden and Singapore: KITLV and ISEAS, 1998); and Ishii Yoneo (ed.), *The Junk Trade from Southeast Asia: Translations from the Tosen Fusetsu-gaki, 1674–1723* (Canberra and Singapore: RSPAS and Institute of Southeast Asian Studies, 1998).
57. Anthony Reid (ed.) *The Last Stand of Asian Autonomies. Responses to Modernity in the Diverse States of Southeast Asia and Korea* (London: Macmillan, 1997).
58. Jennifer Wayne Cushman (1944–1989). Her major works included (ed. with Wang Gungwu) *Changing Identities of the Southeast Asian Chinese Since World War II* (Hong Kong: Hong Kong University Press, 1988); (ed. Craig J. Reynolds), *Family and State: The Formation of a Sino-Thai Tin-mining dynasty, 1797–1932* (Singapore: Oxford University Press, 1991); and *Fields from the Sea: Chinese Junk Trade with Siam during the late Eighteenth and Early Nineteenth Centuries* (Ithaca, New York: Cornell University Southeast Asia Programme, 1993).
59. Anthony Reid and Kristine Ailunas Rodgers (ed.), *Sojourners and Settlers: Histories of Southeast Asia and the Chinese in Honour of Jennifer Cushman* (St Leonards: Allen and Unwin, 1996).
60. Craig J. Reynolds, a graduate of Cornell University's Southeast Asian Studies Programme and a specialist in the cultural, social and intellectual history of Modern Thailand, is now based at the ANU. His works include: *Thai Radical Discourse: The Real Face of Thai Feudalism Today* (Ithaca, N.Y.: Southeast Asia Program, Cornell University, 1987); (ed.) *National Identity and Its Defenders: Thailand, 1939–1989* (Clayton, Vic.: Centre of Southeast Asian Studies, Monash University, 1991); and *Seditious Histories: Contesting Thai and Southeast Asian Pasts* (Seattle and Singapore: University of Washington Press and Singapore University Press, 2006).
61. The Centre for the Study of the Chinese Southern Diaspora (CSCSD) is now

directed by Li Tana. For further details of the Centre and its activities, see <http://rspas.anu.edu.au/cscsd/>.
62. Anthony Reid, 'Early Chinese Migration into North Sumatra', in *Studies in the Social History of China and Southeast Asia. Essays in Memory of Victor Purcell*, edited by Jerome Ch'en and Nicholas Tarling (Cambridge: Cambridge University Press, 1970), pp. 289–320.
63. Anthony Reid, 'The Rise and Fall of Sino-Javanese Shipping,' in *Looking in Odd Mirrors: The Java Sea*, edited by V.J.H. Houben, H.M.J. Maier and W. van der Molen (Leiden: Leiden University Department of Southeast Asian Studies, 1992). pp. 177–211.
64. Anthony Reid, "The Unthreatening Alternative: Chinese Shipping in Southeast Asia 1567–1842", *RIMA* 27 (1994): 13–32.
65. Anthony Reid, 'The Origins of Revenue Farming in Southeast Asia,' in *The Rise and Fall of Revenue Farming: Business Elites and the Emergence of the Modern State in Southeast Asia*, ed. H. Dick and J. Butcher, (London: Macmillan, 1993), pp. 69–79.
66. In Vol. 2 of *The Age of Commerce*, the section on 'Chinese Commerce and Ethic Polarization' begins with a translated quote from Jacques Savary des Bruslons' *Dictionnaire universal de commerce* (1723): "The Chinese are in Asia, like the Jews in Europe, dispersed into every place where there is some profit to be made." See Anthony Reid, *Southeast Asia in the Age of Commerce, 1450–1680*. Vol. II, p. 311.
67. See Blussé and Stolte, "Studying Southeast Asia in and for Southeast Asia", p. 16.
68. Daniel Chirot, *Social Change in a Peripheral Society: The Creation of a Balkan Colony* (New York: Academic Press, 1976); *Social Change in the Twentieth Century* (New York: Harcourt Brace Jovanovich, 1977); *Social Change in the Modern Era* (San Diego: Harcourt Brace Jovanovich, 1986); and *Modern Tyrants: The Power and Prevalence of Evil in Our Age* (New York: Free Press, 1994).
69. D. Chirot and A. Reid (eds.), *Essential Outsiders: Chinese and Jews in the Modern Transformation of Southeast Asia and Central Europe* (Seattle: University of Washington Press, 1997).
70. See Blussé and Stolte, "Studying Southeast Asia in and for Southeast Asia", p. 16.
71. Over the years, Tony's doctoral students and advisees have included: 1) At ANU: Yeo Kim Wah, Ian Black, James Warren, Robert Reece, Alfons van der Kraan, Dennis Shoesmith, Cheah Boon Kheng, Akira Oki, Anton Lucas, Suyatno Kartodirdjo, Robert Day, Twang Peck Yang, Masashi Hirosue, Ariffin Omar, Jane Drakard, Ruurdje Laarhoven, K.C. Wong, Kelly Ward, Maurizio Peleggi, Grayson Lloyd, Yang Tsung-rong, Minako Sakai, Ian Welch and Sally White. 2) At UCLA: Paul Lavy, Roxanna Brown, Catherine Lilly Greene, Bokyung Kim, Nhung Tuyet Tran and Eric Jones. 3) At NUS: Didi Kwartanada, Iioka Naoko and Walter Strach.

72. <http://www.international.ucla.edu/cseas/>.
73. <http://www.ari.nus.edu.sg/article_view.asp?id=1>.
74. Producing *An Indonesian Frontier: Acehnese and Other Histories of Sumatra* (Singapore: Singapore University Press, 2004) and editing *Verandah of Violence: The Historical Background of the Aceh Problem* (Singapore: Singapore University Press, 2006).
75. <http://www.ari.nus.edu.sg/article_view.asp?id=275>.
76. <http://www.ari.nus.edu.sg/article_view.asp?id=881>.
77. <http://www.iseas.edu.sg/nsc/>.
78. See Blussé and Stolte, "Studying Southeast Asia in and for Southeast Asia", p. 13.
79. David Morgan and Anthony Reid (eds.), *The New Cambridge History of Islam*, Vol. 3: *The Eastern Islamic World, Eleventh to Eighteenth Centuries* (Cambridge: Cambridge University Press, 2010).
80. Those familiar with the geography of Canberra will secretly be hoping that the Southside suburbs also get a guernsey and that future grandchildren will be named perhaps 'Narrabundah' and 'Manuka.'

References

Asad-ul Iqbal Latif. *Wang Gungwu, Junzi. Scholar-Gentleman in Conversation with Asad-ul Iqbal Latif*. Singapore: ISEAS, 2010.

Bassett, David K. *British Trade and Policy in Indonesia and Malaysia in the Late Eighteenth Century*. Zug: Inter Documentation Company, 1971.

———. *The British in Southeast Asia during the Seventeenth and Eighteenth Centuries*. Hull: University of Hull, Centre for Southeast Asian Studies, 1990.

Beaglehole, John C. *The Exploration of the Pacific*. London: A. and C. Black, 1934.

———. *The Journals of Captain James Cook on his Voyages of Discovery*. Cambridge: Hakluyt Society, 1955.

Beaglehole, Tim. *A Life of J.C. Beaglehole: New Zealand Scholar*. Wellington: Victoria University Press, 2006.

Blussé, Leonard and Carolien Stolte. "Studying Southeast Asia in and for Southeast Asia. An Interview with Anthony Reid". *Itinerario* 34, no. 2 (2010): 7–18.

Braudel, Fernand. *La Méditerranée et le monde méditerranéen à l'époque de Philippe II*. Paris, A. Colin, 1949.

———. *Civilisation Matérielle, Economie et Capitalisme, XVe-XVIIIe*. Paris : A. Colin, 1979.

Brewster, Jennifer and Anne Booth (comp.). *Bibliography of statistical sources on Southeast Asia, c. 1750–1990*. Canberra: RSPAS, ANU, 1990.

Bulbeck, David, Anthony Reid, Lay Cheng Tan and Yiqi Wu (comp.). *Southeast Asian Exports since the Fourteenth Century: Cloves, Pepper, Coffee and Sugar*. Leiden and Singapore: KITLV and ISEAS, 1998.

Chirot, Daniel. *Social Change in a Peripheral Society: The Creation of a Balkan Colony.* New York: Academic Press, 1976;
———. *Social Change in the Twentieth Century.* New York: Harcourt Brace Jovanovich, 1977.
———. *Social Change in the Modern Era.* San Diego: Harcourt Brace Jovanovich, 1986.
———. *Modern Tyrants: The Power and Prevalence of Evil in Our Age.* New York: Free Press, 1994.
Chirot, Daniel and A. Reid (eds.). *Essential Outsiders: Chinese and Jews in the Modern Transformation of Southeast Asia and Central Europe.* Seattle: University of Washington Press, 1997.
Cowan, C.D. *Nineteenth Century Malaya: The Origins of British Political Control.* London: Oxford University Press, 1961).
———. *The Economic Development of Southeast Asia: studies in economic history and political economy.* London: Allen & Unwin, 1964.
———. *The Economic Development of China and Japan: studies in economic history and political economy.* London: Allen & Unwin, 1964.
———. *Sir Frank Swettenham's Malayan Journals, 1874–1876.* Kuala Lumpur: Oxford University Press, 1975.
Cushman, Jennifer Wayne. *Fields from the Sea: Chinese Junk Trade with Siam during the late Eighteenth and Early Nineteenth Centuries.* Ithaca, New York: Southeast Asia Program, 1993.
———. (ed. Craig J. Reynolds) *Family and State: The Formation of a Sino-Thai Tin-mining Dynasty, 1797–1932.* Singapore: Oxford University Press, 1991.
Cushman, Jennifer Wayne and Wang Gungwu (eds.). *Changing Identities of the Southeast Asian Chinese Since World War II.* Hong Kong: Hong Kong University Press, 1988.
Fernando, M.R. and David Bulbeck (eds.), *Chinese Economic Activity in Netherlands India: Selected Translations from the Dutch.* Singapore: Institute of Southeast Asian Studies, 1992.
Goody, John Rankine. *The Domestication of the Savage Mind.* Cambridge, Cambridge University Press, 1977.
———. *The Logic of Writing and the Organization of Society.* Cambridge, Cambridge University Press, 1986.
———. *The East in the West.* Cambridge, Cambridge University Press, 1986.
Ishii Yoneo (ed.). *The Junk Trade from Southeast Asia: Translations from the Tosen Fusetsu-gaki, 1674–1723.* Canberra and Singapore: RSPAS, Institute of Southeast Asian Studies, 1998.
Jeffrey, Robin. *The Decline of Nayar Dominance: Society and Politics in Travancore, 1847–1908.* London: Chatto & Windus, 1976.
———. *Politics, Women and Well-Being: How Kerala Became 'a Model'.* London: Macmillan; New Delhi: Oxford University, 1992.
———. *India's Newspaper Revolution: Capitalism, Politics and the Indian-Language Press, 1977–97.* London: C. Hurst, 2000.

Kathirithamby-Wells, Jeyamalar. *The British West Sumatran Presidency, 1760–1785: Problems of Early Colonial Enterprise*. Kuala Lumpur: University of Malaya Press, 1977.

———. *Nature and Nation: Forests and Development in Peninsular Malaysia*. Copenhagen: NIAS Press, 2005.

Kathirithamby-Wells, Jeyamalar and John Villiers (eds.). *The Southeast Asian Port and Polity: Rise and Demise*. Singapore: Singapore University Press, 1990.

Khoo Kay Kim. *The Western Malay States, 1850–1873: The Effects of Commercial Development on Malay Politics*. Kuala Lumpur and New York: Oxford University Press, 1972.

———. *Sabah: History and Society*. Kuala Lumpur: Malaysian Historical Society, 1981.

Ladurie, Emmanuel Le Roy. *Les paysans de Languedoc*. Paris: S.E.V.P.E.N., 1966.

———. *Montaillou, village occitan de 1294 à 1324*. Paris: Gallimard, 1975.

Li Tana and Anthony Reid (eds.). *Southern Vietnam under the Nguyen: Documents on the Economic History of Cochinchina (Dang Trong) 1602–1777*. Canberra and Singapore: RSPAS and Institute of Southeast Asian Studies, 1993.

Lieberman, Victor. "An Age of Commerce in Southeast Asia? Problems of Regional Coherence — A Review Article". *The Journal of Asian Studies* 54, no. 3 (Aug. 1995): 796–807.

Marr, David G. *Vietnamese Anticolonialism, 1885–1925*. Berkeley and Los Angeles: UC Press, 1971.

———. *Vietnamese Tradition on Trial 1920–1945*. Berkeley and Los Angeles: UC Press, 1981.

———. *Vietnam 1945: The Quest for Power*. Berkeley and Los Angeles: UC Press, 1995.

Marr, David G. and A.C. Milner (eds.). *Southeast Asia in the Ninth to Fourteenth Centuries*. Canberra and Singapore: RSPAS and ISEAS, 1986.

Maryanov, Gerald Seymour. *Decentralization in Indonesia as a Political Problem*. Ithaca: Cornell University, 1958.

———. *Conflict and Political Development in Southeast Asia*. Athens: Ohio University Centre for International Studies, 1969.

Morgan, David and Anthony Reid (eds.). *The New Cambridge History of Islam*, Vol. 3: *The Eastern Islamic World, Eleventh to Eighteenth Centuries*. Cambridge: Cambridge University Press, 2010.

Parker, Noel Geoffrey. *The Thirty Years' War*. London: Routledge and Kegan Paul, 1984.

———.*The Military Revolution: Military Innovation and the Rise of the West, 1500–1800*. Cambridge: Cambridge University Press, 1988.

Pluvier, Jan M. *Confrontations: A Study in Indonesian Politics*. Kuala Lumpur: Oxford University Press, 1965.

———. *A Handbook and Chart of Southeast Asian History*. Kuala Lumpur: Oxford University Press: 1967).

———. *Southeast Asia from Colonialism to Independence.* Kuala Lumpur & New York: Oxford University Press, 1974.

———. *Historical Atlas of Southeast Asia.* Leiden: Brill, 1995.

Purcell, Victor W.W.S. *The Memoirs of a Malayan Official.* London: Cassell, 1965.

———. *The Chinese in Malaya.* London: Oxford University Press, 1948.

———. *The Chinese in Southeast Asia.* London: Oxford University Press, 1951.

———. *Malaya: Communist or Free.* Stanford: Stanford University Press, 1954.

Rajah, Ananda. "Gehan Wijeyewardene (1932–2000)". *The Asia Pacific Journal of Anthropology* 2, no. 1 (May 2001): 89–108.

Reid, Anthony. "Church & State in New Zealand". *Student* (Wellington, c. Aug. 1961).

———. *The Contest for North Sumatra: Atjeh, the Netherlands and Britain 1858–1898.* Kuala Lumpur and Singapore: Oxford University Press/University of Malaya Press, 1969.

———. "Early Chinese Migration into North Sumatra". In *Studies in the Social History of China and Southeast Asia. Essays in Memory of Victor Purcell*, edited by Jerome Ch'en and Nicholas Tarling, pp. 289–320. Cambridge: Cambridge University Press, 1970.

———. "The Kuala Lumpur Riots and the Malaysian Political System". *Australian Outlook* 23, no. 3 (1970): 258-78.

———. "Trade and the Problem of Royal Power in Aceh, c.1550–1700". In *Pre-Colonial State Systems in Southeast Asia: the Malay Peninsula, Sumatra, Bali-Lombok, South Celebes*, edited by Anthony Reid and Lance Castles, pp. 45–55. Kuala Lumpur: MBRAS, 1975.

———. *The Blood of the People: Revolution and the End of Traditional Rule in Northern Sumatra.* Kuala Lumpur: OUP, 1979.

———. "The Origins of Poverty in Indonesia". In *Indonesia - Australian Perspectives*, edited by J.J. Fox, J.A.C. Mackie & Peter McCawley, pp. 441–54. Canberra: RSPacS, ANU, 1981.

———. (ed.) *Slavery, Bondage and Dependency in Southeast Asia.* St Lucia: Queensland University Press, 1983.

———. *Southeast Asia in the Age of Commerce, 1450–1680.* Vol. I: *The Lands below the Winds.* New Haven: Yale University Press, 1988.

———. "The Rise and Fall of Sino-Javanese Shipping". In *Looking in Odd Mirrors: The Java Sea,* edited by V.J.H. Houben, H.M.J. Maier and W. van der Molen, pp. 177–211. Leiden: Leiden University Department of Southeast Asian Studies, 1992.

———. *Southeast Asia in the Age of Commerce, 1450–1680.* Vol. II: *Expansion and Crisis.* New Haven: Yale University Press, 1993.

———. "The Origins of Revenue Farming in Southeast Asia". In *The Rise and Fall of Revenue Farming: Business Elites and the Emergence of the Modern State in Southeast Asia*, edited by H. Dick and J. Butcher, pp. 69–79. London: Macmillan, 1993.

———. "The Unthreatening Alternative: Chinese Shipping in Southeast Asia 1567–1842". *RIMA* 27 (1994): 13–32.

———. (ed.) *The Last Stand of Asian Autonomies: Responses to Modernity in the Diverse States of Southeast Asia and Korea*. London: Macmillan, 1997.

———. (ed.) *Verandah of Violence: The Historical Background of the Aceh Problem*. Singapore: Singapore University Press, 2006.

———. *An Indonesian Frontier: Acehnese and Other Histories of Sumatra*. Singapore: Singapore University Press, 2004.

Reid, Anthony and Kristine Ailunas Rodgers (eds.). *Sojourners and Settlers: Histories of Southeast Asia and the Chinese in Honour of Jennifer Cushman*. St Leonards: Allen and Unwin, 1996.

Reid, Helen and Anthony Reid. *South Sulawesi*. Berkeley, Periplus Editions, 1988.

Reynolds, Craig J. *Thai Radical Discourse: The Real Face of Thai Feudalism Today*. Ithaca, New York: Southeast Asia Program, Cornell University, 1987.

———. (ed.) *National Identity and Its Defenders: Thailand, 1939–1989*. Clayton: Centre of Southeast Asian Studies, Monash University, 1991.

———. *Seditious Histories: Contesting Thai and Southeast Asian Pasts*. Seattle and Singapore: University of Washington Press and Singapore University Press, 2006.

Roff, William R. *The Origins of Malay Nationalism*. New Haven: Yale University Press, 1967.

———. (ed.) *Kelantan: Religion, Society and Politics in a Malay State*. Kuala Lumpur: Oxford University Press, 1974.

Roosa, John. *Pretext for Mass Murder: The September 30th Movement & Suharto's Coup d'État in Indonesia*. Madison: University of Wisconsin Press, 2007.

Sadka, Emily. *The Protected Malay States, 1874–1895*. Kuala Lumpur: University of Malaya Press, 1968.

Short, Anthony. *The Communist Insurrection in Malaya 1948–1960*. London: Muller, 1975.

———. *The Origins of the Vietnam War*. London: Longman, 1989.

Tilley, Charles. *Coercion, Capital, and European States, AD 990–1990*. Cambridge, Mass.: B. Blackwell, 1990.

———. *Social Movements, 1768–2004*. Boulder: Paradigm Publishers, 2004.

———. *Contention and Democracy in Europe, 1650–2000*. Cambridge: Cambridge University Press, 2004.

Walton, Margery et al. *John Cawte Beaglehole: A Bibliography*. Wellington: Alexander Turnbull Library, 1972.

Wijeyewardene, Gehan. *Place and Emotion in Northern Thai Ritual Behaviour*. Bangkok: Pandora, 1986.

———. (ed.) *Ethnic Groups Across National Borders in Mainland Southeast Asia*. Singapore: ISEAS, 1990.

Wijeyewardene, Gehan and E.C. Chapman (ed.). *Patterns and Illusions: Thai History and Thought*. Canberra: RSPAS, 2000.

Wyatt, David. *The Politics of Reform in Thailand*. New Haven: Yale University Press, 1969.
———. *Thailand: A Short History*. New Haven: Yale University Press, 1984.
Wyatt, David and Aroonrut Wichienkeeo. *The Chiang Mai Chronicle*. Chiang Mai: Silkworm Press: 1995.
Wyatt, David and H. Teeuw. *Hikayat Patani: The Story of Patani* (2 vols.). The Hague: Martinus Nijhoff, 1970.

PART II
The Scholarship of Anthony Reid

2

THE PAST AS THREAT, THE PAST AS PROMISE
The Historical Writing of Anthony Reid

Robert Cribb

In March 2007 the Indonesian Attorney-General, Abdul Rahman Saleh, issued a decree banning some fourteen school history text books and ordering that all copies be withdrawn from use and burned. The grounds which the Attorney-General offered for this drastic action were that the books had failed to mention the 1948 Madiun Revolt by the Indonesian Communist Party (PKI) and had referred to the 1965 coup in Jakarta as G/30/S, omitting the suffix '-PKI', previously used in all official statements to link the coup to the communists. That coup, still poorly understood, involved the murder of six senior anti-communist generals and appears to have been an attempt by junior, leftist officers and leading elements from the Communist Party to forestall a predicted military coup and to shift Indonesian politics decisively to the Left.[1] Just over two years later, in September 2009, a coalition of Islamic and conservative groups joined forces in Surabaya to burn copies of the newly-released memoirs of one of the leaders of the Madiun Revolt.[2]

Some observers have treated these manifestations of anti-Communism as a regrettable relic of the sustained propaganda effort of the Suharto era;[3] others see them as an aspect of Islamist assertiveness against Indonesia's secularist traditions. Nonetheless, hostility to the Indonesian Communist Party, so anomalous now in a world where most Communist parties have either collapsed or embarked unashamedly on a capitalist road, seems to be located at least partly in a deeper Indonesian attitude to history.

The historian John Lukacs has identified historical consciousness as the sense that the present is different from the past in ways that have to do with the outcome of human endeavours. He identifies historical consciousness as supremely characteristic of the modern world, because it leads to (or from) the conclusion that human effort can bring about change for the better in the human condition.[4] Here, however, I am interested in the narrower question of the way in which modern Indonesians recruit the events and conditions of the past to provide lessons for the present. Any attempt to explore the collective historical consciousness is necessarily speculative, but I want to suggest that recent Indonesian attitudes to the historical past have generally constructed it as a source of menace, rather than inspiration. Despite official efforts, especially under Suharto's New Order, to construct an inspiring historical landscape populated by exemplary heroes,[5] Indonesians do not on the whole draw a sense of national pride from their past. Pride lies in what Indonesia is — the fourth most populous country in the world, a leader in Southeast Asia — and in Indonesia's potential to become just and prosperous, not in what it once was.

In the vision which most Indonesians have of their national past, rather, two villains stalk the landscape. One villain is the Communist Party, alleged author of two stabs in the national back — in 1948 at Madiun, when the heartland of the new Indonesian Republic was hemmed into a narrow stretch of central and eastern Java and seemed to face imminent destruction at the hands of Dutch colonial forces; and in 1965, when Partai Komunis Indonesia (PKI) elements murdered six anti-communist generals, allegedly as a prelude to a massive, bloody strike against their political enemies across the length and breadth of Indonesia. The second villain is the Dutch, former colonial masters of the archipelago who are commonly portrayed as having sucked wealth out of the archipelago to fund a Golden Age on the shores of the North Sea, killing any Natives who resisted their rule, callously exploiting labour in a way that drove hundreds of thousands more into early graves, and humiliating the rest in a demeaning, racist colonial social order. The colonial era, in this popular conception, is bracketed by Jan Pieterszoon Coen's genocide of the Bandanese in 1609 and by the terror of 'Turk' Westerling in southern Sulawesi in 1946–47 in which 40,000 people are reputed to have been killed.

The impulse to identify villains is a strong one in Indonesia. It lies at the heart of Pramoedya Ananta Toer's Buru Quartet of historical novels which trace the Indonesian national awakening of the early twentieth century through the life of 'Minke', representing the nationalist Tirtoadisuryo. On the Indonesian side of his narrative, Pramoedya creates strong, complex and admirable characters but his Europeans are cardboard-thin caricatures, reminiscent of the prejudicial representation of Communists in the New Order propaganda film *Pengkhianatan G/30/S-PKI*; there is no hint in his Buru novels of the complexities of the colonial system, of the tangled relationships between exploitation, good intentions, disdain, intolerance, condescension, affection, suspicion, disappointment, compromise and generosity that characterized the colonial order. Indeed, the central events in the first novel of the Quartet — the reclassification of Minke's wife Annelies as a European, the consequent annulment of her marriage (which would have been legal had she remained a Native) and her removal to Europe — had no parallel in the actual history of colonialism but were apparently based on the circumstances of the Maria Hertogh case in Singapore in 1950.[6]

Pramoedya's analysis represents a popular answer to the question identified by Benda in his 1962 review of Feith's *Decline of Constitutional Democracy in Indonesia*. In that review, Benda characterized Feith as asking 'What's wrong with Indonesia?' In the 1950s, this question had seldom arisen, except in the jaded mutterings of old colonial hands. Indonesians and outside observers alike viewed Indonesia's prospects with a fundamental sense of optimism — the country might face enormous problems as a consequence of ethnic and religious diversity and because of lack of infrastructure and human capital, but it seemed that energy, selflessness and ingenious resourcefulness would carry it forward. By the early 1960s, however, the tone of the assessments had changed. Underlying much of what was said about Indonesia was at least a hint and often a powerful assertion that something was seriously wrong with the country. From the point of view of the then-standard analysis, Indonesia had indeed gone wrong — instead of consolidating the democratic order that the nationalist movement had appeared to promise, Indonesia had slid into Sukarno's semi-authoritarian and increasingly ramshackle Guided Democracy.

Benda's suggestion was that Guided Democracy, rather than being dismissed simply as the product of democratic 'decline', might be understood as a return to that he referred to as Indonesia's 'moorings' in its own history.[7] Indonesia had only gone 'wrong', in Benda's view, if the pathway defined by Europe's experience was defined *a priori* as 'right'. Benda's implication that nothing was really wrong with Indonesia, however, could not survive the turmoil of the mid-1960s. As Indonesia slid into the chaos leading to the 1965–66 massacres, the question 'What's wrong with Indonesia?' returned to haunt studies of the country and it has remained in the air ever since.

Throughout the long era of authoritarian developmentalism under President Suharto, many things seemed to be going right for Indonesia, especially in the economy, but it was hard not to see the political order as morally and intellectually warped, and it was not difficult to find serious social and economic problems underlying the apparent developmental successes of the regime.

Although some observers suggested that the flaw might lie in some aspect of Indonesia's cultural make-up, the more common implication was that the answer lay in history. Ben Anderson expressed the mood most eloquently in the colophon to his *Java in A Time of Revolution, 1944–1946*, when he cited Brutus in Shakespeare's *Julius Caesar*:

> There is a tide in the affairs of men,
> Which, taken at the flood, leads on to fortune;
> Omitted, all the voyage of their life
> Is bound in shallows and in miseries.

Anderson's work specifically lamented the failure of the revolutionary leader Tan Malaka to take charge of the Indonesian struggle for independence and to insist on full decolonization rather than compromise with the Dutch. His approach echoed that of the Dutch socialist Jacques de Kadt, who as early as 1949 had described Dutch policy as 'a tragedy of missed chances;' Anne Booth developed the same analytical approach when she characterized the Indonesian economy in the nineteenth and twentieth centuries as 'a history of missed opportunities.'[8] Even scholars who did not explicitly talk of wrong turns taken in the past increasingly implied that Indonesia's chances of success were compromised by its past — by Dutch policies which had shaped the nationalist reaction in undesirable ways and by the very creation of a state straddling so many ethnic groups and so many islands with such uneven levels of many economic development.[9] Indonesians themselves have come to share this sense that their country's real potential has been compromised, perhaps fatally, by its history. It has become surprisingly common to hear from young Indonesians the comment '*kami salah dijajah*', we were colonized by the wrong people; if only Indonesia had been colonized by the British, this line of thought suggests, the country could have ended up as a more powerful version of Malaysia.

It is hard to imagine that a past peopled with villains and punctuated with missed opportunities is an asset for modern Indonesia. On the one hand, a sense of pervasive villainy is deeply antipathetic to the growth of social trust which Fukuyama, most recently in a long line of observers, has identified as a major element in the smooth running of society.[10] On the other hand, a perception of missed opportunities is profoundly discouraging. It implies that one's efforts have already been defeated, or half-defeated, by the mistaken decisions of those who are now long gone. The corollary of missed opportunities is a bleak future, governed by the misfortunes of the past.

Tony Reid, whose work is honoured in this volume, has been one of the most foremost exponents of a very different kind of history, one that invigorates and empowers. Rather than directly addressing policy achievements and policy errors of the independent era, Reid has sought to inform the debate by exploring the rich political, social and cultural repertoires available to the peoples of the archipelago in pre-colonial times. His contribution does not dismiss the possibility that villains, both in the colonial era and after 1950 may have done enormous damage to Indonesia, but it represents a forceful assertion of Indonesia's potential to get its future right. More than anything else, Reid's work is a repudiation of the pessimism which is embedded popularly in the *salah dijajah* comment and academically in the 'missed opportunities' trope.

Reid's earliest work contained only a hint of what was to come. His article 'Indonesian diplomacy: a documentary study of Atjehnese foreign policy in the reign of Sultan Mahmud, 1870–74', which appeared in 1969 along with the book of his Cambridge thesis (*The Contest for North Sumatra: Atjeh, the Netherlands and Britain 1858–1898*), directed the reader's attention to the Indonesian perspective on a diplomatic relationship that was more commonly examined from a European point of view.[11] This attention to an Indonesian perspective was, however, clearly in line with the excitement that had been generated by John Smail's seminal essay of 1961 'On the Possibility of an Autonomous History of Modern Southeast Asia,'[12] which argued for looking at Southeast Asian history from the point of view of Southeast Asians. Smail's argument in turn was partly a re-working of J.C. van Leur's rebuke to historians, written in 1939 but not translated into English until 1955, for shifting their view of Indonesia from indigenous society to 'the high gallery of the trading house' as soon as Europeans appeared on the scene.[13] Reid's research then took a step forward in chronological terms to address the end of colonialism, when Indonesians re-asserted their autonomy by seizing independence in a bloody national revolution. Two books arose from this project: *The Indonesian National Revolution* (1974),[14] which remains the standard academic work on that period, and *The Blood of the People: Revolution and the End of Traditional Rule in Northern Sumatra*,[15] which was one amongst several academic studies by (then) younger scholars of the regional dimension of the Indonesian revolution. His research on this topic also included important contributions to knowledge of the Japanese period in Indonesia.

Even before *Blood of the People* was published, however, Reid's attention had turned to the period immediately before Western colonialism in Indonesia. One of Reid's earliest excursions into the pre-colonial period was a lecture delivered at Flinders University in Adelaide in 1975 entitled ' "Heaven's will and man's fault": The rise of the West as a Southeast Asian dilemma.'[16] The lecture showed Southeast Asians grappling seriously with the analytical problem presented by the rise of Western power in their region; these were not innocent people bewildered as if by the arrival of all-powerful creatures from an unknown realm, but rather canny operators seeking to make sense of a rapid change in the balance of power in their region. Perhaps more important, the lecture also gave empirical flesh to Van Leur's repudiation of the sudden shift of attention from indigenous society to Westerners that he identified as taking place in European history-writing about the region. Using indigenous sources, Reid began to bring to life the world-view of the people of Southeast Asia.

The 'Heaven's will' lecture was a reflective, agenda-setting piece, but Reid had already begun to follow the agenda he set in Adelaide. In 1975, he published a chapter 'Trade and the Problem of Royal Power in Aceh: Three Stages, c.1550–1700'[17] and the bulk of his publications for the next twenty years explored this period, culminating in his magisterial *Southeast Asia in the Age of Commerce* (2 vols, 1988–1993). In contrast with earlier periods, the era extending from about 1450 until the imposition of colonial rule (a highly variable date across the archipelago) represented a window of research opportunity into Indonesian societies before the distorting effects of foreign rule. The research was made possible by the Europeans' unprecedented penchant for documentation, including the preservation of indigenous materials, and Reid's scholarship was marked by close attention to these early texts. An immediate consequence of this focus, moreover, was that Reid's focus broadened from Indonesia to Southeast Asia as a whole. Although the Indonesian archipelago remained the centre of gravity in his writing, his works indicated a growing conviction that the Southeast Asian realm as a whole was the proper frame for scholarly investigation of the pre-colonial period, and he became one of the foremost exponents of the historical reality of Southeast Asia in answer to those who claimed that it was a post-war, and primarily Western, conception.

The central theme of Reid's *Age of Commerce* work was the vibrancy of pre-colonial Southeast Asian society. One of his most inspiring, though relatively little noticed, works was a study of a family in seventeenth century Makassar in the eastern Indonesian archipelago who steered their own and their city's fortunes through the challenges and opportunities of growing Dutch political, commercial and cultural power in the region.[18] This article remains one of very few works that brings to life the experience of Indonesians in the early modern period who were powerful, intelligent figures within their own societies.

Reid's commitment to using the past to inform the present in a way that inspires a feeling of possibility, rather than arousing a sense of dread or lost opportunity, is expressed especially in his exploration of three issues.

First, Reid joined the French historian Denys Lombard in identifying pre-colonial Southeast Asia as an 'Asian Mediterranean,' following the insights of Fernand Braudel into the original Mediterranean as a region of rich commercial, cultural and social interaction.[19] In exploring Southeast Asia's history on the eve of European colonialism, Reid was taken by similarities between his region and the Mediterranean. Braudel's celebrated work *The Mediterranean and the Mediterranean World in the Age of Philip II* had described a region in which islands and jutting peninsulas created a realm that was neither land nor ocean, where the sea both united and divided, where gleaming anecdotes of local particularity set off the deep, richly textured fabric of broad cultural and commercial interaction. This insight went far beyond the commonplace that modern national borders in Southeast Asia, created for the most part on the colonial era and by colonial powers, did not necessarily coincide with either older political structures or with ethnic and cultural distinctions. Rather, in identifying diversity as a characteristic of the Southeast Asian region, it created legitimate spaces for all those communities — small indigenous ethnic groups, hybrid and creole societies, imaginative religious belief groups — that had failed to emerge from the transition to modernity as the core identity of one or more nations. Reid's Southeast Asia was Southeast Asian by virtue of, not despite, its diversity. Reid's insight, moreover, adds depth to the current debate over the relationship between globalization and local identity. Globalization is routinely assumed to imply cultural homogenization in the long term, yet the 'Asian Mediterranean' thesis suggests provocatively that cultural diversity can coexist with economic integration.

Reid's arguments here butted on to the longstanding controversy within Southeast Asian history over the issue of cultural transmission. The first Western scholars to pay attention to Southeast Asia had noted the presence of important elements of Indian civilization in the early history of much of the region and had perceived these elements as signs of an underlying cultural unity with India. Regional terms such as Further India, Indonesia, Insulinde and Indochina reflected the presumption of Southeast Asia's belonging to its great civilizational neighbours. Later scholars such as R.C. Majumdar read the fragmentary evidence from early times as telling the story of Indian colonization of Southeast Asia and there was no doubting the historical record of 1,000 years of Chinese rule in what later became independent Vietnam. The assumption behind these interpretations was that Southeast Asians had been the passive recipients of high culture delivered from elsewhere. Where transmission appeared to have been incomplete, it was attributed to atavism, conservatism and perhaps intellectual inability on the part of Southeast Asians. The same broad assumptions were applied to the arrival of Islam in maritime Southeast Asia and even to the spread of Western culture.

In 1934 Van Leur, initiator of the autonomous approach to Southeast Asian history, had argued that the scholars of Indianization, Sinicization, Islamification and Westernization had all overstated the extent of outside influences. These influences, he argued, were in fact no more than a 'thin and flaking glaze' over deep structural and cultural continuities within Southeast Asian societies.[20] This judgement was clearly echoed Benda's claim concerning politics in the early 1960s: 'The Indonesian river is flowing more and more in an Indonesian bed; the game being played is, once again, Indonesian.'[21]

Important though the autonomist proposition of Van Leur and Benda was as a repudiation of the unsubstantiated and somewhat chauvinist conclusions of Majumdar and the like, it proved to be seriously problematic beyond the level of corrective rhetoric. For one thing, it ran counter to the obvious empirical evidence that indigenous tradition and foreign influences were intimately intertwined in most aspects of Southeast Asian society, and the slightly discomforting discovery that much of what had been regarded as traditional was in fact thoroughly assimilated foreign influence. Recognition of the importance of outside influences was reinforced by the pioneering linguistic and cultural research of Bellwood showing that the great majority of Indonesians and Filipinos were descendants of Austronesian emigrants from Taiwan 5,000 years ago and that Polynesian cultures, relatively unaffected by outside influences, probably held significant clues as to the underlying cultural heritage of maritime Southeast Asia. Moreover, the generation of scholars who trained, like Reid, in the 1960s, began to realize that the autonomist arguments gave comfort to a dangerous local chauvinism within Southeast Asia. This chauvinism was symbolized especially by the reshaping of the Pancasila at the hands of Suharto's New Order. The five principles — belief in God, humanity, nationalism, democracy, and social justice — were incorporated into the preamble of the Indonesian constitution on the basis of a celebrated speech by Sukarno on the eve of the independence declaration. They had clearly been formulated with reference to the ruling ideas in international political discourse, the New Order recast them as a purely Indonesian doctrine, dug from the soil of Indonesia by Sukarno. The same chauvinism was evident in the so-called 'Asian values debate' of the late 1990s, when semi-authoritarian Southeast Asian leaders such as Lee Kuan Yew and Mahathir Mohamad contrasted the allegedly communitarian values of Asia with the supposed individualism of the West.[22]

Under these circumstances, Reid was a pioneer in a movement which developed a sophisticated new analysis of the place of outside influences in Southeast Asian cultures. The essence of this argument was that Southeast Asia's genius lay in its eclectic recruitment of outside ideas. Ideas came from outside, it was true, but they came on terms decided by Southeast Asian themselves, so that, for instance, the broad class categories of Hinduism — *brahmana, ksatriya, vaisya, sudra* — were accepted, but not the system of individual occupational castes and outcaste that bedevil Indian society and not the institutionalized misogyny of classical Hinduism or Confucianism. Just as important, Southeast Asian societies recruited outsiders — Chinese, Turks, Arabs, Japanese, Indians and more — to staff its courts, serve its markets, mine its minerals, till its fields. If U.S. President Ronald Reagan once said 'Every immigrant makes America more American,' Reid argued that outsiders made Southeast Asia more Southeast Asian.

The second issue echoing through Reid's work is his controversial assertion that Southeast Asian women enjoyed a relatively high social standing as well as individual freedom and access to political and economic power in early Southeast Asia. It was a direct, if implicit, challenge to the orthodoxy that Asian civilizations had been hyper-patriarchal. This assertion was widely contested by scholars who felt that it glossed over the extensive evidence of traditional gender inequality in Southeast Asia. These counter-arguments were often apt, but they commonly failed to recognize Reid's broader points: that models for understanding Southeast Asia based on the classical civilizations and cultures of India and China will not necessarily do justice to Southeast Asia's special characteristics, and that the region's past offers material that can be recruited to progressive causes in the present. Reid's insights into the historical position of Southeast Asian women continue to provide a basis for the argument that many of the allegedly customary restrictions on women's autonomy in contemporary Southeast Asia are forms of recently-invented tradition, rather than deep-seated elements in the region's culture.

Reid's third major proposition was that Southeast Asians had developed a 'genius' for managing without powerful states, an issue pursued also by James C. Scott in his recent work. Reid's academic career encompassed the whole of the long New Order in Indonesia, a period of military-based, presidential rule in which authoritarianism was formally justified by its delivery of social and economic benefits. Challenging this official orthodoxy, Reid's work asserted the identity of Southeast Asia as a civilizational region that was distinguished from India, China, the Middle East and indeed Europe by the absence of a tradition of empire. For Reid, part of the Southeast Asian genius lay in this capacity to be one without having to surrender either to cultural uniformity or to the shrill dogmatism of unitarist nationalism which characterized China and India and which came to be a feature of New Order Indonesia. Reid's work implied that colonialism had destroyed or suppressed important elements in what made Southeast Asia a special place in global history, but his point was not to blame colonialism — relatively little of his work focuses on the high colonial periods when the greatest damage to indigenous societies is likely to have been done — but rather to point to the region's home-grown potential for generating creative solutions to its problems. His chapter 'Merdeka: the concept of freedom in Indonesia' exemplifies this approach, arguing that ideas of freedom have deep indigenous roots in the archipelago and cannot be dismissed as a foreign import.[23]

Two contemporary problems have informed Reid's writing in recent years. One is the Aceh conflict, in which a vigorous Acehnese nationalist movement initially sought independence from Indonesia but settled, in the aftermath of the 2004 tsunami, for a high level of autonomy within the Indonesian state. The issue took Reid back to the geographical region of his first Southeast Asian research. His conclusion emphasised Acehnese exceptionalism: Aceh was the last great independent state to be subjugated by the Dutch, the only region of Indonesia to enter the modern era with the historical legacy and political, social and cultural forms to underpin a separate political identity. Although his position was that history identified a distinct Acehnese identity warranting political recognition, he insisted that this recognition should take place within the kind of creative, layered political construction that characterized pre-colonial Southeast Asian polities.

The second contemporary issue engaging Reid is the Chinese in Southeast Asia. Appalled by racist violence against Chinese communities, Reid has endeavoured to develop a historical narrative of Chinese engagement in Southeast Asia which eliminates the stark image of Chinese alien economic beasts and replaces it with a complex picture of rich economic and cultural contribution to the region. Wade in this volume explores the ways in which Chinese contributed to the spread of Islam in Southeast Asia. This assertion of the legitimacy and value of the Chinese presence in Southeast Asia sprang not only from Reid's liberal concern over racist persecution, but also and more profoundly from his understanding of the characteristic pattern in

Southeast Asia of recruiting outside people and ideas to enrich the region culturally and materially.

Taken as a whole, the historical research of Tony Reid is a remarkable body of scholarship. Reid is unusual in combining an enduring professional commitment to the empirical, source-based rigour that is characteristic of the best historical writing and a breadth of vision that makes his writings not just respected and admired but intellectually influential. His work, moreover, shows an underlying commitment to the relevance of history to the present, to the constructive development of historical consciousness. In contrast to the powerful tendency, both in Indonesian public debate and in historical writing on Indonesia, to treat the past as menacing, Reid enriches our vision of the past by unfolding its diversity and complexity. Readers of Reid's work do not need to despair that Indonesia, or Southeast Asia more broadly, has to rise above its past if it is to achieve anything. The past, rather, is a rich resource that holds a promise of what the future can be.

Notes

1. John Roosa, *Pretext for Mass Murder: The September 30th Movement and Suharto's Coup d'etat in Indonesia* (Madison: University of Wisconsin Press, 2006).
2. Soemarsono, *Revolusi Agustus: kesaksian seorang pelaku sejarah* [The August Revolution: the testimony of an agent of history] (Jakarta: Hasta Mitra, 2008).
3. See, for instance, Paige Johnson Tan, 'Teaching and remembering: The legacy of the Suharto era lingers in school history books', *Inside Indonesia* 92 (Apr–Jun 2008). <http://insideindonesia.org/content/view/1077/47/>.
4. John Lukacs, *Historical Consciousness: or the Remembered Past* (New Brunswick: 1994). For some scholars, the term historical consciousness refers rather to the sense of being located in contingent, historically-specific times. This definition is also useful, but I will not explore it further here. See Ryan Holston, 'On the Meaning of Burke's Historical Consciousness', paper presented at the annual meeting of the Southern Political Science Association, Hotel Intercontinental, New Orleans, 9 Jan 2008. <http://www.allacademic.com/meta/p212657_index.html>.
5. Klaus H. Schreiner, "National ancestors: the ritual construction of nationhood", in *The Potent Dead: Ancestors, Saints and Heroes in Contemporary Indonesia*, edited by Henri Chambert-Loir and Anthony Reid (Honolulu: University of Hawai'i Press, 2002), pp. 183–204; and Klaus H. Schreiner, "The making of national heroes: Guided Democracy to New Order, 1959–1992", in *Outward Appearances: Dressing State and Society in Indonesia*, edited by Henk Schulte Nordholt (Leiden: KITLV, 1997), pp. 259–90.
6. See Tom Earnes Hughes, *Tangled Worlds: The Story of Maria Hertogh* (Singapore: Institute of Southeast Asian Studies, 1980); Haja Maideen, *The Nadra Tragedy:*

the Maria Hertogh Controversy (Petaling Jaya: Pelanduk Publications, 2000); and Syed Muhd. Khairudin Aljunied, *Colonialism, Violence and Muslims in Southeast Asia: The Maria Hertogh Controversy and Its Aftermath* (London: Routledge, 2009).

7. Harry J. Benda, "Democracy in Indonesia" (review of Herbert Feith, *The Decline of Constitutional Democracy in Indonesia* [Ithaca NY: Cornell University Press, 1962]), *Journal of Asian Studies* 23, no. 3 (May 1964): 453.

8. Jacques de Kadt, *De Indonesische tragedie: het treurspel der gemiste kansen* [The Indonesian tragedy: the tragedy of missed opportunities] (Amsterdam: G.A. van Oorschot, 1949); and Anne Booth, *The Indonesian Economy in the Nineteenth and Twentieth Centuries: A History of Missed Opportunities* (New York: St. Martin's Press, 1998).

9. J.D. Legge, "Indonesia's Diversity Revisited", *Indonesia* 49 (1990): 127.

10. Francis Fukuyama, *Trust: The Social Virtues and the Creation of Prosperity* (New York: Free Press, 1995), esp. pp. 149–60.

11. Anthony Reid, *The Contest for North Sumatra: Atjeh, the Netherlands and Britain 1858–1898* (Kuala Lumpur: O.U.P., 1969); Anthony Reid, "Indonesian diplomacy: a documentary study of Atjehnese foreign policy in the reign of Sultan Mahmud, 1870–74", *Journal of the Royal Asiatic Society Malaysian Branch* 42, no. 216, pt. 2 (Dec 1969): 74–114.

12. John R.W. Smail, "On the Possibility of an Autonomous History of Modern Southeast Asia", *Journal of Southeast Asian History* 2, no. 2 (July 1961): 72–102.

13. J.C. van Leur, review of volumes 2 and 3 of Stapel, *Geschiedenis van Nederlandsch Indië* (1939), in J.C. van Leur, *Indonesian Trade and Society* (The Hague: van Hoeve, 1967), pp. 261–67.

14 Anthony J.S. Reid, *The Indonesian National Revolution* (Hawthorn: Longman, 1974).

15. Anthony Reid, *The Blood of the People: Revolution and the End of Traditional Rule in Northern Sumatra* (Kuala Lumpur, OUP, 1979).

16. Anthony Reid, ' "Heaven's Will and Man's Fault": The Rise of the West as a Southeast Asian Dilemma' (Flinders University Asian studies lecture, 1975).

17. Anthony Reid, "Trade and the Problem of Royal Power in Aceh: Three Stages, c.1550–1700", in *Pre-colonial State Systems in Southeast Asia: The Malay Peninsula, Sumatra, Bali-Lombok, South Celebes*, edited by Anthony Reid and Lance Castles (Kuala Lumpur, Malaysian Branch, Royal Asiatic Society, 1975), pp. 45–55.

18. Anthony Reid, "A great seventeenth century Indonesian family: Matoaya and Pattingaloang of Makasar", *Masyarakat Indonesia* 8, no. 1 (1981): 1–28.

19. Denys Lombard, *Le carrefour javanais: essai d'histoire globale* (Paris: Editions de l'Ecole des hautes etudes en sciences sociales, 1990), 3 vols; Fernand Braudel, *La Méditerranée et le Monde Méditerranéen a l'époque de Philippe II* (Paris: Librairie Armand Colin. I949), published in English as *The Mediterranean and the Mediterranean World in the Age of Philip II* (Berkeley: University of California Press, 1996).

20. J.C. van Leur, *Indonesian Trade and Society: Essays in Asian Social and Economic History* (The Hague: W. Van Hoeve, 1955), p. 95.
21. Harry J. Benda, "Decolonization in Indonesia: The Problem of Continuity and Change", *American Historical Review* 70, no. 4 (1965): 1073.
22. Michael D. Barr, *Cultural Politics and Asian Values: The Tepid War* (London: Routledge, 2002).
23. Anthony Reid, "Merdeka: the concept of freedom in Indonesia", in *Asian Freedoms: The Idea of Freedom in East and Southeast Asia*, edited by David Kelly and Anthony Reid (Cambridge: Cambridge University Press, 1998), pp. 141–60.

References

Barr, Michael D. *Cultural Politics and Asian Values: The Tepid War*. London: Routledge, 2002.

Benda, Harry J. 'Democracy in Indonesia' (review of Herbert Feith, *The Decline of Constitutional Democracy in Indonesia* [Ithaca NY: Cornell University Press, 1962]), *Journal of Asian Studies* 23, no. 3 (May 1964): 449–56.

―――. "Decolonization in Indonesia: The Problem of Continuity and Change". *American Historical Review* 70, no. 4 (1965): 1058–73.

Booth, Anne. *The Indonesian Economy in the Nineteenth and Twentieth Centuries: A History of Missed Opportunities*. New York: St. Martin's Press, 1998.

Braudel, Fernand. *La Méditerranée et le Monde Méditerranéen a l'époque de Philippe II*. Paris: Librairie Armand Colin. 1949, published in English as *The Mediterranean and the Mediterranean World in the Age of Philip II*, Berkeley: University of California Press, 1996.

Fukuyama, Francis. *Trust: The Social Virtues and the Creation of Prosperity*. New York: Free Press, 1995.

Hughes, Tom Earnes. *Tangled Worlds: The Story of Maria Hertogh*, Singapore: Institute of Southeast Asian Studies, 1980.

Kadt, Jacques de. *De Indonesische tragedie: het treurspel der gemiste kansen* [The Indonesian tragedy: the tragedy of missed opportunities]. Amsterdam: G.A. van Oorschot, 1949.

Legge, J.D. "Indonesia's Diversity Revisited". *Indonesia* 49 (1990): 127–31.

Leur, J.C. van. *Indonesian Trade and Society: Essays in Asian Social and Economic History*. The Hague: W. Van Hoeve, 1955.

―――. Review of volumes 2 and 3 of Stapel, Geschiedenis van Nederlandsch Indië (1939), in J.C. van Leur, *Indonesian Trade and Society*, pp. 261–67. The Hague: van Hoeve, 1967.

Lombard, Denys. *Le carrefour javanais: essai d'histoire globale*. Paris: Editions de l'Ecole des hautes etudes en sciences sociales, 1990. 3 vols.

Lukacs, John. *Historical Consciousness: or the Remembered Past*. New Brunswick: Transaction Publishers, 1994.

Maideen, Haja. *The Nadra Tragedy: The Maria Hertogh controversy*. Petaling Jaya: Pelanduk Publications, 2000.

Reid, Anthony. "Indonesian Diplomacy: A Documentary Study of Atjehnese Foreign Policy in the Reign of Sultan Mahmud, 1870–74". *Journal of the Royal Asiatic Society Malaysian Branch* 42, pt. 2, no. 216 (Dec 1969): 74–114.

———. *The Contest for North Sumatra: Atjeh, the Netherlands and Britain 1858–1898*. Kuala Lumpur: OUP, 1969.

———. *The Indonesian National Revolution*. Hawthorn: Longman, 1974.

———. *"'Heaven's Will and Man's Fault": The Rise of the West as a Southeast Asian Dilemma'*. Flinders University Asian studies lecture, 1975.

———. "Trade and the problem of royal power in Aceh: three stages, c.1550–1700". In *Pre-colonial State Systems in Southeast Asia: The Malay Peninsula, Sumatra, Bali-Lombok, South Celebes*, edited by Anthony Reid and Lance Castles, Kuala Lumpur, pp. 45–55. Kuala Lumpur: Malaysian Branch, Royal Asiatic Society, 1975.

———. *The Blood of the People: Revolution and the End of Traditional Rule in Northern Sumatra*. Kuala Lumpur: OUP, 1979.

———. "A great seventeenth century Indonesian family: Matoaya and Pattingaloang of Makasar". *Masyarakat Indonesia* 8, no. 1 (1981): 1–28.

———. *Southeast Asia in the Age of Commerce, 1450–1680*. Vol. I: *The Lands below the Winds*. New Haven: Yale University Press, 1988.

———. *Southeast Asia in the Age of Commerce, 1450–1680*. Vol. II: *Expansion and Crisis*. New Haven: Yale University Press, 1993.

———. "Merdeka: The Concept of Freedom in Indonesia". In *Asian freedoms: The Idea of Freedom in East and Southeast Asia*, edited by David Kelly and Anthony Reid, pp. 141–60. Cambridge: Cambridge University Press, 1998.

Roosa, John. *Pretext for Mass Murder: The September 30th Movement and Suharto's Coup d'etat in Indonesia*. Madison: University of Wisconsin Press, 2006.

Schreiner, Klaus H. "The Making of National Heroes: Guided Democracy to New Order, 1959–1992". In *Outward appearances: dressing state and society in Indonesia*, edited by Henk Schulte Nordholt, pp. 259–87. Leiden: KITLV, 1997.

———. "National ancestors: the ritual construction of nationhood". In *The Potent Dead: Ancestors, Saints and Heroes in Contemporary Indonesia*, edited by Henri Chambert-Loir and Anthony Reid, pp. Honolulu: University of Hawai'i Press, 2002.

Smail, John R.W. "On the Possibility of an Autonomous History of Modern Southeast Asia". *Journal of Southeast Asian History* 2 no. 2 (July 1961): 72–102.

Soemarsono. *Revolusi Agustus: kesaksian seorang pelaku sejarah* [The August Revolution: the testimony of an agent of history]. Jakarta: Hasta Mitra, 2008.

Syed Muhd. Khairudin Aljunied. *Colonialism, Violence and Muslims in Southeast Asia: The Maria Hertogh Controversy and Its Aftermath*. London: Routledge, 2009.

Tan, Paige Johnson. "Teaching and remembering: The legacy of the Suharto era lingers in school history books". *Inside Indonesia* 92 (Apr–Jun 2008). <http://insideindonesia.org/content/view/1077/47/>.

PART III
Southeast Asia in the World

3

SOUTHEAST ASIA AND EURASIA DURING A THOUSAND YEARS*

Victor Lieberman

In 1792 the French monarchy imploded. Between 1799 and 1815 a new Parisian regime improved administrative efficiency, while dramatically extending French territory. French conquests precipitated imitative reforms across Europe and a permanent reduction in the number of independent states.

Between 1752 and 1786 the Burmese, Siamese, and Vietnamese kingdoms all collapsed. In each realm, a more dynamic leadership succeeded in rebuilding state authority and extending its territorial writ. Ensuing wars between reinvigorated empires accelerated competitive reform and permanently reduced the number of independent mainland Southeast Asian states.

How shall we explain these synchronized parallels between far-flung sectors of Eurasia? Surely, one might reply, no explanation is needed: the cultural contexts were so different, the political and interstate systems so unique, as to render these parallels curious, but basically meaningless coincidence.

Closer consideration, however, suggests that more was involved. In fact, the late 1700s ended the third and initiated the last of four cycles of consolidation which were synchronized between much of Europe and mainland Southeast Asia and which spanned the better part of a millennium. The first synchronized consolidation, marked by extremely rapid economic growth, began in the tenth century and concluded with a generalized political and social breakdown lasting, depending on local context, for much of the period from the mid-thirteenth to the mid-fifteenth century. Political integration resumed in the mid-1400s, but between 1550 and 1610 the chief Southeast Asian states, as well as France and Russia again collapsed. Reforms in the early and mid-seventeenth century inaugurated a third phase of consolidation — one that ended with the late eighteenth century collapse and dramatic revivals with which I opened.

Why, then, should distant regions, with no obvious cultural or economic links, have experienced more or less coordinated cycles? Moreover, why did interregna in both mainland Southeast Asia and much of Europe become ever shorter and less disruptive? In virtually every case, the thirteenth/fifteenth century collapse was longer and more dislocative than the late sixteenth crisis, which was more destructive than late eighteenth century disturbances.

Or to reverse the terms of inquiry so as to pose a yet more basic problem: Why in the second millennium did societies in mainland Southeast Asia as well as Europe grow more politically and culturally coherent? Whereas Europe as a whole in 1450 had some 500 political units, by the late nineteenth century the number was closer to 30. Between 1450 and 1825 some 23 independent Southeast Asian kingdoms collapsed into three. Increased size notwithstanding, each survivor was more effectively centralized than any local predecessor. At the same time in European and Southeast Asian realms alike, the dialect, religion, and ethnicity of capital elites entered into more sustained dialogue with provincial and popular traditions. Only between c. 1400 and 1825 did Burmese, Siamese, Vietnamese, French, and Russian ethnicities cohere and come to dominate extensive territories that bore their name. Why, then, these parallel consolidations between lands at the ends of the earth, as it were? Why too did the Japanese islands exhibit many of these same patterns, including accelerating cultural unity and an unprecedented political consolidation between 1600 and 1850?

In his justly celebrated *Southeast Asia in the Age of Commerce*[1] and in numerous essays, Tony Reid was first to challenge scholars to think about precolonial Southeast Asia as a coherent region and to relate its history to wider global patterns. It is in this spirit of comparative inquiry that I raise these questions. Following on Tony's work, I seek most basically to connect mainland Southeast Asia to world history and thus to continue Tony's critique of Orientalist encapsulation, that assumption of irreducible idiosyncrasy and peculiarity, that long dominated writing on our part of the world. But in exploring extra-regional comparisons, I seek also to influence broader discussions that began in the late twentieth century about the long-term relation between white-skinned peoples and the rest of the world generally. That is to say, in qualifying Orientalism, sustained comparisons promise to weaken Orientalism's inseparable twin, European exceptionalism.[2]

A regnant trope from the 1700s until the 1990s and still enormously influential both in the academy and among the educated public, European exceptionalism claims that the history of Europe, or at least Western Europe, differs fundamentally from that of the rest of mankind. The twin glories of modernity, industrialization and democracy, reflect peculiarly European cultural features — including a stress on individual autonomy, secure property rights, contract, and empirical inquiry — apparent since at least the middle ages.[3]

To date, critics of European exceptionalism have pursued three principal approaches. First, scholars have tried to find Asian analogues to specifically European socio-political institutions, among which feudalism and the public sphere have been most popular. On the whole, these inquiries have borne modest fruit — and in many cases, have been abandoned — because the terms of reference proved too narrow.

A second, more successful line of inquiry pioneered by James Lee and his collaborators has shown that the hallowed dichotomy between high fertility, high mortality regimes in Asia and low fertility, low mortality regimes in Europe is grossly overdrawn.[4]

A third line of inquiry, comparing industrial potential in pre-1850 Europe and Asia, has generated the most lively interest, but has failed to produce a consensus. Although all accept that commerce and handicrafts in pre-1820 Japan, China, India, as well as Southeast Asia, grew more specialized, there is little agreement as to why these movements proved less conducive to industrialization than in Western Europe, or at least Britain.[5]

I attempt to develop a fourth axis of Eurasian comparison, namely, long-term trends to political and cultural integration. To be sure, we already have a modest comparative literature on pre-1850 Eurasian state formation, but none that seeks to explain parallel political and cultural consolidations over widely-dispersed areas for sustained periods, and certainly none that features Southeast Asia. The potential virtue of my approach is two-fold. First, it promises a fresh view of Eurasia during a thousand years as a synchronized ecumene in which European forms of integration constituted local variants on more widespread patterns. This is not to deny European specificities, as in some sense all regions, by definition, were unique. Yet in using Southeast Asia to direct attention to hitherto ignored commonalities, I reject, or qualify substantially, Samuel Huntington's oft-cited dichotomy between the West and the Rest.[6] Second and somewhat ironically given its synthetic vision, my approach promises to enrich local studies by teasing out overarching factors from local variables. For example, if we accept that France, Kiev, Pagan, Angkor, and Vietnam all enjoyed unprecedented economic vitality between

900 and 1250, in each case we are obliged to weigh the relation between local factors and those substantially independent of local context, including climate, global epidemics, and interregional commerce.

The countries on which I focus were all part of what I term the "protected rimlands," protected in the sense that they were insulated against long-term occupation by Inner Asian nomads. As such they experienced a peculiarly autonomous form of political evolution that may be distinguished, in varying degrees, from patterns in Southwest Asia, South Asia, and China. To illustrate these trends, I consider, for Europe, France and Russia (although any number of realms could have served) and, for northeast Asia, Japan. Thus with Burma, Siam, and Vietnam, we have six examples of indigenous-led consolidation around the Eurasian perimeter during roughly a thousand years, 800 to 1800.

Obviously, even this select category contains enormously diverse potentials. For example, if we adopt Charles Tilley's device of arranging states along a continuum from capital-intensive to coercion-intensive,[7] among the six states under review, France, where serfdom effectively disappeared by 1500, lay closest to the capital-intensive pole. Thinly populated and substantially dependent on hereditary bound labour, Russia, Burma, and Siam represented a more coercion-dependent path. Japan and Vietnam lay somewhere in between. Whereas France in 1800 supported an increasingly Weberian bureaucracy with three levels of appointed officials between Paris and the frontiers, Burma and Siam remained patrimonial solar polities, with only one layer of appointees, vast unadministered hill regions, and royal authority ebbing so gradually as to preclude any notion of fixed frontiers.[8]

One could multiply distinctions of this sort indefinitely. How extraordinary, how puzzling, how demanding of explanation, then, is the fact that all these idiosyncratic realms, ranged around the edges of Eurasia and enjoying little or no contact, should have followed broadly comparable developmental trajectories at roughly the same time. I do not pretend that the resultant concentrations of power were similar. I do claim, however, that within each region, judged by local standards, political and cultural cohesion in 1825 exceeded that in 1600, which exceeded that in 1400, and so forth. And within each region integration accelerated markedly from 1600 to 1825.

Let me unpack the argument by considering for all six realms three broad indices of integration, namely, territorial organization, administrative centralization, and cultural homogenization. To be sure, these criteria hardly exhaust the possibilities for Eurasian classification. Different comparative criteria — urbanization, gender relations, literary production, population densities, agrarian productivity, technological creativity, social structure

— would yield very different, but no less valid, alignments of Eurasian realms. Obviously too, here I can provide only the most schematic overview, but I am hopeful that the novelty of these views will compensate for their brevity.

First, then, territorial integration. Lying on the periphery of established civilizations, in the late first or early second millennium all six regions imported from older Eurasian centres world religions and systems of writing and administration that helped generate what I term "charter states," in which category I include Pagan, Angkor, early Vietnam, the Frankish kingdom, Kiev, and *ritsuryo* Japan. That is to say, each state, the first indigenous supra-local polity in its area, provided an institutional, cultural, and territorial charter for all subsequent formations. Bolstered by imported cultural technologies and rapid economic growth, each exerted authority over an unprecedented territory, although by later standards that authority was unstable and spatially limited. Finally, at various times between 1240 and 1470 all six charter polities disintegrated through a combination of factors to be considered shortly.

Post-charter crises differed in frequency and severity. Such differences aside, in each region territorial consolidation resumed between 1450 and 1600 and continued to gain strength into the early 1800s. As noted, the 23 Southeast Asian states of 1450 were reduced to three, the antecedents of Burma, Thailand, and Vietnam, while in Europe 500 dwindled to about 30. Or to view the same process from a different angle, in Vietnam, Burma, Siam, and Russia, imperial territories in 1825 were one-and-a-half to five times larger than in 1600. For Japan, able to expand only in Ryukyu and Hokkaido, the figure was below 25 per cent, and for post-1600 France about ten per cent. Such differences aside, in every realm between 800/900 and 1825 not only did the amount of territory controlled by the dominant regional power rise dramatically, not only did successive eras of collapse become shorter and less catastrophic, but periods of consolidation and fragmentation themselves correlated ever more closely among these six regions.[9]

Along with territorial integration, a second feature shared by all six realms was a sustained trend toward administrative centralization. Because larger domains required more efficient control, while the concentration of resources that flowed from better coordination aided conquest and colonization, external expansion and internal reform reinforced one another and followed a similar cyclic-cum-secular rhythm.

Charter administrations tended to be superficial, personalistic, substantially dependent on religious institutions for local control, and content with a largely ritualistic overlordship. Even after the charter era, most states remained concentric ring systems, that is, closely administered cores surrounded by provinces whose autonomy increased with distance. If Southeast Asian solar polities represented unusually decentralized versions, this basic description applies as well to ancien regime France, Muscovy, and Tokugawa Japan. At the same time, however, and especially after 1450 or 1550, we find in each polity a long-term tendency for peripheral zones and autonomous enclaves to assimilate to the status of core provinces, and for systems of extraction and coordination in the core to grow more efficient. In this extension of central control, moreover, broadly comparable strategies were at work. In the early stages, centralization usually entailed not the destruction, but the subordination of outlying political units, whose loyalty the capital ensured by manipulating patronage and/or by subordinating those units to an overarching network of specialized royal officials. If in the short term this mosaic strategy placed obvious limits on integration, it also reduced the financial costs of integration for the capital and the psychological costs for outlying populations.

In the charter era, religious institutions enjoyed extensive autonomy, but as post-1500 states grew more competent, lay authorities in all six realms moved to reclaim much of the authority and wealth. Revolutionary France was unique in the violence of its anticlerical assault, but not in the principle of state supremacy.

Likewise, especially from the early 1600s, in order to enhance the throne's military power and to restore order after severe upheavals, central authorities in all six societies sought to limit social mobility and to extend censuses and cadastres. Russian serfdom, Burmese and Siamese systems of hereditary royal service, Tokugawa estate divisions and curbs on social and geographic mobility, and French Counter-Reformation controls in city and countryside all testified to this trend.

In Southeast Asian kingdoms and those territories that cohered as Japan, France, and Russia, we also find sustained movements toward vertical and horizontal integration of culture, that is, of language, religion, and ultimately, ethnicity. Dependent on invisible capillary processes as well as public directives, this process exhibited a more gradual trajectory than territorial or administrative change. Along with territorial and administrative consolidation, cultural integration, then, is a third feature shared by all rimlands under review.

Whereas in 1000 each lowland sector of mainland Southeast Asia had supported two to four competing ethnicities and whereas popular religions had been preliterate and animist, in each sector by 1800 a single ethnicity-cum-language — Burmese, Siamese, Vietnamese — had become incontestably dominant, while both elites and peasantry supported basically the same textually-based religious/cultic system. In Japan, according to one authority, if there is one marked characteristic of the post-charter years, it is a clear sense of a coming together for the first time of hitherto distinct subcultures, both regional and class-specific.[10] The vertical penetration of Orthodoxy and the horizontal extension of Great Russian ethnicity from the Volga-Oka heartland to the eastern Ukraine and to the Volga and Don basins testified to similar integrative thrusts, as did the conversion of France from a polyglot empire to a realm in which Parisian French, though hardly universal even in 1825, was incontestably dominant. Tied to a host of practices ranging from dress to literature to nuptiality, Parisian dialect became key to participation in national culture. In Burma, Siam, Vietnam, Japan, Russia, and France, albeit in varying degrees, rising literacy, the development of more popular literary genres, and the displacement of universal languages (Pali, Sanskrit, Chinese, Latin) by capital-based vernacular tongues and syllabaries reflected and facilitated expansion in interregional and interclass communication.

How cohesive were pre-nineteenth century cultures? In many ways, of course, integration remained quite limited. On the one hand, these trends were too weak in that often they breached geographic and social isolates only episodically, leaving identities fluid and situationally contingent. On the other hand, these trends were too strong in the sense that the same dynamics as encouraged amalgamation could nurture countervailing currents. Efforts to impose official culture sparked open resistance, including anti-centralizing revolts, and all manner of hidden subversion. If international circuits increased the power of the state, those same circuits could draw imperial elites away from the traditions of their own peasantries, as happened to varying degrees in Petrine Russia and post-1460 Vietnam. Most critical, market specialization nurtured diversity, hence psychological fracture, in aesthetic and religious expression and in consumer habits. Finally, even in Europe to the mid-1700s, governments continued to conceptualize their authority in primarily dynastic and religious terms that were universalist, polyethnic, and hierarchical, and thus distinct from the modern nationalist exaltation of discrete secular cultures and civic equality.

Nonetheless, not only did such universal ideologies coexist with intensifying, if undertheorized official patronage of secular culture, but in many contexts universal religious and local ethnic identities proved mutually reinforcing. The fact that Muscovites, by definition, were Orthodox while their chief enemies were non-Orthodox encouraged a recurrent, if imperfect, fusion of ethnicity, religion, and political loyalty reminiscent of those cleavages that pitted Khmers against Vietnamese and Burmese against Siamese. If the Japanese faced no obvious external enemy, Tokugawa advocates of "nativist learning" encouraged a sense of Japanese alterity to China. Louis XIV's motto "one king, one law, one faith" expressed protonational aspiration as well as Counter-Reformation fervour. Like modern nationalism, such movements promoted specific symbols — linguistic, sartorial, religious, ritualistic — as badges of political inclusion. So too, long before 1800 the slowly rising proportion of subjects willing to identify culturally with each capital anticipated nineteenth- and twentieth-century trends.

In sum, in Russia, Japan, France, and each of mainland Southeast Asia's three principal corridors, after 1450 and more especially 1700, once self-sufficient entities became more closely linked politically and culturally. The incorporation of local isolates (economic, political, cultural) into larger systems that at the same time were more complex and internally specialized resembled the movement in biology from single-cell to multi-cell organisms. But what dynamics were at work? So far I have said little about underlying pressures for change.

My basic argument is this: Within each region economic expansion, new cultural currents, interstate competition, and state initiatives combined to link local societies and to strengthen emergent imperial cores at the expense of outlying areas. Each phenomenon had a certain autonomy, but all reinforced and modified one another.

In considering economic organization, again we are dealing with wide discrepancies in form and productivity. That said, all six realms experienced cumulative, if episodic increases in population and output. Within 1825 boundaries, between 1300 and 1825 the population of France rose roughly 50 per cent, those of Burma and Siam perhaps 100 per cent, those of Vietnam and Japan some 250 per cent, and of Russia 600 to 900 per cent. Everywhere frontier reclamation entailed extensive growth, but population increase also helped to raise productivity in agriculture and handicrafts. Particularly from the late 1400s to the early 1600s and again in the eighteenth century, international trade powerfully reinforced local Smithian specialization by widening market access, enhancing bullion stocks, and introducing novel crops, technologies, and consumer goods.

Such growth tended to multiply in cumulative fashion the superiority of privileged districts — Southeast Asian lowlands, the Volga-Oka interfluve, the Paris basin, the Kinai-Kanto axis in Japan — over more marginal areas. Even if core and periphery grew at the same pace, the core's initial superiority ensured a self-reproducing absolute advantage. Yet, at least to 1650 in most cases, growth rates in the core tended to exceed those in outer zones. Furthermore, the development of national markets, which usually implied a concentration of higher level functions in each capital region, meant that even where colonization and overseas trade became major engines of growth, the centre retained critical benefits. Such advantages allowed the capital to pyramid its powers of coercion and attraction.

Not only the scale, but the nature of each political economy changed. In all six realms we find a movement from subsistence to market production, from land grants to stipends, and (with the partial exception of Japan) from in-kind to cash taxes, all of which facilitated central control. Frequently the key to centralization lay in the inclination of local elites not only to support, but to create, a coordinating agency that could guarantee commercial privileges, adjudicate disputes, standardize weights, measures, and currency; and share expanded tax revenues. In this sense, integration reflected local initiatives as much as top-down imposition.

Much the same could be said of new cultural currents. Local markets disseminated central dialects, religious practices, and fashions; while along the agricultural frontier, settlers tied more or less closely to imperial culture confronted alien populations. Frequently the initiative for linguistic and ritual standardization came not from the throne, content to rule over a polyglot realm, but from provincial elites eager to boost their prestige by imitating court practices.[11] In all six realms literacy rose sharply after 1500, again through multiple pressures: administrative routinization demanded more literate record-keepers, religious reform bred a hunger for textual authority, while commercial intensification lent numeracy and literacy greater practical value and provided the wherewithal for new educational infrastructures. If, as the Reformation shows, literacy could be deeply subversive, more generally the circulation of texts sanctioned by the centre encouraged identification with its political claims, while literacy by its very nature facilitated what James Scott terms "administrative legibility." Religious/cultic reform frequently had similar standardizing implications. In varying degrees, Theravada and Neo-Confucian reform, Tridentine Catholicism, and Russian Orthodoxy aligned personal salvation with public discipline, instilled respect for hierarchy, pacified peasants without a direct commitment of royal resources, and thus made local governance more feasible.[12]

As polities cohered in response to multiple pressures, as once independent principalities were cannibalized, as warfare grew in scale and expense, would-be survivors were compelled to overhaul their military and fiscal systems. If Darwinian pressures of this sort proved more intense in Europe than in Southeast Asia, in both regions virtually every major administrative change between 1450 and 1800 responded to bellicist imperatives. War also assisted cultural integration by encouraging identification with central norms against those of an alien, minatory "other." Japan was an exception proving the rule: absence of an external threat contributed to Japan's unusually glacial administrative change and, despite dense communication circuits, to a comparatively weak sense of ethnic alterity. Conversely, Japan's period of most rapid administrative change, 1470–1610, was the era of most intense civil war.

As administrative capacity grew, in order to bolster its patronage and military prospects, each state self-consciously sought to strengthen its economic base, whether through colonization and settlement, sponsorship of new crops and technologies, monetary reform, or commercial initiatives. "[O]ne cannot help but be struck," Jan de Vries has written of Europe between 1600 and 1750, "by the seemingly symbiotic relationship…between the state, military power, and the private economy's efficiency…"[13] Consider too the unintended economic impact of government actions. For example, in all six realms, territorial unification, although preeminently a political act, served to lower transaction costs by standardizing measurements, reducing tolls, widening legal jurisdictions, concentrating urban demand, and connecting ports and hinterland more directly.

Similarly, Ava, Ayudhya, Versailles, Moscow, and Edo functioned as cultural arbiters in ways both accidental and deliberate. By appealing to a combination of snobbery and practical ambition, political patronage offered a powerful, if unintended, spur to provincial imitation. The growing circulation of government documents and legal decisions had a similar standardizing effect. More self-consciously, capitals sought to unify aesthetic, linguistic, and above all, religious practices; to organize national pantheons, to integrate local social hierarchies, to standardize legal codes, and to weaken the cultures of refractory minorities.

In short, in France, Russia, Japan, and each of mainland Southeast Asia's three chief sectors, integration reflected a synergy between local movements of economic and cultural change, intensifying warfare, and wider state interventions. As webs of interdependence and specialization grew more dense, as supralocal economic and cultural linkages became more stable, political integration grew more normative, as suggested by the tendency for successive interregna to grow shorter and less disruptive. Tethered, the stallion grew less violent.

But why synchronization across widely-separated Eurasian rimlands? Why did these areas march more or less in tandem? The most obvious agent of coordination, namely long-distance trade, was not invariably most potent.

In the charter era c. 900–1250, the vigorous economic growth that we find in most realms reflected the intersection of local institutional and social factors with global climate, disease, and long-distance exchange. During the Medieval Climate Anomaly (also known as the Medieval Warm Period) of these same centuries, temperatures in the northern hemisphere rose by some 0.8–2 degrees Celsius. In northwestern Europe and Russia by extending the growing season by as much as eight weeks, by permitting the cultivation of rich, hitherto waterlogged bottomlands, and by reducing mortality among draft animals and humans alike, warmer drier weather improved agrarian yields, enhanced nuptiality, and contributed to rapid population increase. In these same centuries, by magnifying the land-sea thermal gradient on which monsoons feed, global warming strengthened monsoon rains, to the benefit of irrigated rice and settlement, in much of South, Southeast, and East Asia. Thus the Medieval Climate Anomaly helped to coordinate charter-era demography in ostensibly independent regions.[14] In this same period, that is c. 900–1250, in several Eurasian rimlands denser populations and more regular contacts with older centres may have begun to convert smallpox and measles from almost uniformly lethal epidemics of adults to less economically and demographically disastrous diseases of children.[15] At the same time, strong population growth not only in rimlands but in South Asia and South China fed long-distance trade, which had cultural as well as economic benefits for initially preliterate rimland cultures.

The political collapse of the late thirteenth to fifteenth centuries in much of Europe and Southeast Asia reflected, in part, strains characteristic of the previous period and reversed critical charter-era processes. In the densely settled cores of Burma, Angkor, Vietnam, and France, by 1250 three centuries of sustained reclamation had created growing shortages of quality arable land. In varying degrees, all four cores suffered ecological strains and intensifying conflicts for control of the surplus. By compressing the north European growing season and severely weakening Southeast Asian monsoons, the onset of the Little Ice Age in the late thirteenth and fourteenth centuries dramatically compounded these problems. So too, in Southeast Asia, Russia, as well as Japan, disproportionately rapid agrarian and/or commercial expansion on the periphery intensified centrifugal political strains. Long-standing institutional fissures, papered over during centuries of prosperity, now widened. The Hundred Years War — pivoting on the contradiction between early Capetian tolerance for overlapping spheres of influence and the more exclusive ambitions of the centralizing Valois and English states — offers perhaps the best known example, but recurrent succession disputes in the Kievan federation and endemic tensions between the throne and wealthy monastic institutions in Pagan proved no less debilitating. Finally, the Mongols intensified Eurasia's crisis in two ways. On the one hand, they transmitted the Black Death from Inner Asia to Europe. This was both a random epidemiological event and an artifact of commercial intensification insofar as it spread along interregional trade routes opened during the antecedent era of prosperity. On the other hand, Mongol attacks destroyed

Kiev, weakened Kamakura Japan, and, in combination with Tai movements, disrupted Southeast Asian charter states.

Political revivals across mainland Southeast Asia, France, Russia, and Japan between 1450 and 1600 benefited from both cyclic and secular shifts. In one region after another, long periods of disorder produced compensatory improvements in finance, transport, industry, and administrative technique — what in Europe has been termed "a harvest of adversity."[16] In other words, we find in widely-separated areas parallel, but quite independent, economic and institutional responses to antecedent crises. Such adjustments allowed fifteenth-century societies to start from a higher technical level than their charter predecessors. Modest post-1480 climatic amelioration and, in Europe, a marked demographic recovery from the plague reinforced this revival.

To such quasi-cyclic factors must be added truly novel elements after 1500. New World crops increased the utility of marginal lands in Southeast and East Asia. More critical, world bullion stocks rose in response to demographic revival and an associated increase in Eurasian trade, especially in China, whose insatiable silver appetite drove up the price for Japanese and then freshly discovered New World bullion to the point where once impractical extraction techniques became profitable. Between 1450 and 1650 the resultant tripling of the world's silver bullion supply lubricated market exchange across Eurasia.[17] In one realm after another monetization and commercial intensification facilitated fiscal extraction and, by spurring literacy, pilgrimage, communications, and the commodification of culture, promoted the vertical and horizontal diffusion of elite and capital norms. In this same period, that is c. 1450 to 1650, European-style firearms spurred political consolidation not only in Europe, but in Japan and Southeast Asia. True, neither of the latter regions experienced the full revolution in infantry training and drill, fort construction, or naval warfare that we find in Europe. Yet after 1550, in Japan, Burma, Siam, and Vietnam, not to mention western and eastern Europe, the high costs of handguns, cannon, and gun-resistant fortifications, and the associated demand for fiscal and logistical experiment, conferred a cumulative advantage on the wealthiest, most innovative polities.

Again, commercial and military advances also carried destabilizing potential. In the late 1500s, rapid population growth and price inflation joined territorial overextension encouraged by the large-scale introduction of firearms to produce a new round of collapse in Southeast Asia, Russia, and France. So too, if Enlightenment notions of secular progress and national community lacked even remote Asian echoes, the European and Southeast Asian crises of the late 1700s with which I opened this inquiry also had common generic roots in rapid commercial and demographic growth. But hopefully enough has been said to outline, if not to prove, my basic thesis that widely separated rimlands shared a pattern of sustained construction punctuated by cyclic collapse and compensatory innovation.

Let me now shift to comment more briefly on other sectors of Eurasia. The concept of "protected rimlands," in which category I have placed most of Europe, mainland Southeast Asia, and Japan, assumes significance only in contrast to what might be termed the "exposed zone" of Eurasia, in which category I include the eastern Mediterranean, Southwest Asia, South Asia, and China.

To be sure, many of the same forces as promoted integration in the protected zone — demographic and agrarian expansion, commercialization, wider literacy, firearms, accumulated institutional expertise and interstate pressures — encouraged integration in the exposed zone as well. I hardly seek to replace the East-West binary with a new dichotomy between protected and exposed zones. In terms of demographic waves and a persistent trend toward more complex political organizations and more rapid cultural circulation, I see no basic distinction between the six realms we have considered, on the one hand, and China and South Asia, on the other.

For example, in China — *locus classicus* of the dynastic cycle — successive imperial breakdowns grew shorter and less institutionally disruptive. Assuming sophisticated form as early as the Song, the late imperial system of civil service examinations, bureaucratic jurisdictions, civilian supremacy, and official-gentry cooperation enjoyed its greatest demographic and territorial reach, and arguably its greatest political stability, in the eighteenth century under the Qing. Between the original Han charter unification and 1800, Chinese imperial territories more than doubled, with particularly dramatic expansion in the late seventeenth and eighteenth centuries, as was also true of Southeast Asian realms and Russia. So too, over an unusually long period but with a marked acceleration from the sixteenth to nineteenth centuries, in what was surely one of Eurasia's most successful examples of cultural homogenization, Chinese writing and ethnicity spread into what is now south, southwest, and western China.[18]

In South Asia, integration was far more fragile and limited than in either the protected rimlands or China, but in South Asia too we find that intervals between successive subcontinental empires diminished. As the most territorially expansive, fiscally penetrating, and culturally hegemonic empire in precolonial Indian history, beneficiary of firearms, bullion flows, new commercial linkages, and cumulative institutional expertise, the Mughal realm of c. 1560–1710 may be compared to such contemporary formations as Toungoo/Konbaung Burma, Late Ayudhya/early Chakri Siam, Nguyen Vietnam, Bourbon France,

Romanov Russia, and Qing China. Likewise the southward diffusion, first, of Sanskritic and, then, of Perso-Islamic culture, the northward spread of *bhakti* devotional cults, the growing post-1650 salience of Brahmanical notions of caste, and the continuous expansion of settled agriculture and commercial circuits encouraged a real, if modest, degree of vertical and horizontal cultural exchange across the subcontinent. Albeit with local twists, economic trends and associated political patterns in South Asia also followed a broadly familiar rhythm, including a surge in population and output between c. 850 and 1300 and again between 1450 and 1700.[19]

How, then, did China and South Asia differ from Southeast Asia and other protected rimlands? I see critical differences in charter chronology, Inner Asian exposure, and imperial scale.

Most obvious, state and literate culture formation in North China and the Indo-Gangetic plain (as well as in Southwest Asia) began one to three thousand years earlier than in the protected zone. This very precocity allowed these areas to serve as civilizational donors to the protected rimlands. As we have seen, the latter, lying on the periphery of older city-based civilizations, underwent charter state formation only in the late first or early second millennium.

Further, as befits my basic distinction between protected and exposed zones, China, India, and other areas lay open to ever more insistent occupation by nomadic cavalry from the steppes and forests of Inner Asia. In western and northern Europe, Japan, and Southeast Asia, forests, inadequate pasture, malarial climate, or ocean barriers inhibited such incursions. Even in Russia, subject to Mongol-Tatar suzerainty from 1240, not only did nomads leave governance entirely to Russian princes, who maintained an ethnic and Orthodox identity distinct from that of their steppe overlords, but Tatar political influence declined sharply after 1380. Thus, in all protected rimlands political and cultural evolution remained in indigenous hands.

By contrast, in India, China, and other parts of the exposed zone, political integration came to rely on Inner Asian conquerors — Khitans, Jurchens, Mongols, and Manchus in China; Turko-Mongols, seconded by Tajiks and Afghans in South Asia — whose growing power throughout most of the second millennium dramatically altered local trajectories. In these areas, Inner Asians became the chief agents if not of early modernity, then certainly of pre-1850 integration. South Asia, for example, between c. 550 and 1200 remained divided among modest regional states whose increasingly coherent personalities suggest that South Asia was headed toward a permanent multistate system not unlike that of Europe. But after 1200 Muslim Turkic invaders imposed a genuinely novel imperial vision that assumed its most awesome form in the Mughal empire. In China, without the Mongols, north and south — which

Marco Polo considered different countries — may never have come together; and without the Manchus, China surely never would have been joined to Manchuria, Mongolia, Xinjiang, and Tibet. Administratively, Inner Asians also brought local governance to unprecedented levels of efficiency, in China by improving indigenous systems (the Manchus were determined to show skeptical Chinese that they could operate Confucian bureaucracy better than the Chinese themselves), in India by introducing substantially novel systems of Persian and Near Eastern origin.

In cultural terms too, Inner Asian rule carried peculiar signatures reflecting the goals and insecurity of tiny conquest elites. Whereas in the protected rimland states, elite and mass, at least in the core, shared a common ethnicity, language, and religion, Inner Asian conquerors, to ensure cohesion, self-consciously sought to preserve a separate identity which Mark Elliott, writing of the Qing, terms "ethnic sovereignty" or "Manchu apartheid."[20] In India Mughal cohesion and self-image had both ethnic and religious bases. Such distinctions endured despite Manchu-Chinese and Turkic-Indian political accommodations and long-term assimilation. Fearful that politicized popular ethnicity would be directed against them, Inner Asian conquest elites looked askance on the sort of protonational mobilization that enjoyed increasing, if still episodic, official sanction in Burma, Siam, Vietnam, France, and Russia. Whereas protected rimland elites disseminated their culture as an aid to stability, the Manchus (although periodically acquiescing in Sinification projects among southwest aboriginals) decided that stability required not only elaborate institutional barriers between themselves and Chinese, but determined efforts to preserve Manchu cultural distinctiveness. And if the Mughals encouraged Islamic conversion among their subjects, their growing insistence on Islamic ritual sovereignty at the expense of non-Muslim faiths and their marked preference for fellow Inner Asians over indigenous warrior elites had somewhat the same insulating effect as Manchu policies. I would note in passing that in island Southeast Asia, Iberian and Dutch conquest elites, coming by sea, played a territorially integrative, culturally encapsulated role similar in some ways to that of Manchus and Mughals, coming overland.[21]

In the case of China and South Asia (as well as Southwest Asia), there is reason to believe that these two features — civilizational precocity and exposure to Inner Asian conquest — were organically related. In the second and first millennia BCE relatively easy intercourse between Eurasian heartlands gave these areas access to cultural, technological, and biological inputs that encouraged state formation far earlier than in the more isolated and impoverished rimlands. But later, this same exposure left the heartlands more or less defenseless against nomadic cavalry.

Along with civilizational precocity and exposure to Inner Asian conquest, a third distinguishing feature of South Asia and China was the vast size of imperial lands and populations. This in turn imposed limits on progressive centralization stricter than in most protected zone realms. At first glance, Russia, with its extensive territories, again would seem to defy inclusion in the rimland category, but in fact Russia's modest population, that population's heavy concentration in the western sector of the empire, and Russia's involvement in the European multistate system proved fully compatible with sustained, long-term, accelerating centralization. By contrast, for most of Indian history, centrifugal geography, pervasive rural militarization, and parcelized sovereignty decreed that the subcontinent would oscillate between relatively short-lived periods of imperial unity and longer eras of polycentrism. As a result, links between successive subcontinental empires were relatively weak, regional literatures luxuriated, and South Asia's linguistic and cultural map remained fragmented much as was true of Europe at large. Like their Delhi Sultanate predecessors (1206–1398), the Mughals failed to secure stable control over the Deccan or South India. Indeed, desultory Mughal campaigns in the Deccan overstrained imperial resources and contributed directly to imperial collapse.[22]

The Qing were more fortunate than the Mughals because Chinese geography was inherently less centrifugal than Indian, because China's logographic script inhibited regional literary cultures even as phonetic Indian alphabets encouraged them, and because civil service examinations, Sinic bureaucracy, and Confucianism provided superb instruments of social and political standardization without close Indian analogue. These were symptom and cause of imperial vigor, and after crushing the Western Mongols in the 1750s, the Qing, unlike the Mughals, faced no credible military threats.

Yet the extraordinary size of Qing territory (some 11,000,000 square kilometres) and population (some 350 million in 1800) precluded the sort of progressive administrative penetration that we find around the protected rimlands. This is not to say that by some absolute standard, levels of local control and extraction in, say, Burma and Siam in 1800 exceeded those in Qing China. But I do claim that Burma and Siam had yet to exhaust the potential of pre-industrial administrative technologies, whereas China had reached those limits substantially by the Southern Song (1127–1279). Thereafter for the bureaucracy to have expanded at the same rate as the Chinese population would have exceeded the centre's capacity for administrative coordination and control, threatening systemic breakdown. Thus, whereas in all six protected rimland states under review the ratio of appointed officials to subjects grew notably between 1000 and 1800, China in the same period was obliged to reduce that ratio sharply, to devolve societal management from officials to local elites, and to compensate with a greater emphasis on cultural instruments of control and on ad hoc understandings between officials, sub-bureaucrats, and gentry. Likewise and again in contrast to rimland states, the absence of credible military rivals reduced Chinese pressures for military innovation — which virtually ceased after 1700 — and for fiscal maximization.[23] By best estimates, the proportion of national wealth that the Qing took in taxes in 1780 was only 26 to 40 per cent of that collected in France, England, or Russia.[24] In truth, fiscal restraint, like bureaucratic self-limitation, may have been less luxury than necessity. For if we accept that imperial size mandated declining official-to-subject ratios and substantial practical devolution, to have attempted European-style taxation might have antagonized independent local elites to such a degree as to imperil central control. By this logic, stable subcontinental dominion and limited taxation were two sides of the same coin.

In conclusion, I have made several large claims, all of which seek to use Southeast Asia's marginal position with Eurasia — a marginality both physical and historiographic — as a leverage point from which to pry open new understandings of Southeast Asia and Eurasia over several centuries. Precisely because mainland Southeast Asian states were relatively small and isolated, their sustained participation in wider patterns shows in particularly dramatic form the functional unity of Eurasia, in particular the coherence of its protected rimlands. Innumerable particularities aside, between c. 800 and 1830 realms in mainland Southeast Asia, Europe, and Japan followed surprisingly synchronized trajectories toward territorial, administrative, and cultural integration. At a workable level of abstraction, the dynamics of integration were comparable. Finally, despite numerous pan-Eurasian features, in chronology, in protection against Inner Asian conquest, in elite-mass cultural configurations, and in problems of scale, the rimlands were in varying degrees distinct from India and China, both part of the exposed zone of Eurasia. Necessarily — and hopefully — these claims will invite debate. But if a consideration of Southeast Asia can help inform wider perspectives, it will have helped to carry forward the comparative work that Tony Reid first summoned us to consider.

Notes

* This paper, with the exception of contextual modifications for the current volume, was first published in *South East Asia Research* 19, no. 1 (March 2011). It is reproduced here by permission of IP Publishing Ltd., Copyright © 2011 SOAS.

1. Anthony Reid, *Southeast Asia in the Age of Commerce 1450–1680. Volume One: The Lands Below the Winds* (New Haven: Yale University Press, 1988); *Volume Two: Expansion and Crisis* (New Haven: Yale University Press, 1993).
2. Many of the arguments in the essay are developed at length in Victor Lieberman, *Strange Parallels: Southeast Asia in Global Context, c. 800–1830, Volume 1. Integration on the Mainland* (Cambridge: Cambridge University Press, 2003) and idem, *Strange Parallels: Southeast Asia in Global Context, c. 800–1830, Volume 2: Mainland Mirrors: Europe, Japan, China, South Asia, and the Islands* (Cambridge: Cambridge University Press, 2009). This essay is intended both as a precis for those unwilling to read the two volumes' 1400 pages and as an encouragement for some brave souls to do so.
3. Well-publicized expositions of this viewpoint include David Landes, *The Wealth and Poverty of Nations* (New York: W.W. Norton, 1998); Lawrence Harrison and Samuel Huntingdon, eds., *Culture Matters* (New York: Basic Books, 2000); David Levine, *At the Dawn of Modernity* (Berkeley: University of California Press, 2001); Jack Goldstone, *Why Europe? The Rise of the West in World History, 1500–1800* (Boston: McGraw Hill, 2008).
4. James Lee and Wang Feng, *One Quarter of Humanity* (Cambridge, MA: Harvard University Press, 1999); Tommy Bengtson, Cameron Campbell, James Lee, et al., *Life Under Pressure* (Cambridge, MA: MIT Press, 2004).
5. For China, see Kenneth Pomeranz, *The Great Divergence* (Princeton: Princeton University Press, 2000), and the lively debate involving Pomeranz, Philip Huang, James Lee, Cameron Campbell, Wang Feng, Robert Brenner, and Christopher Isett in *The Journal of Asian Studies* 61, no. 2 (2002): 501–662. For Southeast Asia, see Reid, *Southeast Asia in the Age of Commerce*, Volume 2, ch. 5 "The Origins of Southeast Asian Poverty."
6. See n. 3 *supra* and Samuel Huntington, *The Clash of Civilizations and the Remaking of World Order* (New York: Simon and Schuster, 1996), ch. 8.
7. Charles Tilly, *Coercion, Capital, and European States AD 900–1900* (Cambridge, MA: Basil Blackwell, 1990).
8. For mainland Southeast Asian realms, see Lieberman, *Strange Parallels, Volume 1*. For Russia, Valerie Kivelson, *Autocracy in the Provinces* (Stanford: Stanford University Press, 1996) and John P. LeDonne, *Absolutism and Ruling Class: The Formation of the Russian Political Order* (New York: Oxford University Press, 1991); for France, William Doyle, ed., *Short Oxford History of France* series (Oxford: Oxford University Press, 2001 et seq.); for Japan, Conrad Totman, *A History of Japan* (Malden, MA: Blackwell, 2000); plus copious citations for Russia, France, and Japan in Lieberman, *Strange Parallels, Volume 2*, chaps. 2–4.
9. See Lieberman, *Strange Parallels, Vol. 1*, Figs. 1.1, 1.2.
10. Barbara Ruch, "The Other Side of Culture in Medieval Japan," in *The Cambridge History of Japan, Volume 3: Medieval Japan*, edited by Kozo Yamamura (Cambridge: Cambridge University Press, 1990), p. 501.

11. See, for example, the origins of French language standardization discussed in Paul Cohen, "Courtly French, Learned Latin, and Peasant Patois" (Princeton Univ. PhD diss., 2001), pp. 75–98, 456–563, 647–747, esp. 730–34; idem, "L'imaginaire d'une langue nationale", *Histoire Epistemologie Langage* 25 (2003): 19–69.
12. See James Scott, *Seeing Like A State* (New Haven: Yale University Press, 1998); and Philip Gorski, *The Disciplinary Revolution* (Chicago: University of Chicago Press, 2003).
13. Jan de Vries, *The Economy of Europe in An Age of Crisis, 1600–1750* (Cambridge: Cambridge University Press, 1976), p. 242, strongly supported by Tilly, *Coercion, Capital*, especially ch. 3
14. Lieberman, *Strange Parallels, Vol. 1*, 101–12, and *Vol. 2*, chs. 2, 5, 6, plus Michael Mann et al., "Global Signatures and Dynamical Origins of the Little Ice Age and Medieval Climate Anomaly", *Science* 326 (2009): 1256–60; Edward Cook et al. "Asian Monsoon Failure and Megadrought During the Last Millennium", *Science* 328 (2010): 486–89; Valerie Trouet et al., "Persistent Positive North Atlantic Oscillation Mode Dominated the Medieval Climate Anomaly", *Science* 324 (2009): 78–80; Willie Soon, Sallie Baliunas et al., "Reconstructing Climatic and Environmental Changes of the Past 1000 Years: A Reappraisal", *Energy and Environment* 14 (2003): 233–96; David Zhang et al., "Global Climate Change, War, and Population Decline in Recent Human History", *Proceedings of the National Academy of Sciences* 104 (2007): 19214–19219; Brendan Buckley et al., "Climate as A Contributing Factor in the Demise of Angkor, Cambodia", *Proceedings of the National Academy of Sciences* 107 (April 13, 2010): 6748–52.
15. Cf. Ann Bowman Jannetta, *Epidemics and Mortality in Early Modern Japan* (Princeton: Princeton University Press, 1987); William Wayne Farris, *Japan's Medieval Population* (Honolulu: University of Hawaii Press, 2006), arguing for such an adjustment only after c. 1280; and Lieberman, *Strange Parallels, Vol. 2*, chs. 2, 4.
16. Edwin Hunt and James Murray, *A History of Business in Medieval Europe, 1200–1550* (Cambridge: Cambridge University Press, 1999); and Lieberman, *Strange Parallels, Vol. 2*, ch. 2.
17. Ward Barret, "World Bullion Flows, 1450–1800", in *The Rise of Merchant Empires*, edited by James Tracy (Cambridge: Cambridge University Press, 1990), pp. 224–54.
18. Lieberman, *Strange Parallels, Vol. 2*, ch. 5.
19. Ibid., ch. 6.
20. Mark Elliott, *The Manchu Way* (Stanford: Stanford University Press, 2001), and Lieberman, *Strange Parallels, Vol. 2*, ch. 5.
21. For discussion of island Southeast Asia's relation to Eurasian themes, a discussion beyond the scope of the present essay, see Lieberman, *Strange Parallels, Vol. 2*, ch. 7.

22. See Catherine Asher and Cynthia Talbot, *India Before Europe* (Cambridge: Cambridge University Press, 2006), chs. 8, 9; and Lieberman, *Strange Parallels, Vol. 2*, ch. 6.
23. Because it too faced no serious military challenges, Tokugawa Japan to 1854 was an exception proving the rule that military demands spurred administrative penetration and fiscal maximization.
24. Late eighteenth-century imperial taxes in China averaged some 5 per cent of national income. Susan Naquin and Evelyn Rawski, *Chinese Society in the Eighteenth Century* (New Haven: Yale University Press, 1987), p. 219. This compared to over 12 per cent in France, 12–15 per cent in Russia, and over 19 per cent in Britain. See Peter Mathias and Patrick O'Brien, "Taxation in Britain and France, 1715–1810," *Jl. of European Economic History* 5 (1976): 608–13; Arcadius Kahan, *The Plow, the Hammer, and the Knout* (Chicago: University of Chicago Press, 1985), p. 345; Richard Hellie, "The Costs of Muscovite Military Defense and Expansion," in *The Military and Society in Russia 1450–1917*, edited by Eric Lohr and Marshall Poe (Leiden: Brill, 2002), p. 66. For a general discussion, see Lieberman, *Strange Parallels, Vol. 2*, ch. 5.

References

Asher, Catherine and Talbot Cynthia. *India Before Europe*. Cambridge: Cambridge University Press, 2006.

Barret, Ward. "World Bullion Flows, 1450–1800," in *The Rise of Merchant Empires*, edited by James Tracy, pp. 224–54. Cambridge: Cambridge University Press, 1990.

Bengtson, Tommy. Campbell Cameron, Lee James, et al., *Life Under Pressure*. Cambridge, MA: MIT Press, 2004.

Buckley, Brendan et al. "Climate as a Contributing Factor in the Demise of Angkor, Cambodia". *Proceedings of the National Academy of Sciences* 107 (April 13, 2010): 6748–52.

Cohen, Paul. "Courtly French, Learned Latin, and Peasant Patois" PhD Dissertation, Princeton University, 2001.

———."L'imaginaire d'une Langue Nationale". *Histoire Epistemologie Langage* 25 (2003): 19–69.

Cook, Edward et al. "Asian Monsoon Failure and Megadrought during the Last Millennium", *Science* 328 (2010): 486–89.

Doyle, William (ed.). *Short Oxford History of France*. Oxford: Oxford University Press, 2001.

Elliott, Mark. *The Manchu Way*. Stanford: Stanford University Press, 2001.

Farris, William Wayne. *Japan's Medieval Population*. Honolulu: University of Hawaii Press, 2006.

Goldstone, Jack. *Why Europe? The Rise of the West in World History, 1500–1800*. Boston: McGraw Hill, 2008.

Gorski, Philip. *The Disciplinary Revolution*. Chicago: University of Chicago Press, 2003.
Harrison, Lawrence and Samuel Huntingdon (eds.). *Culture Matters*. New York: Basic Books, 2000.
Hellie, Richard. "The Costs of Muscovite Military Defense and Expansion". In *The Military and Society in Russia 1450–1917*, edited by Eric Lohr and Marshall Poe. Leiden: Brill, 2002.
Huntington, Samuel. *The Clash of Civilizations and the Remaking of World Order*. New York: Simon and Schuster, 1996.
Hunt, Edwin and Murray James. *A History of Business in Medieval Europe, 1200–1550*. Cambridge: Cambridge University Press, 1999.
Jannetta, Ann Bowman. *Epidemics and Mortality in Early Modern Japan*. Princeton: Princeton University Press, 1987.
Kahan, Arcadius. *The Plow, the Hammer, and the Knout*. Chicago: University of Chicago Press, 1985.
Kivelson, Valerie. *Autocracy in the Provinces*. Stanford: Stanford University Press, 1996.
Landes, David. *The Wealth and Poverty of Nations*. New York: W.W. Norton, 1998.
LeDonne, John P. *Absolutism and Ruling Class*. New York: Oxford University Press, 1991.
Lee, James and Feng Wang. *One Quarter of Humanity*. Cambridge, MA: Harvard University Press, 1999.
Levine, David. *At the Dawn of Modernity*. Berkeley: University of California Press, 2001.
Lieberman, Victor. *Strange Parallels: Southeast Asia in Global Context, c. 800–1830, Volume 1. Integration on the Mainland*. Cambridge: Cambridge University Press, 2003. *Volume 2: Mainland Mirrors: Europe, Japan, China, South Asia, and the Islands*. Cambridge: Cambridge University Press, 2009.
Mann, Michael et al. "Global Signatures and Dynamical Origins of the Little Ice Age and Medieval Climate Anomaly". *Science* 326 (2009): 1256–60.
Mathias, Peter and Patrick O'Brien. "Taxation in Britain and France, 1715–1810". *Journal of European Economic History* 5 (1976): 608–13.
Naquin, Susan and Evelyn Rawski. *Chinese Society in the Eighteenth Century*. New Haven: Yale University Press, 1987.
Pomeranz, Kenneth. *The Great Divergence*. Princeton: Princeton University Press, 2000.
Reid, Anthony. *Southeast Asia in the Age of Commerce 1450–1680. Volume One: The Lands Below the Winds*. New Haven: Yale University Press, 1988. *Volume Two: Expansion and Crisis*. New Haven: Yale University Press, 1993.
Ruch, Barbara. "The Other Side of Culture in Medieval Japan". In *The Cambridge History of Japan, Volume 3: Medieval Japan*, edited by Kozo Yamamura, pp. 500–43. Cambridge: Cambridge University Press, 1990.

Scott, James. *Seeing Like a State*. New Haven: Yale University Press, 1998.
Soon, Willie, Sallie Baliunas et al. "Reconstructing Climatic and Environmental Changes of the Past 1000 Years: A Reappraisal". *Energy and Environment* 14 (2003): 233–96.
Tilly, Charles. *Coercion, Capital, and European States, AD 900–1900*. Cambridge, MA: Basil Blackwell, 1990.
Totman, Conrad. *A History of Japan*. Malden, MA: Blackwell, 2000.
Trouet, Valerie et al. "Persistent Positive North Atlantic Oscillation Mode Dominated the Medieval Climate Anomaly". *Science* 324 (2009): 78–80.
Vries, Jan de. *The Economy of Europe in an Age of Crisis, 1600–1750*. Cambridge: Cambridge University Press, 1976.
Zhang, David et al. "Global Climate Change, War, and Population Decline in Recent Human History". *Proceedings of the National Academy of Sciences* 104 (2007): 19214-19219.

4

A TWO-OCEAN MEDITERRANEAN

Wang Gungwu

Europeans know how important the Mediterranean Sea is in their history. In Asia, historians appreciate that Sea's connection with the powerful civilizations that arose there. But some are likely also to highlight it as the location for millennia of trading and military actions that ended with the division between the Christian West and core Islamic lands. It was that stalemate between the two civilizations from the seventh to the fifteenth century that finally led the Europeans to turn to the Atlantic in search of a new route to India and China. After that, new groups of actors emerged to dominate the modernization narrative for the next five centuries. The West steadily colonized large parts of Asia and brought their brand of imperialism everywhere. During that period, the Mediterranean syndrome of war and division took various shapes and underwent changes arising from relationships that became globalized in increasingly intense ways. Only recently, with the new wars in the Middle East, have we been reminded that the syndrome is alive both within and beyond its original home, and that it remains the seedbed of power struggles that the world faces today.

For Southeast Asia, the region's historians have been inspired by Fernand Braudel's study of the Mediterranean and some have been ready to compare the historical developments in the two regions. The work of Anthony Reid in the 1980s on the "Age of Commerce, 1450–1680" in Southeast Asia led the way. Denys Lombard then took the subject further and organized an international symposium on "La Méditerranée Asiatique" in 1997. Since then, we have also had Heather Sutherland's careful analysis of the very concept of the Mediterranean itself.[1] For most historians, the conditions in Southeast Asia around the Java Sea and the South China Sea (shortened here as "Nanhai") would make a very imperfect match for that Mediterranean. But the insights provided by Braudel's approach were certainly enlightening and using it to elucidate these maritime areas of Asia has certainly been worthwhile. Thus, interest remains and closer comparisons have become thinkable today. This essay honours Anthony Reid for having drawn attention to similarities and differences in Southeast Asia, and seeking to explain some new developments that now hinge on this region. In particular, the relationships among the insular and continental states in the emerging regional structure around the Pacific Ocean that has been extended to the Indian Ocean have become more significant. If they are compared with the Mediterranean syndrome both past and present, there are features that deserve careful examination.

When we simply look at the map, the near-Mediterranean nature of the Nanhai, or Southern Sea, may seem obvious. But when we go beyond maps, the differences stand out. Around the lands of the Mediterranean coasts, for more than two millennia, there were complex struggles for dominance among various civilizations, religions and empires and these struggles dictated developments in every aspect of that region's history. By contrast, for the littoral peoples of the Nanhai, the powerful empires from North China (the Qin dynasty and its successor the Han) had marched south from the great river valleys of the Huang Ho and the Yangzi during the third and second centuries BC, and conquered the small kingdoms and tribal states of the Yue peoples. That empire then stopped at the coasts of modern South China and the Gulf of Tongking, and was content thereafter to control less than half these lands of the northern Nanhai. Thereafter, there were growing but limited trading and cultural contacts across the Nanhai. But the disparity between the imperial states in the north and the small port kingdoms scattered around the Nanhai coasts did not lead to any developments that could be compared to the centuries of intense activities around and across the Mediterranean before and during this period.

It is, however, possible to point to some features that could be described as potentially Mediterranean or semi-Mediterranean, or if I may coin a word, *semiterranean*, but these features were to become apparent only later in the first millennium. I suggest that this word can be applied to the later half of the Tang dynasty (eighth–ninth centuries), especially after the beginning of the tenth century when the southern Chinese of the Nan Han and Min kingdoms began in earnest to trade with the region.

For the next five centuries (tenth–fourteenth centuries), new trading relationships developed for all the littoral states of the South China Sea but they remained no more than *semiterranean*. It was not until the sixteenth century that the political and religious conflicts of the Mediterranean Sea were extended in various directions and arrived in Southeast Asia. By the eighteenth century, these conflicts led to some two centuries of colonial rule, followed in the latter half of the twentieth century by decades of decolonization and the ongoing phenomenon of globalization.[2] The ramifications for the region are still present. In recent decades, seeking a degree of integration through the Association of Southeast Asian Nations (ASEAN), the region faces new challenges that include the larger Mediterranean syndrome encompassing both the Indian and Pacific oceans. The work of integration is still work in progress. If it fails, Southeast Asia may be drawn into power configurations across both those oceans to its east and west that could resemble the historical division of the Mediterranean. This essay suggests why the analogy is thinkable today and why Southeast Asia as a contested region may have critical roles to play in such an extended trans-oceanic Mediterranean.

My interest in the region began with the broad concept of a "Malaysia" from the perspective of the "Malay" peoples of the archipelago, and that of the Dutch and British who sought to rule over them. I compared that concept with the term Nanyang (Southern Ocean) as understood by Chinese settlers and sojourners and used in Chinese documents. It led me to write about the trade that the Chinese conducted with the ports and kingdoms on the coasts of the South China Sea up to the tenth century.[3] For this trade, I used the term Nanhai (Southern Sea), an indeterminate term found in early Chinese writings. One of my conclusions was that, although the geographical features of this Nanhai reminded me of the Mediterranean Sea, the key ingredients in Mediterranean history could not be found there. I did not consider whether the term Nanyang was equivalent to the region we call Southeast Asia. Instead, I simply described what I thought were unique features of the region's relationship with the various Chinese dynasties in the first millennium CE.

Southeast Asia became the term of choice for the emerging region by the time I began to teach at the University of Malaya in 1957. At the new campus in Kuala Lumpur after Malayan independence, the demand was for writing and teaching national history to help build the new state. This history was to be freed from British imperial history and located in a yet to be shaped region in the new Asia. At the core, therefore, was the history of Southeast Asia. That was supplemented by courses on East and South Asian history on the one hand and world history on the other. In the latter, the emphasis was on the rise of the West and its impact on global developments since the nineteenth century. Southeast Asia thus became essential background to the construction of Malaya's national history. Anthony Reid joined the university at the time and played a vital part to ensure that the region's history would be well integrated into the core themes for historical teaching and research.

Since the 1960s, there have been numerous efforts at defining Southeast Asia, justifying its integrity as a region and underlining its significance. There have also been doubts whether everyone is comfortable with Southeast Asia as a regional entity and whether that entity has a secure future. Understandably, the historians of each country tend to present the region's history in their own way and give uneven weight to the major developments that affected the region as whole. Elsewhere, economic and security analysts regularly complain that, despite the establishment and enlargement of ASEAN in 1967, Southeast Asian governments still do not really think regionally and have not done enough to make the new regionalism effective. Many of them are sensitive to these criticisms but, in their belief that the region is of primary importance, continue to encourage work that would put Southeast Asian studies on the map.

This essay comes at Southeast Asia from another angle. It draws inspiration from Anthony Reid's research that emphasizes the maritime core of the region when he identified the Age of Commerce and acknowledged the work of Fernand Braudel on the Mediterranean. Braudel's seminal writings have influenced many others to re-look at Mediterranean-like conditions in the China Seas, the Java Sea, the Baltic, the Caribbean and even in less obvious maritime areas like the two halves of the Indian Ocean to the east and west of the Indian subcontinent. These inquiries have been both stimulating and productive. Tony Reid's two volumes, *The Lands Below the Winds* and *Expansion and Crisis*, testify to the enormous impact that the Mediterranean paradigm has had.

I have written elsewhere about why the Mediterranean complex was not native to the China Seas.[4] It was never the geography of the Mediterranean Sea that interested me, but its history. I identified four ingredients of that history that are central to its distinctiveness, factors that propelled the kingdoms and empires that grew out of the Mediterranean to be enlarged far beyond its shores. The ingredients were: (1) The Mediterranean was a central place for multiple civilizations. (2) Its shores attracted intense migratory and commercial activities. (3) It spawned empires characterized by strong maritime power. (4) It sustained tenets of religion and ideology that have determined the nature of later political and economic changes.[5]

In my early work, I brushed aside the idea that the Nanhai littoral in ancient times, made up of China and various Indianized kingdoms and ports, was in any way comparable to the Mediterranean complex. After the tenth century, however, and progressively to the present, including the centuries that have been seen as the age of commerce, the process of becoming more *semiterranean* can be discerned. South China became economically more active after the end of the Tang dynasty. When that dynasty fell in 907, a number of independent southern kingdoms were established that took new initiatives in the Nanhai. It is possible to date the emergence of *semiterranean* conditions from that time. The powerful kingdoms and empires among the littoral states developed regular trade and tribute relationships, but were only tangentially engaged across what was *geographically* fragmented and one-sided space. They did not produce the forces and compulsions that drove the Mediterranean states and cultures to become an inseparable complex.[6]

In re-examining the history of the peoples and cultures who lived on these shores, we can say that the Nanhai was potentially two smaller *semiterranean* zones, the South China and the Java Seas, that could, given a strong push, have produced Mediterranean characteristics. The Mongol imperial explosion from Eurasia that led to naval attacks on Java and Japan at the end of the thirteenth century, for example, could have produced such a push.[7] But it was not sustained and, in any case, failed to leave any lasting impact on the region. This was still true a century later when the Ming Emperor Yongle sent Zheng He in 1405 on the first of his seven expeditions to the Indian Ocean. The geopolitical situation remained one-sided when, three decades later, the Ming court decided to disband its navy and effectively withdrew to defend its coastal boundaries.[8] For some, that series of imperial displays of overwhelming force may be seen as a preview of what was to come when, after 1498, European naval power began to be applied continuously to most of Asia. But I suggest that would be an anachronistic reading that could be misleading if pursued further. Nothing in the history of the Ming and Qing dynasties from the mid-fifteenth century till the end of the nineteenth could be depicted as having any push towards naval aggression.

What burst out from the Western Mediterranean, however, was a new kind of power that told a different story. It stimulated an increasingly global phenomenon based on the sustained use of aggressive maritime power. The story had begun with alternating power centres that spanned the Mediterranean coasts of the three continents of Europe, Asia and Africa for millennia. There had developed patterns of change that produced the unending struggles between the Greco-Roman-Christian world and the Arab-Islamic *ummah*. The hinterlands of these two forces were united and divided in turn by that inland sea but, across the centuries, the Mediterranean complex did represent an extraordinary example of the balance of power. This was obviously different from the asymmetry found in the Nanhai where China's power and wealth was overwhelming on the rare occasions when the Chinese state took an interest in maritime affairs. Instead, it was the exhilarating but diffuse Indian Ocean cultures that exerted more influence on local populations over the centuries. From the subcontinent, they came to dominate the art and architecture, the languages and scripts, the gods, and rituals, the music and dance in most of the Nanhai. In time, the situation became one of a cultural and commercial asymmetry that led the region's peoples to lean towards the West. It also reflected an asymmetry that was to remain as long as China was focused on overland security threats in the north, and as long as no grouping of Nanhai states appeared that could challenge the power of China.

Thus it was *semiterranean* commerce, migration, and political cultures that characterized the region. The Malay peoples moved around their island world more intensely and laid the foundations for polities that extended the range of Srivijaya and then the Majapahit and Malacca empires. Other migrations overland, by the Viet conquerors of Champa and the Thai rulers of Ayutthaya, pushed southwards, and Ayutthaya developed enough naval power to put pressure on Malacca. Limited numbers of Indian and Muslim merchants continued to come from the west, but the Chola invasions from India, for example, were not sustained. The Chinese, often together with Arabs, traded in larger numbers and, after the arrival of Europeans, the trading activities of the Chinese in particular expanded rapidly to all parts of the Malay Archipelago.[9]

Japanese and Korean traders and sailors joined their Chinese counterparts from time to time. Muslim merchants from the west also extended the trade they had with the Islamic kingdoms in first Sumatra and Malacca and then in Java, Borneo, Sulawesi and beyond.[10] But the nature of their trade did not radically change until they had to deal with new institutions like the Dutch and English East India Companies. These long-distance trading companies had creatively evolved from the merchant guilds and city states that formed the original frontlines in the centuries of struggle between Christian monarchs and the Moors of the Mediterranean. They were increasingly well-organized and difficult for local polities to defend against.

The rapid Islamization of the Malay world also brought new changes. The interactions between Hindu-Buddhist rulers and Islamic merchant enclaves eventually divided the Buddhist mainland from an increasingly Muslim Nusantara, something that could be compared with the divisions that characterized the Mediterranean, albeit on a lesser scale. The coming of the Europeans in the sixteenth century disrupted the early divisions by introducing Christianity, at least on the eastern periphery of Southeast Asia. Later, with the advent of modern scientific and secular values, this European impact became even stronger. Most dramatically, this awakened political forces in Japan and added a modern and powerful naval dimension that was rooted in Asia. By the end of the nineteenth century, the combined power of Japan and the West challenged the ancient values and institutions of China and paved the way to new ideological and nationalist revolutions that totally transformed the region.

Although *semiterranean* Southeast Asia around the Nanhai after the sixteenth century was still unable to balance the power of China, the region had come alive. This vitality encouraged greater multilateral intercourse. The potential for Mediterranean development was there from the time the Portuguese and Spanish kings ousted their Moorish rivals first in Europe and then challenged them in Asia. The way the Spanish led the way across the Atlantic and were confronted by the Dutch, British and the French could be described as extending the Mediterranean complex and turning the Pacific into something of a Spanish lake.[11] The first change came from the Spanish push out of the Mediterranean into the Atlantic and then into the Pacific. When others even better organized and more determined joined them, a new future began to take shape for the Nanhai. The key development hinged on a new power balance between the European powers and the Qing Empire, although the latter was slow to recognize the shift. It took two so-called Opium Wars in the nineteenth century to bring that message home to the Chinese, events that were to change the *semiterranean* nature that the region had so far experienced.

The Europeans then built new centres of countervailing power that linked a strategic network of ports. Out of these came the ring of Western empires that sought to extend their China trade and eventually cooperated among themselves in order to stand up to Qing dynastic power. Beginning from the nineteenth century, the British led the way to break the barriers that the Manchu regime had put up. Finally, strong countervailing power had arrived in the South China Sea. It is possible now to see that these were the first steps towards making local *semiterranean* conditions more comparable to those of the Mediterranean, conditions that British empire-builders had so carefully studied.

The maritime empires that emerged after 1800 ensured that interactions between powerful states on opposite coasts were no longer one-sided. The Qing Empire was counterbalanced by a concert of European powers and this was further strengthened by the power of the United States followed by the belated rise of the maritime Japanese empire. During that time, trade volumes throughout the region increased sharply. The one-sidedness that used to be in China's favour was reversed as foreign imports and investments coming from the powers controlling Southeast Asia began to outstrip economic developments in China. Chinese exports increasingly included the outflow of human resources as Chinese labourers swelled the communities in every major port of the China Seas. By the end of the nineteenth century, the rapid decline in Chinese power and the collapse of the native Chinese economy had become so pronounced that many in China feared that the one-sided reversal would become permanent and result in the carving up of China into many parts. Fortunately, the Western powers saw Japanese ambitions as threatening to their dominance and decided to hold the Japanese back. Eventually, World War II provided them with the opportunity to intervene and restore the balance by helping China in a war that the Chinese could not have won alone. In so doing, that contributed further to create the Mediterranean conditions that local Southeast Asian polities had not been able to develop themselves.

When the Chinese Communist Party united China's imperial territories and took the Soviet Union's side in the Cold War, the ideological division of the world was distinctly modern but not all that different in nature from the religious divides that marked the Mediterranean complex. The new secular religions were new versions of the historic Mediterranean divides, but on a much larger global stage. Although the Cold War is now over and the new divides are more complicated, the prospect of continual division along religious or ideological lines remains. The shape of the division is still unclear. On the one hand, the extended role of Islam in the region is less predictable and, on the other, China confounded all expectations in the 1980s by reversing their revolutionary past and successfully building a new kind of state-sponsored capitalism within three decades. What that means for the secular but still ideological West has become a subject of intense concern. When China re-emerges as a maritime power, Southeast Asia will certainly face further changes in the global struggle.

These changes may be depicted simply as the logical consequences of Great Power rivalries or as realist applications of balance of power strategies. But a deeper change becomes clear by employing the image of the Mediterranean complex. The Mediterranean Sea was the arena where several ancient civilizations contended for power. The sea evoked images of maritime trade and colonization and the waxing and waning of empires down the centuries. Then the Portuguese and the Spanish broke out of the Mediterranean impasse between the Christian and Muslim kingdoms and found new routes to India and China across the Atlantic and via the Indian and Pacific Oceans. The Europeans were tired of being at the mercy of Muslim merchants who dominated the routes to Asian markets. After 1492, and especially after 1498, they could finally compete directly with Muslim traders. The unbearable tensions that had confined them to the Mediterranean Sea for so long finally outgrew the limits of medieval technologies and religious divisions. That enterprise did not represent a rupture in European history but was the result of an expansion of a strong historical complex that had long connected the three linked continents of Africa, Asia and Europe, and now added the continent of the Americas.

Obviously there is no exact fit today between the Nanhai and its oceanic extensions on both sides and the region around the Mediterranean. For example, although there have been more intense migratory and commercial activities that have brought the economies of China and Southeast Asia closer together, the strengths of the economies are still very uneven. While there are new maritime centres in the region, they are, with the exception of Japan, still economically dependent on powers much further away like the United States and its allies. It is possible to identify new versions of religions and ideologies that can shape the direction of future political and economic change. But the region by itself is still *semiterranean* because the hinterland of each of the countries is weaker than that of China, especially during the periods when the Chinese took an interest in building a credible navy.[12] The multiple civilizational developments that characterized the Mediterranean complex may now be present, but they have been introduced and still supported from elsewhere. Southeast Asian cultures that are now exposed to modern civilizational divisions still have to draw their strength from the Indian Ocean or the West. Couched in terms of the ancient conflicts between Christian and Muslim or between Muslim and Hindu-Buddhist, that might appear familiar. But modern secular divisions like the political ideologies of the Cold War have also left deep impressions. And there are advanced technologies that have compressed beyond recognition the geopolitics of the whole world. It is thus possible to view the Nanhai as a frontline for older and newer maritime powers to face the rise of China. If the larger complex based primarily on the Pacific Ocean (and can now include the Indian Ocean) is compared with the idea of an enlarged Mediterranean, the deeply divisive experiences of that historic Mediterranean complex can become part of the entire region's future. That would envisage the formation of a maritime arc from at least Japan to Indonesia that can be backed by powerful hinterlands further away. Distance has become less of a factor as new technologies bring the world closer together. Whether we see all this in the end as a matter of compressing the world to be analogous to the Mediterranean complex, or of enlarging the Mediterranean complex to encompass future geopolitics, is not important. What is interesting is to recognize that the Mediterranean analogy is useful and that studying the long process of historical change between the China Seas and the two Oceans will give us different perspectives on the present and future.

The Nanhai that was divided during the Cold War resembled that between Christian Europe and Muslim Afro-Eurasia. After the Cold War, with globalization and the military technology now available, an extended divide that is based on efforts to balance greatly enhanced naval power is now evolving. On one side are powers that wish to contain China with multiple alliances; on the other, China and its hinterland are trying hard not to be isolated. It is already a more complicated set of power configurations than any in the past. For example, in place of ideology, there are now divisions along religious lines where the borders are unclear. Faced with the extended role of Islam from the Indian Ocean to the eastern limits of Southeast Asia, such divisions will be hard to manage.

In China, Deng Xiaoping's economic reforms transformed the revolutionary agenda by initiating a capitalistic process that depends on strong state initiative and control. This is still evolving and it is too early to say how this will change the distribution of political and economic power in the China Seas. But it is clear that China will never again neglect naval power. It is now determined to become a maritime power if only to ensure its sovereignty, protect its coastal territories and guarantee the sea-lanes that supply the resources essential to its continued economic growth.[13] The impact of such naval power on the nature of the China Seas and beyond is still not clear, but if there is an equivalent countervailing force, however distant across either if not both the Pacific and Indian Oceans, then the comparison between this extended complex and the Mediterranean syndrome will remain valid.

Using the analogy of the Mediterranean complex may not be reassuring to Southeast Asia. From beyond the China Seas, powers like the United States and its allies could employ the image of a maritime arc to support an integrated region and set it against possible future Chinese growth. If ASEAN is not integrated, it could be divided between states that link up the maritime arc and those that choose to maintain a positive relationship with a powerful China. That would lead to divisions that would closely resemble the way the Mediterranean is still divided today.

China has great need for a friendly maritime neighbourhood and is working hard for ASEAN integration as a defense against this region being used as a hostile group. If the region does become fully integrated, ASEAN would be empowered to play a pivotal role in keeping the peace for the larger region beyond the China Seas, including the Pacific Ocean and the Indian

Ocean. If China can convince its neighbours that it is committed to nothing more than the peaceful restoration of its historically secure environment, ASEAN integration would be a valuable development for all concerned.

The nations of Southeast Asia want to maximize their security and ensure economic development under the most advantageous conditions they can get. They have through ASEAN sought to use the organization to persuade interested parties that this represents the most effective route to regional peace. If successful, they can seek to avoid reproducing the fiercely divisive nature of the Mediterranean complex. But they would not want to return to the asymmetrical *semiterranean* condition before the nineteenth century. They can do this only by becoming truly integrated and thus having the capacity to balance the interests of China with those of powers that want to keep China out. Only in that way could they ensure that they will not be the instruments of future rival powers.

Notes

1. Fernand Braudel, *La Méditerranée et le Monde Méditerranéen a l'époque de Philippe II.* (Paris: Libraire Armand Colin, 1949); Claude Guillot, Denys Lombard and Roderich Ptak (eds.), *From the Mediterranean to the China Sea: Miscellaneous Notes* (Wiesbaden: Harrassowitz, 1998); Anthony Reid, *Southeast Asia in the age of commerce, 1450–1680. Vol. 1: The Lands Below the Winds; Vol. 2: Expansion and Crisis* (New Haven: Yale University Press, 1988 and 1993); and Heather Sutherland, "Southeast Asian History and the Mediterranean Analogy", *Journal of Southeast Asian Studies* 34, no. 1 (2003): 1–20.
2. Although this development began with the Portuguese and Spanish monarchs at the end of the fifteenth century, it was not until the nineteenth century that the modern phase of globalization can be said to have started. See K.M. Panikkar, *Asia and Western Dominance: A Survey of the Vasco da Gama Epoch of Asian History, 1498–1945* (London: Allen & Unwin, 1953); Kenneth Pomeranz, *The Great Divergence: China, Europe, and the Making of the Modern World Economy* (Princeton: Princeton University Press, 2000); R. Bin Wong, *China Transformed: Historical Change and the Limits of European Experience* (Ithaca: Cornell University Press, 1997); and Andre Gunder Frank, *ReOrient: Global Economy in the Asian Age* (Berkeley: California University Press, 1998).
3. Wang Gungwu, "The Nanhai Trade: A Study of the Early History of Chinese Trade in the South China Sea", (M.A. Thesis, University of Malaya, 1956) published in *Journal of the Malayan Branch of the Royal Asiatic Society*, Kuala Lumpur, Monograph Issue, Vol. 31, part 2 (1958) (New paperback edition published by Eastern Universities Press in 2003).
4. Wang Gungwu, "The China Seas: Becoming an Enlarged Mediterranean", in

The East Asian 'Mediterranean': Maritime Crossroads of Culture, Commerce and Human Migration, edited by Angela Schottenhammer (Wiesbaden: Harrossowitz Verlag, 2008), pp. 7–22.

5. The four ingredients are drawn from a range of histories of the ancient Mediterranean, including the classical works of Herodotus' *History* and Thucydides' *Peloponnesian War*; and modern studies by M.I. Rostovtzeff, *The Social and Economic History of the Roman Empire* (Oxford: Clarendon Press, 1926); and Max Cary, *The Geographic Background of Greek and Roman History* (Oxford: Clarendon Press, 1949). On later periods, important writings include those by Ibn Khaldun, *The Muqaddimah: an Introduction to History*, translated by Franz Rosenthal (London: Routledge & Kegan Paul, 1986); and the modern studies Henri Pirenne, *Mahomet et Charlemagne*, translated by Bernard Miall (New York: Barnes & Noble, 1939); and Steven Runciman, *A History of the Crusades*. 3 vols. (Cambridge: Cambridge University Press, 1951–1954).

6. Paul Pelliot, "Deux itinéraires de Chine en Inde à la fin du VIIIe siècle", *Bulletin de l'École Française d'Extrême Orient*. Vol. IV (1904): 215–363; 372–73; and George Coedes, *Les états hindouises d'Indochine et d'Indonésie* (Paris: E. De Bocard, 1948).

7. J. J. Saunders, *The History of the Mongol Conquests* (London: Routledge and Kegan Paul, 1971); Tanaka Takeo 田中健夫 (ed.), *Kamakura Bakufu to Moko shurai* 鎌倉幕府と蒙古襲来 (Tokyo: Gyosei, 1986); Yu Changsen, 喻常森 *Yuandai haiwai maoyi*. 元代海外贸易(Xi'an: Xibei daxue chubanshe, 1994); John Andrew Boyle, *The Mongol World Empire, 1206–1370* (London: Variorum Reprints, 1977).

8. Ma Huan, *Ying-yai sheng-lan*. *'The overall survey of the ocean's shores'*. Translated by J. V. G. Mills (Cambridge: Cambridge University Press, for the Hakluyt Society, 1970). Also Roderich Ptak, *China and the Asian Seas: Trade, Travel, and Visions of the Others (1400–1750)* (Brookfield, Vt.: Ashgate, 1998); Edward L. Dreyer, *Zheng He: China and the Oceans in the Early Ming Dynasty, 1405/1433* (New York: Pearson Longman, 2006).

9. W.P. Groeneveldt, *Notes on the Malay Archipelago and Malacca, compiled from Chinese Sources*, Batavia (1876, republished 1880 in *Verhandelingen van het Bataviaasch Genootschap van Kunsten en Wetenschappen*, vol. 39); Henri Cordier, *Bibliotheca Sinica: Dictionnaire bibliographique des ouvrages relatifs à l'Empire chinois*, 2 vols. (Paris: E. Leroux, 1881–1885); Friedrich Hirth, *China and the Roman Orient: Researches into their Ancient and Mediaeval Relations as represented in old Chinese Records* (Shanghai: Kelly and Walsh, 1885); and Friedrich Hirth and W.W. Rockhill, *Chau Ju-kua: His Work on the Chinese and Arab Trade in the Twelfth and Thirteenth Centuries, entitled Chu-fan-chi* (*Zhufan zhi)* (St Petersburg: Imperial Academy of Sciences, 1911). Also, Paul Wheatley, "Geographical Notes on Some Commodities Involved in Sung Maritime Trade", *Journal of Malayan Branch of the Royal Asiatic Society* 32, no. 2 (1959): 1–139; and Paul Wheatley, *The Golden Khersonese: Studies in the Historical Geography*

of the Malay Peninsula before A.D. 1500 (Kuala Lumpur: University of Malaya Press, 1961).
10. Lin Tien-wai 林天蔚 and Joseph Wong 黃约瑟 (eds.), *Gudai Zhong-Han-Ri guanxi yanjiu* 古代中韩日关系研究 [Studies on Relations between China, Korea, and Japan in Ancient Times] (Hong Kong: Centre of Asian Studies, University of Hong Kong, 1987); Charlotte von Verschuer, *Across the Perilous Sea: Japanese Trade with China and Korea from the 7th to the 16th Centuries*. Translated by Kristen Lee Hunter (Ithaca, New York: East Asia Program, Cornell University, 2006); and Wontack Hong, *Korea and Japan in East Asian History: a Tripolar Approach to East Asian History* (Seoul: Kudara International, 2006).
11. O.H.K. Spate, *The Spanish Lake*, Volume 1 of *The Pacific since Magellan* (Minneapolis: University of Minnesota Press, 1979). Chang T'ien-tse, *Sino-Portuguese Trade from 1514 to 1644: A Synthesis of Portuguese and Chinese Sources* (Leiden: E.J. Brill, 1933); K.N. Chaudhuri, *Trade and Civilisation in the Indian Ocean: An Economic History from the Rise of Islam to 1750* (Cambridge: Cambridge University Press, 1985); Anthony Disney and Emily Booth (eds.), *Vasco da Gama and the Linking of Europe and Asia* (New Delhi and New York: Oxford University Press, 2000); Uma Das Gupta (ed.), *The World of the Indian Ocean Merchant, 1500–1800: Collected Essays of Ashin Das Gupta* (New Delhi and New York: Oxford University Press, 2001).
12. Lo Jung-pang, "The Emergence of China as a Sea Power during the Late Sung and Early Yüan Periods", *Far Eastern Quarterly* 14, no. 4 (1955): 489–504; "The Decline of the Early Ming Navy", *Oriens Extremus* 5, no. 2 (1958): 149–68; and "Maritime Commerce and its Relation to the Sung Navy", *Journal of the Economic and Social History of the Orient* 12, no. 1 (1969): 57–101.
13. James C. Hsiung, "Sea Power, Law of the Sea, and a Sino-Japanese East China Sea 'Resource War' ", in James C. Hsiung (ed.), *China and Japan at Odds: Deciphering the Perpetual Conflict* (New York: Palgrave Macmillan, 2007), pp. 133–54; Bruce Swanson, *Eighth Voyage of the Dragon: a History of China's Quest for Seapower* (Annapolis: Naval Institute Press, 1982); Thomas M. Kane, *Chinese Grand Strategy and Maritime Power*. (London: Frank Cass, 2002); Alexandra Chieh-Cheng Huang, "Chinese Maritime Modernization and its Security Implications: the Deng Xiaoping Era and Beyond" (Ph.D. Dissertation, George Washington University, 1994).

References

Boyle, John Andrew. *The Mongol World Empire, 1206–1370*. London: Variorum Reprints, 1977.

Braudel, Fernand. *La Méditerranée et le Monde Méditerranéen a l'époque de Philippe II*. Paris: Libraire Armand Colin, 1949.

Cary, Max. *The Geographic Background of Greek and Roman History*. Oxford: Clarendon Press, 1949.

Chang T'ien-tse. *Sino-Portuguese Trade from 1514 to 1644: A Synthesis of Portuguese and Chinese Sources.* Leiden: E.J. Brill, 1933.

Chaudhuri, K.N. *Trade and Civilisation in the Indian Ocean: An Economic History from the Rise of Islam to 1750.* Cambridge: Cambridge University Press, 1985.

Coedes, George. *Les états hindouises d'Indochine et d'Indonésie.* Paris: E. De Bocard, 1948.

Cordier, Henri. *Bibliotheca Sinica: Dictionnaire bibliographique des ouvrages relatifs a la Empire chinois.* 2 vols. Paris: E. Leroux, 1881–1885.

Disney, Anthony and Emily Booth (eds.). *Vasco da Gama and the Linking of Europe and Asia.* New Delhi and New York: Oxford University Press, 2000.

Dreyer, Edward L. *Zheng He: China and the Oceans in the Early Ming Dynasty, 1405/1433.* New York: Pearson Longman, 2006.

Frank, Andre Gunder. *ReOrient: Global Economy in the Asian Age.* Berkeley: California University Press, 1998.

Groeneveldt, W.P. *Notes on the Malay Archipelago and Malacca, compiled from Chinese Sources.* Batavia: W. Bruining, 1877. Republished in *Verhandelingen van het Bataviaasch Genootschap van Kunsten en Wetenschappen*, vol. 39 (1880).

Guillot, Claude, Denys Lombard and Roderich Ptak (eds.), *From the Mediterranean to the China Sea: Miscellaneous Notes.* Wiesbaden: Harrassowitz, 1998.

Gupta, Uma Das (ed.). *The World of the Indian Ocean Merchant, 1500–1800: Collected Essays of Ashin Das Gupta.* New Delhi and New York: Oxford University Press, 2001.

Hirth, Friedrich. *China and the Roman Orient: Researches into their Ancient and Medieaval Relations as Represented in Old Chinese Records.* Shanghai: Kelly and Walsh, 1885.

Hirth, Friedrich and W.W. Rockhill. *Chau Ju-kua: His Work on the Chinese and Arab Trade in the Twelfth and Thirteenth Centuries, entitled Chu-fan-chi (Zhufan zhi).* St Petersburg: Imperial Academy of Sciences, 1911.

Hong, Wontack. *Korea and Japan in East Asian History: A Tripolar Approach to East Asian History.* Seoul: Kudara International, 2006.

Hsiung, James C. "Sea Power, Law of the Sea, and a Sino-Japanese East China Sea 'Resource War'". In *China and Japan at Odds: Deciphering the Perpetual Conflict*, edited by James C. Hsiung, pp. 133–54. New York: Palgrave Macmillan, 2007.

Huang, Alexandra Chieh-Cheng. "Chinese Maritime Modernization and its Security Implications: the Deng Xiaoping Era and Beyond". Ph.D. Dissertation, George Washington University, 1994.

Kane, Thomas M. *Chinese Grand Strategy and Maritime Power.* London: Frank Cass, 2002.

Khaldun, Ibn. *The Muqaddimah: an Introduction to History*, translated by Franz Rosenthal. London: Routledge & Kegan Paul, 1986.

Lin Tien-wai 林天蔚 and Joseph Wong 黃约瑟 (eds.). *Gudai Zhong-Han-Ri guanxi yanjiu* 古代中韩日关系研究 [Studies on Relations between China, Korea, and

Japan in Ancient Times]. Hong Kong: Centre of Asian Studies, University of Hong Kong, 1987.

Lo, Jung-pang. "The Emergence of China as a Sea Power during the Late Sung and Early Yüan Periods". *Far Eastern Quarterly* 14, no. 4 (1955), pp. 489–504.

———. "The Decline of the Early Ming Navy". *Oriens Extremus* 5, no. 2 (1958): 149–68.

———. "Maritime Commerce and its Relation to the Sung Navy". *Journal of the Economic and Social History of the Orient* 12, no. 1 (1969): 57–101.

Ma Huan. *Ying-yai sheng-lan. 'The Overall Survey of the Ocean's Shores'*. Translated by J. V. G. Mills. Cambridge: Cambridge University Press, for the Hakluyt Society, 1970.

Panikkar, K.M. *Asia and Western Dominance: A Survey of the Vasco da Gama Epoch of Asian History, 1498–1945*. London: Allen & Unwin, 1953.

Pelliot, Paul. "Deux itinéraires de Chine en Inde à la fin du VIIIe siècle", *Bulletin de l'École Française d'Extrême Orient* Vol. IV (1904): 215–363; 372–73.

Pirenne, Henri. *Mahomet et Charlemagne*, translated by Bernard Miall. New York: Barnes & Noble, 1939.

Pomeranz, Kenneth. *The Great Divergence: China, Europe, and the Making of the Modern World Economy*. Princeton: Princeton University Press, 2000.

Ptak, Roderich. *China and the Asian Seas: Trade, Travel, and Visions of the Others (1400–1750)*. Brookfield, Vt.: Ashgate, 1998.

Reid, Anthony. *Southeast Asia in the Age of Commerce, 1450–1680. Vol. 1: The Lands below the winds; Vol. 2: Expansion and Crisis*. New Haven: Yale University Press, 1988 and 1993.

Rostovtzeff, M.I. *The Social and Economic History of the Roman Empire*. Oxford: Clarendon Press, 1926.

Runciman, Steven. *A History of the Crusades*. 3 vols. Cambridge: Cambridge University Press, 1951-1954.

Saunders, J. J. *The History of the Mongol Conquests*. London: Routledge and Kegan Paul. 1971.

Spate, O.H.K. *The Spanish Lake*, Volume 1 of *The Pacific since Magellan*. Minneapolis: University of Minnesota Press, 1979.

Sutherland, Heather. "Southeast Asian History and the Mediterranean Analogy", *Journal of Southeast Asian Studies* 34, no. 1 (2003): 1–20.

Swanson, Bruce. *Eighth Voyage of the Dragon: a History of China's Quest for Seapower*. Annapolis: Naval Institute Press, 1982.

Tanaka Takeo 田中健夫 (ed.). *Kamakura Bakufu to Moko shurai* 鎌倉幕府と蒙古襲来. Tokyo: Gyosei, 1986.

Verschuer, Charlotte von. *Across the Perilous Sea: Japanese Trade with China and Korea from the 7th to the 16th Centuries*. Translated by Kristen Lee Hunter. Ithaca, New York: East Asia Program, Cornell University, 2006.

Wang Gungwu, "The China Seas: Becoming an Enlarged Mediterranean". In *The East Asian 'Mediterranean': Maritime Crossroads of Culture, Commerce and*

Human Migration, edited by Angela Schottenhammer, pp. 7–22. Wiesbaden: Harrossowitz Verlag, 2008.

———. "The Nanhai Trade: A Study of the Early History of Chinese Trade in the South China Sea". M.A. Thesis, University of Malaya, 1956, published in *Journal of the Malayan Branch of the Royal Asiatic Society*, Kuala Lumpur, Monograph Issue, Vol. 31, part 2 (1958) (New paperback edition published by Eastern Universities Press in 2003).

Wheatley, Paul. "Geographical Notes on Some Commodities Involved in Sung Maritime Trade". *Journal of Malayan Branch of the Royal Asiatic Society* 32, no. 2 (1959): 1–139.

———. *The Golden Khersonese: Studies in the Historical Geography of the Malay Peninsula before A.D. 1500*. Kuala Lumpur: University of Malaya Press, 1961.

Wong, R. Bin. *China Transformed: Historical Change and the Limits of European Experience*. Ithaca: Cornell University Press, 1997.

Yu Changsen 喻常森. *Yuandai haiwai maoyi* 元代海外贸易. Xi'an: Xibei daxue chubanshe, 1994.

5

THE CONCEPTS OF SPACE AND TIME IN THE SOUTHEAST ASIAN ARCHIPELAGO*

Denys Lombard (translated by Helen Reid)

Our concepts of space and time are highly useful in our daily lives and are, moreover, ingrained in our history. Hence it seems almost impossible for us to understand any phenomenon in our own culture or any other without first defining it by placing and dating it, thereby relating it to other phenomena while at the same time endowing it with its own unique characteristics. This way of thinking goes back far into the past.

The Greeks already had the idea of progression — and history — as well as an autonomous notion of space that was sufficiently developed to allow for both geometry and geography. Subsequently Christianity made an important contribution towards consolidating our idea of linear time by giving a meaning to the life of the individual (through reflecting on its finality) and by tracing the collective adventure of the human race from a starting point at the creation of the world to a conclusion at the Last Judgment. Since the sixteenth century, scientific thought and the ideology of progress have not challenged the primacy of either concept, and while some of Einstein's ideas clearly called them into question, it is obvious that these ideas have been swept along with the encroaching tide of modernity.

We well know — as research has shown — that our Western societies have not always held such definite opinions on this subject. For a long time there were quite complex views about an afterlife, whether in space or time.

Where did souls go after death? Whereabouts in space could purgatory be situated? The world was only mapped through a long process of trial and error. Pilgrimages were contemporaneous with voyages of exploration and discovery. Europe too has known the millenarian upheavals that can be seen today in certain countries in the throes of decolonization. Not so long ago in the privacy of our homes makeshift shamans used *Ouija* boards in their attempts to communicate with the dead, and we know that astrology and numerology still flourish at the very heart of the most developed urban societies. At this point one could simply accept that different conceptual systems can overlap or exist in juxtaposition, but in general we prefer to consider these concepts as 'residual' aberrations. In contrast with them, our pure concepts of space and time seem all the more precious and indispensable.

There is some interest in trying to look at another way of perceiving things, in a region of the world whose history has been very different. The Southeast Asian Archipelago lies at the crossroads of the great Asian cultures of India, Islam and China, yet it has retained a strong Austronesian identity. Contact with the West was established there with the arrival of the first Portuguese (Afonso de Albuquerque captured Malacca in 1511), but the real confrontation with Western ways of thinking began much later, with the organization of the 'Netherlands Indies' in the nineteenth century, the development of the first religious missions (which had been forbidden by the Dutch Company before that date) and the establishment of the first schools. We are not concerned here with the details of this confrontation, which was rendered even more intense by the achievement of independence (in 1949 for Indonesia, 1957 for Malaysia) and exposure to a much more diversified 'Western' culture. Our main concerns are on the one hand with the first signs of an Islamic 'modernity', which can be discerned fairly clearly from the fifteenth century in the societies of the great sultanates of the port cities, and on the other hand with the retention of a much more archaic concept in the agrarian societies in the interior, notably in Java, in which the notions of space and time still seem to converge.

First of all a few words on the great economic and social changes that affected the Archipelago as well as the rest of Southeast Asia, during the centuries that preceded the arrival of the first Portuguese. No doubt these changes followed in the wake of major transformations that took place in the international exchange networks — disruption of the route through Central Asia that had been so important under the Tang dynasty, and the gradual establishment of the Mongol system. This era saw an unprecedented development of the maritime route linking the China Sea to the Indian Ocean, the abandonment of the great agrarian cities of the interior (Pagan, Angkor,

Majapahit) and the flourishing of a new generation of cities situated on the coast (Malacca, Aceh, Banten) or on a river close to the sea (Pegu, Ayutthaya).[1] This radical change in urban cartography was accompanied by a progressive increase in the use of monetary systems (the import of Chinese copper cash, then the minting of gold or tin coins *in situ*) and of course important social changes: traditional hierarchies began to be challenged and new clienteles were established (together with a new dependency based on debt).

This phenomenon took place over at least three centuries — from the thirteenth to the sixteenth century. It was accompanied by a radical change in ideologies. Hinduism, often associated with Mahayana Buddhism, had inspired the great monuments in the most ancient cities in Cambodia and Java (and as we know, retained its hold in Bali). Now these two ideologies were gradually replaced by two new religions: Theravada Buddhism in most of the countries of Indochina (Burma, Siam, Cambodia and Laos) and Islam in the Southeast Asian Archipelago.

Comparative research has hardly touched this area, but it is striking to note certain parallels between the latter two ideologies, which are so different in other ways. Firstly, in both cases they place importance on the chronological and the topographical, for example giving an eminent role to great historical figures such as Muhammad and Siddhartha, and paramount importance to making pilgrimage to the sources of the belief, whether this be journeying on the one hand to Mecca and Medina, or on the other hand to the holy places in Northern India where the Buddha lived during the major stages in his life. Another significant fact is that in both cases the idea of the person is given greater emphasis. The individual is encouraged to feel responsible and to behave in a moral way in expectation of the judgment which will decide his fate in the afterlife.

The progress made by Islam was particularly marked in the trading sultanates in the west of the archipelago (Malacca, Aceh, Johore, Banten, Demak and Makassar), and inspired a wealth of literature, basically in Malay (written in the Arabic script) but also in Javanese, Bugis and Makassarese. Fairly often these texts were influenced by Arab or Persian models. These could be considered an excellent *corpus* through which to study the changes in mentality at this time, and especially the emergence of a new concept of time and space.

Precise terms can be found in these texts, borrowed from Arabic, to express 'time' (*waktu*), 'the era' (*zaman*), 'the century' (*abad*) and 'the hour' (*jam*). However the most striking novelty is the widespread use of the Muslim calendar. In the epigraphic texts of ancient Java, the year was lunar-solar and as in India and Cambodia was calculated as part of an era, called *shaka*, which began in 78 CE.² From the introduction of Islam, in the coastal sultanates the year consisted of 12 synodical months, each 29 days long, counted from the *Hijra*. This implies adherence to a widespread reckoning system and an effort to establish a relationship between all the events that took place in the Islamic community (*ummah*). Moreover, henceforth the rhythm of the day was marked by the succession of the five prescribed prayers (*subuh, lohor, asar, maghrib* and *isya*), which served as a means of ordering the day's activities. In addition, while minarets were rare in the Archipelago, the *bedug*, large drums made of buffalo hide, would sound out the hours that were important to the community, somewhat like our church bells.

It has been pointed out quite correctly that this lunar calendar which had been introduced by traders is better adapted to the needs of city dwellers than to peasants, who need above all to take note of seasonal changes, in the equator as in more temperate climates. On the other hand the new system had positive, almost modern, aspects. Introducing the unchanging regularity of the rhythm of the months (as well as that of the seven-day week) established the fundamental principle that time is coherent and neutral. Reference to the almanacs (*primbon*) still in use in Java (and Bali) will show that pre-Islamic time was, on the contrary, fragmentary and heterogeneous, consisting essentially of positive and negative moments and days that were lucky or unlucky. Their nature could only be identified by a difficult process of calculation. It was much more important to establish the quality of the moment, its 'density', than to calculate the shortness or length of a period of time, as the success of an enterprise depended entirely on that quality.

In order to evaluate the quality of a given moment, you would need for example to take into account the specific tonality of each of the 30 *wuku*, or combinations of seven days each, which together constituted a cycle.³ Alternatively, taking account of the fact that no fewer than six weeks existed, all of different lengths (seven, three, five, six, eight or nine days), one would need to carefully study the complex interplay arising when days of different cycles coincided. Hence, for example, when *kliwon*, the most important day in the five-day week, fell at the same time as *kajeng* (a day in the three-day week), it was necessary to make offerings to malevolent spirits; but if *kliwon* fell at the same time as *sanescara* (a strong day in the seven-day week) — which happened every 35 days — these circumstances were considered particularly auspicious.

In comparison, the Muslim calendar is extremely simple. It levels all the disparities and, except for Fridays (as well as a small number of major festivals such as the anniversary of the Prophet's birthday) it imposes a regular system of calculating time where man can take the real initiative. This change is even more radical than the Christian system where each day has its 'saint', which to some extent reflects its heterogeneous origins.

The new calendar not only established a homogeneous system for calculating time. In addition, by identifying a beginning and an end to the world, Islamic ideology gave meaning to history. This gave rise to the idea of time moving on, oriented towards a goal, which is found elsewhere in other prophetic religions. There is a strong message about the fleeting nature of material things and the importance of the Last Judgment in a short Muslim moral tract that probably originated in one of the ports on the north coast of Java in the sixteenth century:

> Nothing is eternal in this world (*ora kekel ing dunya*). Be aware that on the Judgment Day (*ari kiyamat*) only a rare few faithful ones will be recognized among the true Muslims.[4]

A similar idea appeared at the beginning of the seventeenth century in an important tract of political philosophy, *The Kings' Crown* (*Tāj us-salatin*) written in Malay in Aceh or Johore:

> Man is a traveller (*musafir*) who must pass through several stages — his father's loins, his mother's breast, then a third stage in this lower world, then the grave, then the Judgment Plain, and finally heaven or hell, where he will remain forever.
> The way open to him is long and difficult, and he can only find provisions on this earth. Once launched, the chariot of his life (*kendaraan umurnya*) rolls on without stopping, and without his being aware of it. Each time he breathes is one more step along the way, each month another league, each year further still.[5]

Probably there is no better illustration of this linear view of time in existence. However in his very fine '*Poem on the Ship*' (*Syair Perahu*), written in Malay in North Sumatra towards the end of the sixteenth century,[6] Hamzah Fansuri compares life in this world to making a sea crossing:

> Ah, young man, know your true self!
> This ship represents your body.
> Your time on this earth will be fleeting;
> You will only know peace on the other side...
>
> There is no God but Allah, and you are following him.
> The wind is roaring, the seas are tempestuous,
> Whales and sharks are pursuing you...
> Make sure you hold tight to the tiller, don't falter!

If you can always be vigilant
All these tempests will die down.
There will be calm after the storm,
You will land safely on the island...

A new concept of the past and a new historiography were developing that were closely related to this new concept of human progress. In particular, there was a marked increase in the number of *silsilah*, or genealogies, that link up the generations in long chains, giving a marvelous visual representation of the idea of linear continuity. The importance of lineage in the Archipelago is certainly much more ancient, but Islam played an important role here by privileging paternal descent. Moreover, following this same model Islam introduced the idea of a 'spiritual chain' through the *tarekat* (brotherhood) linking the current sheikh to the founding sheikh (and the founding sheikh to the Prophet).

In addition, in certain sultanates (Makassar, Bima and the island of Sumbawa) court scribes began to maintain 'daily diaries' where they kept note of the sovereign's main activities, ships departing or embassies arriving. It is true that this practice does not seem to have been very widespread. The other sultanates generally preferred 'chronicles' that were more or less romanticized, where history was often interwoven with mythology in a complex fabric that sometimes drives historians to despair.[7]

A glorious exception to this rule is the *Sultans' Garden* (*Bustan us-salatin*), an ambitious survey of human knowledge in seven volumes written in 1638 in Aceh in Malay. The author, Nuruddin ar-Raniri, a Gujarati, sets out to relate the history of the world from its creation, particularly focusing on Islamic achievements from the time of Muhammad to the Sultanates of the Archipelago.

Parallel to this developing sense of time, the concept of space also became more precise. Here we will not concern ourselves with the effects of new inventions that were certainly instrumental in changing man's relationship with the world. These would, for example, include the role of firearms, which were well-known in Southeast Asia before the arrival of the Portuguese, especially the 'giant' cannon that various sultans had manufactured in the sixteenth and seventeenth centuries. They were used not so much for firing heavier cannonballs at their adversaries as to sound the alarm, or to announce their demands to the farthermost corners of the land.[8] They would also include the first mechanical objects, such as toys or automatons inspired by distant Alexandrian models that are described in Malay texts, or skilful models of animals portrayed in the first European accounts,[9] which show the desire to imitate nature and by this means control it.

Rather, this study is more concerned with the slow but basic move away from cosmological to geographical space, or in other words a move away from the mandala to the map. At the margins of the very simplified diagram (a centre and four cardinal directions) that continued to provide the sedentary with a reassuring explanation of the macrocosm, helping them to harmonize their lives in relationship to that concept, gradually topographical contours were beginning to emerge that certainly gave a less stylized picture of a totality, but instead showed one better adapted to the traveller's needs.

Our information on this subject is still very fragmentary. There seems to be no doubt that the geographical map was in use in the Archipelago before the Portuguese arrived. Unfortunately we have no original examples of this cartography. However we do have a report from Ludovico de Varthema, who states that he travelled from Borneo to Java in 1505 on a native vessel whose pilot had a compass and a map 'where a good many lines were drawn to indicate the winds, in the same way as the maps we use ourselves.'[10] Admittedly one cannot always rely on Varthema. Nevertheless, we also have Albuquerque's detailed account of a superb Javanese map that he had translated and copied by his pilot, Francisco Rodrigues. The original was lost in 1511 with the rest of the treasure that had been seized in Malacca, when the ship taking it back to Portugal was wrecked.[11]

In 1876, moreover, in the little village of Ciela south of Garut in West Java, a Dutch civil servant named Karel Frederik Holle discovered a very interesting map of the region on fabric that possibly dated from 1560. This precious document has since then disappeared, leaving only the account that Holle published at that time. What is all the more remarkable is that it was not a maritime map, but gave a particularly rich toponymy of the whole centre of the Sunda district.[12]

This new sense of geography is also well-illustrated in several Malay literary texts. In the East Javanese Panji stories from the fifteenth and sixteenth centuries we can already see a vogue for adventure and travellers' tales, but the hero, who is setting out to search for his beloved Candrakirana, is still part of a fictional universe ruled by magic.

However the seventeenth-century Malay novel that features the hero Hang Tuah is based in a very realistic world.[13] The task which the Sultan of Malacca gives to his admiral Hang Tuah is to carry out a whole series of diplomatic and military operations in places that mostly have well-known place names from which a reader referring to a map can trace out a certain political horizon. For example, relations with the neighbouring trading ports on the east coast of the Malay Peninsula (Trengganu and Indrapura) are rather tense, and Malacca has to resort to force. On the other hand, relations with Palembang (in Sumatra) and the islands in the Straits (Bintan, Lingga, Singapore) are cordial and always peaceful. Further to the east there are two powers that have to be reckoned with: Brunei (on the north coast of Borneo) and especially Java, where Hang Tuah is sent several times, and which seems to be the most dangerous rival. Beyond the Archipelago properly speaking, contacts are maintained with the distant powers. Embassies are sent to China and Siam, Vijayanagar, South India, Mecca and as far as Egypt and Rum (Constantinople), where the Admiral goes to ask the Great Lord for cannon. The author endeavours to give each of the countries visited its special character by adding a little 'local colour.' In Siam there is a humorous touch in descriptions of the swashbuckling Japanese guards, who saunter about 'with their sabres trailing along the ground'; while in Negapatam the author is concerned about the 'outspoken' traders whose arrogance is second to none.

Another text that is roughly contemporaneous with the Hang Tuah novel conveys a similar impression. It tells of the conquest of the world by King Iskandar, the propagator of Islam.[14] Of course this is the Malay version of the *Novel of Iskandar*, which follows the hero from one end of the inhabited world to the other, introducing a host of details about distant lands to the Malay readers, who had hitherto known nothing about them. Notable examples are Andalusia; Sicily, home of a terrible volcano whose crater is one of Hell's gates; the great desert in Africa, land of giraffes and ostriches; the land of cotton (between Antioch and Aleppo); the gardens of Kashmir; the copper mines of Central Asia; the forays of Gog and Magog, nomadic peoples against whom Iskandar has a great wall built; China, with its musk. Returning to Egypt, in the end the hero establishes Kandariah, a vast city with numerous palaces honeycombed with underground passageways, a bronze fortress and a high tower (*al-Manar*), equipped with mirrors to keep watch on the ships passing by along the coast.

Of course this is a fictional itinerary and in no way geographically accurate, but what is important here is its interest in the global. The conqueror wishes to go from the 'land where the sun sets' to the 'land where it rises'; and once he reaches the eastern limits of the world he decides to venture into the ocean in order to visit the anti-world (or the world upside down, *dunia balik*), which is symmetrical with our world. To do this he orders the construction of a sort of bathyscaphe, a great 'glass container' (*peti kaca*) suspended by a cable, in which he has himself lowered into the ocean. Iskandar's curiosity and his drive to confront the unknown purely for the joy of discovery are reminiscent of some sixteenth century European heroes.

Putting aside all these changes that were informed, if not inspired, by Islam, we now turn to the pre-Islamic system as witnesses saw it in ancient Java and as it still survives in the agrarian societies of the interior, as well as in Bali.

Here, the fundamental principle is fairly simple, even if we often have some difficulty in understanding all the implications. This principle postulates that all concepts and all perception can and must belong to one of four distinct poles, or more precisely five, as the centre is a privileged place where the elements from the four domains on the periphery must be able to converge and become harmonized. According to this principle, then, each of these five points — the centre and the four cardinal directions of North, South, East and West — is associated not only with a deity but also with a basic colour, a metal, a liquid, an animal, a series of letters and one day from the five-day week. Properly speaking it is not space but the totality of Being that is divided up according to a gigantic system linking and harmonizing these five categories (or nine, as sometimes there is the further complication of intermediate directions). To understand this system, a Westerner might think of the language of flowers, the symbolism of precious stones or Rimbaud's 'Sonnet des voyelles.'

A whole technical literature on this subject developed, beginning in the eleventh century with the *Sang Hyang Kamahāyānikan*, followed by the *Korawāsrama* (sixteenth century?) and the *Manikmaya* (eighteenth century) and continues to flourish today, giving rise to the many *primbon* (almanacs) that continue to appear. Basically this literature is intended to provide the keys to these 'correspondences' so that the world can be deciphered or 'read.' In fact the same word, *baca*, is used in Javanese for 'interpreting' a phenomenon and 'reading' a book.

Rather than launch into a host of variations, we shall only consider a few elementary examples here. In general the colour white, silver and coconut milk correspond with the East; the colour red, copper and blood correspond with the South; the colour yellow, gold and honey correspond with the West; the colour black, iron and indigo correspond with the North; and finally the centre, which represents the synthesis of the four directions and embodies all their qualities, is linked with blended colour, bronze (which is an alloy) and boiling water (*wédang*). The days of *pancawara*, the five-day week, are similarly divided up according to the cardinal directions, with *kliwon* at the centre (which is generally held to be the most important day). This seems to suggest that time is not seen as an autonomous category, but simply divided up like the other elements according to the quintuple system:[15]

This study is not the place for a more detailed consideration of the history of this system. Nevertheless it posits some fascinating problems and has inevitably inspired some interesting comparisons.[16] Louis-Charles Damais has clearly shown that this identification of five cardinal directions with the five basic colours was in no way influenced by Indian or Chinese symbolic systems, but originated purely from Nusantara.[17] Some scholars have gone further than this in suggesting that the classification must date back to a period when Javanese society was divided into four complementary clans, and it is certainly possible to see parallels with other societies in the region.

FIGURE 1
Illustration of the Various Affiliations among Directions, Colours and Week Days

	North	
West	Centre	East
	South	

	Black	
Yellow	Multicoloured	White
	Red	

	wagé	
pon	*kliwon*	*legi*
	pahing	

Others again have gone still further, for example in relating it to the cruciform schema, recalling the words of Saint Jerome: *Ipsa species crucis quid est nisi forma quadrata mundi?* (Can this crucifix form represent anything else than the four corners of the world?) Similarly, Saint Irenaeus stated that the four gospels corresponded to the four cardinal points.[18]

The matter in question here concerns the implications of such a classification on a conceptual level. Since we are accustomed to our own idea of a historical, linear time, it requires effort to imagine a 'time' that is motionless and confined within things. From that perspective, society does not seem to be progressing along a certain path, leaving its past behind. Instead, it grows on itself, driving its past out to the periphery somewhat like onion skin. The dead become 'spirits' (*yang*) and go off into the neighbouring forests where they continue to take part in community life. While the coming of Islam puts an end to this wandering, the spirits still continue to intercede on behalf of the living who come to their tombs to appeal to them.

Perhaps the essential point is that the future is contained in the present. People have to learn to interpret the 'signs' (*pralambang*) that can reveal it. There is a very important literature of 'predictions' (*ramalan*) on this subject.[19] Of course these predictions can only be verified after the event, but it is Westerners who feel the need to be skeptical, because their linear view inhibits them, preventing them from interpreting such predictions properly. An interesting study could be undertaken of the 'logic' that is peculiar to this science of deciphering, which is based on etymological interpretation (*keratabasa*) — because words are part of the profound nature of the things that they represent — and on numerological calculation (*petungan*) because numbers too are within things, and reveal their essence.

There is a strange little booklet published in 1965 under the title 'The meaning of the sacred numbers' that might give some idea of this way of thinking.[20] The author sets out to explain the 'underlying significance' of the date 17 August 1945 (17-8-45), which was the date when Sukarno declared the independence of Indonesia. First of all one must calculate a number by multiplying 17 by 8 and then by 45. This gives a number of days (6,120), which corresponds more or less to 17 years. The author then endeavours to build a scale of numbers (periodization) based on the number 17, starting from the 'sacred year' which is 1945. Going backwards in time, this gives 1928 (the year of the Youth Oath) and 1911 (the year of the founding of the Sarekat Islam, an important Islamic movement). Going forwards, 1962 (the year when the Netherlands ceded Western New Guinea) would lead on to 1979, the year when Indonesia would once again become a 'maritime power', and finally 1996, when a socialist regime would be established.

The author's speculations in the area of cartography are even more remarkable than these manipulations of chronology. Here the links between the notions of space and time are still apparent. The author compares Krakatoa (the famous volcano in the middle of the Sunda Strait) and the islands of Sumatra and Java to the axis and two hands of an enormous clock, and states that these two hands point exactly to 10.28 a.m., the moment (in Java time) when Sukarno read the declaration of independence. In another example of this type of speculation, he draws an oblique line on a map of Indonesia, passing through the centre of Kalimantan and cutting through the equator at an angle of 17° (still keeping 17 August in mind), and observes that this

FIGURE 2
Archipelagic Space as a Clock of National History
(after B. Setiadidjaja, *Arti Angka-angka Keramat bagi Bangsa Indonesia dan Dunia Baru,* Bandung 1965, p. 78)

line goes 'exactly' from Sabang to Merauke, that is to say from one end of Indonesia to the other. There is no better illustration of the link between time and matter.

This is a very simplified exposé. It does, however, show that two radically different systems of space and time coexist in the Southeast Asian region. One of these is very close to our own, and can easily coincide with that system, although its origins are in no way the same. The other system is completely foreign to our way of thinking, but far from being merely 'residual,' is part of a very strong tradition that shows no sign of disappearing. In an era where there is much talk of the progress of 'development' (and the Westernization that often accompanies that development), it is worth remembering these two points.

Notes

* This contribution is translated from Denys Lombard, "Les concepts d'espace et de temps dans l'archipel insulindien", *Annales: Économies, Sociétés, Civilisations*, no. 6 (1986): 1385–96.
1. For the rise of these new merchant towns see Denys Lombard, "Pour une histoire des villes du Sud-Est asiatique," *Annales: Économies, Sociétés, Civilisations*, no. 4 (1970): 842–56.
2. Indianists are still divided on the exact nature of the event that put its mark on the year 78 CE. In Java there seems to be no memory of such a moment in history, and the beginning of the *Shaka* era has traditionally been associated with the arrival in Java of a mythical person, Aji Saka, who enriched the culture notably by introducing writing to the island. For a study of the dating system used in the epigraphical texts of ancient Java, see Johannes G. de Casparis, *Indonesian Chronology* (Leiden & Cologne: Brill, 1978).
3. See Louis-Charles Damais, "Le Calendrier de l'ancienne Java," *Journal asiatique*, CCLV (1967): pp. 133–41; also Miguel Covarrubias, *Island of Bali* (New York: A.A. Knopf, 1965. Originally published 1937), pp. 282ff.
4. The Javanese text was translated and published by Gerardus Willebrordus Johannes Drewes, *An Early Javanese Code of Muslim Ethics* (The Hague: Martinus Nijhoff, 1978). Quoted from pp. 14–15.
5. One of the many manuscripts of *The Kings' Crown* was published by Khalid Hussain, *Bukhair Al-Jauhari: Taj us-Salatin* (Kuala Lumpur: Dewan Bahasa dan Pustaka, 1966). A French translation of a different manuscript appeared in the 19th century: Aristide Marre, *Makôta radja-râdja ou La Couronne des rois* (Paris: Maisonneuve, 1878).
6. For Hamzah Fansuri, see J. Doorenbos, *De Geschriften van Hamzah Pansoeri* (Leiden: Batteljee & Terpstra, 1933) and the more recent study by Syed Muhammad Naguib Al-Attas, *The Mysticism of Hamzah Fansurî* (Kuala Lumpur:

University of Malaya Press, 1970). For an Italian translation of the *Poem on the Ship* (*Syair Perahu*), see Alessandro Bausani, *Le Letterature del Sud-Est Asiatico* (Milan: Accademia, 1970), pp. 317–21.

7. In *Archipel*, 20, 1980, the section 'De la philologie à l'histoire' focuses entirely on the problems of 'reading' posed by the Malay manuscripts. This is notably the case in the study by Lode F. Brakel, 'Dichtung und Wahrheit, Some Notes on the Development of the Study of Indonesian Historiography', pp. 35–44.

8. For example Augustin de Beaulieu, who went to Aceh in 1619, remarked: 'Every morning and evening the King has cannon fired as the castle gates opened, and if any neighbouring king decided to do the same thing, he would make war on him, saying that he had invented this custom, and wished to keep it for himself alone, to bear witness to his might.'(Melchisédech Thévenot, ed., *Collections de voyages*, vol. 2 (Paris: 1666), p. 119).

9. For example Edmund Scott, a factor in the English post at Banten, gives a long account of the great pageant organized in June–July 1605 on the occasion of the circumcision of the young prince. He describes the animals, artificial as well as living, that were part of the procession: 'beasts and foules, both alive and also so artificially made that except one has been neere, they were not to be discerned from those that were alive…'(Sir William Foster (ed.), *The Voyage of Sir Henry Middleton to the Moluccas, 1604–1606* (London: Hakluyt Society, 1943), pp. 152–62.

10. The text is quoted by Frederik Caspar Wieder in the article 'Kaartbeschrijving' (Cartography) in D.G. Stibbe (ed.) *Encyclopaedie van Nederlandsch-Indië*, 2nd ed. ('s Gravenhage & Leiden: Martinus Nijhoff & Brill, 1919), vol. 2.

11. See Armando Cortesão, ed., *The Suma Oriental of Tomé Pires and the Book of Francisco Rodrigues*, vol. 1 (London: Hakluyt Society, 1944), Introduction, pp. lxxviii–ix.

12. Karel Frederik Holle, "De Kaart van Tjiëla of Timbangenten," *Tijdschrift van het Bataviaasch Genootschap*, XXIV (1877): 168–76, with separate facsimile. Several Bugis maps have also been preserved, but they seem much more recent.

13. The *Hikayat Hang Tuah* was translated into German by Hans Overbeck *Die Geschichte von Hang Tuah*, 2 vols. (Munich: Georg Müller, 1922), and more recently into Russian by Boris Parnikel, *Povesti o Hang Tuahe* (Moscow: Nauka, 1984).

14. There is not yet a satisfactory edition of the *Hikayat Iskandar Zulkarnain*; nor has it been translated. The first part (372 pp., up to the conquest of Egypt) was published by Khalid Hussain in Latin script (Kuala Lumpur: Dewan Bahasa dan Pustaka, 1967). The most useful work is still the study by P. J. van Leeuwen, *De Maleische Alexander-roman* (Meppel: Ten Brink, 1937), which comprises fairly long extracts.

15. Another sign that gives further evidence of this linking of time with the general system of correspondences is the use of *candrasangkala*, or 'chronograms', which

is still highly regarded in Java. The procedure consists of noting the year of an event not with numbers but with words to which numerical values have been attributed. However these words still retain their original meaning, which allows for an allusion to the dated fact at the same time. It is also noteworthy that the three Indonesian words *empat* (four), *tempat* (place) and *sempat* (occasion, time of an action) are all etymologically linked and originate from the same root, *pat*.

16. Note particularly Patrick Edward de Josselin de Jong (ed.), *Structural Anthropology in the Netherlands* (The Hague: Martinus Nijhoff, 1977), which republished a number of articles on the classifications systems in English translation, notably Frederik Daniel Eduard van Ossenbruggen, "Java's Monca-pat: Origins of a Primitive Classification System", pp. 32–60; and Théodore G.Th. Pigeaud, "Javanese Divination and Classification", pp. 64–82.
17. Louis-Charles Damais, "Etude javanaise III: à propos des couleurs symboliques des points cardinaux," *Bulletin de l'Ecole française de l'Extrême-Orient*, LVI (1969): 75–118.
18. Van Ossenbruggen, "*Java's Monca-pat*," p. 58, refers to Salomon Reinach, *Orpheus, histoire générale des religions* (Paris: A. Picard, 1909), p. 320.
19. Many of these predictions are attributed to King Joyoboyo (twelfth century) but they are in fact much more recent. In the twentieth century, there has been an increase in these predictions during the most troubled times: 1945–49, the period of the so-called 'Physical' Revolution, and 1965–67, the upheavals following the events of September and October 1965. The predictions give the impression of being an attempt to reassure people by showing that all these changes were in the nature of things, and conformed to prophecies.
20. B. Setiadidjaja, *Arti Angka-angka Keramat bagi Bangsa Indonesia dan Dunia Baru* (Bandung: Balebat, 1965).

References

Al-Attas, Syed Muhammad Naguib. *The Mysticism of Hamzah Fansurî*. Kuala Lumpur, Dewan Bahasa dan Pustaka, 1970.

Bausani, Alessandro. *Le Letterature del Sud-Est Asiatico*. Milan: Accademia, 1970.

Brakel, Lode F. "Dichtung und Wahrheit, Some Notes on the Development of the Study of Indonesian Historiography." *Archipel* 20 (1980): 35–44.

Casparis, Johannes G. de. *Indonesian Chronology*. Leiden & Cologne, Brill, 1978.

Cortesão, Armando (ed.). *The Suma Oriental of Tomé Pires and the Book of Francisco Rodrigues*. 2 vols. London: Hakluyt Society, 1944.

Covarrubias, Miguel. *Island of Bali*. New York: A.A. Knopf, 1965 (Orig. publ. 1937).

Damais, Louis-Charles. "Le Calendrier de l'ancienne Java." *Journal asiatique* CCLV (1967): 133–41.

———. "Etude javanaise III: à propos des couleurs symboliques des points cardinaux." *Bulletin de l'Ecole française de l'Extrême-Orient* LVI (1969): 75–118.

Doorenbos, J. *De Geschriften van Hamzah Pansoeri*. Leiden: Batteljee & Terpstra, 1933.

Drewes, Gerardus Willebrordus Johannes. *An Early Javanese Code of Muslim Ethics*. The Hague: Martinus Nijhoff, 1978.

Foster, William (ed.). *The Voyage of Sir Henry Middleton to the Moluccas, 1604–1606*. London: Hakluyt Society, 1943.

Holle, Karel Frederik. "De Kaart van Tjiëla of Timbangenten." *Tijdschrift van het Bataviaasch Genootschap* XXIV (1877): 168–76.

Khalid Hussain (ed.). *Bukhair Al-Jauhari: Taj us-Salatin*. Kuala Lumpur: Dewan Bahasa dan Pustaka, 1966.

Khalid Hussain. *Hikayat Iskandar Zulkarnain*. Kuala Lumpur: Dewan Bahasa dan Pustaka, 1967.

Josselin de Jong, Patrick Edward de (ed.). *Structural Anthropology in the Netherlands*. The Hague: Martinus Nijhoff, 1977.

Leeuwen, J. van. *De Maleische Alexander-roman*. Meppel: Ten Brink,1937.

Lombard, Denys. "Pour une histoire des villes du Sud-Est asiatique." *Annales. Économies, Sociétés, Civilisations* No. 4 (1970): 842–56.

———. "Les concepts d'espace et de temps dans l'archipel insulindien." *Annales. Économies, Sociétés, Civilisations* No. 6 (1986): 1385–96.

Marre, Aristide. *Makôta radja-râdja ou La Couronne des rois*. Paris: Maisonneuve, 1878.

Ossenbruggen, Frederik Daniel Eduard van. "Java's Monca-pat: Origins of a Primitive Classification System." In *Structural Anthropology in the Netherlands*, edited by Patrick Edward de Josselin de Jong, pp. 32–60. The Hague: Martinus Nijhoff, 1977.

Overbeck, Hans. *Die Geschichte von Hang Tuah*. 2 vols. Munich: Georg Müller, 1922.

Parnikel, Boris. *Povesti o Hang Tuahe*. Moscow: Nauka, 1984.

Pigeaud, Théodore G. Th. "Javanese Divination and Classification." In *Structural Anthropology in the Netherlands*, edited by Patrick Edward de Josselin de Jong, pp. 64–82. The Hague: Martinus Nijhoff, 1977.

Reinach, Salomon. *Orpheus, histoire générale des religions*. Paris: A. Picard, 1909.

Setiadidjaja, B. *Arti Angka-angka Keramat bagi Bangsa Indonesia dan Dunia Baru*. Bandung: Balebat, 1965.

Thévenot, Melchisedech (ed.). *Collections de voyages*. Paris: 1666.

Wieder, Frederik Caspar. "Kaartbeschrijving." In the *Encyclopaedie van Nederlandsch-Indië*, 2nd edited by D.G. Stibbe. Vol. 2. 's Gravenhage & Leiden: Martinus Nijhoff & Brill, 1919.

6

DOMINION OVER PALM AND PINE
Early Indonesia's Maritime Reach

Ann Kumar

The first five words of the above title are taken from a poem by Rudyard Kipling which until rather recently was well-known in Australia, where its words were sung every Anzac Day in commemoration of the deaths of many young compatriots in bygone but not forgotten battles of the British Empire.[1] In this poem Kipling reflects on how an excess of imperial pride might see the mighty British Empire pass away like its predecessors, and extols humility and contrition. Kipling's empire was based on British supremacy at sea. So was the much earlier dominion to be described here, which also extended over palm — not just the Indonesian ones, but also the Madagascan ones, so perhaps one should say 'palm and baobab' — and pine, a Japanese one.

In this paper, after briefly sketching Indonesia's maritime reach, I will also argue that it is not simply meaningless to classify Indonesia as 'Southeast Asian' but is in fact a major barrier to any real understanding of its history.

On what criteria might one judge the coherence of a portfolio category such as 'Europe' or 'Southeast Asia'? Some obvious ones suggest themselves: cultural and religious commonality, linguistic commonality, and political unification, of which Europe has the first two, with the great predominance of Indo-European languages, and of Christianity for the last two millennia.

It scores less consistently over time with regards to political unification, since the significant achievements of the Romans were not maintained thereafter, though the constant competitive striving for pan-European empire, especially in the period from Napoleon to Hitler, has allowed historians to pin their narrative to an account of the resultant warfare. Southeast Asia has none of these things.

This lack of any of the unifying factors that make 'Europe' a coherent category causes major problems for historians of Southeast Asia. Attempts are generally made to solve these by one of the following strategies: breaking up Southeast Asia and dealing with the component parts separately;[2] adopting a *pars pro toto* strategy;[3] or attempting to generalize across the whole of Southeast Asia. These generalizations usually have to be very broad indeed to capture all of Southeast Asia and hence are hardly ever peculiar to it. Owen[4] for example oscillates between the first and last strategies, the latter clearly demonstrating the sort of generalization that results. By way of general categories we find, for example ' … when the biggest rogues were overthrown — Thanom in Thailand, Marcos and Estrada in the Philippines, Suharto in Indonesia — most of the reformers who replaced them came from similar backgrounds, so there was little change in the overall trajectory of government policy.'[5] 'Rogue' is hardly specific to Southeast Asia — nor to a particular type of polity, unlike analytical categories of the type of 'feudal lord,' for example, which facilitate productive comparative work. What illuminating comparisons might one make with 'rogue'? Might one ask whether Suharto was a bigger or a different sort of rogue from the other rogues who were contemporaneously, and illegally, saturation bombing Laos? He did rather a lot of bad things but also not a few good things (for example in education and health). This sort of comparison is prejudicial, relying on judgments as to whom one is prepared to stigmatize and whom not.

Southeast Asia not only has many different languages but also a significant array of different language *families*. Indonesia, Malaysia and the Philippines belong to the Austronesian language family — a family unknown on the Southeast Asian mainland with the exception of the Cham languages, whose speakers are relatively recent migrants from Indonesia.[6]

Here I will deal with that part of the Austronesian language family I know best, i.e. the sub-group conventionally referred to as Western Malayo-Polynesian, which includes the languages of Indonesia, Malaysia and the Philippines. The paper will review two case studies from pre-modern history which I hope will be of some interest. But first, some background.

THE AUSTRONESIAN MIGRATION: FROM TAIWAN TO EASTER ISLAND

Horridge points out that the earliest Austronesian colonists in the Pacific were in the same situation as the Vikings on the coast of Norway, and in later times the Portuguese, the English and the Dutch, facing winds they were confident would blow them back close to home — a situation that created a continual stimulus for sailors.[7] These Austronesians were part of an East Asian 'Neolithic Revolution' which had profound implications for many other parts of the world. This particular language family was distinguished from others originating in the same general area in that it had an extraordinary nautical tradition, enabling Austronesians to migrate all across the Pacific. This major population expansion had begun in Taiwan, where Neolithic finds date from 4300 BCE,[8] with some evidence for rice by 3000 BCE. The Austronesian Neolithic was based on agriculture and animal husbandry. It spread rapidly: the earliest Southeast Asian date is from around 3000 BCE, and by 2500 BCE the culture extended all over the region. Neolithic populations occupied the whole region of mainland Southeast Asia, including the Malay Peninsula, by at least 2000 BCE. Bellwood believes that by 1500 BCE Austronesians had reached Indonesia, but it seems to me that a date of 1500 BCE for the *earliest* arrival of Austronesians may be too late. By 1000 BCE we already have highly sophisticated Bronze-Iron societies — not just Neolithic agricultural societies — whose archaeological remains include gold objects, evidence of a wealthy society with an élite class. Such a society would have required some time to develop.

Austronesians reached the Marquesas Islands by about 200 BCE, and by about 500 CE had colonized Hawai'i and Easter Island.[9] This process was so little understood until very recently that the dashing Thor Heyerdahl achieved enormous world-wide fame with his Kon-Tiki voyage, which was based on the premise that early rafts and reed boats *followed* winds and currents, and that Easter Island was settled from South America rather than Asia. Kirch[10] describes the long scholarly debate between those who view Austronesian expansion as resulting from purposive voyages of exploration versus those (such as Sharp[11]) who see it as resulting from accidental drift of canoes being blown off course. Archaeologists however have always favoured the former explanation because of the evidence they have found of *preparedness* — the pigs, dogs, fowl, and crop plants brought along by the settlers. "Drift" also simply does not make sense given Pacific wind and current patterns. Theories concerning drift, shipwreck and chance reflect the fact that modern Europeans tend to think of large solid craft as necessary for trans-oceanic voyages. In

1893 however Norwegians crossed the north Atlantic in a reproduction of the Gokstad Viking ship, taking only 27 days to cross 2,000 miles in bad weather. This feat was repeated in 1958 when seven Norwegians crossed the Atlantic in 22 days in a reproduction Viking ship.[12]

Another factor preventing Western scholars from accepting that the Pacific was settled by purposive voyages of exploration has been that this involves travelling eastwards *against* the prevailing winds and currents. Horridge's response is that the problem of how the Pacific was colonized against prevailing winds and currents is solved if we accept that the earliest pathfinders had boats of similar design to the fast, long-distance single-outrigger with a tilting triangular sail, because these boats sail best a little upwind or with the wind on the beam.[13] Austronesian exploration is considered to have favoured sailing into the wind, with a downwind return. Horridge also remarks that downwind from an undiscovered island there is a scent of land and an interference pattern of the wind-created waves converging behind the island, as well as flotsam on the surface, which numerous sailors have described. Nature thus provides clues of land on the approach side of the island exactly where they are needed.[14] Expert seamen approach land upwind and lay-off until they find a calm landing, as they could certainly do in an outrigger canoe with a tilting triangular sail. Those looking for new land, sons of chiefs in Horridge's hypothesized scenario, had to sail eastwards because that was the direction their boats would naturally take them on the least foolhardy explorations with the expectation of a safe return.

The reality is that the Austronesians developed in early times a precocious command of the sea which many Europeans have been slow and reluctant to realize. As Finney remarks: "Long before the Portuguese and Spanish inaugurated Europe's Age of Exploration, even before the Vikings ventured across the North Atlantic, on the other side of the globe another seafaring race had already spread over two oceans. The geographical spread of these Austronesian-speaking peoples far surpassed that of the world's next largest cultural-linguistic grouping, the Indo-Europeans. Just take Polynesia alone, the easternmost province of the Austronesian world. The Polynesian triangle, bounded by New Zealand, Hawaii and Easter Island, would if cast upon Eurasia stretch from England across Europe and Asia to the Aleutians and then south almost to the tip of India!"[15]

In Indonesia, the Austronesians introduced not only their extraordinary seamanship but also agriculture and advanced craftsmanship, as well as a preference for notably hierarchical societies that made a lasting impact.

JAVANESE MIGRATION TO JAPAN IN THE YAYOI PERIOD

One Austronesian people produced a migration that sailed in the opposite direction — back north, in this case as far north as Japan. The Javanese immigrants who brought about the transformation of Japanese society in the Yayoi revolution were responsible for the greatest migration-induced cultural changes of any that I know. Within the space of a few centuries, a millennia-old hunter-gatherer population (the Jōmon) was not only brought into the 'Neolithic Revolution' which elsewhere in the world saw the introduction of agriculture and all the cultural changes this brought: it was also brought into the bronze-iron age which is attested by the beautifully crafted bells and weaponry of the period. The exuberantly individualistic, ornate and fantastic Jōmon pottery was replaced by a repertoire of simple, function-specific shapes with restrained geometric decoration which constitute the pottery of mass production. Wet-rice agriculture supported a court civilization, the arts, and a hierarchical social order.[16] As in Java, the origin of this revolutionary transformation, we find the establishment of a ruling élite which was immensely preoccupied with distinguishing itself from the rural population, and which brought with them the name of their home kingdom, Taruma. Loanwords which tell the story of this wide-ranging transformation range from specific material items (cloth and plates and rice-cookers in the domestic sphere, fences in the social sphere) through basic everyday vocabulary (for example, words meaning 'to pour', or 'to cover') through to specialized words relating to land usage and notably to leadership, divine kingship, and religion. One such word borrowed was Javanese *matur-*, which became Old Japanese *maturi* and modern Japanese *matsuri*, denoting religious observance. In other words, this migration though in numerical terms small — but nevertheless significantly larger than the Norman migration to England[17] — must have involved no less than the transplanting of a whole society. There would have been farmers, chieftains, highly skilled artisans, women as well as men as is indicated by the mitochondrial DNA, bringing with them their provisions, rice seed, domestic implements, tools and weapons. It seems reasonable to hypothesis that this revolution ultimately derived from the pre-existence of maritime networks of a fluid, and perhaps busy, nature.

Working on this project starkly revealed the immense strength of regional barriers in the academic establishment, with their built-in incentives to create exclusive guilds of experts on 'Southeast Asia' and '[North]East Asia'. It also revealed just how many scholars working on Southeast Asia had very low expectations of the generic Southeast Asian and regarded them as beyond dispute. This attitude is compounded by perhaps the major error for historians, which is to read the present back into the past. Technological and social hierarchies do not remain the same over the centuries, as is amply evidenced by the British example. This one-time Roman colony and backwater went on to become the greatest industrial power in the world, colonizing more of it than any other nation, before losing its empire and de-industrializing.

The Yayoi transformation of Jōmon Japan has obvious similarities to a migration process that took place nearly two millennia later, i.e. the great English migration to the New World, and its impact on the indigenous populations of the various countries affected. There was a huge technological gap between the immigrants and the locals. This English migration partly or completely destroyed indigenous society and culture depending on the capacity for resistance, with varying results for Zulus, American Indians, Maoris, and Australian aborigines, without giving them an entrée into the culture and society of the dominant migrants. In the Yayoi case however the immigrants seem to have drawn most of the Jōmon into the agricultural and hierarchical society that they introduced — suggesting some interesting comparative work for the future.

THE INDONESIO-MALAYAN COLONIZATION OF MADAGASCAR

The Indian Ocean whose wide expanse stretches between Indonesia and Africa was a challenge even to nineteenth-century British sailors, who found it had a much more complicated and difficult system of winds and currents than is found in other parts of the globe.[18] That Southeast Asians could have crossed it in their pre-modern ships seems incredible to many. But there is too much evidence to allow any reasonable doubt that they did.

The Linguistic Evidence

The first mention of a relationship between Malagasy, the language of Madagascar, and Malay languages was by the Portuguese priest Luis Mariano in his description of a voyage to Madagascar in 1613–14: he says that the inhabitants must have come from Malacca.[19]

More than two centuries later William Marsden described the relationship of Malagasy with Indonesian languages as one of the most extraordinary facts in the history of language, when we consider the immensity of the intervening ocean. He remarks, after an examination of the vocabulary on the opposite coasts of Madagascar, that the language had been thoroughly disseminated, in a remarkably uniform way, across this great island. Even in modern times, the difference between dialects is restricted to their phonetic evolution and particularly their vocabulary. Grammar is remarkably uniform, and no dialectical differences are very great.[20] Dahl finds this linguistic uniformity of the world's fourth largest island astonishing when compared with the linguistic diversity of Indonesia.[21] It is in fact astonishing with regard to most of the world, except for such later colonial creations as America and Australia, though these differ significantly in being politically united, whereas Madagascar is not.

Dahl succeeded in narrowing down Madagascar's already recognized affinities with Malay languages and demonstrating that Malagasy was a Southeast Barito language, claiming that Maanyan was its closest relative. This claim has never been successfully challenged, though Dahl has received little recognition for such a major discovery. Linguistic work is ongoing in the Barito area[22] and this may add to the picture. Malagasy also has quite numerous Malay and Javanese loanwords, which belong to all sorts of semantic domains.[23]

The DNA Evidence

Unlike the language, the DNA of Madagascar has only recently been subject to study, by Hurles and his colleagues.[24] This study was able to attribute every maternal and paternal lineage found in the Malagasy to a likely geographic origin, revealing approximately equal African and Indonesian contributions. The most likely origin of the Indonesian ones is Borneo [Kalimantan]. The Island Southeast Asian or Oceanic population closest to the Malagasy (of the relatively small number studied) is that from Banjarmasin. The pooled Borneo population [i.e. including the second sample from Kota Kinabalu] is significantly closer to the Malagasy than is any other Island Southeast Asian population studied — of which there was only one, from the Philippines. No other Indonesian population apart from the two from Kalimantan was sampled, so no light is shed on how many groups from other Indonesian or Malayan populations might have been involved.

Rice and Other Plants

Botanists estimate that 27 per cent of the flora of Madagascar is African and 7 per cent Indonesian.[25] The latter group includes groups of plants sharing a forest or steppe environment, and especially food-producing plants such as rice. Javanese *bulu* (*javanica*) rice is very widely distributed globally and among the places it grows is Madagascar. On this island it is cultivated in part by the wet-rice cultivation mode for which Java is famous. Blench's work demonstrates that some particular Indonesian cultigens of certain plants — especially water-yam (*dioscorea alata*) and taro and some types of banana — were imported into Madagascar in early times.[26] Diamond notes that bananas, Asian yams and taro were already widespread in sub-Saharan Africa in the 1400s.[27] In fact the banana, native to Southeast Asia and New Guinea, had reached Africa a good deal earlier than Portuguese times. A relatively conservative account[28] puts the arrival of plantains, probably accompanied by taro and water-yam at 3,000 years ago in West Africa, while others[29] tentatively suggest 5,000 years ago for Uganda.

Ships and Shipping

The double outrigger is found only a) in Indonesia and its outskirts and b) in Madagascar and East Africa. The centre from which the outrigger spread was Indonesia.[30] Written sources on the early history of Indonesian shipping are few and patchy, with Chinese accounts rather limited before around the seventh century.[31] We do know however that the inhabitants of Southeast Asia already had very large, very fast ships in the early centuries CE. A third century Chinese account says that these large Southeast Asian *po* — to use the Chinese term — are more than 50 metres long and stand out of the water 4 to 5 metres. They carry from six to seven hundred persons, with 10,000 bushels of cargo [according to different interpretations anywhere between 250 to 1,000 tons]. They may have as many as four sails which do not face directly forward but are set obliquely and so arranged that they can all be fixed in the same direction, to receive the wind and to spill it. The pressure of the wind swells the sails from behind and is thrown from one to the other, so that they all profit from its force. If it is violent, they diminish or augment [the surface area of the sails] according to the conditions. This oblique rig, which permits the sails to receive from one another the breath of the wind, obviates the anxiety attendant upon having high masts. Thus these ships can sail without avoiding strong winds and dashing waves, by the aid of which they can make great speed.

An eighth-century account says the *po* can carry more than 1,000 men besides cargo, and are over 60 metres long, lying six or seven feet deep in the water. They are constructed by assembling several thickness of side-planks, for the boards are thin and might break. No iron is used in fastening.[32] We can assume that these ships had no outriggers, as the Chinese would have mentioned such a conspicuous feature. It is important to note that China itself did not possess ocean-going ships before the eighth or ninth centuries CE.

The features mentioned in these Chinese accounts are the same as those of the sixteenth century *jung* as described by the Portuguese, after whose arrival we have rather more descriptions of traditional Southeast Asian craft. The Portuguese found the *jung* were more often than not larger than their own ships and made extensive use of them. One is described as having four super-imposed layers of planks. Wooden dowels were used, there were two masts [other accounts say two to four masts and a bowsprit] and three rudders, and no iron was used. The average burthen was 4–500 metric tons, with a range of 85 to 700 tons; one owned by Pati Unus of Japara may have been 1,000 tons and carried 1,000 men.[33] Multiple sheathing was used for the hull. Sails were made of vegetal matting, and the canted square sail was in common use. Portuguese sources say that the main shipbuilding areas were the north coast of Java, especially around Rembang and Cirebon; the southern coast of Borneo and adjacent islands; and Pegu, which was the largest. The main differences from the Chinese junk were that the Chinese used iron nails and clamps and had different steering — from earliest times they used the single axial stern-post rudder considered one of China's greatest contributions to nautical technology. Southeast Asian ships generally used two lateral quarter-rudders.[34]

The Borobudur Ships

The eleven boats carved in the galleries of the eighth century Buddhist temple Borobudur range from a simple canoe with upturned ends to several large ships with outriggers. There are a number of small ships with upturned stem and stern, a single tall mast, and tilted rectangular sail. Then there are five bas-relief depictions of large vessels with outriggers. They are not five depictions of the same vessel: while the five vessels are obviously similar, and may be seen as illustrating a distinct type of vessel, there are differences in the clearly evident details. These depictions are probably not all by the same artist. The larger boats have two sails, two tripod masts, lateral rudders, and outrigger. They also have a bowsprit on which hung a square sail somewhat similar to the foresail (*artemon*) on a Greek ship of classical times, or on the junk. They are unlike any other ship described from the ancient world; neither are they like any modern sailing ship in Indonesia. The hulls of the best delineated boats at Borobudur have outrigger floats supported on paired outrigger booms. They have tripod masts supporting tilted rectangular sails. They also have lateral rudders and a superstructure built up with poles, which probably were at times covered with mats — all this resembles the *kora-kora*, the fighting ship of the Moluccas encountered by early Western explorers/colonists,[35] a very distinctive and unusual type of outrigger vessel owned by potentates.[36] This Moluccan boat was very thin and long (roughly 10 metres) and carried as many as five rows of oarsmen. It was originally used for raiding and later put to more peaceful purposes. The *perahu konteng* of East Java when planked up to increase the freeboard and cargo capacity also has a profile much like a Borobudur ship. Horridge believes that the Borobudur ships were fighting ships and that there were certainly better cargo boats at that period.

So could Indonesians have sailed to Madagascar on ships like the ones depicted on Borobudur with their 'towering hulls'? Probably they could have, because their remote descendants managed to do so in a replica of a Borobudur ship, called the *Samudra Raksa*, built according to the ratios of a nineteenth century *kora-kora*, which was sailed across the Indian Ocean and around the Cape in 2003–04.[37]

Arab Accounts of Indonesian Attackers

The tenth century *Ajayeb al-Hind* (*Marvels of India*), attributed to Bozorg ibn Shahriyar, a Persian from Ramhormoz, gives an account of an invasion, said to have taken place on the coast of Tanganyika and Mozambique in the mid-tenth century CE,[38] launched by a force of people called the Wakwak or Waqwaq.

This work says that the inhabitants of Waqwaq are numerous. Some of them resemble the Turks. They are the most industrious of all Allah's creatures but are treacherous, cunning and lying. They are said by Ibn Lakis to do incredible things, for example in 334 [945–6 CE] they arrived in 1,000 boats and fought with extreme vigour in an attempt to take the citadel of Qanbaloh,[39] though eventually without success. [Later] some Waqwaq were asked why they had chosen this particular place and they said it was because it had goods suitable for their country and for China, such as ivory, tortoise shells, panther [skins] and ambergris, and because they wanted to get Bantu (known as Zeng or Zenj) who were strong and bore slavery easily.

The name Waqwaq was said by some to come from a wonderful tree called Wakwak, the fruit of which looks like a human and makes a 'wakwak' sound when it falls: Mauny thinks this may be the pandanus tree, called Bakkuwan by the Bataks and grown in Madagascar where it is called Vakwa. Tom Hoogervorst[40] is of the opinion that the Malagasy word *vahoak*, 'people, clan, tribe" — from the Malay *awak-awak*, 'people, crew' — is a more plausible derivation.

Al-Biruni in the eleventh century describes shipping between Sofala, China and island Southeast Asia.[41] Al Idrisi in 1154 speaks of the people of Komr (i.e Madagascar), and the merchants of the land of the Maharaja [Sumatra] visiting the nations of the eastern coast of Africa where they are well-received and trade is conducted. The people of the islands of Zabag are said to visit the land of the Zenj (Bantu) in large and small ships and export merchandise from it, a trade made easier because they understand one another's language.

Music and Culture

It has long been suggested that the xylophone was imported into Africa from Indonesia, and Jones claims that not only the instrument but a whole musical tradition was imported.[42] Other African cultural features which Jones considers to be of Indonesian origin are board games, a particular design of bellows, *plangi* dyeing, patterns and bronzes, some tribal customs, and social organization into kingdoms.[43]

The Wider Context of Indonesian Voyages to Africa

We have surveyed the evidence for Indonesian settlement of Madagascar: the question for many people is why did they 'suddenly think of sailing right across the Indian Ocean to such a remote island?' In fact the voyages to Madagascar and its settlement were not part of an isolated adventure but were intimately linked to old and enduring trade networks that reached beyond the Austronesian domain, to China at one extreme and to Rome at the other. These trade links also had a powerful effect on state formation.

It is most likely that the earliest trade routes of the Indian Ocean developed about 5,000 years ago between the Indus Valley and the Persian Gulf, possibly contemporaneously with initial Austronesian expansion in Southeast Asia. Though there is a lack of good archaeological documentation for the millennium from the fifth century BCE onwards,[44] it is clear that by the last centuries BCE Southeast Asia was already part of a world trading system linking the civilizations of the Mediterranean Basin and Han China.[45] Wisseman Christie describes an 'explosion of trading activity' between about 500 and 200 BCE in the Malacca Straits and in the Java Sea, due to the rise of substantial élites in southern China and parts of India, forming a market for high-status commodities and medicinal substances. This trade stimulated the spread of advanced metallurgical techniques in Southeast Asia, a region already tied into maritime trade networks of considerable antiquity and possessing what was by the standards of the time an advanced marine technology and considerable navigational experience. Trade also led to the growth of states in island Southeast Asia. Wisseman Christie regards trade, not a Marxian Asiatic Mode of Production or Wittfogelian Oriental Despotism, as the mainstay of these early states — even those of Java and Bali.[46] The Javanese states had large-scale distribution systems, exported local crops, handled the spices of the eastern islands, and manufactured bronze axes which were traded to other islands. This trade fed into Indian trade to the West. Cloves were already known in China in the third century BCE and were described by Pliny in the first century CE.[47] In the last centuries BCE Malay sailors were delivering cinnamon from South China Sea ports to East Africa and the Red Sea. Malay sailors were also responsible for opening up an all-sea route to China.[48]

The second stage in the process of state formation in the maritime region seems to have occurred between about 200 BCE and 300 CE when the coastal polities of maritime Southeast Asia were drawn into more direct contact with the major empires of the time and became both a link in the chain and a supplier of the first great Old World trading system, which coalesced in the first century CE. The favoured coasts of this system included the north coasts of Java and Bali and the coast of central Vietnam.[49] Trade continued to expand with the fourth century CE increase in population and wealth in south China, increasing the volume of trade in maritime Southeast Asia.[50] Important early historic polities were Srivijaya, located on the southeast coast of Sumatra, and the state called Ho-ling by the Chinese, probably located on the north coast of central Java (between Pekalongan and Semarang). Ho-ling was the major trading centre linking China with northeast India in the mid-seventh century and must have taken over from the ports of west Java the dominant position in the spice and sandalwood trades. By the late seventh century Srivijaya was dominant, but the balance of economic power shifted back to Java again by the end of the eighth century after Ho-ling merged into the larger central Javanese polity of Mataram.[51]

We can expand this context still further by taking on board perspectives on global history provided by the Wallerstein school. Beaujard[52] points out that Wallerstein created the concept of the world-system in relation to the modern era whereas in fact the emergence of a Eurasian and African world-system can be traced very much further back in time, specifically to the first century CE. It had three sub-systems, the China Sea, the eastern Indian Ocean and the Western Indian Ocean. The maritime historian Alfred Mahan once categorically claimed that both travel and traffic have always been easier and cheaper by water than by land — *pace* the landlubber's acute awareness of the perils of the deep⁵³ — and we can see that the world-system described above is a maritime system. Zones at the intersection of two sub-systems were particularly favoured as they had good opportunities to become a trade nexus — and maritime Southeast Asia is one such zone. Beaujard posits a direct link between Indonesia and Africa/Madagascar in the first to third centuries.⁵⁴ He also concludes that maritime Southeast Asia was relatively proof against the recessions the system periodically suffered (the intervening period might have been as short as 70 years or as long as four centuries), due to climactic stability, to the strategic importance of the Straits of Malacca, and to the high demand for spices from the Moluccas. Traders could also quickly respond when China emerged from a recession and entered upon an upward trend. As is well known, in Wallerstein's core-periphery dichotomy the periphery is exploited, subordinated and dependent, but Beaujard concludes that Southeast Asia, a 'semiperiphery', was not without the power to innovate — notably in the development of navigation around the first century CE. It was in fact a 'pivotal' region that retained a 'primordial' role in the networks throughout history. Hence the settlement of Madagascar. But when did this occur in the long life of this trade system, and how was it settled?

When and How was Madagascar First Colonized by Indonesians and Malays?

A good deal has been written on the date when the first Indonesian colony was planted on Madagascar, but no consensus has yet emerged. The following wide range of dates has been put forward:

- The early centuries BCE, proposed by Blench⁵⁵ on the basis of plant cultigens, and also suggested by the 'explosion of trading activity' to the west between c. 500 and 200 BCE (see above), and by the archaeological work of Ardika and Bellwood.⁵⁶
- Around 400 CE: Marre and much later Dahl pointed out that the number of Sanskrit words in Malagasy is very limited compared with the large number now found in Indonesian languages — which means that the Indonesian settlers must have come at an early stage of Hindu influence.⁵⁷ The *yūpa* post with its Sanskrit inscription of around 400 CE in Muara Kaman, east Kalimantan [one of seven from this area] prompts Dahl to suggest this as the approximate date of the Maanyan migration.⁵⁸
- No earlier than the seventh century: Adelaar's conclusion that the Sanskrit loans in Malagasy must have come from Malay and that Sanskrit influence on Malay cannot be earlier than the seventh century Sumatran Old Malay

inscriptions[59] impel him to date the migration that brought the Maanyan to Madagascar to that time at the earliest.

The situation is complicated by the fact that while some authors envisage only one migration, others envisage two migrations or even waves of migration. Hornell was one of the earliest to suggest two migrations, on rather speculative grounds.[60] Adelaar concludes on the basis of Blench's work on plant cultigens that there may have been some earlier, pre-Barito connection between Indonesia and Madagascar. The very great span of the different dates and the differing opinions concerning how many migrations there may have been reflects, of course, the fact that there is as yet no really conclusive evidence. After all, the fact that Indonesians *could* have colonized Madagascar in the early centuries BCE does not prove that they *did*, and on the other hand the dates provided by the Indonesian inscriptions of the fifth and seventh centuries have no necessary connection at all with the date at which the migration began.

More archaeological work is clearly needed particularly in the coastal areas. Further archaeological work may not be easy, with problems in excavating coastal sites of an early date. Blench remarks that the African coast across from Madagascar lacks archaeological sites even though we know from the Periplus that there was a coastal community there. The traces of this community may have been obliterated by geomorphological change.[61]

As we have seen, the main source of the Indonesian element in Malagasy is Maanyan or a closely-related neighboring language, with smaller contributions from Malay and Javanese. However, the Maanyan and their neighbours are forest-dwelling Dayaks, not sailors. Also, some Malagasy are wet rice farmers, while Dayaks are generally dry rice cultivators. This raises the questions of how and why these inland forest dwellers came to live on a rather inaccessible island at the other side of a great ocean, and establish wet-rice cultivation there. As we have seen, there are Malay and Javanese words in Malagasy. It is also claimed that certain aspects of the administration, culture, and statecraft of the Merina kingdom are strikingly like those of the Indianized Malays and Javanese and unlike anything found in Maanyan society. While Dahl supports the idea of a direct migration of Maanyan, Adelaar suggests, in my opinion more plausibly, that the Maanyan were brought by Malays. This raises the question of why Malays as well as Javanese (given the loan-words and the wet-rice cultivation) took the Maanyan on their trading fleets. It seems unlikely that it was just as extra hands on deck, particularly since they would have had no seagoing experience. It seems more likely that it was to provide labour to grow rice, thus ensuring their masters a local food supply which would enable them to spend more time scouring the African mainland for trade goods. They may well have been slaves, since we know that one of the main things the Indonesians sought from Africa was Bantu slaves. So the whole enterprise must have been highly capitalized, well organized and technologically advanced.

How long did the Indonesian connection last? As we have seen, Mauny reports tenth-century Arab accounts of an Indonesian invasion of the coast between Mombasa and Sofala, which captured Bantu-speaking slaves and presumably took them to Madagascar,[62] and thereafter continuing trade until at least the twelfth century. When al-Idrisi was writing in the twelfth century there were still links between Sumatra and Sofala. It is possible that Indonesian trade declined in this century, which was one of Muslim expansion in Madagascar, with Arabs settling on the south-east coast. However a connection must have endured until much later than this if the Portuguese really did see 'Javanese,' a term which might have also included other Indonesian and Malay peoples, in Madagascar.

CONCLUSION

The concept of Southeast Asia is a good one for numerous purposes: for armies of occupation, for example, and maps for wartime pilots. But as a historical category, particularly for the pre-modern period, it forms a sort of conceptual corral imposed on and bisecting the maritime highway from Japan to Madagascar, cutting off the western and northern parts of the Indonesian world. Within this conceptual corral the pressing agenda is to find similarities, since these are hard to come by. Differences and exceptions, particularly major ones, cause only problems and tend to be brushed aside. Over time they vanish from sight as far as the historical profession is concerned, though they may still be observed by scientists and non-area-based specialists. Yet it is differences that are most stimulating to historical analysis. Can one imagine an analogous neglect of the Industrial Revolution because it was not common to all European countries? Of course not; and the Industrial Revolution has been a testing ground for historical hypotheses, ranging from the ideological 'Protestant Ethic' to the prosaic 'availability of coal and iron,' and the many combinations and permutations of hypotheses. So we have to ask why Indonesia-Malaya alone among 'Southeast Asian' countries has this extraordinary reach from Japan to Madagascar. At present however we do not have the mental space to do this, and ignorance of this reach, and incredulity when it is pointed out, are the usual consequences. Even within the more well-grounded Austronesian grouping, Java in particular is strikingly anomalous, with its combination of land-based and sea-based power: its wealthy wet-rice kingdoms and its enormous ships, so different from Pacific shipping.

So the Indonesian/Malayan world needs to be re-assigned. It might be re-assigned to a different *geographical* category: the world of what Martin Lewis[63] has called the 'Afro-Asian seaway' (and which I might prefer to call the Asia-Africa seaway) whose peoples were part of the same vast maritime trading network. A maritime approach to global studies is certainly needed to complement the usual land-based approach.[64] Or it might be re-assigned to a *conceptual* category of peoples who might be geographically remote and not in direct contact but which are *typologically* the same — expansionist maritime societies, for examples, or colonizing societies: Indonesia/Malaya was not always the colonized area that it was to become. Finally, the Indonesian case would also contribute much light to any study of the global spread of technology and social differentiation. These many contributions of the Indonesian case depend on the adoption of a perspective no longer cabined, cribbed, and confined, but open to an immense maritime world.

Notes

1. Rudyard Kipling, "Recessional", for which see <http://www.bartleby.com/101/867.html>.
2. For instance in David Joel Steinberg (ed.), *In Search of Southeast Asia: A Modern History* (Sydney: Allen & Unwin, 1987).
3. As in Charles Higham, *The Bronze Age of Southeast Asia* (Cambridge: Cambridge University Press, 1996) which actually deals with the Bronze Age of *mainland* Southeast Asia.
4. Norman G. Owen et al., *The Emergence of Modern Southeast Asia: A New History* (Honolulu, University of Hawai'i Press, 2005).
5. Owen et al., *The Emergence of Modern Southeast Asia*, p. 403.
6. See K. Alexander Adelaar, "Where does Malay come from? Twenty years of discussion about homeland, migrations and classifications", *Bijdragen tot de Taal-, Land- en Volkenkunde* 160, no. 1 (2004): 1–30. The diagram on p. 13 includes Chamic in the Malayo-Sumbawan Subgroup, which includes also Madurese, Sundanese, Sasak, Sumbawan, Balinese and Malayic.
7. Adrian Horridge, "The Austronesian Conquest of the Sea — Upwind" in *The Austronesians: Historical and Comparative Perspectives*, edited by Peter Bellwood, James J. Fox and Darrell Tryon (Canberra: ANU E-Press, 1995), p. 157.
8. Peter Bellwood, *Prehistory of the Indo-Malaysian Archipelago*, revised ed. (Honolulu: University of Hawai'i Press, 1997), p. 212.

9. According to Martin Lewis (personal communication) these travellers must actually have reached South America, as otherwise one cannot explain the presence of the sweet potato in New Zealand.
10. Patrick Kirch, *Feathered gods and fishhooks: an introduction to Hawaiian archaeology and prehistory* (Honolulu: University of Hawai'i Press, 1985), pp. 58–66.
11. Andrew Sharp, *Ancient voyagers in the Pacific*, Memoirs of the Polynesian Society No. 32 (Wellington: Polynesian Society, 1956).
12. A.M. Jones, *Africa and Indonesia: the Evidence of the Xylophone and Other Musical and Cultural Factors* (Leiden, E.J. Brill, 1964), p. 183.
13. Horridge, "The Austronesian Conquest of the Sea", pp. 157–58.
14. In contrast, Heyerdahl's square-sailed raft Kon-Tiki ended its journey by crashing helplessly on the windward side of a reef, which is not the way to explore or colonize.
15. Edwin Doran Jr. *Wangka: Austronesian Canoe Origins* (College Station: Texas A&M University Press, 1981), p. 11.
16. For a fuller account, see Ann Kumar, *Globalizing the Prehistory of Japan: Language, Genes and Civilization*, Routledge Studies in the Early History of Asia (London and New York: Routledge, 2009).
17. Masashi Tanaka et al., "Mitochondrial Genome Variation in Eastern Asia and the Peopling of Japan", *Genome Research* 14 (2004): 1832–50.
18. Alexander George Findlay, *A Directory for the Navigation of the Indian Ocean with Descriptions of its Coasts, Islands, etc., from the Cape of Good Hope to the Strait of Sunda and Western Australia; including also the Red Sea and the Persian Gulf; the Winds, Monsoons and Currents and the Passages from Europe to its Various Ports*, third edition (London: Richard Holmes Laurie, 1876), p. 32.
19. Otto Chr. Dahl, *Malgache et Maanjan: une comparaison linguistique*, Egede-Instituttet Avhandlinger, no. 3 (Oslo: Egede-Instituttet, 1951), p. 13.
20. William M. Marsden, *Miscellaneous Works of William Marsden* (London: Parbury, Allen and Co., 1834), pp. 31–32.
21. Dahl, *Malgache et Maanjan*, p. 6.
22. Alexander Adelaar, personal communication.
23. There are also some Sulawesi loanwords, which Adelaar attributes to contact prior to the migration to Madagascar: See K. Alexander Adelaar, "The Indonesian Migrations to Madagascar: Making Sense of the Multidisciplinary Evidence", in Truman Simanjuntak, Ingrid Harriet Eileen Pojoh and Muhammad Hisyam (eds.), *Austronesian Diaspora and the Ethnogeneses of People in Indonesian Archipelago*, (Jakarta: Indonesian Institute of Sciences, 2006), pp. 8–9.
24. M.E. Hurles et al., "The dual origin of the Malagasy in Island Southeast Asia and East Africa: evidence from maternal and paternal lineages", *American Journal of Human Genetics* 76 (2005): 894–901.
25. Michel Mollat du Jourdin, "Les contacts historiques de l'Afrique et de Madagascar avec l'Asie du Sud et du Sud-Est: le rôle de l'Océan indien", *Archipel* 21 (1981): 35–53. See p. 37.

26. Roger Blench, "The Ethnographic Evidence for Long-distance Contacts Between Oceania and East Africa", in *The Indian Ocean in Antiquity*, edited by Julian Reade (London: Kegan Paul/British Museum, 1996), pp. 417–38. See p. 417.
27. Jared Diamond, *Guns, Germs, and Steel: A Short History of Everybody for the Last 13,000 Years* (London: Vintage 1998), p. 381.
28. Roger Blench, "Bananas and Plantains in Africa: Reinterpreting the Linguistic Evidence", *Ethnobotany Research and Applications*, Vol. 7 (2009): 363–80.
29. Tim Denham and Mark Donohue,"Pre-Austronesian dispersal of banana cultivars West from New Guinea: linguistic relics from Eastern Indonesia", *Archaeologica Oceania* 44 (2009): 18–28. See p. 26.
30. James Hornell, *Water Transport: Origins and Early Evolution* (Cambridge: Cambridge University Press, 1946), p. 263.
31. J. Wisseman Christie, "State Formation in Early Maritime Southeast Asia: A Consideration of the Theories and the Data", *Bijdragen tot de taal- land- en volkenkunde* 151, no. 2 (1995): 235–88. See p. 263.
32. Pierre-Yves Manguin, "The Southeast Asian Ship: An Historical Approach", *Journal of Southeast Asian Studies* 11, no. 2 (1980): 266–76. See p. 275.
33. Manguin, "The Southeast Asian Ship", pp. 267–68.
34. Manguin, "The Southeast Asian Ship", pp. 270–72.
35. Adrian Horridge, *Sailing Craft of Indonesia*, Images of Asia Series (Singapore & Oxford: Oxford University Press, 1986), p. 6.
36. Hornell, *Water Transport*, p. 259.
37. For details of the Borobudur Ship Expedition, see the website at <http://www.borobudurshipexpedition.com/>.
38. Raymond Mauny, "The Wakwak and the Indonesian invasion in East Africa in 945 A.D.", *Studia* 15 (May 1965): 7–16. See p. 7.
39. Another place name whose location is a matter of debate, but which appears to have been in or close to Zanzibar. See Georges Loire, *Gens de Mere à Dar-es-Salaam*, (Karthala 1993), p. 67.
40. Personal communication.
41. Mauny, "The Wakwak and the Indonesian Invasion in East Africa in 945 A.D.", pp. 9–10.
42. Jones, *Africa and Indonesia*. See Chapter Ten. Others have cast doubt on the Indonesian origin of the xylophone while suggesting that *other* Indonesian musical instruments *were* imported into Africa.
43. Jones, *Africa and Indonesia*, pp. 227–28.
44. Bérénice Bellina and Ian Glover, "The Archaeology of Early Contact with India and the Mediterranean World, from the Fourth Century BC to the Fourth Century AD", in *Southeast Asia: From Prehistory to History*, edited by Ian C. Glover and Peter Bellwood (London/New York: RoutledgeCurzon, 2004), pp. 68–89. See pp. 69–71.
45. Bellina and Glover, "The Archaeology of Early Contact with India and the Mediterranean World", p. 83.

46. Wisseman Christie, "State Formation in Early Maritime Southeast Asia", pp. 242 and 250–51.
47. Bellina and Glover, "The Archaeology of Early Contact with India and the Mediterranean World", p. 69.
48. Lynda Shaffer, 'Southernization', *Journal of World History* 5 no. 1 (Spring 1994): 1–21. See pp. 4–5.
49. Philippe Beaujard, "The Indian Ocean in Eurasian and African World-Systems before the Sixteenth Century", *Journal of World History* 16, no. 4 (December 2005): 411–65.
50. Wisseman Christie, "State Formation in Early Maritime Southeast Asia", p. 253.
51. Wisseman Christie, "State Formation in Early Maritime Southeast Asia", pp. 263 and 374.
52. Beaujard, "The Indian Ocean in Eurasian and African World Systems", p. 411.
53. Alfred Thayer Mahan, *The Influence of Sea Power Upon History: 1660–1783* (London: Sampson Low, Marston, Searle, & Rivington, 1890). See p. 25.
54. Beaujard, "The Indian Ocean in Eurasian and African World-Systems", Map 1.
55. Blench, "The Ethnographic Evidence for Long-distance Contacts", p. 432.
56. I. W. Ardika & P. Bellwood, "Sembiran: The Beginnings of Indian Contact with Bali", *Antiquity* 65 (1991): 221–32. See also I. W. Ardika, P. Bellwood, I. M. Sutaba & K. C. Yuliati, "Sembiran and the First Indian Contacts with Bali: An Update", *Antiquity* 71(1997): 193–95.
57. Dahl, *Malgache et Maanjan*, p. 367.
58. Dahl, *Malgache et Maanjan*, p. 368.
59. Adelaar, "The Indonesian Migrations to Madagascar", p. 15.
60. Hornell, *Water Transport*, p. 264.
61. Blench, "The Ethnographic Evidence for Long-distance Contacts", p. 432.
62. Mauny, "The Wakwak and the Indonesian invasion", p. 14.
63. Personal communication.
64. See Martin W. Lewis, "Dividing the Ocean Sea." *The Geographical Review* 89, no. 2 (1999): 188–214, and Martin Lewis and Karen Wigen, "A Maritime Response to the Crisis in Asian Studies", *The Geographical Review* 89, no. 2 (1999): 161–68.

References

Adelaar, K. Alexander. "Borneo as a Crossroads for Comparative Austronesian Linguistics". In *The Austronesians: Historical and Comparative Perspectives*, edited by Peter Bellwood, James J. Fox, Darrell Tryon, pp. 81–102. Canberra, ANU E-Press, 1995.

———. "Where does Malay come from? Twenty years of discussion about homeland, migrations and classifications". *Bijdragen tot de Taal-, Land- en Volkenkunde* 160, no. 1 (2004): 1–30.

———. "The Indonesian Migrations to Madagascar: Making Sense of the Multidisciplinary Evidence". In *Austronesian Diaspora and the Ethnogeneses of People in Indonesian Archipelago*, edited by Truman Simanjuntak, Ingrid Harriet Eileen Pojoh and Muhammad Hisyam Jakarta: Indonesian Institute of Sciences, 2006.

Ardika, I. W. & P. Bellwood. "Sembiran: The Beginnings of Indian Contact with Bali". *Antiquity* 65 (1991): 221–32.

Ardika, I. W., P. Bellwood, I. M. Sutaba & K. C. Yuliati. "Sembiran and the first Indian contacts with Bali: an update". *Antiquity* 71 (1997): 193–95.

Beaujard, Philippe. "The Indian Ocean in Eurasian and African World-Systems before the Sixteenth Century". *Journal of World History* 16, no. 4 (December 2005): 411–65.

Bellina, Bérénice and Ian Glover. "The Archaeology of Early Contact with India and the Mediterranean World, from the Fourth Century BC to the Fourth Century AD". In *Southeast Asia: From Prehistory to History*, edited by Ian C. Glover and Peter Bellwood, pp. 68–89. London/New York: RoutledgeCurzon, 2004.

Bellwood, Peter. *Prehistory of the Indo-Malaysian Archipelago.* revised ed. Honolulu: University of Hawai'i Press, 1997.

Blench, Roger. "Bananas and Plantains in Africa: Reinterpreting the Linguistic Evidence". *Ethnobotany Research and Applications* 7 (2009): 363–80.

———. "The Ethnographic Evidence for Long-distance Contacts Between Oceania and East Africa". In *The Indian Ocean in Antiquity*, edited by Julian Reade, pp. 417–38. London: Kegan Paul/British Museum 1996 pp. 417–38.

Dahl, Otto Chr. *Malgache et Maanjan: une Comparaison Linguistique*, Egede-Instituttet Avhandlinger, no. 3. Oslo: Egede-Instituttet, 1951.

Denham, Tim and Mark Donohue. "Pre-Austronesian dispersal of banana cultivars West from New Guinea: linguistic relics from Eastern Indonesia". *Archaeologica Oceania* 44 (2009): 18–28.

Diamond, Jared. *Guns, Germs, and Steel: A Short History of Everybody for the Last 13,000 Years.* London: Vintage, 1998.

Doran, Edwin Jr. *Wangka: Austronesian Canoe Origins*, College Station: Texas A&M University Press, 1981.

Findlay, Alexander George. *A Directory for the Navigation of the Indian Ocean with Descriptions of its Coasts, Islands, etc., from the Cape of Good Hope to the Strait of Sunda and Western Australia; including also the Red Sea and the Persian Gulf; the Winds, Monsoons and Currents and the Passages from Europe to its Various Ports.* Third edition, London: Richard Holmes Laurie, 1876.

Geertz, Hildred. "Indonesian cultures and communities". In *Indonesia*, edited by Ruth T. McVey, rev. ed. New Haven: Human Relations Area Files, 1963.

Higham, Charles. *The Bronze Age of Southeast Asia.* Cambridge: Cambridge University Press, 1996.

Hornell, James. *Water Transport: Origins and Early Evolution*. Cambridge: Cambridge University Press, 1946.

Horridge, Adrian. *Sailing Craft of Indonesia*. Images of Asia series, Singapore/Oxford: Oxford University Press, 1986.

———. "The Austronesian Conquest of the Sea — Upwind". In *The Austronesians: Historical and Comparative Perspectives*, edited by Peter Bellwood, James J. Fox & Darrell Tryon, Canberra: ANU E-Press, 1995.

Hurles M.E., B.C. Sykes, M.A. Jobling and P. Forster. "The dual origin of the Malagasy in Island Southeast Asia and East Africa: evidence from maternal and paternal lineages". *American Journal of Human Genetics* 76 (2005): 894–901.

Jones, A.M. *Africa and Indonesia: the Evidence of the Xylophone and Other Musical and Cultural Factors*. Leiden: E.J. Brill, 1964.

Kirch, Patrick. *Feathered Gods and Fishhooks: An Introduction to Hawaiian Archaeology and Prehistory*. Honolulu: University of Hawai'i Press, 1985.

Kumar, Ann. *Globalizing the Prehistory of Japan: Language, Genes and Civilization*. Routledge Studies in the Early History of Asia, London and New York: Routledge, 2009.

———. "The Single Most Astonishing Fact of Human Geography': Indonesia's Far West Colony". *Indonesia* 92 (October 2011): 59–96.

Lewis, Martin W. "Dividing the Ocean Sea". *The Geographical Review* 89, no. 2 (1999): 188–214.

———. and Karen Wigen. "A Maritime Response to the Crisis in Asian Studies". *The Geographical Review* 89, no. 2 (1999): 161–68.

Loire, Georges. *Gens de Mere à Dar-es-Salaam*. n.p.: Karthala, 1993.

Mahan, Alfred Thayer. *The Influence of Sea Power upon History: 1660–1783*. London: Sampson Low, Marston, Searle & Rivington, 1890.

Manguin, Pierre-Yves. "The Southeast Asian Ship: An Historical Approach". *Journal of Southeast Asian Studies* XI, no. 2 (1980): 266–76.

Marsden, William M. *Miscellaneous Works of William Marsden*. London: Parbury, Allen and Co. 1834.

Mauny, Raymond. "The Wakwak and the Indonesian invasion in East Africa in 945 A.D.". *Studia* 15 (May 1965): 7–16.

Mollat du Jourdin, Michel. "Les contacts historiques de l'Afrique et de Madagascar avec l'Asie du Sud et du Sud-Est: le rôle de l'Océan indien". *Archipel* 21 (1981): 35–53.

Owen, Norman G. et al. *The Emergence of Modern Southeast Asia: A New History*. Honolulu: University of Hawai'i Press, 2005.

Shaffer, Lynda. "Southernization". *Journal of World History* 5 no. 1 (Spring 1994): 1–21.

Sharp, Andrew. *Ancient voyagers in the Pacific*. Memoirs of the Polynesian Society No. 32, Wellington: Polynesian Society, 1956.

Steinberg, David Joel (ed.). *In Search of Southeast Asia: A Modern History*. Sydney: Allen & Unwin, 1987.
Tanaka, Masashi et al. "Mitochondrial Genome Variation in Eastern Asia and the Peopling of Japan". *Genome Research* 14 (2004): 1832–50.
Wisseman Christie, J. "State formation in early maritime Southeast Asia: A consideration of the theories and the data". *Bijdragen tot de taal- land- en volkenkunde* 151, no. 2 (1995): 235–88.

PART IV
Early Modern Southeast Asia

7

SOUTHEAST ASIAN ISLAM AND SOUTHERN CHINA IN THE SECOND HALF OF THE FOURTEENTH CENTURY

Geoff Wade

DEDICATION

Two enduring fields of study for Anthony Reid have been Islam in Southeast Asia — in both historical and contemporary contexts — and the diverse relationships which have long tied Southeast Asia with China. Both aspects found expression in *Southeast Asia in the Age of Commerce*, as well as in a range of articles and other contributions to scholarship. It was through Tony's encouragement that I began exploring the nexus of these two phenomena, particularly as they existed in the fourteenth century. The following article expands on an idea which Tony first conceived and expounded upon in our conversations. This small piece is dedicated to a man of rare qualities — a scholar whose breadth of interests and extensive scholarly endeavours have done nothing to diminish a deep compassion and concern for others.

* * *

INTRODUCTION

Islam came to the polities and societies of Southeast Asia by sea, along the girdle of trade which extended from the Arab and Persian worlds through the ports of South Asia, to Southeast Asia and onwards to the southern extensions of the Chinese world in the East China Sea. Islamic influences extended into Southeast Asia from both ends of this trade route in different periods. In examining such influences, the extension of Islam into Southeast Asia prior to 1500 can be divided into three major stages:

1) The period from the emergence of Islam until the Cōla invasions of Southeast Asia in the eleventh century;
2) The end of the eleventh century until the thirteenth century;
3) The fourteenth and fifteenth centuries, following the establishment of the first Islamic Southeast Asian polities in the thirteenth century.

The present paper will focus attention on the early part of the third period, specifically the second half of the fourteenth century, in order to demonstrate how key were events of this period in the Islamization of Southeast Asia.[1]

There is little doubt that the earliest introduction of Islam to Southeast Asia was by Muslim merchants who travelled along the maritime routes which, for at least a millennium earlier, had connected the two ends of the Eurasian continent. The foundation of the urban centre of Baghdād in 762 C.E. — with Basra as its outlet to the Arabian Sea — was a major impetus in the transformation of trade and the development of commerce between the Persian Gulf and East Asia.[2] The importance of this early maritime vector is still evident today, as it is in maritime Southeast Asia rather than the mainland where reside the major Muslim communities. The specific activities of the early Persian and Arab traders[3] in Southeast Asia are poorly documented, but we can glean some knowledge of them from accounts of the destination ports in southern China. In the eighth century, for example, Ibn Khurdādhbih recorded the trade ports at the furthest distance from the Arab world as *Lūqūn* (likely Loukin, situated in what is today Vietnam), *Khānfū* (Guangzhou/Canton), *Khānjū* (Quanzhou), with *Qānsū* (Yangzhou) marking the end of their maritime route. In the middle of the same century (758/59 CE), following the An Lu-shan rebellion, the major Chinese port of Guangzhou was sacked by persons from "Da-shi," the name which Chinese chroniclers assigned to the Arab world.[4] By a century later, there was evidence in the same city of a quite large Islamic community. Suleimān, who visited Guangzhou in 851, noted that the city had a Muslim community governing itself according to the *sharīa* under a *kādī*, whose appointment had to be confirmed by the Chinese authorities. It is likely that this was the port from which the Arab/Indian ship wrecked off Belitung island in about 826 CE and carrying cargo possibly bound for Western Asia had sailed.[5] That the foreign community in Guangzhou was quite large in the ninth century is affirmed by Abū Zaid, who reported that some 120,000 Muslims, Jews, Christians and Parsees were killed when the city was taken in 878/79 by Huang Chao, a rebel against the ruling Tang dynasty.[6] There is evidence, also from Chinese texts, that Muslim communities had appeared by this period in the ports of Sumatra and of Champa.

ISLAM BETWEEN CHINA AND SOUTHEAST ASIA FROM THE ELEVENTH TO THE THIRTEENTH CENTURIES

It was in the first half of the eleventh century that disruptions to the maritime trade route connecting the two ends of Eurasia resulted from the attacks on and possibly capture of the major peninsular and Sumatran ports in Southeast Asia by Cōla forces. This period also saw a major shift in the region's maritime trade, with the Fujian port of Quanzhou eclipsing the former trade centre of Guangzhou. Quanzhou quickly became the site of mosques[7] and Tamil temples, as the maritime merchants from lands extending all the way to West Asia brought trade products to China and took Chinese products on their return journeys. It is clear that Champa was a major staging post on these voyages, and that Muslim traders led Champa "tribute" missions into China throughout the tenth and eleventh centuries. That the Islamic communities of coastal China and Southeast Asia were intimately tied during the twelfth century is apparent from a comment by al-Idrīsī (1100–65) who stated that when China was convulsed by troubles, the (Muslim) merchants would descend to the harbours of a place they called Zābaj.[8]

Half way around the globe, in and around the Red Sea, the twelfth and thirteenth centuries saw Yemeni ports developing their links with regions to the East under the aegis of the Ayyūbid (1171–1250) in Egypt and subsequently the local Rasulid dynasty (1228–1454). This revitalized the luxury and spice trades both with India and with ports further east, providing increased avenues for Muslims to travel to and interact with people from the Southeast Asian realm, as well as further reasons for Southeast Asians and Chinese to travel to the major Islamic centres in the Middle East.

Quanzhou thus became the end port for the long journey from the Arab and Persian lands, as well as a key port for those Muslims trading from Southeast Asia. From the sources we have available, more than half of the foreign trade into Quanzhou appears to have been controlled by Muslims in this period. By the thirteenth century, when the Mongols ruled over China, it seems that Quanzhou was being administered almost as a Muslim polity, funded through its trade with Southeast Asia and beyond. The boom in maritime trade during the twelfth and thirteenth centuries underwrote Islamic power in Quanzhou, and in this process a figure known as Pu Shou-geng (蒲壽庚) and his family members were major players.

Islamic links between Quanzhou and Brunei during this period are evidenced by material remains. A grave of a Song dynasty official surnamed Pu and likely from Quanzhou has been found in Brunei. Dated to the equivalent of 1264 CE, it is the earliest Chinese-script gravestone in Southeast Asia as well as one of the earliest Muslim gravestones.[9] The Pu clan was a major element in the story of Islam in the maritime realm which connected Southeast Asia and South China. One account suggests that an unnamed Pu ancestor had originally come to Guangzhou from somewhere in the Arab world and had been appointed as the headman of the foreign quarter in that city, eventually becoming the richest man in the entire region. Another version suggests that this person was a noble from Champa which, as noted above, does not preclude him from having been an Arab. Could he have been a descendant of the Pu Luo-e who led his family members to Hainan from Champa in 986 following political disturbance in that place? The fact remains that during the twelfth century a person "surnamed" Pu, a Muslim, was one of the richest men in the city of Guangzhou, and behind his residence stood a giant "stupa," unlike Buddhist ones. This was likely the minaret of the Huai-sheng-si, the famous mosque of Guangzhou. The wealth of the family, however, declined, and the son of the Guangzhou foreign headman, named Pu Kai-zong (蒲開宗), removed the family to Quanzhou[10] as that port rose to dominate the trade with Southeast Asia and beyond. It was his son, Pu Shou-geng who was to become famed in the histories of Quanzhou, Chinese Islam and maritime trade with Southeast Asia.[11] Reputedly for his assistance in suppressing pirates in the region of Quanzhou, Pu Shou-geng was rewarded by the Song court in 1274 with the position of Maritime Trade Supervisor of the port. All maritime trade through Quanzhou was subject to his control, and as this was the major port of the entire polity, the opportunities for gain would have been enormous. He and his brother also operated many ships on their own account. Pu Shou-geng was subsequently appointed to even higher office with a provincial post, only a few years before the Yuan armies crushed the Southern Song capital at Hangzhou and the Song dynasty was brought to an end.[12]

Even before they took Hangzhou in 1276, the Yuan generals had recognized the power of Pu Shou-geng and his brother in south-eastern China and had sent envoys to invite them to side with the Yuan. The Pu brothers knew where their future lay, and they gave their allegiance to the incoming

Mongols. The importance of this to the Yuan was enormous, as it provided the Mongols a local regime with access to the sea, something which the Mongols had never commanded. Their new ally subsequently massacred the Song imperial clansmen who resided in Quanzhou, demonstrating his allegiance to the Mongols. The Yuan rulers richly rewarded those who had assisted them and Pu Shou-geng was appointed as the Grand Commander of Fujian and Guangdong, and subsequently as a vice minister of the Fujian administration. Pu was tasked with assisting the Mongols in both promoting maritime trade and providing ships and personnel for some of the Mongol military expeditions to overseas polities. It is not surprising that the first countries to respond to Pu Shou-geng's invitation to resume trade were Champa in Southeast Asia and Ma'abar, on the subcontinent's Coromandel Coast — both major trading polities with large Muslim populations. One of the latest reports we have of Pu Shou-geng, dating from 1281, notes that he had been ordered by the Yuan emperor to build 200 ocean-going ships, or which 50 had been finished.

The arrival of the Yuan forces in southern China in the 1270s and the violence which accompanied that arrival had apparently spurred some Muslims to leave Chinese ports and, as in the past, flee south. Li Tana has examined the Vietnamese annals on this point and found reference to Muslim refugees from China arriving in the Vietnamese polity in 1274.[13] This date fits well with flight prior to the last-ditch Song defence of Yangzhou during the Yuan attack on that city in 1275. Yangzhou was a very cosmopolitan city and it would not have been surprising if some of the residents there — Muslim and other — would have opted for safer climes to the south prior to the attack.[14]

At approximately the same time, in the Southeast Asian archipelago, we begin to see evidence for the emergence of Muslim rulers. An Islamic gravestone is reported for one Sultān Sulaimān bin Abd Allāh bin al-Basīr of Lamreh dated 608 AH (1211 CE).[15] It remains controversial, but if confirmed this will be the first evidence of a Muslim ruler in the Nusantaran world. Separately, in the account of his return journey by sea from China, Marco Polo reported in the 1290s that the Sumatran city of Pěrlak/Ferlec was Muslim,[16] but neighbouring urban centres named Basman and Samara were not. The latter polity was more than likely Samudera, where a gravestone of the reputed first Islamic ruler of that polity — Sultān Malik al-Sālih — dated 696 AH (1297 CE) has been found.[17] These phenomena manifest a new age in the relationship between Islam and Southeast Asia, with rulers of polities taking on the new religion. That the emergence of these Islamic polities was linked with the rise and expansion of the Mamlūks (1250–1517) in Egypt is suggested by the adoption by Samuderan sultans of the title Al-Malik al-Zahir, an apparent commemoration of the Mamlūk Sultān al-Malik al-Zahir Rukn al-Dīn Baybars al-Bundukdārī (1260–77) of Egypt and Syria, who had defeated the seventh Crusade sent by Louis IX, as well as the Mongol forces at Ayn Jalūt in Palestine in 1260. The indigenous tradition relating to these earliest Islamic polities in Sumatra was later recorded, somewhat anachronistically, in *Hikayat Raja-raja Pasai*.[18]

THE QUANZHOU VIOLENCE AND FLIGHT TO NUSANTARA

Why Islamic polities should have emerged in northern Sumatra in the thirteenth century remains an enigma. It is obvious that Muslim traders had been passing and stopping at these port-polities for centuries before this. It is likely that the rise of Islamic states in Sumatra was linked with the decline of the Cōla dynasty in southern India, the collapse of that country into war and the end of the integrated regional economy which incorporated the northern Sumatran polities. With the rise of the more domestically-oriented Vijayanagara in southern India, the linkages of the Hindu-Buddhist polities of Sumatra with the subcontinent would have declined, as would have the Tamil guilds, the resultant lacuna likely providing new avenues for religious conversion. Moreover, the ports of the Malabar Coast continued to be meeting places and commercial marts for traders from Yemen, Southeast Asia and China. The expansion of Islamic trading networks, and some have suggested Sufi guilds, along these maritime trade routes appears to have thus burgeoned.

From the fourteenth century we see growing evidence of the expansion of Islam in Southeast Asia. In Sumatra (or al-Jāwa as he referred to it), Ibn Battūta recorded what he, or his informants, observed when passing through the port-polity of Samudra in 1345 and 1346. He noted that the ruler — one Sultān Al-Malik Al-Zāhir — was "a Shāfiī in *madhhab* and a lover of jurists" who "often fights against and raids the infidels." It was further noted that "the people of his country are Shāfiī who are eager to fight infidels and readily go on campaign with him. They dominate the neighbouring infidels who pay *jizya* to have peace."[19] Through the account provided, we see a polity whose ruler was engaged in frequent *jihad*, who sent missions to Delhi and to Zaitūn/Quanzhou, and who, at home, was surrounded by wazīrs, secretaries, sharifs, jurists, poets, and army commanders, and who obviously had close links with Islamic societies to the west, and direct sea links with Quilon in India. The Shāfiī school which the sultan followed has remained important throughout Indonesia and in the coastal areas of India. We should not, however, consider this to have been simply a Middle Eastern society or ruling structure transplanted to Southeast Asia. It has been remarked that

Ibn Baṭṭūṭa likely concentrated excessively on the cosmopolitan Arab/Iranian aspects of the court, and ignored the Indic and local elements unfamiliar to him. Certainly, the *batu Aceh* of the period reflect a strong indigenous element in the culture of the polity.[20]

Ibn Baṭṭūṭa then visited Mul Jāwa, the "country of the infidels," which is accepted to mean that Islam had not gained any real foothold in the island of Java by the mid-fourteenth century. The only other major stop on the voyage to China, was Tawālisī, which has never been definitively identified. The long-standing importance of Champa as a stop on the Islamic trade route to China, however, makes it the leading candidate. This supposition is supported by Yamamoto Tatsuro's equation of Kailūkarī, the name of the largest city in Tawālisī according to Ibn Baṭṭūṭa, with the Cham name Klaung Garai.[21]

The West Asian links with Champa are manifested in the princess whom Ibn Baṭṭūṭa met in Tawālisī, who spoke to him in Turkish, who was literate in Arabic, and who wrote out the *bismillāh* in the presence of the visitor. Ibn Baṭṭūṭa, however, considered the polity to be outside Islam. This may well be a manifestation of the diversities of Islam within fourteenth century Southeast Asia. He then travelled on to China, where Ibn Baṭṭūṭa noted the option of staying with Muslim merchants resident there, and that in Zaitun/Quanzhou, the "Muslims live in a separate city." There he met Muslims from Isfahān and Tabrīz. It thus appears that, for Ibn Baṭṭūṭa in the mid-fourteenth century, the areas extending between the Islamic polity at Samudera and the Muslim communities on the Fujian coast remained outside Islam.

Events which occurred in Southern China not long after the visit of Ibn Baṭṭūṭa appear, however, to have had major effects on Islamization in Southeast Asia. As noted, the port of Quanzhou was controlled by Muslims during this period, the Mongol Yuan rulers including them within the *semu*[22] group of Central Asian and Middle Eastern officials who exercised Yuan power over the Chinese inhabitants. The two major groups competing for power over the city and its foreign trade were the locally-born Islamic families, including that of Pu Shou-geng, and the newly-arrived Isfahān group of Persians who had come to the area with the Yuan armies. In the 1350s, a descendant of Pu Shou-geng, named Na-wu-na, controlled the local Maritime Trade Supervisorate for the Yuan court, while the Persians were represented by two persons — Sai-fu-ding and A-mi-li-ding — both holding military positions as brigade commanders. At a time when the Yuan was in steep decline, and when rebellions against the Yuan administration were occurring widely throughout China, it is not surprising that the tensions in Quanzhou also spilled over. The standard *Yuan History* tells us: "In the spring of the seventeenth year of the Zhi-zheng reign (1357), the local brigade commanders Sai-fu-ding and A-mi-li-ding rebelled and took control of Quanzhou." This so-called Isfahān (亦思巴奚)[23] rebellion was to last for ten years. It is possible that the prominent merchant Sharaf al-Dīn of Tabrīz, whom Ibn Battūta met in Quanzhou and of whom he noted that he had borrowed money in India, was the same "Sai-fu-ding" who is mentioned in the Yuan text.[24]

By 1362, the forces of Sai-fu-ding controlled much of the area around the provincial capital Fuzhou, but were then defeated by Yuan forces and fled back to Quanzhou, where it is reported that both Sai-fu-ding and A-mi-li-ding were killed by the Maritime Trade supervisor Na-wu-na, a descendant of Pu Shou-geng. It has been suggested that the members of the Pu Shou-geng clan were Sunni, while the Işfahān forces were Shi'ite. This intra-Islamic struggle in Quanzhou also quickly involved Mongol forces of the Yuan and the Chinese themselves who felt that they had been maltreated under Yuan rule. The breakdown of dynastic order provided an opportunity to a more powerful contender for regional power — Chen You-ding, a former Yuan general. With the assistance of Jin Ji, a general of Persian origin, Chen eliminated Na-wu-na and then began methodically murdering Sunni followers, as well as destroying Sunni graves, mosques and residences. It appears that initially the purge was directed at Sunni followers, but that it later expanded into a broader anti-Islamic campaign, with the depredations lasting for almost a decade after Chen You-ding captured Quanzhou. Those who escaped the purge either fled into the mountains or set sail. This flight of Muslims by sea from Quanzhou and elsewhere in Fujian into Southeast Asia in the 1360s was to greatly stimulate the development of Islam in the Southeast Asian region.

In the 1370s, not much more than a decade after the purges and massacres began in Fujian, Muslim tombs began to appear in Java. Most of these were devoted to elite figures apparently intimately involved with the administration of the Majapahit state. The first of the Islamic gravestones (*maesan*), which are found at Trowulan and Trayala near ancient Majapahit, has an inscription dated to Śaka 1298 (equivalent to 1376 CE) and the dates of subsequent gravestones extend into the third quarter of the fifteenth century.[25] They are inscribed with the Śaka year in ancient Javanese script on one side of the stone, and with pious Islamic inscriptions in Arabic on the other. Given what we know of the situation in Quanzhou in the 1360s and the links already established between Champa and Quanzhou in this period, the existence of the tomb of *Puteri Cempa* (the Campa princess) in Trowulan,[26] dated to 1448 C.E., underlines the likelihood that these graves belong to Muslims who fled the conflagrations in southern China in the 1360s, and were then engaged in various capacities by the Majapahit court, maintaining links with both Champa and the southern Chinese ports. The sudden appearance of a group of Muslims, intimately tied to the Javanese administration is otherwise difficult to explain. It is possible that this *Puteri Cĕmpa* was Haji Ma Hong Fu's wife, whom Parlindungan's "Annals of Semarang and Cirebon" tell us, "had passed away and was buried in Majapahit according to Islamic rites" in or just before 1449.[27] Earlier references in these Annals tell us that Haji Ma Hong Fu, who had his origins in Yunnan, had been married to the daughter of Haji Bong Tak Keng, who had been appointed by the Ming commander Zheng He as a representative to Champa.[28] Separately, at Surabaya, the *Pĕcat tanda*, that is, the "head of the market" at Terung was also a Chinese person employed as an official by the Majapahit court, and it was he who protected the young Muslim man who had come from Champa and who would later become Raden Rahmat.[29]

While Damais and others believe that the persons interred in the graves at Trowulan and Trayala were Javanese,[30] the possibility should also be considered that these were persons from abroad who had given their allegiance to the Majapahit polity. Nascent polities on Java also suggest new arrivals during this period. Demak (淡巴) on the northern Javanese coast first appeared in the Chinese historical record in 1377,[31] and is also recorded as having sent "tribute" to the Ming court in 1394. The founding or expansion of this *pesisir* polity by refugees in the 1360s or 1370s also conforms to all that we know of it. In addition, Javanese texts record Muslim leaders coming to Java from Champa, and settling in the three most important early centres of Islamic propaganda — Surabaya (Ngampel), Gresik (Giri) and Cerbon (Gunung Jati). By the early fifteenth century, with the arrival of further observers on the ships of Zheng He, we read that Gresik had over 1,000 "Chinese" families, likely including the Muslim people of diverse ethnic origins who had fled from Fujian.

Ma Huan, a Muslim who accompanied Zheng He on several voyages, included Java in his first-hand descriptions, later published under the title *Ying-yai sheng-lan* (or "Supreme Survey of the Ocean Shores"). Of Java, which he visited on the 1413–15 mission, he noted:

> The country contains three classes of persons. One class consists of the Muslim[32] people; they are all people from every foreign kingdom in the West who have flowed to this place as merchants; and in all matters of dressing and eating, they are all very clean. One class consists of T'ang people,[33] and they are all people from Guangdong and from Zhangzhou and Quanzhou and such places, who fled away and now live in this country; the food of these people, too, is choice and clean; and many of them follow the Muslim

religion, following the precepts and fasting. One class consists of the local people; they have very ugly and strange appearance, tousled hair, and go in bare feet. They are devoted to devil worship, this country being among the 'devil countries' spoken of in Buddhist books. The food which these people eat is very dirty and bad.[34]

Two major points emerge from Ma Huan's account. The first is that by the early part of the fifteenth century, there was already quite a large number of Muslims, both Chinese and those from further west, resident in Tuban, Gresik, Surabaya and Majapahit on the northern coast of Java, but that the "local people" had not adopted the religion. The second is that many of the Chinese Muslims in Java had "fled" from China, endorsing the thesis that they had fled the repercussions of the "Isfahān rebellion" in Quanzhou.

The likelihood that the earliest Javanese mosques were modelled on Chinese forms has been suggested by De Graaf and Pigeaud, citing the similarity of the top ornament (*mastaka*) of the mosques and the pinnacles of Chinese stupas and pagodas. They note: "It could be expected that the first mosques in Java built by Chinese Muslims were imitations of Chinese pagodas. In their homeland in China or Indo-China pagodas were erected and used by various religions. This supposition is corroborated by the Malay Annals' story about the cooperation of the Chinese shipbuilders of Sĕmarang in the building of the first mosque of Dĕmak." They also note the absence, in the earliest Javanese mosques, of the *surambi*, or front gallery, found in later mosques, and also suggest this as having originated in Chinese architecture.[35]

Evidence from Sumatra also supports the argument for a flight of hybrid Persian-Arab-Cham-Chinese Muslims out of southern China into maritime Southeast Asia during the 1360s. Recent archaeological surveys and excavations in Barus reveal that the earliest Islamic tombstone found there dates from 772 AH/1370 CE,[36] which fits excellently with the chronology proposed above. The name of the woman buried beneath the tombstone — Suy — may be Chinese, while the inscription itself contains Persian grammar and Arabic terms. Thus, the 1360s likely saw the return of an Islamic community to Barus following the driving out of the earlier community in the eleventh century by the Cōlas.

Brunei's adoption of Islam in this period is reflected in the gravestone of a fourteenth-century Sultān, named "Mahārājā Brunī", found in the Residency cemetery in Bandar Seri Begawan. Links between that community and China are indicated by the fact that the gravestone was certainly manufactured in Quanzhou and transported to Brunei, as it is almost identical to those carved in China and, like them, is also made of diabase and inscribed completely in

Arabic. In Terengganu, a stone inscribed in Malay written in Arabic script and dating from the fourteenth century suggests that Islamic law was being practised (or at least promoted) in this estuary of the Malay peninsula. In both these places, there is evidence that Islam had been a recent arrival, and that the process of adjustment was still taking place. The Brunei Sultan, for example, was still being entitled Mahārājā,[37] while the Terengganu inscription referred to the Almighty by the Sanskritic name "Dewata Mulia Raya" alongside the name Allah. In addition, the Terengganu law code provided for differentiated fines depending on social rank, a practice unknown to more orthodox Islam. Kern suggested that "we have here a stone inscription from a convert, undoubtedly assisted by someone learned in the law, among a population yet to be converted."[38] The same phenomenon is manifested in two late fourteenth century gravestones at Minye Tujuh in north Sumatra for the daughter of Sultān Al-Malik Al-Zāhir,[39] which have inscriptions in both Arabic and in Old Malay written in an Indic-inspired Sumatran script.

Thus, the late fourteenth century can certainly be seen as a period of wide extension of Islam within Southeast Asia, as well as of hybridity and synthesis. Apart from those manifestations noted above, Chinese texts note the existence of other Islamic rulers including Sultan "Malik Zāhir", ruler of Samudera in 1383 and Sultān Zayn al-Ābidīn, who had assumed the throne of that polity by 1419; Sultān Husayn, the ruler of Aru in 1411; and Muhammad Shāh, the ruler of Lambri in 1412. We can thereby observe that, by the beginning of the fifteenth century, the northern and eastern coasts of Sumatra were the location of at least three Muslim polities. We remain unsure whether the extension of the presence of Islam in the northern half of Sumatra was the result of the raids by Sultān Al-Malik Al-Zāhir and his successors or other processes.

THE MING MARITIME MISSIONS

By the end of the fourteenth century, it thus appears that the influx of Muslims from Southern China as well as the activities of rulers in the north of Sumatra had already begun to change the religious nature of Nusantara.[40] It was at this juncture, following the coming to power in China of the usurper Ming emperor Yong-le, that another southward push from China was to occur. The voyages of the eunuch Muslim admiral Zheng He, which extended over the period 1405 to 1435, have attracted a wide range of explanations as to their impetus and function. The most appealing is that the usurping emperor Yong-le needed to boost his legitimacy by extending Ming power over as great an area as possible.[41] The sending of these vast armadas under the command of Zheng He and other eunuch officials was intended to bring the known maritime world to submission. Thereby, a *pax Ming* could be established, trade nodes and routes to the West could be controlled, and both political and economic power would come to reside in the hands of the Ming emperor. It was thus that these missions proceeded along the trade routes which the Arabs and Persians had been using for centuries, all the way to the East coast of Africa.

The prominence of Muslim traders and Muslim polities along the existing trade routes may have influenced the decision to have Muslims lead these massive missions, each of which comprised up to hundreds of ships and up to 30,000 troops. Like Zheng He, some of the other senior commanders were Muslims, as were many of the soldiers and seamen who accompanied the missions. It was thus at this time, in an effort to soothe the remaining Muslims of Fujian, to aid the conscription of interpreters and pilots for the eunuch-led armadas and to facilitate links with those who had fled southwards, that the Yong-le emperor issued a proclamation in 1407 that no more violence was to be perpetrated against Muslims. "No official, military or civilian personnel shall despise, insult or bully [Muslims] and whoever disobeys this order by doing so shall bear the consequences."[42]

The Ming missions were certainly not intended by the Ming court to have a religious proselytizing function, but given the religious affiliations of many of the senior members of the missions, it would not have been surprising if there had been efforts to encourage the adoption of a new religion among some of the political leaders met on the voyages. These missions had the added unintentional effect of linking together the major Muslim communities in southern China and those throughout Southeast Asia and India, with the societies of the great Islamic centres of West Asia. Many of the rulers, or at least senior envoys from places visited in Southeast Asia and beyond were carried in the Ming ships to the Chinese capital together with envoys from Islamic polities further west — Cochin, Hormuz, Aden, Dhofar and even Mecca. Awareness of the extent and influence of Islam in these areas may have contributed to the ongoing Islamization in Southeast Asia.

The Ming naval forces definitely became engaged in the politics of Java in the early part of the fifteenth century. Chinese texts inform us that two competing rulers of Java — a Western king and an Eastern king — were engaged with the Ming state in the early years of the century. The Ming naval forces were apparently in close contact with the Eastern ruler before he was killed by the Western ruler in 1406. The Western ruler also killed 170 Ming troops involved with the Eastern kingdom, for which the Ming court demanded 60,000 ounces of gold as compensation. As the Western king was likely the ruler of Majapahit, we might surmise that the Eastern king ruled a newly-emergent coastal polity, probably in the Gresik-Surabaya region, where a new power base had arisen around the Muslim refugees who fled from Fujian to Southeast Asia in the 1360s and 1370s.[43]

This scenario lends credence to the otherwise quite contentious Malay-language *Peranakan* chronicles of Semarang and Cirebon "discovered" and published by Mangaradja Parlindungan in the 1960s. Parlindungan's account, supposedly derived from the Chinese community archives in these cities, depicts a wide-ranging early fifteenth century network of Chinese Hanafi Muslims, spread through polities all over Southeast Asia, and tightly connected to Ming agents such as Zheng He. These Chinese Hanafi communities were supposedly established in Palembang, Sambas, Malacca, and Luzon, as well as all along the north coast of Java — Ancol, Cirebon, Lasem, Tuban, Semarang, Gresik, and Joratan. The account further assigns Chinese origins to some of the Islamic saints of Java, including Sunan Ngampel and Sunan Giri, as well as to Njai Gede Pinatih, the Great Lady of Gresik.[44]

It needs to be affirmed that much of the Parlindungan account is in accord with the evolution of the Chinese Muslim communities overseas as reflected in the foregoing account. People did flee from Quanzhou to various ports in Southeast Asia in the late fourteenth century, and the links which Parlindungan suggests are congruent with other sources he was unlikely to have had access to. The fifteenth-century *Xi-yang fan-guo-zhi* actually stated that all of the Chinese in Java were Muslims,[45] and within Java there are traditions of Chinese participation in the Islamisation of Java.[46] The Sino-Javanese envoy Ma Yong-long (Ma Yong-liang) is well-attested in other sources, but most interestingly, another of the leaders of the Javanese Hanafi community as reported in Parlindungan's work — Gan Eng Cu — is found to have a correlate only in the Ming veritable records (*Ming shi-lu*) which would not have been available to Parlindungan. Of Gan Eng Cu, the Parlindungan account reads:

> 1423: Haji Bong Tak Keng transferred Haji Gan Eng Cu from Manila/Philippines to Tuban/Java to control the flourishing Hanafite Muslim communities in Java, Kukang and Sambas. At that time, Tuban was Java's main port, with the kingdom of Majapahit as hinterland. Haji Gan Eng Cu became a kind of consul-general of the Chinese government, the Ming Emperor, having control of all Muslim Chinese communities in the southern Nan Yang countries including Java, Kukang and Sambas……[47]

In the Ming veritable records, we read of Gong Yong-cai (龔用才 — in Hokkien "Giong Eng-cai"), a Chinese envoy from Java, travelling to the Ming court in 1429, and receiving robes from the Chinese emperor, exactly as was recorded of Gan Eng-cu in Parlindungan's work.[48] This reference opens up the possibility that these annals do provide us with new factual material on Sino-Javanese Islamic networks of the fifteenth century.

Regardless of the veracity of this account, we do observe in this period the beginning of a new age of Islamization along the Javanese northern coast.[49] We have evidence of Islam in Gresik by 1419,[50] and further evidence of the religion's gradual growth along this coast. These *pesisir* communities were to become some of the most powerful agents of Islamic expansion in Southeast Asia both during the fifteenth century and beyond. Demak is depicted in some accounts as having waged *jihad* against other *pesisir* polities through the fifteenth century.[51]

But would any of this have been possible without the southward flow of Muslims out of Quanzhou to Java and elsewhere in Nusantara, as a result or warfare and purges in the last quarter of the fourteenth century? We can never know. What can be affirmed is that that movement of Muslim persons — diverse in ethnicity — to Southeast Asia from the ports of Fujian during this period was a key event in the making of Southeast Asian Islam.

Notes

1. For a fuller discussion of the spread of Islam to Southeast Asia prior to 1500, see Geoff Wade, "Early Muslim Expansion in Southeast Asia, Eighth to Fifteenth Centuries", in *The New Cambridge History of Islam, Volume 3 — The Eastern Islamic World Eleventh to Eighteenth Centuries*, edited by David O. Morgan and Anthony Reid (Cambridge: Cambridge University Press, 2010), pp. 366–408.
2. Pierre-Yves Manguin, "The Introduction of Islām into Champa", in *The Propagation of Islām in the Indonesian-Malay Archipelago*, edited by Alijah Gordon (Kuala Lumpur: Malaysian Sociological Research Institute, 2001), pp. 287–328. See p. 311, n. 12.
3. The "Persian and Arab Traders" referred to here is a generic reference to peoples from the Middle East trading on ships crewed by people of a likely diverse range or ethnicities and religions.
4. Recorded in the *Jiu Tang shu*, or "Older History of the Tang Dynasty", in *juan* 10. The term Da-shi (大食) derives from the Persian name Tazi, referring to a people in Persia. It was later used by the Persians to refer to the Arab lands. The Chinese used it from the Tang dynasty until about the twelfth century to refer to the Arabs.
5. Michael Flecker, "A ninth-century AD Arab or Indian shipwreck in Indonesia: first evidence for direct trade with China", *World Archaeology* 32, no. 3 (February 2001): 335–54.
6. Note, by comparison, the 10,000 Muslim population of Chaul (= Saymur), the main port for the Konkan coast as given by al-Mas'udi. Wink suggests that

the exodus of Arabs from China at this time was responsible for the rise of the major ports in the isthmian region, particularly Kalāh. See André Wink, *Al-Hind, the Making of the Indo-Islamic World*, 3 vols. (Leiden & New York: E.J. Brill, 1990–2004), Vol. I, p. 84.

7. The oldest mosque in Quanzhou reputedly dates from the eleventh century when the port began to rise in importance.
8. Al-Idrîsî, *Opus Geographicum*, edited by E. Cerulli et al., 4 vols. (Naples: Instituto Universitario Orientale, 1970–74, p. 62. Cited in Michael Laffan, *Finding Java: Muslim Nomenclature of Insular Southeast Asia from Śrîvijaya to Snouk Hurgronje*, Asia Research Institute Working Paper Series, No. 52 (Singapore: National University of Singapore, 2005). p. 22, n. 65. This term Zābaj was a generic reference to the ports of Sumatra and surrounding areas, and is the apparent origin of the Chinese name San-fo-qi for Sriwijaya.
9. The assumption is that the official surnamed Pu was, like other members of the Pu clan, a Muslim. There reportedly exists in Leran, East Java an Islamic gravestone dated AH 475 (1082 CE) for a woman, the "daughter of Maimun." However, there is no firm evidence that the gravestone originated in Java, with suggestions that it was possibly being brought there as ballast. See Ludvik Kalus and Claude Guillot, "Réinterprétation des plus anciennes stèles funéraires islamiques nousantariennes: II. La stèle de Leran (Java) datée de 475/1082 et les stèles associées", *Archipel* 67 (2004): 17–36.
10. This is noted in He Qiaoyuan 何喬遠, *Min Shu* 閩書 (Fuzhou: Fujian People's Press, 1994), juan 152.
11. For the most detailed available account of Pu Shou-geng, see Kuwabara Jitsuzo "On P'u Shou-keng", *Memoirs of the Research Department of the Toyo Bunko* II (1928): 1–79 and VII (1935): 1–104.
12. For further details of these events, see Billy K.L. So, *Prosperity, Region, and Institutions in Maritime China: The South Fukien Pattern, 946–1368* (Cambridge, Mass. & London: Harvard University Asia Center, 2000); Hugh Clark, "Overseas Trade and Social Change in Quanzhou through the Song", in *Emporium of the World: Maritime Quanzhou, 1000–1400*, edited by Angela Schottenhammer (Leiden: E.J. Brill, 2001), pp. 47–94; and John Chaffee, "Muslim Merchants and Quanzhou in the Late Yuan-Early Ming: Conjectures on the Ending of the Medieval Muslim Trade Diaspora," in *The East Asian 'Mediterranean': Maritime Crossroads of Culture, Commerce, and Human Migration*, edited by Angela Schottenhammer (Wiesbaden: Harrassowitz Verlag, 2008), pp. 115–32.
13. Personal communication from Li Tana. For original text, see Chen Ching-ho, 陈荆和 (编校) *Đại Việt sử ký toàn thư* (Critical edition) 校合本 <大越史記全書>, 3 vols. (3本). Tokyo: 1985–86. pp. 348–49.
14. One apparent victim of the battles at this time was Pu Ha-ting, a Sayyid of the 16th generation and builder of the Xian-he Mosque in Yangzhou, who died in 1275. See D. D. Leslie, *Islam in Traditional China: A Short History to 1800* (Canberra: Canberra College of Advanced Education, 1986), p. 48.

15. Suwedi Montana, "Nouvelles données sur les royaumes de Lamuri et Barat", *Archipel* 53 (1997): 85–96. See p. 92. There remains much dispute over the dating and other aspects of this gravestone.
16. "This kingdom, you must know, is so frequented by the Saracen merchants that they have converted the natives to the Law of Mahommet — I mean the townspeople only, for the hill people live for all the world like beasts…" Henry Yule (trans. and ed.), *The Book of Ser Marco Polo, the Venetian, Concerning the Kingdoms and Marvels of the East* (London: Murray 1929), Vol. II, p. 284.
17. For further details of the gravestones, see Elizabeth Lambourn, "The formation of the batu Aceh tradition in fifteenth-century Samudera-Pasai", *Indonesia and the Malay World* 32 (2004): 211–48; and Claude Guillot & Ludvik Kalus, *Les monuments funéraires et l'histoire du Sultanat de Pasai à Sumatra* (Paris: Association Archipel, 2008), pp. 177–78.
18. See A.H. Hill, "Hikayat Raja-Raja Pasai", *Journal of the Malayan Branch, Royal Asiatic Society* 33, no. 2 (June 1960).
19. H.A.R. Gibb, *The Travels of Ibn Battuta A.D. 1325–1354*. Translated with revisions and notes from the Arabic text edited by C. Defrémery and B.R. Sanguinetti, completed with annotations by C.F. Beckingham (London: The Hakluyt Society, 1994), Vol. IV, pp. 876–77.
20. See Lambourn, "The formation of the *batu Aceh* tradition".
21. The name of a Cham temple complex (Po Klaung Garai) located at Phanrang in what is today Ninh Thuận Province. It comprises three towers dating back to about 1300, built during the reign of Cham King Jaya Simhavarman II. Yamamoto Tatsuro, "On Tawalisi as Described by Ibn Battuta" in *Memoirs of the Research Department of the Toyo Bunko* VIII (1936): 93–133. See p. 117.
22. Lit: "Diverse peoples."
23. Chen and Kalus suggest an alternative — that the term "yi-xi-ba-xi" should be reconstructed as *ispāh* and that it derives from the Persian term *sepâh*, meaning "great army". See Chen Da-sheng and Ludvik Kalus, *Corpus d'Inscriptions Arabes et Persanes en Chine –1. Province de Fujian (Quanzhou, Fuzhou, Xiamen)* (Paris: Librairie Orientaliste Geuthner, 1991). See p. 45, note 151. However, if their proposal was the case, the final Chinese character would be superfluous. Isfahan is the most feasible origin for this expression, particularly as read in Hokkien, the characters provide "Yik-si-ba-he."
24. It is also likely not coincident that another senior person whom Ibn Battūta met in Quanzhou was Shaykh al-Islām Kamāl al-Dīn, "a pious man" who indeed came from Isfahān. Was he the other leader of the rebellion "A-mi-li-ding" (= Kamāl al-Dīn)?
25. See Louis-Charles Damais, "Études Javanaises: Les tombes Musulmans dates de Tralaya", *Bulletin de l'Ecole Française d'Extrême Orient* 48 (1956): 353–415. See listing and dates of the graves on p. 411.
26. This grave remains today an Islamic pilgrimage site.
27. Hermanus Johannes de Graaf & Theodore G. Th. Pigeaud, *Chinese Muslims in*

Java in the 15th and 16th Centuries: The Malay Annals of Sĕmarang and Cĕrbon, edited by M.C. Ricklefs, Monash Papers on Southeast Asia No. 12 (Melbourne: Monash University, 1984), p. 20. I am assigning this text more veracity than hitherto given to it for reasons detailed below.

28. De Graaf and Pigeaud, *Chinese Muslims in Java in the Fifteenth and Sixteenth centuries*, p. 14. This fits wonderfully with the date of the Trowulan grave, but those who are suspicious of the Parlindungan source might point to the fact that Damais' article on the graves was published in 1956, while Parlindungan's work *Tuanku Rao* within which the "Annals" are contained, was only published in 1964, allowing for the grave date information to be incorporated in the latter work.

29. Denys Lombard and Claudine Salmon. "Islam and Chineseness" in *The Propagation of Islam in the Indonesian-Malay Archipelago*, edited by Alijah Gordon, pp. 181–208 (Kuala Lumpur: Malaysian Sociological Research Institute, 2001), p. 184. See also the correlation in Javanese texts between Champa and the spread of Islam as detailed by Manguin in "The Introduction of Islam into Champa", pp. 294–95.

30. Merle Ricklefs notes of these graves: "The use of the Indian Śaka era and Javanese numerals rather than the Islamic Anno Hijrae and Arabic numerals to date several gravestones leads to the presumption that these mark the final resting place of indigenous Javanese followers of Islam rather than of Muslims from elsewhere. Moreover, on several of these stones are found distinctive sunburst medallions also found on other forms of Majapahit art, suggesting that these were in fact the graves of members of the Majapahit royal family." See M. C. Ricklefs, *Mystic Synthesis in Java: A History of Islamization from the Fourteenth to the Early Nineteenth Centuries* (Abingdon: EastBridge, 2006), p. 13.

31. Geoff Wade (trans.), *Southeast Asia in the Ming Shi-lu: An Open Access Resource* (Singapore: Asia Research Institute and the Singapore E-Press, National University of Singapore, 2005). Entry 1883.

32. The term used was "Hui-hui," likely derived from Hui-gu, the term by which the Chinese knew the Uighurs.

33. Chinese persons.

34. J.V.G. Mills, *Ma Huan, Ying-yai Sheng-lan [1433]: The Overall Survey of the Ocean's Shores* (Cambridge: Cambridge University Press for the Hakluyt Society, 1970).

35. De Graaf and Pigeaud, *Chinese Muslims in Java in the Fifteenth and Sixteenth Centuries*, p. 153.

36. See Ludvik Kalus, "Chap XV: Les Sources Épigraphiques Musulmanes de Barus," in *Histoire de Barus, Sumatra: Le Site de Lobu Tua, II Étude archéologique et Documents*, edited by Claude Guillot, pp. 303–38 (Paris: Association Archipel, 2003). For the tombstone cited, see pp. 305–06. Thanks go to John Miksic for drawing my attention to this tombstone. A recent update on the Islamic vestiges at Barus can be found in Daniel Perret & Heddy Surachman (ed.), *Histoire*

de Barus III: Regards sur une place marchande de l'océan Indien (XIIe-milieu du XVIIe s.) (Paris: Association Archipel & EFEO, 2009), pp. 582–88.

37. The title Maharaja was still in use for the ruler of Brunei in the early fifteenth century.
38. R.A. Kern, "The Propagation of Islam in the Indonesian-Malay Archipelago", in *The Propagation of Islam in the Indonesian-Malay Archipelago*, edited by Alijah Gordon (Kuala Lumpur: Malaysian Sociological Research Institute, 2001), pp. 23–124. See p. 36.
39. Either the same sultan whom Ibn Battuta had met in the 1340s, or his successor.
40. Slametmuljana also examined the role of Chinese Muslims in the Islamization of Nusantara, but included some unconfirmed sources. See Slametmuljana, "Islam before the Foundation of the Islamic State of Demak", *Journal of the South Seas Society* 27, no. 1 & 2 (December 1972): 41–83. My thanks to E. Edwards McKinnon for bringing this source to my attention.
41. The claim that Yong-le and other Ming emperors were closet Muslims is unsubstantiated by any accepted source. For such claims, see Yusuf Chang, "The Ming Empire: Patron of Islam in China and Southeast and West Asia", *Journal of the Malaysian Branch, Royal Asiatic Society* 61, no. 2 (1988): 1–44.
42. Chen Da-sheng 陈达生, *Quan-zhou Yi-si-lan jiao shi-ke* 泉州伊斯兰教石刻 (Islamic Stone Inscriptions from Quan-zhou), (Quanzhou: Fujian People's Press, 1984). See pp. 11–13.
43. Relevant materials can be gleaned from the *Ming Shi-lu*, *Ming-shi* and *Shu-yu-zhou-zi-lu*. The last of these works notes that the majority of Chinese who sojourned in Java were Muslims.
44. See De Graaf and Pigeaud, *Chinese Muslims in Java in the Fifteenth and Sixteenth Centuries*; D.A. Rinkes, *Nine Saints of Java*, translated by H.M. Froger, edited by Alijah Gordon (Kuala Lumpur: Malaysian Sociological Research Institute, 1996); and Rinkes, *Nine Saints of Java*; and Tan Yeok Seong, "Chinese Element in the Islamisation of Southeast Asia — A Study of the Story of Njai Gede Pinatih, the Great Lady of Gresik" *Journal of the South Seas Society* 30, nos. 1 and 2 (1975): 19–27.
45. Lombard and Salmon, "Islam and Chineseness", p. 183.
46. Slametmuljana, *Runtuknja Keradjaan Hindu-Djawa dan Timbulnja Negara-negara Islam di Nusantara* (Jakarta, Bhratara, 1968) as quoted in Lombard and Salmon, "Islam and Chineseness", p. 184.
47. De Graaf and Pigeaud, *Chinese Muslims in Java in the Fifteenth and Sixteenth Centuries*, p. 15.
48. De Graaf and Pigeaud, *Chinese Muslims in Java in the Fifteenth and Sixteenth Centuries*, pp. 15–16.
49. For further details of which, see Lombard and Salmon, *Islam and Chineseness*, pp. 115–17.
50. J.P. Moquette, "De datum op den grafsteen van Malik Ibrahim te Grisse"

Tijdschrift voor Indische Taal-, Land- en Volkenkunde LIV (1912): 208–14. Again the gravestone derived from Cambay.
51. De Graaf and Pigeaud, however, write of a tradition which holds that the first Muslim ruler of Demak (who was of Chinese origin) did not emerge until the last quarter of the 15th century. See Hermanus Johannes de Graaf & Theodore G. Th. Pigeaud, *Islamic States in Java 1500–1700* ('s-Gravenhage: KITLV, 1976), pp. 6–8.

References

Chaffee, John. "Muslim Merchants and Quanzhou in the Late Yuan-Early Ming: Conjectures on the Ending of the Medieval Muslim Trade Diaspora". In *The East Asian 'Mediterranean': Maritime Crossroads of Culture, Commerce, and Human Migration*, edited by Angela Schottenhammer, pp. 115–32. Wiesbaden: Harrassowitz Verlag, 2008.

Chang, Yusuf. "The Ming Empire: Patron of Islam in China and Southeast and West Asia". *Journal of the Malaysian Branch, Royal Asiatic Society* 61, no. 2 (1988): 1–44.

Chen Ching-ho, 陈荆和 (编校) *Đại Việt sử ký toàn thư* (Critical edition) 校合本 <大越史記全書>, 3 vols. (3本). Tokyo: 1985–86.

Chen Da-sheng 陈达生. *Quan-zhou Yi-si-lan jiao shi-ke* 泉州伊斯兰教石刻 (Islamic Stone Inscriptions from Quan-zhou). Quanzhou: Fujian People's Press, 1984.

Chen Da-sheng and Ludvik Kalus. *Corpus d'Inscriptions Arabes et Persanes en Chine –1. Province de Fu-jian (Quanzhou, Fuzhou, Xiamen)*. Paris: Librairie Orientaliste Geuthner, 1991.

Clark, Hugh. "Overseas Trade and Social Change in Quanzhou through the Song". In *Emporium of the World: Maritime Quanzhou, 1000–1400*, edited by Angela Schottenhammer, pp. 47–94. Leiden: E.J. Brill, 2001.

Damais, Louis-Charles. "Études Javanaises: Les tombes Musulmans dates de Tralaya". *Bulletin de l'Ecole Française d'Extrême Orient* 48 (1956): 353–415.

Flecker, Michael. "A ninth-century AD Arab or Indian shipwreck in Indonesia: first evidence for direct trade with China", *World Archaeology* 32, no. 3 (February 2001): 335–54.

Gibb, H.A.R. *The Travels of Ibn Battuta A.D. 1325–1354*. Translated with revisions and notes from the Arabic text edited by C. Defrémery and B.R. Sanguinetti, completed with annotations by C.F. Beckingham. London: The Hakluyt Society, 1994.

Gordon, Alijah (ed.). *The Propagation of Islam in the Indonesian-Malay Archipelago*. Kuala Lumpur: Malaysian Sociological Research Institute, 2001.

Graaf, Hermanus Johannes de and Theodore G. Th. Pigeaud. *Islamic States in Java 1500–1700*. 's-Gravenhage: KITLV, 1976.

———. *Chinese Muslims in Java in the Fifteenth and Sixteenth Centuries: The Malay*

Annals of Sĕmarang and Cĕrbon, edited by M.C. Ricklefs, Monash Papers on Southeast Asia No. 12. Melbourne: Monash University, 1984.

Guillot, Claude (ed.). *Histoire de Barus, Sumatra: Le Site de Lobu Tua, II Étude archéologique et Documents.* Paris: Association Archipel, 2003.

Guillot, Claude and Ludvik Kalus. *Les monuments funéraires et l'histoire du Sultanat de Pasai à Sumatra.* Paris: Association Archipel, 2008.

He Qiaoyuan 何喬遠. *Min Shu* 閩書. Fuzhou: Fujian People's Press, 1994.

Hill, A.H. "Hikayat Raja-Raja Pasai". *Journal of the Malayan Branch, Royal Asiatic Society* 33, no. 2 (June 1960).

Idrîsî, Al-. *Opus Geographicum,* edited by E. Cerulli et al., 4 vols. Naples: Instituto Universitario Orientale, 1970–74.

Kalus, Ludvik. "Les Sources Épigraphiques Musulmanes de Barus". In *Histoire de Barus, Sumatra: Le Site de Lobu Tua, II Étude archéologique et Documents,* edited by Claude Guillot, pp. 303–38. Paris: Association Archipel, 2003.

Kalus, Ludvik and Claude Guillot. "Réinterprétation des plus anciennes stèles funéraires islamiques nousantariennes: II. La stèle de Leran (Java) datée de 475/1082 et les stèles associées". *Archipel* 67 (2004): 17–36.

Kern, R.A. "The Propagation of Islam in the Indonesian-Malay Archipelago". In *The Propagation of Islam in the Indonesian-Malay Archipelago,* edited by Alijah Gordon, pp. 23–124. Kuala Lumpur: Malaysian Sociological Research Institute, 2001.

Kuwabara Jitsuzo 桑原隲藏. "On P'u Shou-kêng: a man of the Western regions, who was the superintendent of the trading ships' office in Ch'üan-chou towards the end of the Sung dynasty, together with a general sketch of trade of the Arabs in China during the T'ang and Sung eras". *Memoirs of the Research Department of the Toyo Bunko,* II (1928): 1–79 and VII (1935): 1–104.

Laffan, Michael. *Finding Java: Muslim Nomenclature of Insular Southeast Asia from Śrîvijaya to Snouk Hurgronje.* Asia Research Institute Working Paper No. 52. Singapore: National; University of Singapore, 2005.

Lambourn, Elizabeth. "The formation of the *batu Aceh* tradition in fifteenth-century Samudera-Pasai". *Indonesia and the Malay World* 32 (2004): 211–48.

Leslie, D. D. *Islam in Traditional China: A Short History to 1800.* Canberra: Canberra College of Advanced Education, 1986.

Liu Xu 劉昫 et al. *Jiu Tang shu* 舊唐書. Beijing: Zhonghua shu ju, 1975.

Lombard, Denys and Claudine Salmon. "Islam and Chineseness". In *The Propagation of Islam in the Indonesian-Malay Archipelago,* edited by Alijah Gordon, pp. 181–208. Kuala Lumpur: Malaysian Sociological Research Institute, 2001.

Manguin, Pierre-Yves. "The Introduction of Islam into Champa". In *The Propagation of Islam in the Indonesian-Malay Archipelago,* edited by Alijah Gordon, pp. 287–328. Kuala Lumpur: Malaysian Sociological Research Institute, 2001.

Mills, J.V.G. *Ma Huan, Ying-yai Sheng-lan [1433]: The Overall Survey of the Ocean's Shores.* Cambridge: Cambridge University Press for the Hakluyt Society, 1970.

Montana, Suwedi. "Nouvelles données sur les royaumes de Lamuri et Barat". *Archipel* 53 (1997): 85–96.

Moquette, J.P. "De datum op den grafsteen van Malik Ibrahim te Grisse". *Tijdschrift voor Indische Taal-, Land- en Volkenkunde* LIV (1912): 208–14.

Parlindungan, Mangaraja Onggang. *Pongkinangolngolan Sinambela gelar Tuanku Rao: terror agama Islam mazhab Hambali di tanah Batak 1816–1833*. Jakarta: Tandjung Pengharapan, 1964.

Perret, Daniel and Heddy Surachman (Ed.). *Histoire de Barus III. Regards sur une place marchande de l'océan Indien (XIIe-milieu du XVIIe s.)*. Paris: Association Archipel & EFEO, 2009.

Ricklefs, M.C. *Mystic Sythesis in Java: A History of Islamization from the Fourteenth to the early Nineteenth Centuries*. Abingdon: EastBridge, 2006.

Rinkes, D.A. *Nine Saints of Java*. Translated by H.M. Froger, edited by Alijah Gordon. Kuala Lumpur: Malaysian Sociological Research Institute, 1996.

Slametmuljana. *Runtuknja Keradjaan Hindu-Djawa dan Timbulnja Negara-negara Islam di Nusantara*. Jakarta: Bhratara, 1968.

———. "Islam before the Foundation of the Islamic State of Demak". *Journal of the South Seas Society* 27, nos. 1 and 2 (1972): 41–83.

So, Billy K.L. *Prosperity, Region, and Institutions in Maritime China: The South Fukien Pattern, 946–1368*. Cambridge, Mass: Harvard University Asia Center, 2000.

Tan Yeok Seong. "Chinese element in the Islamisation of Southeast Asia — A Study of the Story of Njai Gede Pinatih, the Great Lady of Gresik". *Journal of the South Seas Society* 30, nos. 1 and 2 (1975): 19–27.

Wade, Geoff (trans.). *Southeast Asia in the Ming Shi-lu: An Open Access Resource*, Singapore: Asia Research Institute and the Singapore E-Press, National University of Singapore, 2005. <http://epress.nus.edu.sg/msl/>.

———. "Early Muslim expansion in South-East Asia, Eighth to Fifteenth Centuries". In *The New Cambridge History of Islam, Volume 3 — The Eastern Islamic World Eleventh to Eighteenth Centuries*, edited by David O. Morgan and Anthony Reid, pp. 366–408. Cambridge: Cambridge University Press, 2010.

Wink, André. *Al-Hind, The Making of the Indo-Islamic World*. 3 vols. Leiden & New York: E.J. Brill, 1990–2004.

Yamamoto, Tatsuro. "On Tawalisi as Described by Ibn Battuta". *Memoirs of the Research Department of the Toyo Bunko* VIII (1936): 93–133.

Yule, Henry (trans. and ed.). *The Book of Ser Marco Polo, the Venetian, Concerning the Kingdoms and Marvels of the East*. London: Murray, 1929.

8

LANCARAN, GHURAB AND *GHALI*: Mediterranean Impact on War Vessels in Early Modern Southeast Asia[1]

Pierre-Yves Manguin

Until the end of the seventeenth century, galleys remained the backbone of the Mediterranean war fleets. Maritime powers such as Venice, Genoa, the Holy Order of Malta and the Ottoman empire, not to speak of lesser actors in the Middle Sea such as Spain or Portugal, all maintained large fleets of such oared sailing vessels. This tradition went back to Antiquity, and reached its high point at the critical 1571 battle of Lepanto, in which large Ottoman and united European fleets opposed each other, and the Muslim forces were defeated, but far from eliminated.

It has long been known that the conflict between European and Ottoman forces spilled over into the largely Muslim Indian Ocean as the Portuguese entered it. At its eastern borders, the burgeoning Malay world sultanates, after the fall of their major stronghold at Melaka to the hands of the Portuguese, became *de facto* actors of this generalized conflict; by the second half of the sixteenth century, Aceh and some of its allies had secured some help from the Ottomans and from their Indian Ocean allies against European competitors. In the straits area of Southeast Asia, however, the dividing line between the Muslim and Christian camps was far from clear-cut, as local economic and political rivalries often took precedence over the religious divide; the Portuguese found themselves more than once siding with Johor against Aceh, and the final capture of Portuguese Melaka by the Dutch was achieved with Acehnese help.²

When the Portuguese arrived in Southeast Asian waters in 1509, they soon had to deal with local war fleets, whether to fight against them, or to side with them. In fact, as they had already been doing along the Western coast of India and in the Arabian Sea and the Persian Gulf, they would themselves adapt their war tactics at sea to the specific environment of Melaka and neighbouring Muslim polities. One year after taking over the Malay city-state, they engaged in a programme of building their own galleys for local usage, and they appear to have been keen on using Javanese craftsmanship and manpower to build them, and then to man them. All through the sixteenth century, the fleets for the defence of Melaka were constructed locally or in India. In 1601, when the Viceroy in Goa ordered the Melaka captain to fight against the Dutch newcomers, he again instructed him to "take with him an armada of galleys and *fustas* and a few galleons" and he stressed the importance of "oared vessels (…) which are more efficient than tall ships in those Southern Seas."³

As I have argued elsewhere for Southeast Asia, and as has been made obvious for decades by far more numerous studies in the field of European maritime history, a comprehensive investigation of shipbuilding traditions and of their evolution provides a good approach to the overall social and economic history of the area under investigation. Patterns of maritime trade are inextricably correlated with patterns of armed conflict at sea. In an earlier study, after close observation of sixteenth and seventeenth century sources, I documented a radical change in the size of the trading and war fleets of insular and peninsular Southeast Asia and concluded that the rise of belligerence at sea coincided with the disappearance of indigenous high-seas trading and shipping, and the development of a new breed of political powers, with a growing emphasis on territoriality, centralization, cash-cropping economy, and autocracy.⁴ I had not then devoted much space to the war-ships themselves, only to the remarkable growth in overall size of the war fleets, and to the economic cost of such a key development. Here, I will concentrate on the developments of the constitutive elements of these war fleets, showing the evolution from the largely indigenous war fleets of the early sixteenth century, made up of relatively small vessels, to the vast fleets of the late sixteenth and early seventeenth centuries, where heavily-armed, colossal galleys took a prominent place. To do so, I will use both local and European (mainly Portuguese) sources; in such technical matters, both can be profitably put to use, despite some difficulties resulting mainly from the different agendas of the authors of these texts.[5] The principal character of the *Hikayat Hang Tuah*, for instance, could be said to have spent most of his heroic life sailing around the Malay World, thus providing much context for reconstructing the maritime scene in early Sultanate times. While the published manuscript was compiled in the early eighteenth century, the situations described in the text, as well as the terminology used, clearly date back to earlier times.

This article will therefore concentrate on those ships that constituted the backbone of the fleets of the developed states of the western half of insular and peninsular Southeast Asia (the Malay World *lato sensu*) during the sixteenth and early seventeenth centuries, leaving aside ships and fleets of the eastern half of the region. During this period, the historical context in these eastern islands differed profoundly from the Malay and Javanese areas: they were then in an earlier stage of state formation and the Mediterranean impact on ship and warfare technology did not affect them as it did Malay and Javanese polities.[6] I will further single out those vessels that belonged to the universal category of "long ships" (such as the "galleys" of the Mediterranean), as opposed to "round" or "tall ships" (the contemporary Malay world *jongs* and Portuguese *naus*).[7] The fact that long ships were the backbone of Southeast Asian war fleets is expected: these ships were most efficient in small, closed and protected seas, that is, in archipelagic environments. Such long ships, lying low above water, were not readily serviceable on high, open seas, with long rolling waves, where they were rarely used.[8]

PREMODERN WAR FLEETS AND VESSELS

Between the eighth and the thirteenth century, there are multiple references to warfare at sea in Southeast Asian and neighbouring waters, and particularly to fleets manned by *Javaka*, by *Kunlun* (both terms used for the peoples of the Malay world), by Javanese, and by people affiliated to the polity of Srivijaya, all being aggressively active and projecting Malay world power at sea in places as far apart as the coasts of Đại Việt and Champa to the east, and those of Sri Lanka to the west.[9] Cham, Khmer and Indian inscriptions, as well as Sri Lankan, Arabic, Chinese and Vietnamese textual sources tell us about fleets "with thousands of white sails," armed with machines that "shoot poisoned arrows." Zhao Rugua tells us in the thirteenth century that the ruler of *Boni* (Brunei) "has for his protection over a hundred fighting boats and when they have an engagement, they carry swords and wear armour."[10]

The above references, however, provide no information on the types of boats that composed these fleets. Only the Austronesian-speaking Chams and their fleets, constant foes of Angkor, were privileged enough to find themselves portrayed on Angkorian reliefs; the vessels depicted, however, are river boats, not true sea-going, sailing vessels, and fall outside the scope of this paper.[11] For the period, none of the few other boats appearing on graffiti or reliefs (including the famous eighth century Borobudur reliefs) can be readily interpreted as oared, fighting vessels of the kind we will deal with below.

The earliest reference in Malay to a vessel used by Malays comes in a 685 CE inscription of Srivijaya. This Kedukan Bukit inscription was written to celebrate some momentous episode in the life of the newly-founded polity, when the king led his army of 20,000 men, both by boat (*sāmvau*, Modern Malay *sampan*) and by land, in a solemn procession. The inscription being in Old Malay, this is the first time a name for a vessel is given in its vernacular form in the whole of Southeast Asia (and the last one too, unfortunately, in Malay, before Malay manuscripts make their appearance a millennium later). For lack of any other indication, we can only speculate that this indicates a long oared vessel rather than a round one, the inscription having been written in a riverine environment at Palembang, and the occasion being military. Another inscription by the same ruler of Srivijaya, dated to 686 CE, does not mention boats *per se*, but it was erected across the Strait of Bangka, at the newly absorbed site of Kota Kapur, which could only be reached by sea, and it furthermore mentions the fact that "the army of Srivijaya had just set out on an expedition against the land of Java which was not obedient to Srivijaya", an "army" (*vala*) which could of course only have proceeded to Java by sea, as a war fleet.[12] Were the vessels carrying this army to Java the same as the *sampan* of the contemporary Kedukan Bukit inscription? Again, we are left with no definite answer to such questions.

In much later times, the term *sampan* (which the Portuguese always transcribe as *champana*) is often used in classical Malay literature where it is the second most commonly used term for boats (52 times, but far behind the generic term *perahu*, which occurs 853 times). In both Malay and Portuguese sources, however, the term *sampan/champana* is used either to describe the smallest vessels accompanying the fleets, or to designate the boat of larger ships. The *sampan*, by then, do not therefore truly belong to the category of "long ships" that made up the backbone of Southeast Asian war fleets, as we will see. This apparent change in meaning over time is very common in nautical vocabulary: nautical terms travel far and fast, and do not always stay attached to the type of vessel they would have originally indicated.

The only other term of interest to us here which has a long history in the Malay world is *lancang*. It appears, for tax purposes, in two lists of names for various boats in Old Balinese inscriptions from the North coast of Bali, dating from 896 and 923 CE.[13] The inscription does not say what the boat looked like or what it was used for in Bali. *Lancang* reappears in Malay classical texts to designate a sailing boat: it is found 129 times — but 125 times in the *Hikayat Indraputra* alone, in one single passage describing the construction of the mythical hero's extraordinary vessel, capable of flying in the air, a fanciful description that is of little use for our present purpose. The *Hikayat Hang Tuah* is the only other text to use it (three times), and only in episodes referring to pre-Melaka or early Melaka times: it is found among the vessels composing the fleets of Sri Tribuana at the foundation of Singapore, and also in the times of Sultan Mansur Shah (fifteenth century). It is as if the term was felt as being obsolete by the time these narratives were put together in writing during the seventeenth century. Early modern Portuguese sources never use a term such as "lanchão", which would have been a regular transcription of *lancang*; this appears to confirm that the term was obsolete in the sixteenth century.[14] However, it reappears in eighteenth and nineteenth century Malay texts (as evidenced by searches in the MCP[15]), and it is very popular in modern Malay literature, such as in *pantuns*, under the guise of the *lancang kuning*, as a metaphor for the ruler and the state.[16]

EARLY SIXTEENTH CENTURY WAR VESSELS

The Portuguese authors, when they refer to the ship type they found to be a mainstay of early sixteenth century local fleets, and which remained in use well into the seventeenth century, always use the word "lanchara", which is a somehow irregular transcription of Malay or Javanese *lancaran*.[17] The latter, however, is only found eight times in classical Malay texts accessible through the MCP, and all these occurrences are in the *Sejarah Melayu*. Seven out of the eight references to a *lancaran* found in the *Sejarah Melayu* are to three-masted vessels (*lancaran bertiang tiga*), as if, at the time the narrative was composed, this had become a set phrase. It is worth noting also that these references are to episodes contemporary to those of the *Hikayat Hang Tuah* in which the term *lancang* was used (the founding of Singapore and the times of Sultan Mansur Shah). Again, it is as if the term was then felt to be old-fashioned. The reason for this inconsistency between these two textual corpora is not clear, but may be attributed to the fact that Malay narratives, with few exceptions, were written down in the seventeenth century, when such vessels had become somehow obsolete, in comparison with the more prestigious Mediterranean tradition of war ships, by then in full swing. The Portuguese made it clear, though, that *lancaran* were the backbone of the regional fleets before Mediterranean influences became felt, and remained an essential component of all later fleets, alongside the modern, popular galley-type vessels. The traditional local vessels may have then lost popularity, but the repeated mention of "three masted *lancaran*" in Malay sources no doubt also points to sizeable ships, comparable in tonnage to the average galley.

The first Portuguese references to "lancharas", are to those kept at Lingga in 1513–14. The "royal" vessel was the "the size of a large galleass" (i.e. larger than ordinary galleys) and was "strong and beautiful, much armed and martial." Apart from the crew, she carried 200 men, "protected by large shields, and armed with bows, arrows and blow-pipes."[18] The "state lancharas" of Bintan, in 1520, had their bows and sterns beautifully decorated in gold "in the way the princes of these places showed off the dignity of their service."[19] In the 1520s, one regular "lanchara" of Pasai carried 150 men, under the command of a Javanese captain, and the large ones, belonging to the admiral of the fleet, with 300 men aboard, are said to have been Javanese.[20] Still in the 1520s, we are also told of smaller "lancharas" at Bintan and Pahang, with 50 or 60 men only, armed with only one swivel-gun (*berço*), but with arrows, spears and fire-hardened wooden spars.[21] Among the numerous accounts of the 1568 siege of Melaka by an Acehnese fleet, a relation written by Nicolau Pereira S.J. in 1582 states: "In Aceh, the boats are usually *lancharas*. They are taller than galleys, and some have two rows of oars; they are as long as galleys (…); they [in Aceh] also have galleys, galiots and fustas (…)".[22] This last remark is a first clear indication of the new trend at work in Malay world waters, as we shall see below.

The only good depiction of a Malay "lanchara" is the often reproduced drawing by Manuel Godinho de Herédia (Erédia) in the early seventeenth century. The vessel represented appears not to have been very large: it had two masts, square sails made of matting, two quarter rudders, only ten rowlocks on each board (with probably two men per oar, therefore with 40 rowers), and carved figures at bow and stern (Figure 1).[23] Earlier on, we have to rely on the details of an anonymous 1568 bird's-eye view of Melaka during its siege by the Acehnese fleet.[24] A few of the isolated vessels depicted there have discernable details (most are drawn moored side by side, and details are therefore lost): one three-masted vessel, under the Ilha das Naos (Pulau Jawa), clearly sports two quarter rudders, which makes it a local, traditionally-built boat, probably a *lancaran*; others, particularly the large ones with no quarter rudders, may be representations of the "galleys, galiots and fustas" in the large fleet (Figures 2, 3). Two other battle scenes between the Portuguese and the Acehnese off Changi (in modern Singapore) in 1581 and in the Melaka roads

FIGURE 1

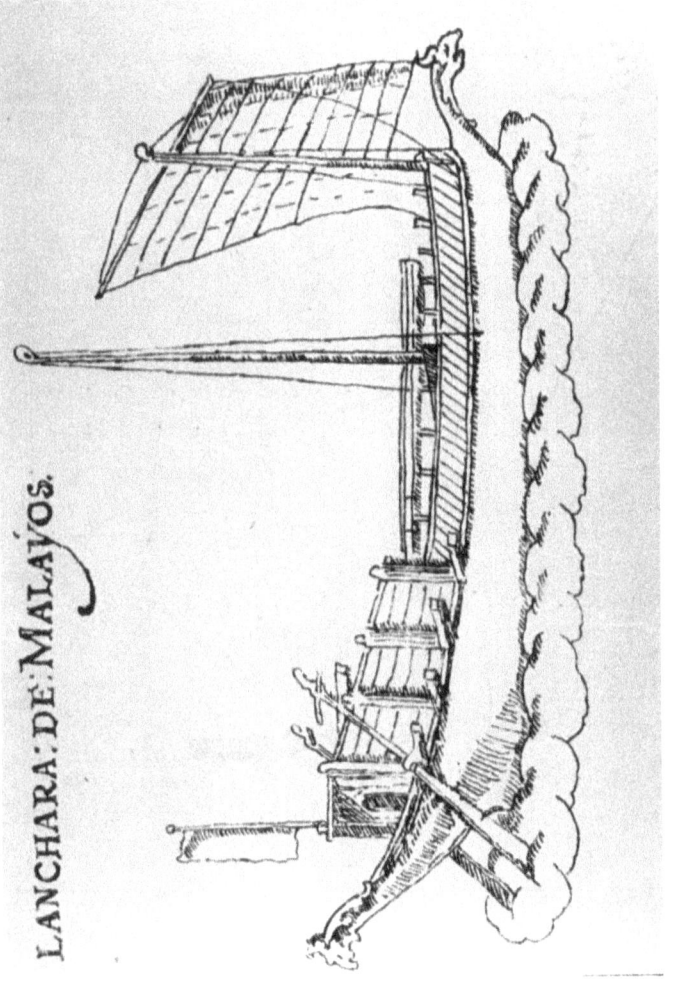

Malay *lancang*, as drawn by Manuel Godinho de Herédia, ca. 1600 (Herédia 1881–82).

FIGURE 2

The Acehnese siege of Melaka, 1568 (two details; courtesy Biblioteca nacional do Brazil).

FIGURE 3

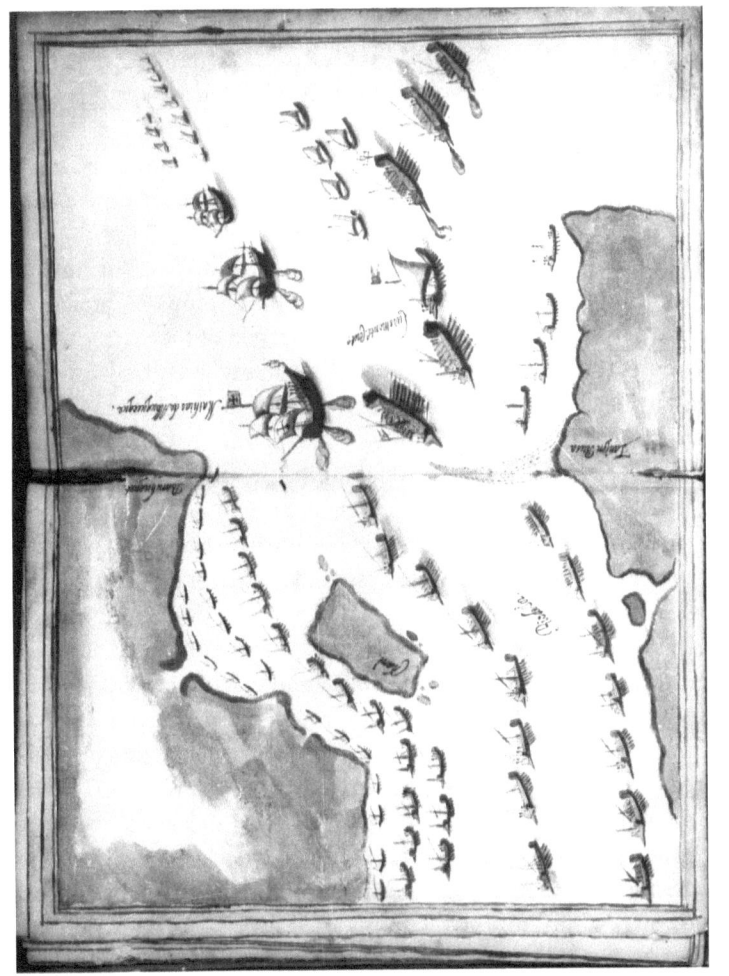

Naval battle off Changi; 1581, the Acehnese and Portuguese fleets (Manuscript by Manuel Godinho de Herédia, *História de serviços com martírio de Luís Monteiro Coutinho...*, 1615, Courtesy Biblioteca nacional de Portugal).

in 1583 were illustrated by Manuel Godinho de Herédia, but his manuscript was written in 1615, and these scenes may not represent exactly the situation in the 1580s (Figures 4, 5).

Contrary to classical Malay literature, the heroes of which appear to spend much of their time at sea, Javanese literature is not rich in references to the sea and to shipping and is therefore of little use to us here.[25] I only found boats mentioned in significant ways in the *Kidung Sunda* and the *Dewa Ruci*, two texts written in Middle Javanese that appear to date from the mid-sixteenth century.[26] The term *(la)lancaran* is found among other names in a list given by the *Dewa Ruci*, with no further details; it is however associated with terms such as *galiyu* and *ghorab*, which again points towards a transition to Mediterranean type fleets of the second part of the sixteenth and seventeenth centuries, and with the term *kelulus*, discussed below.

The Javanese appear to have been more familiar with fleets of large, round ships, which could have only served to transport troops to attack enemy positions overseas. The best known Javanese armada of the sixteenth century is the ill-fated fleet that had been prepared for many years by Patih Unus of Jepara to attack Melaka, and which ended up attacking the city in 1512–13, when it had already fallen into Portuguese hands. It transported 10,000 men aboard 30 large *jong*, and some 70 small sailing vessels, including "calaluzes" (Javanese *kelulus*) and "pangajavas" (Malay *penjajap*). Portuguese sources regarding this event assert that the Javanese learned from this defeat at sea that such unwieldy ships were a weakness and could not be defended against many smaller, manoeuvrable ships; they did however partly go back to their usual tactics in 1551 and 1574: the latter fleet still comprised 80 *jong*, but they were now accompanied by 220 *kelulus* and carried 15,000 men.[27] This emphasis on fleets of large, round ships in Java may have been brought about because their vessels and fleets were often active on the relatively open Java Sea (as compared to the sheltered straits zone where most Malay sultanates operated their fleets). Large fleets from Aceh and Melaka, as described in both Portuguese and local sources, also included a few round ships, but these were clearly not the backbone of the fleets, only complementary means of transport of men, ammunition and supplies.

One name for a long boat that appears in descriptions of Javanese fleets and seems to have been of Javanese origin is *kelulus / kalulus*, transcribed by the Portuguese as "calaluz". It appears in both Javanese and Malay texts of the period. Tomé Pires says they were "a speciality of Java", that they had "figureheads in the shape of snakes", that they were "so clean and ornamental, with so many canopies that the rowers are not seen by the lord; [there are] beautiful apartments for [the prince's] women, other places for the nobles

FIGURE 4

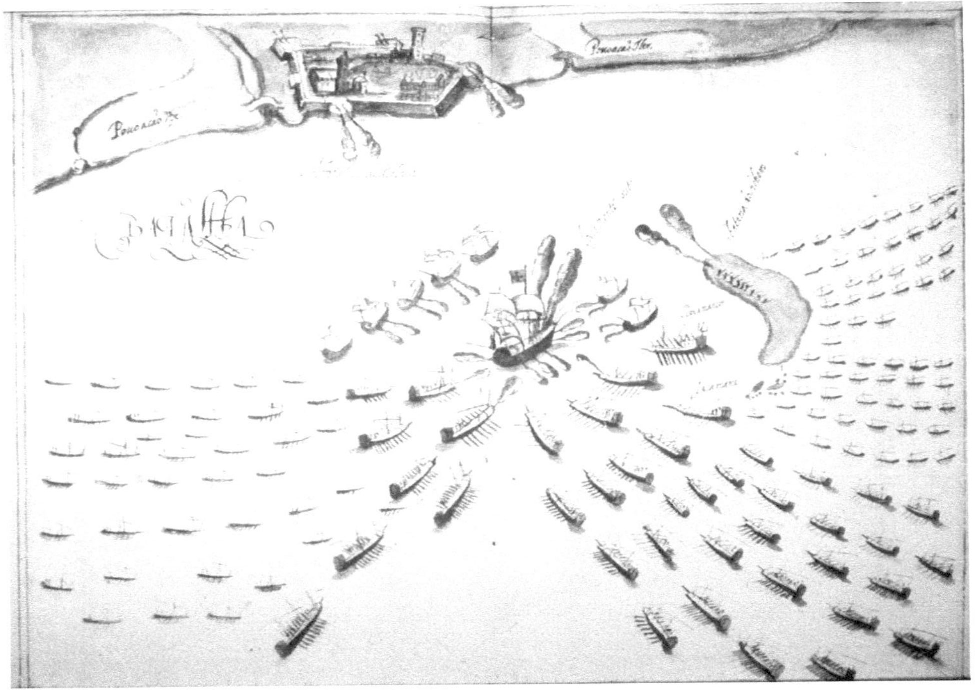

The 1583 siege of Melaka by Aceh (Manuscript by Manuel Godinho de Herédia, *História de serviços com martírio de Luís Monteiro Coutinho...*, Courtesy Biblioteca nacional de Portugal).

Lancaran, Ghurab and Ghali

FIGURE 5

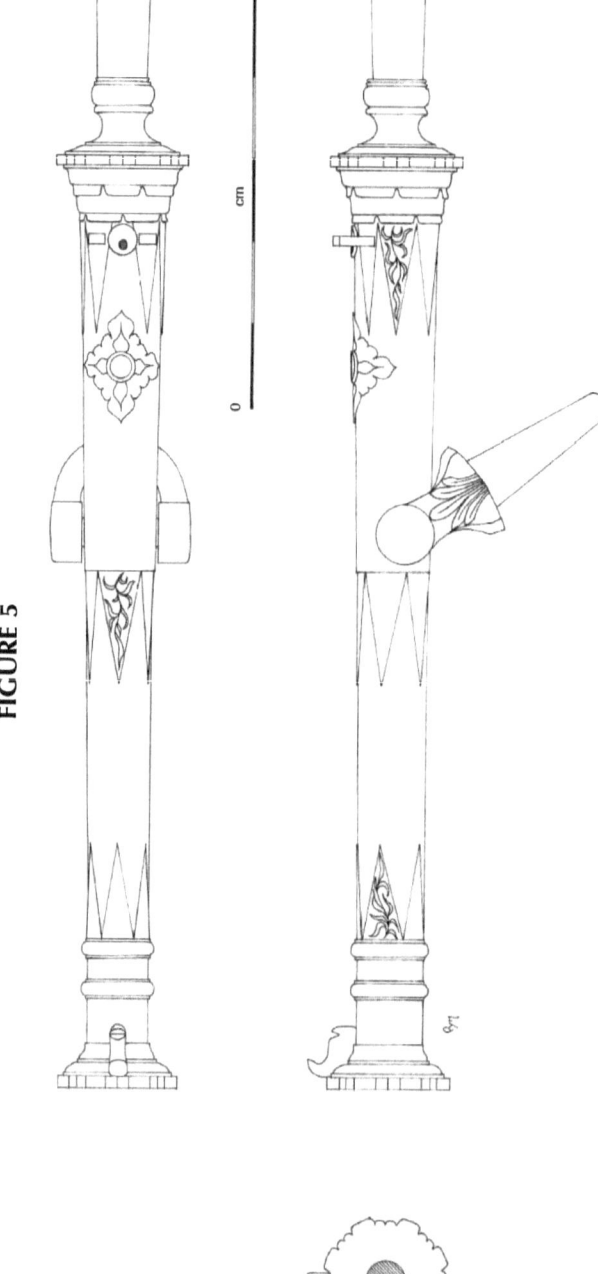

A swivel-gun from Insular Southeast Asia, undated (courtesy Musée du Quai Branly, Paris; drawing by P.-Y. Manguin, first published in Manguin 1976).

who accompany him (…)". In 1537, Javanese *kelulus* encountered in Patani are described as having two rows of oars: one is made of paddles, the other one is "as galleys"; they carried 100 soldiers, much artillery and fire devices. They still appear to have been used in the early seventeenth century: Gonçalo de Souza, in his *Coriosidades*, writes that they have 27 oars (54 rowers?) and 20 soldiers and are armed with small swivel guns ("falconselhos") at bow and stern.[28] All these references point to a boat that was not as large as the contemporary *lancaran*.

One other vessel which is regularly mentioned in Malay, Javanese and Portuguese sources, but appears not to have been of major importance, is the *penjajap*, a term usually transcribed as "pangajao" or "pangajava" and other less regular variations (the phonetics of the term appear to have posed problems to the Portuguese).[29] In 1509, they are said to be "vessels of this land [of Sumatra], long and swift, going very well under sail or oars." These are the only details we could gather about this type of long vessel.[30]

None of the above quotations from local or Portuguese sources referring to long vessels used in Malay and Javanese fleets — before the impact of Mediterranean traditions was felt — provides us with information on shipbuilding techniques *per se*. Nothing is told in contemporary sources of the structural details that marine archaeologists are so keen on observing to classify the boats they study: how were their hulls assembled, and how were their planks joined together and fastened? In sixteenth century European sources, only the large trading *jong* attracted enough attention for some of its authors to pursue this kind of structural detail.[31] No sixteenth century long vessel has yet turned up in an archaeological site. We are thus confined to informed speculation. Like all the local vessels of the time, and of later times too, *lancaran*, *kelulus* and other war vessels must have had carvel-joined hull planks (unlike the clinker-built Northern European galleys): if they had not, the Portuguese would no doubt have remarked it. Planks would most probably have been edge joined with wooden dowels rather than with iron nails, like most contemporary trading vessels (they would no longer have been stitched together with *ijok* ropes as in earlier times).[32] The fact that the *lancaran*, as we have also seen, appear to have sported two side rudders, again point towards a local, enduring tradition, with little influence from the Indian Ocean, where central rudders had been in use for three centuries (large Bugis trading ships of the 1970s still made full use of such quarter rudders).[33]

There are numerous references, starting in the early sixteenth century, to attest the casting of light artillery in Java and other areas of insular Southeast Asia. Javanese *kidung* texts have occasional references to cannon and cannoneers (as in *juru-modya ning bedil besar ing bahitra* in the

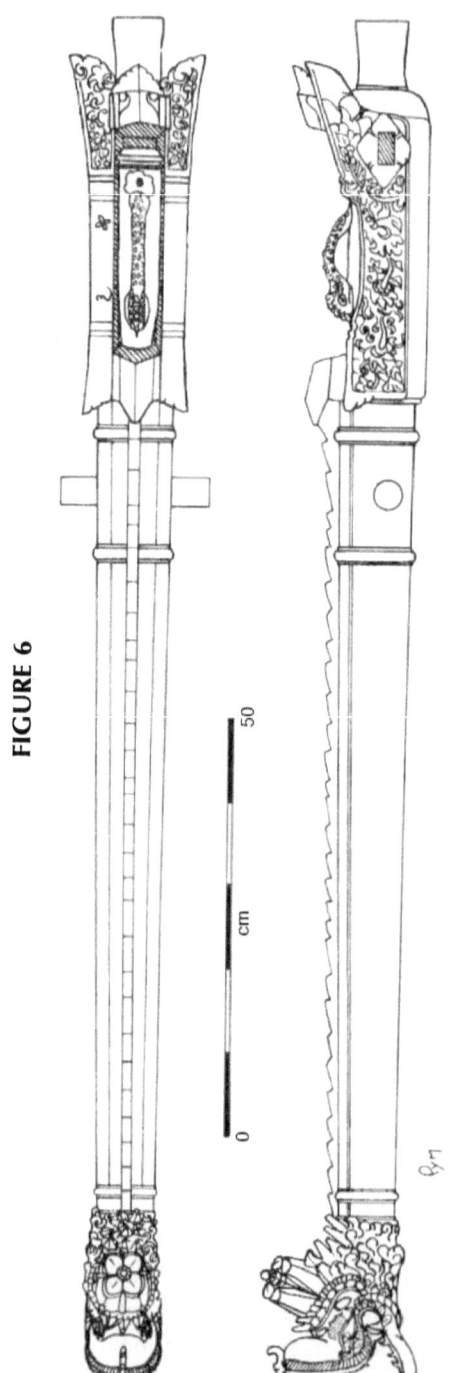

FIGURE 6

A breech-loading Javanese swivel-gun, undated (courtesy Luís de Camões Museum, Macau; drawing by P.-Y. Manguin, first published in Manguin 1976).

FIGURE 7 A "galley" from Banten (Lodewijckz, *Het eerste boek...*, 1598, fols. 35ro–36vo).

FIGURE 8

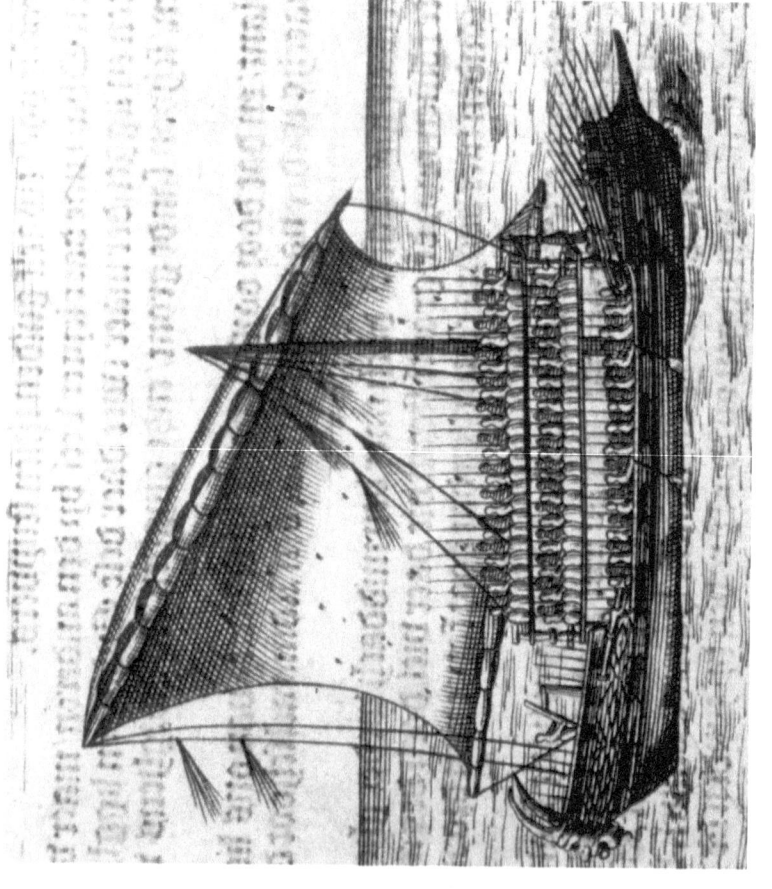

A "galley" from Madura (*Tweede boek...*, 1601, pl. 17).

ca. sixteenth century *Kidung Sunda*).[34] Terms such as *bedil*, or *rentaka* appear repeatedly in contemporary Malay texts, to describe armaments in urban stockades or aboard ships. Portuguese and Spanish sources also often refer to small swivel-guns used on board ships or on top of defensive palisades.[35] The people of Melaka, when the city was taken in 1511, "possessed much copper and tin, and their founders were as good as the Germans". In 1513, the Javanese fleet of Patih Yunus, when it sailed to attack Melaka, "carried much artillery made in Java, for [the Javanese] are excellent founders". Andrés Urdaneta, a Spaniard captured by the Portuguese in Maluku and brought back to Melaka in 1535 via Panarukan confirms such skills: "The Javanese possess much bronze artillery, which they cast on their own."[36] One reference from the 1550s mentions *lancharas* of Johore and Japara carrying "much artillery", which could only mean at the time that they carried many swivel-guns.[37] Many museums in the world hold collections of swivel-guns, almost all of them undated, unfortunately (Figures 5, 6).[38] Dutch engravings of 1598 and 1601 show such swivel-guns mounted on war vessels from Banten and Madura (Figures 7, 8).[39] The relative lightness of most of these fork-mounted swivel-guns made them the ideal firearm for naval combat on board light and fast sailing and rowing long boats. These, however, were used against men as muskets, when boarding, not as the larger cannon used to fire at ships and fortresses, which would only appear later in the sixteenth century. Loaded with scattershot and fired into the rowing benches at close range, swivel guns must have been horribly effective.

None of the available sources for the first half of the sixteenth century mentions heavier artillery being used on *lancharan*. It would have been brash to conclude from such negative evidence alone that no heavier artillery was then mounted on these ubiquitous vessels. However, no cannon larger than swivel-guns could have been mounted on these traditional craft: standard fastening of hull planks in the Malay World did not make use of iron nails, clamps or rivets, only of wooden dowels, and hulls were therefore not sturdy enough to resist the jolts of the recoil of large cannon.[40] The new galley type ships, on the other hand, had been developed earlier in the Mediterranean in parallel with the development of heavy on-board artillery. In Portuguese sources, therefore, references to heavy cannon in the Malay world is principally attached to the newly-adopted shipbuilding tradition.

THE MEDITERRANEAN IMPACT

For the next phase of the history of war ships in the Malay world, the analysis of nautical vocabulary shall turn out to be even more useful. We will now be dealing with a technological revolution which took place under the very eyes of the authors of our main sources, both local and European.

The two key words are now *ghurab* (or *ghurap*, from the Arabic or Persian for galley) and *ghali* (or, rarely, *gali*, from Portuguese "galé").[41] Both are used in Malay and Javanese texts of the sixteenth and seventeenth centuries to describe the galley-type long vessels that now appear on the local scene. Terms for vessels of the galley-type, but larger ("galeaça") or smaller ("galeota") than the regular galley, are also (but rarely) found in local sources and all derive from the European vocabulary, as they did in the Mediterranean (as in *kalyota*, a Turkicisation of Italian "galiotta").[42] *Galiut* appears in the *Hikayat Banjar*; while *ghalias* appears twice in the *Sejarah Melayu* and in the *Hikayat Hang Tuah*, always to describe Portuguese vessels. Turkish craftsmanship is no doubt largely at the origin of the adoption of such new oared-vessel designs; Portuguese, however, who had themselves adopted Mediterranean shipbuilding techniques for their own war fleets in the Indian Ocean, would also have had their share in these innovations, as some of the sources make clear, whether it was done by mere osmosis in cosmopolitan harbour communities, of with the help of Portuguese renegades or mercenaries.[43] It is surprising, at first sight, to find nowhere in local sources the Turkish term *kadīrga*, which was used for the regular Ottoman war galley.[44] However, despite wide-ranging interaction with the Turks in the seventeenth and later centuries, Turkish vocabulary made little or no inroads into Malay.[45] Communication must have mainly been in Arabic, and it is the Arabo-Persian term *ghurab* which became attached to this new boat design.

The term *ghurab* appears for the first time in an early sixteenth century text — Pigafetta's record of his journey with what was left of Magellan's fleet across the Malay world. His Italian-Malay vocabulary list within this work was gathered at Brunei in 1522.[46] This is surprisingly early, as the term, when associated with the operation of the vessel it describes, only reappears in Portuguese sources in the late 1530s. This may be explained by the fact that the word could have been known to literate Malays, who would have learnt it from their readings in Arabic, even if the ship itself was not yet in regular use in the archipelago. This may also explain why the most common transcript of the southern European term for galley is *ghali* (rather than *gali*), with an initial *ghain* ع as in *ghurab*.[47]

Ghurab is found 64 times in pre-eighteenth century Malay texts, mainly in two texts written in Aceh in the 1630s and 1640s, the *Hikayat Aceh* and al-Raniri's *Bustan al-Salatin* (46 times), once only in the *Hang Tuah*, and never in the *Sejarah Melayu*. On the other hand, *ghali* (rarely spelled *gali*) appears 95 times in the same corpus (and once, under the form *galiyu*, in the Javanese *Dewa Ruci*). The *Hikayat Hang Tuah* alone uses it 84 times, and the *Sejarah Melayu* six times. From this we may infer that Aceh and the Malay-speaking sultanates differed in the word they used for referring to the new galley-type vessel, the former preferring the Arabic/Persian form, the latter the Portuguese one, to describe one and the same vessel. Both etymologies, however, are unmistakably of foreign origin.

Starting in the 1530s, Portuguese authors include references to galleys in their descriptions of Malay fleets. What emerges clearly from these narratives and their comparison throughout the sixteenth and the early seventeenth centuries is the fact that, as time passes, the magnitude of the local fleets becomes greater: all documents indicate an increase in the number of galley-type vessels in the fleets, in the number of cannon they carry, and in the size of both the galleys and the cannon themselves. I have shown in an earlier work how the size of fleets had dramatically swollen during this period.[48] The composition of the fleets had likewise undergone many changes.

The first fleets count no galleys in them. Galleys appear only in the late 1530s, in small numbers compared to the accompanying *lancaran*: five, against 100, according to Fernão Mendes Pinto, and the term "galiota" is more often used, which means these are smallish galleys.[49] The single galley in a 1551 joint Johore/Japara fleet with 80 *lancaran* is said to be armed only with one large cannon and many swivel-guns.[50]

The first large fleet where galley type ships figure prominently is the Acehnese fleet which laid siege to Melaka in 1568.[51] By then, the intervention of the Ottomans and their Indian Ocean allies had become a fact, even if no Turkish armada ever made it further east than Hormuz. The 1568 fleet counted three large galiots from Malabar, four "galés bastardas" (i.e. larger than regular galleys), 60 galiots and 200 "lancharas" and "fustas". The large "bastardas" are said to have been different from "lancharas", in length 40 to 50 metres, and to have counted 24 banks with 190 rowers.[52] They were armed with 12 large "camelos" (three on each side of the bow, four at the stern), one basilisk also placed at the bow, 12 falcons, and 40 smaller swivel guns (See Figure 2).

The transition to a heavily armed galley-type vessel comparable to those built in the Mediterranean was therefore by then well under way, particularly in Aceh, from where it appears to have spread to other city-states in the region. We know that cannon, firearms and other war materials had started arriving annually to Aceh from Jeddah, and that the Turks also sent military experts, masters of galleys, and technicians for making and operating other weapons and war material.[53] In 1575, the Acehnese fleet had

40 royal galleys with Turkish captains and 200 to 300 crew (with soldiers), 110 smaller galiots and "lancharas" carrying "old [i.e. experienced] soldiers ("lascharins"), Turks, Arabs, Decanis, Acehnese." They had two masts with square top sails.[54]

To sum up, the average Acehnese galley in the second half of the sixteenth century would have been approximately 50 metres long, have had two masts, with square sails and top sails; it would have been propelled by 24 oars on each side, carry some 200 men aboard, and have been armed with some 20 cannon (two or three large ones at the bow, the rest smaller swivel guns). Like the Mediterranean galley, locally-built *ghurab* appear to have been a rather standardised production in the Malay world.

The *Hikayat Aceh*, describing events of the 1570s, states that among the vessels available at Aceh, Daya and Pedir, there are 120 large *ghurab*, and 230 smaller *fusta*, not counting many smaller boats. The state galley (*ghorab istana*) is said to carry ten *meriam*, 50 Portuguese *lela*, and 120 *cecorong*, not counting the muskets (*ispinggar*). Smaller vessels are said to have carried only five *meriam*, 20 Portuguese *lela,* and 50 *cecorong*.[55] This description in fact matches other descriptions of galleys built in Iskandar Muda's time during the early seventeenth century, when the *Hikayat Aceh* was written, rather than the situation in the 1570s. We also learn from the Gaio manuscript that the Sultan of Aceh, in the 1580s, maintained a war fleet in the river flowing through his capital.[56]

The two frequently published Dutch engravings drawn from information gathered during the first Dutch voyages to Southeast Asian seas bring us rare images. One vessel is from Banten, the other from Madura. They are both smallish. Both have a single mast (though Lodewijcksz' accompanying text on the Banten vessel mentions two masts), and only a few oars and few cannon. The 1601 engraving of a Madurese vessel may be a rather awkward depiction of a *lancaran* or comparable vessel, whereas the 1598 engraving of the Banten war ship has a definitely more Mediterranean look to it, with one major difference: as often noted in other texts and images, local craft appeared to have always carried a raised deck ("baileu", i.e. *balai*), on which stood the fighting men, atop the rowers sitting below, a feature very different from Mediterranean vessels (Figures 4, 5).[57]

Portuguese sources for the following decades are scarce, and bring no new descriptions of local war vessels, as this is a relatively calm period in terms of maritime interactions in the area of our concern. When we enter the splendid reign of Sultan Iskandar Muda of Aceh (1607–36), sources become abundant again, if only because the Portuguese are no longer the only Europeans to report on what they see. Moreover, Europeans have much to report on Aceh in general, particularly when it comes to the maritime scene. The sultanate, at its apogee, embarked on a breathtaking shipbuilding spree, devoting no doubt much of its resources to constructing a war fleet of superb, outsized galleys.

Augustin de Beaulieu, who was at Aceh in 1621, gives us the best description of the vessels.[58] He affirmed that the sultan had 100 galleys available at any time, but that they were spread all over his territory, from Daya on the west coast to Pedir on the east coast. The royal galleys had a keel made from a single piece of timber, 39 metres long. They were thus "one third larger than any Christian galley." They had square sails, as in round ships, not lateen sails like the Portuguese galleys. Acehnese were "good artisans," particularly the galley builders. But these vessels were too heavily built to Beaulieu's taste (too high, too beamy, with planking up to 15 centimetres thick), and the rowing apostis (rowing frames) were too small and weak; each of the oars was manned by only two standing men, as they were not so long or that heavy ("they are mere poles with a board set at their end, well made and nicely decorated"). They carried three main cannon (up to 40 pounders) and many swivel-guns. The larger ones would carry up to 600 or even 800 men. An elephant could also be embarked aboard the larger galleys (as in the galleys sent to Priaman with 300 men aboard when Beaulieu was there). There are unfortunately no detailed images of such large vessels, only represented in depictions of whole fleets, as seen above.

In a rare passage with precise details, the *Hikayat Hang Tuah* mentions one *ghali* with her dimensions. The narrative is of course not of much use to us here in terms of chronology, but the length and beam of the said royal vessel (*ghali kenaikan raja*) matches other seventeenth century sources: she would have been 60 *gaz* in length (approximately 67 metres) and six *depa* (11 metres) in beam (i.e. a regular length to beam ratio of approximately 7:1).[59]

One often-quoted example is that of the Acehnese galley captured in 1629 by the Portuguese (named, according to them, the "Espanto do Mundo", the "Terror of the Universe", probably a free translation of *Cakra Dunia*). There were reported to have been 47 of them. She was "bigger than anything ever built in the Christian world" and was indeed meant to show off the power and wealth of Iskandar Muda. She reached 100 metres in length and 17 metres in breadth, had three masts with three square sails and topsails, was propelled by 35 oars on each side, could carry 700 men aboard and was armed with 18 large cannon (five-55 pounders on the bow; one 25-pounder on the stern; 17-and-18 pounders on the sides; plus 80 falcons and smaller swivel-guns). Her castle could compete with that of Portuguese galleons (i.e. of large, round ships).[60]

CONCLUSION

A military revolution took place in Malay world waters between the mid-sixteenth century and the 1630s. We have seen the local armadas evolving from small fleets of medium-sized, traditionally built, lightly-armed oared vessels in the early sixteenth century (comprising some 30 to 150 vessels, each manned by 50 to 100 men, carrying between 1,500 and 8,000 men), to overgrown fleets after the turn of the seventeenth century (up to 300 vessels, including some fifty huge, heavily-armed Mediterranean-type galleys, carrying up to 15,000 men to war). The huge galleys built in the 1620s to display the grandeur of Iskandar Muda are the last Acehnese or Malay galleys to be described in any detail in seventeenth century Portuguese sources. This is not to say that war fleets disappear after that time in the Malay world or for that matter in Southeast Asia. Makassar, a growing maritime power when the Dutch arrived, would retain some strength at sea and resist the Dutch for some more decades. Powers like Siam, Burma and some Malay states would keep war fleets afloat well into the nineteenth century. The "battle for Junk Ceylon", as narrated in the *Syair Sultan Maulana*, pits three such fleets against each other in 1809.[61]

However, with the arrival of Northern European powers, particularly the Dutch VOC, the historical *conjoncture* was radically modified. The newcomers had by then benefited from another revolution in naval technology: they sailed on heavily armed, large round ship firing broadsides, of the kind that would largely dominate European seas and the Mediterranean during the following centuries, pushing galley fleets aside forever. These tall ships now entered Southeast Asian seas under Dutch and British flags, heralding social developments that would bring about radically transformed interactions between European and Southeast Asian societies. The shipping scene of the Malay world would resist in many ways, and would undergo new transformations to adapt to these new times. It would however no longer be able to compete in such an accomplished way with Western imposed developments.

Notes

1. The first time I dealt with the question of premodern Southeast Asian war fleets was in a lecture I gave at the Australian National University in July 1979. This was also when I first met Anthony Reid. The second occasion I had occasion to use data gathered on this same subject was in a chapter I wrote for his volume *Southeast Asia in the Early Modern Era*, in which I documented and analysed the momentous episode of Southeast Asian maritime history which I called "the

vanishing *jong*" [Pierre-Yves Manguin, "The vanishing jong: Insular Southeast Asian fleets in war and trade (fifteenth–seventeenth centuries", in *Southeast Asia in the Early Modern Era: Trade, Power, and Belief*, edited by Anthony Reid (Ithaca: Cornell University Press, 1993), pp. 197–213]. It therefore occurred to me that it would be fitting to contribute to this festschrift an essay which is a complement to the latter work, and which also touches upon two of Tony's research interests: Aceh and the Ottomans.

2. On sixteenth and seventeenth century Aceh, and its relationships with the Portuguese and the Turks, see Charles Ralph Boxer, "The Acehnese attack on Malacca in 1629, as described in contemporary Portuguese sources", in *Malayan and Indonesian Studies*, edited by J. Bastin and R. Roolvink (Oxford: Oxford University Press, 1964), pp. 105–21; Charles Ralph Boxer, "Asian Potentates and European Artillery in the Sixteenth-Eighteenth Centuries: A Footnote to Gibson-Hill", *Journal of the Malayan Branch, Royal Asiatic Society* 38, no. 2 (1965): 156–72; Denys Lombard, *Le Sultanat d'Atjeh au temps d'Iskandar Muda, 1607–1636*, PEFEO 62 (Paris: EFEO, 1967); Pierre-Yves Manguin, "Of Fortresses and Galleys. The 1568 Acehnese Siege of Melaka, following a Contemporary Bird's-eye View", in *Asian Studies in Honour of Professor Charles Boxer*, edited by P.-Y. Manguin and G. Bouchon, *Modern Asian Studies* 22, no. 3 (1988): 607–28; Anthony Reid, "Sixteenth Century Turkish Influence in Western Indonesia", *Journal of Southeast Asian History* 10, no. 3 (1969): 395–414; Anthony Reid, *The Ottomans in Southeast Asia*, ARI Working Paper 36 (Singapore: Asia Research Institute, National University of Singapore, 2005); Paulo Jorge Sousa Pinto, *Portugueses e malaios: Malaca e os Sultanatos de Johor e Achém, 1575–1619* (Lisboa: Sociedade Histórica da Independência de Portugal, 1997); Jorge M. dos Santos Alves, *O Domínio do Norte de Samatra. A história dos sultanatos de Samudera — Pacém e de Achém, e das suas relações com os Portugueses (1500–1580)* (Lisboa: Sociedade Histórica da Independência de Portugal, 1999); Jorge M. dos Santos Alves and Pierre-Yves Manguin, *O 'Roteiro das cousas do Achem' de D. João Ribeiro Gaio: Um olhar português sobre o norte de Samatra em finais do século XVI*, Colecção Outras Margens (Lisboa: Commissão Nacional para as Comemorações dos Descobrimentos Portugueses, 1997).

3. See Letter of 1512, in Academia das Ciências de Lisboa, *Alguns documentos do Archivo Nacional da Torre do Tombo acerca das navegações e conquistas portuguezas publicados por ordem do governo de Sua Majestade Fidelissima ao celebrar-se a commemoração quadricentenaria do descobrimento da America* (Lisboa: Imprensa Nacional, 1892), pp. 245–50; and Historical Archives, Goa, King's letter to the Viceroy, 1601, *Livro das Monções*, 7: 17ro (unpublished).

4. Manguin, "The vanishing jong."

5. For Malay sources, I would like to emphasize how much this research owes to Ian Proudfoot's Malay Concordance Project (MCP) at the Australian National University: <www.anu.edu.au/asianstudies/proudfoot/MCP/Q/mcp.html>. By providing on-line tools to search simultaneously for boat names and other

nautical terms among dozens of classical Malay texts, and to classify them, with their context, into various orders, including chronological, it made comparisons over time and place possible, an otherwise daunting task. When statistics for usage of classical Malay terms are given below, they are always based on MCP counts. I have arbitrarily only taken into account the pre-1800s texts, which includes all major relevant texts for our purpose: *Hikayat Raja Pasai, Hikayat Indraputra, Hikayat Aceh, Sejarah Melayu, Hikayat Banjar* and *Hikayat Hang Tuah* (MCP query parameters: 1300–1700, prose and verse texts). Such figures, based on only one version of a text, are only indicative. A thorough study of classical Malay usage of nautical terms and of their etymology would need to be pursued by consulting the original manuscripts of the published texts included in the MCP, together with their variants in often unpublished manuscripts. This is beyond the scope of the present study, and it would most probably not modify the general historical conclusions we draw from the data available through the MCP. References to the printed editions used in the MCP will be found on the MCP site. Only when it is relevant are direct quotations from these printed editions given in this article.

6. For recent studies on fleets and armament from the eastern part of Southeast Asia, and comparisons with other Southeast Asian fleets, see Felice Noelle Rodriguez, "Juan de Salcedo Joins the Narrative Form of Warfare", *Journal of the Economic and Social History of the Orient* 46, no. 2 (2003): 143–64; Gerrit Knaap, "Headhunting, Carnage and Armed Peace in Amboina, 1500–1700", *Journal of the Economic and Social History of the Orient* 46, no. 2 (2003): 165–92; Victor Lieberman, "Some Comparative Thoughts on Premodern Southeast Asian Warfare", *Journal of the Economic and Social History of the Orient* 46, no. 2 (2003): 215–25; Laichen Sun, "Gunpowder Technology and Commerce in East and Southeast Asia, c. 1368–1683: Towards Defining an 'Age of Gunpowder' in Asian History", in *Workshop on Northeast Asia in Maritime Perspective: A Dialogue with Southeast Asia*, edited by Yamauchi Shinji, Fujita Kayoko and Piyada Chonlaworn (Osaka and Singapore: Osaka University and Asia Research Institute, 2004), pp. 12–25; and the relevant passages in Michael Charney, *Southeast Asian Warfare*, 1300–1900 (Leiden and Boston: Brill, 2004).

7. The length/beam ratio is one essential parameter in any ship. As a consequence of a fundamental law of sailboat design, all other factors being equal, the longer the boat, the faster. In the Early Modern Era, "long" vessels usually had a length/beam ratio of 6:1 (usual for merchant galleys) to 8:1 (in lighter, swifter, war galleys), whereas "round" ships meant for commerce and carrying bulk cargo had a ratio of 3:1 to 4:1.

8. The literature on the Mediterranean war fleets, both European and Ottoman, is immense. The general works that I used for reference include Roger C. Anderson, *Oared Fighting Ships: From Classical Times to the Coming of Steam* (Kings Langley: Argus Books Ltd, 1976); Carlos M. Cipolla, *Guns, Sails & Empires: Technological Innovation and the Early Phases of European Expansion: 1400–1700* (London and

New York: Collins and Pantheon Books, 1965); J.F. Guilmartin, *Gunpowder and Galleys: Changing Technology and Mediterranean Warfare at Sea in the 16th Century* (London: Cambridge University Press, 1974); Frederic Chapin Lane, *Navires et constructeurs à Venise pendant la Renaissance* (Paris: SEVPEN, 1965) (translated from the 1934 Baltimore edition, and revised by the author); Frederic Chapin Lane, *Venetian ships and shipbuilders of the Renaissance* (New York: Arno Press 1979) (reprint of the 1934 Baltimore edition); Henrique Lopes de Mendonça, *Estudos sobre navios portugueses nos séculos XV e XVI*, Colecção de documentos, 5 (Lisboa: Ministério da Marinha,1892); John H. Pryor, *Geography, Technology, and War: Studies in the Maritime History of the Mediterranean, 649–1571* (Cambridge: Cambridge University Press, 1988); Rhoads Murphey, *Ottoman warfare, 1500–1700* (London: UCL Press, 1999); and Susan Rose, *Medieval Naval Warfare, 1000–1500* (London: Routledge, 2002).

9. Georges Maspero, *Le Royaume de Champa* (Paris: Van Oest, 1928), pp. 155–56, 294; Gabriel Ferrand, "Le K'ouen-louen et les anciennes navigations interocéaniques dans les mers du sud", *Journal Asiatique* 17 (1919): 167–68, 248, 359, 407, 431, 464; Gabriel Ferrand, "L'empire sumatranais de Çrîvijaya", *Journal Asiatique* 20 (1922): 60, 228. George Coedès, *Les Etats hindouisés d'Indochine et d'Indonésie* (Paris: de Boccard, 1964), pp. 173–76, 213, 293, 336–37. R.A.L.H. Gunawardana, "Ceylon and Malaysia: A Study of Professor S. Paranavitana's Research on the Relations between the Two Regions", *University of Ceylon Review* 25, no. 1–2 (1967): 1–64; W.M. Sirisena, *Sri Lanka and South-East Asia. Political, Religious and Cultural Relations from A.D. c. 1000 to c. 1500* (Leiden: E.J. Brill, 1968), pp. 36–57; Gerald Randall Tibbetts, *A Study of the Arabic Texts Containing Material on Southeast Asia* (London: Royal Asiatic Society, 1979), p. 35; Horace Geoffrey Quaritch Wales, *Ancient Southeast Asian Warfare* (London: B. Quaritch, 1952).

10. Friedrich Hirth and William W. Rockhill, *Chau Ju-Kua: His Work on the Chinese and Arab Trade in the Twelfth and Thirteenth Centuries, Entitled Chu-Fan-Chi* (St. Petersburg: Imperial Academy of Sciences, 1911), p. 155.

11. On the Khmer and Cham fleets depicted in Cambodia, see George Groslier, "La battellerie cambodgienne du VIIIe au XIIIe siècle de notre ère", *Revue archéologique*, 5e Série, vol. 5 (1917): 198–204; Pierre Paris, "Les bateaux des bas-reliefs Khmers", *Bulletin de l'Ecole française d'Extrême-Orient* 41 (1941): 335–64; Michel Jacq-Hergoualc'h, *L'armement et l'organisation de l'armée khmère aux XIIe et XIIIe siècles d'après les bas-reliefs d'Angkor Vat, du Bayon et de Banteay Chmar* (Paris, Publications du Musée Guimet, 1979); and Michel Jacq-Hergoualc'h, "L'armée du Campa au début du XIIIe siècle", in *Le Campa et le Monde Malais* (Paris: Publications du Centre d'Histoire et Civilisations de la Péninsule Indochinoise, 1991): 27–46.

12. George Coedès, "Les inscriptions malaises de Çrivijaya", *Bulletin de l'Ecole française d'Extrême-Orient* 30 (1930): 33–37, 48–49, 79. Cognates of *sampan* are to be found in Old Javanese (*sambo*) as well as in most languages of Southeast Asia

(it passed into neighbouring Austroasiatic, Tibeto-Burman and Thai languages of Southeast Asia) and in other languages in the Indian Ocean, all the way to Madagascar. In some of these languages, such as Thai, Burmese or Khmer, it appears to have been used for large trading vessels. This diffusion of a Malay term into so many Southeast Asia and Indian Ocean languages should be better studied, but this broad coverage is most probably related to Srivijaya's considerable outreach. The often quoted Chinese origin of the term is open to doubt, as it does not appear in Chinese texts before the eighth century; see Léonard Aurousseau, "Notes et mélanges: Le mot sampan est-il chinois ?", *Bulletin de l'Ecole française d'Extrême-Orient* 22 (1922): 1–4. Aurousseau did not yet know of its appearance in Malay a century before.

13. Roelof Goris, *Prasasti Bali: Inscripties voor Anak Wungçu* (Bandung: Masa Baru, 1954), 2 vols, I: pp. 54–55, II: p. 121. See also the long etymological footnote on *lanca*, *lancang* and *lancaran* by Louis-Charles Damais (1957: 647, n. 3), where it is demonstrated that the last two terms cannot be of Portuguese origin, as often claimed, but that the contrary holds true. Only Malay *lanca* — attested only once in the *Sejarah Melayu* to refer to a Portuguese boat — may have originated in Portuguese *lancha*. As the term *lancang* is not attested in Old Javanese, Damais suggested that, because it appears in inscriptions of coastal north Bali, in a maritime-oriented context, *lancang* may well have entered Balinese via the Malay lingua franca. The phonetic closeness of the originally unconnected terms built upon Portuguese "lançar" (to launch), which probably gave birth to "lancha", and upon Malay/Javanese *lancar* (swift), which gave birth to *(la)lancaran* and possibly *lancang*, is probably responsible for the contamination of the two series and the ensuing confusion.

14. *Lanchão* is attested in modern Portuguese (as well as in Italian and Spanish), but could well be a regular augmentative of Portuguese *lancha*, and may therefore not be connected with Malay *lancang*.

15. The Malay Concordance Project, for which see note 5 above.

16. On which see, among many others, Pierre-Yves Manguin, "Shipshape Societies. Boat Symbolism and Political Systems in Insular Southeast Asia" in *Southeast Asia in the 9th to 14th Centuries*, edited by D.G. Marr and A.C. Milner (Canberra & Singapore: Research School of Pacific Studies, Australian National University/ Institute of Southeast Asian Studies, 1984), pp. 187–213. See pp. 193–94.

17. One would have expected "lancharão" as a regular rendering of *lancaran*. The multiple and confusing quasi-homophones alluded to in note 13 may be responsible for this irregularity.

18. João de Barros and Diogo do Couto, *Da Ásia de João de Barros e de Diogo do Couto: dos feitos que os portugueses fizeram no descobrimento dos mares e terras do Oriente*, 24 vols. (Lisboa: Na Régia Officina Typografica, 1777–78), Década II/ix/vii, pp. 351 sq.; Fernão Lopes de Castanheda, *História do descobrimento e conquista da Índia pelos Portugueses,3a edição conforme a edição princeps, revista e anotada por Pedro de Azevedo,* Scriptores Rerum Lusitanarum, Série A, 9 "livros"

in 4 vols. (Coimbra: Imprensa da Universidade, 1924–1933), p. 33, livro III/cap. 135: 327–28.
19. A. da Silva Rego (ed.), *Documentação ultramarina portuguesa*, 10 vols. (Lisboa: Centro de Estudos Históricos Ultramarinos, 1960–67) I, pp. 361–62.
20. Rego, *Documentação ultramarina portuguesa*, I: 364; Barros and Couto, *Da Ásia de João de Barros e de Diogo do Couto*, Década III/iii/vi, p. 301; Castanheda, *História do descobrimento*, livro V/cap. 38: 62.
21. Artur Basílio de Sá (ed.), *Documentação para a história das missões do Padroado português do Oriente, Insulíndia*, 6 Vols. (Lisboa: Agência Geral do Ultramar, 1955–58), I: 184, 187; Castanheda, *História do descobrimento*, livro VII/cap. 23: 37.
22. Joseph Wicki, "Lista de moedas, pesos e embarcações do Oriente, composta por Nicolau Perreira S.J. por 1582", *Studia* 33 (1971): 137–48. See pp. 146–47. On the 1568 siege, see Manguin, "Of Fortresses and Galleys", pp. 619–21 for the discussion of the graphic representation of the Acehnese fleet. Beside the larger galleys, both Portuguese and Malay World fleets comprised lighter oared vessels such a galiots and *fustas*.
23. Manuel Godinho de Herédia, *Malaca, l'Inde méridionale et le Cathay. Manuscrit original autographe appartenant à la Bibliothèque royale de Bruxelles, reproduit en fac-simile et traduit par M. Léon Janssen*, 2 vols. (Bruxelles: Bibliothèque royale, 1881–82) and 1930 (English translation by J.V.G. Mills).
24. Anonymous manuscript, Biblioteca nacional do Brazil, Rio de Janeiro (Arc.009,13,006, Cartografia), first published in full and discussed in Manguin, "Of Fortresses and Galleys." In the present essay, we only publish two details of this large drawing, showing the Acehnese war fleets and what is most probably a *lancaran*.
25. On the paucity of Javanese literary references to the sea, see Manguin, "Of Fortresses and Galleys", pp. 192–93, 202. I must admit, though, that I have no access to Javanese texts in their original language, only to their translations; moreover, there is no tool comparable to the *Malay Concordance Project* to easily work on the vocabulary in this repertoire. Petrus Josephus Zoetmulder's *Old Javanese-English Dictionary* ('s-Gravenhage: Koninklijk Instituut voor Taal-, Land- en Volkenkunde, M. Nijhoff, 1982) is valuable, as it is based on a corpus of texts that bridges most of the ancient Javanese literary genres (from Old Javanese to Middle Javanese texts, via *kakawin* literature) and it includes quite a few terms for boats. However, none of the terms for the vessels under consideration here appear in texts earlier than those of the *kidung* and Middle Javanese corpus, hence only in texts roughly contemporary to the European or Malay sources we use in this article.
26. Zoetmulder, *Old Javanese-English Dictionary*, s.v. *lancar* ; see also Poerbatjaraka, "Déwa-Roetji", *Djawa* 20, no. 1 (1940): 5–86; the list is found on str. 9 of the text. When Poerbatjaraka published the *Dewa Ruci*, he dated it to the mid-sixteenth century, but Willem F. Stutterheim, who found it represented on

earlier reliefs, preferred the fifteenth century, as detailed in his "De Ouderdom van de Dewaruci", *Djawa* 20, no. 2 (1940): 131–32. The fact that the text also uses words of Mediterranean origin such as *galiyu* and *gorap*, which I associate with sixteenth century developments, clearly tilts the scale in favour of the mid-sixteenth century for its compilation, unless this particular passage is a later addition. The *Kidung Sunda* has many references to boats and ships, but the terms of interest to us here do not appear. See Cornelis Christiaan Berg, "Kidung Sunda. Inleiding, tekst, vertaling en aanteekeningen", *Bijdragen van het Koninklijk Instituut voor Taal-, Land- en Volkenkunde* 83 (1927): 1–161.

27. See A. de Bulhão Pato and H. Lopes de Mendonça (eds.), *Cartas de Afonso de Albuquerque: seguidas de documentos que as elucidam publicadas de ordem da classe de ciências morais, políticas e belas-letras da Academia das Ciências de Lisboa*, Colleção de monumentos inéditos para a história da conquista dos Portugueses (Lisboa: Academia das Ciências de Lisboa, 1884–1935). III: 58–60, 127; Tomé Pires, *The Suma oriental of Tomé Pires: an account of The East, from the Red Sea to Japan, written in Malacca and India in 1512–1515. The book of Francisco Rodrigues: rutter of a voyage in the Red Sea, nautical rules almanack and maps, written and drawn in the East before 1515*, edited and translated by A. Cortesão. 2 vols. (London: The Hakluyt Society, 1944), pp. 151, 188; and Jorge de Lemos, *Hystoria dos cercos que em tempo de Antonio Monis Barreto gouernador que foi dos estados da India, os Achens & Iaos puserão à fortaleza de Malaca sendo Tristão Vaz da Veiga capitão della* (Lisboa: Manoel de Lyra, 1585), 2a parte, cap I.

28. Zoetmulder, *Old Javanese-English Dictionary*, s.v. *kalulus*; Pires, *The Suma oriental of Tomé Pires*, p. 195 sq.; Barros and Couto, *Da Ásia*, Década IV/ix/xv, pp. 551–52; Castanheda, *História do descobrimento*, livro VIII/cap. 78: 331 and livro VIII/cap. 79: 346; and *Coriosidades de Gonçalo de Sousa (…)*: manuscript in the Biblioteca da Universidade de Coimbra, Ms. 3074, fol. 38vo.

29. Most of the references to *penjajap* in Malay sources appear in post-1700 texts (as queried with the MCP), as if the use of these craft had gone through some later revival.

30. Castanheda, *História do descobrimento*, livro III/cap. 51: 129. Texts, Malay or Portuguese, when describing war fleets, occasionally mention other boat names: *banting, balang, dendang, dadap, jalia, pencalang, pilang, som, sumbuk* that may have belonged to the category of oared vessels. Most appear to have been minor vessels (in numbers and in size) and constraints of space preclude me from examining them all in this article.

31. Pierre-Yves Manguin, "The Southeast Asian Ship: An Historical Approach", *Journal of Southeast Asian Studies* 11, no. 2 (1980): 266–76.

32. Stitching of planks is no longer mentioned in texts for Western Southeast Asia after the fifteenth century, and the most recent stitched plank shipwreck recovered so far dates from the twelfth century. See Pierre-Yves Manguin, "The Southeast Asian Ship: An Historical Approach"; Pierre-Yves Manguin, "Sewn-plank Craft

of Southeast Asia. A Preliminary Survey" in *Sewn Planked Boats: Archaeological and Ethnographic papers based on those presented to a conference at Greenwich in November 1984*, BAR International Series 276, edited by S. McGrail and E. Kentley (Greenwich/ Oxford: National Maritime Museum, 1985), pp. 319–43; and Pierre-Yves Manguin, "Southeast Asian shipping in the Indian Ocean during the 1st millennium AD" in *Tradition and Archaeology. Early Maritime Contacts in the Indian Ocean*, edited by Himanshu Prabha Ray and Jean-François Salles (New Delhi and Lyon: Manohar and Maison de l'Orient méditerranéen, 1996), pp. 181–98.

33. Pierre-Yves Manguin, "Late Mediaeval Asian Shipbuilding in the Indian Ocean: A Reappraisal" in *The Trading World of the Indian Ocean, 1500–1800*, edited by Om Prakash (Calcutta: Centre for Studies in Civilisations, 2011): 597–629.

34. Zoetmulder, *Old Javanese-English Dictionary*, s.v. *bĕḍil*. See also Hendrik Kern, "Oorsprong van het Maleisch word *bĕḍil*", *Bijdragen toot de taal-, land- en volkenkunde van Nederlandsch Indie* 54 (1902): 311–12, for the Tamil etymology of this term.

35. For more details on light artillery and its use in insular Southeast Asia, and for further references and illustrations, see Pierre-Yves Manguin, "L'artillerie légère nousantarienne. A propos de six canons conservés dans des collections portugaises", *Arts Asiatiques* 32 (1976): 233–54.

36. See Afonso de Albuquerque, *Comentários do grande Afonso de Albuquerque capitão geral que foi das Indias Orientais em tempo do muito poderoso Rei D. Manuel o primeiro deste nome* (Lisboa: Na Regia Officina Typografica, 1774), 3ra parte, cap. 28, p. 145; Barros and Couto, *Da Ásia*, Década I/ix/iv, p. 354; The letter to Charles V, dated 1537, published in D. Martín Fernandez de Navarrete, *Coleccion de los viages y descubrimientos que hicieron por mar los españoles desde fines del siglo XV*, 5 vols. (Madrid: Imprenta Real, 1825–37) , vol. V, p. 431. Many references to swivel-guns in sixteenth century Philippines will be found in the texts translated in Emma H. Blair and James A. Robertson, *The Philippine Islands, 1493–1898*, 55 vols. (Cleveland, The A.H. Clarke Company, 1903–09). See index, vol. LV, s.v. *Moros: weapons and warfare* and s.v. *Military affairs: artillery*).

37. Joseph Wicki (ed.), *Documenta indica*, Monumenta Missionum Societatis Jesu. Missionis Orientalis, 18 vols. (Rome: Monumenta Historica Societatis Jesu, 1948–88). See Vol. II, p. 209.

38. The two drawings given here were first published in Manguin, "L'artillerie légère nousantarienne" with additional photographs and full descriptions of the cannon.

39. G.M.A. Willem Lodewijcksz, *D'eerste boeck. Historie van Indien, waer inne verhaelt is de avontueren die de Hollandtsche schepen bejeghent zijn (…)*. (Amstelredam: Cornelis Claesz, 1598), fols. 35ro-36vo, and *Het Tweede Boeck…* 1601: pl. 17.

40. Similarly, locally-made Bugis trading ships of the 1970s, still traditionally edge joined with wooden dowels, had to shift to fastening with iron bolts when they

started carrying large engines the vibrations of which were fatal to their earlier fastenings.

41. On the difficulties encountered when deciding on the Arabic or Persian etymology of loan words in Malay, see Russell Jones, *Loan-words in Indonesian and Malay, compiled by the Indonesian Etymological Project* (Jakarta: KITLV and Buku Obor, 2008): xxv.
42. Pryor, *Geography, Technology, and War*, pp. 67–68.
43. On Portuguese renegades and mercenaries, see Maria Augusta Lima Cruz, "Exiles and Renegades in Early Sixteenth Century Portuguese India", *The Indian Economic Social History Review* 23, no. 3 (1986): 249–62; and the complementary article by Dejanirah Couto, "Quelques observations sur les renégats portugais en Asie au XVIe siècle", *Mare Liberum* 16 (1998): 57–85.
44. On Ottoman shipbuilding technology in the sixteenth–seventeenth centuries, see Idris Bostan, *Ottoman Maritime Arsenals and Shipbuilding Technology in the Sixteenth and Seventeenth Centuries*. Manchester, Foundation for Science, Technology and Civilisation, 2007. A splendid *kadirga* of the early seventeenth century is exhibited in the National Naval Museum at Istanbul.
45. Muhammad Abdul Jabbar Beg, *Persian and Turkish Loan-Words in Malay* (Kuala Lumpur: University of Malaya Press, 1982).
46. Alessandro Bausani, "The First Italian-Malay Vocabulary by Antonio Pigafetta", *East and West* 11, no. 4 (1960): 229–48.
47. The term may have also been used in one pre-sixteenth Malay text, the *Hikayat Raja Pasai*, which is said to have been composed in the 1390s; the version known to us, however, was published on the basis of an early nineteenth century manuscript, which makes it impossible to ascertain if the term *ghurab* was in fact being used as early as the late fourteenth century (See Jones, *Loan-words in Indonesian and Malay* and MCP. The word *ghurab* appears seven times in the MCP concordance of the *Hikayat Raja Pasai*).
48. Manguin, "The vanishing jong". See the tables and the attached bibliographic references.
49. Fernão Mendes Pinto, *Peregrinaçam: texto primitivo, inteiramente conforme a primeira edição (1614) / Peregrinação: versão integral em Português moderno, por Adolfo Casais Monteiro. Seguida das suas cartas*, 2 vols. (Lisboa: Sociedade de Intercambio Cultural Luso-Brasileiro, 1952–53). See vol. I, pp. 101, 122, 142; See also Barros and Couto, *Da Ásia*, Década VI/v/i, p. 345.
50. Wicki, *Documenta indica*, II: 209.
51. On which see Manguin, "Of Fortresses and Galleys" and the numerous sixteenth century references quoted therein.
52. If these figures are correct, we would probably have 23 banks with 4 rowers per oar on each side, and two banks, closer to the narrower part of the ship, with only three rowers per oar. Another royal galley of the time is said to have 29 banks of rowers. The very technical question of the rowing system of oared vessels (diremes, triremes or quadriremes) has produced a considerable literature. With the scant information available in the sources used in this article, it is

practically impossible to bring new data to this debate. Christiaan Nooteboom in his two articles "Eastern Diremes", *Mariner's Mirror* 35, no. 4 (1949): 272–75 and "Galeien in Azie", *Bijdragen van het Koninklijk Instituut voor Taal-, Land- en Volkenkunde* 108 (1952): 365–80, discussed this question for Southeast Asian vessels, on the basis mainly of Eastern Indonesian 19th-century data, without much success.

53. Boxer, "The Acehnese attack on Malacca in 1629", 119–21.
54. *História de serviços com martírio de Luís Monteiro Coutinho, ordenada por Manoel Godinho de Erédia, Anno 1615*: Manuscript, Códice 414, Biblioteca Nacional de Lisboa, fol. 8vo-9ro this illustrated manuscript is now available online at <http://purl.pt/1275>. See also Barros and Couto, *Da Ásia*, Década IX/xvii, p. 122 and Lemos, *Hystoria dos cercos*, 21).
55 Teuku Iskandar (ed.), *De Hikajat Atjeh*, VKI 26 ('s-Gravenhage: KITLV, 1958). See p. 175. The exact identification of these firearms with those mentioned in European, mainly Portuguese sources of the time would need another article, in which contemporary descriptions would be closely compared.
56. See Jorge M. dos Santos Alves and Pierre-Yves Manguin, *O 'Roteiro das cousas do Achem' de D. João Ribeiro Gaio: Um olhar português sobre o norte de Samatra em finais do século XVI* (Lisboa: Commissão Nacional para as Comemorações dos Descobrimentos Portugueses, 1997).
57. Lodewijcks, *D'eerste boeck*, fols. 35ro–36vo, and *Het Tweede Boeck* pl. 17.
58. Reference to Beaulieu's narrative are from the 1696 edition (published by Thévenot); the passage on the galleys is found on pp. 106–07. The EFEO recently republished this text as Augustin de Beaulieu, *Mémoire d'un voyage aux Indes orientales (1619–1622). Un marchand normand à Sumatra*, édité par Denys Lombard, Pérégrinations asiatiques I (Paris: École française d'Extrême-Orient, 1996).
59. Kassim Ahmad (ed.), *Hikayat Hang Tuah* (Kuala Lumpur: Dewan Bahasa dan Pustaka, 1968). See p. 102.
60. The descriptions of these huge Acehnese galleys have often been published: the original Portuguese texts will be found in J.H. da Cunha Rivara, "Victória de Nuno Alvares Botelho em Malaca, 1629", *O Chronista de Tissuary (Nova Goa)* 1 (1866): 6–20; Alfredo Botelho de Sousa, *Nuno Álvares Botelho* (Lisboa: Agência Geral das Colónias, 1940); and in English in Boxer, "The Acehnese attack on Malacca in 1629".
61. Cyril Skinner, *The Battle for Junk Ceylon. The Syair Sultan Maulana*, Bibliotheca Indonesica 25 (Dordrecht: Koninklijk Instituut voor Taal-, Land- en Volkenkunde, 1985).

References

Academia das Ciências de Lisboa. *Alguns documentos do Archivo Nacionale da Torre do Tombo acerca das navegações e conquistas portuguezas publicados por ordem do governo de Sua Majestade Fidelíssima ao celebrar-se a commemoração quadricentenaria do descobrimento da America.* Lisboa: Imprensa Nacional, 1892.

Albuquerque, Afonso de. *Comentários do grande Afonso de Albuquerque capitão geral que foi das Indias Orientais em tempo do muito poderoso Rei D. Manuel o primeiro deste nome.* Lisboa: Na Regia Officina Typografica, 1774.

Alves, Jorge M. dos Santos. *O Domínio do Norte de Samatra. A história dos sultanatos de Samudera — Pacém e de Achém, e das suas relações com os Portugueses (1500–1580).* Lisboa: Sociedade Histórica da Independência de Portugal, 1999.

Alves, Jorge M. dos Santos and Pierre-Yves Manguin. *O 'Roteiro das cousas do Achem' de D. João Ribeiro Gaio: Um olhar português sobre o norte de Samatra em finais do século XVI.* Colecção Outras Margens. Lisboa: Commissão Nacional para as Comemorações dos Descobrimentos Portugueses, 1997.

Andaya, Barbara W. "Aspects of Warfare in Premodern Southeast Asia", *Journal of the Economic and Social History of the Orient* 46, no. 2 (2003): 139–42.

Anderson, Roger C. *Oared Fighting Ships: From Classical Times to the Coming of Steam.* Kings Langley: Argus Books Ltd, 1976.

Aurousseau, Léonard. "Notes et mélanges: Le mot sampan est-il chinois?". *Bulletin de l'Ecole française d'Extrême-Orient* 22 (1922): 1–4.

Barros, João de, and Diogo do Couto. *Da Ásia de João de Barros e de Diogo do Couto: dos feitos que os portugueses fizeram no descobrimento dos mares e terras do Oriente,* 24 vols. Lisboa: Na Régia Officina Typografica, 1777–78.

Bausani, Alessandro. "The First Italian-Malay Vocabulary by Antonio Pigafetta". *East and West* 11, no. 4 (1960): 229–48.

Beaulieu, Augustin de. *Mémoires du voyage aux Indes orientales du général Beaulieu dressés par luy-mesme.* In *Relations de divers voyages curieux, publiées par M. Melchissédec Thévenot,* vol. I. Paris: T. Moette, 1696.

———. *Mémoire d'un voyage aux Indes orientales (1619–1622). Un marchand normand à Sumatra,* édité par Denys Lombard. Pérégrinations asiatiques, I. Paris: École française d'Extrême-Orient, 1996.

Beg, Muhammad Abdul Jabbar. *Persian and Turkish Loan-Words in Malay.* Kuala Lumpur: University of Malaya Press, 1982.

Berg, Cornelis Christiaan. "Kidung Sunda. Inleiding, tekst, vertaling en aanteekeningen". *Bijdragen van het Koninklijk Instituut voor Taal-, Land- en Volkenkunde* 83 (1927): 1–161.

Blair, Emma H. and James A. Robertson. *The Philippine Islands, 1493–1898.* 55 vols. Cleveland, The A.H. Clarke Company, 1903–09.

Bostan, Idris. *Ottoman Maritime Arsenals and Shipbuilding Technology in the 16th and 17th Centuries.* Manchester: Foundation for Science, Technology and Civilisation, 2007.

Boxer, Charles Ralph. "The Acehnese attack on Malacca in 1629, as described in contemporary Portuguese sources". In *Malayan and Indonesian Studies,* edited by J. Bastin and R. Roolvink, pp. 105–21. Oxford: Oxford University Press, 1964.

———. "Asian Potentates and European Artillery in the Sixteenth-Eighteenth Centuries", *Journal of the Malayan Branch, Royal Asiatic Society* 38, no. 2 (1965): 156–72.

Bulhão Pato, A. de and H. Lopes de Mendonça (eds.). *Cartas de Afonso de Albuquerque: seguidas de documentos que as elucidam publicadas de ordem da classe de ciências morais, políticas e belas-letras da Academia das Ciências de Lisboa*. Colleção de monumentos inéditos para a história da conquista dos Portugueses. Lisboa: Academia das Ciências de Lisboa, 1884–1935.

Castanheda, Fernão Lopes de. *História do descobrimento e conquista da Índia pelos Portugueses*, 3a edição conforme a edição princeps, revista e anotada por Pedro de Azevedo (Scriptores Rerum Lusitanarum. Série A). 9 "livros" in 4 vols. Coimbra: Imprensa da Universidade, 1924–33.

Charney, Michael. *Southeast Asian Warfare, 1300–1900*. Leiden and Boston: Brill, 2004.

Cipolla, Carlos M. *Guns, Sails & Empires: Technological Innovation and the Early Phases of European Expansion: 1400–1700*. London & New York: Collins and Pantheon Books, 1965.

Coedès, George. "Les inscriptions malaises de Çrivijaya". *Bulletin de l'Ecole française d'Extrême-Orient* 30 (1930): 29–80.

———. *Les Etats hindouisés d'Indochine et d'Indonésie*. Paris, de Boccard, 1964.

Couto, Dejanirah. "Quelques observations sur les renégats portugais en Asie au XVIe siècle". *Mare Liberum* 16 (1998): 57–85.

Cruz, Maria Augusta Lima. "Exiles and Renegades in Early Sixteenth Century Portuguese India". *The Indian Economic and Social History Review* 23, no. 3 (1986): 249–62.

Damais, Louis-Charles. "[Review of:] Poerbatjaraka, 'Riwajat Indonesia', djilid I, 1952". *Bulletin de l'Ecole française d'Extrême-Orient* 48, no. 2 (1957): 607–49.

Ferrand, Gabriel. "Le K'ouen-louen et les anciennes navigations interocéaniques dans les mers du sud". *Journal Asiatique* 17 (1919): 5–68, 201–41, 239–333, 431–92.

———. "L'empire sumatranais de Çrîvijaya". *Journal Asiatique* 20 (1922): 1–104, 161–246.

Goris, Roelof. *Prasasti Bali: Inscripties voor Anak Wungçu*. 2 vols. Bandung: Masa Baru, 1954.

Groslier, George. "La battellerie cambodgienne du VIIIe au XIIIe siècle de notre ère". *Revue archéologique* (1917): 198–204.

Guilmartin, J.F. *Gunpowder and Galleys: Changing Technology and Mediterranean Warfare at Sea in the Sixteenth Century*. London: Cambridge University Press, 1974.

Gunawardana, R.A.L.H. "Ceylon and Malaysia: A Study of Professor S. Paranavitana's Research on the Relations between the Two Regions". *University of Ceylon Review* 25, no. 1–2 (1967): 1–64.

Herédia, Manuel Godinho de. *Malaca, l'Inde méridionale et le Cathay. Manuscrit original autographe appartenant à la Bibliothèque royale de Bruxelles, reproduit en fac-simile et traduit par M. Léon Janssen*. 2 vols. Bruxelles: Bibliothèque royale, 1881–82.

———. "Eredia's description of Malacca, Meridional India and Cathay" (translated and edited by J.V.G. Mills). *Journal of the Malayan Branch, Royal Asiatic Society* 8, no. 1 (1930): 1–288.

Hirth, Friedrich and William W. Rockhill. *Chau Ju-Kua: His Work on the Chinese and Arab Trade in the Twelfth and Thirteenth Centuries, Entitled Chu-Fan-Chi*. St. Petersburg, Imperial Academy of Sciences, 1911.

Iskandar, Teuku (ed.). *De Hikajat Atjeh*. VKI 26. 's-Gravenhage: KITLV, 1958.

Jacq-Hergoualc'h, Michel. *L'armement et l'organisation de l'armée khmère aux XIIe et XIIIe siècles d'après les bas-reliefs d'Angkor Vat, du Bayon et de Banteay Chmar*. Paris, Publications du Musée Guimet, 1979.

———. "L'armée du Campa au début du XIIIe siècle", in *Le Campa et le Monde Malais*. pp. 27–46. Paris: Publications du Centre d'Histoire et Civilisations de la Péninsule Indochinoise, 1991.

Jones, Russell (ed.). *Hikayat Raja Pasai*. Petaling Jaya, Penerbit Fajar Bakti, 1987.

———. *Loan-words in Indonesian and Malay, compiled by the Indonesian Etymological Project*. Jakarta: KITLV, Buku Obor, 2008.

Kassim Ahmad (ed.). *Hikayat Hang Tuah*. Kuala Lumpur: Dewan Bahasa dan Pustaka, 1968.

Kern, Hendrik. "Oorsprong van het Maleisch word *bĕḍil*". *Bijdragen toot de taal-, land- en volkenkunde van Nederlandsch Indie* 54 (1902): 311–12.

Knaap, Gerrit. "Headhunting, Carnage and Armed Peace in Amboina, 1500–1700". *Journal of the Economic and Social History of the Orient* 46, no. 2 (2003): 215–25.

Lane, Frederic Chapin. *Navires et constructeurs à Venise pendant la Renaissance*. Paris: SEVPEN, 1965 (translated from the 1934 Baltimore edition, and revised by the author).

———. *Venetian Ships and Shipbuilders of the Renaissance*. New York: Arno Press 1979 (reprint of the 1934 Baltimore edition).

Lemos, Jorge de. *Hystoria dos cercos que em tempo de Antonio Monis Barreto gouernador que foi dos estados da India, os Achens & Iaos puserão à fortaleza de Malaca sendo Tristão Vaz da Veiga capitão della*. Lisboa: Manoel de Lyra, 1585.

Lieberman, Victor. "Some Comparative Thoughts on Premodern Southeast Asian Warfare". *Journal of the Economic and Social History of the Orient* 46, no. 2 (2003): 215–25.

Lodewijcksz, G.M.A. Willem. *D'eerste boeck. Historie van Indien, waer inne verhaelt is de avontueren die de Hollandtsche schepen bejeghent zijn (...)*. Amstelredam: Cornelis Claesz, 1598.

Lombard, Denys. *Le Sultanat d'Atjeh au temps d'Iskandar Muda, 1607–1636*. PEFEO 62. Paris: EFEO, 1967.

Manguin, Pierre-Yves. "L'artillerie légère nousantarienne. A propos de six canons conservés dans des collections portugaises". *Arts Asiatiques* 32 (1976): 233–54.

———. "The Southeast Asian Ship: An Historical Approach". *Journal of Southeast Asian Studies* 11, no. 2 (1980): 266–76.

———. "Shipshape Societies. Boat Symbolism and Political Systems in Insular South-East Asia". In *Southeast Asia in the 9th to 14th Centuries*, edited by D.G. Marr and A.C. Milner, pp. 187–213. Canberra and Singapore: Research School of Pacific Studies, Australian National University/Institute of Southeast Asian Studies, 1984.

———. "Sewn-plank Craft of Southeast Asia. A Preliminary Survey". In *Sewn Planked Boats. Archaeological and Ethnographic papers based on those presented to a conference at Greenwich in November, 1984*, edited by S. McGrail and E. Kentley, pp. 319–43. Greenwich/Oxford: National Maritime Museum (British Archaeological Reports Archaeological Series 10/BAR International Series 276), 1985.

———. "Of Fortresses and Galleys: The 1568 Acehnese Siege of Melaka, following a Contemporary Bird's-eye View". In *Asian Studies in Honour of Professor Charles Boxer*, edited by P.-Y. Manguin and G. Bouchon, pp. 607–28 (*Modern Asian Studies* 22, no. 3, special issue/Ecole française d'Extrême-Orient), 1988.

———. "The vanishing jong: Insular Southeast Asian fleets in war and trade (15th–17th centuries)". In *Southeast Asia in the Early Modern Era: Trade, Power, and Belief*, edited by A. Reid, pp. 197–213. Ithaca and London: Cornell University Press, 1993.

———. "Southeast Asian shipping in the Indian Ocean during the 1st millennium AD". In *Tradition and Archaeology. Early Maritime Contacts in the Indian Ocean*, edited by Himanshu Prabha Ray and Jean-François Salles, pp. 181–98. New Delhi and Lyon: Manohar and Maison de l'Orient méditerranéen, 1996.

———. "Late Mediaeval Asian Shipbuilding in the Indian Ocean: A Reappraisal". In *The Trading World of the Indian Ocean, 1500–1800*, edited by Om Prakash, pp. 597–629. Calcutta: Centre for Studies in Civilizations (Project on History of Science, Philosophy and Culture in Indian Civilization), 2011.

Maspero, Georges. *Le Royaume de Champa*. Paris: Van Oest, 1928.

Mendonça, Henrique Lopes de. *Estudos sobre navios portugueses nos séculos XV e XVI*. Lisboa: Ministério da Marinha (Colecção de documentos, 5), 1892.

Murphey, Rhoads. *Ottoman Warfare, 1500–1700*. London: UCL Press, 1999.

Navarrete, D. Martín Fernandez de. *Coleccion de los viages y descubrimientos que hicieron por mar los españoles desde fines del siglo XV*. Madrid: Imprenta Real, 1825–37, 5 vols.

Nooteboom, Christiaan. "Eastern Diremes". *Mariner's Mirror* 35, no. 4 (1949): 272–75.

———. "Galeien in Azie". *Bijdragen van het Koninklijk Instituut voor Taal-, Land- en Volkenkunde* 108 (1952): 365–80.

Paris, Pierre. "Les bateaux des bas-reliefs Khmers". *Bulletin de l'Ecole française d'Extrême-Orient* 41 (1941): 335–64.

Pinto, Fernão Mendes. *Peregrinaçam: texto primitivo, inteiramente conforme a primeira edição (1614) / Peregrinação: versão integral em Português moderno, por Adolfo Casais Monteiro. Seguida das suas cartas.* 2 vols. Lisboa: Sociedade de Intercambio Cultural Luso-Brasileiro, 1952–53.

Pinto, Paulo Jorge Sousa. *Portugueses e malaios: Malaca e os Sultanatos de Johor e Achém, 1575–1619.* Lisboa: Sociedade Histórica da Independência de Portugal, 1997.

Pires, Tomé. *The Suma oriental of Tomé Pires: an account of The East, from the Red Sea to Japan, written in Malacca and India in 1512–1515. The book of Francisco Rodrigues: rutter of a voyage in the Red Sea, nautical rules almanack and maps, written and drawn in the East before 1515*, 2 vols. edited and translated by A. Cortesão. London: The Hakluyt Society, 1944.

Poerbatjaraka. "Déwa-Roetji". *Djawa* 20, no. 1 (1940): 5–86.

Pryor, John H. *Geography, Technology, and War: Studies in the Maritime History of the Mediterranean, 649–1571.* Cambridge: Cambridge University Press, 1988.

Rego, A. da Silva (ed.). *Documentação ultramarina portuguesa.* 10 vols. Lisboa: Centro de Estudos Históricos Ultramarinos, 1960–67.

Reid, Anthony. "Sixteenth Century Turkish Influence in Western Indonesia". *Journal of Southeast Asian History* 10, no. 3 (1969): 395–414.

———. *The Ottomans in Southeast Asia.* ARI Working Paper 36. Singapore: Asia Research Institute National University of Singapore, 2005.

Rivara, J.H. da Cunha. "Victória de Nuno Alvares Botelho em Malaca, 1629". *O Chronista de Tissuary (Nova Goa)* 1 (1866): 6–20.

Rodriguez, Felice Noelle. "Juan de Salcedo Joins the Narrative Form of Warfare". *Journal of the Economic and Social History of the Orient* 46, no. 2 (2003): 143–64.

Rose, Susan. *Medieval Naval Warfare, 1000–1500.* London: Routledge, 2002.

Sá, Artur Basílio de (ed.). *Documentação para a história das missões do Padroado português do Oriente, Insulíndia.* 6 vols. Lisboa: Agência Geral do Ultramar, 1955–58.

Sirisena, W.M. *Sri Lanka and Southeast Asia. Political, Religious and Cultural Relations from A.D. c. 1000 to c. 1500.* Leiden: E.J. Brill, 1968.

Skinner, Cyril. *The Battle for Junk Ceylon. The Syair Sultan Maulana.* Bibliotheca Indonesica, 25. Dordrecht, Koninklijk Instituut voor Taal-, Land- en Volkenkunde, 1985.

Sousa, Alfredo Botelho de. *Nuno Álvares Botelho.* Lisboa: Agência Geral das Colónias, 1940.

Stutterheim, Willem F. "De Ouderdom van de Dewaruci". *Djawa* 20, no. 2 (1940): 131–32.

Sun Laichen. "Gunpowder Technology and Commerce in East and Southeast Asia, c. 1368–1683: Towards Defining an 'Age of Gunpowder' in Asian History". In *Workshop on Northeast Asia in Maritime Perspective: A Dialogue with Southeast Asia*, edited by Yamauchi Shinji, Fujita Kayoko and Piyada Chonlaworn. Osaka and Singapore: Osaka University and Asia Research Institute, 2004: 12–25.

Tibbetts, Gerald Randall. *A Study of the Arabic Texts Containing Material on Southeast Asia*. London and Leiden: Royal Asiatic Society, 1979.

Het tweede Boeck, journael oft dagh-register, inhoudende een warachtich verhael ende historische vertellinghe vande reyse gedaen door de acht schepen van Amstelredamme, gheseylt inden maent martij 1598 onder 't beleydt vanden admirael Iacob Cornelisz Neck ende Wybrant van Warwijck als vice-admirael etc. Amstelredamme: Cornelis Claesz, 1601.

Wales, Horace Geoffrey Quaritch. *Ancient Southeast Asian Warfare*. London: B. Quaritch, 1952.

Wicki, Joseph. "Lista de moedas, pesos e embarcações do Oriente, composta por Nicolau Perreira S.J. por 1582". *Studia* 33 (1971): 137–48.

Wicki, Joseph (ed.). *Documenta indica*. 18 vols. Monumenta Missionum Societatis Jesu. Missionis Orientalis. Rome: Monumenta Historica Societatis Jesu, 1948–88.

Zoetmulder, Petrus Josephus. *Old Javanese-English Dictionary*. 2 vols. 's-Gravenhage, Koninklijk Instituut voor Taal-, Land- en Volkenkunde, M. Nijhoff, 1982.

9

WEATHER, HISTORY AND EMPIRE
The Typhoon Factor and the Manila Galleon Trade, 1565–1815

James Francis Warren

INTRODUCTION

This paper describes and analyses how the Manila galleon trade and Spain's efforts to colonize the Philippines were frequently placed in jeopardy by the uncontrollable and unpredictable power of cyclonic storms. It highlights the significance of the devastating impact of typhoons on the history of the Spanish galleons trading between Manila and Acapulco as an unexplored aspect of the history of the Philippines under Spain. The Manila galleon trade was one of the most persistent, perilous and profitable trans-oceanic enterprises in the annals of colonial economic history. Between 1565 and 1815, the galleons or "China ships", the largest and wealthiest merchant ships of their age, carried the treasures of China and other parts of Asia to the West via Mexico. To the peoples of the Philippines, China and Japan they were the "silver argosies," returning from Mexico with silver ingots, Mexican and Peruvian pesos and the manufactured goods of Europe. However, more than forty galleons were lost over the course of 250 years, many of them to typhoons and storms at sea. The sudden loss of these huge vessels in the storm-tossed waters between the Philippines and Mexico had dire economic and social consequences in the seventeenth and eighteenth centuries as the Spanish colony was utterly dependent on a financial administrative grant in aid (the *situado*) and trade with Mexico.[1]

FOUNDING MANILA

Ferdinand Magellan, the Portuguese navigator who sailed under the flag of Castille *y* Leon, in an effort to make the vision of a new Spanish empire over the Pacific a reality, set out from Spain in 1519 with five ships and a complement of 264 crew to find a way to the fabled Spice Islands by sailing westward. At a time when few believed in the theory of the spherical form of the earth, the renowned mariner sought a passage by the south of America in order to circumnavigate the globe.[2] On this first epic-making voyage around the world, Magellan successfully navigated across the Pacific and sighted the island of Samar on 16 March 1521.[3] A year later, and three years after the expedition set out from Spain, only the ship *Victoria* returned, with just 18 men, but its hold was filled with 26 tons of cloves. Despite the huge losses in men and ships, the expedition proved an enormous financial success: the spices returned the 20,000 ducats the venture had cost, plus a 105 per cent profit.[4]

More expeditions followed that of Magellan. But the Philippines — set against this background of early Spanish attempts to establish a global Pacific network of trade and communications — was not formally organized as a colony until 1565 when Philip II appointed Don Miguel de Legaspi, who had distinguished himself in Mexico, the first Governor-General. In that same year, Andres Urdaneta navigated the first European eastward passage from Manila to Mexico by sailing north to Japan and catching the downward current to the southeast coast of California.[5]

In 1571 Legaspi chose the site of Manila as the capital because of its excellent natural harbour and the rich hinterland surrounding the city, which could supply it with the necessary produce and natural resources.[6] Located at the rear of one of the best bays in the world in the age of sail — a bay of approximately 39 kilometres in diameter and 193 kilometres in circumference — it could hold all the fleets of Europe.[7] Manila, like Melaka, Makassar, Gresik and other major port cities of the early modern era that were engaged in commerce, was situated both against the sea at the mouth of a deltaic plain and beside a large navigable river.[8] Legaspi's planned settlement of Manila rose from the eastern shores of a delta on the mouth of the Pasig River. Over the first two centuries, settlements radiated from both sides of the Pasig, separated by tributaries and creeks and joined together by several bridges.

The Spanish quickly took advantage of Manila's commanding position to improve and transform the landscape, employing typical models of town life taken from Spain and which accompanied them from their American colonies. Corvée labour on a grand scale was used to build Intramuros, or the "walled city": which included royal houses (*casas reales*), fortifications, port facilities, warehouses, shipyards, foundries, churches, convents, private residences and roads. Outside the massive stone walls was a surrounding moat constructed in 1603. Found inside the walled city — which had seven gates, closed by drawbridges at night — were narrow cobbled lanes, streets and plazas and the tiled roof houses with their standard *azoteas*, or balconies on which the Spaniards congregated. The heart of this enclosed city was the square-shaped Plaza Royal, surrounded by the old Cathedral, the palace of the Governor-General and other government buildings. Residences surrounding the town square were located further back within blocks framed by a grid pattern of streets.[9]

Intramuros, the city of Manila by the bay, was the heart and soul of the islands, the centre of the Spanish civil, religious, military and commercial activity in the islands, and the seat of civil and ecclesiastical authority. Its location, at the southern end of the fertile central Luzon plain and on the large and protected bay, rapidly made the city and port area a centre of cross-cultural commerce and trans-oceanic economic activity between Asia and the Americas that brought the Chinese and Japanese to the Philippines. Intramuros was a formidable, well-planned city that was to act as the western terminus of the galleons that bound Manila and the Philippines to Spain, and early became the centre of the highly lucrative galleon trade that carried Chinese silk, porcelain and Philippine products to Mexico.

THE CITY AND COMMERCE

When the Spanish arrived in the Philippines in 1565 the resident Chinese population was small, but there existed already well-established lines of inter-island trade and communication with southeast China. The Chinese junk trade was established in the Ming era and provided both commercial and cultural contacts for the Chinese already residing in the Philippines. From 1405 to 1433, Chinese fleets, including leviathan treasure junks, and hundreds of war junks that dwarfed the later Spanish and Portuguese caravels, had projected the Ming empire's power far beyond its shores, reaching Southeast Asia and the coasts of East Africa. However, conservative Confucian mandarins managed to gain control of Chinese foreign policy and halt the astonishing voyages, imposing an austere isolationism that prevented the Chinese from possibly bringing the Indian Ocean and eastern Pacific within their sphere of influence. The arrival of the Spanish in the Philippines provided the missing link for the Chinese to expand their trade across the Pacific Ocean. Eight years later, in 1573, a Spanish galleon arrived in Acapulco laden with all the fabulous treasures of late fifteenth-century Ming China.[10] The world's longest voyage of trade and navigation had been completed: the Pacific maritime silk-road was born.

The trans-oceanic voyages of the galleons from Acapulco to Manila and back enabled markets to be linked together and their commodities soared in value as the vessels criss-crossed the ocean in opposite directions. The pattern of exchange in this commerce was for Manila to import silk, ceramics and other manufactures from China, in exchange for its exports of local marine and forest products and silver from the Spanish mines in Mexico and Peru.[11] Chinese junks brought their goods from Canton and other ports to Manila, where the cargoes were reloaded in the galleons bound for Acapulco and the Spanish markets of the Americas. The coveted Chinese silks and brocades, Indian and Philippine cottons, and oriental porcelains were exchanged for Mexican and Peruvian silver. The galleons carried silver and gold ingots, Spanish coins and European manufactures back across the Pacific to Manila.

Unless the Pacific crossing had been unusually difficult, the galleons arrived in Acapulco before the end of the year, in time for the great fair. Similarly, when the galleons were refitted and departed in the early months of the next year they were met at the end of the voyage at the Manila market by the merchants and artisans representing the interests of Chinese long-distance traffic. The earlier arrival of the Chinese trading junks in Manila carrying precious stocks for Acapulco signalled the beginning of the annual fair in the city.

For 250 years, until 1815, the Philippines would have no other means of communication and support from Spain except the trans-Pacific crossing of the *nao de la china* or "ships of China", the great merchant vessels plying between Manila and Acapulco, which linked the Philippines with China and the vice royalty of New Spain or Mexico. The Philippines was administered from Mexico and its commerce centred on the galleon trade in which Manila functioned as an *entrepôt* between two continents. As said, Manila was perfectly situated on the eastern shore of a great bay, a natural ample harbour, to serve Spain's bid for an Asian-Pacific trading empire in the seventeenth century. The well-defended inlet, on which the arsenal with its fortifications stood, afforded the best anchorage in the bay and was the refuge of ships during typhoons and severe storms that frequented the region.[12]

Manila thus became the homeport of the great China ships, the hub for the Spanish-Chinese galleon trade. By 1630, at the peak of its prosperity, Manila would have a population of about 40,000, largely drawn to the Philippines by the trade conducted by "the richest ships in all the oceans".[13] For Spain, Manila was the key to dealing directly with China. This of course placed

Spanish officials, members of the church hierarchy, and merchants in Manila in an enviable, if not awkward, position that they jealously guarded, always worrying about the possible loss of a lucrative source of income if Manila were to be suddenly bypassed on the route to China. Manila's geographical location and the singular character of the galleon trade helped the city's merchants and commerce not only survive, but prosper, and the Manila Bay area quickly became the major site of Chinese settlement and the retail and wholesale trades.[14]

The Chinese state had begun to license junks to trade legally in southern waters in the late 1560s, and by 1588 the galleon trade in American silver was attracting 16 junks a year to Manila, guaranteeing the rapid development and commercial success of the city.[15] The end of the sixteenth century was marked by the phenomenal development of the trade between the Philippines and Mexico. It also saw the feverish settlement and construction of Manila, and its commercial metamorphosis into a European walled *entrepôt* of commercial warehouses, government buildings and a sprawling Chinese quarter and nearby residences situated outside the walls of the city. The landscape and the people featured a cosmopolitan blend of Asiatic and Spanish features, with a population made up mostly of Chinese, Japanese and Spaniards, and to a lesser extent of the different neighbouring ethno-linguistic groups, especially the Tagalogs.

The building of Intramuros largely as a stone city with massive ramparts, moats and walls required an immense labour force of public workers, masons, carpenters and blacksmiths. In Manila and elsewhere the widespread use of stone and tile for government buildings, churches and convents was accomplished by coercion rather than subsidy.[16] The construction of lime and stone stucco structures also required vast forest resources to fire the kilns and an equally vast supply of limestone and coral to produce the lime. This building technique was to accelerate the degradation of both the forest and the coastal reef systems.[17] Major shipbuilding sites were established at Cavite, several on the Camarines coast, on the Gulf of Sorsogon at Bagatao and at other places in Albay Province, Marinduque, Mindoro, Masbate, Iloilo and the east coast of Samar.[18] The escalation of galleon-building activity at these sites, especially during peak periods of trading activity, attracted population and led to the clustering of settlements and the stripping of the fragile tropical environment.

As the scale of the galleon trade grew, the Chinese population of Manila expanded quickly to the point where it outnumbered the resident Spanish. Their prime reason for being there was that they were all somehow involved in the Chinese junk trade to Mexico. The Spanish authorities viewed the Chinese as an economic necessity in the larger scheme of things, but felt threatened by their size and martial strength. Therefore, as Spain's policy of Chinese containment took shape, methods were applied in the Philippines similar to those used against the Jews in Spain: onerous taxation, legal restrictions and expulsions. After 1582, the city authorities required all non-Catholic Chinese to reside in a walled compound beyond the city called the *Parian*, the Tagalog word for marketplace. The location of the *Parian* would move from time to time and persist until 1790. This officially designated Chinese quarter outside the walls of the capital soon became the commercial heart of the city.

Despite laws passed in Spain between 1594 and 1627 to protect the interests of the Chinese, Manila, situated at the opposite end of the empire, was so far away that such laws were poorly enforced. Taxation remained high, extra levies had to be met, and headmen were expected to provide rowers for the galleys.[19] Manila was wracked by troubles internally, and in 1603 a series of misunderstandings led the Chinese community around it to rise against the Spanish. As a result the entire Chinese population was massacred. But the Spanish quickly realized — much to their chagrin — that the well-being and maintenance of the city and its commerce was utterly dependant on the Chinese merchants and artisans. Spain consequently tried to limit the size of the Chinese population to 6,000, but was unable to do so. By 1630, there was a population of about 20,000 Chinese in Manila.

There would be further violent uprisings in 1639, 1662, and 1686 as the Spanish continued to repress and exploit the Chinese, as well as expel them. But despite these extreme measures the Chinese population was maintained around the 20,000 mark. By the middle of the eighteenth century, Chinese Catholic mestizo merchants and traders, who were finally given freedom to travel throughout the islands, were significant trans-shippers of goods collected and forwarded to Manila from different parts of the archipelago. These merchants had an edge on their local indigenous counterparts as they had the necessary connections both in the *Parian* and in Manila proper, as well as locally, to meet the increased demand in China for particular commodities that could be exchanged as part of the commerce of the galleon trade.

The galleon trade flourished in the first few decades after its inception, based largely on Chinese goods brought to Manila for transhipment to Mexico. In those early decades when the trade ran unfettered by laws, the galleons returned the next year with the cash profits from the sale of the goods in the Acapulco market and additional Mexican silver to meet the requirements of the government in Manila.[20] The first *permiso*, or restriction on the trade was established in 1593, limiting the value of the annual cargo to New Spain. The value of the cargo was not to exceed 250,000 pesos at Manila, with a sales worth in Mexico not over double that amount.[21] The same maximum was extended by further decrees in 1604 and 1619. However, by 1702 the *permiso* had risen to 300,000 pesos, by 1734 to 500,000 pesos and in 1776 it was increased to 750,000 pesos. The return value of the cargo remained the same, in each case fixed at double the *permiso*.[22] The limited lading space was divided into *piezas* (pieces), and *boletas* (permits) were issued as a certificate of ownership for each *pieza*. For the merchants and the *boleteros* wishing to convert their papers into as much cash as possible, sizeable quick returns on their investments were possible.

Corruption in the trade between Manila and Acapulco began with the introduction of the first *permiso* in 1593. Henceforth, the galleons regularly carried tons of cargo that included contraband. The value of the cargo invariably far exceeded the officially set amount. The merchants, clergy, and government servants maintained a vice-like grip over all Spanish trade between Manila and Mexico and enjoyed immense profits from the annual voyages to Acapulco. Corruption among these high officials, friars and merchants was widespread. The prescribed division of lading space of 4,000 shares, each representing a *pieza* usually worth 1,500 to 2,000 thousand pesos, was never adhered to: the cargo space of galleons was normally crammed with 6,000 to 7,000 *piezas*, and one heavily laden galleon sunk with 12,000 *piezas* in her hold.[23]

THE JOURNEY, STORMS AND SHIPWRECKS

The possibility of navigating the Pacific Ocean bound the two continents together and linked Mexican, Chinese, Filipinos, and Japanese and their wares to one another, advancing their views and knowledge of other places and themselves. The navigation remained fixed till the end of the trade in 1815 along the track that Urdaneta had sailed in 1565. At the height of the trade, these giant vessels, built in different parts of the Philippines with draft labour, could transport as many as 400 passengers and an enormous cargo. The eastbound galleons departing Manila were in principle scheduled to leave in July of each year and were ideally to sail from Acapulco in January of the next year. The voyage back to the Philippines was relatively quick and often required only three months. The duration of the average voyage to New Spain, however, was long and difficult, taking five to seven months.[24]

The journey of the Spanish galleons across the Pacific to Mexico and back during the seventeenth and eighteenth centuries was perilous. The difficulties began as soon as the galleon left Manila from the port of Cavite. The Philippine Archipelago for length and irregularity of shoreline, and for the large number of major islands, reefs and shoals, presented more visible and submerged hazards to the galleons and inter-island vessels than any other nation or archipelago in that part of the world. The Philippine waters were almost completely uncharted and woefully lacking in navigation aids to guide the navigators of the galleons through dangerous waters. Such charts as did exist were with few exceptions of questionable value because of inaccuracies and a lack of much necessary navigational data about Philippine and adjacent waters.[25]

Added to these fixed natural hazards was the fact that the northern and central islands of the Philippines lie squarely within the typhoon belt of the western Pacific Ocean and the China Sea; an area where strong winds and heavy seas occur during certain times of the year.[26] There are only five places in the world where the right combination of temperatures, moisture, pressure, and wind patterns enable the birth of cyclonic storms and then keep them going, namely the tropical and subtropical North Atlantic Ocean, the Pacific Ocean, the Indian Ocean and the Caribbean and China Seas. Each area has historically coined its own name for these cyclonic storm systems. They are called typhoons in the Asian-Pacific basin, or *baguio* in the Philippines, cyclones in the Indian Ocean and hurricanes in the northern hemisphere.[27]

Typhoons, as the offspring of water and air, are powered by heat from the sea, high planetary winds, and their own violent energy. They move as giant whirlwinds in a large tightening spiral around a centre of extreme low pressure, the air reaching a maximum velocity in a circular band extending outward between thirty and fifty kilometres from the rim of the eye. The circulations of the cyclonic winds near the eye may gust to more than 200 kilometres per hour, and the entire typhoon covers the ocean's surface and dominates the lower atmosphere over thousands of square kilometres, with the giant whirlwinds covering tens of thousands of square kilometres.

Typically, the Philippine typhoon season follows a fairly regular pattern, beginning around mid-year and hitting its peak with the strongest typhoons occurring between September and November.[28] Each year, an average of nineteen tropical cyclones work their way west from the Caroline Islands and the Marianas, their spirals of wind and rain forming at sea several thousand kilometres away before moving towards the Philippines. The typhoon belt, in which Manila and a major portion of the Philippines lies, stretches right across the Pacific through the track of the galleons to the Marianas, an appointed port of call and storm incubator. This made the trade route reaching out from China through Manila to Mexico one of the most difficult passages to navigate in the world.

There was no intensive study of the typhoon and western Pacific weather at that time and galleon pilots and navigators had to compile their own charts over the years to create reliable information about the incidence and movement of typhoons and the role of winds and ocean currents to help navigation between Manila and Acapulco. For 250 years a galleon's survival on the crossing depended on the competence of her pilot and crew and their constant vigilance and awareness of changes in the weather. Usually the force and direction of the wind and the appearance of the sea and sky were all the information the early galleon sailors had to tell them when to strike particular sails and spars and snug a vessel down under close reefs or storm sails.[29] To be caught unawares with a full spread of sail by a passing squall or sudden high wind could mean the loss of spars or canvas, while to sail close to the centre of a typhoon could spell disaster.

When a galleon sailed through the Strait of San Bernardino and moved out into the big ocean, the long journey to Acapulco of approximately 9,000 nautical miles commenced. Sailing out of sight of land required local knowledge of northern waters: of depths, rocks, reefs, the position of shifting shoals and sandbanks. Extremely important for the Spanish mariners was familiarity with the strong currents running along the Pacific coast and through the major chokepoint of the Balintang channel, which separates the China Sea from the Pacific Ocean. The currents in this passage are treacherous and when combined with high winds and sudden squalls could drag a ship far off course and even wreck it.

The navigators found it extremely difficult to sail eastward almost the length of the Pacific Ocean because the galleons could not sail straight into the trade wind, or close to the direction the wind was coming from. The best position for the navigators was to have the trade wind that pushed their sails to Mexico blowing from behind the large ship but slightly to the side. These eastbound galleons sailed far north to use the westerlies. They usually crossed the meridian of the Marianas near the Bonin Islands, ran southeast of Japan, rose to a northern parallel between 30 degrees and 40 degrees before heading eastward into the wind, and passed north of the — still unknown to the Europeans — Hawaiian Islands to a point near the Californian coast. The galleons then veered south along the American west coast for Acapulco, usually reaching the port before the end of the year in time for the great fair.[30] The annual cost of taking the "plunge" was prodigious in terms of vessels, cargo, crew, and passengers, but the prize for crossing the ocean and making landfall in Acapulco was victory over the longest, loneliest, most dangerous, and lucrative water route of the globe.

The galleons ideally sailed from the port of Cavite for Acapulco in late June or early July in order to clear the San Bernardino Strait by August when poor weather and high winds could be expected. They headed northeast. It was important for the Acapulco-bound galleons to have taken in their cargo during the month of May, in order to take advantage of the first *vendavals* (southwest monsoon) which was well established by June.[31] By sailing then, the ships ran less risk of encountering storms and would reach Acapulco one or even two months earlier.[32] Archbishop Manuel Antonio de Rojo y Vieyra, writing in the middle of the eighteenth century, also stressed late June or early July at the latest as an auspicious time for galleons to sail from the Philippines to avoid typhoons from the China Sea:

> ... the pilots believed that the course by way of Cabo Bojeador [Ilocos Norte province] was more expeditious and advantageous, if the ships left at the latest by the beginning of July; but, if it were dispatched, as usually happened, at the end of July, or in August, it was to be feared that the terrible typhoons or hurricanes of the China Sea would reach as far as the said cape and farther, and would carry it away. Consequently, it was more advisable for the said ship to pursue its voyage through the Embocadero, and the *vendavals* would be favourable to it until they left it, and farther until they reached the Marianas.[33]

As the vessel headed north-east in the months between August and September after a timely departure from Manila, there was nevertheless an extreme risk of losing the vessel and cargo in a shipwreck on the coast or at sea. Lack of rain, bone-chilling winds, heavy seas, and persistent fog and mist in certain spots on the northern leg of the journey were a hazard to galleon shipping. Rainwater was scarce on the trip northward, into the regions of severe cold and storms below Japan, and galleons that set sail for Mexico took the necessary precaution of hanging from the riggings hundreds of red clay waters jars, filled to the brim. The absolute necessity of making sure that there was enough water on board was a constant source of anxiety before the galleon reached the northern parallels and encountered the westerlies and the rainstorms that brought relief. Fresh supplies of water were collected by using large mats and bamboo tubes to funnel the rain into jars, casks and wooden barrels.[34] The icy chill and fog that could hug the waters for days turned the northern horizon into a killing ground as many crew and passengers, who were only inured to the tropical climate of the Philippines, died of pneumonia.

Typhoons and storms were often an essential part of the galleon experience, albeit frequently terrifying. Historically, typhoons have only sporadically occurred in the area five degrees on either side of the equator. But up to as many as thirty tropical cyclones have occurred annually in the western Pacific Ocean and South China Sea, due to the strong sustained winds and extreme low pressure that builds up in the Pacific Ocean.[35] It was not always possible to avoid the paths of typhoons, particularly *en route* from Manila to the annual fair in Mexico. Thirteen out of the nineteen galleons mentioned between 1568 and 1797 in Father Selga's *Charts of Remarkable Typhoons in the Philippines* were lost on the outward-bound trek to New Spain.[36] Typhoons happened quite regularly after mid-year, and much just depended on the departure time and how the crew handled the vessel in a storm.

A galleon that left Manila after the middle of July was 'practically certain' to run into rough weather within the following three months.[37] The difficulties encountered in trying to reach the meridian of the Marianas after a late departure from Cavite at the end of July was set out in an account of a fateful voyage and storm, written on the coast of Ilocos by Don Pedro de Anriondo in early November 1602. Toward the end of July, the galleon *San Antonio*, the flagship *El Espiritu Santo*, and the vice-admiral's ship *Jesus Maria* set off for New Spain. Only the galleon *San Antonio* was to complete the voyage because the other two vessels were forced to return to Cavite, battered beyond belief by typhoons. In particular, the *Espiritu Santo* encountered a strong cyclonic storm in the Pacific below Japan. Don Pedro's account of this '*baguio*' reads:

> At 25° degrees, we encountered a storm that forced us to unload everything that was on deck, and below it, up to 300 bundles and boxes. This storm lasted from 21–23 August when we were at 28° and a half. The sails were ripped and we cut the mainmast; and there were nearly 20 hand-spans of water.[38]

With the decks awash and fearing that they were going to sink, valuable cargo was jettisoned and the rapidly rising water gradually began to drain from the dark, smelly rat-infested lower decks. With great difficulty, the beleaguered galleon limped back into Cavite on 18 November 1602.

Nearly two decades later, in Geronimo de Silva's long letter to the King, dated 1 August 1621, that ranges over many topics — including the 'scandalous' adultery and death (or murder) of Governor Fajardo's wife at the hand of the Governor — the first thing that De Silva comments on is the 'many hurricanes and bad weather' that were affecting the shipping and trade between the Philippines and Mexico. The letter mentions seven typhoons in a row that pounded two outward-bound galleons on their way northeast the previous year. One ship seems to have been lost and the other returned to Manila with the crew severely traumatized:

> Last year two ships sailed out of a strait where these islands come to an end, encountered seven hurricanes, so furious that it seemed as if the sea would swallow it up; and those who were aboard gave themselves up a thousand times for lost. They tried to make port in Japan, but it was impossible; and they finally arrived at Manila, rounding Cabo de Bojeador. The men arrived in very bad condition, and many of them blinded with the salt water which had dashed into their eyes. Three days before these tempests commenced they sighted the *capitana*, but never saw her again.[39]

Juan Medina, in his history of the Augustinian order in the Philippines, tells the story of an Augustinian religious who throughout eleven typhoons "lashed to the mizzen mast, with a crucifix in his hands, consoled the crew and animated and encouraged them." Medina writes of the difficulties of keeping the galleons afloat on the eastbound track linking Manila to Acapulco because of the spate of typhoons and frightful storms, "in such a plight that they agreed to return, suffering destructive hurricanes, so that, had not the ship been so staunch, it would have been swallowed up by the sea a thousand times."[40]

In 1646, the *San Luis* sailed from Cavite with a rich cargo, the crew and passengers having ignored the bad omen signified by a raven hovering about the vessel shortly before it prepared to sail for Acapulco. But while rounding the northern coast of Luzon, before the *San Luis* had gained her altitude, a typhoon was gathering itself to deliver a fatal blow. The enveloping darkness of the storm stalked closer and closer and suddenly dashed the galleon back upon the rocky shores of Cagayan, with loss of her cargo, crew and most of her passengers.[41]

On the other hand, the wreck of the galleon *Santo Cristo de Burgos* illustrates the navigational hazards the galleons leaving the Philippines regularly encountered in the southern waters of Bikol. On 23 July 1726, the crew of the *Santo Cristo de Burgos* found themselves caught in a typhoon. Mallari describes the changing weather pattern and wind directions and the damage done to the galleon. When the vessel started to drag its anchors, it was clear to all on board that they were to be run aground on Ticao Island. According to experienced gunners Andres Philipe and Fernando de los Reyes:

> The galleon continued dragging its toothless anchors across a soft and sandy seabed. There was still hope for safety, either by weighing anchors or cutting the cables and steering into open sea and riding the storm in search of refuge in any port. But this was impossible. The galleon would be a wreck in a short time because it was close to the shore and the wind was unyielding.[42]

If a galleon left Acapulco too late it was likely to run into bad weather from the Ladrones upward.[43] A classic example of the considerable misfortune that could occur due to a late departure from Acapulco was the loss of the galleon *Nuestra Señora de la Encarnacion* in 1649 under the command of General Don Lopez Colindrico. It was overtaken by a typhoon in the San Bernardino Strait on 5 October, and wrecked on the shores of Bulan, Sorsogon, resulting in 200 deaths and the loss of all the cargo. The Augustinian Casimero Diaz bluntly stated the shipwreck occurred because "it left Acapulco too late" and "lost the better season of the brisas."[44]

One badly-battered galleon that managed to arrive after a stormy voyage from Acapulco barely could make port in Borongan, Samar. In 1655, she landed her passengers and was held by two stout cables while her cargo of 100,000 Mexican pesos was being transferred to another vessel. With the crew still on board, the cables parted in the choppy sea and the galleon drifted on the strong tide and high wind, running aground on a jagged coral reef at the mouth of the cove and breaking up, the silver going to the bottom with her. Ironically, Samareño divers were able to recover the silver but refused to give much of it to the Crown. Instead, they defiantly claimed it — and rightfully so — as their back pay for building the galleon, which had been constructed in that very same harbour. The local salvage operation flooded the Samar coast with so much Mexican silver that the price of fighting cocks rose to twenty pesos and bets at cock fights to as high as a thousand pesos.[45]

In June 1690, the galleon *Señora del Pilar de Zaragosa y Santiago* also hit a reef, but at Cocos Island on Guam's southern coast. The galleon struck the southern reef of the one hundred acre island, *en route* to the annual fair in Manila, with a shipment of silver swords and artefacts. With its bottom torn open in a typhoon, the galleon sunk in water up to twenty-seven metres deep. Its crew and some Franciscan missionaries managed to escape before it slipped off the edge into the ocean shelf.[46]

Over two and a half decades, more than forty ships were either wrecked or lost at sea, fifteen of which were westbound silver galleons, while countless other ships had to put back to port.[47] This had far-reaching consequences as all of Philippine commerce centred on the galleon trade. The islands were totally reliant on this trade and the financial aid, or *situado*, brought by the galleons from Mexico. A return to port was financially nearly as disastrous to the islands' commerce as a shipwreck. Usually, the cargo had deteriorated or had been totally ruined if much water had entered the ships' hold. It was also customary to throw goods overboard in order to lighten the ship. Even if the merchandise was saved and could be kept in good condition until next year's crossing, it could often not be transported. In some cases this was due to a lack of ships, but in most cases because a double lading was not permitted.⁴⁸

An unsuccessful voyage had a profound economic and social impact. Testimonies of contemporaries reveal how strongly the people felt the islands depended on the galleon trade, and the nervousness a non-arrival or return to port caused. The sources emphasize the importance of a timely departure to avoid storms and typhoons, and the economic impact of an unsuccessful voyage and the social anxiety it caused, with people worrying about their livelihoods and the future of the islands. When ships were lost or wrecked there was added uncertainty and grief because of family, relatives and friends that had been on board.

Jaspar Ayala, in a letter written from Manila in 1589 to Philip II, provided important early information about the possible critical impact the non-arrival of the galleons from New Spain would have on the future prosperity and well-being of Manila and the fledgling colony. He also stressed that the window of opportunity to get the ships into the archipelago before the advent of the typhoon season was quite small:

> Moreover, as I write this clause, we have had thus far no news of ships from Nueva Espana, although this is the seventh of July. The entire support of this land depends on the coming and going of the ships; and if they are not here by May or the middle of June, by delaying longer they run a great risk of being lost, and with them the welfare and support of this land. Sailing from the port of Acapulco at the beginning of March they would arrive here in good time and without risk from storms. As this is of much importance, I beseech your Majesty to be pleased to order your viceroy of Nueva Espana to exercise the utmost diligence in the early dispatch of the ships which are to come to this land, in order that they may accomplish the purpose of the voyage.⁴⁹

In his 1621 letter to the king, De Silva noted that 'God was pleased' that the year before the mastless and badly racked *Almirante* had managed to put back to Manila in distress, but lamented the fact that the typhoons had precipitated an economic crisis between Manila and Acapulco:

> That was a most severe loss for this city, since the chief sinew of its support at present is nothing but the trade of those two ships; for as the times go, there is now no other recourse. It is considered as certain that the flagship made the voyage, although there is no more certainty than trust that God had taken it to safety .... That is no little cause for anxiety to this wretched city, in addition to the ravages of enemies and other disasters that ordinarily afflict it.⁵⁰

Juan Nino de Tavora, in a 1629 letter to the King about the slowness of the ships which came from New Spain and the disadvantages of the *vendavals* for Manila-bound ships in relation to storms and the disruption to the trade, wrote:

> I shall briefly mention some general points of the government, for which I take pen in hand today, 19 July, before the arrival at this port of Cavite of the ships from Nueva Espana, or news that they have entered the islands. Consequently, we (I and all this city) are as anxious as can be imagined, as it is now so late and the *vendavals* have already set in with some vehemence. May God, in his mercy, have pity on us; and will your Majesty be pleased to urge the Viceroy of Nueva Espana, by ordering him to have the aid for these islands leave Acapulco at least by the middle of March. By that the voyage will be made certain; but if it is delayed until the last of the same month or the first of April, as has been done these last years, these islands are in evident danger or remaining without aid, and that would mean their total ruin.[51]

An unsigned letter from Cavite in 1639 recounts what happened to two ill-fated *nao* which disappeared the year before. The uncertainty regarding whether a trading ship was lost is evident in this passage. Wreckage washed up on shore gives clues to the possible fate of two galleons — but hope remains until such time as the ships are well overdue for arrival at Manila:

> We received news here, on the twenty-fifth of June, that the sea of Camarines is continually floating ashore more fragments of the wrecked ship, which some think that they recognize as belonging to the flagship .... But others are of the opinion that the wreckage shows unmistakable signs of the two ships, both flagship and *Almirante*. That casts a gloom over all the land. If that has happened (may God not have permitted), it is thought that it will be impossible for these islands to recover in many years .... Because of this, and because many have been persuaded that the two ships of the past year have been wrecked — not only because of the signs that the sea has thrown up, but because news of their arrival is so belated — there is a universal gloom and sorrow over all the country, such as it has never had before. May God in his mercy console the land.[52]

In the same year that the two ships coming from Acapulco were wrecked, 1638, the flagship *Nuestra Señora de Concepcion* sailed from Manila. It was the largest ship built up to that time. On her voyage to Acapulco she was caught by a typhoon and wrecked with a total loss of cargo and the death of nearly all the passengers near the island of Saipan in the northern Marianas. The *Sucesos de las Filipinas* describes the reaction to this news in Cavite:

As soon as the tidings were told in this port of Cavite, the sobs and cries were so many that all were stunned, for there is no one who has not lost a son, a father, a brother, a brother-in-law, a father-in-law or a husband. The loss has been one of the greatest that has ever visited these islands, because of the loss of the men and the poverty of the islands.[53]

Although almost all died when the *Nuestra Señora de Concepcion* wrecked, a few survived, as happened in other cases. It is interesting to briefly examine the consequences of such an event. In the vast expanses of the Pacific, Spanish shipwrecked survivors, perhaps with a few score of Filipino and Chinese passengers, split up into groups of castaways, hoping beyond hope to return to Manila or Acapulco. Did galleon survivors and castaways influence Polynesians? Certainly, some unknown Spanish and Chinese survivors did bring about an early and perhaps significant union of Europeans, Chinese, and Polynesians. Diaz states that the few castaways who survived the disaster of the *Concepcion* were all eventually taken back to Manila — all except one, a Chinese blacksmith, who chose to spend the rest of his life there. He acquired great influence because of his technical skills as a smith among the tiny isolated group of outer islands in the northern Marianas.

In the aftermath of the typhoon, stranded survivors made contact with distinct groups of Polynesian people in the Marianas and elsewhere and began to develop new ethnic identities and lifestyles, and possibly contributed towards fostering the creation of a Hispano-Polynesian culture in some places. The sudden presence of Spanish and Chinese castaways with their skills, inventiveness and cultural achievements, originating from a totally alien maritime world and culture, perhaps, over time, enabled cultural accommodation and borrowing, which penetrated all of the neighbouring islands.[54]

THE MANILA GALLEON TRADE AND THE TYPHOON FACTOR

The galleon trade played an all-important role in the Philippine economy and society under the Spanish. From the beginning of the seventeenth century until the mid-1760s, the export trade of the Philippines was largely restricted to the cargoes of galleons trading between Manila and Acapulco. Unlike in the Americas, the Spanish did not develop the trade potential of the agricultural or mineral resources of the islands before the nineteenth century. Instead, the Philippines was administered from Mexico and its commerce centred on the galleon trade between southeast China and Acapulco in which Manila functioned as an *entrepôt* between two continents and two vast economic empires and cultural worlds. The colonial government moreover depended on the subsidies from Mexico — transported by the galleons — for its operating costs.

The failure to exploit indigenous resources, and the investment of nearly all official, private, and church capital in the galleon trade were mutually reinforcing. Schurz, speaking about the enormous significance surrounding the trading and trafficking of this busy, bustling and sordid Manila by those who governed it notes that: 'Their only occupation and source of income were the Acapulco trade. The character of Manila society, in the wider sense of that word, was determined, beyond the circumstance of climate and situation, by conditions incidental to the all-important galleon commerce.'[55]

Loss of galleons *en route* to Manila represented financial disaster for the colony as it meant a loss of the *situado*. But whether the destination was Manila or Acapulco, an unsuccessful voyage, caused by the wrecking, capture or return to port of a ship, meant loss of trade, income and often people. Typhoons formed a major threat to the galleon trade. These storms, sometimes in combination with other factors, were responsible for a large part of the more than forty wrecks and the uncountable times ships had to return to port over the 250-year period of galleon commerce. Time and again, this caused great harm to the colony.

Six galleons were lost between 1600 and 1609. In 1603, the year of the Chinese uprising and consequent burning of the *Parian* by the Spanish in Manila, one Acapulco-bound galleon was shipwrecked and another had to return to port. The *Capitana, Nuestra Señora de los Remedios*, was driven back without a mast and jettisoned much of her cargo after having encountered severe storms. The *Almirante, San Antonio*, was lost at sea. It had carried the most valuable cargo up to that time as well as many prominent people.[56] The economic losses and the destruction of the city led many Spaniards to leave the Philippines.[57]

The period from the 1630s to the 1680s was one in which the galleon trade and thereby the Philippines suffered greatly. In the 1630s the galleon trade was not only disrupted by typhoons but also by the interfering Governor Corcuera and the overzealous cargo inspector Quiroga who "by his rigorous measures reduced the permission to terms so restricted that it was rather taking away the permission entirely than carrying out its intent."[58] On several occasions during that decade ships were not allowed to or could not sail from Manila. The departure of the great *Nuestra Señora de Concepción* in 1638 should have brought relief but ended in disaster as it was wrecked in a typhoon. The next year, two ships coming from Acapulco suffered the same fate, and although the *situado* was saved, the property of the citizens was lost, amounting to 550,000 pesos. The consequences of these interferences and losses were disastrous for the junk traffic and the commercial life of the *Parian*. At the same time, there was no relaxation of the level of taxation, which caused the 1639 Chinese uprising.[59]

Already, the galleon trade was affected by the collapse of the silver mines of Potosi after 1630 and the reduced number of Chinese trading ships reaching Manila a decade later. Speculation and investment in the galleon trade had risen dramatically in the sixteenth century and peaked in 1597, after which there were occasional lapses. A major downward trend followed in the period between the 1640s and 1680s. The Chinese junk trade to Southeast Asia in the boom years between 1570 and 1630 was followed by a slump as China slid into decline, marked by a succession crisis that ended with the overthrow of the Ming dynasty by rebels and Manchu invaders. In 1639, sixteen registered junks still sailed for Manila, while at least that many unsanctioned junks were also recorded in the Spanish port. But an average of only seven vessels a year arrived in Manila from Chinese ports in the period between 1644 and 1681.[60]

The problems confronting the Philippines as a result of the downward trend in the galleon trade between the 1640s and 1680s were compounded by the many galleon losses. In a period of fifteen years, beginning in 1638, eleven galleons were lost due to typhoons and poor seamanship. And in the three-year period from 1655 to 1657 alone, four galleons were lost.[61] These factors resulted in a state of chronic financial crisis as silver reserves were drained to pay Chinese merchants and artisans and the capital was not replaced by fresh shipments from Mexico. The repeated losses of vessels and liquid capital forced the financially-beleaguered government to increase the scale and intensity of the taxation and draft labour on the rural societies of Luzon and the Visayas.[62]

At the same time, the colonial government desperately needed for the *situado* to arrive safely from Mexico in order to survive in times marked by conflict. The Spanish colonial government was involved in a long war with the Dutch in the seventeenth century as well as in an intermittent conflict with the Iranun within the Philippines. This nearly bankrupted the colonial treasury and it relied on the *situado* to make up the annual deficits.

In the eighteenth century, typhoons again exacerbated problems for the Philippines with regards to the galleon trade. In the seven years after the capture of the *Covadonga* by Admiral Anson in 1743, there were at least three years in which no *situado* was sent. During that same period galleons leaving Manila in 1747 and 1748 had to return to port due to bad weather and another was wrecked *en route* to Acapulco in 1750 (see Appendix: Losses of the Manila–Acapulco Trade 1586–1797). A year later, wherein again no subsidies were sent, a major war broke out between Spain and Sulu, with the Iranun carrying out extensive raids, which once more caused serious financial difficulties for the Spanish colony.

In 1761, on the eve of the British occupation of Manila, the galleon *Concepcion* was lost in a storm at sea on its way to Manila. Lost with her were the 500 persons on board and the financial aid for the colony. As had been the case with typhoon sinkings a century earlier during the war against the Dutch, the sinking of the *Concepcion* left the royal treasury in Manila virtually empty and the country and people prostrate, leading Father Juan de la Concepcion to describe the wretched state of the islands as like "*un desmuyado cuerpo, sin espiritu y sin sangre*" [an unconscious body, bereft of life and spirit].[63] The following year, the galleon *Santisima Trinidad* fell into the hands of the British when putting back to Manila due to storms.[64]

Throughout time, the coffers of the Manila government were repeatedly emptied and Philippine society suffered through warfare with the Dutch or the English, the incessant struggle with the Iranun raiders, and the periodic loss or return to port of a Manila galleon due to storms and typhoons. Vessels continued to be lost at regular intervals in destructive typhoons up to 1811, when the last galleon set sail for Acapulco, while losses due to typhoons coincided with key turning points and/or helped trigger events leading to turning points in the history of the Philippines under Spain.

CONCLUSION

Manila and a major portion of the Philippines lay in a huge typhoon belt stretching right across the Pacific through the track of the galleons to the Marianas Islands, an appointed port of call, and storm incubator. In the vast uncharted reaches of the Pacific basin, an absolutely enormous area that had hardly any contact with the outside world, the giant galleons simply disappeared, never to return to Manila. Many of them either sunk in cyclonic storms at sea or were dashed to pieces along the irregular eastern coastline of the archipelago or on some far-flung Pacific reef by a typhoon.

The sudden sinking in a storm of a Manila Galleon carrying the *situado* repeatedly highlighted the chronic, albeit critical, nature of the Philippine's vulnerability and dependence, foreshadowing possible economic disaster for the colony. Some of the most acute moments in the early history of the Spanish colonial project in the Philippines coincided with the tightly-spaced losses of a series of galleons in cyclonic storms. The impact of these destructive typhoons immediately erased all signs of communication and commerce between Mexico, China and the Philippines and left colonial society in the Philippines impoverished, facing calamity.

Notes

1. I am indebted to Maaike Mintjes, my research assistant, for her valuable comments, criticisms and encouragement in helping me revise this paper for the Festschrift. There are few published sources of information on the subject of the Manila Galleons. The standard work first published in 1939 is William Lytle Schurz, *The Manila Galleon* (New York: E.P. Dutton, 1959); Rafael Arenas Diaz, *Memoria sobre el Comercio y Navegacion de las Islas Filipinas* (Cadiz: Imprenta de D. Féros, 1838); John D. Hayes, "The Manila Galleons", in *United States Naval Institute Proceedings*, LX (1934): 1689–96; *Métode que se observa constantemente en México, Acapulco y Manila para recibir y despachar todos los años el galeon de filipinas.* (Cadiz: 1763). See also Justin Winsor, ed., *Narrative and Critical History of America, Vol. 2 Discoveries of the Pacific Coast of North America* (Cambridge: Haughton, Mifflin and Company, 1886). Articles on galleons shipwrecked trading between Manila and Acapulco have become an essential source of information. See Eugene Lyons, "Track of the Manila Galleons", *National Geographic Magazine* 178, no. 3 (September 1990): 5–37; and William Mathers, "The *Nuestra Senora de la Concepcion*," *National Geographic Magazine* 178, no. 3 (September 1990): 39–52.
2. W. Cameron Forbes, *The Philippine Islands* (Cambridge MA.: Harvard University Press, 1945), pp. 20–21. See also Francis Henry Hill Guillemard, *The Life of Ferdinand Magellan and the First Circumnavigation of the Globe, 1480–1521* (London: G. Philip and son, 1890); Stefan Zweig et al, *Conqueror of the Seas: The Story of Magellan* (New York: Viking Press, 1938); and Laurence Bergreen, *Over the Edge of the World: Magellan's Terrifying Circumnavigation of the Globe* (Hammersmith: Harper Perennial, 2003).
3. Horacio de la Costa, S.J., *Readings in Philippine History* (Manila: Bookmark, 1965), pp. 16–17. See also Antonio Pigafetta, "Primo Viaggio Intorno al Mondo", in *The Philippine Islands* 55 vols, edited by E.H. Blair and J.A. Robertson (Cleveland: Clark, 1903-9) (henceforth *BRPI*) 33, pp. 175–81.
4. Guillermard, *Life of Ferdinand Magellan*, pp. 297, 310; Schurz, *The Manila Galleon*, pp. 20–21.
5. Eugene Lyon notes in his 1990 article on the route of the Manila Galleons that the navigator of the *San Lucas* had already found the successful track shortly before Urdaneta piloted the *San Pablo* along the route, but that the Spanish court credited Urdaneta with the discovery of the track. See Schurz, *The Manila Galleon*, pp. 219–20.
6. "Verdadero relacion de la grandeza del Reyno de China, con las cosas mas notables de ella, por Miguel de Loarca, soldado, uno de dos que fueron alla desde las Islas de Luzon que aora llaman Philipinas; ano de 1575," in *Catálogo*

de los documentos relativos a las Islas Filipinas existentes en el Archivo de Indias de Sevilla. Por D. Pedro Torres·y Lanzas ... Precedido de una ... Historia general de Filipinas desde los primeros descubrimientos ... hasta la muerte de Legazpi, edited by Pablo Pastells (Barcelona: Imprenta Viuda de Luis Tasso, 1925), Vol. I, pp. 27–29.

7. Fedor Jagor, *Travels in the Philippines* (Manila: Filipiniana Book Guild, 1965), p. 4.
8. Frederick L. Wernstedt and Joseph E. Spencer, *The Philippine Island World: A Physical, Cultural and Regional Geography* (Berkeley: University of California Press, 1967), p. 384; Nick Joaquin, *Manila My Manila* (Manila: Bookmark, 1999), pp. 3–8.
9. Robert R. Reed, "Hispanic Urbanism in the Philippines: A Study of the Impact of Church and State", in *Journal of East Asiatic Studies* 2, no. 1 (March 1967): 1–222; Joaquin, *Manila My Manila*, pp. 55–60; Manuel A. Caoili, *The Origins of Metropolitan Manila: A Political and Social Analysis* (Quezon City: University of the Philippines Press, 1999).
10. Schurz, *The Manila Galleon*, p. 251.
11. Ibid., pp. 154–92; Anthony Reid, *Southeast Asia in the Age of Commerce 1450–1680, vol. 2* (New Haven: Yale University Press, 1993), pp. 22–23.
12. José Algue, S.J., *The Cyclones of the Far East* (Manila: Department of the Interior, Bureau of Public Printing, 1904); Wernstedt and Spencer, *The Philippine Island World*, p. 384.
13. Schurz, *The Manila Galleon*, p. 13.
14. Ibid., pp. 79–83; Jaquet Amyot, S.J., *The Manila Chinese* (Manila: Ateneo de Manila University Press, 1973); Edgar Wickberg, *The Chinese in Philippine Life* (New Haven: Yale University Press, 1965), pp. 3–44; Joaquin, *Manila My Manila*, pp. 65–70.
15. Reid, *Southeast Asia in the Age of Commerce, vol. 2*, p. 273.
16. Caoili, *The Origins of Metropolitan Manila*, p. 25; see also Fernand Braudel, *Civilization and Capitalism 15th–18th Centuries*, vol. 1 (New York: Harper and Row, 1979), pp. 267–68.
17. For example, on the advent of stone and lime structures in the Philippines with particular reference to the Batanes Islands, see Florentino H. Hornado, *Taming the Wind: Ethno-Cultural History on the Ivatan of the Batanes Isles* (Manila: University of Santo Tomas Publishing House, 2000), pp. 62–66; Norma I. Alarcon, *Philippine Architecture during the Pre-Spanish and Spanish Periods* (Manila: University of Santo Tomas Publishing House, 1991). See also, René B. Javellana, "The Colonial Townscape" in *Kasasayan: The Story of the Filipino People, Vol. 3: The Spanish Conquest*, edited by José S. Arcilla (Manila: Asia Publishing House, 1998).
    José S. Arcilla, S.J., "The Colonial Townscape", in *Kasaysayan* 3 (Manila: Asia Publishing Company, 1998), pp. 66–79.
18. Schurz, *The Manila Galleon*, pp. 195–96.

19. Ibid., pp. 83–90; Wickberg, *The Chinese in Philippine Life 1850–1898*, pp. 9–10.
20. Schurz, *The Manila Galleon*, p. 182; Lyon, "Track of the Manila Galleon", pp. 11–14.
21. Schurz, *The Manila Galleon*, p. 155.
22. Ibid.
23. Galleons sometimes carried 6000–7000 *piezas*, while the *San Jose* sunk with 12,000 "packages" in her hold (ibid., p. 158).
24. Schurz, *The Manila Galleon*, pp. 216–50; Lyon, "Track of the Manila Galleon", pp. 28–34.
25. "Aids to Navigation in Philippine Waters", in *Manila Harbour Board Report, 1934* (Manila: Government of the Philippine Islands, 1934), p. 5; Commander Robert F. Luce, "Brief History of Hydrographic Survey Work in the Philippine Archipelago", in *Manila Harbour Board Annual Report 1934*, p. 9.
26. Algue, *The Cyclones of the Far East*, pp. 16–23, 90–91, 237–68; Wernstedt and Spencer, *The Philippine Island World*, pp. 50–52.
27. See Isaac Monroe Cline, *Tropical Cyclones* (New York: The MacMillan Co., 1926); Henry Piddington, *The Sailors Hornbook for the Law of Storms* (London: F. Norgate, 1876); Ivan Ray Tannehill, *Hurricanes: Their Nature and History* (Princeton: Princeton University Press, 1956).
28. Algue, *The Cyclones of the Far East*, pp. 86–88.
29. Letter from Fleet Admiral Chester W. Nimitz to Pacific Fleet and Naval Shore Activities, 13 February 1945, "Damage in a Typhoon, Lessons of", Archives of the Manila Observatory (AMO), Fr Miguel Selga's Papers, Box 57, item 7.
30. Schurz, *The Manila Galleon*, pp. 216–46; Lyon, "Track of the Manila Galleon", pp. 12–13.
31. Schurz, *The Manila Galleon*, p. 217.
32. Antonio de Morga, "Sucesos de las Islas Filipinas" (Mexico, 1609), in *BRPI* 15, p. 174.
33. Archbishop Manuel Antonio de Rojo y Vieyra, "Rojo's Narrative, Manila 1763", in *BRPI* 49, p. 198.
34. Percy A. Hill, *Romance and Adventure in Old Manila* (Manila: Filipiniana Book Guild, 1964), p. 178; Lyon, "Track of the Manila Galleon", p. 38.
35. Algue, *The Cyclones of the Far East*.
36. Miguel Selga, *Charts of Remarkable Typhoons in the Philippines 1348–1934* (Manila: Bureau of Printing, 1935).
37. Schurz, *The Manila Galleon*, p. 252.
38. Selga, *Charts of Remarkable Typhoons in the Philippines 1348–1934*, 21–22 August 1602.
39. "News from the Province of Filipinas, this Year, 1621, Alonso Roman", in *BRPI* 20, p. 34.
40. Juan de Medina, O.S.A., "History of the Augustinian Order in the Filipinas Islands, 1630" (printed at Manila, 1893), in *BRPI* 24, pp. 53, 160–61.

41. Hill, *Romance and Adventure in Old Manila*, p. 110.
42. Francisco Mallari, "The Wreck of Santo Cristo De Burgos", in *Vignettes of Bicol History* (Quezon City: New Day Publishers, 1992), pp. 72–73.
43. Schurz, *The Manila Galleon*, p. 281.
44. Casimiro Diaz, O.S.A., "The Augustinians in the Philippines, 1641–1670", extracts from his *Conquests of the Filipinas Islands and Chronicle of the Religious of our Father St. Augustine* (Manila: 1718) in *BRPI* 37, p. 180.
45. William Henry Scott, *Barangay: Sixteenth Century Philippine Culture and Society* (Manila: Ateneo de Manila Press, 1994), p. 112.
46. The government of Guam has a claim on the 300 year-old wreck. The salvaging rights to the *Pilar* were awarded to a marine archaeologist Duncan Mathewson. The story of the Spanish Galleon and the marine archaeologists that have been excavating the sunken hull of the *Pilar* has been a regular feature in a documentary for the Science Frontier series by the Discovery Channel.
47. Schurz, *The Manila Galleon*, pp. 251–83; Lyon, "Track of the Manila Galleon", p. 18.
48. Schurz, *The Manila Galleon*, p. 261.
49. Letter from Santiago de Vera to Philip II, Manila, 13 June 1589, in *BRPI* 7, pp. 134–35.
50. Letter from Geronimo de Silva to the King, Manila, 1 August 1621, in *BRPI* 20, p. 106.
51. Letter from Juan Niño de Tavera to Philip II, Cavite, 1 August 1629, in *BPRI* 23, p. 47.
52. "Events in Philipinas, 1638–39" (unsigned, probably Juan Lopez, 1639), in *BPRI* 29, pp. 166–68.
53. Selga, *Charts of Remarkable Typhoons in the Philippines 1348–1934*, 20 September 1638; William Mathers and his team successfully salvaged the galleon, *Nuestra Senora de la Concepción*, which foundered on 20 September 1638 in the Saipan Channel in the northern Marianas. See Mathers, "Nuestra Senora de la Concepción", pp. 40–53. The article includes remarkable close-up photographs of recovered gold jewellery.
54. Robert Langdon has explored the possible impact of sixteenth century Spanish castaways on the pre-Cook history of the eastern Pacific. See Robert Langdon, *The Lost Caravel* (Sydney: Pacific Publications, 1975).
55. Schurz, *The Manila Galleon*, p. 38.
56. Ibid., pp. 258–59.
57. Lyon, "Track of the Manila Galleon", p. 17.
58. "Commerce between the Philippines and Nueva Espana" (from the *Extracto Historial*), in *BRPI* 30, p. 50.
59. Juan de la Concepcion, *Historia General de Philipinas* (Manila: A. de la Rosa y Balagtas 1788) 5, p. 429. See also "Relation of the Insurrection of the Chinese" in *BRPI* 29, pp. 208–58.
60. Reid, *Southeast Asia in the Age of Commerce, vol. 2*, p. 273.

61. Lyon, "Track of the Manila Galleon", p. 18.
62. See J. H. Parry, *The Spanish Seaborne Empire* (Penguin, 1973), p. 222; and C.R. Boxer "Plata es Sangre: Sidelights on the Drain of Spanish-American Silver in the Far East", in *Philippine Studies* 18 (1970): 457–75.
63. Juan de la Concepcion, *Historia General de Philipinas* 7, pp. 3–11.
64. Schurz, *The Manila Galleon*, p. 261.

References

Alarcon, Norma I. *Philippine Architecture during the Pre-Spanish and Spanish Periods*. Manila: University of Santo Tomas Publishing House, 1998.

Algue, José, S.J. *The Cyclones of the Far East*. Manila: Department of the Interior, Bureau of Public Printing, 1904.

Amyot, Jaques. *The Manila Chinese*, Manila: Ateneo de Manila University Press, 1973.

Archives of the Manila Observatory, Fr. Miguel Selga's Papers, Box 57.

Bergreen, Laurence. *Over the Edge of the World: Magellan's Terrifying Circumnavigation of the Globe*. Hammersmith: Harper Perennial, 2003.

Boxer, C.R. "Plata es Sangre: Sidelights on the Drain of Spanish American Silver in the Far East". *Philippine Studies* 18 (1970): 457–75.

———. *The Dutch Seaborne Empire*. London: Penguin, 1973.

Blair, E.H. and J. Robertson, eds. *The Philippine Islands, 1493–1803*, 55 vols. Cleveland: Arthur H. Clark, 1903–9.

Burt, Wayne V. "The Search for the Manila Galleon Log Books", *Bulletin of the American Meteorological Society* 71, no. 11 (November 1990): 1630–1630.

Cano, Gaspar O.S.A., *Catalogo de los religiosos de N.P.S. Agustin de la Provincia del Smo Nombre de Jesus de Filipinas desde su estabilcimiento en estas islas hasta nuestros dias*, vol. XXXX (Manila: 1864.

Caoili, Manuel A. *The Origins of Metropolitan Manila: A Political and Social Analysis*. Quezon City: University of the Philippines Press, 1999.

Cline, Isaac Monroe. *Tropical Cyclones*. New York: The MacMillan Co., 1926.

Concepcion, Juan de la. *Historia General de Philipinas*, 14 vols. Manila: A. de la Rosa y Balagtas, 1788.

Costa, Horacio de la. *Readings in Philippine History*. Manila: Bookmark, 1965.

———. *The Jesuits in the Philippines, 1581–1768*. Cambridge, MA: Harvard University Press, 1967.

Diaz, Rafael Arenas. *Memoria sobre el Comercio y Navegacion de las Islas Filipinas*. Cadiz, Imprenta de D. Féros, 1838.

Forbes, Cameron W. *The Philippine Islands*. Cambridge: Harvard University Press, 1945.

Garcia, Rolando R. et al, "Atmospheric Circulation Changes in the Tropical Pacific Inferred from the Voyages of the Manila Galleons in the Sixteenth-Eighteenth Centuries", in *Bulletin of the American Meteorological Society* 82, no. 11 (November 2001): 2435–56.

Guillemard, Francis Henry Hill. *The Life of Ferdinand Magellan and the First Circumnavigation of the Globe, 1480–1521*. London: G. Philip and son, 1890.

Hayes, John D. "The Manila Galleons". *United States Naval Institute Proceedings*, LX (1934): 1689–96.

Hill, Percy A. *Romance and Adventure in Old Manila*. Manila: Filipiniana Book Guild, 1964.

Hornedo, Florentino. *Taming the Wind: Ethno-Cultural History on the Ivatan of the Batanes Isles*. Manila: University of Santo Tomas Publishing House, 2000.

Jagor, Fedor. *Travels in the Philippines*. Manila: Filipiniana Book Guild, 1965.

Javellana, René B. "The Colonial Townscape". In *Kasasayan: The Story of the Filipino People Vol. 3: The Spanish Conquest*, edited by José S. Arcilla. pp. 66–74. Manila: Asia Publishing House, 1998.

Joaquin, Nick. *Manila My Manila*. Manila: Bookmark, 1999.

Langdon, Robert. *The Lost Caravel*. Sydney: Pacific Publications, 1975.

Lyon, Eugene. "Track of the Manila Galleons". *National Geographic Magazine* 178, no. 3 (1990): 5–37.

Mallari, Francisco. "The Wreck of *Santo Cristo De Burgos*". In his *Vignettes of Bicol History*. Manila: New Day Publishers, 1999.

Manila Harbour Board Report 1934. Manila: Bureau of Public Printing, 1934.

Mathers, William. "The *Nuestra Senora De La Concepción*". *National Geographic Magazine* 178, no. 3 (1990): 39–52.

Métode que se observa constantamente en México, Acapulco y Manila para recibir y despachar todos los años el galeon de filipinas. Cadiz: 1763.

Moyano, Jose Cosona. *Filipinas y su real Hacienda (1750–1800)*. Cordoba: Montre de peidad y Caya de Aborros de Cordoba, 1986.

Noone, Martin J. *General History of the Philippines, Part 1, Vol. 1, The Discovery and Conquest of the Philippines (1521–1581)*, Manila: Historical Conservation Society, 1984.

Pastells, Pablo et al. *Catálogo de los documentos relativos a las Islas Filipinas existentes en el Archivo de Indias de Sevilla. Por D. Pedro Torres·y Lanzas ... Precedido de una ... Historia general de Filipinas desde los primeros descubrimientos ... hasta la muerte de Legazpi*. Barcelona: Imprenta Viuda de Luis Tasso, 1925).

Piddington, Henry. *The Sailors Hornbook for the Law of Storms*. London: F. Norgate, 1876.

Quirino, Carlos and Abraham Laygo. *Regesto Guion Catalogo de los Documentos Existantes en Mexico sobre Filipinas*. Manila: El Comite de Amsitad Filipino-Mexicana, 1965.

Reed, Robert R. "Hispanic Urbanism in the Philippines: A Study of the Impact of Church and State". *Journal of East Asian Studies* 2, no. 1 (1967): 1–222.

Reid, Anthony. *Southeast Asia in the Age of Commerce 1450–1680: Vol. Two, Expansion and Crisis*. New Haven: Yale University Press, 1993.

Scott, William Henry. *Barangay: Sixteenth Century Philippine Culture and Society*. Manila: Ateneo de Manila Press, 1999.

Schurz, William Lytle, *The Manila Galleon*. New York: E.P. Dutton & Co., 1959.
Selga, Miguel. *Charts of Remarkable Typhoons in the Philippines 1902–1934: Catalogue of Typhoons 1348–1934*. Manila Bureau of Printing, 1935.
Díaz-Trechuelo Spinola, María Lourdes, "Dos Nuevos Derroteros del Galeon de Manila (1730 y 1773)", in *Annuario de Estudios Americanes* 13 (1956): 1–83.
Tannehill, Ivan Ray. *Hurricanes: Their Nature and History*. Princeton: Princeton University Press, 1956.
Wernstedt, Frederick L. and J.E. Spencer. *The Philippine Island World: A Physical, Cultural and Regional Geography*. Berkeley: University of California Press, 1967.
Wickberg, Edgar. *The Chinese in Philippine Life 1850–1898*. New Haven: Yale University Press, 1965.
Winsor, Justin (ed.). *Narrative and Critical History of America*. Cambridge MA.: Haughton, Mifflin and Company, 1886.
Zweig, Stefan et al. *Conqueror of the Seas: The Story of Magellan*. New York, Viking Press, 1938.

APPENDIX: LOSSES OF THE MANILA-ACAPULCO TRADE 1568–1806

Year	Embarkation Date	Place	Ship(s) affected	Commander	Affected by	Fate of ship(s)/crew and passengers/cargo
1568	1 June	Cebu	Nao capitana	Felipe de Salcedo	Typhoon on 15 August	Heavy storm carried ship out of port of Guam and dashed it against the coast, smashing it to pieces. Commander and majority of the passengers (ship had 130 persons on board) had landed. Total loss of cargo, including great quantity of cinnamon[1]
1572	13 August	Manila	*Santiago* and *San Juan*		Typhoon	Returned to port because of stormy weather.[2]
1576		Acapulco				Lost *en route*, all people killed.[3]
1576	Early in year		*Espiritu Santo*		Typhoon	Wrecked at Catanduanes Island (could be the same incident as above).[4]
1578		Manila				Lost *en route*.[5]
1580		Manila	*San Juanillo*	Don Juan Ronquillo del Castillo	Unknown	Returned to Manila in very bad condition.[6]
1590	1 March	Acapulco			Typhoon between March and June	Dismasted by typhoon and wrecked on coast of Marinduque. No lives were lost.[7]
1591	25 March	Acapulco	*San Idelfonso*			Lost at sea.[8]
1593		Manila	*San Felipe* and *San Francisco*			Ships put back in distress, one in Manila, one at island of Zebre, very much crippled and wrecked.[9]

Year	Embarkation Date	Place	Ship(s) affected	Commander	Affected by	Fate of ship(s)/crew and passengers/cargo
1596	12 July	Manila	Galleon *San Felipe*	General D. Matias de Sandecho	Typhoons on 18 & 25 September, and 3–8 October in latitude of Japan	The ship was diverted from its course by typhoons. On 18 September hurricane waves carried away the binnacle, steering gear and galley, destroying the sails and helm main. On 25 September the lower deck was damaged. On 3 October a typhoon of 5-day duration "forced the galleon without masts and sails, towed by 200 *funcas*, to the dangerous shores of Chopongame, where she was stranded and filled with water up to the first deck." It fell into the hands of the enemies on the coast of Japan. There were 300 persons on board, among them 7 clergy. Six persons drowned on 18 September. Chaplain Fray Felipe de Jeses o de las Casas and companions of the same Institute were put to death at Nagasaki. Cargo would have been worth more than 1.3 million pesos in Mexico.[10]
1600		Manila	*San Geronimo*, *Santa Margarita*		Typhoon	Ships lost their mast in a storm. *Santa Margarita* drifted to island of Ladrones. *San Geronimo* drifted to Luzon, near Catanduanes Island, and was driven ashore on 1 February 1601.[11]

1601	Acapulco	*Santo Tomas*		Typhoon on 1 May	Missed San Bernardino Strait, carried by currents towards Catanduanes, while lying at anchor in a bay a hurricane tore the ship away from its moorings.[12]
1602	Manila	Captain's ship, *El Espiritu Santo*, Admiral's ship, *Jesus Maria*		Typhoon in the Pacific, 21–23 August	Ships had to return to Cavite much damaged by storms. The sails of *El Espiritu Santo* were destroyed and they had cut down the mast. Both ships returned almost without crew or cargo. *El Espiritu Santo* had to lighten the ship of everything on top deck and 300 boxes and bales from below deck.[13]
1603	Manila	*Magdalena*		Bad conditions, uneven load	Ship turned over on her side at her moorings before leaving Cavite as she was ready to clear from port.[14]
1603 June	Manila	*Capitana Nuestra Senora de los Remedios, Almiranta San Antonio*		Typhoons	The capitana was driven back to Manila mastless, the almiranta was lost at sea. All on board, including many prominent people, were lost on *San Antonio*. Huge wealth lost with *San Antonio*, the capitana also lost much of her cargo.[15]
1604	Acapulco	Almiranta (*San Diego?*)			Did not manage to follow flagship into Cavite and remained on the shoal of Mindoro for a month which caused great loss."[16]
1608	Manila	Flagship	Juan Tello de Aguirre		Ship was wrecked 100 leagues from Manila.[17]

Year	Embarkation Date	Place	Ship(s) affected	Commander	Affected by	Fate of ship(s)/crew and passengers/cargo
1609	July	Manila	Almiranta *San Andres*, flagship *San Francisco*, *Santa Ana*	Juan Ezquerra	Typhoons	All three ships encountered storms, only the almiranta completed the voyage, the *Santa Ana* reached Japan almost entirely dismantled and the *San Francisco* was wrecked on the coast of Japan.[18]
1616–7		Manila				All four galleons returned to port.[19]
1620	4 April	Acapulco	*San Nicolas de Tolentino*, patache *Nuestra Senora del Rosario*	Fernando de Ayala on *San Nicolas*	Encounter with Dutch and a typhoon near Samar on 2 August	*San Nicolas* was wrecked near Borongan by storm, after battle with the Dutch, the patache foundered near Palapag. Little of the cargo of *San Nicolas* was lost.[20]
1620	Aug.	Manila	Flagship *Nuestra Senora de la Vida*, almiranta	Don Fernando Centeno	Bad pilot on flagship, typhoons	The flagship was lost on reef through the fault of the pilot, who was then hanged by the passengers. The almiranta returned to port badly racked and dismasted — many hurricanes and bad weather on high seas.[21]
1621		Manila	*San Nicolas*			Lost with 330 persons.[22]
1629	4 August[23]	Manila	Almiranta and *San Juan*		Typhoons	The almiranta had to cut down its mast, lost the rudder, and returned to Cavite. The *San Juan* made it to Valdebanderas: 99 died.[24]
1631		Manila	*Santa Maria Magdalena*			Sank in port of Cavite, 13 drowned and all cargo was lost.[25]

Year	Port	Ship	Event	Description
1638	Manila	Flagship *Nuestra Señora de la Concepción*	Typhoon in the Pacific on 20 September	Wrecked near the island of Rota, Mariana Islands. Death of almost all passengers, people drowned or were killed by the natives, one of the greatest losses in men. Flagship was largest ship built till then, total loss of cargo. Ship "contained the greatest wealth of the islands," great loss because of the poverty of the islands.[26]
1638 Aug.	Manila	Almiranta *San Ambrosio*		Wrecked on coast of Paracali (could have belonged to the flagship *Concepción*, above).[27]
1639	Manila	2 ships	Typhoon over China Sea and western Luzon, on 5 August	Out of 5 ships, 2 foundered near Cavite, 600 Chinese died.[28]
1639	Acapulco	*San Ambrosio* and another ship	Typhoon over China Sea and western Luzon, on 5 August	Both ships wrecked on the coast of Vigan, Cagayan; 150 persons lost. The *situado* was saved as it had been taken out earlier, but the property of the citizens was lost, amounting to 550 thousand pesos.[29]
1643	Manila	Flagship *San Luis*		Flagship returned to port dismasted.[30]
1646	Manila			Wrecked on coast of Cagayan on 25 July 1646.[31]
1649	Acapulco	Nao *Nuestra Señora de la Encarnación*	Typhoon in San Bernardino Strait on 5 October	Overtaken in San Bernardino Strait, wrecked on shores of Bulan, Sorsogon. Over 200 persons lost and all cargo.[32]
1650	Manila			Returned to port.[33]

Year	Embarkation Date	Place	Ship(s) affected	Commander	Affected by	Fate of ship(s)/crew and passengers/cargo
1650	1 April	Acapulco	Nuestra Senora de Guia			Almost wrecked, great loss and damage to goods carried.[34]
1651		Manila	San Diego			Put back to port.[35]
1654	22 February	Acapulco	San Diego		Typhoon between San Bernardino Strait and Manila, on 29 or 30 May.	Wrecked not far from Manila. "The storm lasted 15 days and caused unbelievable sufferings to the survivors." All people and cargo saved.[36]
1655		Acapulco	San Francisco Xavier			Wrecked in Borongan on 19 October 1655.[37]
1656		Manila	2 ships			Put back to port.[38]
1663		Manila	San Sabiniano			Reached Manila again after 7 months.[39]
1666		Manila	2 ships			Returned to port, failed to make the voyage.[40]
1669		Cavite & Lampon	Almiranta Nuestra Senora del Buen Socorro, flagship San Diego	Almiranta: Diego de Arevalo; flagship: Don Francisco Vizcarra		Both ships returned to port. The Almiranta sailed from Cavite and put back at Lampon, the flagship sailed from Lampon and put back at Cavite.[41]
1672		Manila	San Telmo	General Antonio Nieto	Probably typhoons	Put back to port.[42]
1681		Manila	Santa Rosa			Returned to port.[43]
1682		Manila	Santa Rosa		Typhoons	Ship forced back to Manila because of storms and consequent damage.[44]
1687		Manila	Santo Nino	Lucas Mateo Urquina	Typhoons	Ship was not very strong, fierce storms compelled it to seek port and it wintered in Bagatoa. Returned with cargo half rotten.[45]

Year	Date	Origin	Ship	Captain	Cause	Notes
1690	20 March	Acapulco	Almiranta Nuestra Senora del Pilar de Zaragoza			Ship lost in Marianas, all people saved, cargo partly lost.[46]
1692		Manila	Santo Christo de Burgos	General Don Bernardo Ignacio del Bayo	Typhoons	Ship had to put back to Sorsogon 'after having endured great tempests.'[47]
1693		Manila	Santo Christo de Burgos			Ship was wrecked (according to Schurz it burned in the open sea, other sources say cause is unknown).[48]
1694		Manila	San Jose, the largest galleon built in the Philippines		Typhoon on 3 or 4 July near Mariveles	Ship ran aground on island of Luban, shattered to pieces. Over 400 people died, among them Fr Predo de Cassanova, old missionary of Visayas, bound for Madrid and Rome as Procurator General of the Philippines. Total loss of very valuable cargo, over 12,000 *piezas* destroyed.[49] Never seen again, everything lost.[50]
1705		Manila	San Francisco Xavier galleon Santo Cristo de Burgos			
1726		Manila			Typhoon on 23 July	Wrecked on rocks of Ticao Island, it could not be repaired and crew burnt the ship and its contents of which a great part had been ruined by water. 'This was a great loss to the citizens of Manila, as all their investments for this year were thus destroyed.'[51]
1730	9 March	Acapulco	Sacra Familia			Lost in Mindoro on 9 November 1730.[52]
1735		Acapulco	San Cristobal			Wrecked near entrance of San Bernardino Strait on 29 or 30 June 1735.[53]
1750	June/July	Manila	Nuestra Senora del Pilar	Ignacio Martinez de Faura	Bad conditions.[54]	

Year	Embarkation Date	Place	Ship(s) affected	Commander	Affected by	Fate of ship(s)/crew and passengers/cargo
1762	1 August	Manila	Santisima Trinidad alias Nuestra Senora del Buen Fin		Storms and English	Had to return to Manila and was captured by the English in the San Bernardino Strait. Ship was sold by the English in 1763.[55]
1768	3 August	Manila	San Carlos		Typhoons on 8–10 September and 29 September	Ship was buffeted by two typhoons in the Pacific, forced to return to Cavite. "The sufferings on board ship were unbelievable." One of the 64 exiled Jesuits on board died.[56]
1770	17 August	Manila	Frigata San Jose			Awaited favourable winds in San Jacinto, Ticao, but had to return to Cavite on 29 October 1770.[57]
1772	14 July	Manila	San Carlos alias A. Burro Mio			Ship returned to port after 105 days.[58]
1775	17 April or 19 April	Manila	Nuestra Senora de la Concepcion			Wrecked in Marianas.[59]
1782	June	Manila	San Pedro alias el Caviteno			Lost north of Luzon.[60]
1795		Manila	San Andres boat			Returned to port.[61]
1797		Acapulco			Typhoon of 21–22 April	Caught in storm.[62]
1797		Manila	Frigate Santa Maria		Typhoon of 21–22 April	Ship sunk, cargo saved.[63]

Year	Date	Location	Ship	Owner	Event	Notes
1797 or 1798		Manila	Ship *San Andres*	D. Manuel Lecaroz, merchant of Manila	Typhoon in October	*San Andres* wrecked on the Naranjo Islands, near San Bernardino Strait, between Ticao and Capul Islands. Crew saved but (part of) the valuable cargo lost.[64]
1806	11 December	Manila	*Esperanza*			Ship sunk, people saved but cargo lost
1806		Manila	*El Magallenes* alias *San Fernando*	Angel Crespo		Ship had to retreat to Manila.[65]

Notes: With the exception of that from Selga's *Charts of Remarkable Typhoons in the Philippines 1902–1934* and Noone's *General History of the Philippines*, the data was taken from the citations and sources found on <www.mrcstudios.com/bruce>, accessed 27 September 2003. This website is no longer available, but has been updated as <http://home.windstream.net/cr33856>. While I have relied on the quotations and sources as listed on the site, the conclusions I have drawn from these occasionally differ from the conclusions on the site.

Notes

1. Selga, *Charts of Remarkable Typhoons*.
2. *BRPI*, pp. 239–41; 34, p. 256; Schurz, *The Manila Galleon*, p. 251.
3. Gaspar Cano, O.S.A., *Catalogo de los religiosos de N.P.S. Agustin de la Provincia del Smo Nombre de Jesus de Filipinas desde su estabilcimiento en estas islas hasta nuestros dias*, Manila, vol. XXXX, 1864: p. 14; Schurz, *The Manila Galleon*, p. 258.
4. Martin J. Noone, S.S.C., *General History of the Philippines, Part 1, Vol. 1, The Discovery and Conquest of the Philippines (1521–1581)*, Manila: Historical Conservation Society, 1984, p. 444, from *The United States and Its Territories, 1870–1925: The Age of Imperialism*, The University of Michigan Collection, online <www.hti.umich.edu/p/philamer>, accessed 5 April 2007.
5. *BRPI* 27, p. 187.
6. Ibid.
7. Horacio de la Costa, S.J., *The Jesuits in the Philippines, 1581–1768*, Cambridge, MA: Harvard University Press, 1967, p. 121.
8. Rolando R. Garcia et al, "Atmospheric Circulation Changes in the Tropical Pacific Inferred from the Voyages of the Manila Galleons in the Sixteenth-Eighteenth Centuries", in *Bulletin of the American Meteorological Society* 82, no. 11 (November 2001): 2435–56, p. 2439, online <http://ams.allenpress.com>, accessed 5 April 2007.
9. *BRPI* 27, p. 190; Schurz, *The Manila Galleon*, p. 261.
10. Selga, *Charts of Remarkable Typhoons in the Philippines*.
11. Ibid.
12. Ibid.
13. Ibid; *BRPI* 27, p. 192; Schurz, *The Manila Galleon*, p. 261.
14. Schurz, *The Manila Galleon*, p. 257.
15. Schurz, *The Manila Galleon*, pp. 258–59, *BRPI* 16, p. 45, *BRPI* 27, p. 193.
16. *BRPI* 13, p. 221.
17. *BRPI* 27, p. 194.
18. *BRPI* 17, pp. 132–37; *BRPI* 27, p. 194.
19. Schurz, *The Manila Galleon*, p. 261.
20. Selga and Schurz say the patache foundered, other sources say it was safe. See Selga, *Charts of Remarkable Typhoons in the Philippines*; *BRPI* 19, pp. 91–93; R.R. Garcia et al., "Atmospheric Circulation Changes in the Tropical Pacific", pp. 11–12; Schurz, *The Manila Galleon*, p. 348.
21. *BRPI* 20, p. 106; *BRPI* 27, p. 194; Schurz, *The Manila Galleon*, p. 258.
22. Schurz, *The Manila Galleon*, p. 259.
23. Selga, *Charts of Remarkable Typhoons in the Philippines*: Ships left on 1 August 1629, returned to Philippines after 7 months of unsuccessful efforts to cross the Pacific, due to typhoons.
24. *BRPI* 24, pp. 160–61.
25. *BRPI* 27, p. 197.
26. Selga, *Charts of Remarkable Typhoons in the Philippines*; Schurz, *The Manila Galleon*, p. 259.
27. *BRPI* 29, p. 157.
28. Selga, *Charts of Remarkable Typhoons in the Philippines*.
29. Schurz, *The Manila Galleon*, p. 259 states the *San Ambrosio* lost 150 persons. According to Steve Singer, 2 million silver pesos were lost. See Singer, "The Manila Galleons",

in *Treasure Expeditions*, 1999–2007, online <http://www.treasureexpeditions.com/The-Manila-Galleons.htm>, accessed 5 April 2007. See also Selga, *Charts of Remarkable Typhoons in the Philippines*; BRPI 29, p. 196; Garcia et al, "Atmospheric Circulation Changes in the Tropical Pacific", p. 2446.

30. *BRPI* 35, p. 176.
31. Garcia et al., "Atmospheric Circulation Changes in the Tropical Pacific", p. 19.
32. Selga, *Charts of Remarkable Typhoons in the Philippines*; BRPI 36, p. 51; Schurz, *The Manila Galleon*, p. 259.
33. *BRPI* 36, p. 51.
34. Ibid; Garcia et al., "Atmospheric Circulation Changes in the Tropical Pacific", p. 19.
35. Garcia et al., "Atmospheric Circulation Changes in the Tropical Pacific", p. 20.
36. Selga, *Charts of Remarkable Typhoons in the Philippines*; BRPI 37, p. 207; Garcia et al., "Atmospheric Circulation Changes in the Tropical Pacific", p. 20.
37. Garcia et al., "Atmospheric Circulation Changes in the Tropical Pacific", p. 2246.
38. *BRPI* 47, p. 69.
39. Schurz, *The Manila Galleon*, p. 261.
40. Ibid.
41. *BRPI* 37, pp. 274–75.
42. *BRPI* 42, p. 133; Schurz, *The Manila Galleon*, p. 261, discusses ships returning to port due to storms and mentions there was such a case in 1672. This could refer to the *San Telmo*.
43. *BRPI* 42, pp. 205–6.
44. Schurz, *The Manila Galleon*, p. 261.
45. *BRPI* 42, p. 260; Schurz, *The Manila Galleon*, p. 261.
46. *BRPI* 47, p. 75; Garcia et al., "Atmospheric Circulation Changes in the Tropical Pacific", p. 8.
47. *BRPI* 42, p. 309.
48. Ibid; *BRPI* 41, p. 36; Schurz, *The Manila Galleon*, p. 259.
49. Selga, *Charts of Remarkable Typhoons in the Philippines*; Schurz, *The Manila Galleon*, pp. 259–60.
50. Schurz, *The Manila Galleon*, p. 260; *BRPI* 44, p. 142.
51. Selga, *Charts of Remarkable Typhoons in the Philippines*.
52. Garcia et al., "Atmospheric Circulation Changes in the Tropical Pacific", p. 33.
53. Garcia et al., "Atmospheric Circulation Changes in the Tropical Pacific", p. 34; Schurz, *The Manila Galleon*, p. 260.
54. *BRPI* 48, p. 154, n. 77; Jose Cosona Moyano, *Filipinas y su real Hacienda (1750–1800)*, Cordoba, Spain: Montre de peidad y Caya de Aborros de Cordoba, 1986, p. 263.
55. Schurz, *The Manila Galleon*, p. 261.
56. Selga, *Charts of Remarkable Typhoons in the Philippines*; de la Costa, *The Jesuits in the Philippines*, pp. 588–91.
57. María Lourdes Díaz-Trechuelo Spinola, "Dos Nuevos Derroteros del Galeon de Manila (1730 y 1773)", in *Annuario de Estudios Americanes* 13 (1956).
58. Wayne V. Burt, "The Search for the Manilla Galleon Log Books", in *Bulletin of the American Meteorological Society* 71, no. 11 (November 1990): p. 1633; Moyano, *Filipinas y su real Hacienda*, pp. 280, 299.
59. Two different dates are given: 17 April in Garcia et al., "Atmospheric Circulation Changes in the Tropical Pacific", p. 42; 19 April in Schurz, *The Manila Galleon*, p. 281.
60. Spinola, "Dos Nuevos Derroteros del Galeon de Manila", p. 51.

61. Schurz, *The Manila Galleon*, p. 261.
62. Selga, *Charts of Remarkable Typhoons in the Philippines*.
63. Ibid.
64. Selga and Singer state that the *San Andres* departed in 1797, Schurz and Quirino & Laygo say it was 1798. Selga reports the cargo saved, all three other sources report it (partly) lost. See Selga, *Charts of Remarkable Typhoons in the Philippines*; Schurz, *The Manila Galleon*, p. 260; Carlos Quirino and Abraham Laygo, *Regesto Guion Catalogo de los Documentos Existantes en Mexico sobre Filipinas*, Manila: El Comite de Amsitad Filipino-Mexicana, 1965, p. 270.
65. Schurz, *The Manila Galleon*, p. 261; Quirino & Laygo, *Regesto Guion Catalogo de los Documentos Existantes en Mexico*, p. 80.

10

INTERRACIAL MARRIAGES AND THE OVERSEAS FAMILY
The Case of the Portuguese Topasses in Timor

Barbara Watson Andaya and
Leonard Y. Andaya

In historiographical terms, the publication of the first volume of *Southeast Asia in the Age of Commerce* in 1988 marked a watershed in the study of the region's premodern history. In this pioneering work Anthony Reid touched on many aspects of daily life, but he remains one of the few historians to think seriously about the ways in which social and economic changes of the period affected understandings of what constituted a family.[1] In particular, Tony drew attention to the growing visibility of sexual relations between foreign traders and local women, remarking that "interracial unions were a feature of all the commercial cities of Southeast Asia".[2] Such unions had long been customary, but the presence of individuals born of "mixed" parentage became more noticeable in early modern times because so many European men arrived in Asia without women. As terminologies were expanded to include new words such as *mestiço* and half-caste, European desire for demographic classification of the areas that came under their control raised questions about the place of such individuals in the social system. These very classifications, and the invidious prejudice that privileged a white skin, meant that even influential families of mixed ancestry found it difficult to place their sons in positions of authority in European-dominated administrations, despite the obvious need for linguistically qualified people as cultural bridges. Acceptance by European society was always qualified, always contingent upon individual abilities, and it could never be assumed that a *mestiço* son would inherit any status or advantage acquired by his father. In this context, the territorial control and political power wielded by certain *mestiço* families in Timor, and the standing they attained in the local environment, represents an intriguing exception.

MAINTAINING THE HOME CULTURE IN THE OVERSEAS FAMILY

Although miscegenation was increasingly common from the sixteenth century, the earliest records suggest that traders arriving in Southeast Asia had long been aware of the advantages that followed their acceptance by a local woman and her family as a legitimate sexual partner. Even a brief liaison could create a whole network of adoptive kin and thus become a significant means of strengthening economic relationships. "The people of Tun Sun [probably on the Malay Peninsula]," noted a Chinese encyclopaedia in the tenth century, "practice the Brahmin's doctrine and give them their daughters in marriage. Consequently many of them do not go away."[3]

The presence of an identifiable group of people, the offspring of these unions, only gradually began to receive linguistic recognition, itself an indication of their growing numbers. It is noteworthy that the Malay term *peranakan*, referring to those of mixed descent (Malay-Chinese or Malay-Indian), does not occur in written sources before the seventeenth century. Even before this, however, physical appearance would in most cases have indicated the dual heritage that marked the children of these cross-cultural families. The *peranakan* children of a Malay mother and a Chinese father, for instance, were likely to be distinguished by their relatively fair skin, often compared to the colour of the *langsat* fruit (*lansium domesticum*). This was considered an important measure of female beauty, and Malay rulers frequently selected *peranakan* women as *gundik*, or secondary wives. Similarly, physique and personal appearance could also reveal Indian ancestry. In Aceh, said one commentator, "many people from Nagore intermarry and reside, their progeny are known by the name of *orang dangan* (sic. *dagang* = trader)". William Marsden (1754–1836) thus invoked the intermarriage associated with Indian trading connections to explain the fact that Acehnese were generally "taller, stouter and of darker complexion" than other Sumatrans.[4]

Despite their genetic heritage, these "mixed" children would normally have been more comfortable with the language and cultural practices of their mother and her relatives, since their paternal kin were far away and the trading activities of a foreign father usually meant that his domestic presence was intermittent. Indeed, in returning to his homeland, where he might maintain an "official" wife and family, he could permanently disappear from the lives of his "foreign" children. On the other hand, those fathers who chose to remain but who wanted something of their own culture passed on to their "mixed" children faced real obstacles because of the localization of the domestic milieu. Visitors from China were particularly outspoken in their disapproval of the household environment found among overseas Chinese communities, and deplored the cultural dilution that occurred when their countrymen took non-Chinese wives. In southwest China, Han intermarriage with non-Han peoples was in fact outlawed in the 1720s.[5] Such policies were impossible to enforce in the more distant Nanyang, the "southern seas," but observers became optimistic about the feasibility of replicating the "Chinese" family as permanent trading communities developed along the Southeast Asian coasts. A retired merchant, Xie Qing'gao (1765–1822), thus noted approvingly that although the first waves of Chinese males reaching Borneo had taken Dayak women as sexual partners, "when the population had grown" they began "to arrange marriages among themselves and then rarely took Dayak women for their wives."[6] By contrast, the Hadhrami sayyids of the same period, conscious of the expanding diaspora in Southeast Asia, generally accepted the idea that a man could take a non-Arab wife. Nonetheless, concern was frequently expressed about the morality of the *muwallad*, the children born of foreign mothers. Sayyid families in Southeast Asia were thus intent on affirming their separate status by intermarrying only with high-ranking local women, by living in a specific urban locality (like Acheen Street in Penang), by maintaining a specific dress and life-style, by a more self-conscious display of Islamic piety, and by providing an education for their sons.[7]

From the perspective of a well-to-do but "mixed" family now domiciled in Southeast Asia, a correct upbringing for locally-born sons was especially important. If youths were to follow their fathers in business, it was essential that they be not merely verbally competent but also literate in the paternal language. More particularly, familiarity with their father's culture would make them a desirable son-in-law, one demonstrably capable of heading a household grounded in approved values. Such knowledge, however, could not be attained without instruction, especially when a boy was surrounded by female relatives and servants who were ill-versed in the culture of the father's homeland. The extent to which foreign fathers sought to inculcate what they considered appropriate and unchanging values is itself illustrative of the sense of absence from "home" so crucial in shaping the mobile diasporic experience.[8] Parents desirous of raising their sons to be more "Chinese," for instance, might well offer attractive remuneration to recruit a teacher who had been unsuccessful in China's rigorous examination system. Cheng Xunwo thus spent five months in Batavia as a tutor around 1740, and Wang Dahai, who lived for ten years in Java between 1783 and 1793, also taught at one of the city's two Chinese schools.[9] The acquisition of Indian languages used in trade could be equally valuable, for a youth equipped with business skills would be more likely to make an advantageous marriage. The origins of the "Melaka Chittys" can be traced to the fifteenth century, but through interaction with their home communities and careful nurturing of language and religion, they were able to retain their Tamil Hindu identity, as did the Muslim Tamils, the Chulia. A Hindu temple built in 1781 by the Chitty community still survives, and in the late eighteenth century Tamil children were customarily taught their father's language, with most of the town's schoolteachers reportedly Tamil.[10]

EUROPEAN ATTITUDES TO 'OVERSEAS FAMILIES'

In Chinese and Indian societies, cultural acceptance of the "overseas family" was complicated by deep-rooted objections to migration and miscegenation that intensified the feeling of "absence". Despite a long tradition of maritime trade, Hindus held fast to the belief that "crossing the black sea" was polluting to higher castes. The caste system itself posed problems to intermarriage, even for those who were engaged in ocean-borne trade, since Hinduism's cultural boundaries excluded foreign-born wives. Again, notwithstanding generations of emigration, Chinese who left their homeland were considered disloyal to their ancestors, and the wholesale killing of Chinese in Manila in 1603 and in Java in 1740 was deemed an appropriate punishment.[11] Although Arab migration was ennobled by its association with the spread of Islam, "Java" (meaning island Southeast Asia) was commonly depicted as a region of moral corruption, and popular sayings exhorted young men to "forget Java; stay home and water the fields ... the satisfied stay with their folk".[12]

The Portuguese arrival in Asia in the sixteenth century introduced rather different attitudes towards migration and the overseas family. In order to service its expanding empire in Africa and Asia, the Portuguese Crown actively encouraged the annual departure of hundreds of healthy and unmarried young men.[13] Since their numbers were never sufficient to fulfil the demands placed on them, the conqueror of Melaka, Afonso de Albuquerque, conceived the revolutionary idea of an officially condoned and interracial family, where the father was a Portuguese soldier or official and the mother a Christianized local woman. The ultimate goal was to maintain an adequate supply of manpower by producing offspring who would feel "Portuguese" through a shared religion and language.

One could well argue that Portuguese efforts in Southeast Asia were successful, at least in the opinion of contemporaries. As William Dampier (1651–1715) remarked wryly, "The breed of them is scattered all over India; neither are there any People of more different Complexions than of that Race, even from the Coal-black to a light Tawney."[14] Less tangible, but ultimately more significant was an inculcation of the idea of "Portuguese-ness," a self-identity that persisted long after Portugal itself had become a minor European power. Yet despite *mestiço* acceptance of Catholicism and their ability to speak at least a creole Portuguese, Portugal's administrators harboured basic doubts about the capacity of the *mestiço* family to act as a conduit for the transmission of Christian values. In this regard, it was considered that Crown and Church should ideally work in close alliance, since schooling was seen as integral to the missionary project; it is significant that the Malay word "sekolah" is itself derived from Portuguese. Indeed, one of the first steps of António Galvão following his appointment as governor of Ternate was to establish a seminary in which native children could receive an education and be taught Christianity.[15] Perhaps the most well-known product of an "Asian" schooling was Manuel Godinho de Erédia (1563–1623), who was born in Melaka, his father Portuguese and his mother a Makassar woman of good birth who had adopted Christianity. Educated in Melaka and at the Jesuit seminary at Goa, Erédia became a geographer and cartographer of considerable repute and the author of one of the best early accounts of the Malay Peninsula.[16]

By the beginning of the seventeenth century, despite the weakening of the Portuguese Asian empire (*Estado da India*), the influence of Portuguese *mestiços* could be tracked in courts throughout the Malay-Indonesian archipelago and in coastal Southeast Asia as well. Neither was there a major linguistic shift following the capture of Portuguese Melaka in 1641 by the VOC (Dutch East India Company) and the Portuguese retreat in eastern Indonesia. The Dutch language never displaced the creole Portuguese heard in the streets of many port cities in maritime Southeast Asia, and for much of the period Portuguese was used in diplomatic correspondence and negotiations between the Dutch and local rulers. In the 1780s teachers in Batavia's VOC schools still used Portuguese, and when Governor Petrus van der Parra (1761–75) published the Psalms and Gospels at his own expense, the text was in Portuguese.[17] Those *mestiços* who acquired Dutch were in a particularly strong position as intermediaries, with a prime example being the "dark Portuguese" Tomas Diaz, sent as a VOC envoy to central Sumatra in 1684.[18]

While the Dutch and English East India Companies were less forthright in promoting the growth of overseas communities through sexual unions between European fathers and local mothers, the expansion of the "Eurasian" population was a natural outgrowth of their presence.[19] In 1630 and in 1642 VOC regulations gave implicit approval of marriages between European men and Asian women, and in Dutch-controlled towns wealthy Christian *mestiço* families could wield considerable influence. Nonetheless, the social status of even the most prominent was always tainted by their "native" origins, and by the localization of their professed Christianity. VOC officials who wanted their Eurasian sons to grow up as Netherlanders commonly sent them back to Europe, sometimes as early as at two or three years-old.[20] Most of these youths then identified with Dutch culture and remained in Europe, although those who returned were well-placed to make used of their linguistic skills. One example is Samuel Baron, who was born of a Dutch father, head of the Dutch factory at Hoi An, and a mother described as "Vietnamese," whom Baron later implied was also of Portuguese descent. His father sent him to Europe in 1659, probably as a teenager, but he later came back to Vietnam, where he operated as a trader. Baron's ability to straddle two worlds is indicated in his description of himself as "a native of Tonqueen," in the fact that he was adopted by one of the local princes, and in the deep knowledge of local customs evident in his well-known account of Vietnam. Undoubtedly with an eye to his future career, however, this account was written in English and was submitted to his patron, the governor of Madras.[21]

Individuals like Baron who could exploit the advantages of their local connections can be located in many different contexts. In contrast to British India, the permeability of ethnic relationships in the English East India Company post of Bengkulen was often compared to Batavia and, by the end of the eighteenth century, Eurasians occupied some of the most important administrative positions.[22] Edward Coles, for instance, was the son of an Englishman and a Malay woman. His mother and his wife were both apparently individuals of some status, for he was said to be related "by birth and marriage ... to all the Malay chiefs". Coles served as Governor of Bengkulen between 1781 and 1785, and even an unsympathetic observer said he was "clever and sensible ... a perfect Malay with the advantage of a European education".[23] He went so far as to challenge the delicate social order of the English factory by claiming that he had "not a drop of English blood in his veins." Yet his very standing among the local Malay community, which led some to call him "the king of the Malays," could also be the basis for accusations of disloyalty. Evidently angered when men of Malay-English parentage "gave orders to a Bengal (i.e. English) officer," the Commissioner of Bengkulen in 1800 foreshadowed later attitudes when he requested that Calcutta send "no more half castes."[24]

THE "MESTIÇO FAMILY": THE PORTUGUESE CONTEXT

The idea of the *mestiço* family as the bulwark of Portugal's trading empire was fundamentally flawed because it failed to appreciate the extent to which skin colour would determine social classification in overseas communities. Afonso de Albuquerque, who promoted the idea of "mixed marriages", was very much a product of his times and had in fact expressed the hope that Portuguese would marry only local women of "Aryan origin." In 1514 he even wrote to the King of Portugal with the assurance that he had not allowed marriages with "dark and dissolute women", but only with the "chaste and fair."[25] To overcome such entrenched attitudes, Portuguese rulings emphasized that Christianity, not colour, should be the guiding principle determining Portuguese citizenship, and that Asian converts should be regarded as the equal of white Portuguese Christians, particularly if they were more or less assimilated to Portuguese culture and had been baptized.[26] Laws to this effect passed between 1562 and 1582, however, were never fully implemented, and in Southeast Asia, "Portuguese" society became divided into "white" (fairer-skinned, more European in lifestyle) as opposed to those deemed "black" (darker, more local, and thus of lower status).[27] These differences were exacerbated because although the Dutch population lists did maintain a "*mestiezen*" category, darker Portuguese mestiços were often equated with "native Christians" or became merged with the local population.[28]

One of the distinctive features of the so-called "black Portuguese"[29] was the adoption of European dress, particularly by the men, who were noted for their European-style silk shirts, pantaloons, and particularly for their hats, often of bright colours and decorated with plumes and gemstones. So conspicuous was this feature that the Portuguese called the entire community "*gente dos chapeos*", or the "hat people", and in eastern Indonesia the black Portuguese were called "*Topasses*", said to be derived from the Hindustani word *topi* (hat).[30] Johan Nieuhof's seventeenth-century illustration of a Topasses man thus pays careful attention to his European-style hat, while a Malay poem depicts an umbrella (a mark of high rank in Malay society) and a hat "worn at a jaunty angle" as distinguishing features of the *anak Peranggi*, the "Portuguese" Sinyor Kosta.[31] The prestige associated with the Portuguese hat is apparent in its incorporation into the rituals of some Timorese groups; one

Timor ruler was in fact called "*Sobe Kase*" ("strange hat") because he wore a hat given to him by the Portuguese.[32]

Dispersed across Asia, this separate but vaguely-defined Portuguese *mestiço* population gave rise to the unique Topasses community in the "Solor archipelago" of eastern Indonesia (including Flores, Solor, Adonara, Lembata, Timor, and some of the smaller offshore islands). It was here, at the edges of the *Estado da India*, that the "white" and the "black" Portuguese struggled for dominance. Yet despite ongoing conflict, the Topasses community successfully evolved by affirming its links to the Portuguese Crown while establishing family networks with indigenous societies. Leading Topasses families continued to play a crucial intermediary role between the white Portuguese and the local communities, thereby assuring Portuguese success in maintaining a foothold in eastern Timor while the remainder of the eastern archipelago ultimately succumbed to the Dutch.

In the Solor archipelago the term "black Portuguese" was synonymous with the "Topasses" or the "Hat People", differentiating them from the native Christians who, though relatively numerous, did not link themselves to the Portuguese. But the Topasses were also clearly distinguished from the "white" Portuguese, especially those born in Portugal, who regarded themselves as quite separate from the *mestiço* communities. A primary determinant in establishing these boundaries was skin colour, which, despite royal ordinances, presented a major barrier to acceptance of native Christians or *mestiços* as equals by the higher status white Portuguese. In a major departure from the earlier attitudes, white Portuguese men actively avoided taking a bride who might jeopardize their privileged status. Even as they insisted on racial superiority, however, white Portuguese officialdom was gradually losing authority in the eastern archipelago because of the steady weakening of the *Estado da India*. Although private Portuguese traders remained, *mestiços* became politically more prominent in the region. The story of these *mestiços*, particularly the rise of their two leading families, the Hornays and the da Costas, demonstrates the success of the Topasses in providing a bridge between the cultural world of the European and the indigenous communities. It also explains why the word "Portuguese" continues to evoke images of physical and spiritual power in eastern Indonesia.

TWO TOPASSES FAMILIES: THE HORNAYS AND DA COSTAS

In 1562 the Portuguese built a fort in Solor, which became the major centre of Portuguese activities before the establishment of posts in Timor. It was probably at this time that a *mestiço* society began to develop as Portuguese sailors and traders cohabited with or married local women.³³ By 1613, the Topasses population was already considerable, being concentrated on the island of Solor and at Larantuka at the eastern end of the island of Flores, which formed part of the Lamaholot cultural area.³⁴ A striking feature of the Lamaholot region, and one typical of numerous societies in the eastern archipelago, was the existence of an ancient duality manifested in the rivalry of two groups, the Demon (loosely associated with the interior and agriculture, and subsequently with Christianity) and the Paji (linked to the coast and trade, and then Islam).³⁵ In time the Demon became larger and more dominant, and it was with these Christianized groups that the Topasses eventually allied. Aided by their native Demon allies, the Topasses were able to maintain strongholds at Larantuka against a strong Paji challenge. Within this protective environment, and with wealth drawn from their dominance in the sandalwood and *cassia lignea* trade, the Topasses developed into a formidable entity in the Solor archipelago.

In the early seventeenth century the most prominent family in Topasses society went by the name of Hornay. The progenitor was Jan de Hornay, a Dutch commander of the Solor fort who fled to Larantuka in 1629, converted to Catholicism, and married a low-born Christianized Timor woman, previously the slave of Portuguese Dominican monks. Supported by the Demon groups, de Hornay was eventually pardoned by the VOC in 1643 because Batavia recognized the economic value of an alliance with a powerful local clan. Jan's son, Gonsalvo de Hornay, established his own kingdom on Timor, and was regarded as one of the most powerful individuals on the island. In turn, Gonsalvo's sons, António and Francisco, also became important Timor rajas.³⁶ At the same time, the Hornays were adamant in their pledge of loyalty to the abstract idea of "Portugal," perhaps inspired by missionary accounts of João IV (1640–56) as the universal redeemer king.³⁷ Because of his loyalty to the Portuguese captain in Larantuka, António was nominated as the new Captain-Major (*Capitão Mor*). Strong opposition from another Topasses leader, Mateus da Costa, who had distinguished himself in battles against the Dutch on Timor, marked the beginning of a protracted struggle between the Hornay and the da Costa families for dominance in the Solor archipelago, and particularly in Timor.³⁸

The strength of these families can be traced not merely to their control of the sandalwood trade, but to their continuing intermarriage with Timor's numerous chiefly families. In one such union, António Hornay wed the daughter of the ruler of the kingdom of Ambeno, and their offspring contributed to increased Topasses influence.³⁹ In forming their own kingdoms and themselves becoming independent rajas, the Hornays and the da Costas became an integral part of Timor's political, economic, and cultural landscape. When William Dampier arrived in Lifao, the nominal centre of Portuguese authority on Timor in 1699, he described the Topasses as:

> a sort of Indians, of a Copper-colour ... [who were] already so mixed that it is hard to distinguish whether they are Portugueze or Indians. Their Language is Portugueze; and the Religion they have, is Romish. They seem in Words to acknowledge the King of Portugal for their Sovereign; yet they will not accept of any Officers sent by him... Of this mixt Breed there are some thousands ... They value themselves on the account of their religion and descent from the Portugueze; and would be very angry if a man should say they are not Portugueze.

Dampier himself saw only three or four "right" (meaning "white") Portuguese while he was in Timor, and this situation remained essentially unchanged for another fifty years or more.[40]

The strength of Topasses identity lay not only in their retention of some aspects of Portuguese language and culture, but in their veneration of the distant Portuguese King (to whom António Hornay promised to bequeath all his possessions) and their proclaimed adherence to the Catholic faith. Since the women of the Topasses community were generally products of the local environment, it is unlikely that even a creole Portuguese was used in the domestic domain; it can be argued, therefore, that in eastern Indonesia professed religion rather than language became a determining feature of the "Topasses" identity. This identity, however, incorporated numerous indigenous elements. Christian banners and symbols may have been carried into battle, but animal sacrifices and the drinking of blood were also performed to ensure success.

Although we know little of the practice of Christianity in Topasses families, women in charge of household management would have been key agents in this process of localization. Dampier commented, for instance, that the Topasses did not observe Catholic dietary restrictions (presumably fish on Friday, for instance), "but take the liberty to eat flesh when they please." The influence of local mothers must have similarly guaranteed the retention of many local customs.[41] A visitor to Timor in the 1770s thus noted that although "Portuguese Catholics" knew little more than a few prayers, they never failed to wear a rosary or a cross around their necks as a form of protection. Missionaries appeared every twelve months or so to baptize children, a ritual critical in any claim to be "Portuguese". It is likely, however, as in areas under Dutch control, that baptism was only carried out after certain rituals had been performed to ensure that the time was auspicious and that no harm would come to the family.[42] In sum, then, although the Topasses retained their "Portuguese" identity, with its particular stress on adherence to the Catholic faith, they were also children of native mothers and a part of their mothers' communities. While a small number of individuals may have had some sense of what "being Portuguese" entailed in Macao or Goa, life in Portugal itself could only be imagined. With little sense of a home-culture that should be preserved through imitating family management in white households, the reputation of Topasses leaders and their status as clan heads was built less on a "correct" home environment than on prowess in battle, skill with weapons, or a reputation for extra-human powers.

REDEFINING PORTUGUESENESS

The authority of leading Topasses families on Timor in the seventeenth and early eighteenth centuries was in great measure due to their role in repelling the VOC challenge to the Portuguese position. In 1656 Batavia dispatched a large force to the island, but it was overcome by a Topasses army led by António Hornay and Mateus da Costa. Though "white" Portuguese also assisted in subsequent victories against Dutch troops, it became increasingly evident that Portuguese control in Timor, Solor and Flores was fundamentally dependent on the support of the far more numerous "black" Portuguese communities. With Topasses control over most of the important sandalwood-producing areas of Timor, António Hornay was able to act as an independent lord even while formally acknowledging the authority of the white Portuguese. The rapid pace of Topasses indigenization contributed to growing friction with the white Portuguese as the substantial numbers and strength of the Topasses in the Lamaholot area and in Timor allowed them first to ignore and later to challenge the authority of Portuguese officials sent from Portugal, Goa, and Macau. By the latter part of the seventeenth century many of the Topasses had been born in the Solor archipelago, including Timor, and were truly "*mestiço*" in blood, attitudes, and loyalties. Topasses communities were found in different areas in the eastern part of Timor, and some came to play important roles as bodyguards to local rulers. Acting as indigenous rulers, the Hornays and da Costas contracted marriages with the many royal families, several of whom incorporated the name "da Costa" and "Hornay" into their own titles and honorifics. In addition, earlier rivalries between the Hornays and the da Costas had been laid aside as they eventually agreed to alternate leadership between the two families. Collected in more recent times, a local legend gives some sense of how this very Asian solution was incorporated into Timor's mythology. According to this legend, a quarrel broke out between two sons of the ruler of Melaka, the well-known Malay kingdom. One son, Hornay, decides to leave with his nephew Costa. They eventually land in Flores, and Costa goes farther to Timor. Here he marries the daughter of the Raja Ambeno, eventually succeeds his father-in-law, but ultimately names his uncle Hornay as his heir.[43]

The cooperation between the da Costas and the Hornay families after 1670 gave them a distinct advantage over white Portuguese governors whose tenure was usually short and who were therefore far less able to develop the same network of alliances, and far less likely to put down family roots. For around a hundred years, from the mid-seventeenth century, the white Portuguese garrison in Lifau was periodically besieged by the Topasses and their native allies, and its survival was dependent on the goodwill of Topasses leaders. The white Portuguese were always at a disadvantage because the Topasses forces were as proficient as they in the use of firearms and were far more numerous than any force that the Portuguese authorities could marshal.

Captain-Major António Hornay, whom C.R. Boxer has called the "uncrowned king of Timor," was also quick to crush any resistance by native kings while establishing lucrative alliances with others. His forces controlled much of the island, especially along the coasts, and he was thus far more powerful and influential than the enclave of white Portuguese sheltering within their fortification at Lifau.[44] Hornay's death in 1697 was seen by the white Portuguese as an ideal opportunity to appoint one of their own, but the appointment was flatly rejected by the Topasses. Instead, they installed Domingo da Costa, the son of a previous Captain-Major, as Hornay's successor.[45] In 1702 a more serious threat came from a white Portuguese, António Coelho Guerreiro, who was appointed Captain-Major at Lifau. He sought to assert his authority by compelling Domingo da Costa to relinquish his position, but the Portuguese force sent against the Topasses stronghold was badly defeated and retreated back to Lifau in disarray. Guerreiro's expulsion of all Topasses living in Lifau simply compounded his difficulties, since the majority immediately joined da Costa. Guerreiro himself was eventually discharged from office to be replaced by another white Portuguese governor.[46]

In 1707, the white Portuguese suffered a major setback when a force sent against Domingo da Costa was again routed by a superior Topasses army. This led to a change of tactics. Instead of further hostilities, the white Portuguese sought instead to incorporate da Costa into the governing administration, and in 1708 he was made Vice-Governor at Lifau.[47] The subsequent arrangement, whereby the highest post was held by a white Portuguese and the second-in-command by a Topasses, was only intermittently workable, and the periodic agreements made between white and black Portuguese remained uneasy. In finally concluding peace with the white Portuguese in 1728, for example, the people of the Timorese kingdom of Belu demanded that they be placed under "their lawful lord," the Topasses leader Francisco Hornay (1722–1730).[48]

By 1729, the Dutch estimated that there were approximately 40,000 Topasses scattered through the whole Solor archipelago. This was a considerable force when compared to the gradually diminishing numbers of both white Portuguese and Dutch in these islands. So dominant were the Topasses that only the Dutch and their Timorese allies remained as obstacles to their total supremacy on the island. In a combined effort to oust the Dutch, the entire Topasses community united under the combined leadership of the Hornays, the da Costas, and other major Topasses families in the battle of Penfui in 1749.[49] Though the Topasses defeat ensured the continuing presence of the Dutch in Timor, Topasses influence remained extensive well into the nineteenth century. The leading families like the Hornays and da Costas had become part of the indigenous kinship network and were never absorbed by the white Portuguese. Nonetheless, they remained loyal to the distant Portuguese ruler and, as Dampier had perceptively remarked, "would be very angry if a Man should say they are not Portugueze". The historical evolution of the Topasses in eastern Indonesia thus remains an instructive case study of the complexity of being "Portuguese" at the edges of empire.[50]

With well-respected rulers, a formidable fighting force, and strong cultural links to the area, the Topasses families were regarded in much the same way as the numerous chiefdoms dotting the landscape of Timor and other islands of the Solor archipelago. By the early seventeenth century, this capacity to develop a truly indigenous family network enabled the Topasses to operate as a group with ascribed leadership based on continuity rather than simply the achievements of particular individuals. Yet they continued to maintain a Portuguese identity despite their increasing adaptation to indigenous values, language, and culture. Even as their colour and localized culture redefined what it meant to be "Christian" and "Portuguese," the Topasses also resisted efforts to make them a subordinated and less important part of an overseas Portuguese society dominated by those with fair skin.

Afonso de Albuquerque's vision of *mestiço* offspring sustaining the far-flung Portuguese Asian empire had been achieved, although the society that emerged was rather different from that which he had envisaged. The Topasses were crucial in maintaining Timor for the Portuguese, but they were able to do so because of their adaptation to indigenous culture and values. By invoking Portuguese prestige and exploiting their own local family networks, the Hornays and da Costas succeeded in mobilizing a range of different chiefdoms, thwarting Dutch attempts to conquer the whole island of Timor.

CONCLUSION

Southeast Asian history throws up many examples of individuals — men and women of "mixed birth" — who exploited new opportunities open to them and gained a place in history. For the most part, however, children of the "irregular and shifting unions" between European men and local women were relegated to the margins of colonial society.[51] Afonso de Albuquerque's goal of developing a coherent and legitimate overseas population from a base of Christian Indo-Portuguese families never became a reality. Yet the general characterization of *mestiço* communities in early modern Southeast Asian history as being marginal did not apply to the Topasses.

Mestiço-hood (Port. *mestiçagem*) by its very nature requires access to two or more cultures. In the case of the Topasses in Timor, the steadily diminishing numbers of white Portuguese and the demise of the *Estado da India* ultimately made their link to Portuguese culture and language far less useful than the ties to indigenous cultures. As the reputation of this distant but highly successful *mestiço* community spread throughout the former Portuguese Asian empire, other black Portuguese joined the Topasses. This flow of other *mestiço* communities to Timor, added to the natural increase of Topasses families, and assured the survival of the Topasses as an influential ethnic entity in the entire Solor archipelago, including Timor.

Unlike other smaller *mestiço* communities elsewhere in Southeast Asia, which eventually merged with the European or the native community based on colour, the large numbers and military strength of the Topasses made their special identity both enviable and desirable. The criteria for achievement and the standards for comparison were generated from within their own society, rather than being received from a "home country" such as China or the Hadhramaut. The Topasses experienced no sense of cultural separation like that attributed to many diasporic groups, and saw no need to renew familial or other links with a distant homeland. Still controlling a substantial part of Timor in the late eighteenth century, they retained the political and religious symbols that justified their claim to be Portuguese even as the kinship ties that bound them to indigenous communities became increasingly valuable. In consequence, this society was able to operate as the centre of its own world, successfully challenging the accepted hierarchy of "white" over "non-white" and claiming an identity infused with a unique confidence and self-assurance.

Notes

1. Jean Gelman Taylor, *The Social World of Batavia: European and Eurasian in Dutch Asia* (Madison: University of Wisconsin Press, 1983) is a pioneering study. The

reconstitution of family relationships is also implicit in Hendrik E. Niemeijer, *Batavia: Een kolonial samenleving in de 17de eeuw* (Amsterdam: Balans, 2005).
2. Anthony Reid, *Southeast Asia in the Age of Commerce 1450–1680. Volume One: The Lands Below the Winds* (New Haven and London: Yale University Press, 1988), p. 155.
3. Paul Wheatley, "Desultory Remarks on the Ancient History of the Malay Peninsula", in *Malayan and Indonesian Studies: Essays Presented to Sir Richard Winstedt on His Eighty-Fifth Birthday*, edited by J. Bastin and R. Roolvink (Oxford: Clarendon Press, 1964), pp. 45–46.
4. Lee Kam Hing, *The Sultanate of Aceh: Relations with the British 1760–1824* (Kuala Lumpur: Oxford University Press, 1995), pp. 162, 189 fn. 25; William Marsden, *The History of Sumatra* (Kuala Lumpur: Oxford University Press, 1975; Reprint of 1811 edition), p. 398.
5. C. Pat Giersch, "'A Motley Throng': Social Change on Southwest China's Early Modern Frontier, 1700–1880", *Journal of Asian Studies* 60, no. 1 (February 2001): 86.
6. Leonard Blussé, "*Kongkoan* and *Kongsi*: Representations of Chinese Identity and Ethnicity in Early Modern Southeast Asia", in *Shifting Communities and Identity Formation in Early Modern Asia*, edited by Leonard Blussé and Felipe Fernández-Armesto (Leiden: Research School of Asian, African and Amerindian Studies, Leiden University, 2003), p. 98.
7. Huub de Jonge and Nico Kaptein, eds. *Transcending Borders: Arabs, Politics, Trade and Islam in Southeast Asia* (Leiden: KITLV Press, 2002); Engseng Ho, *The Graves of Tarim: Genealogy and Mobility Across the Indian Ocean* (Berkeley and Los Angeles: University of California Press, 2006), pp. 68, 72, 124.
8. For a masterly study of this concept, see Ho, *The Graves of Tarim*, especially pp. 17–22.
9. Claudine Salmon, "Wang Dahai and His View of the 'Insular Countries' (1791)", in *Chinese Studies in the Malay World*, edited by Ding Choo Ming and Ooi Kee Beng (Singapore: Times Media, 2003), pp. 31–33, 61 fn. 8.
10. Anne Bulley, *Free Mariner: John Adolphus Pope in the East Indies, 1786–1821* (London: British Association for Cemeteries in South Asia, 1992), p. 103; Samuel S. Dhoraisingam, *Peranakan Indians of Singapore and Melaka. Indian Babas and Nonyas-Chitty Melaka* (Singapore: Institute of Southeast Asian Studies, 2006), p. 121; A.H. Hill, ed. and trans., *Hikayat Abdullah* (Kuala Lumpur and London, 1970), p. 45.
11. Pál Nyíri, "From Class Enemies to Patriots: Overseas Chinese and Emigration Policy and Discourse in the Peoples Republic of China", in *Globalizing Chinese Migration: Trends in Europe and Asia*, edited by Pál Nyíri and Igor Saveliev (London: Ashgate, 2002), pp. 208–41.
12. Ho, *The Graves of Tarim*, pp. 67, 82.
13. C.R. Boxer, *The Portuguese Seaborne Empire 1415–1825* (New York: Alfred A. Knopf, 1969), p. 52.

14. William Dampier, *Voyages and Discoveries* (London: Argonaut 1931), p. 111.
15. B.J. Visser, *Onder Portugeesch-Spaansche Vlag: De Katolieke Missie van Indonesië 1511–65* (Amsterdam: N.V. de R.K. Boek Centrale, 1925), p. 18.
16. O.H.K. Spate, "Erédia, Manuel Godinho de (1563–1623)", *Australian Dictionary of Biography* (Melbourne: Melbourne University Press, 1966) I: 357–58.
17. Taylor, *The Social World of Batavia*, pp. 18–19, 85.
18. Timothy Barnard, "Mestizos as Middlemen: Tomas Días and his Travels in Eastern Sumatra", in *Iberians in the Singapore-Melaka Area (Sixteenth to Eighteenth Century)*, edited by Peter Borschberg (Wiesbaden: Harrassowitz, 2004), pp. 147–60.
19. The term Eurasian is used here anachronistically, since it did not come into use in India until the nineteenth century.
20. Taylor, *The Social World of Batavia*, pp. 43–45, 75, 80.
21. Olga Dror and K.W. Taylor, eds., *Views of Seventeenth Century Vietnam: Christoforo Borri on Cochinchina and Samuel Baron on Tonkin* (Ithaca, NY: Cornell Southeast Asia Program, 2006), pp. 74–83.
22. John Bastin, *The British in West Sumatra (1685–1825)* (Kuala Lumpur: University of Malaya Press, 1965), p. xxii.
23. Bastin, *The British in West Sumatra*, pp. 98n.303; 101, 105.
24. Bastin, *The British in West Sumatra*, pp. 105, 109
25. Boxer, *Portuguese Seaborne Empire*, pp. 302–06; António da Silva Rego, *Portuguese Colonization in the Sixteenth Century: A Study of Royal Ordinances* (Johannesburg: Witwatersrand University Press, 1957), pp. 39-40.
26. Da Silva Rego, *Portuguese Colonization in the Sixteenth Century*, p. 66.
27. *Documentação para a História das Missões do Padroado Português do Oriente*, edited by Artur Basílio de Sá (Lisboa: Agencia Geral do Ultramar, 1956), IV.
28. Nordin Hussin, *Trade and Society in the Straits of Melaka: Dutch Melaka and English Penang, 1780–1830* (Copenhagen: NIAS Press, 2007), pp. 163–65; Niemeijer, *Batavia*, pp. 400–01; Johan Nieuhof, *Voyages and Travels to the East Indies 1653–1670*. Introduction by Anthony Reid (Kuala Lumpur and London: Oxford University Press, 1988. Reprint of 1704 edition), p. 277; Taylor, *The Social World*, pp. 46–47.
29. The term "black Portuguese" was commonly used by Europeans to distinguish the European Portuguese from an ever-changing and motley community of Portuguese mestiços, native mercenaries, freed native Christian slaves, native Christians, etc. Leonard Y. Andaya, "The Portuguese Tribe in the Malay-Indonesian Archipelago in the Seventeenth and Eighteenth Centuries", in *The Portuguese and the Pacific*, edited by Francis A. Dutra and João Camilo dos Santos. Santa Barbara: Center for Portuguese Studies, 1995, pp. 129–45.
30. Another less convincing origin of the term is from the Tamil *tuppasi* or "interpreter". C.R. Boxer, "The Topassesses of Timor", *Koninklijke Vereeniging Indisch Instituut* Mededeling no. 73, Afdeling Volkenkunde no. 24 (1947), p. 1.

31. Nieuhof, *Voyages and Travels*, p. 37; A. Teeuw, R. Dumas, Muhammad Haji Salleh, R. Tol and M.J. van Yperen, eds. and trans., *A Merry Senhor in the Malay World: Four Texts of the Syair Sinyor Kosta* (Leiden : KITLV Press, 2004) I: 67, 139, 145, 175.
32. Even in the twentieth century a ruler of Sikka in eastern Flores is depicted in a photograph proudly wearing a version of the Portuguese hat. H.G. Schulte Nordholt saw the ruler of Sikka with this hat in 1939. H.G. Schulte Nordholt, *The Political System of the Atoni of Timor* (The Hague: Nijhoff, 1971), p. 165, fn. 25.
33. Schulte Nordholt, *The Political System*, p. 166.
34. Boxer, "The Topassesses of Timor," p. 3.
35. A fuller account of the Demon and Paji is in P. P. Arndt, "Demon und Padzi, die feindlichen Brüder des Solor-Archipels," *Anthropos* 33 (1938): 1–58.
36. Arend de Roever, *De jacht op sandelhout: de VOC en de tweedeling van Timor in de seventiende eeuw.* (Zutphen: Walburg Pers, 2002), pp. 239–40, 256.
37. Boxer, *The Portuguese Seaborne Empire*, p. 371.
38. C.R. Boxer, *Francisco Vieira de Figueiredo: A Portuguese Merchant-Adventurer in Southeast Asia, 1624–1667* (The Hague: Nijhoff, 1967), pp. 46–47; G.P. Rouffaer, "Chronologie der Dominikaner Missie op Solor en Flores, vooral Poeloe Ende ca. 1556–1638; en bibliografie over het Ende-fort", *Nederlandsch-Indië Oud en Nieuw* 8 (1923–24): 216.
39. R.H. Barnes, "Avarice and Iniquity at the Solor Fort", *Bijdragen tot de Taal-, Land- en Volkenkunde* 143, nos. 2 and 3 (1987), p. 230.
40. William Dampier, *A Voyage to New Holland: The English Voyage of Discovery to the South Seas in 1699*, edited by James Spencer (Gloucester, UK: Alan Sutton, 1981), pp. 176, 183; Boxer, *The Portuguese Seaborne Empire*, pp. 143–44.
41. Jean-Baptiste Pelon, *Description de Timor occidental et des îles sous domination hollandaise (1771–1778)*, edited by Anne Lombard-Jourdan (Paris: Association Archipel, 2002), pp. 19–20 offers an intriguing description of Timor women, especially in regard to their extensive tattooing.
42. Pelon, *Description de Timor occidental*, pp. 8, 42; Dampier, *A Voyage to New Holland*, p. 183.
43. Roever, *De jacht*, pp. 65–66.
44. C.R. Boxer, *Fidalgos in the Far East* (The Hague: Nijhoff, 1968), p. 181; W. Ph. Coolhaas, ed., *Generale Missiven van Gouverneurs-generaal en Raden aan Heren XVII der Verenigde Oostindische Compagnie* (The Hague: Nijhoff, 1960–1997), 4: 273, 13 February 1679 *Generale Missiven*, 5: 459, 31 January 1692.
45. *Generale Missiven*, 5: 841, 30 November 1697.
46. *Generale Missiven*, 6: 196–97, 30 November 1702; 240–41, 1 December 1703; 291, 299, 354, 30 November 1704.
47. *Generale Missiven*, 6: 486, 539, 30 November 1707.
48. *Generale Missiven*, 8: 199, 8 December 1728.
49. For a recent overview of this period, see Hans Hägerdal, "Rebellions or

Factionalism: Timorese Forms of Resistance in an Early Colonial Context, 1650–1769", *Bijdragen tot de Taal-, Land- en Volkenkunde* 163, no. 1 (2007): 1–33.
50. Leonard Y. Andaya, "'The 'Informal Portuguese Empire' and the Topasses in the Solor Archipelago and Timor in the Seventeenth and Eighteenth Centuries", *Journal of Southeast Asian Studies* 41, no. 3 (2010): 391–420.
51. Boxer, *The Portuguese Seaborne Empire*, pp. 314–15.

References

Andaya, Barbara Watson. *To Live as Brothers: Southeast Sumatra in the Seventeenth and Eighteenth Centuries*. Honolulu: University of Hawai'i Press, 1993.

Andaya, Leonard Y. "The 'Informal Portuguese Empire' and the Topasses in the Solor, Archipelago and Timor in the Seventeenth and Eighteenth Centuries". *Journal of Southeast Asian Studies* 41, no. 3 (2010): 391–420.

Andaya, Leonard Y. "The Portuguese Tribe in the Malay-Indonesian Archipelago in the Seventeenth and Eighteenth Centuries." In *The Portuguese and the Pacific*, edited by Francis A. Dutra and João Camilo dos Santos, pp. 129–48. Santa Barbara: Centre for Portuguese Studies, University of California at Santa Barbara, 1995.

Arndt, P. P. "Demon und Padzi, die feindlichen Brüder des Solor-Archipels". *Anthropos* 33 (1938): 1–58.

Barnard, Timothy. "Mestizos as Middlemen: Tomas Días and his Travels in Eastern Sumatra". In *Iberians in the Singapore-Melaka Area (16th to 18th Century)*, edited by Peter Borschberg, pp. 147–60. Weisbaden: Harrassowitz, 2004.

Barnes, R.H. "Avarice and Iniquity at the Solor Fort". *Bijdragen tot de Taal-, Land- en Volkenkunde* 143, nos. 2 and 3 (1987): 20–36.

Bastin, John. *The British in West Sumatra (1685–1825)*. Kuala Lumpur: University of Malaya Press, 1965.

Blussé, Leonard. "*Kongkoan* and *Kongsi*: Representations of Chinese Identity and Ethnicity in Early Modern Southeast Asia". In *Shifting Communities and Identity Formation in Early Modern Asia*, edited by Leonard Blussé and Felipe Fernández-Armesto, pp. 93–106. Leiden: Research School of Asian, African and Amerindian Studies, Leiden University, 2003.

Boxer, C.R. *Francisco Vieira de Figueiredo: A Portuguese Merchant-Adventurer in Southeast Asia, 1624–1667*. The Hague: Martinus Nijhoff, 1967.

———. "The Topasses of Timor". *Koninklijke Vereeniging Indisch Instituut Mededeling* no. 73, Afdeling Volkenkunde no. 24 (1947): 1–22.

———. *Fidalgos in the Far East*. The Hague: Nijhoff, 1968.

———. *The Portuguese Seaborne Empire 1415–1825*. New York: Alfred A. Knopf, 1969.

Bulley, Anne. *Free Mariner: John Adolphus Pope in the East Indies, 1786–1821*. London: British Association for Cemeteries in South Asia, 1992.

Da Silva Rego, A. *Portuguese Colonization in the Sixteenth Century: A Study of the Royal Ordinances (Regimentos)*. Johannesburg: Witwatersrand University Press, 1959.

Dampier, William. *Voyages and Discoveries* London: Argonaut 1931.

Dampier, William. *A Voyage to New Holland: The English Voyage of Discovery to the South Seas in 1699*, edited by James Spencer. Gloucester, UK: Alan Sutton, 1981.

Dhoraisingam, Samuel S. *Peranakan Indians of Singapore and Melaka. Indian Babas and Nonyas-Chitty Melaka*. Singapore: Institute of Southeast Asian Studies, 2006.

Documentação para a História das Missôes do Padroado Português do Oriente, edited by Artur Basílio de Sá. Lisboa: Agencia Geral do Ultramar, 1956.

Dror, Olga and K.W. Taylor (eds.). *Views of Seventeenth-Century Vietnam: Christoforo Borri on Cochinchina and Samuel Baron on Tonkin*. Ithaca, NY: Cornell Southeast Asia Program, 2006.

Generale Missiven van Gouverneurs-generaal en Raden aan Heren XVII der Verenigde Oostindische Compagnie, edited by W. Ph. Coolhaas. The Hague: Martinus Nijhoff, 1960–1997.

Giersch, C. Pat. "'A Motley Throng': Social Change on Southwest China's Early Modern Frontier, 1700–1880". *Journal of Asian Studies* 60, no. 1 (February 2001): 67–94.

Hägerdal, Hans. "Rebellions of factionalism: Timorises forms of resistance in an early colonial context, 1650–1769". *Bijdragen tot de Taal-, Land- en Volkenkunde* 163, no. 1 (2007): 1-33.

Hill, A.H. (ed. and trans.). *Hikayat Abdullah*. Kuala Lumpur and London: Oxford University Press, 1970.

Ho Engseng. *The Graves of Tarim: Genealogy and Mobility Across the Indian Ocean*. Berkeley and Los Angeles: University of California Press, 2006.

Jonge, Huub de and Nico Kaptein (eds.). *Transcending Borders: Arabs, Politics, Trade and Islam in Southeast Asia*. Leiden: KITLV Press, 2002.

Lee Kam Hing. *The Sultanate of Aceh: Relations with the British 1760–1824*. Kuala Lumpur: Oxford University Press, 1995.

Marsden, William. *The History of Sumatra*. Kuala Lumpur: Oxford University Press, 1975; Reprint of 1811 edition.

Niemeijer, Hendrik E. *Batavia: Een koloniaal samenleving in de 17de eeuw*. Amsterdam; Balans, 2005.

Nieuhof, Johan. *Voyages and Travels to the East Indies 1653–1670*. Introduction by Anthony Reid. Kuala Lumpur and London: Oxford University Press, 1988. Reprint of 1704 edition.

Nordin Hussin. *Trade and Society in the Straits of Melaka: Dutch Melaka and English Penang, 1780–1830*. Copenhagen: NIAS Press, 2007.

Nyíri, Pál. "From Class Enemies to Patriots: Overseas Chinese and Emigration Policy and Discourse in the Peoples Republic of China". In *Globalizing Chinese Migration: Trends in Europe and Asia*, edited by Pál Nyíri and Igor Saveliev. London: Ashgate, 2002, pp. 208–41.

Pelon, Jean-Baptiste. *Description de Timor occidental et des îles sous domination hollandaise (1771–1778)*, edited by Anne Lombard-Jourdan. Paris: Association Archipel, 2002.

Reid, Anthony. *Southeast Asia in the Age of Commerce 1450–1680. Volume One: The Lands Below the Winds.* New Haven and London: Yale University Press, 1988.

Roever, Arend de. *De jacht op sandelhout: de VOC en de tweedeling van Timor in de seventiende eeuw.* Zutphen: Walburg Pers, 2002.

Rouffaer, G.P. "Chronologie der Dominikaner Missie op Solor en Flores, vooral Poeloe Ende (ca. 1556–1638): en Bibliografie over het Ende-Fort." *Nederlandsch-Indië Oud en Nieuw* 8 (1923–24): 204-22, 256–60.

Salmon, Claudine. "Wang Dahai and His View of the "Insular Countries" (1791)". In *Chinese Studies in the Malay World*, edited by Ding Choo Ming and Ooi Kee Beng. Singapore: Times Media, 2003, pp. 31–67.

Schulte Nordholt, H.G. *The Political System of the Atoni of Timor.* The Hague: Martinus Nijhoff, 1971.

Spate, O.H.K. "Erédia, Manuel Godinho de (1563–1623)". *Australian Dictionary of Biography.* Melbourne: Melbourne University Press, 1966. I: 357–58.

Taylor, Jean Gelman. *The Social World of Batavia: European and Eurasian in Dutch Asia.* Madison: University of Wisconsin Press, 1983.

Teeuw, A., R. Dumas, Muhammad Haji Salleh, R. Tol and M.J. van Yperen (ed. and trans.). *A Merry Senhor in the Malay World: Four Texts of the Syair Sinyor Kosta.* Leiden: KITLV Press, 2004.

Visser, B.J. *Onder Portugeesch-Spaansche Vlag: De Katolieke Missie van Indonesië 1511–65.* Amsterdam: N.V. de R.K. Boek Centrale, 1925.

Wheatley, Paul. "Desultory Remarks on the Ancient History of the Malay Peninsula". In *Malayan and Indonesian Studies: Essays Presented to Sir Richard Winstedt on His Eighty-Fifth Birthday*, edited by J. Bastin and R. Roolvink. Oxford: Clarendon Press, 1964, pp. 33–86.

Tony as a university student in the late 1950s. *Source*: Helen Reid.

Wedding photo with Helen in front of King's College Chapel, Cambridge in 1963. *Source*: Helen Reid.

With graduates and colleagues at a University of Malaya graduation ceremony, late 1960s. *Source:* Helen Reid.

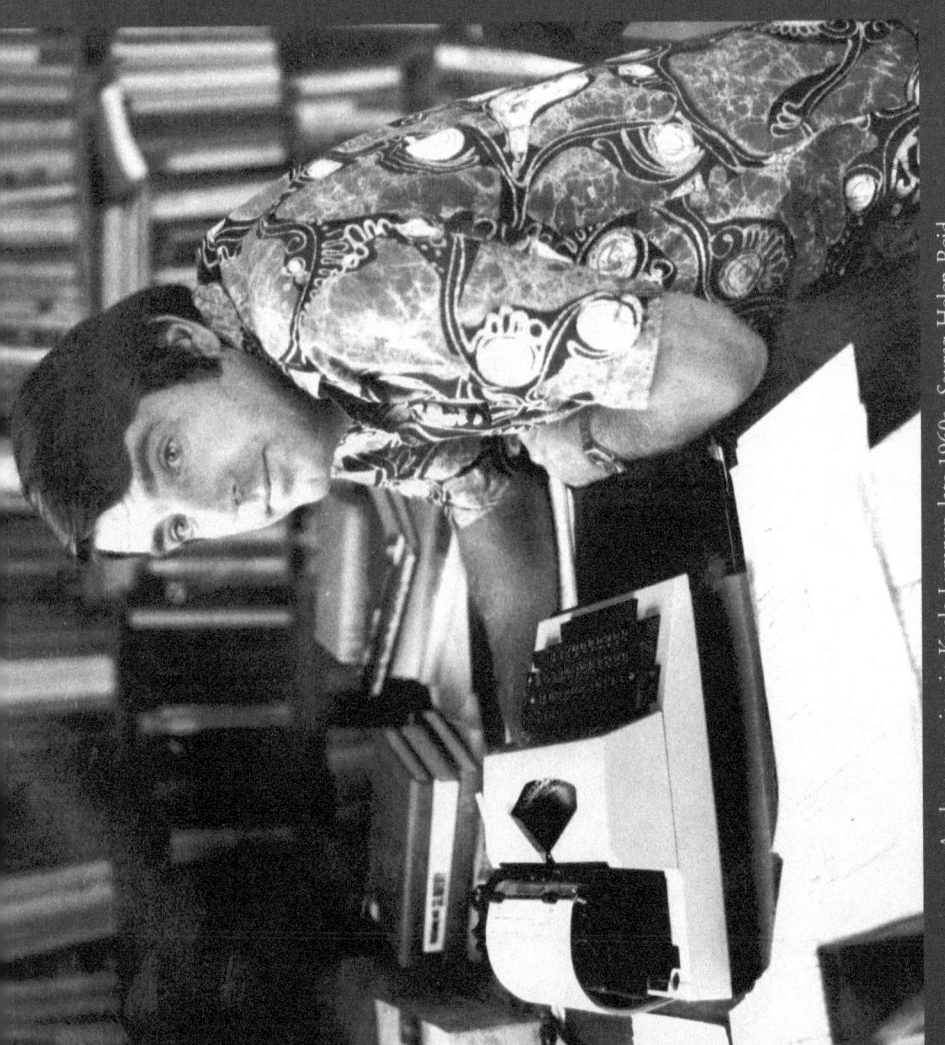

At the typewriter in Kuala Lumpur, late 1960s. *Source*: Helen Reid.

Attending the International Association of Historians of Asia conference in Manila in 1983. *Source*: Helen Reid.

With colleagues at the University of California Los Angeles in 2000. *Source*: Helen Reid.

Fukuoka Asian Culture Prize winner in 2002. *Source*: Helen Reid.

Launch of the Asia Research Institute at NUS in Singapore, 2003. *Source*: Helen Reid.

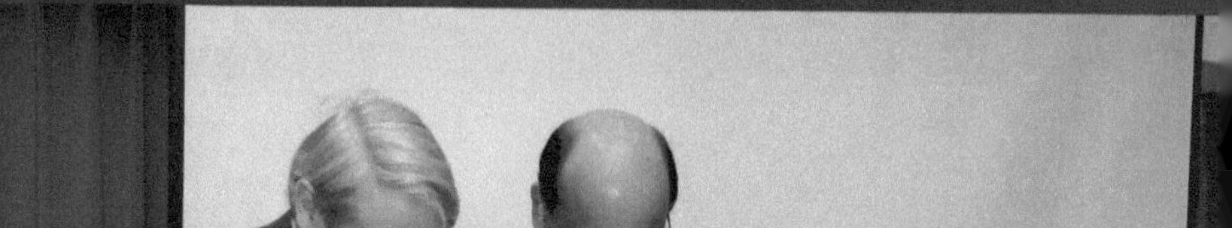

Celebrating the 5th Anniversary of Asia Research Institute in 2006 with Singapore Education Minister Tharman Shanmugaratnam and NUS President Shih Choon Fong. *Source*: Asia Research Institute (ARI) National University of Singapore (NUS).

The pensive scholar at 70. *Source*: Helen Reid.

11

A NOTE ON THE *ČHĀM* DIASPORA IN THE AYUTTHAYAN KINGDOM

Ishii Yoneo

The kingdom of Ayutthaya (1351–1767) is counted as one of the most successful port-polities in Southeast Asia. Through her twin access both to the Bay of Bengal on the one hand and to the South China Sea on the other, Ayutthaya flourished in the early modern period as one of the most important *entrêpots* of the region. The prosperity of this kingdom greatly depended upon the success of her external trade administered by the king himself, who was known as the "Great Merchant" to the contemporary European observers.[1] Among the variety of bureaucratic machinery which existed, one of the most powerful offices, therefore, was the *phrakhlang* or the Royal Treasury whose function was to deal with incoming foreigners, diplomats as well as merchants.

Nidhi Eoseewong has noticed that the Ayutthayan kings had two kinds of officials, namely *khunnāng fāi pokkhrong* or administrative officials and *khunnāng fāi phūchamnānkān* or officials with special capabilities, the latter being under the direct control of the king.[2] It is to be noted that almost all of the latter groups were non-Siamese immigrants. One example can be seen in the case of *Krom Āsā Yīpun* or Japanese Volunteers who were, from time to time, mobilized to suppress local rebellions. In this note an example of seafarers from among the *khunnāng fāi phūchamnānkān* shall be taken up for consideration.

The Siamese are sometimes said to be "aquatic in their disposition."[3] However, this does not mean that they are good at maritime navigation: the sphere of their activities seems to be limited to freshwater environments such as rivers. Operations at sea seem to have been exclusively in the hands of non-Siamese. Simon de la Loubère writes in his *The Kingdom of Siam* that "the Officers and Seamen, on whom he confides, are Foreigners."[4] This is known from the case of royal junk trade which was exclusively managed by the Chinese.[5] Each of the Chinese seamen on board a royal junk was given a *sakdinā* grade in accordance with their respective roles on board. It started at 400 for a captain of a junk of more than eight metres width down to 25 for minor crew members such as a sweeper.

In this note we take up for consideration the case of the *Krom Āsā Čhām* or *Čhām* volunteers, found in *Tamnaeng Nā Thahān Hua Müang*[6] within *The Laws of the Three Seals*.[7] Judging from existing circumstantial evidence, it was most likely a naval force. According to the list of officials given in the law, the commander of the *Čhām* volunteers was given a title of *Phra* with *sakdinā* of 2000. Though this was lower than that of the commander of the *Krom Dang Thōng Khwā* composed of Mon volunteers, who was given *sakdinā* 3000, it is still higher than most other *krom āsā*, such as Japanese. This might imply its importance in the Ayutthayan military bureaucracy.

The structure of the *Krom Āsā Čhām* is detailed in Figure 1. From the list, we see that the *Krom Āsā Čhām* consisted of two departments of left (*krom āsā sāi*) and right (*krom āsā khwā*), governed by *Phra*-rank high officials called *Čhāng Wāng* or a commander[8] with *sakdinā* grade 2000. Under each of the two commanders, there were left and right directors called *čhao krom sāi* (left) and *čhao krom khwā* (right) each having *sakdinā* 1600. And each of the departments had deputy directors with *sakdinā* 800, which gave a total of eight deputy directors. Below these levels there were minor officials with the rank of *Khun* and *Mün*, the number of whom are not mentioned in the Law.

The structure of the *Krom Āsā Čhām* was smaller than the *Krom Dang Thōng Khwā*, which was supposed to be another naval force composed of the Mon. However it was as large the *Krom Phratamruat* or Royal Police Department. The *Krom Āsā Čhām* was one of the *Thahān Āsā* which was composed of "foreign language speaking immigrants to Ayutthaya who, having enjoyed exemption from corvée labour, in the case of war served for the Siamese king with their individual expertise".[9] It was likely that it was due to their cultural background as seafarers that they were highly valued by the king of Ayutthaya. As for their seamanship, R.C. Majumdar writes:

> The Chams were hardy fearless mariners and boldly plied the ocean for the purpose of trade and war. There were mercantile vessels as well as ships of war. We often hear of Cham fleets harassing the coasts of Annam and Cambodge and pillaging the seacoasts towns and ports.....

FIGURE 1
Official Positions and *Sakdinā* among the
Krom Āsā Čhām (*Čhām* Volunteers)

Official Position	*sakdinā*
Left Commander, *Čhām* Department *(Phra)* พระราชวังสรร จางวางกรมอาษาจามซ้าย	2000
Right Commander, *Čhām* Department *(Phra)* พระราชวังสรร จางวางกรมอาษาจามขวา	2000
Left Deputy Commander *(Luang)* หลวงวิสุทธรายา ปลัดจางวางซ้าย	800
Right Deputy Commander *(Luang)* หลวงวิสุทธรายา ปลัดจางวางขวา	800
Right Director, *Čhām* Department *(Luang)* หลวงษรเสนี เจ้ากรมอาษาจามขวา	1600
Deputy Director, Left Department *(Khun)* ขุนรามฤทธิไกร ปลัดซ้าย	800
Deputy Director, Right Department *(Khun)* ขุนไชยภักดี ปลัดขวา	800
Secretary *(Khun)* ขุนไชยเสนี สมุบาญชีย	400
Left Director, *Čhām* Department *(Luang)* หลวงศรีมหาราชา เจ้ากรมอาษาจามซ้าย	1600
Left Deputy Department Director *(Khun)* ขุนรามเดช ปลัดกรมซ้าย	800
Right Deputy Department Director *(Khun)* ขุนนเรนภักดี ปลัดกรมขวา	800
Secretary *(Khun)* ขุนพลเสนี สมุบาญชีย	400
Right Director, *Čhām* Department *(Luang)* หลวงลักษมาณา เจ้ากรมอาษาจามขวา	1600
Left Deputy Department Director *(Khun)* ขุนวิสุทสงคราม ปลัดกรมซ้าย	800
Right Deputy Department Director *(Khun)* ขุนนเรนภักดี ปลัดกรมขวา	800
Left Director, *Čhām* Department *(Luang)* หลวงสุรินทเสนี เจ้ากรมอาษาจามซ้าย	1600
Deputy Director, Left Department *(Khun)* ขุนวิสุทเดช ปลัดซ้าย	800
Deputy Director, Right Department *(Khun)* ขุนวิชิตสงคราม ปลัดขวา	800
Čhām Volunteer *(Khun)* ขุนอาษาจาม	400
Čhām Volunteer *(Mün)* หมื่นอาษาจาม	200

An infamous activity of the Cham mariners was the systematic piracy in which they were engaged. Not only did they pillage defenseless towns and ports on the sea-coast by a sudden raid but they also captured and plundered vessels which passed along their coast. The vessels going to or coming from China which had of necessity to sail close to the shores of Annam, were their special victims, and for some time the Annamese waters came to be regarded with terror by the trading people of the east.[10]

It is known that when the modern Siamese navy was started it was based upon the traditional Mon "*marin*" in 1858, and members of *Āsā Čhām* were recruited as seamen to help the Mon.[11]

The ancient kingdom of Champa was destroyed by the invading Vietnamese army in 1471 A.D. This might have been instrumental in accelerating the diaspora of the Cham population to various parts of Southeast Asia including Ayutthaya. In sixteenth century Portuguese documents, *Čhām* are mentioned as being active in external trade along the Bay of Siam. And in 1662, a missionary reported the existence of a colony of the *Čhām* in Ayutthaya.[12]

In recent years the study of the *Čhām* diaspora in Southeast Asian history has been growing, although little has been done so far on their activities in Ayutthaya. It is hoped that this brief note could encourage a further study of the *Čhām* diaspora in the Thai kingdom of Ayutthaya.

Note: Professor Ishii Yoneo died unexpectedly on 12 February 2010, leaving his unfinished draft intended for the Reid festschrift. We include this incomplete submission both as a token of great respect for Professor Ishii and also because of the close relationship which Tony enjoyed with Ishii *sensei*. Koizumi Junko helped to prepare the manuscript for publication.

Notes

1. George Finlayson, *The Mission to Siam and Hué, the Capital of Cochin China in the Years 1821–22* (London: J. Murray, 1826), p. xvi; Simon de la Loubère, *The Kingdom of Siam*, with an introduction by David K. Wyatt, Oxford in Asia Reprints (Singapore and Oxford: Oxford University Press, 1986), p. 71.
2. Nidhi Eoseewong, *Kānmüang Thai Samai Phra Nārāi*. Bangkok: Thammasat University, 1980, pp. 7–8.
3. Finlayson, *The Mission to Siam and Hué*, p. 212.
4. De la Loubère, *The Kingdom of Siam*, p. 92.
5. See Yoneo Ishii (ed.) *The Junk Trade from Southeast Asia: Translations from the Tôsen Fusetsu-gaki, 1674–1723* (Singapore: ISEAS, 1998).

6. The *Tamnaeng Nā Thahān Hua Müang* is dated 1298 of an unidentified calendar, but is thought to probably date from 1466 CE.
7. This collection of laws was compiled and promulgated in 1805 in the reign of King Rama I. (Editor's Note: Prior to his death, Professor Ishii was engaged in a computerization project for the *Kotmai Trā Sām Duang* [Laws of the Three Seals]. See <http://gissv.cseas.kyoto-u.ac.jp/ktsd/01three_seals/01outline_e.html>).
8. Traditional Thai titles are, from higher to lower: *Čhaophyā, Phyā, Phra, Luang, Khun* and *Mün*.
9. Prince Naritsarānuwattiwong and Prince Damrongrāchānuphāp, *Sān Somdet vol. 5*. (Bangkok: Khurusaphā, 1961), p. 49.
10. R.C. Majumdar, *Champā, History and Culture of an Indian Colonial Kingdom in the Far East 2nd–16th Century A.D.* reprint. (Delhi: Gian Publishing House, 1985), p. 224.
11. Suporn Ocharoen, *Mōn nai Müang Thai* [The Mons in Thailand] Bangkok: Samnakngan Kongthun Sanapsanun Kānwičhai: Mūnnithi Khrōngkān Tamrā Sangkhommasāt lae Manutsayasāt, 1998), p. 134.
12. Pierre-Bernard Lafont, "Aperçu sur les relations entre le Campā de l'Asie du sud-est," in *Actes du seminaire sur le Campā organizé à l'Univerité de Copenhague le 23 mai 1987*. (Paris: Centre d'histoire et civilisations de la péninsule indochinoise, 1988), pp. 78–79.

References

Eoseewong, Nidhi. *Kānmüang Thai Samai Phra Nārāi*. Bangkok: Thai Khadi Institute, Thammasat University, 1980.

Finlayson, George. *The Mission to Siam and Hué, the Capital of Cochin China in the Years 1821–22*. London: J. Murray, 1826.

Ishii, Yoneo (ed.). *The Junk trade from Southeast Asia: Translations from the Tôsen Fusetsu-gaki, 1674–1723*. Singapore: ISEAS, 1998).

Lafont, Pierre-Bernard. "Aperçu sur les relations entre le Campā de l'Asie du sud-est," in *Actes du seminaire sur le Campā organizé à l'Univerité de Copenhague le 23 mai 1987*. pp. 71–82. Paris: Centre d'histoire et civilisations de la péninsule indochinoise, 1988.

Loubère, Simon de la. *The Kingdom of Siam*. With an introduction by David K. Wyatt, Oxford in Asia Reprints. Singapore and Oxford: Oxford University Press, 1986.

Majumdar, R.C. *Champā, History and Culture of an Indian Colonial Kingdom in the Far East 2nd–16th Century A.D.* reprint. Delhi: Gian Publishing House, 1985.

Naritsarānuwattiwong, Prince and Prince Damrongrāchānuphāp. *Sān Somdet vol. 5*. Bangkok: Khurusaphā, 1961.

Ocharoen, Suporn. *Mōn nai Müang Thai* [The Mons in Thailand]. Bangkok: Samnakngan Kongthun Sanapsanun Kānwičhai: Mūnnithi Khrōngkān Tamrā Sangkhommasāt lae Manutsayasāt, 1998.

12

TONGKING IN THE AGE OF COMMERCE

Li Tana

Studies on the premodern history of Vietnam owe much to Tony Reid, whose concept of the "Age of Commerce" has enlightened and inspired a generation of younger scholars. The "traditional" Vietnam had hitherto been portrayed as an undifferentiated swamp of peasantry living in closed and identical villages — "the Vietnamese village" — which stretched from north to south and throughout the centuries. Reid's representation of premodern Southeast Asia in relation to the rest of the world re-shaped the study of Southeast Asia and threw powerful new light onto facets of Vietnamese history and society which had previously not been properly investigated. For the first time, commerce was seen as an index of power and prosperity in premodern Vietnam like in its other Southeast Asian counterparts. If, over the last twenty years, scholars on Vietnam have more or less demolished the image of "a united Vietnam, a village Vietnam, a Confucian Vietnam, and a revolutionary Vietnam", this owes much to Reid for providing powerful weapons and frameworks within which new ground could be opened.

Over the last 10 years, our knowledge of seventeenth century northern Vietnam (Tongking, or Dang Ngoai) has grown remarkably.[1] In a way this is indicative and a result of the acceleration of researches on Vietnamese history over this period. Scholars in Vietnam, sometimes in collaboration with foreign scholars, have also contributed important work to the field, and much of this is based on stele inscriptions collected from northern and central Vietnam.[2] This article will build on these new findings and explore the relations between

Tongking's overseas trade and social changes, particularly the cultural and religious changes in seventeenth century Tongking society.

THE SIZE OF SEVENTEENTH CENTURY TONGKING'S OVERSEAS REVENUE

The role of commerce in changing societies has been recognized almost everywhere in Asia, but Tongking until recently retained the image of being comprised of classic autonomous villages, with deeply-rooted Confucian values and centred of an agricultural economy. If there was any sign of significant commercial growth here, it was but a "capitalist sprout," incidentally grown out of the soil of a typical subsistence economy. Although the existence of foreign trade was acknowledged, it was treated as an affair between the king, mandarins and foreign merchants, with little or nothing to do with the ordinary people, their petty trade, or the society. This approach of viewing foreign trade and domestic society as isolated compartments was partly due to the lack of systematic economic data.

The greatly improved field of historical studies over the last five years has shed valuable light on seventeenth century Tongking. If we were not so sure about the importance of foreign trade before this, the new researches indicate with little doubt that it was indeed significant to Tongking's economy, comparable to the effects in other Southeast Asian countries during the Age of Commerce. Between 1637 and 1680, a yearly average of 278,900 guilders or about 90,000 *taels* of silver were brought into Tongking by the VOC,[3] and another 43,500 *taels* were brought in by the Chinese merchants.[4] This meant that about 4.3 tons of silver was flowing into the country each year from these two sources alone. George Souza points out that Portuguese ships or *chos* yearly brought silver or coins (*caixas*) to Tongking between 1626 and 1669, at about 2–3 tons per year.[5] Before the VOC and Portuguese factors came into existence, there had been a constant inflow of silver between 1604 and 1629, when Japanese silver export to Tongking was around 2.5 tons per year.[6] We have good reason to believe that Chinese investment in Tongking remained constant or increased in the early seventeenth century, one of the peaks of commercial growth in Chinese history. In the light of the work of Souza, Hoàng Anh Tuấn and Iioka on Tongking, among others, we can now safely conclude that, for roughly 80 years of the seventeenth century, Tongking yearly had an inflow of around six to seven tons of silver.[7]

This suggests that around 450,000 *quan* of copper cash were being annually injected into Tongking's economy, throughout most of the seventeenth century.[8] This figure is significant, because it means that the foreign silver income was eight times the taxes derived from passes, ferries and markets of Tongking in the 1730s.[9] This income from exports was thus also comparable to Tongking's southern rival Cochinchina, or Đàng Trong. The Nguyễn's annual revenue during the mid-eighteenth century was an average of 380,700 *quan*,[10] and two-thirds of that would have come from overseas trade.[11] The Trịnh's silver income was more than the state revenue of the eighteenth century Nguyễn.

We have thus in recent years come to know that a large volume of silver flowed into Tongking society, significant enough to influence some of the policies. But once it came into the country, where did the silver go? Are we able to trace this from the surviving evidence, in order to see the impact of this foreign silver?

A set of figures about the religious life of seventeenth century Tongking suggests one direction. There are still thousands of *đình* or village halls in contemporary Vietnam and the few hundred oldest ones have steles indicating their founding years. None of these indicates that it had existed prior to the seventeenth century.[12] Another set of figure is also interesting: among the 411 Certificates granted to the local deities (*thần sắc*) by different Vietnamese courts, none of the documents was done before the seventeenth century.[13]

If the income from overseas trade gives a rough idea of the size of the seventeenth century Tongking economy and the share of its export sector, the emergence of the communal halls and a dazzling number of deities suggest a series of lively and significant changes occurring in Tongking society overlapping with the commercial boom of the seventeenth century. The following is an attempt to trace the path of the silver in exchange, production, and consumption, so as to present seventeenth century Tongking as a "coherent arc of change"[14] through the interactions between foreign and domestic trade, between commerce and the state, and between commerce and the society.

WAS 1550–1680 A GOLDEN ERA?

Contrary to the long-held view that the sixteenth century was a regressive and desolate era in Vietnamese history, which saw the country ruled by a usurping Mạc family, who constantly fought against the Lê-Trịnh, recent scholarship suggests a quite different picture of Vietnamese society in this period. According to Trần Quốc Vượng, it was during this period that the suffocating atmosphere of Confucian domination under Lê Thánh Tôn was significantly alleviated. It was also the Mạc, according to Đinh Khắc Thuận, after coming to power in 1527, who reformed the country's rapidly declining economy. Agriculture was extensively developed, and an irrigation system was built around the Mạc capital region in Hải Dương. At least 15 new bridges were built, according to the existing stele inscriptions; while revived handicrafts production stimulated the need for more markets, and overseas trade flourished.[15]

This renewed vigour was also manifested in the constructions of this period. A survey of the 2000 steles of the period shows that, in terms of building or renovating temples, communal halls, markets, bridges and ferries, the construction projects under the half century of Mạc rule in the sixteenth century were more numerous than the projects from c.1680 to c.1840 combined (see Figure 1 below).

The civil wars of the sixteenth and seventeenth centuries seem to have stimulated the two Đại Việt societies. When the war with the Mạc ended in 1593, the Lê-Trịnh continued to carry out the Mạc's open-door policies, encouraging handicrafts production and foreign trade, which offered the quickest source of income to repair the damaged agricultural infrastructure in the post-war era. The early seventeenth century thus saw Tongking picking up the momentum and development of the Mạc of the sixteenth century.

But Tongking also benefitted greatly from the broader background of the booming late Ming economy, one of the greatest economic expansions in Chinese history. By the late sixteenth century, China was intimately a part of the growing global economy. The Chinese traded actively in the South China Sea commercial trading networks with silk and porcelain in exchange for silver. These two exports were precisely the same staples of Tongking. It seemed therefore, while Tongking shared the boom years of the Southeast Asian economies between 1570 and 1630, as noted by Reid,[16] it shared the same export markets and products with China. Different from other Southeast Asian countries during the Age of Commerce, whose export items were spices, pepper, and luxury trade items such as aromatics and gold, Tongking's main export items were silk and porcelain. Tongking's strength, in other words, rested on manufacturing, which was the most important silver earner and one of the main engines of the seventeenth century Tongking economy.

The demand for silk from Tongking first by the Japanese and then by the Dutch must have stimulated the expansion of silk production. By the late 1640s the size of raw silk production was considerable. In 1648, for example, although the Chinese offered a high price and brought 6,000 *piculs* of Tongking raw silk to Nagasaki, the VOC was still able to buy 522 *piculs* of raw silk, and a good amount of *pelings*, velvet and other silk products to Japan, worth over 300,000 guilders. Again in 1650, while junks from China brought a total of 930 *piculs* of raw silk to Nagasaki, Chinese junks from

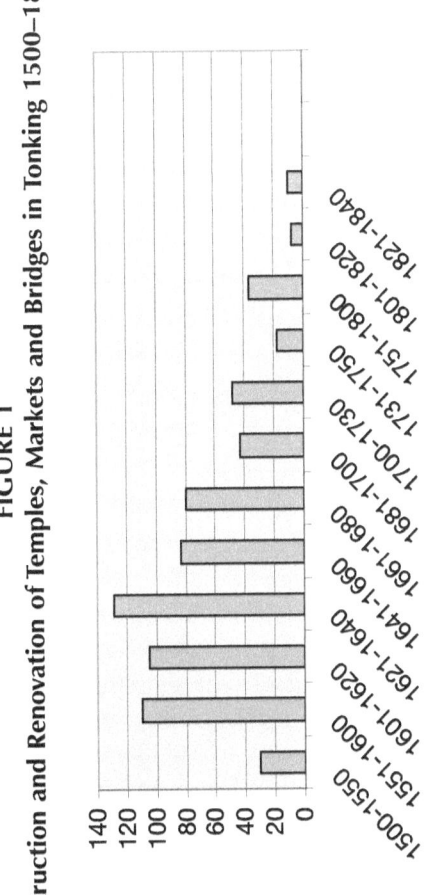

FIGURE 1
Construction and Renovation of Temples, Markets and Bridges in Tonking 1500–1840

northern Vietnam carried 820 *piculs* of Tongking raw silk, plus large amounts of silk piece goods.[17] This indicates that Tongking raw silk was competitive in Japan markets and thus was an attractive alternative to Chinese silk, both in terms of quantity and price.

The capacity of silk production of Tongking averaged 130–150 tons of raw silk and around 10,000 piece-goods a year. It would have required no less than 20,000 households or 100,000 labourers to produce the amount.[18] But since 90 per cent of silk production was women's work and silk was a sideline production, the households involved in the silk production would have been three or four times the 20,000 figure. In response to the demand for silk, and the silver flowing in, the number of Vietnamese peasants involved in silk production in the seventeenth century would have been considerable. Raw silk production is a labour-intensive business. A study of the silk-producing areas in China indicates that if the cycle of rice-planting on an acre of land requires 76 days, tending an acre of mulberry trees needs 196 days. Silkworm tending is equally labour-intensive and labour is usually 30–50 per cent of the total production cost.[19] If we are not clear whether silkworm tending, cocooning, and spinning were done by the same family, we do know that dying operations were performed by specialized villages,[20] and silk piece-good producers definitely bought raw silk rather than producing their own. So there were layers in the silk production, circulation and export sectors, each relying on the other, and all demanding some coordination. These in turn relied on agricultural productivity, transport and commerce, as these provided the necessary materials, food, transport and commercial links.

Under such circumstance cutting taxes to encourage domestic trade was to the government's advantage, as the enormous silver revenue derived from foreign trade had made the income from the domestic trade sector less important anyway. It was no coincidence therefore that the Trịnh abolished tax collecting passes in the country in 1658, and in 1660 further forbade officers from charging high fees on ferries and markets.[21] In the same year the government ordered the whole country to build highways (đương thiên lí, "roads of a thousand *lí*"), in order "to facilitate travel."[22]

The half-century war with Cochinchina seems to have stimulated silk production and given it more focus, as this was the most important means for obtaining hard cash to finance the more advanced weapons from the West. Silk manufacturing in Tongking thus developed to a higher level and numerous silk-producing centres flourished in and around Thăng Long. New villages emerged and the seventeenth century thus was an important period in the history of settlement of the Red River Delta. Archaeological findings in a ten-year Japanese project on the history of village formation in the Nam Định area reveals that a new landscape was made during the seventeenth century, possibly by both land expansion of the older villages and establishment of new settlements.[23]

New cash crops were introduced and became rapidly popular. Tobacco was brought into Tongking in the early 1660s from Laos and soon became an essential part of ordinary people's life. "Officers, common people and women all compete to get addicted to it, so much so that there is a saying that, 'one can do without eating for three days but cannot do without smoking for one hour'".[24] The method of brewing rice wine came from Guangdong but was originally from Siam, according to Lê Quý Đôn. This involved "adding aromatics to the wine which was called a-la-ke (arrack)."[25] Corn was also brought in during the seventeenth century. Although its Vietnamese name is *Lúa Ngô* (the crop of Ngô, i.e. the Chinese), the method of planting using a knife to dig a hole and plant the seed suggested that it might have been introduced into Tongking from the mountain peoples. The Sơn Tây region even came to rely on corn as its staple food. Both corn and sorghum became important crops in the bordering provinces with China.[26] The seventeenth century was in many ways a "'golden era' and gave birth to an unprecedented commercial system", as described by Hoang Anh Tuan.[27] The next sections examine this golden era.

THE FIRST INDICATOR: EXPANDED CONSTRUCTION

There is no doubt that a large percentage of the silver earned in the seventeenth century went to the war effort. According to De Rhodes, Tongking had at least 500 galleys, three times more than Cochinchina, and superior to those of Cochinchina in their size, armaments and decorations. The soldiers were well trained and disciplined, and skillfully used all weapons, as was shown by the pistols and arquebuses which they fired with admirable skill.[28]

I will concentrate here however, on the expanded consumption resulting from this unprecedented inflow of silver. To begin with, the court spent considerably on the building and renovation of the capital, particularly the palaces. In 1630 alone, three palaces were built for the Lê king, together with another sixteen new buildings.[29] The funds spent on the Trịnh lord's palaces were carefully not recorded but must have been comparable to those used for the king's residence. Government offices were enlarged and renovated. An example was the enlargement of the Chiêu Sự Hall of the Trịnh lord in 1663, where gold and red lacquer was extravagantly utilized.[30] Together the Vietnamese capital made an impressive sight for De Rhodes, who described Kẻ Chợ as "a very large, very beautiful city where the streets are broad, the people numberless, the circumference of the walls at least six leagues around".[31]

Because the Trịnh lord did not monopolise the silk trade, enough space was left for ordinary people to make profits. In 1644, for example, among the raw silk the VOC purchased from Tongking, only 21 per cent was bought from the Trịnh lord and the local mandarins, and about 80 per cent was bought from the local people.[32] Income from silk production was about 39 *piculs* (or 2,331 kg.) of rice, enough for a household of five to live on.[33] The silk income mainly flowed from the coast to the regions around the capital area, and these were the areas where concentrated construction occurred. In the absence of information on civilian residence construction, the steles recording constructions and renovations of temples (*chùa*), communal halls (*đình*), markets, bridges and ferries suffice to show that there was a construction boom in Tongking between 1500 and 1680.

What was also remarkable is that the most rapid growth in construction occurred in the neighbouring provinces of two major urban centres — Hanoi and Phố Hiến — rather than in the two centres themselves. Construction in Hải Dương and Hưng Yên provinces was five times more than that of Hanoi, while Bắc Ninh province doubled Hanoi, and Hà Tây equalled that of Hanoi.[34] This suggested that there was fairly large volume of capital available in the society. Tongking's urbanization in the Age of Commerce thus was represented more by the mushrooming village markets, more extensive market networks and more frequent exchanges, than the construction of large cities. The reason that these provinces saw the most remarkable growth was the handicraft industry. An important characteristic of seventeenth century silk production in Tongking was that the producers were not producing household surplus but were manufacturing for the overseas markets. Although the producers continued to live in farming households, they specialised in parts of the production process, relying on markets. The markets will be the focus of the section below.

THE SECOND INDICATOR: THE EXTENSION OF MARKETS

Although the people of Tongking did not generally engage in sea commerce, the trade on ports and rivers was frequent, and profit considerable, according to De Rhodes.

> Yet without leaving the Kingdom ... merchants do a lot of business, thanks to the convenience and multitude of the ports, and in a manner so advantageous for them that they double their capital two or three times in a year without running the risks so common everywhere at sea. For along all

the coast of the Kingdom of Annam, extended for more than 350 French leagues, you count a goodly fifty ports, able to welcome at least ten or twelve large ships, at the mouths of so many rivers.[35]

Markets proliferated around the country — village markets, district markets, morning and afternoon markets — when the pace of production was quickened. Most of them appeared around the ports and rivers. On the Red River, according to Nguyễn Đức Nghinh, in a distance of mere 10 kilometres, "there was a whole string of riverside markets."[36] The dense network of waterways in the Red River Delta facilitated travel, trade, and transport of heavy and cumbersome merchandise.

Travel by land also became frequent and easy, facilitated by many inns or guesthouses which mushroomed during this Age of Commerce. A map of the mid-seventeenth century was accompanied by an interesting description of the routes and suggestions for places to stay, not unlike the *Lonely Planet* these days:[37]

> Find a nice day to start your journey from the capital, in the early morning. Travel for a day and you stay in the (*quán*) Lễ Inn, second day in the Cót Inn, third day in Cát Inn, fourth day in Vạn Inn, fifth day in Bồ tục Inn, sixth day in Hoàng Mai, seventh day in Sò Inn, eighth day in Vĩnh Market (Chợ), and the ninth day at Nhà Bridge (Cầu). On the tenth day you stay in Lạc Inn, eleventh day in Khe-lau Inn; twelfth day in Phù-lưu Market, and on the fifteenth day and a half you stay in Lũ-đăng Inn.

These inns seemed to suggest the existence of fairly dense and evenly distributed regional marketing networks. This contrasts with the density of the markets in northern and central Vietnam in the year 1417, recorded by the Ming documents. According to this source, there was a rough average of one market in every 50 villages, with great variation between the coast and the upland regions. On the coast where markets were more easily found, the density of markets was an average of one market per 10 villages.[38] A great many village markets emerged and thrived in the seventeenth century. According to Nguyễn Đức Nghinh, the surviving documents suggest that 15 out of 17 temple markets came into being in the seventeenth century.[39] Phạm Thị Thủy Vinh, a Vietnamese scholar who has done research on 1063 inscriptions found in Kinh Bắc (today's Bắc Ninh and Bắc Giang provinces), also points out that the majority of markets in Kinh Bắc recorded in steles were established in the seventeenth century, during this "peak of the commercial economy in pre-modern Vietnam."[40] The average of village markets of her data gives us one market per 4.4 villages in this province.[41]

Village markets mushroomed because of the rapidly growing need for exchange. Producers of raw silk, cotton and cotton thread for example needed markets to sell the products, and some markets were established to cater to that need.[42] Establishing a market was also a relative quick way to obtain cash income. According to a seventeenth century inscription of a market in Hanoi suburb, textile sellers were to pay 5 *tiền* (60 cash) per head, and each pork stall had to pay 2 *quan* (1,200 cash). These rules however were applied to the traders from outside only, while the host villagers enjoyed a total or partial tax exemption.[43] Since a market was an income generator for the village in which it was located and the main purpose was to attract traders from the outside, villagers were keen to set up markets in their own villages but careful to avoid overlapping with the market days of the nearby villages. The folkloric saying in the region near Nam Định thus goes:

On the first and seventh days go to Luong market,
On the second and sixth, to Ninh Cuong, on the fifth and ninth to Dong Bien.
The fourth and tenth are market days at Con Cham,
On the third and eighth days, it's the turn of Don and Trung.
At Hom Dinh, the market is crowded in the morning,
While Phe Sau is full toward noon and so is Cau on the riverside.
Nearby is Phuong De, while Dau opens in the morning.
On odd days let's go to Con Coc, and on even days to Dong Cuong.
O traders, Quan Anh is full of markets where you can buy and sell![44]

The development of handicraft villages, together with advantageous land and water transportation, gave rise to many trade markets and trade villages in Kinh Bắc. The Đoan Minh pagoda in 1693 said that "we had a Buddhist market from the previous dynasty [i.e. Mạc] which met 12 times a month to sell earthen wares and ceramics. Traders piled up their stocks in mounds, wealth and goods were always in circulation. Each and every household had its own kiln to make utensils, and each autumn there was a festival for celebration".[45]

Because of the financial benefit the village markets brought in, conflicts occurred frequently over the possession of a certain market. For example, when the villagers of Cổ Loa determined to fight a lawsuit over the ownership of the market against the neighbouring village of Duc Tu, they agreed that "the population of Cổ Loa unanimously pledged to see the lawsuit through to the end, whatever the costs." Should the lawsuit be lost and the representatives of Cổ Loa were flogged at the court, "the population of the village would raise money to indemnify them, at the rate of 2 *tiền* (or 120 cash) for each lash he received."[46]

The number of vendors must have mushroomed. Again De Rhodes had a unique way to measure them, by way of counting the betel-nut traders in Thăng Long:

> The more comfortable people have servants who prepare the packet [of betel nuts], but to supply the rest of the people … who have no one in their service to prepare it for them, we count up to 50,000 dealers who for a modest price sell it in various parts of the town; from which it is necessary to conclude that the number of people who buy it is inestimably great.

Most, if not all of these betel-nut vendors would have been women. To have good business, as a Vietnamese proverb goes, the best place is close to the market, and the second best is close to a river (*Nhất cận thị, nhị cận giang*), so travel became important. A government edict of 1663, which issued 47 rules to maintain social order, confirms that travel had become an important part of life for ordinary people. These rules include Number 20, "Inns should be careful not to provide venues for illicit sexual activities, while not rejecting guests who are seeking accommodation". Rule Number 18 also related to lifestyle in the public space: "Men and women are not to indulge themselves in sexual debauchery (肆淫风)."[47]

The picture of women busy along the rivers or crossing on ferries was portrayed by Tú Xương, a Vietnamese writer of the late nineteenth century, when he described his wife as follows:

> All year round you are busy trading at the riverside,
> Earning enough to feed 5 children and one husband.
> Sleeping alone, you toss and turn in bed,
> Crossing on the ferry, you chat happily on the river.[48]

The more relaxed atmosphere and more important role in silk production and commerce "gives great liberty to the young women, who offer themselves of their own account to any strangers, who will go to their price (from 5 to 100 dollars)."[49] This was not unlike, in the eyes of the VOC factors, their colleagues in Japan who enjoyed Japanese wives, or the company employees in Ayutthaya who courted and lived with the Siamese and Mon women. As Reid points out, interracial unions were a feature of all the commercial cities of Southeast Asia.[50] It was those women traders, according to Olga Dror, who were able to travel around the country protected by Liễu Hạnh's cult.[51] This female deity, a singing girl, a *geisha*, or a prostitute when she was alive, emerged from the coast as a most powerful female spirit in the seventeenth century, at least as potent as other male deities.

THE THIRD INDICATOR: THE THRIVING *ĐÌNH*

While the impact of silver was reflected in many aspects of the society, it is even easier to trace the silver used for the founding of *đình*. The *đình*, we are told, was a communal hall, and both a product and the symbol of the ancient and autonomous villages in which they were situated. Yet, the earliest stele inscriptions found in a *đình* only goes back to the sixteenth century, and most of the *đình* were founded from the seventeenth century onward. This contrasts sharply with Buddhist temples, where stele inscriptions go as far back as 618 AD.[52] The stele inscriptions of the *đình*, in other words, indicate their rather late founding dates, and can hardly support the view that these symbolise the ancient villages.

There were indeed *đình* before the sixteenth century but they were shelters for travellers, which reflect the true meaning of the Chinese character 亭 (pavilion),[53] built along the route to allow travellers to rest. The *Annam chi lược* (a brief history of Annam), compiled in 1333 CE, lists a *đình* called Phấn Dịch (粉驛亭, "A courier station/pavilion in pink colour or painted"). Under this entry it explains:[54]

> Because the [country] is hot, there are often pavilions (*đình*) built along the big roads (通衢) to rest the travellers. Before the first Tran king became a king as was still but a teenager, he met a Buddhist monk who predicted that he would become influential when he grew up…when he became the king, he ordered that every *đình* in the country build a statue of Buddha in thanks to the monk.[55]

From the above information we can glean that before the sixteenth century the *đình* was a simple building combining the functions of resting-place for travellers and courier station. The official Ming documents in the year 1417 recorded 339 courier stations 驛 in northern and central Vietnam.[56] Some of them likely overlapped with pavilions (*đình*) or indeed were the pavilions themselves.[57] It also suggests that no deity had existed in the *đình* or pavilions before the Trần Dynasty. The fundamental and earlier function of *đình*, in other words, was to assist in linking different places through travel and trade. This extroversive nature of the early *đình* was overwritten by the scholars from the seventeenth century, who emphasised the nature of the *đình* as a property possessed by only the villagers within a certain community, as against other communities. The locations of the *đình* however betray such a view. According to Hà Văn Tấn, they were often built along the rivers, and faced towards the river,[58] rather than being in the heart of the village.

The *đình* had its second incarnation in the seventeenth century. While the earlier *đình* was a simple building with 4 rows of pillars, from the seventeenth century on they grew larger and began to have six rows of pillars. While inscriptions of the sixteenth century indicate that there were *đình* with thatched roofs, from the seventeenth century onwards a tiled roof was the norm.[59] Most importantly, where there was no deity in the *đình*, from the seventeenth century on most of the *đình* started to house the *thành hoàng*. This *thành hoàng* is a collective name for thousands of local deities or spirits, so each village could have a different *thành hoàng* in their *đình*. It was from this time that we began to have the earliest sign of the worshiping of tutelary spirits in the *đình*. It was this religious function that attracted followers, and importantly, donations. This led to the further widespread building of *đình*, and from then on the *đình* and their founding dates were recorded in the steles. Phạm Thị Thủy Vinh's data, for example, suggests that 58 per cent of the *đình*s in Bắc Ninh province were built in the seventeenth century and the rest were built later.[60]

The reason that *đình* suddenly became so popular in the seventeenth century was that it opened a glorious way to make a living person, his wife and dead family members, an object of worship as *thành hoàng*. A large number of big donors or their mothers became the *phúc thần* (deity of fortune or happiness) of the *đình* to which they made the donation.[61] Many eunuchs also thus became the "deity of fortune" or the protector of the *đình*, because they donated a large amount of silver to establish *đình* in their native villages. A senior eunuch Nguyễn Thái Duong, for example, donated some 500 *taels* of silver in 1657 to his village so that a *đình* could be built, and more importantly, his ancestors could be worshipped alongside the local deity.[62] Before he died in 1667, he donated another large amount of money and land to the three villages nearby, and thus was made the "*thành hoàng*" or the tutelary guardian of the three villages.[63] In 1670 another eunuch Trương Tho Kien donated 120 *taels* of silver together with land to build a *đình* for the same purpose. The Eunuch General Ngô Lệnh Công also enthusiastically donated money to build two *đình*s in 1697.

Here we can clearly see how VOC silver passed into the *đình*s. The *capados* or eunuchs were the most feared and hated people of the VOC factors in Tongking. They had the ears of the Trịnh lord and were the ones directly involved with collecting taxes and engaging in negotiations. This put them into the best position to squeeze silver out of the VOC. In 1650 alone, other than the 25,000 taels paid to the Trịnh lord and 10,000 to the Crown Prince, the VOC paid 10,000 taels to the five chief eunuchs.⁶⁴

Not surprisingly eunuchs became the richest people after the Lê-Trịnh rulers, if we take the donations of Bắc Ninh province as examples. Among the donations made to *đình*s, temples and other public properties, 44 were made by queens and court women, 71 were made by Lê-Trịnh government officers, and 99 were made by the eunuchs. What is really telling however was the quantity of donations. While no officer's donation was more than 8 *mẫu* of land, and the total land of 71 donations by the officers was below 200 *mẫu*, in 1655, one eunuch alone donated 44 *mẫu* and 300 *taels* of best silver, plus 210 strings of copper coins.⁶⁵

Here we see a crucial income flow from overseas trade feeding almost directly into the founding of *đình*s. Much wealth generated or squeezed from the foreign merchants came to the court, to government officials and particularly to the eunuchs. A considerable amount in turn flowed from them to serve religious purposes, particularly building and renovating temples and communal halls. Many *đình*s could not have been founded without the direct involvement of some of the eunuchs, as the examples above indicate. The most visible avenues of silver disbursement were to two destinations. One went to the constructions of *đình*, and the other to the building of temple markets. Many new temple markets were built in the seventeenth century, although it was one of the oldest forms of market in Vietnam.⁶⁶

A large amount of silver flowed into the pockets of the rich and powerful, in other words, was directly involved in the restructuring of the *đình* and the local religion of *thành hoàng* worship, and in the flourishing of temple markets. Remarkably both establishments were created to generate more financial income to serve religious functions. What is also important here is that Tongking in the Age of Commerce did see the flourishing of a universal religion, in this case Buddhism, as pointed out by Anthony Reid, but along with this development, the worship of local spirits mushroomed, many of them housed under the roof of the *đình*, in this age of religious revolution. In fact, if there was anything remarkable in the religious aspect of Tongking society, it was not the revival of Buddhism or Confucianism, but the emergence and worship of hundreds of spirits. Although about a dozen deities had been worshipped before the fifteenth century in Đại Việt,⁶⁷ the seventeenth century saw the flourishing of hundreds of deities, and none had been heard of before. A seventeenth century Chinese traveler thus reported:"[Vietnamese] read fairly widely, and are literate, but they fancy strange and wield things….[They] worship shamans and spirits, not the two religions [Confucianism and Buddhism]."⁶⁸

THE FORMATION OF VILLAGE LITERATI

It is puzzling that the rather rapid commercialization, easier travel, more frequent mobility, width of choice in local religion and more relaxed social relations which were displayed in seventeenth century Tongking society, it was to develop into a much more village-based society by the late seventeenth century. Here a view by a well-known Vietnamese scholar Phan Đài Doãn is worth pondering. He noted that Confucianism of seventeenth- and eighteenth-century Tongking was typically rural, which made it different from its contemporary and more urban-based Confucianist counterpart in southern China.[69] Tongking's literati of this period also contrasted sharply to their forefathers of the Lý and Trần periods. In those earlier periods the aristocrats were mostly aristocrats and more urban-based.

The dramatic political upheavals of the sixteenth century brought drastic changes at the elite level — Lê to Mạc, and Mạc to Lê-Trịnh within half a century, each producing a different group of aristocrats. Here "social disorder" literally and repeatedly occurred. When the Mạc fell, the temples owned by them became the property of villages, as did the temples privately owned by the aristocrats.[70] These village temples played important roles in binding villagers together.

The easier access to wealth and to cheap, printed books brought into Tongking by Chinese merchants expanded the size of village-based literati. From the late sixteenth century onwards the cost of printing in the Yangzi River Delta dropped dramatically. Different from other Southeast Asian countries, where the Chinese junks that visited were predominantly from Guangdong and Fujian, the Chinese junks visiting Tongking most frequently in the late seventeenth century were those from Ningbo, the port of the Yangzi River delta and the centre of print culture.[71] Cheap and abundant Chinese books therefore played an important role in raising literacy levels and enlarging the base of the literati. From this point of view, the literati revival of the late seventeenth century in northern Vietnam cannot be separated from the print culture flourishing in the Yangzi River delta. Nor can it be separated from the Japan trade, which was the main driver of the Asian trade in general, and book export in particular.[72] In other words, the "traditional" "Confucian" "village" values of the Vietnamese elites was built precisely upon the mass production of the Chinese print industry from the late sixteenth century onward. The books brought into Vietnam by the merchants formed the stock of knowledge, and served as important sources for the newly-developed approaches to textual interpretation, biography and historiography in the eighteenth century.[73]

Although the conventional view tends to put literati and merchants at two poles far apart from each other and sharing little, the stele inscriptions indicate that most scholars who passed examinations were from Hải Dương and Kinh Bắc, the two provinces that had the highest level of commercialization. The places where the largest percentage of stele inscriptions is found were villages with a more developed economy of handicrafts and trade,[74] rather than purely agriculture-based villages.[75] The material foundation of the village-based literati was to a large extent the trade and commercialisation of the society during this period.

Notes

1. Hoàng Anh Tuấn, "Silk for Silver: Dutch-Vietnamese Relations, 1637–1700" (Ph.D. dissertation, University of Leiden, 2006); Iioka Naoko, "Literati Entrepreneur: Wei Zhiyan in the Tonkin-Nagasaki Silk Trade" (PhD dissertation, National University of Singapore, 2009); Olga Dror, *Cult, Culture, and Authority: Princess Lieu Hanh in Vietnamese History* (Honolulu: University of Hawaii Press, 2007); for new studies on Vietnamese villages, see Philippe Papin and Olivier Tessier (eds.), *Làng ở vùng châu thổ sông Hồng: Vấn đề còn bỏ ngỏ* [The village in questions] (Hanoi: Ecole française d'Extrême-Orient/Trung tâm Khoa học xã hội và Nhân văn Quốc gia, 2002).
2. Phạm Thị Thủy Vinh, *Văn bia thời Lê xứ Kinh Bắc và sự phản ánh sing hoạt làng xã* [The Stelae of the Kinh Bac Region during the Lê Period: Reflections of Village Life], (Hanoi: Bibliotheque vietnamienne-VIII and Ecole française d'Extrême-Orient, 2003); Đinh Khắc Thuân, *Lịch sử triều Mạc qua thư tịch và văn bia* [A history of the Mac through books and inscriptions] (Hanoi: Nhà xuất bản Khoa học xã hội, 2001).
3. Hoàng Anh Tuấn, "Silk for Silver", Appendix 3. Hoàng's estimation of average was based on the period between 1637 and 1699, while the annual average would be much higher for the period 1637 and 1680, the period to which this article refers.
4. Hoàng Anh Tuấn, "Silk for Silver", p. 181. My calculation is again based on the annual average between 1637 and 1680.
5. George Bryan Souza, *The Survival of Empire: Portuguese Trade and Society in China and the South China Sea, 1630–1754* (Cambridge: Cambridge University Press, 2004), pp. 111–15. The figure of 2–3 tons came from personal communications with Prof. Souza. My deep gratitude to him for his advice.
6. Japanese exports of silver to Southeast Asia were 20 tons per year between 1604 and 1629, and the percentage of Red Seal ships which sailed to Tonking was 12.4 per cent. See Anthony Reid, *Southeast Asia in the Age of Commerce 1450–1680. Volume Two: Expansion and Crisis* (New Haven and London: Yale University Press, 1993), pp. 18, 24.

7. This did not include the investment of the English and the French during the last quarter of the seventeenth century.
8. The silver/cash ratio fluctuated between 1 tael: 2,000 cash and 1: 1,300 cash, and sometimes dropped to as low as 1 tael: 500 cash in the 1650s, when there was a high inflow of silver from the VOC. See Hoàng Anh Tuấn, pp. 178–79. The average ratio was still around 1 tael: 2 quan, as recorded by Phan Huy Chú. See Phan Huy Chú, *Lịch triều hiến chương loại chí* [A reference book of the institutions of successive dynasties], 3 volumes (Hanoi: Nhà xuất bản khoa học xã hội, 1992), 2: 243.
9. Taxes collected from passes (1732): 26,731 *quan*; taxes from ferries (1732): 2,737 *quan*; Taxes from markets (1727): 1,660 *quan*. Total: 31,128 *quan*. Phan Huy Chú, *Lịch triều hiến chương loại chí*, 2: 268–70.
10. Li Tana and Anthony Reid (eds.), *Southern Vietnam under the Nguyễn: Documents on the Economic History of Cochinchina (Dang Trong), 1602–1777*, Economic History of Southeast Asia Project (Canberra and Singapore: ANU/ISEAS, 1993), p. 118. Silver: cash ratio 1:2 *quan*.
11. Li Tana, *Nguyễn Cochinchina: Southern Vietnam in the Seventeenth and Eighteenth Century* (Ithaca: Cornell University Southeast Asia Program, 1998), pp. 87–89.
12. *Văn khắc Hán-Nôm Việt Nam* [Steles in Han-Nom characters in Vietnam] (Hanoi: Social Science Publishing House, 1993), pp. 27–192.
13. Liu Chun Yin, Lin Qing Zhao and Tran Nghia (eds.), *Yuenan hannan wenxian mulu tiyao* [Catalogue and Abstracts of Han-Nom textual material in Vietnam] (Taipei: Asia-Pacific Studies Centre, Academic Sinica, 2004), Supplement vol. 1, pp. 1–127.
14. Timothy Brook, *The Confusions of Pleasure: Commerce and Culture in Ming China* (Berkeley: University of California Press, 1999), p. xvii.
15. Đinh Khắc Thuân, *Lịch sử triều Mạc*, pp. 198–207.
16. Anthony Reid, *Southeast Asia in the Age of Commerce, 1450–1680*, vol. 2, pp. 17–24.
17. Hoàng Anh Tuấn, "Silk for Silver", pp. 141–42.
18. The VOC's exports comprised 90 tons of raw silk and 6,000 piece-goods in a good year in the mid-seventeenth century; Chinese export were equivalent to two-thirds of the VOC figures; the yield and income are based on Hoàng Anh Tuấn, *Silk for Silver*, pp. 181–82.
19. John Lossing Buck, *Land Utilization in China* (Chicago: University of Chicago Press, 1937), p. 302.
20. Cotton thread was made by some specialized villages to supply the textile-weaving villages. Vũ Đức Thơm, "Bước đầu tìm hiểu về cây bông trong đời sống của người nông dân trước năm 1945 ở Quỳnh Côi" [Towards an understanding of cotton planting in peasants' livelihood before 1945], in *Hội thảo khoa học người dân Thái Bình trong lịch sử* [Proceedings of the conference on the people of Thai Binh], (Thái Bình: Bộ phần lịch sử dân tộc, ban nghiên cứu lịch sử Đảng tỉnh Thái Bình, 1986), p. 417.

21. Phan huy Chú, *Lịch triều hiến chương loại chí*, 2: 267.
22. *Đại Việt sử ký toàn thư* [The Vietnamese Annals] (Tokyo: Tokyo University Institute of Oriental Culture, 1984–86), p. 965. Hereafter *Toàn Thư*.
23. Nishimura Masanari and Nishino Noriko, "Archaeological study of the settlement formation in the Red River Plain: a case of Bach Coc and the surrounding" (Paper presented at the conference 'Vietnamese Peasant Activity: An Interaction between Culture and Nature', Leiden, 28–31 August 2002), p. 10.
24. Lê Quý Đôn. *Vân Đài Loại Ngữ* [Classified talk from the study], (Saigon: Phủ quốc vụ khanh đặc trách Văn hóa, 1973), vol. 3, pp. 34b–35a.
25. Lê Quý Đôn. *Vân Đài Loại Ngự*, p. 40a.
26. Lê Quý Đôn. *Vân Đài Loại Ngự*, p. 49b.
27. Hoàng Anh Tuấn, "Silk for Silver", p. 47.
28. Alexandre de Rhodes, *Histoire du royaume du Tonkin*, edited by Jean-Pierre Duteil (Paris: Éditions Kimé, 1999), pp. 33–36. My thanks to Nola Cooke for translating the relevant sections for me.
29. *Toàn Thư*, p. 941.
30. *Toàn Thư*, p. 975; see also the stele "Nam Giao điện bi ký", no. 161, Han-Nom Institute.
31. See Solange Hertz (trans.), *Rhodes of Vietnam: The Travels and Missions of Father Alexander de Rhodes in China and Other Kingdoms of the Orient* (Westminter, Maryland: The Newman Press, 1966), p. 64.
32. Hoàng Anh Tuấn, *Silk for Silver*, p. 140.
33. The VOC exported 90 tons of raw silk and 6,000 piece-goods in a good year in the mid-seventeenth century; Chinese exports were two-thirds of those of the VOC; the yield and income are based on Hoàng Anh Tuấn, *Silk for Silver*, pp. 181–82.
34. Interestingly, this pattern is repeated in contemporary Vietnam. The 2006 growth rates of Hưng Yên, Vĩnh Phúc, Hải Dương and Hà Tây near Hanoi were between 23 per cent and 28.3 per cent; while Bình Dương and Đồng Nai provinces near Ho Chi Minh City were 23.4 per cent and 21.2 per cent respectively. The GDP growth rates of the two major cities were 12 per cent and 11 per cent respectively.
35. Alexandre de Rhodes, *Histoire du royaume du Tonkin*, p. 58.
36. Nguyễn Đức Nghinh, "Markets and Villages", in *The Traditional Village in Vietnam*, edited by Phan Huy Lê et al. (Hanoi: The Gioi, 1993), p. 353.
37. *Thien Nam Tứ chí lộ đồ* [The map of Thiên Nam] compiled between 1630 and 1653, according to Truong Bao Lam. *Hồng Đức bản đồ* [Maps of the Hong Duc reign] (Saigon: Bộ quốc gia Giáo dục, 1962), pp. XII, 72.
38. *Ngannan tche yuan* (Hanoi: Imprimerie d'Extreme-Orient, 1932), vol. 2, pp. 61–63.
39. Nguyễn Đức Nghinh, "Markets and Villages", p. 331.
40. Phạm Thị Thủy Vinh, *Văn bia thời Lê xứ Kinh Bắc*, p. 166.
41. Phạm Thị Thủy Vinh, *Văn bia thời Lê xứ Kinh Bắc*, pp. 166–70. See "谅江府安勇县玉林社福严寺", "集市碑记", "二社共论碑记", and "开市立碑".

42. "They sell cotton thread to people outside the county, even those from Hà Đông would come and buy cotton thread here. "Vũ Đức Thơm". "Bước đầu tìm hiểu", p. 417.
43. Nguyễn Đức Nghinh, "Markets and Villages", pp. 328–29.
44. Nguyễn Đức Nghinh, "Markets and Villages", p. 324.
45. Phạm Thị Thủy Vinh. *Văn bia thời Lê xứ Kinh Bắc*, p. 221.
46. Cited from Nguyễn Duc Nghinh, "Markets and Villages", pp. 326–27.
47. *Toàn Thư*, p. 974.
48. "Thương vợ", Tú Xương (1870–1907):
    Quanh năm buôn bán ở mom sông,
    Nuôi đủ năm con với một chồng.
    Lặn lộn thân cô khi quãng vắng,
    Eo sèo mặt nước lúc đò đông.
    Một duyên hai nợ âu đành phận,
    Năm nắng mười mưa há quản công.
    Cha mẹ thói đời ăn ở bạc,
    Có chồng hờ hững cũng như không".
49. Quoted from Hoàng Anh Tuấn, p. 174.
50. Anthony Reid, *Southeast Asia in the Age of Commerce, 1450–1680. Volume One: The Lands Below the Winds* (New Haven and London: Yale University Press, 1988), p. 155.
51. Dror, *Cult, Culture, and Authority*, p. 81.
52. Not even one earlier stele inscriptions was collected from a *dinh*. See Phan Văn Các and Claudine Salmon, *Épigraphie en chinois du Viêt Nam = Văn kh'ac Hán Nôm Việt Nam* (Paris: Presses de l'École française d'Extrême-Orient; Hà Nôi: Vien nghiên cuu Hán Nôm, 1998).
53. Hà Văn Tấn and Nguyễn Văn Kự, *Đình Việt Nam: Community Halls in Vietnam* (Ho Chi Minh City: Nhà xuất bản Thành phố Hồ Chí Minh, 1998), p. 75.
54. Lê Trắc, *Annam Chí lược*, p. 27.
55. The practice of placing statues of Buddha in the pavilions seemed to have disappeared in the fifteenth century, perhaps during Lê Thánh Tôn's reign. The oldest *dinhs* existing in Vietnam still do not have any deity. See Hà Văn Tấn and Nguyễn Văn Kự, *Đình Việt Nam*, p. 83.
56. *Ngannan tche yuan*, vol. 2, pp. 61–63.
57. Hà Văn Tấn insists that two types of *đình* existed before the sixteenth century: one was resting pavilions and the other communal halls. His evidence was that the former did not have accommodation facilities. But as the name "Phấn Dịch Đình" recorded in 1333 for a *đình* attests, pavilions (*đình*) and courier stations (*dịch* or *tram*) were one and the same thing. Courier stations in the Ming period did provide free accommodation, food and transport labour to those bearing travel permits, and were spaced along routes every 60 to 80 *li* (35–45 kilometres). See Timothy Brook, *The Confusions of Pleasure*, p. 35.
58. The *Toàn Thư* records that in 1522 the Lê king stopped at a *đình* on his way

into exile. *Toàn Thư*, vol. 2, p. 828. Hà Văn Tấn and Nguyễn Văn Kự, *Đình Việt Nam*, p. 80.

59. Hà Văn Tấn and Nguyễn Văn Kự, *Đình Việt Nam*, p. 82.
60. My calculations are based on Phạm Thị Thủy Vinh, *Văn bia thời Lê xứ Kinh Bắc*, pp. 573–87.
61. For example, the "Hau than bia ky" in the year 1682, in Mai Dinh village, Hiep Hoa district, Bac Ha prefecture, see Phạm Thị Thủy Vinh, *Văn bia thời Lê xứ Kinh Bắc*, p. 574; the "Phùng sự hầu thần", of 1694, No. 3905-3912-13; the "Cẩm ơn duc bi" of 1683 in An Tru village, Lương Tài district, Bắc Ninh province, no. 6008-11; "Phùng sự hầu thần bi", No. 3905; 3912-13 in Hán-Nôm Institute.
62. No. 2355-56, Hán-Nôm Institute, "Hung tao Minh dinh bi"; also see Phạm Thị Thủy Vinh, *Văn bia thời Lê xứ Kinh Bắc*, p. 610.
63. No. 2345-47, Hán-Nôm Institute, "Vinh tran am bi"; Phạm Thị Thủy Vinh, *Văn bia thời Lê xứ Kinh Bắc*, p. 612.
64. Hoàng Anh Tuấn, "Silk for silver", p. 90.
65. Phạm Thị Thủy Vinh, *Văn bia thời Lê xứ Kinh Bắc*, p. 610.
66. In 1632, for example, the marquis of Van Nghien from Hải Hưng founded a market and offered it to a pagoda; in 1650 another marquis named Võ also bought a plot of land to set up a market which was later donated to a pagoda. Nguyễn Đức Nghinh, "Markets and Villages", p. 333.
67. See Lý Tế Xuyên, *Yuedian youling ji* [Việt điện U Linh tập, Compilation of the potent spirits in the Realm of Viet], in *Collection Romans & Contes du Vietnam écrits en Han* (Paris-Taipei: Ecole Française d'Extrême-Orient/Student Book Co. Ltd, 1992), serie II, vol. 2.
68. [Qing dynasty] Li Xiangen 李仙根, "Annan zaji" 安南雜記 [Miscellaneous notes on Annam], collected in *Congshu jicheng chubian: Annan zhuan ji qita erzhong* (Shanghai: Shangwu Press, 1937), p. 2.
69. Phan Đài Doãn, "Introduction", in Phạm Thị Thủy Vinh, *Văn bia thời Lê xứ Kinh Bắc*, p. 208.
70. Đinh Khắc Thuân. *Lịch sử triều Mạc*, p. 237.
71. 1689: April 28 (ship no. 42): statement of Lin Ganteng: There were two ships which visited Tongking from Ningpo in the March–April period. Another statement by Jiang Chouquan from Xiamen (ship no. 44) said that the two ships would soon head back to Ningpo. See Chen Chingho, "Chinese Junk Trade at Nagasaki at the Beginning of the Qing Dynasty", *New Asia Journal*, no. 1, vol. 3 (1960): 273–332. 250. For other references to ships trading to Nagasaki from Tonking, see *Kai-hentai* 華夷変態 (Tokyo: Toyo Bunko, 1958):

1690: ship no. 87 (June 22) Ningpo ship, came from Tongking. (vol. 2, pp. 1285–86)

1691: ship no. 18 (January 27), Ningpo ship from Tongking (vol. 2, pp. 1316–17)

1692: ship no. 59, (May 27), Tongking-Tongking (vol. 2, pp. 1471–72)

1693: ship no. 58, (June 3), Ningpo ship from Tongking (vol. 2, pp. 1565–66)
1698: ship no. 70 (June 16), Ningpo ship from Tongking. (vol. 3, pp. 2022)
1699: ship no. 37 (May 16), Ningpo ship from Tongking. (vol. 3, pp. 2065–66)
1708: ship no. 101 (June 5), Guangdong ship from Tongking (vol. 3, p. 2580)
1710: ship no. 52 (July 10), Ningpo ship from Tongking (vol. 3, p. 2680)
1711: ship no. 55 (June 22), Ningpo ship from Tongking. (vol. 3, pp. 2689–90)
1712: ship no. 62 (July 16), Tongking ship via Putuo Shan. (vol. 3, p. 2690)

72. Keith Taylor, "The Literati Revival in Seventeenth-Century Vietnam", *Journal of Southeast Asian Studies* XVIII, no. 1 (March, 1987): 1–23.
73. Victor Lieberman, *Strange Parallels: Southeast Asia in Global Context, c. 800–1830*. (Cambridge: Cambridge University Press, 2003), pp. 404–05.
74. Phạm Thị Thủy Vinh, *Văn bia thời Lê*, p. 228. See also Thinh Liet village in Shaun Malarney, "Ritual and Revolution in Vietnam", Ph.D. dissertation, University of Michgan, 1993, p. xiv.
75. "The chief riches, and indeed the only commodity, is silk, raw and wrought" from Samuel Baron, "A Description of the Kingdom of Tonqueen" (1685), in *Views of Seventeenth-Century Vietnam: Christoforo Borri on Cochinchina, and Samuel Baron on Tonkin*, introduced and annotated by Olga Dror and K.W. Taylor (Ithaca: SEAP, 2006), p. 210. According to Hoàng Anh Tuấn, the main silk-producing areas were Sơn Tây, Bắc Ninh, Hải Dương and Sơn Nam. These were also the places from where the highest number of persons passing examinations came. See Hoàng Anh Tuấn, *Silk for Silver*, p. 41.

References

Brook, Timothy. *The Confusions of Pleasure: Commerce and Culture in Ming China*. Berkeley: University of California Press, 1999.

Buck, John Lossing. *Land Utilization in China*. Chicago: University of Chicago Press, 1937.

Chen Chingho. "Chinese Junk Trade at Nagasaki at the Beginning of the Qing Dynasty". *New Asia Journal* 1, no. 3 (1960): 273–332.

Đại Việt sử ký toàn thư [The Vietnamese Annals]. Tokyo: Tōkyō Daigaku Tōyō Bunka Kenkyūjo Fuzoku Tōyōgaku Bunken Sentā, 1984–86.

Đinh Khắc Thuân. *Lịch sử triều Mạc qua thư tịch và văn bia* [A history of the Mac through books and inscriptions]. Hanoi: Nhà xuất bản Khoa học xã hội, 2001.

Dror, Olga. *Cult, Culture, and Authority: Princess Lieu Hanh in Vietnamese History*. Honolulu: University of Hawaii Press, 2007.

Dror, Olga and K.W. Taylor (Intro. and Annot.). *Views of Seventeenth Century Vietnam:*

Christoforo Borri on Cochinchina and Samuel Baron on Tonkin. Ithaca: Cornell University Southeast Asia Program, 2006.

Hà Văn Tấn and Nguyễn Văn Kự. *Đình Vietnam: Community Halls*. Ho Chi Minh City: Nhà xuất bản Thành phố Hồ Chí Minh, 1998.

Herz, Solange (trans.). *Rhodes of Vietnam: The Travels and Missions of Father Alexander de Rhodes in China and Other Kingdoms of the Orient*. Westminster, Maryland: The Newman Press, 1966.

Hoàng Anh Tuấn. "Silk for Silver: Dutch-Vietnamese Relations, 1637–1700", Ph.D. Dissertation, University of Leiden, 2006.

Hồng Đức bản đồ [Maps of the Hong Duc reign]. Saigon: Bộ quốc gia Giáo dục, 1962.

Iioka Naoko. "Literati Entrepreneur: Wei Zhiyan in the Tonkin-Nagasaki Silk Trade". Ph.D. dissertation, National University of Singapore, 2009.

Kai-hentai 華夷変態. Tokyo: Toyo Bunko, 1958.

Lê Quý Đôn. *Vân Đài Loại ngữ* [Classified talk from the study]. Saigon: Phủ quốc vụ khanh đặc trách Văn hóa, 1973.

Lê Trắc. *Annam Chí lược* [A brief history of Annam]. Hue: Viện đại học Huế, Uỷ ban phiên dịch sử liệu Việt Nam, 1961.

Li Tana. *Nguyen Cochinchina*. Ithaca: Cornell University Southeast Asia Program, 1998.

Li Tana and Anthony Reid (eds.). *Southern Vietnam under the Nguyen: Documents on the Economic History of Cochinchina (Dang Trong), 1602–1777*. Canberra and Singapore: Economic History of Southeast Asia Project, ANU/ISEAS, 1993.

Li Xiangen. "Annan zaji" 安南雜記 [Miscellaneous notes on Annam]. In *Congshu jicheng chubian: Annan zhuan ji qita erzhong*. Shanghai: Shangwu Press, 1937.

Lieberman, Victor. *Strange Parallels: Southeast Asia in Global Context, c. 800–1830*. Cambridge: Cambridge University Press, 2003.

Liu Chun Yin, Lin Qing Zhao and Tran Nghia (ed). *Yuenan hannan wenxian mulu tiyao* [Catalogue and Abstracts of Han-Nom textual material in Vietnam]. Taipei: Asia-Pacific Studies Centre, Academia Sinica, 2004.

Ly Tê Xuyên. *Yuedian youling ji* [Viet dien U Linh tap, Compilation of the potent spirits in the Realm of Viet]. In *Collection Romans & Contes du Vietnam écrits en Han* (Paris-Taipei: Ecole Française d'Extrême-Orient/Student Book Co. Ltd, 1992.

Malarney, Shaun. "Ritual and Revolution in Vietnam". Ph.D. dissertation, University of Michigan, 1993.

Ngannan tche yuan. Hanoi: Imprimerie d'Extrême-Orient, 1932.

Nguyễn Đức Nghinh. "Markets and Villages". In *The Traditional Village in Vietnam*, edited by Phan Huy Lê et al. Hanoi: Thế Giới, 1993.

Nishimura Masanari and Nishino Noriko. "Archaeological study of the settlement formation in the Red River Plain: a case of Bach Coc and the surroundings." Paper presented at the conference "Vietnamese Peasant Activity: An Interaction between Culture and Nature", Leiden, 28–31 August 2002.

Papin, Philippe and Olivier Tessier (eds.). *Làng ở vùng châu thổ sông Hồng: Vấn đề còn bỏ ngỏ* [The village in questions]. Hanoi: Ecole française d'Extrême-Orient/ Trung tâm Khoa học xã hội và Nhân văn Quốc gia, 2002.

Phạm Thị Thủy Vinh. *Văn bia thời Lê xứ Kinh Bắc và sự phản ánh sing hoạt làng xã* [The Stelae of the Kinh Bac Region during the Lê Period: Reflections of Village Life]. Hanoi: Bibliotheque vietnamienne-VIII and Ecole française d'Extrême-Orient, 2003.

Phan Huy Chú. *Lịch triều hiến chương loại chí* [A reference book of the institutions of successive dynasties] 3 volumes. Hanoi: Nhà xuất bản khoa học xã hội, 1992.

Phan Văn Các and Claudine Salmon. *Épigraphie en chinois du Viêt Nam = Văn khắc Hán Nôm Việt Nam*. Paris: Presses de l'École française d'Extrême-Orient; Hà Nội: Viện nghiên cứu Hán Nôm, 1998.

Reid, Anthony. *Southeast Asia in the Age of Commerce 1450–1680, Volume One: The Lands Below the Winds*. New Haven and London: Yale University Press, 1988.

———. *Southeast Asia in the Age of Commerce 1450–1680, Volume Two: Expansion and Crisis*. New Haven and London: Yale University Press, 1993.

Rhodes, Alexander de. *Histoire du royaume du Tonkin*. edited by Jean-Pierre Duteil (Paris: Éditions Kimé, 1999).

Souza, George Bryan. *The Survival of Empire: Portuguese Trade and Society in China and the South China Sea, 1630–1754*. Cambridge: Cambridge University Press, 2004.

Văn khắc Hán-Nôm Việt Nam [Steles in Han-Nom characters in Vietnam]. Hanoi: Social Sciences Publishing House, 1993.

Vũ Đức Thơm. "Bước đầu tìm hiểu về cây bông trong đời sống của người nông dân trước năm 1945 ở Quỳnh Côi" [Towards an understanding of cotton planting in peasants' livelihood before 1945]. In *Hội thảo khoa học người dân Thái Bình trong lịch sử* [Proceedings of the conference on the people of Thai Binh]. Thái Bình: Bộ phần lịch sử dân tộc, ban nghiên cứu lịch sử Đảng tỉnh Thái Bình, 1986.

PART V
Modern Southeast Asia

13

HADHRAMI PROJECTIONS OF SOUTHEAST ASIAN IDENTITY

Jeyamalar Kathirithamby-Wells

"Paradoxically, the diversity of Southeast Asia and its openness to outside influences were among the defining characteristic of the region" — Anthony Reid.[1]

DIASPORIC NETWORKS AND SOUTHEAST ASIAN INTEGRATION

Anthony Reid's *Southeast Asia in the Age of Commerce*[2] has contributed hugely to stimulating an ongoing discourse on exploring imaginative ways of defining regional identity.[3] Contrary to perceptions of regional and national identities as being potentially divergent, Reid in his more recent study, *Imperial Alchemy*,[4] points to their common subscription to plurality.

The task of Southeast Asian nation-building, laying emphasis on centralizing state power and territorial consolidation, has been at the expense of more salient impulses of regional integration. Pre-eminently, networks of trade, religious discourse and inter-personal relations, mediated by nodal centres of power rather than state structures, have projected a shared regional identity. Providing a lead in this direction, Tony Day and Heather Sutherland have explored the concept of informal social ties in terms of genealogy, gender and familial relations as sources of social integration, with the latter focusing specifically on the linkages between trade, cities and kinship.[5] Fluid and amoebic, these configurations, transcending space and time, mediated relations between centre, periphery and the external world.

Integral to the functioning of the nodal centres of power was the Southeast Asian 'big man' whose charismatic leadership and talent were rooted not in formal structures, but informal familial and clan relations. These networks of loyalties, through which the 'man of prowess' could accumulate wealth and clientage, generated circles of influence and power.[6]

The same personal ties and communal networks that defined social reality within the region's autochthonous societies proved relevant to the vitality of diasporic communities[7] and their important subscription to the institution of the 'big man'. Conspicuous the regional trade network, the Southeast Asian 'big man' was synonymous with the *orang kaya* (rich man) or "man of wealth and influence."[8] In this regard, I intend in this essay to highlight the unique circumstances that privileged the 'big men' of the Hadhrami diasporic network in shaping history and identity in the Malay-Indonesian region.

SEEKERS OF DIASPORIC FORTUNES

Sāda Influence and Charisma

Traceable to the commercial prosperity of Melaka, the *orang kaya* as a class emerged through the accumulation of wealth-related influence by state officials and especially foreign merchants favoured by the state.[9] The latter were ideal agents for strengthening external links and raising the international profile of a port-polity. As a 'stranger' he could also be better trusted and disciplined and frequently earned the coveted position of royal trader (the Malay *saudagar raja*).[10]

By the eighteenth century, when indigenous power was enfeebled, displaced communities of Malays, Bugis, Makassarese, Minangkabaus and sea-gypsies, came to the fore as diasporic networks to bolster the regional economy. Operating in conjunction were networks of a trans-oceanic order, of which the Nanyang Chinese diaspora was numerically and economically the most distinctive. But by far the most politically and socially influential was the Hadhrami diaspora, its members constituting the bulk of the region's Arab population. From within their small number[11] emerged some of the most dynamic *orang kaya* of the period. Their influence, though arguably limited to the Malay-Indonesian sector, played no small part in reinforcing the role of the Southeast Asian 'big man' in trans-regional integration.

Though expanding Southeast Asian monarchies ended arguably with the close of the age of 'Age of Commerce',[12] international trade and scriptural religion remained key elements in shaping change and continuity.[13] This had significant implications for diasporic communities which were fundamentally tightly-knit clan and familial networks of shared religious beliefs and social norms. The ethnic identities especially of communities of an extra-regional provenance were thereby perpetuated, though some local assimilation through marriage was not uncommon. In the case of the Hadhramis, however, shared faith with the indigenes in the form of Sunni Islam of the Shāfiʿī judicial school of law (*madhhab*) provided a common reference point for inter-ethnic interactions. Especially at an advantage were the Hadhrami *sāda* (singular: *sayyid*) or ʿAlawī[14] by virtue of their claims of descent from Prophet Muhammad. Among them a significant number were *muwalladūn* (singular *muwallad*), locally-born to indigenous mothers.

The ʿAlawī ethos proved remarkably adaptable to Southeast Asian concepts of power and leadership.[15] A charismatic ʿAlawī, operating within robust familial and clan networks, replicated the Southeast Asian 'big man', bolstered by kinship and patron-client relations.[16] Moreover, *sāda* contribution to religious thought, scholarship and entrepreneurial innovation reflected Southeast Asian 'genius' in its receptivity to external influences since the early phase of Indian influence.

Sufi and Shaman

The *ṭarīqa* (*tarikat*) ʿAlawiyya, which marked the self-identity of the Hadhrami — understood by some scholars as being 'historical *shiʿa*' because of its *sufi* basis[17] — was partial to Southeast Asia's syncretic tradition. Pre-existing Indic notions of *sakti*, accessed through religious devotion (*bakti*) and meditation (*tapa*),[18] were enhanced by the Islamic concept of *ilmu*, encompassing all knowledge — religious, esoteric and secular. The association between knowledge and power added to the veneration the *sāda*, universally respected as transmitters of *ilmu*.[19]

Believed to be endowed with the spiritual powers to bestow *berkat* (blessing, favour), the *sāda* were co-opted by Malay rulers for strengthening their status and legitimacy. In eighteenth-century Perak the al-Faradz served as the ruler's spiritual mentors and stepped into the role of *pawang* or the practitioners of herbal and shamanistic skills. In the latter role, the *sayyid* founder-ruler of Pontianak ostensibly exorcized a female ghost, who had preyed on infants and pregnant women, and under whose name the new settlement prospered.[20] Furthermore, extra-scriptural ʿAlawī practices, such as visits to the graves of *walī* (*Ṣufī* saints) on feast days (*ziyāra*),[21] overlapped indigenous traditions of ancestor worship in the cult of the *keramat / punden* (a spiritually potent object or person).[22] Directly related to state-making were the royal graves and mausoleums of the charismatic *sāda* rulers. The tombs of Sayyid Abd al-Rahman al-Qadri (r. 1771–1809) in Pontianak and Sultan Taha Safiuddin (r. 1855–1904) of Jambi in Muara Tebu were the sites of popular pilgrimage and worship. Among the graves of *sāda* still visited are those of Tuan Guru (Shaykh Sayyid Gani of Madura) in Penang, and Habib Noor in Singapore.

Valour, linked to the supernatural power of Arab holy men, factored into power politics, which colonial regimes could ill-afford to ignore. In the Minang district of Naning in Melaka, Dol Sayyid, when installed as *penghulu* by the British in 1802 inherited the sacred sword, *baju* (coat) and ornamental stick believed to bestow special sanctity and power to its possessor. Faith in the efficacy of his power led to diseased clients drinking water in which his foot had been dipped. His subsequent defiance of the British, supported by his mystical grip on the people, culminated in the Naning War (1831–32).[23] Similarly, the charismatic holy man Sayyid Paluh of Terengganu (see below) duly impressed the British official, Hugh Clifford who noted: "He is a man who is certainly possessed of an extraordinarily strong personality and of immense personal magnetism".[24]

Knowledge and Power

Encapsulated in the *sufi* concept of the 'Perfect Man' was the "psychology of human potentialities"[25] identifiable with the multiple talents and achievements of the *sayyid* as the Southeast Asian 'man of prowess.' The downgrading of lineage within a cognate system of kinship in the region emphasized individual achievement through the resourceful use of 'prowess' for forging and manipulating alliances.[26] Power was fluid and impermanent and opportunity ever present for aspirants with the appropriate talent and personality.[27] 'Prowess,' an integral part of charisma, merged with the Islamic concept of sovereign authority. To quote A.H. Johns, "[W]hile Caliph is a title which connotes religious authority by a 'valid' line of succession, anyone can be a Sultan if he is in the right place at the right time and has sufficient force of personality — which is what charisma in this sense means."[28]

In the Acehnese poem, the *Hikajat Potjut Muhamat*, the 'Alawī adventurer Jamal al-Alam Badr al-Munir (Poteu Jeumaloj) is depicted as the archetypal 'man of prowess' who rose from merchant to ruler. Ousted from power in 1726, he raised a resistance against his Bugis rival, mirroring the very characteristics of "plotting," "resourcefulness" and "skilfulness" attributed to the divine by the *sufi* poet, Hamza Fansuri.[29] Despite the unprecedented levels of taxes he imposed, the charismatic and magical powers ascribed to him as a *sayyid* guaranteed tacit, if not open grassroots support. In contrast, the powerful *ulèebalang* (military leader) Bèntara Keumangan who took up the cause against Jamal al-Alam, met his death "struck by divine wrath" for going against a *sayyid*. The final defeat of Jamal al-Alam himself was not by human agency but the mysterious onslaught of cholera.[30]

Fundamental to the "'Alawī way" (path or travel towards divinity) were journeys in search of knowledge through pilgrimage and the narrative of mobility.[31] The expansion of the Hadhrami Indian Ocean network into east Africa and the Indian subcontinent (principally Kerala and Hyderabad) saw a parallel development in Southeast Asia. According to 'Alawī folklore, Hadhrami migration was pioneered by four youths from Tarim. Following tutelage under one Muhammad b. Hamid in Malabar, they pioneered the settlement of Siak, Terengganu, Pontianak and Kubu.[32] In a region where the indivisible link between trade and religion defined political power, the Hadhrami migrant found a comfortable niche within the rich resource pools of the Outer Islands and the Malay Peninsula, crucial for provisioning the region's expanding trade with China.[33]

The renewed phase of Islamic influence under the Hadhrami trader-predicants of the seventeenth and eighteenth centuries had distinct scholarly overtones. Nur al-Din al-Raniri (d. 1658), a *muwallad* from Gujarat who served at the court of Iskandar Thani (r. 1636–41) of Aceh, was perhaps the best known of the early scholars who contributed to the diasporic Hadhrami transmission of knowledge.[34] Again, Sayyid Abd al-Samad al-Palimbani b. Abd al-Rahman al-Jawi (1704–89), the foremost Malay-Indonesian scholar of the period, established Palembang's place within the lively 'Alawī scholarly network.[35]

Elite Synergy

Gendered alliances — a key factor in Southeast Asian state-making — lent *sāda* adventurers legitimacy and status within the host community. It, moreover, neutralized potential rivalry with existing power-holders and allowed ready access to economic and political opportunities. The well-calculated marriage of the strong man, Sayyid Uthman of Siak, to Tengku Embong Badariah set the seeds for the growth of the Shihab dynasty. As she was both the daughter of Raja Alam, claimant to the Johor throne and granddaughter of the Bugis warrior, Daeng Perani, the marriage brought the Shihab into the grand Malay-Minangkabau-Bugis royal alliance.[36]

In southwest Kalimantan, Sayyid Abdul al-Rahman al-Qadri married Utin Candera Midi, daughter of Daeng Menanbun, brother of the first Bugis under-king Daeng Merewa. This alliance formed the linchpin of Pontianak's relations with the Bugis in Mempawah and Riau. The centrality of familial ties to state-making was highlighted in the close relations between Sayyid Abd al-Rahman and Chandera Midi's cousin Raja Haji, the fourth *yang dipertuan muda* of Riau. It was the latter who formally installed the ruler of Pontianak as Sultan after helping him conquer Sanggau, which gave access to the gold-rich upper Kapuas River.[37] In Palembang, the marriage of a certain Sayyid al-Aydarus to a sister of Sultan Mahmud Badaruddin (r. 1724–57) and another *sayyid* to the daughter of the Sultan Ahmad Tajuddin (r. 1757–74), spoke for the high standing of the Palembang Arab community, the second largest after Aceh.[38]

Exogamous matrimonial alliances admitted the *sāda* into the game of "playing relatives"[39] while, at the same time, the endogamous marriage of their female counterparts (*sharīfa*) preserved 'Alawī status. The resulting ambiguous 'insider-outsider' identity, combining distance and closeness, detachment and involvement, was played to advantage by the *sāda* at a time of beleaguered indigenous power. 'Alawīs such as the Shihab in Siak and the al-Aydarus in Terengganu brought new vigour to quintessential Malay concepts of kinship and kingship rooted in the illustrious legacy of the Riau-Johor sultanate. The intra-regional networks of aristocratic Malay and 'Alawī bloodlines intermeshed, mutually reinforcing status and prestige. By this process the *sāda* became custodians, in some instances, not only of diasporic 'Alawī but also of Malay-Bugis bloodlines.[40]

RULER AND MERCHANT CAPITALIST

Trade and Marauding

Whereas seventeenth century royal absolutism had placed severe restraints on the emergent class of '*orang kaya*' or men of wealth and influence,[41] *sāda* initiative, underpinned by Hadhrami social and entrepreneurial ethos, resuscitated the politics of trade. Within the ambit of the diasporic network, the *sāda* enjoyed conditions of security and stability for entrepreneurial activity independent of the state, with clan dominance in particular geographical and investment sectors. The popular *mufāwaḍa* or 'universal partnership' that reflected the family or clan nature of joint entrepreneurial activity[42] reduced rivalry and gave maximum opportunity for investment, whether of political or commercial capital.

Sāda commercial adventurism was focused on bolstering faltering states, pre-empting colonial intrusions into the resource rich peripheral areas of east Sumatra, the Malay Peninsula and west Kalimantan. Here the families, predominantly of the al-Jufri, al-Aydarus, al-Shihab, al-Qadri and al-Aydid clans, breathed new life into the institution of *orang kaya* using their *sāda* status to good effect. Whether engaged as trader-*ulama* or merchant-marauders, their religious credentials, access to influential marriages and commercial acumen proved valuable passports to the elite institution of *orang kaya*.

The trans-regional receptivity of *sāda* among fellow believers transcended ethnic and political borders. Unlike *orang kaya* under previous strong regimes, the *sāda* were not subjected to the severe restrictions and whims of local rulers. Indeed, their patronage and collaboration were courted. By and large, immunity from state control allowed for freedom of individual action and initiative, supported by 'Alawī clan loyalties and group spirit ('*aṣabīya*). With social and commercial advantage on their side, the *sāda* were ideally equipped to steer the politics of trade within a robust commercial network that spanned the Archipelago from Aceh to New Guinea. Equally, their reputation as custodians of Islamic law and jurisprudence was a passport to political influence. An eighteenth-century example was the founding of the commercial settlement of Mempawah[43] in Southwestern Kalimantan by Habib Husayn b. Ahmad al-Qadri, one of the pioneer 'Alawī migrants. His reputation as a theologian and a man of peace and justice, and not least his wide experience as a trader, evoked trust in his authority and contributed to the attraction and rapid rise of the settlement.[44]

At a time of fragmented indigenous power and a general upsurge in sea-raiding, *sāda* were not averse to exploiting their moral authority to capitalize on the links between trade and marauding. Both Siak and Pontianak were built on the material and social capital accrued from the trading-cum-marauding activities of its *sāda* founders.[45] So deeply entrenched were Hadhrami *orang kaya* in the socio-political ramifications of maritime raiding that colonial authorities, guided by their own vested interests, were reluctant to prosecute those resident within their jurisdiction. In 1816 the Penang government was embarrassed by the long arm of its judiciary that imprisoned Sayyid Husayn al-Aydid (d. 1840) on a charge of piracy. The *sayyid*, reputedly the island's richest individual who had strong political and economic connections with Aceh and links with British private traders, was promptly released upon the governor's intervention.[46]

British commercial interests in Kalimantan similarly privileged Pontianak's ruler Sayyid Kasim b. Abdul Rahman al-Qadri (r. 1808–19), notwithstanding his subscription to piracy and slave trading. Hadhrami entrepreneurs, in turn, while remaining closely wedded to disaporic networks and family business, adapted readily to profitable partnerships with European business houses. Hussain al-Aydid of Penang collaborated with John Palmer and Company in Calcutta in the distribution of opium and weapons as did Sultan Kasim of Pontianak.⁴⁷ In Singapore, the *sāda* who formed a significant component of the prosperous Arab merchant community, colluded with European mercantile firms in Surabaya in counterfeiting coinage for circulation in the Netherlands Indies.⁴⁸

The *sāda* collaborated, moreover, with European merchants and sea captains in importing contraband into the Netherlands Indies, principally from Singapore. In 1884, the al-Jufri-owned *SS Vidar*, on which Joseph Conrad once served as navigating officer, was one of 10 steamships engaged in suspect transports. Sailing under the flag of the British marine to Berau, in northeast Kalimantan, the vessel carried weapons and slaves. The latter, destined for labour and human sacrifice, were exchanged with the Dayaks for forest produce.⁴⁹

The customary exemption of *sayyid* from taxes and duties on trade gave them a clear advantage for forging the trans-regional commercial networks, their success affirmed in their distinction as the biggest ship-owners. Based mainly in Gresik, Semarang, Pekalongan and Surabaya, as well as in Palembang, they operated the largest private vessels covering the longest distances.⁵⁰ This, as well as their readiness to take physical and financial risks accounted for their maritime pre-eminence till the last quarter of the nineteenth century. Information gathering on natural resources, which underpinned expertise in trade, herbal medicine and ship-building, took Hadhramis to pioneer frontiers.

In the Outer Islands, rivers servicing coast-interior trade and communication formed vital extensions of Hadhrami maritime networks. Merchants, investors and shippers at down-river assembly points and export centres attracted intrepid Arab traders, often clan members. The same riverine commercial routes served as conduits for religious ideas via the market place, mosque and *madrasah* (religious schools). Knowledge of places and produce and the confidence the Arabs evoked among fellow Muslim traders and middlemen accounted for their distinction as major players in the assembly of forest produce, as well as Minangkabau gold, tin and, later, gambier and coffee.

In Siak, the bigger vessels like the *chialoup* and *gonting*⁵¹ were predominantly Arab-owned and the merchant princes, Raja Muhammad Ali and Sayyid Ali al-Shihab traded through agents with Melaka, Palembang and Java.⁵² Trade at important upriver junctions (*pengkalan*) was often managed by an Arab *syahbandar*. During the mid-eighteenth century, Sayyid Muhammad Ba Husayn of the al-Saqqaf family, a prominent trader with a shrewd appreciation of inland resources, was *syahbandar* at Senapelan, strategically located on the upper Siak River within reach of Patapahan's tin and gold.⁵³ Al-Shihab economic power came to full flowering when Sayyid Ali became Sultan Syaifuuddin (r. 1791–1811) of Siak. The new ruler placed his brother, Sayyid Ahmad, at the prosperous commercial centre of Tebing Tinggi, below Pekan Bahru, and his nephew Tengku Kasim at Palalawan, the main bulking station in the adjacent river valley of Kampar.[54]

In southwest Kalimantan, the ruler of Pontianak invested in the profitable Arab and Bugis commercial network that stretched into the Dayak interior little known to Europeans.[55] British country traders such John Palmer of Calcutta and Captain Joseph Burn, based in Penang, relied on partnerships with Sayyid Kasim of Pontianak.[56] Arab trade into the interior continued to flourish and, according to oral sources, Sayyid Salim b. Muhammad (d. 1937), a member of the Bin Talib family and originally based in Surabaya, began his career engaged in 'silent trade' with the Dayaks. The profits accrued paved the way for his subsequent entrepreneurial success in Singapore, on a par with the al-Saqqaf, al-Kaf and al-Junayd clans.[57]

The Toraja interior of Sulawesi was yet another area where a *sayyid* rose to be *orang kaya*. From the 1860s to the 1880s, the Sulawesi-born Sayyid Ali b. Muhammad al-Sjafi who married into the local court, developed a strategy for undermining Bugis trade in Pare-Pare. Establishing a rival commercial foothold further north at Palopo, he operated a complex network of internal markets supported by his own private army, exchanging arms for coffee and slaves with the ruler of Luwu.[58] Local prestige, superior commercial strategy and a flair for knowledge gathering, including geographical information, would appear to have given Sayyid Ali, like other *sāda*, a clear edge over competitors.[59]

Dual Identity and Ambiguous Loyalties

Knowledgeable, influential and holding considerable economic power, the *sāda* used their 'insider-outsider' status and their traditional role as adjudicators in disputes to act as communicators and intermediaries in interactions between power-holders. With their wide leverage for independent action, they made ideal European agents. The Pontianak prince, Sharif Hamid, acted as chief agent in the Dutch political transactions of the mid-nineteenth century with Bali and Lombok.[60] *Sāda* traded their diplomatic skills, urbanity and superior knowledge of regional affairs for Dutch confidence and favour. During the 1820s, Hasan al-Habshi, a Batavian wholesaler engaged in the distribution of rice, represented Dutch interests on diplomatic missions to Siam, Brunei, Bali and Surakarta.[61] In 1822/3 when a Riau mission arrived in Batavia headed by Sayyid Muhammad Zain al-Kudsi, it was a fellow ʿAlawī, Sayyid Hasan al-Habshi, who was entrusted with protocol and care of the visitors.[62] The various services he rendered, particularly the valuable report he submitted in 1830 to the Governor General on piracy, based on local intelligence, earned him the title of *pangeran* (prince/lord) in addition to a handsome annuity of 4,800 florins.[63] Several other *sāda* served as headmen, Arabic translators and interpreters in the coastal cities of Java.[64]

The potential for independent thinking and action was demonstrated by Sayyid Uthman b. Aquil al-Alawi (1822–1914). His role as 'Honorary Advisor on Arab Affairs' and his Dutch-backed print propaganda against the *ṭarīqa* Naqshbandiya found critics among fellow *sāda*. But it did little to diminish his status as a respected *ulama* and *mufti* of Batavia committed to the preservation of ʿAlawī identity and orthodoxy.[65] Indeed his intellectual and scholarly collaboration with Dutch scholar-administrators, his concern for law and order and his anti-*jihad* stance may well have influenced the government's policy of winning the collaboration of "educated" Arabs.[66] Likewise, the part played by his son-in-law Muhammad b. Aquil b. Yahaya (1863–1931) as a British informant was independent of his pro-Ottoman stance.[67]

Reconciling God and Mammon

Among *sāda*, "[c]ombining a religious career with a business career was the norm rather than the exception and had the aura of a time-honoured tradition."[68] Thus, trade nourished both secular and religious influence. One of the many religious teachers of comfortable means and high status in the Malay Peninsula was Habib Hasan al-Attas (b. 1832?), whose entrepreneurial father from Hadhramaut had settled in Pahang and established close relations with the royalty. Educated at al-Azhar University, Habib Hasan taught at the Madrasah al-Saqqaf in Singapore and at Priangan in west Java. With an equal flair for business, he later invested in 14,000 acres of land in Pahang, committing the profits to various social projects, among them the construction of a *madrasah* in Johor.[69]

The widespread religious endowments and charitable acts of the ʿAlawī (see below) starkly contradicted the subscription by some to indigenous forms of wealth formation through corvée extraction and bonded labour.[70] Singapore's successful entrepreneur, Sayyid Muhammad b. Ahmad al-Saqqaf (d. 1906), used his shipping facility to repatriate hundreds of stranded pilgrims from Jeddah to Kukub Island, off Johor, only to have them work as contract labourers on the 10,000-acre Constantinople Estate, notoriously dubbed the "Monster Estate."[71]

Again, participation in slave-raiding, marauding and smuggling — conventional methods of raising capital and manpower in the region — was not deemed to be an ethical issue.[72] Again, profit-seeking was not incompatible with the 'Alawī way of self-endeavour and enterprise, endorsed by twentieth-century Islamic reformism, which had material improvement well within its agenda.[73]

Notorious was the Arab practice of capital formation through money-lending. To circumvent Islamic prohibitions against *ribā* or interest, loans were made purportedly as 'rent,' with the right to repurchase (*'uhda*). As patron within the resident Muslim community, a *sayyid* was in a position to offer flexible lending rates through knowing his creditors, their problems and money needs as they related to religious and social obligations.[74] In transactions involving commercial loans, the *sayyid* similarly found ways of avoiding usury. In Pontianak, Sultan Kasim al-Qadri refused to make loans to the private trader Captain Daniel Smith, because "interest was contrary to his religion."[75] However, Islamic law offered avoidance of *ribā* through the institution of *al-mudarabah* or *al-muqaradah*, involving the services of an agent-manager with the investor's share of the profit fixed at the time of the contact.[76] It is likely that the ruler resorted to this arrangement in his dealings with "the prince of merchants", John Palmer of Calcutta.[77] However when prejudicial to profit maximization, Islamic law was compromised, apparently without the loss of spiritual authority. A case in point was the venerated status of Sultan Abd al-Rahman of Pontianak who abstained from opium consumption but traded freely in it.[78]

Sāda merchant capitalists shared a common ethos with the classical *sāda* saint-personalities who combined scholarship with action and the sacred with the mundane.[79] *Sāda* linguistic skills, which facilitated commercial and social interaction, complemented knowledge of Islamic jurisprudence (*fiqh*), herbal medicine and *ṭarīqa* practices. Manuscripts and books were among prized possessions in well-furnished merchant dwellings.[80] Like Weber's modern entrepreneur of the Protestant persuasion, the *sayyid* merchant accumulated wealth through frugality but expended it on conspicuous consumption and hospitality for supporting clan, clientage and business interests. Sayyid Hasan of Gresik, reputedly the richest merchant and ship-owner in early nineteenth century Java, maintained a well-appointed home fit for the reception of his European merchant contacts; but his personal needs were modest.[81] The lavish parties laid at their island mansions by Sayyid Husayn al-Aydid of Penang and Umar b. Muhamad al-Saqqaf of Singapore combined traditional hospitality with urban sophistication becoming of the new breed of *orang kaya*.[82]

REIMAGING IDENTITY

Finding a Niche

When, in the last quarter of the nineteenth century, Chinese and European competition outpaced Hadhrami shipping and trade, the entrepreneurial *sāda* rapidly adjusted. Responding to the challenge posed by the powerful European cartels in the shipment of pilgrims, Sayyid Umar al-Saqqaf formed a syndicate in 1896 in partnership with European investors and the Sharif of Mecca.[83]

Loss in inter-island shipping, particularly to the government-backed *Koninklijke Paketvaart Maatschappij* (KPM) founded in 1880,[84] was offset by pioneering profitable niches for trade in rice, spices, forest produce, slaves and livestock, substituting the more manoeuvrable schooners and small *perahu* for the square-rigged vessels. By thus specializing in the inter-island movement of cargo along routes inaccessible to steamers, the *sāda* arrived at a comfortable accommodation with Dutch economic interests. By pioneering settlements within the eastern Indonesian trade network, in Buru, Ternate and Manado in addition to those existing in Ambon and Banda,[85] the *sāda* successfully bolstered the institution of *orang kaya*.[86] In the substantial Arab settlement in Banda, Sayyid Abdullah Ba Adillah, Captain of the Arabs, augmented his fortunes through gaining Dutch permission in 1897 to collect pearls off the Aru Islands.[87] Sayyid Abd Rahman b. Abu Bakr al-Qadri, banished from the court in Pontianak, lived in Sumbawa during 1842–1878, surrounded by some 200 family members. His economic clout, based on a prosperous trade in horses and wide credibility as an arbitrator, enhanced his role as an intermediary between the Dutch and the indigenes, earning recognition as the Raja of Waingapu.[88]

The accreditation of *sāda* 'big men' as *tengku* (princes) in the Malay courts of the Peninsula and Sumatra was duly matched by the Dutch conferral of the title of *pangeran* (prince/noble/chief) on the shipping magnates, Sayyid Hasan and Sayyid Alwi of the al-Habshi in Surabaya.[89] The recipient of a similar honour was their contemporary, Sayyid Ali b. Abu Bakr b. al-Shaykh Abu b. Bakr Salim, Captain of the Arabs in Palembang (1833–78).[90]

In Java and the western Archipelago the decline in shipping business was compensated for by diversified investment in land and real estate as well as in the retail, coffee export and batik manufacturing sectors.[91] Likewise, in Palembang, *sāda* enterprise focused on external trade and urban enterprise, in consequence of the Dutch political advance and restrictions on Arab access into the interior, which struck at the very heart of their earlier success. Sayyid Alwi Shaykh al-Saqqaf, in partnership with Alimunar, engaged in shipping timber to the Middle East and the West, while Shaykh Shihab(?) Arsitek invested diversely in the rice and rubber industries, the manufacturing of ice and the construction business.[92]

The beginning of the twentieth century witnessed a still-thriving *sāda* merchant elite in the Javanese ports. In the commercial hub of Singapore the *sāda orang kaya* exerted greater political influence than their Chinese counterparts. Overall, the increased urban orientation of Hadhrami economic activity and associated maritime and international connections had important implications for Southeast Asian links with the wider Islamic world.

Internationalizing Southeast Asian Islam

In accordance with the 'Alawī way, the *sāda* lent a religious dimension to entrepreneurial activity. *Sāda* urban entrepreneurs built mosques and established charitable foundations (*wakafl waqf*) for the support of *madrasah* and other public projects. The financing of these institutions by Sayyid Husayn al-Aydid in Penang and the al-Junayd and al-Saqqaf families in Singapore enhanced personal status and enlarged Muslim interconnections.[93] Vested interest notwithstanding, al-Saqqaf investment in the transportation of pilgrims contributed to drawing the "Jawi ecumene"[94] closer within the fold of the *umma*.

Given the shared channels of commerce and religion that defined the Hadhrami diasporic network, the involvement of the Penang and Singapore Arab merchant community in the Aceh War (1873–1903) was a natural outcome. The Dutch Consulate in Singapore was powerless against the collusion of the pro-Acehnese party in the Straits led by Sayyid Muhammad al-Saqqaf, Sayyid Umar b. Ali al-Junayd and Shaykh Ahmad b. Abdullah Baschaib who had a stake in the pepper trade in Aceh.[95] All were intent on recruiting Ottoman protection against the Dutch. *Sāda* political leanings towards Turkey were unequivocal. Two members of the al-Junayd family during the 1880s, as well as Sayyid Muhammad al-Saqqaf, according to the family, acted as unofficial Ottoman Consuls.[96] The same *sāda* business elite in Singapore proved indispensible to the British as power-brokers on the wider canvas of Middle-Eastern politics and socio-political ferment in Hadhramaut.[97]

The invitation extended to three wealthy Kathiri leaders from Singapore and Java to participate in the negotiations leading to the 1918 'Aden Agreement' attested to the wide political influence wielded by their *sāda* merchant allies.[98] Whether in the context of the British-Ottoman tension or the ensuing 'Alawī-Irshādi conflict, *sāda* men of substance continued to display the same initiative, creative response and astute judgements in making their ideological and political choices, significant for entrepreneurial success and social standing.

Strategically poised at the hub of international trade and pilgrim shipping in the Straits Settlements, the Hadhramis used the colonial protection they enjoyed to nurture Muslim solidarity and the pan-Islamic project.[99] *Sāda* funding and individual talent in the promotion of print and journalism (see below)[100] were seminal in drawing the region within the wider world of Islamic discourse.

As in Aceh, the increased pace of Western intrusion into upriver resource pools provoked reaction under the religious inspiration and charismatic power of men of 'Alawī descent. In Jambi the strained relations between the Dutch Resident and Sultan Taha, a man of Arab descent,[101] culminated in the ruler's retreat to the interior to foment resistance.[102] Unsuccessful in his attempt to recruit Turkish aid, Taha succumbed in 1904 to Dutch forces. His charismatic hold on the popular imagination fed smouldering resentment against Dutch intervention, earning him a place among Indonesia's *Palawan Nasional*.[103]

In Terengganu, dissatisfaction over British-introduced laws that curbed free access to the forest and increased royalty on forest produce triggered the 1928 rebellion.[104] Projected as a *jihad* (holy war), it condemned the new laws and the introduction of vaccination as inconsistent with the *syariah*. The leader, Drahman Limbong (Haji Abd Rahman b. Abd Hamid), had been a pupil of the then-deceased holy man, Sayyid Paluh (Abdul Rahman b. Muhammad al-Aydarus, ? c. 1817–1918) whose charismatic power, which extended beyond the borders of Terengganu, had provided spiritual inspiration for the 1891 Pahang uprising triggered by British intervention.[105] The saint's magical powers and esoteric knowledge, purportedly inherited by his son Sayyid Sagap, a trader and businessman, lent inspiration for the movement. Though local in origin, the raising of the "Bendahara Stambul" (the Turkish flag) and public declaration by the Terengganu rebels that all land belonged to God, symbolized its appeal to the wider commonwealth of the *umma*, transcending the sovereign authority of Terengganu's ruler.[106] The British resolution to dispatch Haji Drahman on a pilgrimage to Mekka,[107] with no action being taken against Sayyid Sagap,[108] subscribed to the prevailing colonial consensus that the Arabs who made dangerous enemies, were best cultivated as friends.[109]

Religious and Social Reform

As agents for the transference of reformist ideas from Cairo and Istanbul to the 'land below the winds' the *sāda* were a force for social change. Religion and commerce colluded in Singapore's emergence as the regional print capital linked to Cairo.[110] The journal *al-Imam* (*the Leader*) (1906–08), initiated by the Hadhramis on the island and funded principally by Sayyid Muhammad b. Aquil,[111] was a conduit for the modernist ideas of Jamal al-Din Afghani (1838/39–97) and Muhammad Abduh (1849–1905) as propagated by the Cairo-Based *al-Manār* (*The Beacon*).[112] One of *al-Imam*'s editors and contributors was Sayyid Shaykh Ahmad b. Hasan b. Saqqaf al-Hadi (1867–1934). Raised on Penyengat island near Bintan, he came under the influence of Jamal al-Din al-Afgani and Muhammad Abduh whom he reputedly met during his visit to the Middle East. His novels, such as *Faridah Hanom* (1925), became a mouthpiece for reform at the grassroots.[113] Based in the much freer journalistic environment of Singapore than Batavia, Shaykh al-Hadi's contemporary, Sayyid Muhammad b. Aquil, attacked Dutch colonial policies and 'Arabaphobia' in the Egyptian journal *al-Mu'ayyad*.[114] Such criticism levelled both directly and anonymously spoke for a new liberal mentality fomented by international Islam.

Within the mix of secular and religious activity which preoccupied *sāda* in the Malay-Indonesia world, three broad categories of *orang kaya* are discernable: the ubiquitous entrepreneur-*ulama* with an enduring grassroots appeal; the merchant ruler/merchant aristocrat; and the urbane merchant capitalist of the colonial enclave. On the rise by the beginning of the twentieth century was a fourth category: the trans-regional, cosmopolitan *sayyid* intellectual, distinct from the *alim*, who cut across 'Alawī-Irshādi divisions that afflicted contemporary Hadhrami society. A prototype was the historian and man of letters, Sayyid Muhammad b. Hashim (1882–1960). His commercial activities, like those of his contemporaries, Sayyid Muhammad b. Aquil and Shaykh al-Hadi, financed journalistic and reformist ambitions. Following his arrival in the Netherlands Indies in 1907, he edited the pioneer Arab journal, *al-Bashir* founded in Palembang in 1885. Proficient as well in Malay and English, he recognized their importance as essential tools for his broader commitment to reforming and modernizing Muslim education. Having distinguished himself as a teacher in Palembang and Java, he succeeded Muhammad al-Surkitti al-Ansari as principal instructor at *Jam'iat al-Khayr* (Association of Welfare). The organization, established in 1901, pioneered the modern *madrasah*.[115]

Notwithstanding the cosmopolitan and secular dimensions of the reform movement, it was the intermeshing of entrepreneurial energy and spiritual life at the core of 'Alawī identity that legitimised the *sāda* 'big man' as the agency for change within the *jawi* community. Typical of this class of *orang kaya* was Habib Abdullah b. Muhsin al-Attas of Bogor who was attributed the supernatural powers of a *wali* (Sufi saint). A successful trader in batik, he built the *Majlis al-Nur* in Bogor, fashioned after the *masjid* in Hadhramaut and was a founder member of the *Jam'iat al-Khayr*.[116] Although originally established almost exclusively by Hadhramis for the purpose of bolstering Arab culture, the organization's emphasis on modern-style education — a core feature of *al-Manar*'s programme of reform emulated by the *al-Irshād* schools — placed the Hadharami *orang kaya* at the helm of modernization.[117]

CONCLUSION

Unlike the *orang kaya* of an earlier era who mediated between court and port, the activities of their Hadhrami counterparts were, both functionally and geographically, more wide-ranging. An 'insider-outsider' status, a robust diasporic infrastructure and the congruence of 'Alawī and indigenous clan and familial relations were factors that privileged Hadhrami initiatives. Above all, the *sāda* by virtue of their religious status, were spared the insecurity and fluid fortunes suffered by 'unbelievers' whether in the insular Muslim or mainland Buddhist states. Thus, by revitalizing and renovating the institution of *orang kaya* the Hadhrami 'big men' helped postpone for almost a century the full surrender of Muslim leadership and initiative to Western hegemony. At the same time, *sāda* material, spiritual and intellectual capital played an indispensible part in reinforcing the region's international identity. By the early twentieth century this was reflected in the *sāda* receptivity to an eclectic mix of modernist ideas from the Middle East, Japan and the Chinese community in Java.[118]

Nativistic nationalism ultimately replaced *sāda* cosmopolitism as a potent response to colonial challenge in the Malay-Indonesian world. More enduring, however, was the outstanding model set by the *sāda orang kaya* for the "layering or nesting of identities" involved in the "alchemy" which, as Reid has convincingly argued, produced the gold of Southeast Asian nationhood.[119]

Notes

1. Anthony Reid, "Introduction: A Time and A Place", in *Southeast Asia in the Early Modern Era: Trade, Power, and Belief*, edited by Anthony Reid (Ithaca, NY: Cornell University Press, 1993), p. 3.
2. Anthony Reid, *Southeast Asia in the Age of Commerce*, vol. I, *Land Below the Winds*; vol. II, *Expansion and Crisis* (New Haven: Yale University Press, 1988–1993).
3. See Victor Lieberman, "Local Integration and Eurasian Analogies: Structuring Southeast Asian History", *Modern Asian Studies* 27, no. 3 (1993): 475–80,

569–72; Victor Lieberman, "An Age of Commerce in Southeast Asia? Problem of Regional Coherence — A Review Article," *Journal of Asian Studies* 54, no. 3 (1995): 798–805; Sanjay Subrahmanyam, "Connected Histories: Notes Towards a Reconfiguration of Early Modern Eurasia", *Modern Asian Studies* 31, no. 3 (1997): 297; Denys Lombard, "Networks and Synchronisms in Southeast Asian History," *Journal of Southeast Asian Studies* 26, no. 1 (1995): 10, 15; Ruth McVey, "Globalization, Marginalization, and the Study of Southeast Asia, Southeast Asian Studies: Reorientations," *The Frank H. Golay Memorial Lectures 2 & 3* (Ithaca, NY: Southeast Asian Program Publications, 1998), p. 53; Heather Sutherland, "Contingent Devices", in *Locating Southeast Asia: Geographies of Knowledge and Political Space*, edited by Paul Kratoska, Rebco Raben and Henk Schulte Nordholt (Leiden: KITLV Press, 2005), pp. 22–24.
4. Anthony Reid, *Imperial Alchemy: Nationalism and Political Identity in Southeast Asia* (Cambridge: Cambridge University Press, 2010).
5. Tony Day, "Ties that Unbind: Families and States in Premodern Southeast Asia," *Journal of Asian Studies* 55, no. 2 (1996): 404–05; Tony Day, *Fluid Iron: State Formation in Southeast Asia* (Honolulu: University of Hawai'i Press, 2000) pp. 38–89; Sutherland, "Contingent Devices", pp. 43–49; Heather Sutherland, "Ethnicity, Wealth and Power in Colonial Makassar: A Historiographical Reconsideration", in *The Indonesian City: Studies in Urban Development and Planning*, edited by P. J. M. Nas, Verhadelingen Koninklijk Instituut voor Taal- Land- en Volkenkunde, no. 117 (Dordricht: Floris, 1986) pp. 37–55; see also Peter Boomgaard, Dick Kooiman and Henk Schulte Nordholt (eds.), *Linking Destinies: Trade, Towns and Kin in Asian History*, Verhadelingen Koninklijk Instituut voor Taal- Land- en Volkenkunde, no. 256 (Leiden: KITLV, 2008).
6. O.W. Wolters, *History, Culture and Religion in Southeast Asian Perspectives*, Revised edition (Ithaca and Singapore: Cornell University Southeast Asia Program Publications and Institute of Southeast Asian Studies, 1999), pp. 18–19, 27–28.
7. Here I use Dobbin's and Freitag's reference to Abner Cohen's definition of a trading diaspora as the commercial organization of "a nation of socially interdependent, but spatially dispersed, communities." Christine Dobbin, *Asian Entrepreneurial Minorities: Conjoint Communities in the Making of the World Economy, 1570–1940* (London: RoutledgeCurzon, 1996), p. xi; and Ulrike Freitag, *Indian Ocean Migrants and State Formation in Hadhramaut: Reforming the Homeland* (Leiden: Brill, 2003), p. 3.
8. Reid has defined the *orang kaya* during c. 1450–1680 as "wealthy aristocrats" or "merchant elite", the latter often foreigners. See Reid, *Age of Commerce*, vol. II, p. 115.
9. For an account of the origin and development of the institution within the apparatus of the Malay-Indonesian trading state see Reid, *The Age of Commerce*, vol. II, pp. 114–23; and Jeyamalar Kathirithamby-Wells, "Royal Authority and the *Orang Kaya* in the Western Archipelago 1500–1800," *Journal of Southeast*

Asian Studies 17, no. 2 (1986): 256–67. The relevance of the institution to the development of merchant capitalism during the eighteenth and nineteenth centuries is discussed briefly in Jeyamalar Kathirithamby-Wells, *The Politics of Commerce in Southeast Asia: An Historical Perspective*, An Inaugural Lecture, University of Malaya, Kuala Lumpur (Kuala Lumpur: University of Malaya, 1992), pp. 7–8, 10–11.

10. Barbara Andaya, "The Indian 'Saudagar Raja' in traditional Malay Courts", *Journal of the Malaysian Branch of the Royal Asiatic Society* 51, no. 1 (1978): 13–35; Dhiravat na Pompejra, "Crown Trade and Court Politics during the Reign of King Narai (r.1656–88)," in *The Southeast Asian Port and Polity: Rise and Demise*, edited by Jeyamalar Kathirithamby-Wells and John Villiers (Singapore: Singapore University Press, *Port and Polity*), p. 134.

11. The number of Arabs living in the Netherlands East Indies in 1859 was estimated at over 17,000. By 1885 the number had risen to c. 20,500 and had more than doubled, to 45,000, by 1929. The number classified as Arab rose sharply during the subsequent decade, totalling 71,335 in 1940. Natalie Mobini-Kesheh, *Hadhrami Awakening: Community and Identity in the Netherlands Indies, 1900–1942* (Ithaca, NY: Southeast Asia Publications Program, Cornell University, 1999), p. 21.

12. Reid, *The Age of Commerce*, vol. II, p. 323.

13. According to the census of the *Maktab Daimi* (established by the conservative *al Rābiṭa al-'Alawiyya* formed in 1927 and committed to preserving 'Alawī identity), in c. 1930 there was a total of 17,764 persons from 'Alawī families resident in British Malaya and the Netherlands East Indies. See Sayyid Abubakar b. Ali b. Abubakar Syahbuddin (trans. Ali Yahaya), *Rihlatul Asfar: Otobiografi*, n.p.p., 2000, pp. 107–08.

14. The 'Alawī derived their name from the first jurist and initiator of the Sufi " 'Alawī way" (d. 1255 CE). He was the great-grandson of Ahmad b. Isa, descendant of the Prophet, who migrated from Basra and arrived in 932 CE in Hadhramaut where he established the ancestral line of the *sāda*. See Engseng Ho, *The Graves of Tarim: Geneology and Mobility Across the Indian Ocean* (Berkley: University of California Press, 2006), pp. 37–39.

15. Craig J. Reynolds, "A New Look at Old Southeast Asia", *Journal of Asian Studies* 54, no. 2 (1995): 423.

16. For a discussion of the diasporic status of the Hadhramis see Freitag, *Indian Ocean Migrants*, pp. 1–7.

17. Freitag, *Indian Ocean Migrants*, pp. 90–93; Peter Riddell, *Islam and the Malay-Indonesian World* (London: Horizon Books, 2001), p. 114.

18. Wolters, *History, Culture, and Religion*, pp. 9–11.

19. Tony Day and Craig J. Reynolds, "Cosmologies, Truth Regimes and the State in Southeast Asia", *Modern Asian Studies*, 34, no. 1 (2000): 1–55.

20. Jeyamalar Kathirithamby-Wells, " 'Strangers' and 'Stranger-Kings': The *Sayyid* in Eighteenth-Century Maritime Southeast Asia", *Journal of Southeast Asian Studies* 40, no. 3 (2009): 573–74, 586.

21. Daniel van der Meulen, *Aden to Hadhramaut: A Journey to South Arabia* (London: John Murray, 1947), pp. 153–54; Alexander Knysh, "The Cult of Saints in Hadramawt: An Overview," *New Arabian Studies* 1 (1993): 137–52.
22. James J. Fox, "Ziarah Visits to the Tombs of the Wali, The Founders of Islam in Java," in *Islam in the Indonesian Social Context*, edited by M.C. Ricklefs, Annual Lecture Series, No. 15, 1989 (Clayton, Victoria: Centre for Southeast Asian Studies, Monash University, 1991) p. 19.
23. P.J. Begbie, *The Malay Peninsula*, reprint of 1834 Madras edition (Kuala Lumpur: Oxford University Press, 1967), p. 150; For accounts of the Naning War see Mary C. Turnbull, *The Straits Settlements, 1826–67: Indian Presidency to Crown Colony* (Singapore: Oxford University Press, 1972), pp. 261–66; L.A. Mills, *British Malaya, 1824–64*, introduction by D.K. Bassett (Kuala Lumpur: Oxford University Press, 1966), pp. 149–50; and Begbie, *The Malay Peninsula*, pp. 137–51.
24. Quoted in Shaharil Talib Robert, "The Trengganu Ruling Class in the late Nineteenth Century", *Journal of the Malaysian Branch of the Royal Asiatic Society* 50, no. 2 (1977): 39.
25. John Bousfield, "Islamic Philosophy in Southeast Asia", in *Islam in Southeast Asia*, edited by M.B. Hooker (Leiden: Brill, 1983), p. 116, *passim*.
26. Wolters, *History, Culture and Region*, pp. 112–15.
27. Patricio Abinales, "From *Orang Besar* to Colonial Big Man: The American Military Regime and the Magindano Muslims", Ph.D dissertation, Cornell University, Ithaca, 1998, p. 151.
28. Anthony H. Johns, "Political Authority in Islam: Some Reflections Relevant to Indonesia," in *The Making of an Islamic Political Discourse in Southeast Asia*, edited by Anthony Reid, Monash Papers on Southeast Asia, no. 27 (Clayton, Victoria: Monash University, 1993), p. 23.
29. Quoted in Day, "Ties that Unbind", p. 404. Interestingly, these were the very characteristics that constituted pejorative colonial portrayals of the Arab in Southeast Asia.
30. G. W. J. Drewes (ed. & trans.), Hikajat *Potjut Muhamat: An Acehnese Epic* (The Hague: Martinus Nijhoff, 1979), pp. 16-27, 43, 54, 61, 75, 119.
31. Engseng Ho, "Genealogical Figures in an Arabian Indian Ocean Diaspora", Ph.D. dissertation, University of Chicago, Illinois, 2000, pp. 162–63.
32. "Cacatan Sejarah Sharif Ahmad b. Sultan Abd al-Rahman al-Qadri, Pangeran Bendahara, Pontianak, 1852", Kalimantan West, No. 41, Arsip Nasional Indonesia, Jakarta; Ho, *The Graves of Tarim*, p. 28; Engseng Ho, "Before Parochialization: Diasporic Arabs Cast in Creole Waters", in *Transcending Borders: Arabs, Politics, Trade and Islam in Southeast Asia* edited by Huub de Jonge and Nico Kaptein (Leiden: KITLV, 2002), pp. 21–22.
33. Anthony Reid, "A New Phase of Commercial Expansion in Southeast Asia, 1760–1850," in *The Last Stand of Asian Autonomies: Responses to Modernity in the Diverse States of Southeast Asia, Asia and Korea, 1750–1900*, edited by Anthony Reid (London: Macmillan, 1997), pp. 57–81.

34. Riddell, *Islam and the Malay-Indonesian World*, p. 116.
35. Sayyid Abd al-Samad's father, himself a religious scholar, came from Sana, Yemen, and having married a woman from Palembang took his son to Kedah where he was *mufti*. Educated in Kedah and in the long-established centre of Islamic learning in Patani, Sayyid Abd al-Samad proceeded to the Middle East never to return to the Archipelago. But his influential neo-Sufi scholarly legacy was shared, venerated and mythologized within the disapora. See Azyumardi Azra, *The Origins of Islamic Reformism in Southeast Asia: Networks of Malay-Indonesian and Middle-Eastern 'Ulamā' in the Seventeenth and Eighteenth Centuries* (Leiden: KITLV Press, 2004), pp. 112–14, 130; Riddell, *Islam and the Malay-Indonesian World*, pp. 184–86; Barbara W. Andaya, *To Live as Brothers: Southeast Sumatra in the Seventeenth and Eighteenth Centuries* (Honolulu: University of Hawai'i Press, 1993), pp. 220, 235; Mestika Zed, *Kepialangan Politik dan Revolusi Palembang 1900–1950*, introduced by Audrey Kahin (Jakarta: Pustaka LPES, 2003), pp. 38–39.
36. Kathirithamby-Wells, "'Strangers' and 'Stranger-Kings'", p. 580.
37. Raja Ali Haji ibn Ahmad, *The Precious Gift (Tuhfat al-Nafis)* (trans. and anno.) Virginia Matheson and Barbara Watson Andaya (Kuala Lumpur: Oxford University Press, 1982), pp. 154–57; Elisa Netscher, "Geschiedenis der eerste al-Qadris", *Tijdschrift voor Indische Taal-, Land, en Volkenkunde van het Bataviaasch Genootschap van Kunsten en Wetenschappen* 4 (1855): 299–300.
38. Andaya, *To Live as Brothers*, p. 220.
39. Henk Maier, "'We are Playing Relatives': Riau, the Cradle of Reality and Hybridity," *Bijdragen tot de Taal-, Land en Volkenkunde* 153, no. 3 (1997): 672–98; Kathirithamby-Wells, "'Strangers' and 'Stranger-Kings'", pp. 582–83.
40. Virginia Matheson, "The Tuhfat al-Nafis: Structure and Sources", *Bijdragen tot de Taal-, Land en Volkenkunde* 127 (1971): 381.
41. See Kathirithamby-Wells, "Royal Authority and the *Orang Kaya*", pp. 263–65; Jeyamalar Kathirithamby-Wells, "Forces of Regional and State Integration in the Western Archipelago, c. 1500–1700", *Journal of Southeast Asian Studies* 18, no. 1(1987): 3–34; Reid, *The Age of Commerce*, vol. II, pp. 262–88.
42. A.L. Udovitch, "Commercial Techniques in Early Medieval Islam", in *Islam and the Trade of Asia: A Colloquium*, edited by D.S. Richards (Oxford: Bruno Cassirer, 1970), pp. 42–43.
43. The capital of the Bugis settlement was previously further upriver at Si Bukit.
44. Kathirithamby-Wells, "'Strangers' and 'Stranger-Kings'", pp. 584–85.
45. Ibid., pp. 577–81, 585.
46. John Anderson, *Acheen and the Ports on the North Coast of Sumatra* reprint of 1840 London edition, introduction by Anthony Reid (Kuala Lumpur: Oxford University Press, 1971), pp. 80–81; Lee Kam Hing, *The Sultanate of Aceh: Relations with the British, 1760–1824* (Kuala Lumpur: Oxford University Press, 1995), pp. 252–56.

47. Letters of John Palmer, Calcutta to J. Money, Bombay, 20 March 1813; Palmer to W. Patries, 4 June 1813, Add. 7391; Palmer, Calcutta to Sultan of Pontianak, 24 February 1813; Add. 7392, *Wurtzburg Collection*, Cambridge University Library; Andrew Webster, *The Richest East Indian Merchant: The Life and Business of John Palmer of Calcutta, 1767–1836* (Suffolk: Boydell Press, 2007), p. 96; Lee, *The Sultanate of Aceh*, p. 224.
48. Eric Tagliacozzo, *Secret Traders, Porous Borders: Smuggling and Trade along a Southeast Asian Frontier* (Yale University Press, 2005), p. 214.
49. Norman Sherry, *Conrad's Eastern World* (Cambridge: Cambridge University Press, 1966), pp. 107–10; J.N.F.M. à Campo, "A Profound Debt to the Eastern Seas: Documentary History and Literary Representation of Berau's Maritime Trade in Conrad's Malay Novels", *International Journal of Maritime History* 12, no. 2 (2000): 122, 116–25.
50. *Almanak van Nederlandsch-Indië* (Batavia: Ter Lands Drukkerij, 1830), pp. 108–12; Clarence-Smith, "Hadhrami Entrepreneurs in the Malay World", pp. 298–99; Clarence-Smith, "The rise and fall of Hadhrami shipping", pp. 230–37; Jarom Peeters, "Kaum Tuo-Kaum Mudo: Sociaal-Religieuze Verandering in Palembang, 1821–1942", Ph.D dissertation, Leiden University, 1994, p. 188 n. 124.
51. The "chialoup", a fore-and-aft rigged vessel of European origin, usually with one mast and, on average 55–75 feet long and 20 feet wide, was important in coastal and insular trade. The *gonting*, a larger version of the *mayang*, which derived from the traditional fishing boat, was flat-bottomed and, unlike the "chialoup", served overseas connections in the private sector. Gerrit J. Knaap, *Shallow Waters, Rising Tide, Shipping and Trade in Java Around 1775* (Leiden: KITLV, 1996), pp. 33–35.
52. Jeyamalar Kathirithmby-Wells, "The long eighteenth century in the new age of commerce" in *The Eighteenth Century as a Category of Asian History: Van Leur in Retrospect*, edited by Leonard Blussé and Femme Gaastra (London: Ashgate, 1998), pp. 65, 69–70; Jeyamalar Kathirithamby-Wells, "Siak and its Changing Strategies for Survival, c. 1700–1870", in *The Last Stand of Asian Autonomies: Responses to Modernity in the Diverse States of Southeast Asia, Asia and Korea, 1750–1900*, edited by Anthony Reid (London: Macmillan, 1997), pp. 224, 230.
53. Brian Harrison (trans.), "Malacca in the Eighteenth Century: Two Dutch Governors' Reports", *Journal of the Malayan Branch of the Royal Asiatic Society* 27, no. 1 (1954): 29; Kathirithamby-Wells, "'Strangers' and 'Stranger Kings'", p. 582.
54. Elisa Netscher, "De Nederlanders in Djohor en Siak, 1602 tot 1865", *Verhandelingen Bataviaasch Genootschap* 35 (1870): 146–47.
55. Joseph Burn, "Mr Burn's Account of Pontianak," 12 February and 12 March 1811, *India Office Records, Private Papers, Raffles Collection, XI, MSS Eur. E109,* British Library, London, ff. 132–33; Kathirithamby-Wells, "'Strangers' and 'Stranger-Kings'", pp. 587–88.

56. Webster, *The Richest East Indian Merchant*, pp. 90–91; Bob Reece and F. Andrew Smith, "Joseph Burn and Raffles's Plan for a British Kalimantan", *Borneo Research Bulletin* 37 (2006): 28–29.
57. See below and Ulrike Freitag, "Arab Merchants in Singapore: Attempt of a Collective Biography", in *Transcending Borders*, edited by De Jonge and Kaptein, pp. 116–17.
58. Terance W. Bigalke, *Tana Toraja: A Social History of an Indonesian People* (Leiden: KITLV, 2005), pp. 22–24, 40–42, 75; Terance Bigalke, "Dynamics of Torajan Slave Trade in South Sulawesi," in *Slavery, Bondage and Dependency in Southeast Asia*, edited by Anthony Reid (St Lucia: University of Queensland Press, 1983), pp. 345–46; A. P. van Rijn, "Tocht naar de Boven-Sādang (Midden-Celebes), *Tijdschrift Koninklijk Nederlandsch Aardrijkskundig Genootschap* 19 (1902): 347–49.
59. Van Rijn, "Tocht naar de Boven-Sādang (Midden-Celebes)", pp. 326, 335; G. Teiler, A. M. C. Dissel and J. N. F. M. à Campo, *Zeeroof en Zeeroofbestrijding in de Indische Archipel (19de Eeuw)*, (Amsterdam: De Bataafsche Leeuw, 2005), p. 49; à Campo, "A Profound Debt to the Eastern Seas", p. 89; Burn, "Mr Burn's Account of Pontianak", ff. 34–35.
60. Alfons van der Kraan, "Bali: 1848", *Indonesia Circle* 62 (1994): 29–30.
61. R. Broersma, "Koopvaardij in de Molukken", *Koloniaal Tijdschrift* 23 (1934): 133–34; W. G. Clarence-Smith, "Hadhrami Entrepreneurs in the Malay World, c. 1750–c. 1940" in *Hadhrami Traders, Scholars and Statesmen in the Indian Ocean, 1750s–1960s*, edited by Freitag and Clarence-Smith (Leiden: Brill, 1997), p. 308; L.W.C. van den Berg, *Le Hadhramout et les Colonies Arabes dans l'Archipel Indien* (Batavia: Imprimerie du Gouvernement, 1886) p. 181.
62. Raja Ali Haji, *Tuhfat al-Nafis*, pp. 233–35.
63. Van den Berg, *Le Hadhramaut*, p. 181.
64. Sumit Kumar Mandal, "Finding Their Place: A History of Arabs in Java during Dutch Rule, 1800–1924," Ph.D. dissertation, Columbia University, 1994, pp. 79–81. See Tables 4 & 5 for the impressive number of *sāda* in the service of the Dutch.
65. Mandal, "Finding Their Place," pp. 127–28; M. F. Laffan, *Islamic Nationhood and Colonial Indonesia: The Umma Below the Winds* (London: RoutledgeCurzon, 2003), pp. 87–88, 107.
66. Azyumardi Azra, "A Hadhrami Religious Scholar in Indonesia: Sayyid 'Uthān", in *Hadhrami Traders and Scholars*, edited by Freitag and Clarence-Smith (Leiden: Brill, 1997), pp. 252–55; Nico J. G. Kaptein, "Arabophobia and *Tarekat*: How Sayyid 'Uthmān Became Advisor to the Netherlands Colonial Administration," in *The Hadhrami Diaspora in Southeast Asia: Identity Maintenance or Assimilation?* edited by Ahmed Ibrahim Abushouk and Hassan Ahmed Ibrahim (Leiden: Brill, 2009), pp. 38–42.
67. Mohammad Redzuan Othman, "Conflicting Political Loyalties of the Arabs in Malaya before World War II," in *Transcending Border*, edited by De Jonge and

Kaptein, see pp. 45–48; Sumit K. Mandal, "Forging a Modern Arab Identity in Java in the Twentieth Century", ibid., pp. 169, 176.
68. Beshara Doumani quoted in Freitag, "Indian Ocean Migrants," p. 118.
69. Mohammad Redzuan Othman, "The Middle Eastern Influence on the Development of Religious and Political Thought in Malay Society", Ph.D dissertation, University of Edinburgh, 1994, pp. 92, 108.
70. Van der Kroef, "The Arabs in Indonesia", p. 307; Reid, *Slavery, Bondage and Dependency*, pp. 18–21.
71. J. M. Gullick, "The Entrepreneur in Late Nineteenth Century Malay Peasant Society", *Journal of the Malaysian Branch of the Royal Asiatic Society* 58, no. 1 (1985): 67, 70 n. 69; Van den Berg, *Le Hadhramout*, p. 137.
72. Jeyamalar Kathirithamby-Wells, "Ethics and Entrepreneurship in Southeast Asia, c. 1400–1800", in *Profit Maximization, Ethics and Trade Structure, c. 1300–1800*, edited by Karl A. Sprengard and Roderich Ptak (Wiesbaden: Harrassowitz Verlag, 1994), pp. 175–81.
73. Freitag, *Indian Ocean Migrants*, p. 268.
74. Van der Kroef, "The Arabs in Indonesia", p. 313.
75. F. Andrew Smith, "Hardships in country trade in the East Indies in the early nineteenth century: Seven years in the life of Captain Daniel Smith". Unpublished paper presented at the International Congress of Asian Studies, Kuala Lumpur, August 2007; H. R. C. Wright, *East-Indian Economic Problems of the Age of Cornwallis and Raffles* (London: Luzac, 1961), pp. 287–88.
76. Jeyamalar Kathirithamby-Wells, "Restraints on the Development of Merchant Capitalism in Southeast Asia before c. 1800", in *Southeast Asia in the Early Modern Era: Trade, Power and Belief*, edited by Anthony Reid (Ithaca, NY: Cornell University Press, 1993), pp. 139–40.
77. F. Andrew Smith, "Missionaries, Mariners, and Merchants: Overlooked British Travellers to West Kalimantan in the Early Nineteenth Century," *Borneo Research Bulletin* 33 (2002): 54.
78. Kathirithamby-Wells, "'Strangers' and 'stranger Kings'", pp. 587–88; Van den Berg, *Le Hadhramout*, p. 128.
79. Ho, "Genealogical Figures in an Arabian Indian Ocean Diaspora", p. 56.
80. Van den Berg, *Le Hadhramout*, p. 120.
81. Kathirithamby-Wells, "'Strangers' and 'Stranger-Kings'", pp. 587, 590; G.W. Earl, *The Eastern Seas*, reprint of London 1937 edition (Kuala Lumpur: Oxford University Press, 1971), pp. 76–78.
82. C.E. Wurtzburg, *Raffles of the Eastern Isles* (London: Hodder and Stoughton, 1954), pp. 49–50; Harold Parker Clodd, *"Malaya's First British Pioneer: The Life of Francis Light* (London: Luzac, 1948), pp. 119–20; Freitag, "Arab Merchants in Singapore", p. 125.
83. Janet Ewald and William G. Clarence-Smith, "The Economic Role of the Hadhrami Diaspora in the Red Sea and Gulf of Aden, 1820s to 1930s," in *Hadhrami Traders, Scholars and Statesmen*, edited by Freitag and Clarence-

Smith, p. 288; Clarence-Smith, "Hadhrami Entrepreneurs in the Malay World", pp. 300–01; and Laffan, *Islamic Nationhood and Colonial Indonesia*, p. 105.
84. Van den Berg, *Le Hadhramout*, p. 148; J. N. F. M. à Campo, "Steam Navigation and State Formation", in *The Late Colonial State in Indonesia: Political and Economic Foundations of the Netherlands Indies, 1880–1942*, edited by Robert B. Cribb, (Leiden: KITLV Press, 1994), pp. 11–30. See pp. 7–8.
85. William G. Clarence-Smith, "Economic Role of the Arab Community in Maluku, 1816–1940", *Indonesia and the Malay World* 26 (1988): 32–38; Roy Ellen, "Arab Traders and Land Settlers in the Geser-Gorom Archipelago", *Indonesia Circle* 70 (1996): 239–40; R.Z. Leirissa, "Revivalism in Early Modern Maluku: 'Raja Jailolo'". Unpublished paper presented at the 14th International Association of the Historians of Asia Conference, Bangkok, 20–23 May 1996, p. 12.
86. John Villiers, "The Cash-Crop Economy and State Formation in the Spice Islands in the Fifteenth and Sixteenth Centuries", in *The Southeast Asian Port and Polity: Rise and Demise*, edited by J. Kathirithamby-Wells and J. Villiers (Singapore. Singapore University Press, 1990), p. 91; William G. Clarence-Smith, "The Rise and Fall of Hadhrami Shipping in the Indian Ocean, c. 1750–c. 1940", in *Ships and the Development of Maritime Technology in the Indian Ocean*, edited by David Parkin and Ruth Barnes (London: RoutledgeCurzon, 2002) pp. 237–38.
87. Clarence-Smith, "Rise and Fall of Hadhrami Shipping", p. 238.
88. William G. Clarence-Smith, "Horse Trading: The Economic Role of Arabs in the Lesser Sunda Islands", in *Transcending Borders*, edited by De Jonge and Kaptein, pp. 146–47, 155; Mandal, "Finding Their Place", pp. 42–43; Van den Berg, *Le Hadhramout*, pp. 180, 194; I Gde Parimartha, "Perdagangan dan Politik di Nusa Tenggara 1815–1915", Ph.D. dissertation,Vrije Universiteit, Amsterdam, 1995, pp. 245–47.
89. Frank Broeze, "The Merchant Fleet of Java 1820–1850: A Preliminary Survey", *Archipel* 18 (1978): 265.
90. W. G. Clarence-Smith, "Middle-Eastern Entrepreneurs in Southeast Asia", in *Diaspora Entrepreneurial Networks: Four Centuries of History*, edited by I. B. McCabe, G. Harlaftis and L. P. Minoglou (Oxford: Berg, 2005), p. 230.
91. Clarence-Smith, "Hadhrami entrepreneurs", pp. 305–10.
92. Zed, *Kepialangan Politik dan Revolusi*, pp. 100–02.
93. Khoo Su Nin, *Streets of George Town, Penang* (Penang: Janus Print Resources, 1993), pp. 26, 27; C. B. Buckley, "An Anecdotal History of Old Times in Singapore (Kuala Lumpur: University of Malaya Press, 1962) pp. 563–64; Freitag, "Arab Merchants in Singapore", p. 115.
94. For a discussion of this term as used by Laffan see his *Islamic Nationhood and Colonial Indonesia*, pp. 2–3.
95. Anthony Reid, *The Contest for North Sumatra: Atjeh, the Netherlands and Britain* (Kuala Lumpur: Oxford University Press, 1969), pp. 130–31, 148–49.
96. Freitag, "Arab Merchants in Singapore", p. 128.

97. The al-Saqqaf family, in particular, had strong links with Mecca, close relations with the Sharif and marital connections with the Ottomans. Thus, when an Ottoman warship arrived in Singapore in 1890 at the height of the Aceh War, it was Sayyid Muhammad b. Ahmad al-Saqqaf who represented the local appeal for help. Freitag, "Arab Merchants in Singapore", p. 128; Anthony Reid, "Nineteenth Century Pan-Islam in Indonesia and Malaysia", *Journal of Asian Studies* 26, no. 2 (1967): 278.
98. By this treaty the Kathiris acknowledged Quayti sovereignty and the British protectorate. Freitag, "Hadhramis in International Politics, 1760s–1957", in *Hadhrami Traders, Scholars and Statesmen*, edited by Freitag and Clarence-Smith, pp. 122–24; Freitag, "Arab Merchants in Singapore", p. 129; Freitag, *Indian Ocean Migrants*, pp. 180–82.
99. See Reid, "Nineteenth Century Pan-Islam", pp. 279–83.
100. About a third of the 22 periodicals published in Arabic and Malay between 1876 and 1910 in British Malaya was under Hadhrami auspices. See W.R. Roff, "The Ins and Outs of Hadhrami Journalism in Malaya, 1900–1941: Assimilation or Identity Maintenance", in *The Hadhrami Diaspora in Southeast Asia*, edited by Abushouk and Ibrahim, p. 193.
101. Sultan Taha's mother and first wife were both of Arab descent, most probably from the influential al-Jufri clan of Jambi's *suku kraton*, as was his son-in-law, Sayyid Idrus al-Jufri, Pangeran Wira Kesumo. See Elsbeth Locher-Scholten, *Sumatran Sultanate and Colonial State: Jambi and the Rise of Dutch Imperialism, 1830–1907* (Ithaca: Southeast Asia Programme Publications, Cornell University Press, 2003), pp. 115–39.
102. Locher-Scholten, *Sumatran Sultanate and Colonial State*, pp. 123–24.
103. Ibid., pp. 116, 231–32, 272–73, 285.
104. Jeyamalar Kathirithamby-Wells, *Nature and Nation: Forests and Development in Peninsular Malaysia* (Copenhagen: NIAS Press, 2005), pp. 139–40.
105. W. Linehan, "A History of Pahang", *Journal of the Malayan Branch of the Royal Asiatic Society* 14, no. 2 (1936): 161–62, 166–67.
106. For a detailed account of the uprising see Shaharil Talib, *After Its Own Image: The Trengganu Experience, 1881–1941* (Singapore: Oxford University Press, 1984) Chapter 6, pp. 134–75; Heather Sutherland, "The Taming of the Trengganu Elite", in *Southeast Asian Transitions: Approaches Through Social History*, edited by Ruth T. McVey (New Haven: Yale University Press, 1978), pp. 42–80.
107. Shaharil Talib, *After Its Own Image*, pp. 134–61.
108. Ibid, p. 146.
109. Clodd, *Malaya's First British Pioneer*, pp. 55–56.
110. Laffan, *Islamic Nationhood and Colonial Indonesia*, p. 10.
111. Roff, "The Ins and Outs of Hadhrami Journalism in Malaysia", p. 197.
112. Laffan, *Islamic Nationhood and Colonial Indonesia*, pp. 114–16.
113. Virginia Matheson Hooker, *Writing a New Society: Social Change Through the Novel in Malay* (Leiden: KITLV, 2000), pp. 20–42.

114. Roff, "The Ins and Outs of Hadhrami Journalism in Malaya", p. 197.
115. Freitag, *Indian Ocean Migrants*, pp. 258–59, 270–73; Sayyid Abubakar Syahbuddin, *Rihlatul Asfar*, pp. 92–93.
116. Sayyid Abubakar Syahbuddin, *Rihlatul Asfar*, pp. 101–07.
117. Laffan, *Islamic Nationhood and Colonial Indonesia*, p. 190; Freitag, *Indian Ocean Migrants*, pp. 243–44; Mobini-Kesheh, *Hadhrami Awakening*, pp. 36, 73–74.
118. See Mona Abaza, "Southeast Asia and the Middle East: *Al-Manār* and Islamic Modernity" in *From the Mediterranean to the China Sea: Miscellaneous Notes*, edited by Claude Guillot, Denys Lombard and Roderich Ptak (Wiesbaden: Harrassowitz Verlag, 1998), pp. 102–03.
119. Reid, *Imperial Alchemy*, pp. 2–3, 12.

References

Abaza, Mona. "Southeast Asia and the Middle East: *Al-Manār* and Islamic modernity". In *From the Mediterranean to the China Sea: Miscellaneous Note*s, edited by Claude Guillot, Denys Lombard and Roderich Ptak, pp. 93–113. Wiesbaden: Harrassowitz Verlag, 1998.

Abinales, Patricio. "From *Orang Besar* to Colonial Big Man: The American Military Regime and the Magindano Muslims". Ph.D dissertation, Cornell University, Ithaca, 1998.

Ahmad, Raja Ali Haji ibn. *The Precious Gift (Tuhfat al-Nafis)* (trans. and annot.) V. Matheson and B. Watson Andaya. Kuala Lumpur: Oxford University Press, 1982.

Andaya, Barbara Watson. "The Indian 'Saudagar Raja' in traditional Malay Courts". *Journal of the Malaysian Branch of the Royal Asiatic Society* 51, no. 1 (1978): 13–35.

———. *To Live as Brothers: Southeast Sumatra in the Seventeenth and Eighteenth Centuries*. Honolulu: University of Hawai'i Press, 1993.

Anderson, John. *Acheen and the Ports on the North Coast of Sumatra*, reprint of 1840 London edition, introduction by Anthony Reid. Kuala Lumpur: Oxford University Press, 1971.

Anon. *Almanak van Nederlandsch Indië*. Batavia: Ter Lands Deukkrij, 1830.

Anon. "Catatan Sejarah Sharif Ahmad b. Sultan Abd al-Rahman al-Qadri, Pangeran Bendahara", Pontianak, 1852", Jakarta, Kalimantan West, no. 41, Arsip Nasional Indonesia.

Azra, Azyumardi. "A Hadhrami Religious Scholar in Indonesia: Sayyid 'Uthān". In *Hadhrami Traders, Scholars and Statesmen in the Indian Ocean*, edited by Ulrike Freitag and William G. Clarence-Smith, pp. 249–63. Leiden: Brill, 1997.

———. *The Origins of Islamic Reformism in Southeast Asia: Networks of Malay-Indonesian and Middle-Eastern "Ulamā" in the Seventeenth and Eighteenth Centuries*. Leiden: KITLV Press, 2004.

Begbie, P. J. *The Malay Peninsula*. Reprint of 1834 Madras edition. Kuala Lumpur: Oxford University Press, 1967.

Bigalke, T. W. *Tana Toraja: A Social History of an Indonesian People*. Leiden: KITLV, 2005.

———. "Dynamics of Torajan Slave Trade in South Sulawesi". In *Slavery, Bondage and Dependency in Southeast Asia*, edited by Anthony Reid, pp. 341–63. St Lucia: University of Queensland Press, 1983.

Boomgaard, Peter, Dick Kooiman and Henk Schulte Nordholt (eds.). *Linking Destinies: Trade, Towns and Kin in Asian History*, Verhadelingen Koninklijk Instituut voor Taal- Land- en Volkenkunde, 256. Leiden: KITLV, 2008.

Bousfield, John. "Islamic Philosophy in Southeast Asia". In *Islam in Southeast Asia*, edited by M. B. Hooker, pp. 92–139. Leiden: Brill, 1983.

Broersma, R. "Koopvaardij in de Molukken". *Koloniaal Tijdschrift* 23 (1934): 129–47, 320–50.

Broeze, Frank. "The Merchant Fleet of Java 1820–1850: A Preliminary Survey". *Archipel* 18 (1978): 251–69.

Buckley, C. B. *An Anecdotal History of Old Times in Singapore*. Kuala Lumpur: University of Malaya Press, 1962.

Burn, Joseph. "Mr Burn's Account of Pontianak," 12 February and 12 March 1811, *India Office Records, Private Papers, Raffles Collection, XI, MSS Eur. E109*, British Library, London.

Campo, J. N. F. M. à. "Steam Navigation and State Formation". In *The Late Colonial State in Indonesia: Political and Economic Foundations of the Netherlands Indies, 1880–1942*, edited by R.B. Cribb, pp. 11–30. Leiden: KITLV Press, 1994.

———. "A Profound Debt to the Eastern Seas: Documentary History and Literary Representation of Berau's Maritime Trade in Conrad's Malay Novels". *International Journal of Maritime History* 12, no. 2 (2000): 85–125.

Clarence-Smith, William G. "The Economic Role of the Arab Community in Maluku, 1816–1940". *Indonesia and the Malay World*, no. 26 (1988): 32–38.

———. "Hadhrami Entrepreneurs in the Malay World, c. 1750–c. 1940". In *Hadhrami Traders, Scholars and Statesmen in the Indian Ocean*, edited by Ulrike Freitag and William G. Clarence-Smith, pp. 297–314. Leiden: Brill, 1997.

———. "The Rise and Fall of Hadhrami Shipping in the Indian Ocean, c. 1750–c. 1940". In *Ships and the Development of Maritime Technology in the Indian Ocean*, edited by David Parkin and Ruth Barnes, pp. 227–58. London: RoutledgeCurzon, 2002.

———. "Horse Trading: The Economic Role of Arabs in the Lesser Sunda Islands, c. 1800–1940," in *Transcending Borders: Arabs, Politics, Trade and Islam in Southeast Asia*, edited by Huub de Jonge and Nico Kaptein, pp. 143-62.

———. "Middle-Eastern Entrepreneurs in Southeast Asia". In *Diaspora Entrepreneurial Networks: Four Centuries of History*, edited by I. B. McCabe, G. Harlaftis and L. P. Minoglou, pp. 217–44. Oxford: Berg, 2005.

Clodd, Harold Parker. *Malaya's First British Pioneer: The Life of Francis Light*. London: Luzac, 1948.
Day, Tony. "Ties that Unbind: Families and States in Pre-Modern Southeast Asia". *Journal of Asian Studies* 55, no. 2 (1996): 384–407.
——. *Fluid Iron: State Formation in Southeast Asia*. Honolulu: University of Hawai'i Press, 2000.
—— and Craig J. Reynolds. "Cosmologies, Truth Regimes and the State in Southeast Asia". *Modern Asian Studies* 43, no. 1 (2000): 1–55.
Dobbin, Christine. *Asian Entrepreneurial Minorities: Conjoint Communities in the Making of the World Economy, 1570–1940*. London: RoutledgeCurzon, 1996.
Drewes, G. W. J. (edited and translated). *Hikajat Potjut Muhamat: An Acehnese Epic*. The Hague: Martinus Nijhoff, 1979.
Earl, G. W. *The Eastern Seas*. Reprint of 1937 London edition. Kuala Lumpur: Oxford University Press, 1971.
Ellen, Roy. "Arab Traders and Land Settlers in the Geser-Gorom Archipelago". *Indonesia Circle*, 70 (1996): 237–52.
Fox, James J. "Ziarah Visits to the Tombs of the Wali, The Founders of Islam in Java". In *Islam in the Indonesian Social Context*, Annual Lecture Series, edited by M.C. Ricklefs, no. 15, pp. 19–31. Clayton, Victoria: Centre for Southeast Asian Studies, Monash University, 1991.
Freitag, Ulrike. *Indian Ocean Migrants and State Formation in Hadhramaut: Reforming the Homeland*. Leiden: Brill, 2003.
——. "Arab Merchants in Singapore: Attempt of a Collective Biography". In *Transcending Borders: Arabs, Politics, Trade and Islam in Southeast Asia*, edited by Huub de Jonge and Nico Kaptein, pp. 109–42. Leiden: KITLV, 2002.
Gullick, J. M. "The Entrepreneur in Late 19th Century Malay Peasant Society". *Journal of the Malaysian Branch of the Royal Asiatic Society* 58, no. 1 (1985): 59–70.
Harrison, Brian (trans.). "Malacca in the Eighteenth Century: Two Dutch Governors' Reports". *Journal of the Malaysian Branch of the Royal Asiatic Society* 27, no. 1 (1954): 24–34.
Ho, Engseng. "Genealogical Figures in an Arabian Indian Ocean Diaspora". Ph.D dissertation, University of Chicago, Illinois, 2000.
——. "Before Parochialization: Diasporic Arabs Cast in Creole Waters". In *Transcending Borders: Arabs, Politics, Trade and Islam in Southeast Asia*, edited by Huub de Jonge and Nico Kaptein, pp. 11–36. Leiden: KITLV, 2002.
——. *The Graves of Tarim: Geneology and Mobility Across the Indian Ocean*. Berkley: University of California Press, 2006.
Hooker, Virginia Matheson. *Writing a New Society: Social Change through the Novel in Malay*. Leiden: KITLV, 2000.
Johns, Anthony H. "Political Authority in Islam: Some Reflections Relevant to Indonesia". In *The Making of an Islamic Political Discourse in Southeast Asia*, edited by Anthony Reid, pp. 18–33. Monash Papers on Southeast Asia, no. 27. Clayton, Victoria: Monash University, 1993.
Kaptein, Nico. "Arabophobia and *Tarekat*: How Sayyid 'Uthmān Became Advisor

to the Netherlands Colonial Administration". In *The Hadhrami Diaspora in Southeast Asia: Identity Maintenance or Assimilation?*, edited by Ahmed Ibrahim Abushouk and Hassan Ahmed Ibrahim, pp. 33–44. Leiden: Brill, 2009.

Kathirithamby-Wells, Jeyamalar. "Royal Authority and the *Orang Kaya* in the Western Archipelago 1500–1800". *Journal of Southeast Asian Studies* 17, no. 2 (1986): 256–67.

———. "Forces of Regional and State Integration in the Western Archipelago, c. 1500–1700". *Journal of Southeast Asian Studies* 18, no. 1 (1987): 3–34.

———. *The Politics of Commerce in Southeast Asia: An Historical Perspective*. Inaugural Lecture, University of Malaya, Kuala Lumpur. Kuala Lumpur: University of Malaya, 1992.

———. "Restraints on the Development of Merchant Capitalism in Southeast Asia Before c. 1800". In *Southeast Asia in the Early Modern Era: Trade, Power and Belief*, edited by Anthony Reid, pp. 123–48. Ithaca, NY: Cornell University Press, 1993.

———. "Ethics and Entrepreneurship in Southeast Asia, c. 1400–1800". In *Profit Maximization, Ethics and Trade Structure, c. 1300–1800*, edited by K. A. Sprengard and Roderich Ptak, pp. 171–87. Wiesbaden: Harrassowitz Verlag, 1994.

———. "The long eighteenth century in the new age of commerce". In *The Eighteenth Century as a Category of Asian History: Van Leur in Retrospect*, edited by Leonard Blussé and Femme Gaastra, pp. 217–43. London: Ashgate, 1998.

———. *Nature and Nation: Forests and Development in Peninsular Malaysia*. Copenhagen: NIAS Press, 2005.

———. "'Strangers' and 'Stranger-Kings': The *Sayyid* in Eighteenth-Century Maritime Southeast Asia". *Journal of Southeast Asian Studies* 40, no. 3 (2009): 567–91.

Khoo Su Nin. *Streets of George Town, Penang*. Penang: Janus Print Resources, 1993.

Knaap, Gerrit J. *Shallow Waters, Rising Tide: Shipping and Trade in Java Around 1775*. Leiden: KITLV, 1996.

Knysh, Alexander. "The Cult of Saints in Hadramawt: An Overview". *New Arabian Studies* 1 (1993): 137–52.

Laffan, M. F. *Islamic Nationhood and Colonial Indonesia: The Umma Below the Winds*. London: RoutledgeCurzon, 2003.

Lee, Kam Hing. *The Sultanate of Aceh: Relations with the British, 1760–1824*. Kuala Lumpur: Oxford University Press, 1995.

Lieberman, Victor. "Local Integration and Eurasian Analogies: Structuring Southeast Asian History". *Modern Asian Studies* 27, no. 3 (1993): 475–572.

———. "An Age of Commerce in Southeast Asia? Problems of Regional Coherence: A Review article". *Journal of Asian Studies* 54, no. 3 (1995): 796–815.

Leirissa, R. Z. "Revivalism in Early Modern Maluku: 'Raja Jailolo'". Unpublished paper presented at the 14th International Association of the Historians of Asia Conference, Bangkok, 20–23 May 1996.

Linehan, W. "A History of Pahang". *Journal of the Malayan Branch of the Royal Asiatic Society* 14, no. 2 (1936): pp. 1–256.

Locher-Scholten, Elsbeth. *Sumatran Sultanate and Colonial State: Jambi and the Rise of Dutch Imperialism, 1830–1907.* Ithaca: Southeast Asia Programme Publications, Cornell University Press, 2003.

Lombard, Denys. "Networks and Synchronisms in Southeast Asian History". *Journal of Southeast Asian Studies* 26, no. 1 (1995): 10–16.

Maier, Henk M. "'We are Playing Relatives': Riau, the Cradle of Reality and Hybridity". *Bijdragen tot de Taal-, Land en Volkenkunde* 153, no. 3 (1997): 672–98.

Mandal, Sumit Kumar. "Finding Their Place; A History of Arabs in Java during Dutch Rule, 1800–1924," Ph.D dissertation, Columbia University, 1994.

Matheson, Virginia. "The *Tuhfat al-Nafis*: Structure and Sources". *Bijdragen tot de taal-, Land- en Volkenkunde van het Koninklijk Instituut* 127, no. 9 (1971): 375–92.

McVey, Ruth T. "Globalization, Marginalization, and the Study of Southeast Asia, Southeast Asian Studies: Reorientations". *The Frank H. Golay Memorial Lectures 2 & 3.* Ithaca, NY: Cornell University Southeast Asian Program, 1998.

Mills, L. A. *British Malaya, 1824–64.* Kuala Lumpur: Oxford University Press, 1966.

Mobini-Kesheh, Natalie. *Hadhrami Awakening: Community and Identity in the Netherlands Indies, 1900–1942.* Ithaca, NY: Cornell University Southeast Asia Program, 1999.

Mohammad Redzuan Othman, "The Middle Eastern Influence on the Development of religious and Political Thought in Malay Society". Ph.D. dissertation, University of Edinburgh, 1994.

———. "Conflicting Political Loyalties of the Arabs in Malaya before World War II". In *Transcending Borders: Arabs, Politics, Trade and Islam in Southeast Asia*, edited by Huub de Jonge and Nico Kaptein, pp. 37–52. Leiden: KITLV, 2002.

Netscher, E. "Geschiedenis der eerste al-Qadris". *Tijdschrift voor Indische Taal-, Land, en Volkenkunde van het Bataviaasch Genootschap van Kunsten en Wetenschappen*, no. 4 (1855): 285–304.

———. "De Nederlanders in Djohor en Siak, 1602 tot 1865". *Verhandelingen Bataviaasch Genootschap* 35 (1870).

Parimartha, I Gde. "Perdagangan dan Politik di Nusa Tenggara 1815–1915", Ph.D. dissertation, Vrije Universiteit, Amsterdam, 1995.

Peeters, Jeroen. "Kaum Tuo-Kaum Mudo: Sociaal-Religieuze Verandering in Palembang, 1821–1942". Ph.D. dissertation, Leiden University, 1994.

Pompejra, Dhiravat Na. "Crown Trade and Court Politics during the Reign of King Narai (r.1656–88)". In *The Southeast Asian Port and Polity: Rise and Demise*, edited by Jeyamalar Kathirithamby-Wells and John Villiers, pp. 127–42. Singapore: Singapore University Press, 1990.

Reece, Bob and F. Andrew Smith. "Joseph Burn and Raffles's Plan for a British Kalimantan". *Borneo Research Bulletin* 37 (2006): 27–49.

Reid, Anthony. "Nineteenth Century Pan-Islam in Indonesia and Malaysia". *Journal of Asian Studies* 26, no. 2 (1967): 267–83.

———. *The Contest for North Sumatra: Atjeh, the Netherlands and Britain*. Kuala Lumpur: Oxford University Press, 1969.

———. *Southeast Asia in the Age of Commerce*. Vol. I, *Land Below the Winds*; vol. II, *Expansion and Crisis*. New Haven: Yale University Press, 1988–1993.

———. "Introduction: A Time and a Place". In *Southeast Asia in the Early Modern Era: Trade, Power, and Belief*, edited by Anthony Reid, pp. 1–19. Ithaca, NY: Cornell University Press, 1993.

———. "A New Phase of Commercial Expansion in Southeast Asia, 1760–1850". In *The Last Stand of Asian Autonomies: Responses to Modernity in the Diverse States of Southeast Asia, Asia and Korea, 1750–1900*, edited by Anthony Reid, pp. 57–81. London: Macmillan, 1997.

———. *Imperial Alchemy: Nationalism and Political Identity in Southeast Asia*. Cambridge: Cambridge University Press, 2010.

Reynolds, C. J. "A New Look at Old Southeast Asia". *Journal of Asian Studies* 54, no. 2 (1995): 419–46.

Riddell, Peter. *Islam and the Malay-Indonesian World*. London: Horizon Books, 2001.

Roff, William R. "The Ins and Outs of Hadhrami Journalism in Malaya, 1900–1941: Assimilation or Identity Maintenance". In *The Hadhrami Diaspora in Southeast Asia: Assimilation or Identity Maintenance?*, edited by Ahmed Ibrahim Abushouk and Hasan Ahmed Ibrahim, pp. 191–202. Leiden: Brill, 2009.

Shaharil Talib. *After Its Own Image: The Trengganu Experience, 1881–1941*. Singapore: Oxford University Press, 1984.

Shaharil Talib Robert. "The Terengganu Ruling Class in the late Nineteenth Century". *Journal of the Malaysian Branch of the Royal Asiatic Society* 50, no. 2 (1977): 25–47.

Sherry, Norman. *Conrad's Eastern World*. Cambridge: Cambridge University Press, 1966.

Smith, F. Andrew. "Hardships in country trade in the East Indies in the early nineteenth century: Seven years in the life of Captain Daniel Smith." Unpublished paper presented at the International Congress of Asian Studies, Kuala Lumpur, August 2007.

———. "Missionaries, Mariners, and Merchants: Overlooked British Travellers to West Kalimantan in the Early Nineteenth Century". *Borneo Research Bulletin* 33 (2002): 45–61.

Subrahmanyam, Sanjay. "Connected Histories: Notes Towards a Reconfiguration of Early Modern Eurasia". *Modern Asian Studies* 31, no. 3 (1997): 288–309.

Sutherland, Heather. "The Taming of the Trengganu Elite". In *Southeast Asian Transitions: Approaches Through Social History*, edited by Ruth T. McVey, pp. 32–85. New Haven: Yale University Press, 1978.

———. "Ethnicity, Wealth and Power in Colonial Makassar: A Historiographical Reconsideration". In *The Indonesian City: Studies in Urban Development and Planning*, edited by P. J. M. Nas, pp. 337–55. Dordricht: Floris, 1986.

———. "Contingent Devices". In *Locating Southeast Asia: Geographies of Knowledge and Political Space,* edited by Paul Kratoska, Rebco Raben and Henk Schulte Nordholt, pp. 20–59. Leiden: KITLV Press, 2005.

Syahbuddin, Sayyid Abubakar b. Ali b. Abubakar (trans. Ali Yahaya). *Rihlatul Asfar: Otobiografi,* n.p.p., 2000.

Tagliacozzo, Eric. *Secret Traders, Porous Borders: Smuggling and Trade along a Southeast Asian Frontier.* New Haven: Yale University Press, 2005.

Turnbull, C. Mary. *The Straits Settlements, 1826–67: Indian Presidency to Crown Colony.* Singapore: Oxford University Press, 1972.

Udovitch, Abraham L. "Commercial Techniques in Early Medieval Islam". In *Islam and the Trade of Asia: A Colloquium,* edited by D.S. Richards, pp. 37–65. Oxford: Bruno Cassirer, 1970.

Van den Berg, L.W.C. *Le Hadhramout et les Colonies Arabes dans l'Archipel Indien.* Batavia: Imprimerie du Gouvernement, 1886.

Van der Kraan, Alfons. "Bali: 1848". *Indonesia Circle* 62 (1994): 1–57.

Van der Meulen, Daniel. *Aden to Hadhramaut: A Journey to South Arabia.* London: John Murray, 1947.

Van Rijn, A. P. "Tocht naar de Boven-Sādang (Midden-Celebes)". *Tijdschrift Koninklijk Nederlandsch Aardrijkskundig Genootschap* 19 (1902): 347–72.

Villiers, John. "The Cash-Crop Economy and State Formation in the Spice Islands in the Fifteenth and Sixteenth Centuries". In *The Southeast Asian Port and Polity: Rise and Demise,* edited by Jeyamalar Kathirithamby-Wells and John Villiers, pp. 83–105. Singapore. Singapore University Press, 1990.

Webster, Andrew. *The Richest East Indian Merchant: The Life and Business of John Palmer of Calcutta, 1767–1836.* Suffolk: Boydell Press, 2007.

Wolters, O. W. *History, Culture and Religion in Southeast Asian Perspectives.* Revised edition of 1982 first edition. Ithaca and Singapore: Cornell University Southeast Asia Program and Institute of Southeast Asian Studies, 1999.

Wright, H. R. C. *East-Indian Economic Problems of the Age of Cornwallis and Raffles.* London: Luzac, 1961.

Wurtzburg, C. E. *Raffles of the Eastern Isles.* London: Hodder and Stoughton, 1954.

Zed, Mestika. *Kepialangan Politik dan Revolusi Palembang 1900–1950.* Introduced by Audrey Kahin. Jakarta: Pustaka LPES, 2003.

14

ABSENT AT THE CREATION
Islamism's Belated, Troubled Engagement with Early Indonesian Nationalism[1]

R.E. Elson

When reflecting on the career of a historian with a published repertoire as sweeping, diverse, deep, and influential as that of Anthony Reid, one marvels, at one level, at a lone scholar's capacity to confront, explicate and interpret with such sureness and imaginativeness so many different sets of circumstances, contexts, and periods of time. At a deeper level still, one is set to thinking of questions of historical technique and historical explanation, and in particular of the interplay of diverse individuals and larger forces and ideas and how they engage and collide in making history. Reid's own rich corpus gives of many such examples of the interchange between broad shaping forces of the Braudellian kind ("all the major forms of collective life, economies, institutions, social structures in short and above all, civilizations")[2] and the historical specificity of an individual's or group's conscious and unconscious behaviour. In seeking to pay Reid tribute, I was drawn, as he himself has often been, to looking at an old, perhaps ignored problem, inspired both by the new agendas for understanding the past which the contemporary always throws at the historian, and by Reid's easy mastery of the interplay of the individual and larger social forces through time. The problem I have chosen is a simple one: why did Indonesian Islamism (by which I mean that understanding which demands that the exercise of politics be grounded upon Islam above all else) fail to have a significant, consequential impact on the course of Indonesia's twentieth century history? In beginning to address it — that is all space allows me here — I will restrict myself purely to an analysis of Islamism's engagement with the discourses and directions of early Indonesian nationalism.

ISLAM AND THE NATIONALIST NARRATIVE

The received orthodoxy of Indonesia's coming to be as a modern nation-state is, we all know, a determinedly secular one; the narrative traces the emergence and struggles of a modernizing young elite increasingly captured with and entranced by Westernized visions of nation, progress and prosperity. After some encouraging but ultimately false starts grounded successively in ethnicity, religion and international communism, the nationalist narrative takes flight with the inclusivist affirmation of the nation-ness of the whole archipelago which, the narrative goes, reaches its natural and necessary goal in Sukarno's proclamation of the independence of the Republic of Indonesia in August 1945.

Scholars and commentators have questioned whether the political shape which Indonesia eventually took might have taken other forms — perhaps a federal state, perhaps a multiplicity of states, perhaps different constitutional architecture — but there has been surprisingly sparse analysis of the possibilities of an outcome in which Indonesia shaped its sense of self by virtue of the dominance, or even the significant input, of the Islamic impulse. The question may be put in variously graded ways, ranging from asking why Indonesia did not assume the form of an Islamic state to inquiring into why specifically Islamic thinking of any kind had such marginal input and importance in the final national outcome. Laffan has written of Anderson's "heroic invocation" of the secular nationalist endeavour in Indonesia, remarking that "Anderson was not speaking of a project that identified in any substantial way with the faith of the majority of the inhabitants of the archipelago", and asserting the "real need for a re-examination of the place of religion in guiding the footsteps of some of Anderson's heroes."[3] For Laffan, "the vision of a linear development of an Indonesian nationalism evolving from diverse regional nationalism all tied to the Western metropole and class struggle is neither simple nor completely satisfying."[4] This piece takes up Laffan's challenge and, in so doing, attempts to explain the failure of Islam's champions to interrupt or divert the trajectory of secularized thinking about the emerging Indonesian state.

INDONESIAN MUSLIMS

Scholars generally agree that the rise of modern varieties of thinking about indigenous identity in this region was occasioned by the Netherlands' final success in melding a new, archipelago-wide political entity which it called the Netherlands Indies. That creation, moreover, was imbued with the essential characteristics of a modern state: a centralized form of governance, an efficient bureaucracy staffed by the products of modern Western education, and integrating physical and communications infrastructures — roads, railways, shipping lines, banks, newspapers. An advertisement for the newspaper *Soerabajasch Handelsblad* in the 1907 edition of *De Indische Gids*, effusively describing it as "the greatest daily newspaper of the Netherlands Indies, read from Sabang to Merauke,"[5] was one small indicator of a growing sense of Indies identity/community.

Most of the inhabitants of this newly-fabricated state were Muslims, as indeed their forerunners had been. Ricklefs observes of Java in the later eighteenth and earlier nineteenth centuries that "nothing in the records of this period ... implies that it was possible to be Javanese without being Muslim".[6] But Islam, like the country itself, was changing. Ricklefs has argued vigorously and industriously, if not altogether compellingly, that in Java from about the mid-nineteenth century there had begun a process of polarization of an earlier "mystic synthesis," grounded in Islam,[7] resulting in the emergence of "two groups defined by their Islamic commitment",[8] devout and pious Muslims (*putihan* or *santri*) and, in the great majority, *abangan*, those much less strongly attached to orthodox belief and practice. Moreover, he claims, there began to develop a striking if limited sense of outright opposition to Islam's ascendancy.[9]

The motor of this change in Java, Ricklefs argues, was the increasing prosperity brought into domestic commercial circles — "a native bourgeoisie of Islamic bent"[10] — by the transformative operation of the Dutch system of forced cultivations, allowing some Muslims enhanced status and even the chance to avail themselves of the ever-opening opportunities to travel to Mekka. There they encountered the reforming winds gusting through Middle Eastern Islam, and brought that thinking home with revivalist enthusiasm. Its vigorous introduction may well have excited a deep adverse reaction which took gradual shape in the emergence of the *abangan*, with all the potential for misunderstanding and conflict that entailed.[11]

The Islam lived by Indonesians, then, expressed itself in multiple manifestations, influenced by both imported and locally-forged experience, including varieties of Middle Eastern reformism (notably turn-of-the-century modernist Islam) and indigenized mystical varieties soaked with Sufistic accommodations and selective borrowings. There were, as well, Javanese Christians — a new phenomenon — and even "Javanese intellectuals who wrote works of literature saying that the Islamization of Java was a great mistake."[12] Many late-nineteenth century observers, indeed, cast doubts on the depth of Islamic attachment, especially in Java. The Dutch missionary Poensen, while admitting that "the people on the outside are very certainly Mohammedan", thought that "in the depths of the soul there still works a religious life that expresses itself in all kinds of non-Mohammedan ideas and forms."[13] Another observer noted that though "the native people profess Islam ... most of them are not Mohammedans in the real sense, far from that. The Javan, the ordinary villager, is much more attached to making offerings for various spirits than to the prescriptions of the Koran, which he very seldom observes, indeed he often pokes fun at the *santri* who does this".[14]

That "thin and flaking glaze" conception of Indonesian Islam, sometimes entertained to encourage the prospects for Christian missionary activities, was staunchly rejected by others. Cipto Mangunkusumo, Dutch-educated medico, intellectual, and free spirit, remarked that "our fathers and forefather have believed in that religion for centuries, whether they understood it or not, with their lips and with their hearts — that says it all ... . The fact that we are 'syncretists' ... changes nothing: we go about our business in the holy understanding that we are Muslims!"[15] Famed Dutch Islamologist Christian Snouck Hurgronje, in speaking of Java's Princely Territories, acknowledged that "what [the mass of the population] possess in religious and other beliefs indeed goes by the name 'Islam,' but actually consists in a mixture of Indonesian, Hindu and Chinese elements."[16] Nonetheless, thought Snouck, "this does not take away the fact that chiefs and people there are mostly very attached to Islam, that they see in it a palladium of their nationality, which becomes all the more dear to them according to the measure that it is exposed to attacks from outside."[17] Nor, Snouck noted elsewhere, was that behaviour exceptional; "one comes across such a compromise between the earlier and the later civilizational situation in all Mohammedan lands, including in the stem land of Arabia."[18] Only "superficial observers," he asserted, might be moved to wonder how truly Muslim the Javanese were.[19] Van Ronkel, reporting on Islam in West Sumatra, thought that "all without exception want to be nothing other than Muslims, almost all perform the prayers, be it defectively ... most see in performing the *hajj* or dying in the holy city the fulfilment of their dearest wishes."[20]

REFORMIST THEN MODERNIST ISLAM

The most significant new force in Indonesian Islam was sourced half a world away in the Middle East, where Islam had been gripped by renewal. Those reformist waves sought more authentic expressions of Islam — involving "sharply articulated visions of the self-sufficiency of scripture and the moral responsibility of the individual"[21] — which might dispense with the thick crust of human accretion on religious belief and practice and return to a more firmly-grounded, intellectualized reliance on the original sources of Muslim tradition. Reformist, though not modernist, tendencies were typified in people like Ahmad Khatib, the Minangkabau *madzhab* scholar who left for Mekka in 1876 never to return. His thinking, best known through his fundamental criticism of the Minangkabau custom of matrilineal inheritance as contradicting the law of God and his opposition to Minangkabau mystical *tariqah* orders,[22] was propagated through his pupils returning home and the strong links he maintained with them.[23]

Reformism's modernist turn involved a deep aversion to misguided human innovation (*bid'ah*), but its privileging of the exercise of human rationality exhibited a new confidence in human capacity to interpret old traditions in ways that took better account of and sought to benefit from the reality of modernity. Such sentiments, propagated by such major figures as Jamal al-Din al-Afghani and Muhammad 'Abduh, began to lap upon the island shores of the Indies at the very end of the nineteenth century, partly in consequence of technological advances such as cheap printing and steamships.[24] They expressed themselves institutionally in the early years of the twentieth century in efforts at religious regeneration and the introduction of modern ways of knowing and learning. The champions of these tendencies saw themselves as a *kaum muda* (young group) of Muslim devotees, to be contrasted with the old group (*kaum tua*), still tied to traditional Islamic practices and techniques.[25]

Just after the turn of the century, Indonesian Arabs formed a modern organization, the *Jamiat Khair* (The Benevolent Society), aimed at keeping pace with the rate of modern change especially through modern, Westernized education, which included religious education.[26] A reformist segment of that society created the *al-Irsyad* education movement in 1913.[27] The Muslim scholar Ahmad Dahlan, himself a former student of Khatib in Mekka,[28] and profoundly influenced by the thinking of 'Abduh and his disciple Rashid Rida, formed the Yogyakarta-based modernist *Muhammadiyah* movement in 1912; it focussed on meeting deeply-felt indigenous educational and social needs and on selfless, rational piety as the means for Muslim salvation.[29] *Muhammadiyah*, on a sound footing in Java by the early 1920s, was imported to Minangkabau in 1925 by the uncompromising Haji Abdul Karim Amrullah (Haji Rasul). That Minang connection was to prove central to *Muhammadiyah*'s larger elaboration, and the organization spread quickly into other regions outside Java thereafter.[30]

Notwithstanding its internal divisions and the shades of its manifestation, Islam dominated the terrain of indigenous perceptions of self and community at the turn of the twentieth century. Although indigenous identity sometimes expressed itself in local terms, and sometimes more broadly in ethnic terms (Javanese, Balinese, Acehnese, for example), most of all it found expression in religious terms, that is, in a shared sense of Muslim-ness that transcended any privileged attachment to a specific place.[31] That sense was strengthened by fear of an enhanced and potentially dangerous Christian missionary outreach — often deeply resented as the offensive, aggravating, demeaning and rapacious tool of Christianizing Dutch authority.[32] But Islam remained remote from the levers that guided the flow of political events, a result of the confluence of three factors: a reticence about nation, new, vital and competing cultural imaginings, and its own belated politicking.

MUSLIM DIFFIDENCE ABOUT NATION

Islamic thinking, however, remained essentially a function of self-regarding pious thought, directed more towards right individual and social behaviour and ritual than to political architecture. Within the realm of specifically Muslim thinking — of whatever stripe — notions of territorial belonging or attachment were hardly in evidence. In that sense, Noer notes, "in the political field, the ideas from the Middle East among the reformists in Indonesia were less influential than those in the basically religious arena."[33]

Outside the narrowly Islamic world, though, the new reality of the Indies, together with the confused and confusing experience of epochal change — the call of modernity — began to impress itself on the minds of the few. As Cipto remarked, "Without any doubt, the present day Indies is passing through a particularly pregnant period of evolution."[34] That sense expressed itself in an entirely new conception of belonging; community no longer meant only attachment to a specific village, town, city or even ethnic territory, nor to a broad religious solidarity. Now, with the creation of the Netherlands Indies, it involved a consciousness of the new togetherness of nation. The linking of modernity with the sense of the need for urgent reform and an expanded understanding of political place brought the realization that the essential vehicle through which the problems posed by modernity might be solved was the nation.

That was to have serious implications for those of a seriously Muslim bent, because Islamic expressions of consciousness, even the reforming consciousness of the *kaum muda*, were slow to frame their thinking in terms of a politico-territorial community. Some, like Ahmad Ripangi in mid-nineteenth century Java, asserted their religious authority in opposition to the operations and policies of an infidel government.[35] Others, a little later, expressed deep regret that local Muslim disunity had allowed infidel conquest in the first place.[36] But it was pan-Islamism, not territorial assertiveness, that became the focus of Muslim concern, just as it was that of an increasingly suspicious colonial government.[37] As Snouck remarked, "thirty-five million Netherlands subjects in the Far East are Mohammedans ... consequently, pan-Islamism must be for us something rather more than 'interesting'."[38]

Islam as religion has not often attached itself to notions of place with the concentrated fixity that has come to underline modern national sensibility. But Indies Muslims were not entirely unconscious of homeland. The *Jâwah* communities maintained in Mekka and Cairo by the large and rapidly growing number of Indies pilgrims, disjointed and riven as they were, had a strong sense of Malayo-Muslim identity even if, as Laffan remarks, they expressed their "sense of imagined community above all else as a function of Islam."[39] When they began to join place and religion, the latter was always dominant. Slowly, very slowly, the sense of place began to take sharper focus, partly through a developing print network built upon long traditions of scholarly contact between Southeast Asian students of Islam and the Middle East itself, which took its inspiration from an increasingly restive, politically charged and relatively free religious centre in Cairo, itself increasingly conscious of attachment to homeland (*watan*).[40]

In that context the Singapore Jawi-script journal *al-Imam* (1906–08), "the first channel of Cairene discourse in the *bilad al-jawa*",[41] containing "the first really serious presentation of the Modernist analysis of social, religious and economic issues,"[42] began publication under the leadership of Shaykh Muhammad Tahir bin Jalaluddin al-Minangkabawi al-Azhari from Bukittinggi. Derivative of the Egyptian *al-Manar*, itself under the editorial hand of Rida, *al-Imam* spoke in vague terms of the identity created by the Malay homelands, but without any closer national specificity, and of the Muslim need to progress in tune with modernity's demands.[43]

But Indonesian Islam's slowly formulating sense of territoriality was already hopelessly behind the game. Around the same time, the popular journal

Bintang Hindia had espoused the Netherlands Indies as its specific site of identity. Japan's victory over Russia, underlining notions of national or even racial solidarity rather than religious community, had sounded "the new period for the whole East."[44] Within a few years E. F. E. Douwes Dekker and his colleagues in the Indische Partij (IP) (1912) would drive the idea of the nexus of nation and modernity to its logical conclusion: there is an Indies, we are its citizens, and we demand proprietorial control from the foreign government that currently controls it; "we need here a revolution .... Revolution means THE INDIES STOPS BEING A COLONY AND BECOMES A STATE."[45] The only basis for unity amongst so diverse a collection of peoples was the nation itself; indeed, "social unity is ... only possible where political equality exists among the uniting parts."[46] Religion, then, was peripheral to IP's main concerns and its attitude to religion disinterested; its only religious task, claimed Douwes Dekker, was "to struggle against every expression of sectarianism, to oppose every attempt to nurture religious hatred, and to preach the religion of brotherliness."[47]

While place was important for devout Muslims, it was certainly not the all-consuming entity it was for Douwes Dekker and his fellows. If there was, as Laffan claims, a sense that already "the ultimate goal was the independence (Ar. *istiqlal*) of their various lands (*tanah*),"[48] it was born of a certain frustration that these Muslim lands were under the sway of Dutch and British. "Does all this not make one's heart heavy or indeed wound it?"[49] remarked *al-Imam* in 1906, with the strong implication that loss of territory to these powers was a function of religious negligence. That message was continued by *al-Imam*'s successor publication, *al-Munir* (1911–16), "the first Modernist journal in Indonesia,"[50] a Jawi fortnightly published in Padang by the Minangkabau reformist Haji Abdullah Ahmad.[51] Its masthead contained the motto "For the advancement of Islam, knowledge and news."[52] "We plan," it proclaimed, "to establish true Islam among the people of our nation (*bangsa*) ... and to show them the way to the field of advancement and the life of the world which will bring us perfection in the next life ... [We aim to bring our people] to the field of love for the homeland and its people ... and the way of love for the community."[53] That *bangsa* was in the first instance the Minangkabau homeland, an understanding that gradually expanded to include all of the Muslim inhabitants of the Indies.[54] There was, however, no sense of opposition to Dutch rule, generally seen as sound, efficient and protective of Muslim interests, nor indeed any sense that the journal prescribed any kind of political activism.[55] The masthead of the West Sumatran weekly *al-Akbar*, appearing in 1912, carried the sentiment, "Long live the Dutch Kingdom."[56]

A more specific engagement with territoriality had to await the emergence, then maturity, of the great Java-based mass organization, *Sarekat Islam* (SI). In 1916 — the year of SI's first "national congress" (so designated because SI's leader Cokroaminoto declared, "the popular movement is striving for the formation of a strong unity for all the people of the Indies Archipelago")[57] — *al-Munir*'s manager, together with Cokroaminoto, founded an *al-Islamiyah* Association which produced a Jawi-script journal *al-Islam*, an "organ for Indies-Muslim nationalists,"[58] as its subtitle proclaimed, which explicitly perceived of the nation as "the Muslim people of the Indies."[59]

Despite these developments, however, the reformists were still far from centring their attention and core sense of identity on local place; for them it remained at the periphery in a world centred on the Middle East. They saw their task, accordingly, in a typically missionary sense which tended to denigrate the local as derivative and insubstantial, and its improvement as a matter of more assiduous piety, of re-engineering religious belief and practice in such a way that Muslims might no longer suffer the humbling subordination that their religious laxity had visited upon them in the first place.

NEW MODES OF THINKING ABOUT MODERNITY

While devout Muslims focussed on the demands of reviving and revitalizing their faith, entirely new strains of thinking which gave little space to purely Islamic thought were grasping at other Indonesians' minds. The bureaucratic requirements of the developing Dutch colonial state meant that those members of the indigenous elite drawn into Dutch service needed to blend their lifestyles to accord better with Dutch expectations. That included a wariness, and occasionally a fearful paranoia, about the political effects of a more pious, sometimes more militant, profession of Islam, and a general diminution in the importance of Islamic attachment in their lives.[60] The Regent of Malang, for example, earned the hatred of SI leaders because of "his hostile attitude towards the movement,"[61] while Cipto remarked that Javanese officials were generally opposed to SI, "at least in public."[62] Moreover, the indigenous bureaucratic elite had no interest in admitting new competition to their positions of leadership,[63] sensing the threat presented by the emergence of a middle class of "traders, tradesmen, supervisors ... who continually come to the foreground and take an autonomous position over against the *priyayi*."[64] Accordingly, Snouck could remark in 1904 that "the Javanese aristocracy ... as a rule is *not* strongly Islamic."[65]

The Dutch provided a solidly Western education for their modernizing indigenous officials — secular, modern, and embossed with a strong sense of the superiority of Western civilization and the consequent need for stabilizing social hierarchy. In Snouck's eyes, "all available means" should be employed "to hasten the association of Natives craving for development with our national civilization."[66] This new knowledge, the key to indigenous bureaucratic success, gave them a strong stake in that Westernized world and its continued success; "in our Indonesia", remarked a reminiscing nationalist, "people at the beginning of this century were busy putting out their hands for Western development."[67] The rise of print in the last decades of the nineteenth century as a medium for the spreading and exchange of information and ideas evoked a cosmopolitanism which itself stimulated elite intellectual curiosity.[68] Thus, for the musicologist and Theosophist Suryoputro, "the Javanese have taken on the ideal of developing themselves under the guidance of Dutch intellect."[69] The goal of those Indonesians who had come to the Netherlands to study, Ratu Langie proclaimed, was "to gather knowledge and strive for higher position," but it was also "to pursue an ideal, namely to serve their land."[70] Achmad Jayadiningrat, educated in both Western and Islamic traditions but choosing the Western one with subsequent great success, was a manifestation of the way in which the Western discourse of knowledge, increasingly concerned at what it saw as the immobilizing, deadening and politically dangerous tendencies of the Islam propagated in the Indies,[71] captured its targets and turned them into humane, cosmopolitan, loyal (though often still Muslim), servants of the status quo.[72]

That sense of distance from any intimate connection with Islam and a corresponding attachment to modern Western thinking was exemplified in the thinking of Raden Ajeng Kartini. She called herself "a child of Buddha",[73] and claimed ignorance of Islam; "in truth, I am a Moslem only because my ancestors were. How can I love a doctrine which I do not know — may never know?"[74] She thought polygamy "an evil of gigantic proportions ... under the protection of Mohammedan teaching."[75] More broadly:

> We have for a long time turned our backs totally against religion because we see so much lovelessness under the banner of religion .... The most beautiful and the most elevated religion we think is: Love. And does one absolutely have to be a Christian to be able to live according to that divine commandment? The Buddhist, the Brahmin, the Jew, the Mohammedan, even the Heathen, can also live a life of love.[76]

Kartini exhibited a kind of open, cultured, faintly liberal humanism rather than any specific attachment to Islamic belief or devotion or, indeed, any religion as such. Thus, she wrote, "true culture lies not in the colour of the skin, not in the clothes, not in the outward behaviour, not in the language of the speaker, nor in the name of the religion one confesses. True culture resides in the heart. It is a matter of character and nobility of the soul."[77]

Such emerging styles of thought gave birth of *Budi Utomo* (BU) (1908), an association which sought, under the inspiration of the modernizing journalist Wahidin Sudirohusodo, to refashion Javanese society by combining the best of the (Western) new with (timeless, great, thus pre-Islamic) Javanese culture — itself busily being rediscovered and foregrounded by Dutch scholarship — and to create a new sense of identity amongst those broadly construed as belonging to the Javanese cultural heritage. BU sought, however vaguely, a broader sense of community, "forming as it were a National Fraternity, without differentiating on the basis of race, sex or belief;"[78] it contained a number of Muslim teachers close to the Yogyakarta court, including Haji Fachruddin, while one of its founders, Sutomo, later enjoyed membership of the *Muhammadiyah* executive.[79] "For the Javanese elite," notes Ricklefs, "European-style modernity was a means of embracing pre-Islamic culture,"[80] itself, indeed, a spiritual and intellectual option to revivalist Islam.[81] The power of these new styles of thinking and their relation to notions of modernity and progressivity was reflected in the attachment of some members of the aristocratic elite to such currents as Freemasonry and Theosophy. While Freemasonry held little general appeal for Indonesians (though BU's first president, R.A. Tirtokusumo, Bupati of Karanganyar, was also a Freemason, as were a number of other bupati),[82] Theosophy, with a similar hankering for a kind of synthesized, harmonious human brotherliness that superseded divisions of race and religion, proved rather more attractive to many Javanese aristocrats. One-third of the total membership of the Theosophical Society in the Indies in 1913 comprised "natives," including members of Javanese royal blood;[83] members also included the Surakarta court physician, Javanese culturalist, and influential BU leader Rajiman, as well as senior SI leaders and Cipto Mangunkusumo and even for a time Haji Agus Salim.[84]

Indies society was, then, increasingly deeply divided by two separate but interconnected ideological fault lines. On the one hand were the Islamic modernists, the *kaum muda*, often the products of a Middle Eastern education, spreading their reforming and emancipating religious ideas, over against the traditionalist *kaum tua*, tied to precedent and tradition, enmeshed in cultural constructions of indigenous identity and distrustful that change might unbalance society's harmony. On the other was the Islamic tradition per se, either modernist or traditionalist, against a newly emergent secularising tendency which, while often retaining its cultural attachment to Islam, was not ruled by it, was often critical of what it saw as Islam's constraining, conserving tendencies, and sometimes wanted to forget the "Mohammedan" period in Javanese cultural history;[85] it stretched out to capture and master the new knowledge now increasingly available from the West and to put it at its service.

That emerging tendency's critique of Islam was often expressed in terms of the heights Java had reached in the pre-Islamic period, "the high civilization ... the high level of industry and art in the pre-Islamic period."[86] For Cipto, the Hindu-Javanese Majapahit era was "the period in our history which lives on in our memory as the golden age of our people," notable for "the already existing tolerance of the Javanese in the arena of belief." The subsequent decline he attributed to the meeting of an aging religion — Islam — with a declining civilization.[87] For Rajiman, Majapahit was a "period of glory."[88] Cipto's brother Gunawan thought that "in many respects the Mohamedan religion displays so little obligingness that it ... is inimical to our character." "The Koran is our holy book, we believe in it", he asserted but, he asked, "do we love it? Do we cherish it in our heart as we do Javanese books, which tell us of Majapahit's greatness?" Indeed, "our popular entertainment par excellence, the *wayang*, is an abomination for the true Islamite," and "no matter how high the cultural value of Islam may be, it cannot reach the heart of the people." In the end, Gunawan feared the capacity of religion to divide, and that it stood in the way of his country's resurrection should it be employed as a political weapon.[89] The Javanese nationalist Suriokusumo thought that "religion as a means of unity is finished. Islam cannot tie us to the Sumatran, much less to the Ambonese or Menadonese who are not Muslims. Religion as a means of unity is very unwise if not dangerous."[90] An Indonesian writer took the Prophet to task for his "actions against the Jews and his attitude towards his women;" others criticized Islam in general for its alleged propensity for "holding back progress," for being a "hindrance to the lifting up of the native," for its "false" beliefs about the nature of the afterlife and the fearful destiny of non-believers, and for its tendency to promote intolerance.[91] The Javanese elitist Satiman Wiryosanjoyo was characteristically direct: he saw religious zealotry as inimical to national development, and the pilgrimage as a waste of money.[92]

BELATED ISLAMISM

The territorial agnosticism exhibited by Muslim leaders ignored the political implications of the gathering, consolidating unity of the Netherlands Indies. As we have seen, by the early years of the twentieth century some indigenous intellectuals had began to express a sense of Indies identity, of being part of the new state of the Indies, based on a specific sense of territory and with no particular attachment to Islamic thinking. *Bintang Hindia* spoke of a *bangsa Hindia* (Indies nation) that needed reform and renovation, and exemplified the notion that the key to advancement was modern knowledge.[93] Its masthead proclaimed: "May the kingdom of the Netherlands endure forever, may the land of the Indies (*tanah Hindia*) be famous." Its editor, Abdul Rivai, spoke of a time when the native people of Java "would turn their face in prayer no longer to the ka'abah but to The Hague."[94] Douwes Dekker's IP concretized and gave intellectual substance to that turning away from the primordial.

Islam did provide the basis for SI, the first mass political movement in the Indies — "[SI] unites everything by using the word Islam and it seems straight away that men were equal"[95] — but it was a diffuse and shifting foundation. Broad-based but locally-rooted, with a vague egalitarianism which stood in opposition to demeaning aristocratic hierarchy,[96] SI was a "great folk movement which linked Islamic revival with anti-colonialism."[97] It was, in the words of Governor-General Idenburg, "an expression of what can be called the Native becoming self-conscious."[98] It sought social and material welfare and mutual assistance, making an explicit claim for Muslim solidarity in pursuit of those goals, aiming at enhanced religious knowledge, piety and observance, and devoting itself to the progress and emancipation of the native peoples.[99] An early, non-Muslim observer thought that "the all-inclusive goal that it seeks [is] the improvement of the economic situation of native society and promotion of the religious life."[100] It operated as society's sounding board, its crisis and grievance centre.[101] Islam, indeed, was SI's identifying, communitarian motif, bringing together people of variously different understandings of Islam but — notwithstanding an evident increase in piety, Islamized social behaviour, clubbish solidarity and assertiveness[102] — not just for specifically Islamic purposes. SI in its early great phase never gave specific prominence to Islamic thought or teaching.[103] In Alkema's words, "it was not meant to be a specifically Islamic association. Islam was what tied it together, not its foundation."[104] Suwardi Suryaningrat, scion of the house of Paku Alam, sought in 1913 to remove the requirement that SI members be Muslims because the real solidarity needing expression was that of the inhabitants of the Indies, a spatial rather than religious tie.[105]

Although being Muslim was framed as the badge of indigeneity — for Suwardi, the Islamic label was the means whereby the people associated themselves as being "anti-domination"[106] — SI originally had no specific political agenda. Cokroaminoto asserted in 1912 that "according to the Sjari'ah of Islam, we must obey the command of the Dutch government, we must strictly and loyally follow the laws and regulations of the Dutch."[107] Nonetheless, SI's astonishingly rapid growth and its size and weight necessitated, soon enough, that it engage in politics frontally. In doing so, it found itself inevitably drawn into nationalist politics, the framing of indigenous improvement through enhanced political autonomy. As Suwardi pointed out, SI had decided "in future to accept not only religion but also and especially Indies nationalism as the bond of unity."[108] SI leader Abdul Muis remarked in 1917 that "the basis of our movement … is nationalist,"[109] asserting as well that "as long as the indigenous people of the Indies do not have a true nation and country, the feeling of love for that country and nation must be developed in the hearts of that people. Because a nation which does not have that feeling will not progress and will in fact decline."[110] SI embraced the idea of representational politics ("the administration of the Indies by its own people, without there being any discrimination on the basis of race, colour or religion"),[111] as well as strains of socialism, even as it proclaimed that Islam was "the religion par excellence for the moral education of the people."[112] For the formidable SI intellectual, Haji Agus Salim, the connection between religion and politics remained one essentially of enhanced private behaviour for the social good, proclaiming that "the state should remain outside religious affairs and handle all religions on an equal basis".[113] Cokroaminoto thought likewise: "Currently many bad usages and customs dominate amongst us, while we do not give enough of our attention to religious matters. We always feel ourselves of lesser worth and are convinced of our weakness. This has to change, and it shall, if we truly know the teaching of our religion and carry it out."[114] SI had become political, but not (yet) Islamist. In deploying nationalist discourse, SI would face three great problems. The first was the blowtorch of increasing government opposition. The second was a test of its Muslim credentials. The third was the enduring problem of maintaining the centrality of Islam in a multicultural and multireligious society.

As government suspicion and repression of SI's political pretensions grew — fuelled by reports of SI-sponsored violence and intrigue — conservative members ("quiet, settled citizens of native society")[115] fell away. Many Hadramis, previously highly prominent in the organization but discouraged by growing leftism and reports of systematic corruption, and increasingly marginalized because of their lack of "nativeness" and their "annoying inclination to place themselves and their 'nation' above the Javanese,"[116] also took their leave.[117] Already by 1915, SI was in noticeable decline,[118] especially in rural areas, and in response it turned its attention more strongly to its urban bases, and began involving itself strongly in the burgeoning union movement.[119]

That served to entwine SI with the developing Communist movement which, in a purely tactical move that involved no effort to arrive at a meaningful meeting of ideas, sought to capture SI from within and shunt it in more radical, politically purposeful directions.[120] That stimulated a reaction, an effort by more self-consciously Islamic forces within SI, centred around Haji Agus Salim and the invigorated Yogyakarta SI branch, to push the movement along more determinedly Muslim lines as a hedge against Communist influence spearheaded from Semarang.[121] That heightened Muslim sensitivity expressed itself, for example, in the fevered reaction to a 1918 article in a Yogyakarta newspaper, *Djawi Hisworo*, which had labelled the Prophet as a consumer of opium and jenever.[122] In this Muslim turn, the role of Salim, whose earlier experience as an employee at the Netherlands' consulate in Jeddah (1906–11) had brought him religious revivification as well as a close relationship with 'Abduhist thinking,[123] became ever more important, and Cokroaminoto became ever more a figurehead. Salim, with his knowledge of Arabic and his Middle Eastern experience (gained as an employee at the Netherlands' consulate in Jeddah from 1906–11), enjoyed much greater authority in his Islamic discourse than did Cokroaminoto, whose Islam was partly learned from English-language books since he knew little Arabic.[124] It was, in the end, Salim "who gave an Islamic stamp to the political character of the Sarekat Islam".[125] It was now clear that Islam, under Salim's guiding hand, was to be the driver of SI's policy and politics in a way that had never been evident before.[126] That position had the virtue of excluding Communists (achieved by virtue of the imposition of party discipline in 1921), and emphasising Islam as the bond of all Indonesians, containing the essential elements, economic, social, and spiritual, for Indonesia's uplift.[127] The 1921, the SI congress affirmed the organization's "Muslim-socialist" character and foreshadowed the establishment of a party grounded in specifically Islamic principles, the Partai Sarekat Islam (PSI).[128] In that same year, Snouck could refer to a phenomenon called "Indonesian Islam."[129]

Salim was the first Muslim politician to attempt explicitly and systematically to relate his Islam ("Islam provides a perfect compass and road-map for humanity for its life in the world")[130] to the political problems facing his country and people. It was he who "brought the colour of Islam to SI."[131] Hitherto, Islamic thinking had generally been of a single-dimensional quality, the process of determining how specific issues might be understood — better, adjudicated — from an Islamic perspective. Salim sought to develop from Islam a political approach of a general kind. For him, "there is no need to look for other 'isms' to treat the sickness of the movement. The medicine is in the foundation itself, a foundation which is ancient and enduring ... that foundation is Islam."[132] Thus, the basic principles he drafted for SI included the conviction that "genuine freedom for the people of the Indies, that is, what will really release all the people from every kind of subjection" would be achieved "by means of the road to freedom based upon Islam."[133] For Salim, "all virtues of the other principles can be found in Islam while all defects, faults and evils of the other principles are absent in Islam."[134]

That intellectual trajectory had its natural conclusion in the convening of the first *Al-Islam* congress in Cirebon late in 1922 which indelibly marked SI's shift from a Catholic movement of progress and protest to a more narrowly confined emphasis on the Islamic base of the movement and the unity which Islam brought.[135] Cokroaminoto himself, as well as focussing on Islamic morality — "the necessity that Islam become a living force in people, so that they become better people inside"[136] — began further to develop his thinking on the relationship of Islam to socialism.[137] That thinking sought to find in the Qur'an and the Islamic tradition principles of freedom, equality and brotherhood, as well as opposition to the rapacity of capitalism.[138] Around the same time came the promised, slowly-gestated emergence of the PSI,[139] an organizational overhaul of SI that formally recognized the reality and centrality of contestation for the territory of the Indies (now increasingly called Indonesia) and at the same time indulged in Pan-Islamic pretensions (even if these were essentially directed towards domestic purposes of Islamic solidarity-making).[140] PSI sought to represent in a more disciplined and controlled way devout Muslim political interests rather than, as SI had done, bridging a multiplicity of interests; it strove for "the freedom of the fatherland and of the whole people … true freedom according to the principles and practice of Islam."[141] It sought "to have Islam prevail in all the particulars of life and in the way of life of the people of this country (the East Indies), the greatest number of whom are adherents to the Islamic religion."[142] Cokroaminoto, indeed, proclaimed that Indonesia "shall fall into the hands of SI, for God has promised to support true Muslims if they act in accordance with his orders as laid down in the Qur'an."[143]

Many SI members were dismayed at SI's conversion into a deeply religiously-grounded political organization and one, moreover, that appeared (especially when compared to *Muhammadiyah*) to be unable or unwilling to respond to their everyday concerns.[144] One East Java member thought that "as soon as politics and religion separate from each other, the SI shall undoubtedly progress and unity can quickly be organized."[145] In 1927 a government report noted that "in Surabaya the members of the old SI movement want to know nothing of the PSI. Efforts were afoot to revive the old SI sections."[146] *Kaum tua* supporters saw themselves increasingly marginalized and exposed and sought to improve their status by establishing a rival association, *Nahdlatul Ulama*, in 1926 — traditionalist in orientation but modern in its methods and pragmatically flexible in its political practice.[147]

Even *Muhammadiyah* found itself a victim of PSI party discipline, partly a consequence of *Muhammadiyah*'s view that "those who use religion for political purposes are infidels"[148] — a reflection of *Muhammadiyah*'s disdain for PSI's increasingly isolationist and combative approach — and its preparedness to accept subsidies from the government.[149] Other critics, especially Communists, saw the defining Islamist turn as a rejection and a retreat from the task of opposition and confrontation: "In the practical politics of the far left wing Islam plays no role."[150] Communist popularity, a function of its activism, grew, while that of the PSI receded further, deflating SI hopes that overt secularism would inevitably invite popular rejection. Haji Misbach, preaching an idiosyncratic synthesis of Islam and Marxism which sought to "oppose all oppression" (including that visited upon the people by rapacious Muslim religious officials under Government auspices) and to maintain a brotherly attitude to other associations, "provided they travel in the right direction,"[151] finally threw in his lot with the PKI.

At the same time there emerged a florescence of national consciousness that trenchantly focussed on the national — on national identity and culture, and on national deliverance from foreign domination — and in which Islamically-tinged ideas had little traction. The young Sukarno, though he had lived in Cokroaminoto's house for many years and married his daughter, had clearly opted not to ally himself with the revised SI and under the influence of secularists like Cipto had, in the words of a Dutch official, "let Islam go."[152] In his view, "the Islamic movement ... essentially denies the nation."[153] In the Netherlands, a small, vigorous and increasingly radically-minded group of young Indonesian students was creating an unambiguous sense of a new nation, Indonesia, and the fact that it must be granted — or seize — its freedom. It is arresting to recognize that as one leafs through the pages of its journals *Hindia Poetra* and later *Indonesia Merdeka*, one finds scarcely any mention of Islam; the students celebrated *lebaran*, but they wanted "to make this feast not so much a Muslim one but a general *Indonesian* one, so that our Christian, Buddhist or 'Heathen' compatriots will be just as welcome."[154] Men like these, according to a Dutch report, "are more or less hostile to Islam, and see this religion, with its regulations in the sphere of marriage, the levying of interest etc as an obstacle to progress."[155] By contrast, while Indies students in Cairo, conscious of anti-British political action in Egypt,[156] could move relatively easily to a sense of the freedom of their own homeland, theirs was a distinctly muted, derivative and still strangely vague and now dated sense of pan-Malay Islamic identity.[157]

Not for the first, and not for the last time, Indonesian Muslim politicians were travelling in directions different from those of their fellows. Cipto was characteristically blunt; after its split with the Communists, SI "threw itself on Islam, promoting the interests of which it made its single goal. Thereby it is chained to the great world Islam movement, centred on Arabia and or Egypt."[158] SI was increasingly embracing exclusivity. A leader of the Bangil branch remarked in 1923 that "an organization based on Islam may not mix with non-Muslim associations."[159] Salim made the same point when he remarked that PSI was "independent of any other association or body,"[160] something also evident in his later suspicion of Sukarno's federation of political parties, PPPKI (Permufakatan Perhimpunan Politik Kebangsaan Indonesia).[161] The claim aired at one PSI meeting — "as soon as freedom is attained no one shall be named Regent who is not a good Muslim" — might have been expected to create enmity and opposition.[162] Laffan is certainly overstating his case when he remarks that "the seeds of what would become Indonesian nationalism germinated in two of the Central Lands of Islam as much as in Leiden and Batavia."[163] Islam was always and increasingly marginal to developing Indonesian thinking about the nation. The idea of Indonesia, as it emerged, had almost nothing to do with Islam, which provided little more than a vague incipient sense of solidarity in some places, and its opposite in others.

The idea of Indonesia stood for nothing more than a free, united Indonesian nation, based upon the central pillar of popular sovereignty manifested in a "form of government which is responsible to the people in the true sense of the word."[164] That idea subordinated everything else to its service. Its champions frequently derided Islam as being opposed to modernity and progress and serving only partial or sectional interests rather than those of the nation as a whole. Gatot Mangkupraja thought that "in our struggle towards the freedom of Country and Nation, we nationalists do not wish to be caught up in disputes relating to religion."[165] Gradually through the 1920s, association and sentiment based on ethnic or regional affiliation was forced to cede centrality to the increasingly dominant idea of Indonesia.[166] Religion suffered the same fate. The fact that much of the debate about Indonesian identity went to matters of race — for example, Mohammed Hatta's idea that "nativeness" rested upon ethnicity[167] rather than religion was indicative of Islam's weak political power. Unity, thought Iwa Kusumasumantri, must rest on "the national idea."[168] Within that new nation, Islam should have no more or no less an important role than any other religion. That ruling sense was captured as well in the deeply-felt notion, itself anti-Islamic in fact if not in intention, that Indonesia had always existed, that Islam was just one of many external influences continually reshaping that Indonesia, and that modern nationalism was simply a natural awakening from a long sleep.[169]

By the early and mid-1920s, SI/PSI had become just one of many parties, and its reach and influence were in serious ebb, especially outside Java.[170] The general impression given by reports on its status was one of declining morale, lack of funds, mistrust of leaders and sagging membership.[171] It had definitively admitted the decisive power of the idea of Indonesia, but not the cluster of populist, pluralist, inclusivist ideas that underpinned it. In Cokroaminoto's view, nationalism needed to be based upon the unifying power of Islam, which carried none of the divisive baggage of race, status and region — ignoring the fact that Islamism itself was a wedge against true national unity. "We strive," he said, "for the salvation of Indonesia, if possible of all of its people".[172] Salim was himself even more explicit. Asserting that "denying nationalism … is certainly not Islamic,"[173] and that "the nationalism of the Muslim neither divides nor excludes,"[174] he saw Islam as "our national religion, which is certainly not the least factor in our common Indonesian national culture."[175] In the end, Islam was supreme; the real problem with colonialism was that "people cannot properly confess Islam, as long as they are still governed by a non-Muslim Government."[176] The PSI's 1927 congress at Pekalongan emphasized the importance of Indonesian nationalism, but laid down as its goal "the striving for national freedom on the basis of Islam."[177] To govern the state, Salim proposed at a congress in Yogyakarta in early 1928 an "Islamic democracy" that was not "the Western one of half plus one, but this, that those who are capable and inclined to carry on the tasks of the state must have the opportunity and the power for it."[178] In all of this Salim was keen to oppose what he saw as the heresy of the chauvinistic, aggressive, expansionist and divisive worship of nation above all else. "Our love for the people causes us to honour and respect our fellow-countrymen but it will not elevate *kebangsaan* [nation] to an idol to be worshipped and adored."[179] Islamic democracy, by contrast, was the work of the people's representatives, themselves imbued with Islamic principles.[180] The emerging gulf between the notion of "bangsa kita Islam (our Islamic nation)"[181] and the popular idea of Indonesia was confirmed.

By the end of the 1920s, the dominant political paradigm was inescapably that of the totalizing, unifying Indonesian nation-state. Muslim politicians, too, had fallen under its power, and had to begin to contrive ways in which they could better accommodate their religious sensibilities under its umbrella. They sought them, though, in a self-defeating emphasis on independent religious specificity — even when they no longer thought of their Islam "as an heirloom which blocks progress … as a place to run because we are frightened of the threat of the world hereafter."[182] They could not wholeheartedly embrace a context where national, not religious, unity had become the dominant currency; "it is clear", a Dutch intelligence report remarked in 1929, "that the slogan at the moment is *freedom*, and *not* Islam."[183] The problem for Indonesian Islamists, late to the table, was that they had no hope of popularizing their ideals in circumstances where the larger force capturing and shaping popular thinking was the idea of Indonesia (notwithstanding stubbornly insular efforts by Islamists to frame things differently), where the nation, not religion, was sovereign.

Notes

1. I am grateful for the comments of John Butcher, Akh. Muzakki, Kees van Dijk, Michael Laffan and David Jenkins on an earlier draft of this paper, and for research funding generously provided by the Australian Research Council. A version of this article was previously published in the *Journal of Indonesian Islam* 1, no. 2 (2007): 231–66.
2. Fernand Braudel, *On History*, trans. Sarah Matthews (Chicago: University of Chicago Press, 1980), pp. 11–12.
3. Michael Francis Laffan, *Islamic Nationhood and Colonial Indonesia: The Umma Below the Winds* (London: RoutledgeCurzon, 2003), p. 2.
4. Ibid., p. 166.
5. *De Indische Gids* [*IG*] 29 (1907), n.p.
6. M.C. Ricklefs, *Mystic Synthesis in Java: A History of Islamization from the Fourteenth to the Early Nineteenth Centuries* (Norwalk CT: EastBridge, 2006), p. 225.
7. Ibid., pp. 151, 216–17, 223, 230.
8. Ibid., p. 6.
9. M.C. Ricklefs, *Polarising Javanese Society: Islamic and Other Visions (c. 1830–1930)*, (Singapore: NUS Press, 2007), p. 86.
10. Ibid., p. 28.
11. Ibid., pp. 95, 103–04.
12. Ricklefs, *Mystic Synthesis*, p. 231. For more detailed discussion, see also Ricklefs, *Polarising Javanese Society*, pp. 46, 175, 177, 181–82, 212.
13. C. Poensen, *Brieven over den Islam uit de Binnenlanden van Java* (Leiden: E.J. Brill, 1886), p. 6.
14. Boeka [P.C.C. Hansen Jr], "De Inlander, een Studie", *De Indische Gids* 25 (1903): 1137.
15. Tjipto Mangoenkoesomo, "Dr Kuyper te Laat", *Het Tijdschrift* 2 (1912): 574.
16. C. Snouck Hurgronje to Director of Education, Worship and Industry [DEWI], 21 March 1892, in *Ambtelijke Adviezen van C. Snouck Hurgronje 1889–1936*, edited by E. Gobée and C. Adriaanse (The Hague: Martinus Nijhoff, 1957–65), vol. 2, p. 1077.

17. Snouck Hurgronje to DEWI, 16 October 1894, in Gobée and Adriaanse, *Ambtelijke*, vol. 2, p. 1080.
18. Snouck Hurgronje to Minister of Colonies [MC], 28 October 1910, in Gobée and Adriaanse, *Ambtelijke*, vol. 2, p. 1099.
19. Snouck Hurgronje, "Over Panislamisme" [1910], in *Verspreide Geschriften van C. Snouck Hurgronje*, edited by J. Wensinck, vol. 1 (Bonn: Kurt Schoeder, 1923), p. 375.
20. Ph. S. van Ronkel, *Rapport betreffende de Godsdienstige Verschijnselen ter Sumatra's Westkust* (Batavia: Landsdrukkerij, 1916), p. 14.
21. John R. Bowen, *Muslims Through Discourse: Religion and Ritual in Gayo Society* (New Jersey: Princeton University Press, 1993), p. 22.
22. See Snouck Hurgronje to DEWI, 29 September 1894, in Gobée and Adriaanse, *Ambtelijke*, vol. 3, pp. 1846–48; Murni Djamal, "The Origin of the Islamic Reform Movement in Minangkabau: Life and Thought of Abdul Karim Amrullah", *Studia Islamika [StI]* 5, no. 3 (1998): 6.
23. Deliar Noer, *The Modernist Muslim Movement in Indonesia 1900–1942* (Kuala Lumpur: Oxford University Press, 1973), pp. 31–32; Mahmud Junus, *Sedjarah Pendidikan Islam di Indonesia* (Jakarta: Pustaka Mahmudiah, 1960), pp. 131, 136–37, 141, 144; Djamal, "The Origin of the Islamic Reform Movement in Minangkabau", p. 6.
24. Ahmed Ibrahim Abushouk, "A Sudanese Scholar in the Diaspora: Life and Career of Ahmad Muhamad al-Surkitti in Indonesia (1911–1943)", *Studia Islamika* 8, no. 1 (2001): 59.
25. Noer, *The Modernist Muslim Movement*, p. 6.
26. Ibid., pp. 58, 92; Natalie Mobini-Kesheh, *The Hadrami Awakening: Community and Identity in the Netherlands East Indies, 1900–1942* (Ithaca: Cornell Southeast Asia Program, 1999), pp. 36–37; Adjunct Advisor for Native Affairs [ANA] to Governor-General [GG], 13 May 1913, in *De Opkomst van de Nationalistische Beweging in Nederlandsche-Indië*, edited by S.L. van der Wal (Groningen: J.B. Wolters, 1967), p. 202.
27. Noer, *The Modernist Muslim Movement*, pp. 62–63.
28. Achmad Jainuri, *Muhammadiyah: Gerakan Reformasi Islam di Jawa pada Awal Abad Kedua Puluh* (Surabaya: PT Bina Ilmu, 1981), p. 25.
29. Fauzan Saleh, *Modern Trends in Islamic Theological Discourse in 20th Century Indonesia: A Critical Study* (Leiden: Brill, 2001), pp. 120–21; Takashi Shiraishi, *An Age in Motion: Popular Radicalism in Java, 1912–1926* (Ithaca: Cornell University Press, 1990), p. 137.
30. Jainuri, *Muhammadiyah*, p. 42; Bowen, *Muslims through Discourse*, p. 56.
31. Laffan, *Islamic Nationhood*, p. 99.
32. Snouck Hurgronje to DEWI, 19 January 1894, in Gobée and Adriaanse, *Ambtelijke*, vol. 2, p. 1079; Snouck Hurgronje to DEWI, 16 October 1894, in Gobée and Adriaanse, *Ambtelijke*, vol. 2, p. 1080; Snouck Hurgronje, "Over Panislamisme" , p. 377. See also Adjunct ANA to GG, 13 May 1913, in Anon.

[D.A. Rinkes], *Bescheiden betreffende de Vereeniging 'Sarekat Islam'* (Batavia: Landsdrukkerij, 1913), pp. 22–23. For an example of the dismissive attitude of some Christian missionaries towards Islam, see H. Dijkstra, "De Tweede Wereldgodsdienst", *De Macedoniër* 17 (1913): 65–73.
33. Noer, *The Modernist Muslim Movement*, p. 299.
34. Tjipto Mangoenkoesomo, "Geestelijke Immobiliteit Geeischt", *Het Tijdschrift* 1 (1912): 17.
35. Laffan, *Islamic Nationhood*, p. 32.
36. The Sumatran Ahmad Lampung, paraphrased by Snouck Hurgronje in Laffan, *Islamic Nationhood*, p. 67.
37. Snouck Hurgronje, "Over Panislamisme", p. 366; Laffan, *Islamic Nationhood*, p. 126.
38. Snouck Hurgronje, "Over Panislamisme", p. 366.
39. Laffan, *Islamic Nationhood*, p. 2.
40. Ibid., pp. 10, 20, 129, 131, 133.
41. Ibid., p. 148.
42. M.C. Ricklefs, *A History of Modern Indonesia since c. 1200*, 3rd ed. (Basingstoke: Palgrave, 2001), p. 214.
43. Laffan, *Islamic Nationhood*, p. 153; Noer, *The Modernist Muslim Movement*, p. 34; Azyumardi Azra, "The Transmission of *al-Manar's* Reformism to the Malay-Indonesian World: the Cases of *al-Imam* and *al-Munir*", *Studia Islamika* 6, no. 3 (1999): 79–84, 87, 91.
44. Noto Soeroto, "De Eendracht van Indië en Nederland", *Indische Vereeniging: Voordrachten en Mededeelingen [IVVM]* 5 (1913): 3–4.
45. Quoted in Anon. [D.A. Rinkes], *Bescheiden Betreffende de Vereeniging "De Indiche Partij"* (Batavia: Landsdrukkerij, 1913), p. 1.
46. E.F.E. Douwes Dekker, *Aansluiting tusschen Blank en Bruin. Rede, Uitgesproken door den heer E.F.E. Douwes Dekker in een Openbare Bijeenkomst, Gehouden te Batavia op 12 December 1911* (Batavia: G. Kolff, 1912), p. 13.
47. E.F.E. Douwes Dekker, *De Indische Partij: Haar Wezen en Haar Doel* (Bandung: Fortuna, 1913), p. 25.
48. Laffan, *Islamic Nationhood*, p. 157.
49. *Al-Imam*, vol. 1, no. 3 (19 September 1906), quoted in Laffan, *Islamic Nationhood*, p. 158.
50. Ricklefs, *A History*, p. 214.
51. Noer, *The Modernist Muslim Movement*, p. 39; Azra, "The Transmission", pp. 92–93; Junus, *Sedjarah*, pp. 68–72.
52. Adjunct ANA to GG, 19 February 1912, in Van der Wal, *De Opkomst*, p. 76.
53. *Al-Munir* 1, no. 1 (1 April 1911), quoted in Laffan, *Islamic Nationhood*, p. 174.
54. Laffan, *Islamic Nationhood*, pp. 174–75, 178, 234.
55. Azra, "The Transmission", p. 96.

56. Van Ronkel, *Rapport*, p. 16.
57. Paraphrased in J. Th. Petrus Blumberger, *De Nationalistische Beweging in Nederlandsch-Indië* (Dordrecht: Foris Publications, 1987 [1931]), p. 63.
58. Extract in Anon., *Sarekat-Islam Congres (1e Nationaal Congres) 17–24 Juni 1916 te Bandoeng* (Batavia: Landsdrukkerij, 1916), p. 62.
59. *Al-Islam*, 15 June 1916, quoted in Laffan, *Islamic Nationhood*, p. 179.
60. Snouck Hurgronje to DEWI, 29 September 1894, in Gobée and Adriaanse, *Ambtelijke*, vol. 3, p. 1991. That was not true in every case, of course; the Regent of Temenggung was lauded for the way in which he and his wife "maintained the religion" and for the example of religious practice and enthusiasm he set for his people (*Kaoem Moeda* 4 June 1918, *Overzicht van de Inlandsche en Maleisch-Chineesche Pers* [IPO] 22/1917).
61. Anon., "Sarikat Islam en Onrust in Ned.-Oost-Indië", *De Indische Gids* 35, no. 2 (1913): 1521–22.
62. Tj. Mk [Cipto Mangunkusumo], "De Heer van Kol en de Indische Partij", *De Indiër*, 3 November 1913, p. 38. See also *Kaoem Moeda* 10 December 1917, *Overzicht van de Inlandsche en Maleisch-Chineesche Pers [IPO]* 50/1917; *Padjadjaran* 23 November 1918, *Overzicht van de Inlandsche en Maleisch-Chineesche Pers* 47/1918.
63. Noer, *The Modernist Muslim Movement*, p. 209. Noer adds that "in this connection they found ready support from traditionalist *ulama* ... whose position was also shaken because of the spread of reformist ideas."
64. M. Lindenborn [Director, Netherlands Missionary Association] *Zendingslicht op den Islam* (Den Haag: Den Boekhandel van den Zendingstudie Raad, 1918), p. 141.
65. Snouck Hurgronje to GG, 19 April 1904, in Gobée and Adriaanse, *Ambtelijke*, vol. 1, p. 673 (emphasis in original).
66. Snouck Hurgronje, "Over Panislamisme", p. 379.
67. Anon., "Terugblik", in Anon., ed., *Gedenkboek 1908–1923 Indonesische Vereeniging* (n.p.: n.p., n.d [1924]), p. 3.
68. Ahmat B. Adam, *The Vernacular Press and the Emergence of Modern Indonesian Consciousness (1855–1913)* (Ithaca: Southeast Asia Program, Cornell University, 1995), p. 36.
69. Paraphrased in Anon., "Algemeene Vergadering op den 22ste Mei 1915", *Indische Vereeniging: Voordrachten en Mededeelingen* 10 (1916): 54.
70. Anon., "Bespreking over Gemengde Huwelijken in de Vergadering der Indische Vereeniging op 30 Juni 1915", *Indische Vereeniging: Voordrachten en Mededeelingen* 10 (1916): 57.
71. See Snouck Hurgronje, "Over Panislamisme", pp. 378–79.
72. Laffan, *Islamic Nationhood*, pp. 91, 94; Ricklefs, *Polarising*, pp. 151–53.
73. Letter to Mrs Abendanon, 27 October 1902, in Joost Coté (trans.), *Letters from Kartini: An Indonesian Feminist, 1900–1914* (Clayton: Monash Asia Institute in association with Hyland House, 1992), p. 319.

74. Kartini to Stella Zeehandelaar, 6 November 1899, in Hildred Geertz, ed., *Letters of a Javanese Princess: Raden Adjeng Kartini* (New York: W.W. Norton & Company, 1964), p. 44.
75. Letter to Mrs Abendanon, August 1900, in Coté, *Letters*, p. 26.
76. Letter to Mrs Abendanon, 27 December 1902, in Coté, *Letters*, p. 346.
77. "Give the Javanese Education!", in Coté, *Letters*, p. 541.
78. Soewarno, "Circulaire" [facsimile of the call for the first Java congress], in Anon., *Soembangsih: Gedenkboek Boedi-Oetomo: 1908–20 Mei 1918* (Amsterdam: Tijdschrift Nederl. Indië Oud & Nieuw, 1918), p. 15.
79. Harun Nasution, "The Islamic State in Indonesia: The Rise of the Ideology, the Movement for its Creation and the Theory of the Masjumi", M. A. dissertation, McGill University, 1965, p. 19.
80. Ricklefs, *Polarising*, p. 149.
81. Ibid., pp. 177, 219.
82. C.G. van Wering, *The Freemasons in Budi Utomo* (n.p.: n.p., n.d.), pp. 6, 24.
83. Herman Arij Oscar de Tollenaere, *The Politics of Divine Wisdom: Theosophy and Labour, National, and Womens' Movements in Indonesia and South Asia, 1875–1947* (Nijmegen: Uitgeverij Katholieke Universiteit Nijmegen, 1996), p. 107.
84. See also Hans van Miert, *Een Koel Hoofd en een Warm Hart: Nationalisme, Javanisme en Jeugdbeweging in Nederlands-Indië, 1918–1930* (Amsterdam: De Bataafsche Leeuw, 1995), pp. 102–05.
85. See "Nota over het Congres voor Javaanse Cultuurontwikkeling van B.J.O Schrieke, 27 juli 1918", in *De Ontwikkeling van de Nationalistische Beweging in Nederlandsch-Indië*, edited by R.C. Kwantes, vol. 1 (Groningen: H.D. Tjeenk Willink, 1975), p. 66.
86. *Darmo Kondo* 6 November 1918, *Overzicht van de Inlandsche en Maleisch-Chineesche Pers [IPO]* 45/1918.
87. Tjipto Mangoenkoesoemo, *Iets over den Javaan, Zijn Geschiedenis en Zijn Ethiek* (Semarang: n.p., 1913), pp. 5, 6, 11.
88. Radjiman, "De Maatschappelijke Loop van de Javaansche (Indonesische) Bevolking", *Indisch Genootschap: vergadering van 27 February 1920*: 66. See also his "Het Psychisch Leven van het Javaansch Volk", *Indisch Genootschap: Algemeene vergadering van 14 February 1911*: 154.
89. Goenawan Mangoenkoesoemo, "Ons Standpunt Tegenover den Godsdienst", in Anon., *Soembangsih*, pp. 106, 107, 109, 111.
90. R.M.S. Soeriokoesoemo, "Javaansch Nationalisme", in R.M.S. Soeriokoesoemo, A. Muhlenfeld, Tjipto Mangoenkoesoemo, and J.B. Wens, *Javaansche of Indisch Nationalisme? Pro en Contra* (Semarang: Semarang Drukkerij en Boekhandel H.A. Benjamins, 1918), pp. 3–4.
91. *De Expres* 19 February 1913, quoted in Anon., *Vervolg der Nota I, Betreffende de Geschriften van Douwes Dekker* (Batavia: Landsdrukkerij, 1913), p. 23; *Oetoesan Hindia* 10 May 1917, *Overzicht van de Inlandsche en Maleisch-Chineesche Pers*

[IPO] 19/1917; *Neratja* 19 September 1917, *Overzicht van de Inlandsche en Maleisch-Chineesche Pers* 38/1917; *Sinar Djawa* 25 September 1917, *Overzicht van de Inlandsche en Maleisch-Chineesche Pers* 29/1917; *Soeara Ra'jat* 15 November 1918, *Overzicht van de Inlandsche en Maleisch-Chineesche Pers* 46/1918. For other similar statements see *Islam Bergerak*, 1 August 1917, *Overzicht van de Inlandsche en Maleisch-Chineesche Pers* 51/1917; *Oetoesan Hindia* 17 August 1917, *Overzicht van de Inlandsche en Maleisch-Chineesche Pers* 33/1917; *Oetoesan Hindia* 19 December 1918, *Overzicht van de Inlandsche en Maleisch-Chineesche Pers* 51/1918; *Kaoem Moeda* 25 June 1918, *Overzicht van de Inlandsche en Maleisch-Chineesche Pers* 26/1918;

92. Petrus Blumberger, *De Nationalistische Beweging*, p. 198.
93. Ahmad Adam, *The Vernacular Press*, p. 105; see, for example, *Bintang Hindia* 11 (1906), pp. 140–41, and 18 (1907), pp. 227–28.
94. Quoted in Harry A. Poeze, "Early Indonesian Emancipation: Abdul Rivai, Van Heutsz, and the *Bintang Hindia*", *Bijdragen tot de Taal-, Land- en Volkenkunde* 145 (1989): 91.
95. Verslaggever Hindia-Poetra, "De Deputatie-Indië-Weerbaar als Gasten der Indische Vereeniging", *Hindia Poetra* (1916–17) [*HP*]: 250.
96. *Kaoem Moeda* 19 November 1918, *Overzicht van de Inlandsche en Maleisch-Chineesche Pers [IPO]* 47/1918.
97. David E.F. Henley, *Nationalism and Regionalism in a Colonial Context: Minahasa in the Dutch East Indies* (Leiden: KITLV Press, 1996), pp. 84–85.
98. GG to MC, 2 July 1913, Archive of the Minister of Colonies [AMK], Exhibitum 31 July 1913/U22, Verbaal [V] 9 August 1913/B13, Nationaal Archief, The Hague [NADH].
99. See, for example, Secret Nota Bupati Rembang to Resident Rembang, 13 April 1913, Assistant-Resident Tangerang to Resident Batavia, 7 May 1913, Resident Surakarta to GG, 24 May 1913, in Sartono Kartodirdjo et al., eds., *Sarekat Islam Lokal* (Jakarta: Arsip Nasional Republik Indonesia, 1975), pp. 13, 190, 339; Anon., *Sarekat-Islam Congres (1e Nationaal Congres)*, pp. 58–60.
100. Gerungan S.S.J. Ratu-Langie, *Serikat Islam* (Baarn: Hollandia Drukkerij, 1913), p. 3.
101. A. P. E. Korver, *Sarekat Islam 1912–1916: Opkomst, Bloei en Structuur van Indonesië's Eerste Massabeweging* (Amsterdam: Historisch Seminarium van de Universiteit van Amsterdam, 1982), pp. 116–17.
102. Adjunct ANA to GG, 13 May 1913; ANA to GG, 30 November 1915, both in Van der Wal, *De Opkomst*, pp. 201–02, 430; Resident Surakarta to GG, 24 May 1913, Assistant Resident Meester-Cornelis to Resident Batavia, 26 July 1914, in Kartodirdjo et al., *Sarekat Islam Lokal*, pp. 340–41, 48; Advisor for Administrative Matters in the Outer Possessions to GG, Mail report [MR] 1738/915, V 27 November 1915/13, NADH; Official assisting Attorney-General to Attorney General, 3 February 1919, AMK, MR 1358/1919, NADH; Ratu-Langie, *Serikat Islam*, pp. 18, 21.

103. Bernhard Dahm, *Sukarno and the Struggle for Indonesian Independence* (Ithaca: Cornell University Press, 1969), p. 174; Harry A. Poeze, "Inleiding", in *Politiek-Politioneele Overzichten van Nederlandsch-Indië* [*PPO*], edited by Harry A. Poeze, vol. 1 (The Hague: Martinus Nijhoff, 1982).
104. B. Alkema, *De Sarikat Islam* (Utrecht: G. J. A. Ruys, 1919), p. 38.
105. Shiraishi, *An Age in Motion*, p. 59.
106. Surya Ningrat [Suwardi Suryaningrat], "Het Javaansch Nationalisme in de Indische Beweging", in Anon., *Soembangsih*, p. 33.
107. *Oetoesan Hindia*, 24 March 1912, quoted in Noer, *The Modernist Muslim Movement*, pp. 111–12.
108. Surya Ningrat, "Het Javaansch Nationalisme", p. 33.
109. Abdoel Moeis, "Hindia Boeat Anak Hindia" [1917], in *Permata Terbenam; Capita Selecta Keempat*, edited by Pitut Soeharto and A. Zainoel Ihsan (Jakarta: Aksara Jayasakti, 1982), p. 74.
110. Abdoel Moeis, "Nasionalisme" [1917], in Soeharto and Ihsan, *Permata Terbenam*, p. 79.
111. Paraphrased in Anon., *Sarekat-Islam Congres (2e Nationaal Congres) 20–27 October 1917 te Batavia* (Batavia: Landsdrukkerij, 1919), p. 2.
112. "Beginselverklaring en Werkprogramma", Bijlage IV of ibid., p. 103.
113. H.A. Salim, *Neratja*, 25 October 1917, quoted in Nasution, "The Islamic State in Indonesia", p. 23.
114. Paraphrased in "Meeting over den Mohammedaanschen Godsdienst in het Sirenepark (Vrijdag 25 October 1917", Bijlage VI of Anon., *Sarekat-Islam Congres (2e Nationaal Congres)*, p. 115.
115. "Overzicht van den inwendigen politieken toestand [1922]", AMK, MR 141*/1923, NADH.
116. Haji Fachruddin quoted in "Vergadering van het Comité 'Tentara (Kandjeng) Nabi Moehammad' in den Ochtend van Vrijdag 4 October 1918 in het Lokaal der Arabische Societeit 'al-Djoem'ijah al-Cheirijah' te Soerbaja, Voorgezeten door den heer O.S. Tjokroaminoto", bijlage I of Anon., *Sarekat-Islam Congres (3e Nationaal Congres) 29 Sept.– 6 Oct. 1918 te Soerabaja* (Batavia: Landsdrukkerij, 1919), p. 42.
117. Mobini-Kesheh, *The Hadrami Awakening*, pp. 33, 46, 48, 50–51.
118. ANA to GG, 30 November 1915, in Van der Wal, *De Opkomst*, p. 450.
119. Ruth T. McVey, *The Rise of Indonesian Communism* (Ithaca: Cornell University Press, 1965), p. 25; Korver, *Sarekat Islam*, p. 121.
120. Including a puzzling effort, apparently supported by Douwes Dekker, to open SI to entry by all races and religions and rename the organisation Sarekat Hindia (Indies Association) (Nota P. J. Gerke [1919], in Kwantes, *De Ontwikkeling*, vol. 1, pp. 219–20; Anon. [B. J. O. Schrieke], *Overzicht van de Gestie der Centraal Sarekat Islam in het Jaar 1921* (Weltevreden: Landsdrukkerij, 1921), p. 1. See also Robert Van Niel, *The Emergence of the Modern Indonesian Elite* (The Hague: Van Hoeve, 1960), pp. 152–53; Paul W. van der Veur, *The Lion*

and the Gadfly: Dutch Colonialism and the Spirit of E. F. E. Douwes Dekker (Leiden: KITLV Press, 2006), pp. 407–09; McVey, *The Rise*, p. 64.

121. It is interesting to note that the Yogyakarta group included Suryopranoto, the famous "strike king" and leader of the sugar factory workers' union, the Personeel Fabrieks Bond (PFB), who was not regarded as a fierce champion of religion. Indeed, a report of the PFB congress 1 January 1921 contained not a single direct mention of religion, let alone Islam, and the aims of the PFB included no reference to religion. "P.F.B. actie — Sidoardjo Soerjopranoto. Extract Geheim Rapport van 8 tot en met 14 Juni 1921", AMK, MR 659*/1921, NADH; "Congres P.F.B. gehouden ten huize van Karijoredjo, Toego koelon, op den 31 Dec. 1920 and 1 Januari 1921", AMK, MR 360*/1921, NADH).

122. See *Koloniaal Weekblad*, 6 June 1918, 20 June 1918, 27 June 1918, 4 July 1918, 11 July 1918, 11 August 1918, 22 August 1918; *Oetoesan Hindia* 31 January 1918, 15 February 1918, 18 February 1918, 19 February 1918, 25 February–2 March 1918, in *Overzicht van de Inlandsche en Maleisch-Chineesche Pers [IPO]* 5/1918, 7/1918, 8/1918, 9/1918; Attorney-General's interview with Tjokroaminoto (November 1920–January 1921), AMK, MR 184*/1921, V 2-5-1923-D6, NADH; Shiraishi, *An Age*, pp. 106–07.

123. De Tollenaere, *The Politics*, p. 165; Erni Haryanti Kahfi, "Haji Agus Salim: His Role in Nationalist Movements in Indonesia during the Early Twentieth Century", M.A. dissertation, McGill University, 1996, p. 22.

124. Hasnul Arifin Melayu, "Islam as an Ideology: the Political Thought of Tjokroaminoto", *Studia Islamika* 9, no. 3 (2002): 54; Noer, *The Modernist Muslim Movement*, p. 298.

125. Noer, *The Modernist Muslim Movement*, p. 298.
126. Melayu, "Islam as an Ideology", p. 58.
127. See McVey, *The Rise*, p. 100.
128. Kwantes, *De Ontwikkeling*, vol. 1, p. 511.
129. Snouck Hurgronje to MC, 22 June 1921, in Gobée and Adriaanse, *Ambtelijke*, vol. 2, p. 1702.
130. *Dunia Islam*, 23 March 1923, in Panitia Peringatan Hadji A. Salim Genap Berusia 70 Tahun [Mohamad Roem et al.], *Djedjak Langkah Hadji A. Salim: Pilihan Karangan, Utjapan dan Pendapat Beliau dari Dulu sampai Sekarang* (Jakarta: Tintamas, 1954), p. 4.
131. Suradi, *Haji Agus Salim dan Konflik Politik dalam Sarekat Islam* (Jakarta: Pustaka Sinar Harapan, 1997), p. 54.
132. *Neratja*, 18 October 1921, quoted in Suradi, *Haji Agus Salim*, p. 52.
133. Ibid., p. 54.
134. *Neratja*, 18 October 1921, quoted in Noer, *The Modernist Muslim Movement*, p. 124.
135. Shiraishi, *An Age*, p. 237; H. Aboebakar, *Sedjarah Hidup K. H. A. Wahid Hasjim dan Karangan Tersiar* (Jakarta: Panitya Buku Peringatan Alm. K. H. A. Wahid Hasjim, 1957), p. 309.

136. Cokroaminoto's paraphrased remarks in "Verslag van het 2e al-Islam-Hindia Congres gehouden te Garoet van 19–21 Mei 1924", AMK, MR 460*/1924, NADH.
137. H. O. S. Tjokroaminoto, *Islam dan Sosialisme* (Jakarta: Bulan Bintang, 1950 [1924]).
138. Paraphrased remarks of Cokroaminoto in "Verslag van het 2e al-Islam-Hindia Congres".
139. "Overzicht van den inwendigen politieken toestand [1922]".
140. "Verslag van het buitengewoon Al-Islam Kongres gehouden te Soerabaja op 24, 25, 26 December 1924", AMK, MR 204*/1925, V 15-12-1925-A18, NADH; "PPO" March 1927, in Poeze, *Politiek-Politioneele Overzichten van Nederlandsch-Indië*, p. 24. See also Snouck Hurgronje to MC, 2 February 1926, in Gobée and Adriaansee, *Ambtelijke*, vol. 2, p. 1716; Suradi, *Haji Agus Salim*, p. 41.
141. From the inscription on the reverse side of a PSI identity card, cited in AMK, MR 1015*/1926, V 15-11-1927-L18, NADH.
142. "Maksoed. Toedjoean dan Azas2nja 'Partai Sarekat Islam'", *Bandera Islam*, 26 October 1925.
143. "Vertaling van het verslag van de besloten vergdering van de Partij Sarekat Islam gehouden vrijdag-avond 8 April 1927 in de Islamijah-School op Pakoe-Alaman te Jogjakarta", AMK, MR 646*/1027, V 15-11-1927-L18, NADH.
144. PPO November 1927, PPO July 1928, both in Poeze, *Politiek-Politioneele Overzichten van Nederlandsch-Indië*, pp. 174, 361; "Revolutionnaire richting van de Partij Sarekat Islam", AMK, MR 1084*/1027, V 15-11-1927-L18, NADH.
145. *Kemadjoean Hindia* 5–11 December 1925, *Overzicht van de Inlandsche en Maleisch-Chineesche Pers [IPO]* 51/1925. For comments of a similarly critical kind, see also PPO June 1927, PPO November 1927, PPO December 1927, all in Poeze, *Politiek-Politioneele Overzichten van Nederlandsch-Indië*, pp. 68, 174, 197.
146. PPO June 1927, in Poeze, *Politiek-Politioneele Overzichten van Nederlandsch-Indië* , p. 68.
147. Gregory John Fealy, "Ulama and Politics in Indonesia: a History of Nahdlatul Ulama, 1952–1967", Ph.D dissertation, Monash University, 1998, pp. 25–27; Junus, *Sedjarah*, pp. 209–10; Laffan, *Islamic Nationhood*, p. 235; Giora Eliraz, "The Islamic Reformist Movement in the Malay-Indonesian World in the First Four Decades of the 20th Century: Insights Gained from a Comparative Look at Egypt", *Studia Islamika* 9, no. 2 (2002): 68.
148. SI leader Sastroatmojo, quoted in "Neutraliseering en bestrijding van revolutionnaire propaganda onder de inheemsche bevolking, in het bijzonder van Java en Madoera", AMK, MR 457*/1928, V 1 May 1929 C9, NADH. See also Noer, *The Modernist Muslim Movement*, pp. 137, 235–37.
149. SI had also adopted a policy of non-cooperation with the government, partly out of frustration with what it saw as an increasingly unsympathetic attitude on the part of the government.

150. "Overzicht van den inwendigen politieken toestand [1922]". See also Shiraishi, *An Age in Motion*, p. 245.
151. "Vertaling van een verslag eener vergadering der Sarekat Hindia (N.I.P.) [21 March 1920]", AMK, MR 508*/1920, NADH.
152. Report Ch. O van der Plas, September 1927/March 1928, in Kwantes, *De Ontwikkeling*, vol. 2 (Groningen: Wolters-Noordhof, 1978), p. 715.
153. Soekarno, *Nationalism, Islam and Marxism*, trans. Karel H. Warouw and Peter D. Weldon, with an introduction by Ruth T. McVey (Ithaca: Southeast Asia Program, Cornell University, 1969 [1926]), p. 38.
154. Anon., "Lebaran-viering", *Hindia Poetra* 1 (1923): 33.
155. "Overzicht van den inwendigen Politieken Toestand van Maart 1928 tot December 1928", AMK, MR 260/1929, V 11-3-1930-6, NADH.
156. Consul at Jeddah to Minister of External Affairs, 15 December 1928, AMK, MR 113*/1929, V 23 April 1929/N8, NADH.
157. Laffan, *Islamic Nationhood*, pp. 220–21, 234. For correspondence between Perhimpunan Indonesia in the Netherlands and Cairo students, see AMK, V 9 August 1927/G13, NADH.
158. Tjipto Mangoenkoesoemo, *Het Communisme in Indonesië: Naar Aanleiding van de Relletjes* (Bandung: Algemeene Studieclub, 1927), p. 13.
159. *Oetoesan Hindia*, 9–15 January 1923, *Overzicht van de Inlandsche en Maleisch-Chineesche Pers [IPO]* 3/1923.
160. Quoted in "Verslag van wd. adviseur voor inlandsche zaken (E. Gobée) van het 14e P.S.I.-congres te Pekalongan, 28 sept.–2 okt. 1927", in Kwantes, *De ontwikkeling*, vol. 2, p. 619.
161. PPO December 1928, in Poeze, *Politiek-Politioneele Overzichten van Nederlandsch-Indië*, p. 490.
162. PPO July 1927, in Poeze, *Politiek-Politioneele Overzichten van Nederlandsch-Indië*, p. 84.
163. Laffan, *Islamic Nationhood*, p. 2.
164. "Beginselverklaring en werkprogram" [Kusuma Sumantri's speech on becoming chairman PI, 1923], AMK, V 9 August 1927-G13, NADH.
165. Gatot Mangkoepradja, "Kebangsaan Indonesia" [1932], in Soeharto and Ihsan, *Permata Terbenam*, p. 297.
166. See, for example, Petrus Blumberger, *De Nationalistische Beweging*, pp. 298, 299.
167. Hatta to Soejadi, 2 March 1926, AMK, V 9 August 1927-G13, NADH.
168. "Beginselverklaring en werkprogram", AMK, V 9 August 1927-G13, NADH.
169. See, for example, Moehammad Jamin, "Bangsa dan kebangsaan" [1931], in Soeharto and Ihsan, *Permata Terbenam*, p. 259.
170. "Overzicht van den inwendigen politieken toestand [1922]". See also Shiraishi, *An Age*, pp. 243, 245; McVey, *The Rise*, pp. 166, 177.
171. PPO July 1928, PPO September 1928, PPO November 1928, PPO December 1928, all in Poeze, *Politiek-Politioneele Overzichten van Nederlandsch-Indië*, pp. 361, 418, 472, 498.

172. "Verslag van de wd. adviseur voor inlandsche zaken (R.A. Kern) van het 11e congres van de Centrale Sarekat Islam te Soerabaja, 8–10 aug. 1924", in Kwantes, *De ontwikkeling*, vol. 2, p. 194.
173. *Het Licht* 1, no. 2 (March 1926), quoted in Panitia, *Djedjak Langkah Hadji A. Salim*, pp. 98–99.
174. Quoted in "Verslag van wd. adviseur voor inlandsche zaken (E. Gobée)", p. 623.
175. *Het Licht* 1, no. 2 (1926), quoted in Panitia, *Djedjak Langkah Hadji A. Salim*, p. 102. See also *Hindia Baroe*, 9 January 1925, in Hazil Tanzil, ed., *Seratus Tahun Haji Agus Salim* (Jakarta: Sinar Harapan: 1996 [1984]), pp. 292–93.
176. Sentiment attributed to PSI leaders in Attorney-General to GG, 28 October 1927, in Kwantes, *De Ontwikkeling*, vol. 2, p. 641.
177. Petrus Blumberger, *De Nationalistische Beweging*, pp. 314–15.
178. Quoted in report Ch. O van der Plas, September 1927/March 1928, pp. 724–25.
179. Salim, *Hindia Baru*, 10 May 1925, quoted in Noer, *The Modernist Muslim Movement*, p. 254. See also *Fadjar Asia*, 29 July 1928, in Tanzil, *Seratus tahun*, pp. 347–50. The Singapore-born Ahmad Hassan of the modernist organisation Persis was even more fervent in his denunciation of nationalism as a contradiction of Islam (Fauzan Saleh, *Modern Trends in Islamic Theological Discourse in Twentieth Century Indonesia: A Critical Study* (Leiden: Brill, 2001), p. 138n). For a broader discussion of Salim's ideas on nationalism, and his subsequent polemic with Sukarno, see Erni Haryanti Kahfi, "Islam and Indonesian Nationalism: the Political Thought of Haji Agus Salim", *Studia Islamika* 4, no. 3 (1997), pp. 46–57.
180. Melayu, "Islam as an ideology", p. 67.
181. Bilimaaf, "Tahoen manakah bangsa kita Islam di kota Medan bisa mendjadi madjoe?", *Doenia Bergerak* 35 (1924), pp. 12–13.
182. Mohamad Roem, "Haji Agus Salim", in Tanzil, *Seratus Tahun*, p. 188.
183. "Overzicht van den inwendigen Politeken Toestand" [1929].

References

Abushouk, Ahmed Ibrahim. "A Sudanese Scholar in the Diaspora: Life and Career of Ahmad Muhamad al-Surkitti in Indonesia (1911–1943)". *Studia Islamika* 8, no. 1 (2001): 55–86.

Alkema, B. *De Sarikat Islam*. Utrecht: G.J.A. Ruys, 1919.

Anon. [D.A. Rinkes]. *Bescheiden Betreffende de Vereeniging "De Indiche Partij"*. Batavia: Landsdrukkerij, 1913.

Anon. *Sarekat-Islam Congres (1e Nationaal Congres) 17–24 Juni 1916 te Bandoeng*. Batavia: Landsdrukkerij, 1916.

Anon. *Sarekat-Islam Congres (2e Nationaal Congres) 20–27 October 1917 te Batavia*. Batavia: Landsdrukkerij, 1919.

Anon. ed., *Gedenkboek 1908–1923 Indonesische Vereeniging* (n.p.: n.p., n.d [1924]).

Anon. "Sarikat Islam en Onrust in Ned.-Oost-Indië". *De Indische Gids* 35, no. 2 (1913): 1521–22.

Anon. "Bespreking over Gemengde Huwelijken in de Vergadering der Indische Vereeniging op 30 Juni 1915". *Indische Vereeniging: Voordrachten en Mededeelingen* 10 (1916): 56–73.

Anon. "Maksoed, Toedjoean dan Azas2nja 'Partai Sarekat Islam'". *Bandera Islam*, 26 October 1925.

Anon. "Nota over het Congres voor Javaanse Cultuurontwikkeling van B.J.O. Schrieke, 27 juli 1918", in *De Ontwikkeling van de Nationalistische Beweging in Nederlandsch-Indië*, edited by R.C. Kwantes, vol. 1. Groningen: H.D. Tjeenk Willink, 1975.

Ahmat B. Adam. *The Vernacular Press and the Emergence of Modern Indonesian Consciousness (1855–1913)*. Ithaca: Southeast Asia Program, Cornell University, 1995.

Azra, Azyumardi. "The Transmission of *al-Manar*'s Reformism to the Malay-Indonesian World: The Cases of *al-Imam* and *al-Munir*". *Studia Islamika* 6, no. 3 (1999): 75-100.

Boeka [P.C.C. Hansen Jr]. "De Inlander, een Studie". *Indische Gids* 25 (1903): 1137–83.

Bowen, John R. *Muslims Through Discourse: Religion and Ritual in Gayo Society*. New Jersey: Princeton University Press, 1993.

Braudel, Fernand. *On History*, trans. Sarah Matthews. Chicago: University of Chicago Press, 1980.

Coté, Joost. (trans.) *Letters from Kartini: An Indonesian Feminist, 1900–1914*. Clayton: Monash Asia Institute in association with Hyland House, 1992.

Dahm, Bernhard. *Sukarno and the Struggle for Indonesian Independence*. Ithaca: Cornell University Press, 1969.

De Tollenaere, Herman Arij Oscar, *The Politics of Divine Wisdom: Theosophy and Labour, National, and Womens' Movements in Indonesia and South Asia, 1875–1947*. Nijmegen: Uitgeverij Katholieke Universiteit Nijmegen, 1996.

Dijkstra, H. "De Tweede Wereldgodsdienst". *De Macedoniër* 17 (1913): 65–73.

Fealy, Gregory John. "Ulama and Politics in Indonesia: A History of Nahdlatul Ulama, 1952–1967". Ph.D dissertation, Monash University, 1998.

Geertz, Hildred. (ed.) *Letters of A Javanese Princess: Raden Adjeng Kartini*. New York: W.W. Norton & Company, 1964.

Gobée, E. and C. Adriaanse. (eds.) *Ambtelijke Adviezen van C. Snouck Hurgronje 1889–1936*. The Hague: Martinus Nijhoff, 1957–65.

Henley, David E.F. *Nationalism and Regionalism in a Colonial Context: Minahasa in the Dutch East Indies*. Leiden: KITLV Press, 1996.

Hindia-Poetra, Verslaggever. "De Deputatie-Indië-Weerbaar als Gasten der Indische Vereeniging". *Hindia Poetra* (1916–17) 243–52.

Junus, Mahmud. *Sedjarah Pendidikan Islam di Indonesia*. Jakarta: Pustaka Mahmudiah, 1960.
Jainuri, A. *Muhammadiyah: Gerakan Reformasi Islam di Jawa pada Awal Abad Kedua Puluh*. Surabaya: PT Bina Ilmu, 1981.
Kahfi, Erni Haryanti. "Haji Agus Salim: His Role in Nationalist Movements in Indonesia during the Early Twentieth Century". M.A. dissertation, McGill University, 1996.
———. "Islam and Indonesian Nationalism: The Political Thought of Haji Agus Salim", *Studia Islamika* 4, no. 3 (1997): 46–57.
Korver, A.P.E. *Sarekat Islam 1912–1916: Opkomst, Bloei en Structuur van Indonesië's Eerste Massabeweging*. Amsterdam: Historisch Seminarium van de Universiteit van Amsterdam, 1982.
Laffan, Michael Francis. *Islamic Nationhood and Colonial Indonesia: The* Umma *Below the Winds*. London: Routledge Curzon, 2003.
Lindenborn, M. *Zendingslicht op den Islam*. Den Haag: Den Boekhandel van den Zendingstudie Raad, 1918.
McVey, Ruth T. *The Rise of Indonesian Communism*. Ithaca: Cornell University Press, 1965.
Mangoenkoesoemo, Tjipto. *Iets over den Javaan, Zijn Geschiedenis en Zijn Ethiek*. Semarang: n.p., 1913.
———. "Dr. Kuyper te Laat". *Het Tijdschrift* 2 (1912): 571–74.
Melayu, Hasnul Arifin, "Islam as an Ideology: the Political Thought of Tjokroaminoto". *Studia Islamika* 9, no. 3 (2002): 35–81.
Miert, Hans van. *Een Koel Hoofd en een Warm Hart: Nationalisme, Javanisme en Jeugdbeweging in Nederlands-Indië, 1918–1930*. Amsterdam: De Bataafsche Leeuw, 1995.
Mobini-Kesheh, Natalie. *The Hadrami Awakening: Community and Identity in the Netherlands East Indies, 1900–1942*. Ithaca: Cornell Southeast Asia Program, 1999.
Moeis, Abdoel. "Hindia Boeat Anak Hindia" [1917], in *Permata Terbenam; Capita Selecta Keempat*, edited by Pitut Soeharto and A. Zainoel Ihsan. Jakarta: Aksara Jayasakti, 1982.
Nasution, Harun. "The Islamic State in Indonesia: The Rise of the Ideology, the Movement for its Creation and the Theory of the Masjumi". M. A. dissertation, McGill University, 1965.
Noer, Deliar. *The Modernist Muslim Movement in Indonesia 1900–1942*. Kuala Lumpur: Oxford University Press, 1973.
Noto Soeroto, "De Eendracht van Indië en Nederland". *Indische Vereeniging: Voordrachten en Mededeelingen* 5 (1913): 3–40.
Panitia Peringatan Hadji A. Salim Genap Berusia 70 Tahun [Mohamad Roem et al]. *Djedjak Langkah Hadji A. Salim: Pilihan Karangan, Utjapan dan Pendapat Beliau dari Dulu sampai Sekarang*. Jakarta: Tintamas, 1954.
Petrus Blumberger, J.Th., *De Nationalistische Beweging in Nederlandsch-Indië* (Dordrecht: Foris Publications, 1987 [1931]).

Poeze, Harry A. "Inleiding", in *Politiek-Politioneele Overzichten van Nederlandsch-Indië*, edited by Harry A. Poeze, vol. 1. The Hague: Martinus Nijhoff, 1982.

———. "Early Indonesian Emancipation: Abdul Rivai, Van Heutsz, and the *Bintang Hindia*". *Bijdragen tot de Taal-, Land- en Volkenkunde* 145 (1989): 87–106.

Poensen, C. *Brieven over den Islam uit de Binnenlanden van Java*. Leiden: E. J. Brill, 1886.

Ratu-Langie, Gerungan S.S.J. *Serikat Islam*. Baarn: Hollandia Drukkerij, 1913.

Ricklefs, M. C. *A History of Modern Indonesia since c. 1200*. 3rd ed. Basingstoke: Palgrave, 2001.

———. *Mystic Synthesis in Java: a History of Islamization from the Fourteenth to the Early Nineteenth Centuries*. Norwalk CT: East Bridge, 2006.

———. *Polarising Javanese Society: Islamic and Other Visions, c. 1830–1930*. Singapore: NUS Press, 2007.

Ronkel, Ph. S. van, *Rapport betreffende de Godsdienstige Verschijnselen ter Sumatra's Westkust*. Batavia: Landsdrukkerij, 1916.

Saleh, Fauzan. *Modern Trends in Islamic Theological Discourse in Twentieth Century Indonesia: A Critical Study*. Leiden: Brill, 2001.

Soeriokoesoemo, R.M.S. "Javaansch Nationalisme", in *Javaansche of Indisch Nationalisme? Pro en Contra*, edited by R. M. S. Soeriokoesoemo, A. Muhlenfeld, Tjipto Mangoenkoesoemo, and J.B. Wens. Semarang: Semarang Drukkerij en Boekhandel H.A. Benjamins, 1918.

Shiraishi, Takashi. *An Age in Motion: Popular Radicalism in Java, 1912–1926*. Ithaca: Cornell University Press, 1990.

Snouck Hurgronje, Christiaan. "Over Panislamisme" [1910], in *Verspreide Geschriften van C. Snouck Hurgronje*, edited by A.J. Wensinck, vol. 1. Bonn: Kurt Schoeder, 1923.

Suradi, *Haji Agus Salim dan Konflik Politik dalam Sarekat Islam*. Jakarta: Pustaka Sinar Harapan, 1997.

Tanzil, Hazil. (ed.) *Seratus Tahun Haji Agus Salim*. Jakarta: Sinar Harapan: 1996 [1984].

Tj. Mk [Cipto Mangunkusumo]. "De Heer van Kol en de Indische Partij". *De Indiër*, 3 November 1913: 3740.

Tjipto Mangoenkoesoemo, *Het Communisme in Indonesië: Naar Aanleiding van de Relletjes* (Bandung: Algemeene Studieclub, 1927).

Tjokroaminoto, H.O.S. *Islam dan Sosialisme*. Jakarta: Bulan Bintang, 1950 [1924].

Wal, S. L. van der. (ed.) *De Opkomst van de Nationalistische Beweging in Nederlandsch-Indië*. Groningen: J.B. Wolters, 1967.

15

CHINESE SHRINES CONTESTED
Power and Politics in Chinese Communities in Bangkok in the Early Twentieth Century*

Koizumi Junko

INTRODUCTION

Today, more than 650 Chinese shrines are officially registered with the Ministry of Interior, Thailand.[1] The legal grounds for this registration system is the Ministerial Regulations on Chinese Shrines (*sanchao*) enacted on 15 March 1921.[2] The regulations, jointly issued under the names of the Minister of Local Government and the Minister of Interior, laid the legal groundwork for the government control and "protection" of these religious institutions, by obliging all the Chinese shrines situated on government land or on donated land to have their title deeds made out in the names of the local authorities and their names entered into the list of registered shrines.

Seen from a present-day perspective, the regulations appear to have been favourably received in Thailand. The Ministry of Interior, for instance, recently launched a project to select excellent shrines of the year from among the registered shrines and grant them a pair of royal photos of the king and the queen.[3] However, if we look back in history, the Chinese in Bangkok strongly opposed these regulations at their promulgation. The Siamese government legitimized the introduction of the regulations by explaining that their purpose was to prevent the use of the premises occupied by shrines for illegal purposes such as gambling and meetings of secret societies and to prevent misuse of shrine funds by certain individuals so that the benefits of the great majority of law-abiding Chinese could be protected. Despite this, the regulations evoked strong objections from the Chinese communities in Bangkok.

Based on unpublished Thai archival materials, this essay examines the background and ramification of the regulations. In doing so, it reveals the politics and political strategies of the Chinese in Bangkok and the role of shrines in their communities, which extended beyond religious activities, in the early twentieth century.

THE MINISTERIAL REGULATIONS ON CHINESE SHRINES OF 1921

On 6 August 1920, Chaophraya Yommarat, the Minister of Local Government (*Krasuang Nakhonban*) in charge of the administration of Bangkok, submitted a draft of the Ministerial Regulations on Chinese Shrines to King Wachirawut and asked for his royal endorsement. Expressing strong concern about the disorder which a number of disputes over management of shrines had brought to the courts and the activities of secret societies found at many Chinese shrines in Bangkok, he delineated the following three points as the purpose for the introduction of the regulations: first, to maintain the land donated by individual(s) to a shrine as *khong klang*[4] so that the premises could be maintained as a site of worship by the masses; second, to manage and use the profits gained from donations for the benefit of the masses; and third, to let government officials exercise control over people's gatherings at shrines.[5]

The draft regulations, allegedly sanctioned by Article 123 of the Local Administration Act of B.E. 2456 (1914), which empowered local officials to inspect and support the guardians of temples and places for charity in order to prevent trespassing, comprised twenty-five articles.[6] Among them, the most important provisions, which afterwards were the cause of grave concern among the Chinese, were Articles 4 and 13.

In the draft of the regulations, Article 4 prescribed that all Chinese shrines in Bangkok built on government land or on privately-owned land that had been donated to shrines must have a title deed (*chanot*) in the name of the Prefectural Department (*Krom Phranakhonban*) of the Ministry of Local Government. This government control of shrine land, moreover, was complemented by additional relevant articles. Article 5, for instance, obliged anyone who wished to make a gift of a piece of land for creating and erecting a shrine, or to erect a new shrine upon such land, to send an application in writing with full proof of ownership of the land to be donated. Similarly, Article 6 compelled those desirous of constructing new buildings on the premises of existing shrines to get permission from the Prefectural Department.

Thus placing the land and buildings of such Chinese shrines under government control, the draft regulations also placed management of these shrines under government supervision. Article 13 granted the head of the Prefectural Department the power to appoint a governing manager and an inspector of a shrine at will, allowing anyone, even an outsider, with certain qualifications, to apply for such positions. The primary duty of a manager was to look after the activities of the shrine(s) in his charge for the sake of the shrine's interests, while the inspector was responsible for checking the activities and registered properties of the shrine as well as overseeing the manager (Article 14). The qualifications for manager and inspector were designated as follows: respectful of the beliefs concerned, twenty years-old or over; having a good basis in terms of occupation and property; never indicted for fraud, theft, or plundering, or associated with secret societies, or engaged in any dispute concerning landownership of any shrine; and under Siamese jurisdiction (Article 12).

Based on these provisions, all shrines were required to be entered into the list of registered shrines by providing the name and address of the shrine as well as the details about both the manager and the inspector of the shrine, including their names, ages, "nationality," and occupations (Article 10). Thus placed under government control, these shrines were also required to keep proper account books, and have them always open to the local officials.

The king ordered the draft sent to the ministers of Agriculture, Interior, and Law for further consultation mainly on the following points: whether the legal provisions exceeded the scope authorized by Article 123 of the Local Administration Act; whether the regulations should cover other religions and provincial areas beyond Bangkok; and whether the Prefectural Department should be regarded as a judicial person if the name of the department appeared in title deeds.[7]

After receiving comments from the three ministries, King Wachirawut ordered the Ministry of Local Government to make revisions by duly considering the suggestions. The revised version expanded coverage of the regulations across the whole kingdom, made necessary adjustments to ensure that the regulations were consistent with the relevant provisions in the Penal Code, and added a few new provisions including the one that obliged the managers and inspectors to report to the local officials if they found anyone possibly engaging in illegal activities such as gambling and secret societies.

This revised version was again sent to the king for approval. On 15 March 1921, the regulations were officially issued with a royal endorsement.[8]

DISPUTES OVER HOKKIEN SHRINES IN BANGKOK (1916–1920)

Why did such ministerial regulations specifically target Chinese shrines? Immediately prior to the introduction of the regulations, two sets of court cases concerning the major Hokkien shrines in Bangkok were brought against Phraya Chodukratchasetthi [hereafter abbreviated as Phraya Choduk], the head of *Krom Tha Sai*,[9] by several leaders of the Hokkien community. It seems that these incidents, which dragged on more than three years and could not be settled even by a Supreme Court ruling, made the Siamese government realize that Chinese shrines could be sites of serious disputes.

Case 1: Five Hokkien Shrines in Bangkok

In mid-1917, three Hokkiens in Bangkok, Khun Sawatdiphokhakon [hereafter abbreviated as Khun Sawat], Tieo Seng Ke, and Lim Seng Kit, filed a case against Phraya Choduk over the landownership of and misappropriation of economic gains at five Hokkien shrines: Sun Heng Keng [順興宮], popularly known as Cho Su Kong, located in the Talat Noi district; Kuan Im Teng [観音亭], located adjacent to Kanlayanamit Temple; Kian An Keng [建安宮] or Pun Thao Ma [本頭媽廟] in the Talat Noi district; Hok Lian Keng [福蓮宮], located on Chakkraphet Road; and Sin Heng Keng [新興宮] in the Ban Thawai district.[10]

According to accusations filed by the three plaintiffs and nine other individuals who claimed to be members of the administrative committee of these shrines elected by a meeting of 200 Hokkiens, Phraya Choduk, who was not a committee member, had requested that the Ministry of Agriculture issue title deeds for these five shrines and entered his name as lawful landowner without obtaining permission from the committee.

Strongly denouncing Phraya Choduk, who had been custodian of these shrines, for past misconduct such as embezzlement of 800 *baht* from the shrines' fund and misappropriation of the land of Hok Lian Keng Shrine, the plaintiffs demanded insertion of their names in the title deeds and repayment of 500 *baht* a month that Phraya Choduk had been earning from shrine activities.

Phraya Choduk, on the other hand, denied the allegations, as follows: First, he defended his position as legitimate custodian of the shrines, he explained that he had duly inherited the position from his father, who had been officially entrusted by the Hokkien communities in Bangkok with the task of custodian to look after shrine properties and the income they generated, when he died about twenty years earlier. In addition, when the Hokkiens in Bangkok established the Hokkien Association five or six years earlier, Phraya Choduk had been elected president of the association and assigned to manage the shrines, and he claimed to be performing his duties to the satisfaction of Hokkien people in Bangkok to the present day.

Regarding the question of title deeds for the shrines, Phraya Choduk admitted that he had requested that the Ministry of Agriculture put his name on the title deeds, and he justified this request as a necessity to verify the proper ownership of these premises so the activities of the shrines could be permanently guaranteed. As for the question of embezzlement and concealment of the account books, moreover, Phraya Choduk denied the accusations and claimed that he had never doctored the books, which had always been open to anyone for inspection.

In the deliberation process, the plaintiffs again explained that about two years earlier, they had convened a meeting of those discontented with the way Phraya Choduk had managed the shrines over the past twenty years or so and elected the three plaintiffs and nine other individuals as members of the shrines' administrative committee. It was alleged that more than a hundred individuals out of 60,000 Hokkiens in Bangkok attended the meeting and also requested that Phraya Choduk add the names of a few more individuals to the title deeds, which, however, Phraya Choduk refused to do.

However, this account was seriously questioned when the two policemen, as witnesses for the plaintiffs, attested that only forty-plus people had attended the meeting, and that it had been a surreptitious meeting without Phraya Choduk. In addition, it was also revealed that Phraya Choduk had originally committed 1,300 *baht* for the construction of the shrines, and that 800 *baht* of this was still to be repaid to Phraya Choduk when the shrines collected sufficient donations.

In the end, the court denied the plaintiffs' claim to be legitimate representatives of the Hokkien communities on the grounds that they were selected by only a very limited group of forty-plus individuals, and ruled that they should have no right to administer the shrines. The plaintiffs appealed to the higher court. Two months later, on 15 October 1917, the court of appeal also ruled against the plaintiffs on the same grounds as those given by the lower court.[11] Still dissatisfied with the decision, the plaintiffs further appealed to the Supreme Court, only to meet with another dismissal on 5 December 1919.[12]

Case 2: Pun Thao Ma Shrine in Trok Wat Yuan

Soon after the appeal court delivered the judgement in favour of Phraya Choduk in Case 1, the Civil Court also delivered a judgement on another case filed by a Chinese named Chian against Phraya Choduk in November 1917. Chian claimed ownership of the land of the Pun Thao Ma Shrine, located in the Tambon (sub-district) Trok Wat Yuan, one of the five Hokkien shrines in dispute in Case 1.[13]

According to Chian's accusations, Chian had originally owned the shrine's land and built a row of linked houses with thirteen rooms in the premises. In March 1911, when Chian barrowed 6,000 *baht* from Phraya Choduk, he gave Phraya Choduk the title deed for the land and the row of linked houses as collateral for the debt. At the same time, he also made an agreement with Phraya Choduk, allowing Phraya Choduk to collect the rent from the row of linked houses at the rate of 104 *baht* a month for repayment of the debt. Since then, for six years and two months, Phraya Choduk had collected the rent, the total of which already amounted to 7,696 *baht*. Phraya Choduk, however, instead of returning the title deed to Chian, requested the Ministry of Agriculture officials to survey the land and put his name on the title deed as owner. Chian thus decided to sue Phraya Choduk for repayment of 1,696 *baht* and suspension of rent collection.

According to Phraya Choduk, however, the piece of land in question was originally donated to the shrine by two Chinese named Phuak and Tao. But when a fire had broken out some thirty years earlier, the shrine and buildings in the compound burnt down. Since no one had rebuilt the shrine after the fire, people thought the land was owned by Uphairatchabamrung Temple (hereafter Uphai Temple) and came to settle there by renting the land from the temple. When another fire broke out, a Chinese named Lek, who had come to know that a Chinese shrine had previously been there, collected donations from people to rebuild a shrine and the row of linked houses to let. However, Uphai Temple contended that the land was theirs and took the matter to court. Chian, Phraya Choduk, and Lek pleaded against the temple by asserting the land had been owned by the shrine, and the court dismissed the claim by the temple. When the matter was settled, Chian asked the Ministry of Local Government to issue a certificate for the land so it would be formally acknowledged as the shrine's land. Although the certificate was made out in the name of Chian, it was also a common understanding then that Chian was not the owner but a representative of the shrine.

When the shrine and a row of linked houses with thirteen rooms were finally reconstructed in 1907 or 1908, Chian calculated the amount of money he had spent for the reconstruction work. Finding that his expenses totalling 10,951.75 *baht*, could not be paid off by donations i.e. with only 2,599 *baht* received, Phraya Choduk and others made an arrangement with Chian to allow Chian to receive the rent from the row of linked houses to reimburse him for the 8,352.82 *baht* that he had advanced for construction. However, right after this arrangement was made, Chian brought the shrine's land certificate to the Ministry of Finance as collateral for an unpaid liquor tax owed by another Chinese tax farmer to the ministry. Two years later, when Chian found he had no money with which to redeem the certificate from the ministry, he asked Phraya Choduk and the Hokkien Association to redeem it by paying 8,384 (*sic*) *baht* for him. Since then the certificate was in the hands of Phraya Choduk, and he had been collecting rents from the row of linked houses as reimbursement for the money he had lent Chian to redeem the land certificate. Phraya Choduk had then concluded that Chian had no right to claim landownership of the shrine land in question.

After deliberating over testimony from both sides, the court confirmed the following points. First, although the land certificate was made out in plaintiff's name, his name was written in as representative, not the land-owner, of the shrine. Second, when Uphai Temple claimed the land in question, the plaintiff himself defended it by asserting the land was owned by the shrine; thus there should be no way for the land to be returned to the plaintiff. Third, when the plaintiff assigned the land and row of linked houses to the shrine, his expenses were thoroughly calculated, indicating his full intention of conveying the building and land to the shrine. Thus the court dismissed Chian's claim and concluded that the land in dispute was the land of Pun Thao Ma Shrine.

Chian quickly appealed the decision. In the appeal court, evidence produced by both sides was examined in further detail.[14] Phraya Choduk presented a contract in Chinese which allegedly had been made by Chian when he borrowed 8,380 *baht* from Phraya Choduk to redeem the land certificate, and the balance for reconstruction of the shrine and row of linked houses that Chian had prepared when he was reimbursed for his expenditures from donations. The former also stated clearly that Chian would later make a formal title deed to endorse sale of the land to Phraya Choduk, and the latter was understood as evidence confirming that Chian had accepted the arrangement to return the shrine's land.

Chian, on the other hand, denied the document was in his handwriting, and produced another document, allegedly written by himself, stating that he had received 6,000 *baht* from Phraya Choduk to redeem the land [certificate] deposited with the Ministry of Finance as collateral.

However, the appeal court did not go into these points at issue. Instead, while accepting that Phraya Choduk had duly proved that the land was owned by the shrine, the court simply rejected Chian's claim on the ground that Chian failed to produce clear evidence of a contract obliging Phraya Choduk to return the certificate when the principal was fully repaid by rents from the row of linked houses.

Chian appealed to the Supreme Court. The court gave a decision on 28 February 1920 that, to the surprise of Phraya Choduk, overruled the decisions of both the lower and appeal courts.[15]

How did the Supreme Court come to this conclusion? The record of the decision indicates that what mattered was the validity of the contract document presented by Phraya Choduk and the legitimacy of Phraya Choduk's guardianship of the shrine as chairman of the Hokkien Shrine Association.[16]

As for the contract document presented by Phraya Choduk, allegedly written by Chian when he borrowed 8,380 *baht* from Phraya Choduk to redeem the land certificate from the Ministry of Finance, the court rejected it on the grounds that Phraya Choduk had failed to present a valid witness to support his refutation of Chian's denial of his handwriting. Condemning Phraya Choduk for not drawing up such a document in front of proper officials, the court concluded the document should be invalid. Regarding the question of Phraya Choduk's legitimacy as manager of the Pun Thao Ma Shrine, the court also rejected this as there was no evidence to support it except his own testimony and that of a follower of his. Without presenting clear evidence as to how, by whom, and on what authority and legal procedures Phraya Choduk had been appointed to such position, the court judged his appointment as illegitimate.

However, this was still not the end of the dispute. One month later, a petition dated 30 March 1920, signed by five representative Chinese and accompanied by an attachment bearing 181 signatures and seals of supporters was submitted to the king.[17] The petitioners, three of whom were British subjects, explained how Hokkien people had maintained these five shrines, namely — Cho Su Kong [順興宮], Sin Heng Keng [新興宮], also known as Pun Thao Ma [本頭媽廟], Kian An Keng [建安宮], Hok Heng Keng [福興宮], and Hok Lian Keng [福蓮宮] — by helping each other.[18] They then strongly objected to the Supreme Court decision acknowledging Chian as the legitimate administrator of the shrine located behind Uphai Temple, despite his fraud in using the shrine's land certificate as collateral when he was merely a representative and not the landowner of the shrine. Strongly supporting the legitimacy of Phraya Choduk, on the other hand, the petitioners claimed that these five Hokkien shrines had been administered by the Phraya Chodukratchasetthi family as a hereditary role with no trouble whatsoever until the present day. In contrast to Chian, who was merely a commoner, Phraya Choduk, who had assumed his position by succeeding his father, had had the honourable rank of *phraya* conferred upon him and, as head of *Krom Tha Sai*, was responsible for the administration of Chinese communities in Siam, and the maintenance of those shrines was considered as part of his official duties. To prevent the Hokkiens from further splitting into factions, they also emphasized the importance of placing the five shrines under unified overseership.

THE MINISTERIAL REGULATIONS CONTESTED

Unfortunately, as far as I searched, there is no record of the final decision by the king on this petition. Nevertheless, the fact that the draft of the Ministerial Regulations on Chinese Shrines was prepared only a few months after submission of this petition implies that frequent disputes over Chinese shrines in Bangkok prompted the Ministry of Local Government to introduce tighter control of these religious institutions.[19] However, this did not settle the matter at all; on the contrary, the Chinese communities in Bangkok strongly opposed government control of Chinese shrines, which caused further problems for the government.

Reaction of the Teochiu Chinese in Bangkok

Objections to the regulations began among Teochiu [Chaozhou 潮州] communities, the largest dialect group of Chinese in Bangkok. Luang Phakdiphatthrakon and his followers, a total of 678 Teochiu Chinese in Bangkok, submitted a lengthy petition dated 22 December 1921 requesting revision of the Ministerial Regulations on Chinese Shrines issued on 15 March 1921.[20] According to the petitioners, Teochiu people in Bangkok had been maintaining their shrine, San Chao Kao [literally "the old shrine"], for more than a hundred years. In the mid-1910s, when the shrine building became old and needed repairing, they collected 200,000 *baht* in donations, and decided to erect a new shrine building and a school called Phuai Eng School [培英学校], in the same compound. They claimed that the newly-promulgated regulations would seriously threaten the autonomy of the shrine and the freedom of religion that they had so far maintained.

The criticism was directed at two points: landownership and the appointment and power of the shrine managers. They feared that if the title deed to the shrine's land was issued under the name of the

Prefectural Department, the land would be regarded as government land [*thi luang*, literally royal land] and the power to decide on its utilization or even abandonment or sale to someone else would fall into the hands solely of the Department head. Compared with the cases involving other religions practised in Siam and other countries, they claimed such intervention would be an unprecedented violation of religious freedom and also diverge from traditional policies of the Siamese government toward Chinese shrines.

Similarly, the petitioners also criticized the provisions empowering the head of the Prefectural Department to appoint as a manager someone from outside the community without the consent of the shrine supporters, feeling this to be a serious infringement of their religious autonomy. They insisted on the necessity of choosing their own representative by proper electoral procedure as had been their customary practice and also allowed by the state under the Local Government Act. In conclusion, they demanded the revision of Articles 4 and 13 so that the title deed to shrine land could be issued in the name of the shrine and they could maintain the right to appoint and dismiss their own shrine managers.

The Minister of Local Government, however, proposed to the king that the petitioners' request should be rejected for the sake of keeping peace and order.[21] In the Minister's opinion, the requested revisions were unnecessary because under Article 4, the land would already be understood to be the shrine's land as the name of the shrine would appear in the title deed, while Article 13 should also be understood as an endorsement of existing practice that had already allowed for the appointment of managers and trustees through the same procedures. Believing that some Chinese shrines were strongholds of Chinese secret societies, which had repeatedly provoked untoward incidents such as the general strike of 1910 and the recent boycott of Japanese products, and seriously concerned about the situation of some shrines where the proceeds from the activities and properties were monopolized by a small group of influential people to the detriment of the interests of other groups and the general public, the minister saw it as absolutely necessary to exercise government control over Chinese shrines. Otherwise it was feared that frequent court cases would continue, causing problems for the local officials as well. The king rejected the petition, deeming that the requested revisions were unnecessary.[22]

Campaigns by the Hakka under Foreign Jurisdictions

However, before this royal decision was announced, groups of Hakka Chinese under various foreign jurisdictions started sending petitions to their consulates, which then forwarded the petitions to the Siamese government. In early March 1922, the Siamese Ministry of Foreign Affairs received a letter from the Dutch Consulate in Bangkok along with a petition submitted by a group of twenty-three Hakka who were "Chinese Netherland subjects."[23] The petition described the problems regarding a Chinese shrine named Kwan Oo [関帝廟] located on the Phat Sai Road in Samphen District and requested revisions to the Ministerial Regulations on Chinese Shrines.[24]

According to their account, the Hakka in Bangkok had collected donations and bought a piece of land in Bang Khun Phrom Sub-district and erected a shrine named Rong Lek Shrine there. However, in the mid-1910s, the Privy Purse Department requested this piece of land in order to build a palace for a prince in the area. The Hakka accepted the request in exchange for a piece of empty land on Phat Sai Road and 12,000 *baht* for constructing a new shrine, both being granted by the Ministry of Local Government. The ministry accordingly made out a contract and the paper was kept by the manager of the shrine at that time.

When the transfer of landownership was completed, the Hakka decided to promote both religious activities and education for their offspring so they would become good citizens under royal protection. They thus collected additional donations and erected a three-storeyed building on the new piece of land. This new building housed a Chinese school called Chin Tek School [進德學校] on the ground and first floors, while the top floor, which could be reached by a separate stairway, was used for the Kwan Oo Shrine. Since then, the Hakka had helped each other keep the place in good condition.

After thus reviewing the historical background of the shrine to demonstrate that the shrine had been built on their land with their own money, the petitioners then discussed issues in the new regulations. First, they strongly asserted that the newly-introduced regulations, which gave the ministry ownership of shrine land were an unfair exercise of their power, seriously violating existing landownership rights and freedom of religious activities. Refuting the explanation that the purpose of introducing the regulations was to protect the premises from trespassing, they claimed that the real intention of the ministry was to control the land, properties, interests, and activities of Chinese shrines. They also complained that the need to request prior permission from the Prefectural Department in order to repair shrine buildings was unfair treatment compared with the treatment of other religions in the country.

Another issue was the right of appointment and dismissal of the manager. The petitioners argued that empowering only the head of the Prefectural Department to exercise such right would be highly detrimental to their religious autonomy, and they also expressed regret that those under foreign jurisdictions like themselves were not allowed to be the manager, which they also regarded as unfair in the light of freedom of religion.

Moreover, the legal grounds for the regulations also had to be questioned. They argued many of the provisions were illegal and undue extensions of the Article 123 of the Local Administration Act, which prescribed only the duties of *amphoe* officials in supporting the protectors of religious institutions such as Buddhist temples to prevent trespass and oppression.

Prince Devawongse, the Minister of Foreign Affairs, forwarded this petition to Chaophraya Yommarat, the Minister of Local Government, requesting that he examine the signatures to determine whether the petitioners were really Dutch subjects ("*nai bangkhap holanda*").[25]

Two weeks later, a letter from the Portuguese Consul-General dated 17 March 1922 reached Prince Devawongse. Attached was a similar petition concerning the same Chinese shrine signed by five Portuguese-protected Chinese ("portuguese proteges").[26] This was followed by another petition dated 17 March 1922, submitted by a group of seven Chinese British subjects and forwarded from J. Crosby, the British Consulate-General in Bangkok, to Prince Traidos at the Ministry of Foreign Affairs.[27]

Though all these petitions were quite similar to each other, the one presented by British subjects took on a more forceful tone than the others, asserting not only that the regulations violated the friendship treaty under which freedom of religion for all citizens residing in the country was supposed to be guaranteed by the Siamese government, but also that the registration of the land of this particular shrine with the government would be a violation of Articles 1 and 4 because the land was owned by themselves; thus the shrine was located on private land.[28]

After consulting both the Local and Provincial Administration Act of 1914 and the Ministerial Regulations on Chinese Shrines of 1921, Prince Devawongse replied to the Dutch and Portuguese legations on 25 April 1922, and another reply was sent from Prince Traidos to the British legation the next day.[29] In their replies, both princes emphasized that the purpose of the regulations was to prevent the premises occupied by Chinese shrines from "being used for improper and illegal purposes", and "to insure that the temple funds and premises were used for bona fide religious purposes in the interest of the great majority of law-abiding Chinese". They also claimed that it was necessary to control the administration of shrines in various ways such as "registration of temples", "the election of approved Governing Managers and Inspectors" with certain qualifications, and "the inspection of premises and books of accounts."

Regarding title deeds to the land occupied by shrines, on the other hand, Prince Traidos, denied the petitioners' claim by pointing out that "the petition is in error in stating that the title deeds to temples are required to be made out in the name of the Ministry of Local Government," stating that they should be "made out in the name of the temples." He thus confirmed that it would be impossible for the ministry to sell the land or deal with it improperly. The conclusion was that the same questions had already been raised by other Chinese groups, and the king had already declined to accede.[30]

However, this did not stop the Chinese from submitting petitions. Following another petition by seven Hakka Chinese allegedly French-protected persons (protégés français) at the beginning of May 1922,[31] Crosby at the British Legation informed Prince Traidos that he had received another petition dated 7 June 1922.[32]

The second memorial attached to Crosby's letter was much longer and more detailed than the one submitted in March and again discussed various points.[33] Concerning the interpretation of Article 4 given by Traidos in his letter to Crosby stating that title deeds were in fact to be made out in the name of the shrine, not the Ministry of Local Government, the petitioners argued that this understanding was erroneous and asserted that the correct understanding was that the title deeds must be made out in the name of the Prefectural Department (not the Ministry of Local Government). Moreover, they even sarcastically welcomed the erroneous interpretation forwarded by the Ministry of Foreign Affairs by noting that it would indeed be just and fair to revise the stipulation as they said and make out the deeds in the name of the shrine.

Another point they raised was the purpose of the regulations. In refuting Traidos' explanation that the purpose of the regulations was "to prevent the use of the premises occupied by temples for illegal and improper purposes, such as gambling and the meetings of illegal secret societies," the petitioners pointed out that this explanation was inconsistent with the purpose of the regulations stated in the preface, i.e. to support the guardians of shrines in keeping the premises orderly and safe and preventing any trespassing. They also pointed out that if the purpose given by the Ministry of Foreign Affairs was correct, it would mean the regulations were unnecessary because other laws were already in place for suppressing those illegal activities in Siam, which also covered Chinese shrines.

The third point was freedom of religion. By citing the provision (Article 6) requiring prior permission from the Prefectural Department for construction or repairs of shrine buildings, the petitioners rejected Traidos' explanation that the government had no intention of interfering with freedom of worship. In their eyes, with no criteria for granting permission, this provision could easily be applied in an arbitrary manner. In addition, the power of the head of the Prefectural Department to appoint or dismiss managers and inspectors of shrines was another provision that would be against the principle of religious autonomy. Since no such restrictions were placed on other religions, moreover, it would be unfair discrimination against the Chinese.

Thus strongly refuting the explanations given by the Ministry of Foreign Affairs, they then pointed out that the Ministerial Regulations were in fact *ultra vires* of the Local Administration Act of 1914 in various ways. Noting, for instance, that Articles 5 and 123 of the Local Administration Act, which allegedly provided the legal basis for the Ministerial Regulations, vested only *amphoe* (district) officials with the authority to check, give support to, and protect the guardians of shrines to prevent trespassing, the Ministerial Regulations gave the head of the Prefectural Department full authority to govern the shrines. Indeed, such power as to appoint and dismiss the guardians and inspectors of shrines or to grant permission for the erection or repair of shrines was not prescribed in the Local Administration Law. Another example was the extent of punishment. The regulations prescribed imprisonment not exceeding three years, while ministerial regulations in general could prescribe punishment of only six months maximum imprisonment.

After thoroughly examining the problems of both the reply from the Ministry of Foreign Affairs and the provisions of the Ministerial Regulations themselves, they again confirmed that the premises of Kwan Oo Shrine had always been in their hands, and thus the shrine land should be considered as privately-owned and that the school occupying the ground and first floors should be regarded as a separate institution duly placed under authorization of the Ministry of Education. Drawing on the last points, the petitioners asked the British legation to protect their school against any intervention by the head of the Provincial Department as well.

A few days later, on 16 June 1922, the petition was again forwarded to Chaophraya Yommarat by Prince Devawongse, who requested further clarification on the matter.[34] About a month later, Chaophraya Yommarat replied to Prince Dewavongse that according to Article 4 of the Ministerial Regulations, title-deeds to Chinese temples situated on government land or donated land must be made out in the name of the Prefectural Department of the Ministry of Local Government followed by the name of the shrine to prevent any confusion.[35]

Following this response, Prince Traidos of the Ministry of Foreign Affairs admitted to W. W. Coultas, acting consul-general of Britain, that his previous statement "was in error in asserting that the title-deeds to Chinese temples are required to be made out in the name of the Ministry of Local Government," explaining that title deeds "must be made out in the name of the Prefectural Department" and the name of the temple would appear in the title deed after that of the Prefectural Department.[36]

As for the question of the regulations being *ultra vires*, he agreed to Crosby's suggestion to the petitioners to bring the matter to court if they wished, as the Ministry of Foreign Affairs could not make a statement. A similar reply was also sent out from Prince Devawongse to the French legation in mid-September.[37] Since no record exists of other petitions being submitted by Chinese foreign subjects thereafter, it seems that the series of objections by the Chinese came to an end at this time.[38]

CONCLUDING REMARKS

Serious disputes over the major Chinese shrines in Bangkok in the early twentieth century made the Siamese government realize that these shrines were not just a place for religious practices but a focus of economic interest and a source of serious conflict. Some shrines owned properties of high value both in terms of the land itself and the rows of linked houses that generated a substantial income for maintaining the buildings and activities of the shrine. Further, if the price of land increased, competition for economic gains among factions would become intense.[39] In addition, it was revealed that Chinese communities in Bangkok were not a monolithic entity but comprised multifaceted groups embracing both division and collaboration within and beyond dialect groups. While they were often involved in conflicts of interest among themselves, they also became firmly united and strategically collaborated when they faced interventions from the Siamese government they regarded as unfair. The logical, forceful arguments they gave in rebuttal to the government upon introduction of the Ministerial Regulations on Chinese Shrines demonstrated they had multiple faces such as Chinese, Hokkien or Hakka or Teochiu, Siamese citizens, and even foreign subjects, identities which they tried to manipulate to their advantage.

Chinese shrines and temples are often understood as places representing Chinese culture and thus have been an important subject of research in examining the beliefs and religious activities of overseas Chinese in Thailand.[40] For historians, on the other hand, written records such as inscriptions, wooden tablets, and iron bells, and even architecture and rituals found in Chinese shrines and temples, are also valued as important source materials for tracing the historical traditions of Chinese settlements.[41] But as the cases above suggest, we also need to pay more attention to the political and economic aspects of those shrines and place them in historical contexts, a perspective that views shrines not as something isolated and static, but as something closely interconnected with the dynamism of surrounding communities.

Notes

* This is an abridged and edited English translation of my article originally written in Japanese: "Shamu ni okeru chugoku byo ni kansuru ichikosatu: 'Byo ni kansuru shourei' (1921) wo megutte シャムにおける中国廟に関する一考察—「廟に関する省令」(1921年) をめぐって [Chinese Shrines in Historical Perspective: A Study on the Ministerial Regulations on Chinese Shrines (1921)]," *Toyobunka kenkyujo Kiyo* 東洋文化研究所紀要 150 (March 2007): 310 (17)–275 (52).

1. Krom kanpokkhrong, Krasuang mahatthai, ed., *Thamniap thabian sanchao thua ratcha-anachak* [Directory of registered Chinese shrines, whole kingdom] (Bangkok: n.p., n.a.), p. 9.
2. "Kot senabodi wa duai thi kuson sathan chanit sanchao pho.so. 2463", in *Prachum kotmai pracham sok* [Collected annual laws], edited by Sathian Lailak et al., vol. 33 (Bangkok: Nitiwet, 1935): 404–13. Although the contemporary documents in English use the term "temple(s)" for the Thai term *sanchao*, I use, except in cases of direct quotation, "shrine(s)" for *sanchao* in order to make a distinction from Chinese Buddhist temples designated in Thai as *wat chin*.
3. Krom kanpokkhrong, *Thamniap thabian sanchao*, pp. 45–52.
4. Here *khong klang* means something over which no one could exercise absolute ownership. See D. B. Bradley, *Nangsu akkharaphithansap, Dictionary of the Siamese Language* (Bangkok: Khurusapha Lat Phrao, 1971), p. 79.
5. Chaophraya Yommarat to Phraya Chakkrapanisisinwisut [hereafter referred as Phraya Chakkrapani] (6 August 1920), in National Archives of Thailand [hereafter abbreviated as NA.], the six reign documents, the Ministry of Local Government [hereafter abbreviated as R.VI. N.] 2/79: Ruang kot senabodi nakhonban wa duai sanchao (pho.so. 2463) [Regarding the ministerial regulations of the Ministry of Local Government on Chinese shrines, 1920/1].
6. Kot senabodi krasuang nakhonban wa duai thi kuson sathan chanit sanchao, [NA.R.VI.N.2/79].
7. *Thi* 155/63, Yo rian phraratchapatibat by Phraya Chakkrapani [NA.R.VI.N.2/79].
8. Phraya Chaiyayotsombat to Phraya Chakkrapani (8 September 1920); Chaophraya Surasi to Phraya Chakkrapani (4 October 1920); Chaophraya Aphairacha to Phraya Chakkrapani (26 October 1920); R. Guyon, "Memorandum concerning the Draft Ministerial Regulations on the places of religious institution submitted by the Ministry of Local Government," (25 September 1920); *Thi* 330/63, Yo ruang senabodi nakhonban kho phraborommarachanuyat ok kot wa duai

kuson sathan chanit sanchao by Phraya Chakkrapani; Chaophraya Yommarat to Phraya Chakkrapani (12 February 1921); the Department of Royal Private Secretary to Chaophraya Yommarat (15 March 1921) [NA.R.VI.N.2/79]. Although the Ministry of Agriculture advised that the name of the shrine was to appear in brackets after the Department of Local Government on title deeds, something to which the Ministry of Local Government agreed, this was not stated in Article 4 of the Regulations.

9. Literally translated as the Department of Left Ports, responsible for the administration of Chinese communities.
10. Palat thun chalong krasuang nakhonban to Phraya Prachachip-boriban (26 April 1917) and khamphiphaksa san phaeng (11 August 1917), in NA.R.VI.N.25.1/1: Nai hong hi tanwetchakun kap phuak thun klao thawai dika kho phramahakaruna prot klao tang hai phraya chodukratchasetthi pen phu pokkhrong sanchao hok lian keng (pho.so. 2461–2462) [Mr. Hong Hi Tanwetchakun and his group submitted a petition to the king requesting the appointment of Phraya Chodukratchasetthi as manager of Hok Lian Keng Shrine, 1918/9–1919/20].
11. Khamphiphaksa san utthon (15 October 1917) [NA.R.VI.N.25.1/1].
12. Khamphiphaksa dika thi 1064 (5 December 1919) [NA.R.VI.N.25.1/1].
13. Khamphiphaksa san phaeng (27 November 1917) [NA.R.VI.N.25.1/1].
14. Khamphiphaksa san utthon (8 August 1918) [NA.R.VI.N.25.1/1].
15. Khamphiphaksa thi 1440 (28 February1920) [NA.R.VI.N.25.1/1].
16. *Prathan haeng samoson samrap bamrung sanchao khong phuak chin chat hokkian.*
17. Petition submitted by Hutseng Sibunruang and four other Chinese to the king (30 March 1920) [NA.R.VI.N.25.1/1].
18. The names and locations of these five shrines differ slightly from the ones in dispute in Case 1.
19. Banthuk khwam hen nai khadi thi 440/2464, 617/2464, 618/2464, and 619/2464, in NA.R.VI.N.1/49: Kammakan san dika kho phraratchathan phraborommaratchawinitchai nai ruang kot senabodi thi wa duai thi kuson sathan chanit sanchao (pho.so. 2466) [The supreme court committee members seek royal judgment regarding the Ministerial Regulations on Chinese Shrines, 1923].
20. *Dika thi* 641 (22 December 1921) in NA.R.VI.N.1/46: Dika luang phakdiphatthrakon kap phuak kho hai loek kot senabodi wa duai thi kuson sathan chanit sanchao (pho so 2464) [Petition by Luang Phakdiphattrakon and his followers requesting the abolition of the Ministerial Regulations on Chinese Shrines, 1921/2].
21. Chaophraya Yommarat to Phraya Chakkraphani (22 February 1922) [NA.R.VI.N.1/46].
22. *Thi* 54/497 (23 March 1922) [NA.R.VI.N.1/46].
23. Huber to Devawongse (4 March 1922), in National Archives of Thailand, Ministry of Foreign Affairs (hereafter referred to as NA.KT.) 24/7: Phu thaen nana prathet song ruangrao chin nai bangkhap rong khatkhan kot senabodi ruang

sanchao, (pho.so. 2464–2466) [Foreign representatives send petitions submitted by the Chinese under their jurisdictions expressing objections to the ministerial regulations on Chinese shrines, 1921/22–1923/24]; and NA.R.VI.N.1/49.

24. Ruangrao chin mi chu 23 khon thung thut wilanda (4 March 1922) [NA.KT.24/7].
25. Devawongse to Chaophraya Yommarat (10 March 1922) [NA.KT.24/7]. It was later found that among the 23 Hakka Chinese calling themselves Netherland subjects, 2 were Siamese subjects, 1 was a Portuguese subject, and 5 were unknown, while the 5 Hakka who claimed themselves as Portuguese-protected persons, 3 were under Portuguese jurisdiction ("*nai bangkhap potuket*") and 2 were unknown. See Chaophraya Yommarat to Devawongse (7 April 1922) [NA.KT.24/7].
26. Geffredo Bovo to Devawongse (17 March 1922). The petition was seemingly dated 22 February 1922 [NA.KT.24/7; NA.R.VI.N.1/49].
27. Crosby to Traidos (25 March 1922) [NA.KT.24/7; NA.R.VI.N.1/49].
28. *Samnao thi* 22121 (17 March 1922) [NA.KT.24/7].
29. Devawongse to P.J. Schmidt (25 April 1922); Devawongse to Goffredo Bovo (25 April 1922); and Traidos to Crosby (26 April 1922) [NA.KT.24/7].
30. Traidos to Crosby (26 April 1922) [NA.KT.24/7].
31. *Chabap thi* 2125 (March 1922) and Fern Pila to Devawongse (6 May 1922) [NA.KT.24/7].
32. Crosby to Traidos (12 June 1922) [NA.KT.24/7].
33. *Chabap thi* 4227 (7 June 1922) [NA.KT.24/7].
34. Devawongse to Chaophraya Yommarat (16 June 1922) [NA.KT.24/7].
35. Chaophraya Yommarat to Devawongse (27 July 1922) [NA.KT.24/7].
36. Traidos to W. W. Coultas (21 August 1922) [NA.KT. 24/7].
37. Devawongse to M. Topenot (19 September 1922) [NA.KT.24/7].
38. Devawongse to Chaophraya Mahithon (31 May 1923) [NA.KT.24/7]. However, this was still not the end of the whole story. The Siamese government, alarmed by the issue of the Regulations possibly being *ultra vires* as suggested by the Chinese, started jurisprudence discussions regarding the matter [NA.R.IV.N.1/49].
39. This point was indicated in a petition submitted by Hutseng Sibunruang and four other Chinese to the king (30 March 1920) [NA.R.VI.N.25.1/1].
40. See, for instance, Liu Lifang 劉麗芳 and Mak Lau Fong 麥留芳, Mangu yu xinjiapo huaren miaoyu ji zongjiao xisu de diaocha 曼谷與新加坡華人廟宇及宗教習俗的調查 *MinzuxueYanjiusuo Ziliao Huibian* 民族學研究所資料彙編 9, Zhongyang yanjiuyuan minzuxue yanjiusuo 中央研究院民族學研究所 (Pornpan Juntaronanong and Mak Lau Fong, A Survey on Temples and Religious Practices of Ethnic Chinese in Bangkok and Singapore, *Field Materials Institute of Ethnology, Academia Sinica, Occasional Series*, No. 9, December 1994).
41. See, for instance, Wolfgang Franke 傅吾康主編 and Liu Lifang 劉麗芳合編 eds. *Taiguo huawen mingke huibian* 泰國華文銘刻彙編 [Chinese epigraphic materials in Thailand, collected, annotated and edited by Wolfgang Franke in

collaboration with Pornpan Juntaronanont, with the assistance of Hu Chün-Yin and Teo Lee Kheng], (Taibei 台北: Xinwenfeng chuban gongsi 新文豐出版公司, 1998); Ho Chuimei, "Chinese Temples in Bangkok: Sources of Data for 19th-Century Sino-Thai Communities", *The Journal of the Siam Society* 83, parts 1 and 2 (1995): 25–43; Duan Lisheng 段立生, *Taiguo de zhongshi simiao* 泰國的中式寺廟 [Chinese-styled temples and shrines in Thailand] (Bangkok 曼谷: Taiguo datongshe chuban youxian gongsi 泰國大同社出版有限公司, 1996).

References

Unpublished Archival Documents, National Archives of Thailand
Ministry of Foreign Affairs (Krasuang kantangprathet):
NA.KT. 24/7: Phu thaen nana prathet song ruangrao chin nai bangkhap rong khatkhan kot senabodi ruang sanchao (pho.so. 2464–2466) [Foreign representatives send petitions submitted by the Chinese under their jurisdictions expressing objections to the Ministerial Regulations on Chinese shrines, 1921/22–1923/24]

Ministry of Local Administration (Krasuang nakhonban), the Sixth Reign:
NA.R.VI.1/46: Dika luang phakdiphatthrakon kap phuak kho hai loek kot senabodi wa duai thi kuson sathan chanit sanchao (pho.so. 2464) [Petition by Luang Phakdiphattrakon and his followers requesting the abolition of the Ministerial Regulations on Chinese shrines, 1921/2]
NA.R.VI.N.1/49: Kammakan san dika kho phraratchathan phraborommaratchawinitchai nai ruang kot senabodi thi wa duai thi kuson sathan chanit sanchao (pho.so. 2466) [The Supreme Court Committee members seek royal judgment regarding the Ministerial Regulations on Chinese Shrines, 1923]
NA. R.VI. N.2/79: Ruang kot senabodi nakhonban wa duai sanchao (pho.so. 2463) [Regarding the Ministerial Regulations of the Ministry of Local Government on Chinese shrines, 1920/1]
NA.R.VI.N.25.1/1: Nai hong hi tanwetchakun kap phuak thun klao thawai dika kho phramahakaruna prot klao tang hai phraya chodukratchasetthi pen phu pokkhrong sanchao hok lian keng (pho.so. 2461–2462) [Mr. Hong Hi Tanwetchakun and his group submits a petition to the king requesting the appointment of Phraya Chodukratchasetthi as manager of Hok Lian Keng Shrine, 1918/9–1919/20]

Books and Articles
Bradley, D. B. *Nangsu akkharaphithansap, Dictionary of the Siamese Language*. Bangkok: Khurusapha Lat Phrao, 1971.
Duan, Lisheng 段立生. *Taiguo de zhongshi simiao* 泰國的中式寺廟 [Chinese-styled temples and shrines in Thailand]. Bangkok 曼谷: Taiguo datongshe chuban youxian gongsi 泰國大同社出版有限公司, 1996.

Franke, Wolfgang 傅吾康 (主編) and Liu Lifang 劉麗芳 (合編). eds. *Taiguo huawen mingke huibian* 泰國華文銘刻彙編 [Chinese epigraphic materials in Thailand, collected, annotated and edited by Wolfgang Franke in collaboration with Pornpan Juntaronanont, with the assistance of Hu Chün-Yin and Teo Lee Kheng]. Taibei 台北: Xinwenfeng chuban gongsi 新文豐出版公司, 1998.

Ho Chuimei. "Chinese Temples in Bangkok: Sources of Data for 19th-Century Sino-Thai Communities." *The Journal of the Siam Society* 83, parts 1 and 2 (1995): 25–43.

Krom kanpokkhrong, Krasuang mahatthai. (ed.) *Thamniap thabian sanchao thua ratcha-anachak* [Directory of registered Chinese shrines, whole kingdom]. Bangkok: n.p., n.d.

Lailak, Sathian et al. (ed.) *Prachum kotmai pracham sok* [Collected annual laws]. Bangkok: Nitiwet, 1935.

Liu Lifang 劉麗芳 and Mak Lau Fong 麥留芳, Mangu yu xinjiapo huaren miaoyu zongjiao xisu de diaocha 曼谷與新加坡華人廟宇及宗教習俗的調查 *MinzuxueYanjiusuo Ziliao Huibian* 民族學研究所資料彙編 9, Zhongyang yanjiuyuan minzuxue yanjiusuo 中央研究院民族學研究所, 1994 (Pornpan Juntaronanong and Mak Lau Fong, A Survey on Temples and Religious Practices of Ethnic Chinese in Bangkok and Singapore, *Field Materials Institute of Ethnology, Academia Sinica, Occasional Series*, No. 9, December 1994).

APPENDIX

PUBLICATIONS BY ANTHONY J. S. REID

A. MAJOR BOOKS AUTHORED

The Contest for North Sumatra: Atjeh, the Netherlands and Britain, 1858–1898. Kuala Lumpur, OUP/UMP, 1969. 333pp.
— reissued by University of Malaya Press, 1974.
— Indonesian translation by Masri Maris, Jakarta, Yayasan Obor, 2004

The Indonesian National Revolution, 1945–1950. Hawthorn, Vic. Longmans Australia, 1974. 193pp.
— reprinted by Greenwood Press, Westport, Conn., 1986.
— Indonesian translation Jakarta, Sinar Harapan, 1996.

The Blood of the People: Revolution and the End of Traditional Rule in Northern Sumatra. Kuala Lumpur, OUP, 1979. 288pp.
— Indonesian translation, Jakarta, Sinar Harapan, 1986.

Southeast Asia in the Age of Commerce, 1450–1680. Vol. I: *The Lands Below the Winds.* New Haven, Yale University Press, 1988. 275pp. [7th printing by 1999]
— Indonesian translation as *Asia Tenggara dalam Kurun Niaga,* trans. Mochtar Pabotinggi (Jakarta, Yayasan Obor, 1992).
— Southeast Asia edition Trasvin Publications [Silkworm Books], Chiang Mai, 1995, reprinted 1999.
— Japanese translation by Hirano Hideaki and Tanaka Yūko as *Daikōkai Jidai no Tōnan Ajia* I *Bōekifū no Shita de.* Tokyo: Hosei University Press, 1997.
— Thai translation by Dr Phongsri Lekawatana, Silkworm Books, Chiang Mai, for 5 Area Studies Project, 2004
— Chinese translation by Wu Xiao An and Sun Lai Chen, Beijing: The Commercial Press, 2010.
— Korean translation forthcoming from Simsan Munhwa Publishing Co.

Southeast Asia in the Age of Commerce, 1450–1680. Vol. II: *Expansion and Crisis.* New Haven, Yale University Press (1993). 390pp.
— Southeast Asia edition Chiang Mai, Trasvin Publications [Silkworm Books], 1995, 1999.
— Indonesian translation by R.Z. Leirissa (Jakarta: Yayasan Obor Indonesia, 1999).
— Japanese translation by Hirano Hideaki and Tanaka Yūko as *Daikōkai Jidai no Tōnan Ajia* II *Kakuchō to Kiki*. Tokyo: Hosei University Press, 2002.
— Thai translation by Dr Pongsri Lekawatana, Silkworm Books, Chiang Mai, 2004.
— Chinese translation by Sun Laichen and Li Tana, Beijing: The Commercial Press, 2010.
— Korean translation forthcoming from Simsan Munhwa Publishing Co.

Charting the Shape of Early Modern Southeast Asia. Chiang Mai: Silkworm Books, 1999, 298pp. Indonesian translation, Jakarta, LP3ES, 2004.

An Indonesian Frontier: Acehnese and Other Histories of Sumatra. Singapore: Singapore University Press, 2004; 439pp.
— reprinted 2005

Imperial Alchemy: Nationalism and Political Identity in Southeast Asia. Cambridge: Cambridge University Press, 2009. Xiii + 248pages.

To Nation by Revolution: Indonesia in the Twentieth Century, forthcoming with NUS Press.

B. BOOKS EDITED

Reid, Jubb & Jahmin, *Indonesian Serials, 1942–1950, in Yogyakarta Libraries.* Oriental Monograph Series 15. Canberra, Faculty of Asian Studies with ANU Press, 1974. 133pp.

Reid & Castles, *Pre-Colonial State Systems in Southeast Asia: the Malay Peninsula, Sumatra, Bali-Lombok, South Celebes.* Monograph 6 of Malaysian Branch of the Royal Asiatic Society, Kuala Lumpur, 1975.
— reprinted 1979.

Reid & Marr, *Perceptions of the Past in Southeast Asia.* Singapore, Heinemann for ASAA Southeast Asia Publications Series, 1979.
— reprinted 1983
— Indonesian translation as *Dari Raja Ali Haji Hingga Hamka*, Jakarta, Grafitipers, 1983.

Reid, *Slavery, Bondage and Dependency in Southeast Asia.* St Lucia, Queensland University Press, 1983.
— US edition New York, St Martin's Press, 1983.

Reid & Oki, *The Japanese Experience in Indonesia: Selected Memoirs of 1942–1945.* Athens, Ohio, Ohio University Center for International Studies, 1986. 411pp.

Snooks, Reid & Pincus, *Exploring Southeast Asia's Economic Past*, special issue of *Australian Economic History Review* 31, Pt. 1, 1991.

Reid, *Southeast Asia in the Early Modern Era: Trade, Power and Belief.* Ithaca, Cornell University Press, 1993. 286pp.

Reid, *The Making of an Islamic Political Discourse in Southeast Asia*, Melbourne, Monash University Centre for Southeast Asian Studies, 1993, 132pp.

Li & Reid, *Southern Vietnam under the Nguyen: Cochinchina in the Seventeenth and Eighteenth Centuries.* Singapore, ISEAS, 1993, 161pp.

Reid, *Witnesses to Sumatra: A Traveller's Anthology.* Singapore, OUP, 1994, 314pp.

Reid, *Sojourners and Settlers: Histories of Southeast Asia and the Chinese in Honour of Jennifer Cushman*, Sydney, Allen & Unwin, 1996, 232pp..
— North American edition Honolulu: University of Hawai'i Press, 2001, 216pp.
— Italian translation 2000

Reid, *Indonesia Heritage: Early Modern History.* Singapore: Archipelago Press, 1996, 148pp.

Reid, *The Last Stand of Asian Autonomies. Responses to Modernity in the Diverse States of Southeast Asia and Korea.* London, Macmillan, 1997, 458pp.

Chirot & Reid, *Essential Outsiders: Chinese and Jews in the Modern Transformation of Southeast Asia and Central Europe.* Seattle, University of Washington Press, 1997, 335pp.

Kelly & Reid, *Asian Freedoms: The Idea of Freedom in East and Southeast Asia*, Cambridge, Cambridge University Press, 1998. 228pp.

Reid, *Southeast Asian Studies: Pacific Perspectives*, Tempe, Az: Program in Southeast Asian Studies, Arizona State University, 2003; 375pp.

Reid, *Verandah of Violence: The Historical Background of the Aceh Problem*. Singapore: Singapore University Press, 2006; 397pp.

Reid, *Chinese Diaspora in the Pacific,* (Pacific World: Lands, Peoples and History of the Pacific, 1500–1900, no. 16) [Selected readings]. Aldershot, UK: Ashgate, July, 2008.

Reid, *Chineseness Unbound: Boundaries, Burdens and Belongings of Chineseness outside China*. Special issue in journal *Asian Ethnicity*, Vol. 10, no. 3 (October 2009)

C. MONOGRAPHS & PUBLISHED LECTURES

'Heaven's Will and Man's Fault': The Rise of the West as a Southeast Asian Dilemma. Flinders Asian Studies Lecture 6. Adelaide, Flinders University, 1975. 43pp.

Europe and Southeast Asia: The Military Balance. Townsville, James Cook University Southeast Asian Studies Committee, Occasional Paper 16, 1982. 11pp.

Reid & E. Drysdale, *AAUCS and AUIDP: A Survey of Resource Allocation 1969–1983*. Canberra, International Development Program of Australian Universities and Colleges, 1986. 57pp.

Helen Reid & Anthony Reid, *South Sulawesi*. Berkeley, Periplus Editions, 1988. 122 pp.

O'Hare & Reid, *Australia dan Perjuangan Kemerdekaan Indonesia: Australia and Indonesia's Struggle for Independence* [Indonesian/English], Jakarta, Gramedia for Australia-Indonesia Institute, 1995, 98pp. Reprinted Gramedia, 2005.

Approaching "Asia" from the Southeast: Does the Crisis Make a Difference?, Asian Studies Institute Inaugural Lecture, Wellington: Victoria University of Wellington Asian Studies Institute, 1998. 17pp.

Chinese and Malay Identities in Southeast Asia. PROSEA Research paper No.34. Taipei: Academia Sinica Program for Southeast Asian Studies, 2000.

Aceh and Indonesia: A Stormy Marriage, PROSEA Research paper No.42. Taipei: Academia Sinica Program for Southeast Asian Studies, 2001.

'War, Peace and the Burden of History in Aceh', *Asia Research Institute Working Paper* no. 1, June 2003, <www.ari.nus.edu.sg/publications>.

'Completing the Circle: Southeast Asian Studies in Southeast Asia', *Asia Research Institute Working Paper* no. 12, September 2003, <www.ari.nus.edu.sg/publications>.

'Cosmopolis and Nation in Central Southeast Asia', *Asia Research Institute Working Paper* no. 22, April 2004, <www.ari.nus.edu.sg/publications>.

'The Ottomans in Southeast Asia', *Asia Research Institute Working Paper* no. 36 (Feb 2005), <www.ari.nus.edu.sg/pub/wps2005.htm>.

(with Jiang Na) 'The Battle of the Microbes: Smallpox, Malaria and Cholera in Southeast Asia', *Asia Research Institute Working Paper* no. 62 (April 2006), <www.ari.nus.edu.sg/pub/wps2006.htm>

'Hybrid Identities in the Fifteenth Century Straits', *Asia Research Institute Working Paper* no. 67 (May 2006), <www.ari.nus.edu.sg/publications>.

'Is there a Batak History?' *Asia Research Institute Working Paper* no. 78 (Nov 2006), <www.ari.nus.edu.sg/publications>.

Malaysia/Singapore as Immigrant Societies: The Fifteenth James C. Jackson Memorial Lecture 2008 Armidale: The University of New England for the Malaysia and Singapore Society of Australia, 2008. 22 pages, ISBN 1 921208 34 1.
— Also distributed as Asia Research Institute Working Paper no. 141 (July 2010), <http://www.ari.nus.edu.sg/publication_details.asp?pubtypeid=WP&pubid=1625>.

World History for our Time and Place: The Historian's Contemporary Responsibility, Global History and Maritime Asia Working and Discussion Paper no. 13 (November 2009), Osaka University, Osaka.

D. CHAPTERS IN BOOKS

1970   'Early Chinese Migration into North Sumatra', in *Studies in the Social History of China and Southeast Asia. Essays in Memory of Victor Purcell*, ed. Jerome Ch'en and Nicholas Tarling. Cambridge University Press, 1970, 289–320.

1973   'Some current and projected Southeast Asian research needs', in *Symposium on Southeast Asian Library Resources*. Canberra, The Library, ANU, 36–40.

1975   'Trade and the Problem of Royal Power in Aceh, c.1550–1700', in Reid & Castles 1975 (see B. above), 45–55.

1979 'Indonesia: From Briefcase to Samurai Sword', in *Southeast Asia under Japanese Occupation,* ed. A.W. McCoy. New Haven, Yale University Southeast Asia Studies Monograph Series 22, 16–32.

'The Nationalist Quest for an Indonesian Past', in Reid & Marr, 1979 (see B. above), 281–98.

'Trade and State Power in Sixteenth and Seventeenth Century Southeast Asia', in *Proceedings, Seventh IAHA Conference, 22–26 August 1977,* Bangkok, International Association of Historians of Asia, 391–419.

1981 'The origins of poverty in Indonesia', in *Indonesia-Australian Perspectives,* ed. J.J. Fox, J.A.C. Mackie & Peter McCawley. Canberra, RSPacS, ANU, 441–54.

'Indonesia: Revolution without Socialism', in *Asia — The Winning of Independence,* ed. R. Jeffrey (London/Basingstoke, Macmillan, 1981) 107–57.

1983 'Introduction: Slavery and Bondage in Southeast Asian History', in Reid, 1983 (see B. above), 1–43.

'"Closed" and "Open" Slave Systems in Pre-Colonial Southeast Asia', in Reid, 1983 (see B. above), 156–87.

1984 'The Islamization of Southeast Asia', in *Historia: Essays in Commemoration of the 25th Anniversary of the Department of History, University of Malaya,* ed. Muhammad Abu Bakar et al. Kuala Lumpur, Malaysian Historical Society, 13–33.

1985 (Ito & Reid), 'From Harbour Autocracies to "Feudal" Diffusion in Seventeenth Century Indonesia: The Case of Aceh', in *Feudalism: Comparative Studies,* ed. Edmund Leach, S.N. Mukherjee and John Ward. Sydney, Sydney Association for Studies in Society and Culture, 197–213.

'Trade Goods and Trade Routes in Southeast Asia, c.1300–1700', in *Final Report. Consultative Workshop on Research on Maritime Shipping and Trade Networks in Southeast Asia.* Bangkok, SPAFA Coordinating Unit, 249–72.

1986 'Australia's Hundred Days in South Sulawesi', in *Nineteenth and Twentieth Century Indonesia: Essays in Honour of J.D. Legge,* ed. D.G. Chandler & M.C. Ricklefs. Clayton, Vic., Monash University Centre of Southeast Asian Studies, 201–24.

'The Revolution in Regional Perspective', in *The Indonesian Revolution*, ed. J. van Goor (Utrecht, Utrechtse Historische Cahiers, Jrg. 7, 1986), pp. 183–199.

'Fase Kedua: Kemenangan Terachir, Juli 1947 sampai 1950 [Second Phase: Final Victory July 1947 to 1950]', in *Gelora Api Revolusi: Sebuah Antologi Sejarah*, ed. C. Wild & P. Carey. Jakarta, Gramedia, 181-87.

1987 'Low Population Growth and its Causes in Pre-Colonial Southeast Asia', in *Death and Disease in Southeast Asia: Explorations in Social, Medical, and Demographic History*, ed. Norman Owen. Singapore, OUP for ASAA Southeast Asia Publications Series, 33–47.

1988 'The Identity of "Sumatra" in History', in *Cultures and Societies of North Sumatra*, ed. R. Carle. Berlin, Dietrich Reimer Verlag, 25–42.

'The Victory of the Republic', in *Born in Fire: The Indonesian Struggle for Independence*, An Anthology, ed. C. Wild & P. Carey. Athens, Ohio, Ohio University Press, 178–83.

1989 'The Organization of Production in the Pre-Colonial Southeast Asian Port City', in *Brides of the Sea: Asian Port Cities in the Colonial Era*, ed. P. Broeze. Sydney, University of NSW Press for ASAA, 54–74.

(Brewster & Reid), 'A.W. Hamilton and the Origins of Indonesian Studies in Australia', in *Observing Change in Asia: Essays in Honour of J.A.C. Mackie*, ed. R.J. May & W.J. O'Malley. Bathurst, Crawford House Press, 22–32.

1990 'Dutch Hegemony', 32-5; 'Independence', 36-7; 'Old Makassar', 66-7; 'Ujung Pandang', 68-73; 'Sidetrips from U.P.', 74-9; 'West Coast', 90-1; 'South Coast', 94-9; 'Selayar Island', 100-01; 'Bone and Soppeng', 102-5; 'Luwu', 106-9, all in *Sulawesi: The Celebes*, ed. Toby Volkman and Ian Caldwell (Berkeley, Periplus, 1990).

'A Portrait of Sumatra', in *Indonesia West: Sumatra, Java, Bali, Lombok*, n.p., Robertson McCarta/Nelles Verlag, 1990, pp. 61–73.

"Islamic Kingdoms", pp. 34–37; "Impact of the West", pp. 38–41; and "Modern History", pp. 42–43; in Indonesia Travel Guide: Sumatra, ed. Sindhu Suyana (Berkeley, Periplus, 1991).

1992 'Indonesian Fishermen detained in Broome: A Report on the Social and Economic Background', in *Illegal Entry!* (Darwin, Centre for Southeast Asian Studies, Northern Territory University, 1992), pp. 1–12.

'The Rise and Fall of Sino-Javanese Shipping', in *Looking in Odd Mirrors: The Java Sea,* ed. V.J.H. Houben, H.M.J. Maier and W. van der Molen. Leiden: Leiden University Department of Southeast Asian Studies, pp. 177–211.

'Economic and Social Change, c.1500–1750', in *Cambridge History of Southeast Asia,* ed. Nicholas Tarling, 2 vols. Cambridge, Cambridge University Press (1992), I, pp. 460–507. Chinese translation 2002.

'Southeast Asia: A Region and a Crossroad', in *Cultures at Crossroads: Southeast Asian Textiles from the Australian National Gallery,* Canberra, Australian National Gallery, 1992, pp. 8–17.

'Some Effects on Asian Economies of the European Maritime Discoveries', in *Economic Effects of the European Expansion, 1492–1824* ed. Jose Casas Pardo, Beitrage zur Wirtschafts- und Sozialgeschichte (Stuttgart, Franz Steiner Verlag), pp. 435–62.

1993 'Introduction: A Time and a Place', in Reid, *Southeast Asia in the Early Modern Era* (Ithaca, Cornell U.P., 1993), pp. 1–19.

'Islamization and Christianization in Southeast Asia: The Critical Phase, 1550–1650', in Reid, *Southeast Asia in the Early Modern Era* (Ithaca, Cornell U.P.), pp.151-79.

'Introduction' in Reid (ed.), *The Making of an Islamic Political Discourse in Southeast Asia* (Monash Papers on Southeast Asia, 1993), pp. 1–15.

'Kings, Kadis and Charisma in the 17th Century Archipelago', in Reid (ed.), *The Making of an Islamic Political Discourse in Southeast Asia* (Monash Papers on Southeast Asia, 1993), pp. 83–107.

'The Origins of Revenue Farming in Southeast Asia', in *The Rise and Fall of Revenue Farming: Business Elites and the Emergence of the Modern State in Southeast Asia,* ed. H. Dick and J. Butcher, London, Macmillan, 1993, pp. 69–79.

[Li Tana & Reid], 'Introduction: The Vietnamese Southern Frontier', in Li & Reid 1993 [see above], pp. 1–5.

'The End of Dutch Relations with the Nguyen State, 1651–52', in ibid. pp. 33–37.

[Anne Booth & Reid], 'Trade and Economic Growth in Southeast Asia, 1400–1990', in *Economic Growth and Structural Change. Comparative Approaches over the Long Run on the Basis of Reconstructed National Accounts.* Research Paper: 93.02, Centrum voor Economische Studies, Katholieke Universiteit Leuven, 1993, 13pp.

'The Decline of Slavery in Nineteenth Century Indonesia', in *Breaking the Chains: Slavery, Bondage and Emancipation in Modern Africa and Asia,* ed. Martin Klein (Madison, University of Wisconsin Press, 1993), pp. 64–82.

'John Smail, J.C. van Leur, and the Trading World of Southeast Asia', in *Autonomous Histories, Particular Truths: Essays in Honor of John Smail,* ed. Laurie Sears, Madison, University of Wisconsin-Madison, The Center for Southeast Asian Studies, pp. 87–97.

1994 "Afterword", in *Democracy in Indonesia: 1950s and 1990s,* ed. David Bourchier and John Legge. (Melbourne, Monash University Centre of Southeast Asian Studies, 1994) pp. 313–18.

'Early Southeast Asian Categorizations of Europeans', in *Implicit Ethnographies: Encounters between Europeans and Other Peoples in the Wake of Columbus,* ed. Stuart Schwarz, New York, Cambridge University Press, 1994, pp. 268–94.

[Anne Booth & Reid], 'Population, Trade and Economic Growth in Southeast Asia in the Long-term: An Exploratory Analysis', in *Economic Growth and Structural Change. Comparative Approaches over the Long Run,* ed. Angus Maddison and Hermann Van der Wee. Volume B13 in Proceedings, Eleventh International Economic History Congress, Milan: Universita Bocconi, 1994, pp. 9–21.

1995 "Recent Trends and Future Directions in Southeast Asian Studies (Outside Southeast Asia)", in *Toward the Promotion of Southeast Asian Studies in Southeast Asia,* ed. Taufik Abdullah and Yekti Maunati, Jakarta: Indonesian Institute of Sciences, 1994, pp. 256–76.

1996 'Flows and Seepages in the Long-term Chinese Interaction with Southeast Asia', in Reid (ed), *Sojourners and Settlers* (1995), pp. 15–49.

"Chains of Steel; Chains of Silver: Forcing politics on geography, 1865–1965", in *Historical Foundations of A National Economy in Indonesia, 1890s–1990s,* ed. Thomas Lindblad. Amsterdam: North-Holland for Royal Netherlands Academy of Arts and Sciences, 1996, pp. 281–96. Indonesian translation 2002.

"Continuity and Change in the Austronesian Transition to Islam and Christianity", in *The Austronesians: Historical and Comparative Perspectives*, ed. Peter Bellwood, James J. Fox and Darrell Tryon. Canberra, ANU Department of Anthropology, pp. 314–31.

1997 'Introduction', in Reid (ed), *The Last Stand of Asian Autonomies* (above), pp. 1–25.

'A New Phase of Commercial Expansion in Southeast Asia', in Reid (ed), *The Last Stand of Asian Autonomies* (above), pp. 57–82.

'Merchant Imperialist: W.H. Read and the Dutch Consulate in the Straits Settlements', in *Empires, Imperialism and Southeast Asia: Essays in Honour of Nicholas Tarling*, ed. Brook Barrington. Clayton, Vic.: Monash Asia Institute, 1997), pp. 34–59.

Chapter 2. 'Entrepreneurial Minorities, Nationalism and the State', in *Essential Outsiders*, ed. Daniel Chirot and Anthony Reid (above), pp. 33–71.

Chapter 5. "Humans and Forests in Pre-colonial Southeast Asia", in *Nature and the Orient: The Environmental History of South and Southeast Asia*, ed. Richard Grove, Vinita Damoidaran & Satpal Sangwan. Delhi: Oxford University Press, 1997, pp. 107–26

'Anthony Hearle Johns: a vocation', in *Islam: Essays on Scripture, Thought and Society. A Festschrift in Honour of Anthony H. Johns*, ed. Peter Riddell and Tony Street. Leiden: Brill, 1997, pp. xix–xxxiii

1998 'Inside-Out: the Colonial Displacement of Sumatra's Population', in *Paper Landscapes: Essays in the Environmental History of Indonesia*, ed. Peter Boomgaard, Freek Columbijn and David Henley. Leiden: KITLV Press, 1998, pp. 61–89.

'Four Key Exports and the Trade Cycle of Southeast Asia', in Bulbeck, Reid et al, *Southeast Asian Exports since the 14th Century* (above), pp. 1–16.

'Cloves', pp. 17–21, and 'Pepper', pp. 60–69', in ibid.

'Merdeka: The Concept of Freedom in Indonesia', in Kelly & Reid (eds) *Asian Freedoms* (above), pp. 141–60.

'Globalization and the Asian Cultural Dimension', pp. 44–47 (Japanese) and 130–33 (English); and 'In Search of a New International Order', pp. 86–89 (Japanese) and 167–69 (English), in *International Forum: Asia--Looking to the Future* (Osaka: Osaka International House Foundation, 1998).

'National and Ethnic Identities in a Democratic Age: Some Thoughts of a Southeast Asian Historian', in *Religion, Ethnicity and Modernity in Southeast Asia*, ed. Oh Myung-Seok and Kim Hyung-jun. Seoul, Seoul National University Press, 1998, pp. 11–43.

'Explorings and Reflections on Southeast Asian History', in *Our Cultural Heritage*, ed. John Bigelow. Papers from the 1997 Symposium of the Australian Academy of the Humanities. Canberra: Australian Academy of the Humanities, 1998, pp. 179–82. ISBN 0-909897-42-5.

'Documenting the Rise and Fall of Indonesia as a Regional Trade Centre', in *Proceedings for the International Workshop, Ayudhya and Asia, 18–20 December 1995*, ed. Kajit Jittasevi. Bangkok: Printing House of Thammasat University, n.d. [1998?], pp. 5–15. ISBN 974-572-591-9.

1999 [in Japanese], 'Komento III Ajia no bōeki nettowāku [Comment III Trading networks of Asia]' translated by Kanda Sayako in *Kindai Ajia no Ryūtsū Nettowaku*, ed. S. Sugiyama and Linda Grove. Tokyo: Sobunsha, 1999, pp. 316–21.

Sections of panel discussion, 'Japan as a Maritime Nation — from the Past to the Future', 29.7.1999, published in International Ocean Symposium '99: The Ocean, Can She Save Us? at pp. 116–39 (Japanese) and 252–76.

2000 '*Negeri*: The Culture of Malay-speaking City-States of the Fifteenth and Sixteenth Centuries', in *A Comparative Study of Thirty City-State Cultures* ed. Mogens Herman Hansen. Copenhagen: The Royal Danish Academy of Sciences and Letters, 2000, pp. 417–29.

'The Effect of Violence on Two Sino-Southeast Asian Minorities', in *Intercultural Relations, Cultural Transformation, and Identity: Selected Papers presented at the 1998 ISSCO Conference*', ed. Teresita Ang See. Manila: Kaisa Para Sa Kaunlaran, Inc, 2000, pp. 413–30.

'Five Centuries: Five Modalities. European Interaction with Southeast Asia, 1497–1997', in *Vasco da Gama and the Linking of Europe and Asia*, ed. Anthony Disney. New Delhi: Oxford University Press, 2000, pp. 168–78.

'Professor Denys Lombard: A Tribute', in ibid., pp. 8–10.

'Pluralism and progress in seventeenth-century Makasar', in *Authority and Enterprise: Transactions, Traditions and Texts among the Bugis, Makasarese and Selayarese*, ed. C. van Dijk and Roger Tol, Leiden, KITLV Press, 2000, pp. 55–71. Simultaneously published in *Bijdragen tot de Taal-, Land-. en Volkenkunde* 156, no. 3 (2000), pp. 433–49.

— Indonesian translation as 'Pluralisme dan Kemajuan Makassar Abad ke-17', in *Kuasa dan Usaha di Masyarakat Sulawesi Selatan,* ed. Roger Tol, C. van Dijk and Greg Acciaioli (Jakarta: Ininnawa, 2009), pp. 73–94

2001 'Southeast Asian Population History and the Colonial Impact', in *Asian Population History*, ed. Ts'ui-jung Liu, James Lee, David Reher, Osamu Saito and Wang Feng. Oxford: Oxford University Press, pp. 45–62.

'Asian Trade Networks', in *Commercial Networks in Modern Asia*, ed. S. Sugiyama and Linda Grove (Richmond: Curzon, 2001) pp. 261–64.

'"Outsider" Status and Economic Success', in *Perspectives on the Chinese Indonesians,* ed. Michael Godley and Grayson Lloyd. Adelaide: Crawford House Publishing, 2001, pp. 67–82.

2002 'Island of the Dead: Why do Bataks erect Tugu?', in *The Potent Dead*, ed. Chambert-Loir & Reid, 2002 (above), pp. 88–102. Indonesian translation in *Kuasa Leluhur,* 2006 (above)

2003 'Technology and Language: Negotiating the Third Revolution in the Use of Language', in *Babel or Behemoth: Language Trends in Asia*, ed. Jennifer Lindsay and Tan Ying Ying (Singapore: Asia Research Institute, 2003), pp. 11–20. Indonesian translation as 'Teknologi dan Bahasa: Menyiasati Revolusi Ketiga dalam Penggunaan Bahasa' in *Selarong: Merekam Pemikiran dan Ekspresi Kebudayaan* (Bantul, Yogyakarta), Vol. 6, year 3 (2006), pp. 127–37.

'Globalization, Asian Diasporas and the Study of Southeast Asia in the West: A Changing Perspective from California', in *Asian Migrants and Education: The Tensions of Education in Immigrant Societies and Among Migrant Groups*, ed. Michael Charney, Brenda Yeoh and Tong Chee Kiong (Dordrecht: Kluwer Academic Publishers, 2003), pp. 15–26.

'Southeast Asian Studies: Decline or Rebirth', in *Southeast Asian Studies: Pacific Perspectives*, ed. Reid [above], pp. 1–23.

Reid and Maria Serena I. Diokno, 'Completing the Circle: Southeast Asian Studies in Southeast Asia', in *Southeast Asian Studies: Pacific Perspectives*, ed. Reid [above], pp. 93–107.

2004 'Understanding *Melayu* (Malay) as a Source of Diverse Modern Identities', in *Contesting Malayness: Malay Identity Across Boundaries*, ed. Timothy Barnard (Singapore: Singapore University Press), pp. 1–24.

'Chinese Trade and Southeast Asian Economic Expansion in the Later Eighteenth and Early Nineteenth Centuries: An Overview', in *Water Frontier: Commerce and The Chinese in the Lower Mekong Region, 1750–1880*, ed. Nola Cooke and Li Tana (Lanham, MD: Rowman & Littlefield, and Singapore: Singapore University Press, 2004), pp. 21–34

2005 'Remembering and Forgetting War and Revolution', in *Beginning to Remember: The Past in the Indonesian Present*, ed. Mary Zurbuchen, Geoffrey Robinson and Henk Maier (Singapore: Singapore University Press in association with University of Washington Press, 2005), pp. 168–91.

'Writing the History of Independent Indonesia', in *Nation-Building: Five Southeast Asian Histories*, ed. Wang Gungwu (Singapore: ISEAS, 2005), pp. 69–89.

'Diaspora Networks in the Asian Maritime Context', in *Diaspora Entrepreneurial Networks: Four Centuries of History* ed. Ina Baghdiantiz McCabe, Gelina Herlaftis & Ionna Pepelasis Minoglou (Oxford: Berg, 2005), pp. 353-8.

'Regional Networks of Knowledge in Eastern Asia: Interrupted Histories', in *The Harmony and Prosperity of Civilizations. Selected Papers of the Beijing Forum (2004)*. Beijing: Peking University Press, 2005, pp. 235–46.

2006 'Chapter 1: Introduction', in *Verandah of Violence: The Background to the Aceh Problem*, ed. Anthony Reid (Singapore: Singapore University Press, 2006), pp. 1–21

'Chapter 3: The Pre-modern Sultanate's View of its Place in the World', in ibid., pp. 52–71.

'Chapter 6: Colonial transformation: A bitter legacy', in ibid., pp. 96–108.

[Nhung Tuyet Tran and Reid], 'Introduction: The Construction of Vietnamese Historical Identities', in *Viet Nam: Borderless Histories*, ed. Nhung Tuyet Tran and Anthony Reid. Madison: University of Wisconsin Press, 2006), *ibid.* pp. 3–22.

2007 'Aceh between Two Worlds', in *Cross Currents and Community Networks: The History of the Indian Ocean World*, ed. Himanshu Ray and Edward A. Alpers (New Delhi: OUP, 2007), pp. 100–22. ISBN-13: 978-0-19-567705-8.

'Indonesia's Post-Revolutionary Aversion to Federalism', in *Federalism in Asia*, ed. Baogang He, Brian Galligan and Takashi Inoguchi, Cheltenham,UK and Northampton MA: Edward Elgar Publishers, 2007, pp. 144–64.

'Introduction: Muslims and Power in a Plural Asia', in *Islamic Legitimacy in a Plural Asia*, ed. Anthony Reid and Michael Gilsenan, Abingdon: Routledge, 2007, pp. 1–13.

'Onghokham Memories', in *Onze Ong: Onghokham dalam kenangan*, ed. David Reeve, JJ Rizal, Wasmi Alhaziri, Jakarta: Komunitas Bambu, 2007, pp. 33–35.

2008 'A Plural Peninsula', in *Thai South and Malay North: Ethnic Interactions on a Plural Peninsula*, ed. Michael Montesano and Patrick Jory. Singapore: NUS Press, 2008, pp. 25–38.

'Introduction', in *Chinese Diaspora in the Pacific* (Pacific World: Lands, Peoples and History of the Pacific, 1500–1900, No. 16, ed. Anthony Reid. Aldershot, UK: Ashgate, 2008, pp. xv–xxxiv.

'The Bandung Conference and Southeast Asian regionalism', in See Seng Tan and Amitav Acharya (eds), *Bandung Revisited: A Conference's Legacy and Relevance for International Order*. Singapore: NUS Press, 2008, pp. 19–26.

2009 'Introduction: Negotiating Asymmetry', in *Negotiating Asymmetry: China's Place in Asia*, ed. Anthony Reid and Zheng Yangwen (Singapore: NUS Press, 2009), pp. 1–25.

'Indonesia, Aceh and the Modern Nation-state', in *The Politics of the Periphery in Indonesia: Geographical and Social Perspectives*, ed. Minako Sakai, Glenn Banks and John Walker. Singapore: NUS Press, 2009, pp. 84–100.

[With Charles MacDonald], 'Introduction', in *Personal Names in Asia: History, Culture and Identity*, ed. Zheng Yangwen and Charles Macdonald, NUS Press. pp. 1–18.

'Family Names in Southeast Asian History', in *ibid.* pp. 21–36.

'Is there a Batak History?' in *From Distant Tales. Archaeology and Ethnohistory in the Highlands of Sumatra*, ed. Dominick Bonatz, John Miksic, J. David Neidel and Mei-lin Bonatz, Cambridge: Cambridge Scholars Publishing, 2009, pp. 104–19.

'Southeast Asian consumption of British and Indian cotton cloth, 1600–1850', in *How India Clothed the World: The World of South Asian Textiles, 1500–1850*. Ed. Om Prakash, Giorgio Riello, Tirthankar Roy, and Kaoru Sugihara. The Hague: Brill, 2009, pp. 31–52. ISBN 978 90 04 17653 9 <http://www.lse.ac.uk/collections/economicHistory/GEHN/GEHNPDF/PUNEReid.pdf>.

2010 'Revolutionary State Formation and the Unitary Republic of Indonesia', in *Multination States in Asia: Accommodation or Resistance*, ed. Jacques Bertrand and André La Liberté (Cambridge: Cambridge University Press, 2010), pp. 29–50.

'Hybrid Identities in the Fifteenth Century Straits', in *The Fifteenth Century in Southeast Asia: The Ming Factor*, ed. Geoff Wade and Sun Laichen (Singapore: NUS Press, 2010), pp. 307–32. ISBN 978-9971-69-448-7 paper). Also Hong Kong, Hong Kong University Press.

'Violence at Sea: Unpacking "Piracy" in the Claims of States over Asian Seas', in *Pirates, Pervasive Smugglers: Violence and Clandestine Trade in the Greater China Seas*, ed. Robert J. Anthony (Hong Kong: Hong Kong University Press, 2010), pp. 15–26. ISBN 978-988-8028-11-5

Chapter 12: 'Islam in Southeast Asia and the Indian Ocean Littoral, 1500–1800: Expansion, Polarization, Synthesis', in *The New Cambridge History of Islam*, Vol. 3: *The Eastern Islamic World, Eleventh to Eighteenth Centuries*. ed. David Morgan and Anthony Reid (Cambridge: 2010), pp. 427–69. ISBN 978-0-521-85031-5.

(with David Morgan), 'Introduction: Islam in a Plural Asia, 1200–1800', in David Morgan and Reid (eds.), *The New Cambridge History of Islam*, Vol. 3: *The Eastern Islamic World, Eleventh to Eighteenth Centuries*. Cambridge: Cambridge University Press, 2010, pp. 1–18. ISBN 978-0-521-85031-5,

'Singapore between Cosmopolis and Nation', in *Singapore from Temasek to the 21st Century: Reinventing the Global City*, ed. Karl Hack and Jean Louis Margolin, with Karine Delaye (Singapore: National University of Singapore Press, forthcoming 2010), pp. 37–54. ISBN 978-9971-69-515-6.

'Aceh and the Turkish Connection', in *ACEH: History, Politics and Culture*, ed. Arndt Graf, Susanne Schröter and Edwin Wieringa (Singapore: ISEAS, 2010), pp. 26–38. ISBN978-981-4279-12-3.

Annotations for chapters 21–32 in *Fernão Mendes Pinto and the Peregrinação: Studies, Restored Portuguese Text, Notes and Indexes*, Directed by Jorge Santos Alves (Lisbon: Fundação Oriente, 2010), Vol. III, pp. 61–74.

F. INTRODUCTIONS AND PREFACES TO BOOKS

'Introduction' to reprint of John Anderson, *Acheen* (1840), Kuala Lumpur, OUP, 1971, v–xvi.

'On the Importance of Autobiography', in special issue on Indonesian autobiographies, *Indonesia* 13 (April 1972), 1–3.

'Introduction' to reprint of Ladislao Szekely, *Tropic Fever. The Adventures of a Planter in Sumatra* (1936), Kuala Lumpur, OUP, 1979, v–xv.

'Preface' to Wang Gungwu, *Community and Nation: Essays on Southeast Asia and the Chinese*. Singapore, Heinemann for ASAA, 1981, vii–viii.

'Foreward' to reprint of Madelon Szekely-Lulofs, *Coolie* (1936). Kuala Lumpur, OUP, 1982, v–vii.

'Introduction' to reprint of Johan Nieuhof, *Voyages and Travels to the East Indies 1653–1670* (1703). Kuala Lumpur, OUP, 1988, v–ix.

'Preface', to *Chinese Economic Activity in Netherlands India: Selected Translations from the Dutch*, ed. M.R. Fernando and David Bulbeck, Singapore, ISEAS for ECHOSEA, 1992, pp. xi–xii.

'Preface', to Scot Barmé, *Luang Wichit Wathakan and the creation of a Thai Identity*. Singapore, ISEAS, 1993, pp. ix–x.

'Preface', to *The Junk Trade from Southeast Asia: Translations from the Tosen Fusetsugaki, 1674–1723*, ed. Yoneo Ishii, Singapore: ISEAS for ECHOSEA, 1998.

'Preface' to *Imagining the Chinese Diaspora: Two Australian Perspectives*, by Wang Gungwu and Annette Shun Wah. Canberra: CSCSD, ANU, 1999. Pp. 2–3.

'Preface', pp. vii–viii, in *The Imperial Archives of the Nguyen Dynasty, the Sixth and Seventh Years of Minh Mang Reign (1825–1826), tomes 11–20*, ed. Phan Huy Le. Ha Noi: The Gioi Publishers, 2000, 790pp.

'Preface', pp. v–vi, to Amitav Acharya, *The Quest for Identity: International Relations of Southeast Asia*. New York: Oxford University Press, 2000.

'Preface: Asian Studies in Asia', in *The Directory of Asian Studies in Asia: A summary of reports presented at the 'Asian Studies in Asia' Workshop, held in Hua Hin, April, 1998*. Canberra: ASAA, 2000, pp. 5–9. ISBN 0 909524 42 4.

'Preface' to *Asian Travel in the Renaissance*, ed. Daniel Carey (Oxford: Blackwell, 2004), pp. ix–x.

G. JOURNAL ARTICLES

1961   "Church & State in New Zealand", *Student* (Wellington, c. Aug. 1961)

1964   'The Economic Background to Indonesia's "Confrontation"', *Political Science* (Wellington) 16: 2, 3–6.

1966   'A Russian in Kelantan?', *Peninjau Sejarah* (Kuala Lumpur) I: 2, 42–47.

1967   'Nineteenth Century Pan-Islam in Indonesia and Malaysia', *Journal of Asian Studies* 26: 2, 267–83. Indonesian translation in *Kekacuan dan Kerusuhan: Tiga Tulisan tentang Pan-Islamisme di Hindi-Belanda Timor pada Akhir Abad Kesembilan Belas dan Awal Abad Kedua Puluh*, ed. Nico Kapten (Leiden/Jakarta: INIS, 2003).

"The Agony of Indonesia", in *Opinion* (Kuala Lumpur), I, ii (Sept. 1967), pp. 24–26.

1968   'Tengku Mohamed Arifin — Envoy Extraordinary', *Peninjau Sejarah* III: 2, 31–40.

'Gestapu: A Hesitant Assessment', *Journal of the Historical Society, University of Malaya* VI (1968) 97–104.

1969   'Sixteenth Century Turkish Influence in Western Indonesia', *Journal of Southeast Asian History* X: 3, 395–414. Reprinted in *Profiles of Malay*

Culture: Historiography, Religion and Politics, ed. Sartono Kartodirdjo, Jakarta: Ministry of Education, 1976.

'Indonesian Diplomacy. A Documentary Study of Atjehnese Foreign Policy in the Reign of Sultan Mahmud, 1870–1874', *Journal of the Malaysian Branch, Royal Asiatic Society* 42 Part 2, 74–114. Indonesian translation incorporated in *Surat-Surat Lepas yang berhubungan dengan Politik Luar Negeri Kerajaan Aceh menjelang Perang Belanda di Aceh*, ed. Aboe Bakar, Banda Aceh: Pusat Dokumentasi dan Informasi Aceh, 1982.

'The Kuala Lumpur Riots and the Malaysian Political System', *Australian Outlook* 23: 3, 258–78.

"Atjeh — a Sultanate that Gained Special Status", in *Hemisphere* (Canberra) 13, no. 5 (May 1969), pp. 34–37.

1971 'The Birth of the Republic in Sumatra', *Indonesia* (Ithaca) 12, 21–46.

"Towards a New Indonesian History", *Hemisphere* 15, no. 9 (Sept 1971), pp. 34–37.

1972 'Habib Abdur-rahman az-Zahir (1833–1890)' (edited translation from Dutch), *Indonesia* 13 (April 1972), 37–60.

'The Affair of the Tjumbok Traitors' (edited translation of Indonesian text by Abdullah Arif), *Review of Indonesian and Malayan Affairs* 4/5, 29–65.

1973 'The French in Sumatra and the Malay World 1760–1890', in *Bijdragen tot de Taal-, Land- en Volkenkunde* (Leiden) 129, Parts 2/3, 195–238.

'The Catholics of Indonesia', *Catholic Worker* 439 (June 1973), 10–12.

1974 'Marxist Attitudes to Social Revolution, 1946–1948', *Review of Indonesian and Malayan Affairs* 8, i, 45–56.

1975 'The Japanese and Rival Indonesian Elites: Northern Sumatra in 1942', *Journal of Asian Studies* 35: 1, 49–61.

1976 (with Shiraishi Saya), 'Rural Unrest in Sumatra, 1942: A Japanese Report', *Indonesia* 21 (April 1976), 115–33.

'The Asian Studies Association of Australia', *NZASIAN* (Auckland), No. 3, pp. 30–31.

1977 'Sukarno and the nature of Indonesian political society: a review of the literature', *New Zealand Journal of History* 11, Part 1, 76–83.

'Relating to Asia', *ASAA Review* 1, no. 2 (Nov. 1977), pp. 1–4.

'La Structure des Villes du Sud-est Asiatique (XVIeme-XVIIeme siècles)' in *Urbi* (Paris) 1 (October 1979).

1980 'The Structure of Cities in Southeast Asia, 15th to 17th Centuries', *Journal of Southeast Asian Studies* XI: 2, 235–50.
— reprinted in *European Intruders and Changes in Behaviour and Customs in Africa, America and Asia before 1800*, ed. Murdo J. MacLeod and Evelyn S. Rawski. Variorum Expanding World Series, Vol. 30 (Aldershot/Brookfield/Singapore/Sydney: Ashgate, 1998), pp. 347–62.

1981 '"Alterity" and "Reformism": the Australian frontier in Indonesian studies', *Archipel* 21, 7–18.

'A Great Seventeenth Century Indonesian Family: Matoaya and Pattingalloang of Makassar', *Masyarakat Indonesia* 8: 1, 1–28.

'Karaeng Matoaya dan Karaeng Pattingalloang: pelopor-pelopor pembangunan di abad Ketujuhbelas', *Lontara* (Ujung Pandang) 21: 7, 22–30.

'Social Revolution — National Revolution', *Prisma: The Indonesian Indicator* 23, December 1981, 64–72.

1983 'The Rise of Makassar', *Review of Indonesian and Malaysian Affairs*, Winter/Summer 1983, 117–60.

1984 'The Pre-Colonial Economy of Indonesia', *Bulletin of Indonesian Economic Studies* 20: 2, August 1984, 151–67.

'Southeast Asian Cities before Colonialism', *Hemisphere* 28, Nov./Dec. 1983, 144–49.

'Islamization and Colonial Rule in Moroland: Some Common Responses to the Introduction of New Cultures in East Indonesia and the Philippines', *Solidarity* (Manila) 100, 64–74.

1985 'From Betel Chewing to Tobacco Smoking in Indonesia', *Journal of Asian Studies* 44, iii, 529–48.
— reprinted 1998, see section E

1987   'Southeast Asia and the "Indian Ocean" Enterprise', *ASAA Review* 11, 1, 4–6.

1988   'Female Roles in Pre-Colonial Southeast Asia', in *Asian Studies in Honour of Professor C.R. Boxer*, ed. Geneviève Bouchon and Pierre-Yves Manguin, *Modern Asian Studies* 22: 3 (1988), 629–65.
— reprinted 1998, see section E

1989   'Elephants and Water in the Feasting of Seventeenth Century Acheh', *Journal of the Malaysian Branch, Royal Asiatic Society*, LXII, Pt. i, 25–44.

"Why Economic History", in *ECHOSEA Newsletter* 1, i (January 1989), pp. 1–2.

1990   'An "Age of Commerce" in Southeast Asian History', *Modern Asian Studies* 24: 1 (1990), 1–30.

(with David Kelly) 'Weathering a Political Storm: The Chinese Academy of Social Sciences, 1990', *The Australian Journal of Chinese Affairs* 24: 347–55.

'Australia's Discovery of Indonesia, 1945', *Journal of the Australian War Memorial* 17: 30–40.

'The "Seventeenth Century Crisis" as an approach to Southeast Asian History', *Modern Asian Studies* 24: 4: 639–59.

"Duit Ayam (Chicken Coins)", *ECHOSEA Newsletter* 4 (March 1990), p. 5.

"The 10th International Economic History Congress, Leuven, Belgium, August 1990", *ECHOSEA Newsletter* 5 (Sept. 1990), pp. 1–2.

1991   "Report on a Visit to Dili, 22–24 June 1991", *Asian Studies Review* 15, no. 2 (Nov. 1991), pp. 181–82.

1993   [Reid & Trocki], "The Last Stand of Autonomous States in Southeast Asia and Korea, 1750–1870: Problems, Possibilities, and a Project", *Asian Studies Review* 17: 2 (November 1993), pp. 103–20.

"The Unthreatening Alternative: Chinese Shipping in Southeast Asia, 1567–1842", *Vietnamese Studies* 1993, no. 4 (110 of whole series), pp. 60–90.
— Vietnamese translation published in *Pho Hien: Ky Yeu Hoi Thao Khoa Hoc*, Hanoi, 1994.

1994 "The Unthreatening Alternative: Chinese Shipping in Southeast Asia 1567–1842" *RIMA* 27 (scheduled for 1993), 13–32.

'Historiographical Reflections on the Period 1750–1870 in Southeast Asia and Korea', *Itinerario* (Leiden), 1994, i: 77–88.

1995 "Humans and Forests in Pre-colonial Southeast Asia", *Environment and History* 1 (1995), pp. 93–110.

1996 (Reid & Radin Fernando), "Shipping on Melaka and Singapore as an Index of Growth, 1760–1840", in *South Asia*, Special Issue Vol. XIX (1996), pp. 59–84.

1997 'New Directions for New Times', *Asian Studies Review* 20, no. 3 (April 1997), pp. 149–52.

'Endangered Identity: Kadazan or Dusun in Sabah (East Malaysia)', in *Journal of Southeast Asian Studies* (Singapore), Vol. 28, No. 1 (March 1997), pp. 120–36.

1998 'President's Message: Moving On', *Asian Studies Review* 22, no. 1 (February 1998), pp. 1–2.

'Political "Tradition" in Indonesia: The One and the Many', *Asian Studies Review* 22, no. 1 (February 1998), pp. 23–38.

'Who Made Southeast Asia', in *The Asia-Pacific Magazine*, pp. 64–68.

'Studying "Asia" Internationally', *IIAS Newsletter* 17 (Dec. 1998), pp. 5 & 53.

1999 'A Saucer Model of Southeast Asian Identity', in *Southeast Asian Journal of Social Science*, Vol. 27 no. 1 (1999), pp. 7–23.

'Studying "Asia" in Asia', *Asian Studies Review* 23, no. 2 (June 1999), pp. 141–51.

'Balancing Act', in *Far Eastern Economic Review* Vol. 162, no. 23 (10 June 1999), pp. 56–60.

(with Takeshi Ito), 'A Precious Dutch map of Aceh, c.1645', in *Archipel* 57 (1999), pp. 191–208.

2000 'Which Way Aceh' [The 5th Column], in *Far Eastern Economic Review* Vol. 163, no. 11 (16 March 2000), p. 36.

2001 'Globalisation, Asian Diasporas and the Study of Southeast Asia in the West' [in Chinese], in *Southeast Asian Affairs* no. 1 (Xiamen, March 2001).

'Understanding *Melayu* (Malay) as a source of Diverse Modern Identities', *Journal of Southeast Asian Studies* 32, 3 (October 2001), pp. 295–313.

2003 'Charismatic Queens of Southern Asia', *History Today* 53, vi (June 2003), pp. 30–35.

'Perlawanan dalam Sejarah Nanggroe Aceh Darussalam', *Tempo* (Jakarta) Special Edition 24 August 2003, pp. 38–39.

2004 'Global and Local in Southeast Asian History', *International Journal of Asian Studies* Vol. I, no. 1 (Tokyo, 2004), pp. 5–21.

'War, Peace and the Burden of History in Aceh', *Asian Ethnicity* 15, no. 3 (October 2004), pp. 301–14.

Baogang He and Reid, 'Special Issue Editors' Introduction: Four Approaches to the Aceh Question', *Asian Ethnicity* 15, no. 3 (October 2004), pp. 293–300.

'Global and Local in Southeast Asian History', *International Journal of Asian Studies* Vol. I, no. 1 (Tokyo, 2004), pp. 5–21.

'Studying Southeast Asia in a Globalized World', *Taiwan Journal of Southeast Asian Studies* (Puli, Taiwan), I, no. 2 (October 2004), pp. 3–18.

2006 'Southeast Asia's Powerful Queens', *Heritage Asia* 3, no. 4 (July–September 2006), pp. 62–63.

(with Helen Reid) 'A Voice for Southeast Asian Muslims in the High Colonial Era: The Third Baron Stanley of Alderley,' *Education about Asia* 11, no. 3 (Winter 2006), pp. 4–6.

2007 'Internationalising knowledge in Asia: Problems and Progress', in *Asia: Magazine of Asian Literature* (Seoul), Vol. II, no. 3 (September 2007), pp. 165–83 (Korean) and 184–205 (English)

2008 'Stranger *Orangkaya* and Magic Mediators: Outsiders and Power in Sumatra and Beyond', in special issue of *Indonesia and the Malay World*, ed. David Henley and Ian Caldwell, Volume 36, Issue 105 (July 2008), pp. 253–67.

2009 'Indonesian Studies at ANU: Why so Late?' for special issue in honour of Herb Feith, of *Review of Indonesian and Malayan Affairs* 43, part 1 (2009), pp. 51–74.

'Introduction: Chineseness Unbound', in *Asian Ethnicity* special issue, 10, no. 3 (October 2009), pp. 197–201

'Indonesia: Escaping the Burdens of Chineseness', in *Asian Ethnicity* special issue, 10, no. 3 (October 2009), pp. 267–78.

2010 'Studying Southeast Asia in and for Southeast Asia: An interview with Anthony Reid, by Leonard Blussé and Carolien Stolte', *Itinerario* 34 (2010), pp. 7–18.

'Jewish-Conspiracy Theories in Southeast Asia: Are Chinese the target?' for special issue on Jews in Indonesia, ed. Ronit Ricci, in *Indonesia and the Malay World* 38, no. 112 (November 2010), pp. 373–85.

Review Articles

"Maluku Revisited", in *Bijdragen tot de Taal-, Land-, en Volkenkunde* 151, 1e. afl (1995), pp. 132–35.

'The Regional Thing' (review of Stephen Fitzgerald's *Is Australia an Asian Country?*), *Eureka Street* 7, no. 7 (Sept. 1997), pp. 40–42.

H. ENCYCLOPEDIAS

Eighty entries on Malaysia and the Malay World for *Dictionary of World History*, ed. G.D.M. Howatt, London, Nelson. 1973.

Entries on Soeharto for *Collier's Encyclopedia* (450 words) and *Merit Students Encyclopedia* (300 words), both New York, Macmillan, 1980.

Eleven entries for *Encyclopedia of Asian History*, ed. Ainslie T. Embree, 4 vols, New York, Scribner's; London, Macmillan, 1988.

Academic Advisor, *Atlas of World History*, ed. John Haywood (Oxford Cassell [Andromeda Book], 1997.

Advisory Editor for *A Global Encyclopedia of Historical Writing*, ed. D.R. Woolf. 2 vols, New York & London, Garland Publishing Inc., 1998), and author of 'Indonesian Historiography — Modern', Vol. I, pp. 465–67.

Adviser, *A Historical Guide to World Slavery*, ed. Seymour Drescher and Stanley Engerman. New York: Oxford University Press, 1998, 429pp.

'Migration: Chinese and Southeast Asian Interactions', in *The Encyclopedia of the Chinese Overseas,* ed. Lynn Pan (Singapore: Chinese Heritage Centre, 1998), pp. 50–52.

'The Indonesian National Revolution, 1945–50', pp. 236–38, and 'Indonesian Upheaval. 1965–66', pp. 239–40 in *The Encyclopedia of Political Revolution*, ed. Jack Goldstone (Washington, Congressional Quarterly, 1998).

Adviser, *Encyclopedia of Historians and Historical Writing*, ed. Kelly Boyd (Chicago: Fitzroy Dearborn, 1999), 2 vols.

'Historiography of Southeast Asia', pp. 6808–13 in *International Encyclopedia of the Social and Behavioral Sciences,* ed. Neil Smelser and Paul Baltes. Oxford: Pergamon (Elsevier Science), 2001. ISBN 0 08 0430767.

Advisory Board, *Encyclopedia of Women in Islamic Cultures* (EWIC), ed. Suad Joseph. Leiden, Brill, (in preparation from 1999). 6 vols, 2003–. Also wrote 'Slavery: East Asia and Southeast Asia', for Vol. IV (2006), pp. 504–06.

'Women Traders of Southeast Asia' (1100 words) and 'Melaka' (800 words) for *Encyclopedia of World Trade Since 1450*, ed. John J. McCusker (Macmillan, 2004?)

'Aceh' (4000 words), in *The Encyclopaedia of Islam*, Third Edition, Part 1 (Leiden: E.J. Brill, 2007), pp. 26–32. also at <http://www.ari.nus.edu.sg/docs/Aceh-project/EI3-1-Reid.pdf>.

'Ala'ud-din Ri'ayat Shah al-Kahar' (500 words); in *The Encyclopaedia of Islam*, Third Edition, Part 2 (Leiden: E.J. Brill, 2007), pp. 90–91.

'Fujiwara Iwaichi'; 'F-kikan'; 'Said Abubakar'; 'Dr M. Amir'; 'Inoue Tetsuro' for *Encyclopaedia of World War II in Indonesia.* (Amsterdam: NIOD, forthcoming).

I. GUIDEBOOKS, ETC.

'Dutch Hegemony', 32-5; 'Independence', 36-7; 'Old Makassar', 66-7; 'Ujung Pandang', 68-73; 'Sidetrips from U.P.', 74-9; 'West Coast", 90-1; 'South Coast', 94-9; 'Selayar Island', 100-01; 'Bone and Soppeng', 102-5; 'Luwu', 106-9, all in

Sulawesi: The Celebes, ed. Toby Volkman and Ian Caldwell (Berkeley, Periplus, 1990).

'A Portrait of Sumatra', in Indonesia West: Sumatra, Java, Bali, Lombok, n.p., Robertson McCarta/Nelles Verlag, 1990, pp. 61–73. New edition as *Nelles Guide Indonesia: Sumatra, Java, Bali Lombok, Sulawesi*, by David E. Henley, James J. Fox, Putu Davies, and Anthony J. S. Reid, 2000.

"Islamic Kingdoms", pp. 34–37; "Impact of the West", pp. 38–41; and "Modern History", pp. 42–43; in Indonesia Travel Guide: Sumatra, ed. Sindhu Suyana (Berkeley, Periplus, 1991).

INDEX

A

Abduh, Muhammad, 285, 307
al-Abidin, Sultan Zayn, 135
Acapulco, 183, 185, 191
Aceh
    in de Beaulieu's accounts, 98n8, 166
    European powers and, 146–47, 151
    in Hadhrami network, 275, 283
    literature, 89–90, 163–64, 274–75
    maritime cities, 87
    mixed racial ancestries, 222
    naval fleet, 147, 151, 153f, 156f, 164–65
    Reid and, 6, 12–13, 40
Aceh War, 283, 295n97
Adelaar, K. Alexander, 113, 114, 117n23
Aden Agreement, 283
al-Afgani, Jamal al-Din, 285, 307
Ahmad, Haji Abdullah, 310
Ahmad, Sayyid, 279
Ajayeb al-Hind, 110
Aji Saka, 97n2
al-Akbar (journal), 310
Alam, Raja, 275
al-Alawi, Sayyid Uthman b. Aquil, 280
'Alawi-Irshadi conflict, 283, 285

Albay Province, 187
Alimunar, 282
Alkema, B., 315
Alwi, Sayyid, 282
Ambeno, 229
Ambon, 282
A-mi-li-ding, 131–32, 140n24
Amrullah, Haji Abdul Karim (Haji Rasul), 308
Ancol, 137
Anderson, Benedict R.O., 34, 304
Angkor, 51, 86, 149
An Lu-shan rebellion, 126
"Annals of Semarang and Cirebon," 133, 137–38, 141n28
Annam chi luoc, 257
Anriondo, Pedro de, 193
al-Ansari, Muhammad al-Surkitti, 285
Anson, George, 1st Baron Anson (Admiral), 200
Arab traders, 74, 126, 138n3, 279, 288n11
Ardika, I.W., 113
Arsitek, Syeikh Syihab, 283
Aru, 135, 282
ASEAN (Association of Southeast Asian Nations), 71, 72, 78–79

Asian Studies Association of Australia (ASAA), 9, 14
"Asian values" debate, 39
Asia Research Institute (ARI), 12, 13
Association of Asian Studies, 13
Association of South-East Asian Studies, 16n15
al-Attas, Habib Abdullah b. Muhsin, 285
al-Attas, Habib Hasan, 280
Australia, 3, 11, 101
Australian Academy of the Humanities, 13
Australian National University (ANU), 8, 11, 14, 17n24, 19(nn37, 39), 21n60, 168n5
Austronesian diffusion, 38, 101–16, 117n9
Ayala, Jasper, 196
al-Aydarus clan, 276
al-Aydarus, Sayyid, 276
al-Aydid, Sayyid Husayn, 277, 281, 283
al-Aydid clan, 276
Ayutthaya, 74, 87, 241–44. *See also* Siam
Ayyubid dynasty, 127
al-Azhar University, 280
al-Azhari, Shaykh Muhammad Tahir bin Jalaluddin al-Minangkabawi, 309

B
Ba Adillah, Sayyid Abdullah, 282
Bac Giang province, 254
Bac Ninh province, 253, 254, 258, 259, 266n75
Badariah, Tengku Embong, 275
Badaruddin, Sultan Mahmud, 276
Bagatao, 187
Baghdad, 7, 126
Ba Husain, Sayyid Muhammad, 278
Bali, 87, 88, 112, 149–50, 171n13, 279

Balintang channel, 191
Banda, 282
Bandar Seri Begawan, 134
Bangka Strait, 149
Banjarmasin, 107
Banten, 87, 98n9, 160f, 162, 165
Bantu slaves, 110, 115
Baron, Samuel, 226
Barus, 134
Baschaib, Shaykh Ahmad b. Abdullah, 283
al-Bashir (journal), 285
al-Basir, Sultan Sulaiman bin Abd Allah bin, 129
Bassett, David, 7, 16n15, 17n22
Bataks, 110
Beaglehole, John Cawte, 4
Beaujard, Philippe, 112–13
Belitung shipwreck, 126
Bellwood, Peter S., 38, 103, 113
Belu, 233
Benda, Harry, 15n4, 33, 38
Bengal, Bay of, 241
Bengkulen, 226
Bèntara Keumangan, 275
Bima, 90
Bin Talib family, 279
Bintan, 151
Bintang Hindia (journal), 310, 315
Al-Biruni, 111
Black Death, 57
Blench, Roger, 108, 113, 114
Blood of the People: Revolution and the End of Traditional Rule in Northern Sumatra, 35
Bogor, 286
Bong Tak Keng, Haji, 133, 137
Bonin Islands, 191
Booth, Anne, 15n4, 34
Borneo, 74, 107, 109, 223
Borobudur, 109–10
Boxer, C.R., 232
Braudel, Fernand, 9, 37, 69–70, 72

Britain, 63, 66n24, 75, 101
British Academy, 13
Brunei, 92, 128, 134, 142n37, 148, 279
Buddhism, 55, 87
Budi Utomo (BU), 313
Bugis, 87, 174n40, 272, 276, 279
Bukittinggi, 309
Burma, 47, 50, 54, 56–57, 59, 62, 87, 167
Burn, Joseph (Captain), 279
Buru, 282
Buru Quartet, 32–33
Bustan us-salatin, 90, 163

C
Cairo, 285, 309, 319
Calcutta, 277
California, 184
Cambodia, 87
Cambridge University, 5, 16n13, 20n53
Candera Midi, Utin, 275, 276
candrasangkala, 98n15
Caribbean Sea, 190
Caroline Islands, 190
cartography, 91
Catholicism, 55
Cavite, 187, 189, 192, 193, 197–98
Centre for Southeast Asian Studies, UCLA, 12
Centre for the Study of the Chinese Southern Diaspora (CSCSD), 11, 21n61
Cham languages, 102
Champa
  conquest by Vietnam, 74, 244
  in Islamic trading networks, 127, 129, 131, 133
  naval fleets, 148–49
  origin of Pu family, 128
  volunteers in Ayutthaya, 241–44
Chaophraya Yommarat, 337, 349

Charts of Remarkable Typhoons in the Philippines, 193
Chen Da-sheng, 140n23
Cheng Xunwo, 224
Chen You-ding, 132
chialoup, 278, 291n51
China. *See also individual dynasties*
  attitudes to overseas communities, 223, 224
  Opium Wars, 75
  silver trade and, 183, 249
  in the spread of Islam, 125–38
  taxation in, 62–63, 66n24
  territorial integration, 59, 60–61, 70
  trade with Southeast Asia, 70–71, 74, 110, 111–12, 185–87, 260
China Sea, 190, 191
Chinese Communist Party, 76
Chinese communities in Southeast Asia
  in the Philippines, 185–89, 199, 224
  Reid and, 40–41
  scholars working on, 6, 11, 16n19
  shipwreck survivors, 198
  in Siam/Thailand, 242, 336–51
Chinese language, 53
Chin Tek School, 346
Chirot, Daniel, 11
Chola dynasty, 74, 126, 127, 130, 134
Cho Su Kong shrine, 339, 343
Christianity, 85, 89, 227, 229, 230, 308
Ciela, 91
Cirebon, 109, 133, 137
Clark, Margaret, 15n4
Clifford, Hugh, 274
Cochinchina, 248, 251
Cocos Island, 195
Coen, Jan Pieterszoon, 32
Cokroaminoto, Omar Said, 311, 315–19, 321

Cold War, 76, 78
Coles, Edward, 226–27
Colindrico, Don Lopez (General), 195
College of Asia and the Pacific, 14
Co Loa village, 255
Colombo Plan, 5, 15n8
Columbia University, 15n4, 17n24
Concepcion (ship), 201
Confucianism, 39, 55, 62
Conrad, Joseph, 278
Constantinople Estate, 280
Contest for North Sumatra: Atjeh, the Netherlands and Britain 1858–1898, 6, 35
Cook, James (Captain), 4
Corcuera, Sebastián Hurtado de, 199
Coriosidades, 158
Cornell University Southeast Asia Program, 11, 18n26, 19n37, 21n60
Coromandel Coast, 129
Coultas, W.W., 349
Covadonga (ship), 200
Cowan, Charles Donald (Jeremy), 6, 16n15
Crosby, J., 347, 348
Cushman, Jennifer Wayne, 11, 21n58

D

da Costa, Domingo, 232
da Costa, Mateus, 229, 231
Dahl, Otto Chr., 107, 113, 114
Dahlan, Ahmad, 307
Damais, Louis-Charles, 94, 133, 141n28, 171n13
Dampier, William, 225, 230, 233
Day, Tony, 271
Dayaks, 114, 223, 278, 279
de Albuquerque, Afonso, 86, 91, 224–25, 227, 233, 234
de Beaulieu, Augustin, 98n8, 166
Decline of Constitutional Democracy in Indonesia, 33

de Erédia, Manuel Godinho, 151, 152f, 155, 156f, 225
de la Concepcion, Juan, 201
de Legaspi, Don Miguel, 184
Delhi, 130
de los Reyes, Fernando, 194
Demak, 87, 133, 138, 143n51
Demon, 229
Deng Xiaoping, 78
de Silva, Geronimo, 193, 196
de Souza, Gonçalo, 158
Devawongse Varoprakar, Prince of Siam, 347, 349, 350
Dewa Ruci, 155, 164, 172n26
Diamond, Jared, 108
Diaz, Casimero, 195, 198
Diaz, Tomas, 226
al-Din, Shaykh al-Islam Kamal, 140n24
al-Din Sharaf, 132
dinh, 257–59
Đinh Khac Thuan, 248
di Tiro, Tengku Cik, 16n17
di Tiro, Tengku Hasan Muhammad, 6, 13, 16n17
Djawi Hisworo (newspaper), 317
Đoan Minh pagoda, 255
Dobbin, Christine, 287n7
Douwes Dekker, E.F.E., 310, 315, 328n120
Dror, Olga, 256
Duc Tu village, 255
Dutch colonial power
  Aceh and, 40, 147, 283
  attitudes to, 32
  decolonization process, 34
  Hadhramis and, 279–80, 282, 283, 284, 285
  historical sources, 162, 165, 306
  Indonesian nationalism and, 305, 308, 310, 311–12, 315
  Makassar and, 167
  mixed marriages and, 226, 227, 229, 230

Index

other European powers and, 75,
  147, 200, 228, 231
territorial integration and, 61
Timor and, 228, 229, 233
Dutch East India Company. *See* VOC
  (Dutch East India Company)
Dutch language, 225

E
East Africa, 108
Easter Island, 103, 104
East India Company, 74, 226
ECHOSEA Project, 10–11
Edinburgh University, 17n24
Egypt, 127, 129–30
Elliott, Mark, 61
El Spiritu Santo (ship), 193
Eoseewong, Nidhi, 241
Estrada, Joseph, 102
Eurasians, 226, 236n19

F
Fachruddin, Haji, 313
Fajardo de Entenza, Alonso
  (Governor), 193
Fansuri, Hamzah, 89, 274
al-Faradz, 273
Faridah Hanom (novel), 285
Feith, Herbert, 33
Finney, Ben R., 104
Fisher, Charles, 16n15
Flores, 229, 237n32
Food and Agriculture Organization
  (FAO), 14n2
France, 50–54, 56, 57, 59, 63,
  66n24
Free Aceh Movement, 12–13, 16n17
Freedman, Maurice, 16n15
Freitag, Ulrike, 287n7
Fujian, 129, 132, 137, 260
Fukuoka Asian Culture Prizes, 13
Fukuyama, Francis, 34–35
Fuzhou, 132

G
galleys, 146, 160f, 161f, 163, 164
Galvão, Antonio, 225
GAM (Gerakan Aceh Merdeka),
  12–13, 16n17
Gan Eng Cu, 137–38
Gani, Shaykh Sayyid, 274
Garut, 91
ghali, 163–64
ghurab, 163–64, 175n47
Giri, Sunan, 137
Gokstad Viking ship, 104
Gong Yong-cai, 137–38
gonting, 278, 291n51
Goody, John (Jack) Rankine, 10,
  20n53
Graaf, Hermanus Johannes de, 134,
  143n51
Greeks, 85
Gresik, 133, 134, 137, 138, 184, 278
Guam, 195, 205n46
Guangdong, 129, 252, 260
Guangzhou, 126–27, 128
Guerreiro, António Coelho, 232

H
al-Habshi, Sayyid Alwi, 282
al-Habshi, Sayyid Hasan, 279, 280,
  282
Hadhramaut, 280
Hadhrami diaspora, 223, 271–86,
  288n14
al-Hadi, Sayyid Shaykh Ahmad b.
  Hasan b. Saqqaf, 285
Hai Duong province, 249, 253, 261,
  266n75
Hainan, 128
Haji, Raja, 276
Hakka community in Bangkok,
  345–50, 353n25
Hamid, Haji Abd Rahman b. Abd,
  284
Han dynasty, 59, 70, 111

Hangzhou, 128
Hanoi, 253, 263n34
Hasan, Sayyid, 281, 282
Hamid, Sharif, 279
Ha Tay, 253
Hatta, Mohammed, 320
Hà Van Tan, 258, 264n57
Hawaii, 103, 104, 191
Heinemann, 9, 19n40
Henry Luce Foundation, 10
Hertogh, Maria, 33
Heyerdahl, Thor, 103, 117n14
Hikajat Potjut Muhamat, 274
Hikayat Aceh, 163, 165, 169n5
Hikayat Banjar, 163, 169n5
Hikayat Hang Tuah, 91–92, 148, 150, 163, 164, 166, 169n5
Hikayat Indrapura, 150, 169n5
Hikayat Raja-raja Pasai, 130, 169n5, 175n47
Hindia Poetra (journal), 319
Hinduism, 39, 87, 224
Hoàng Anh Tuan, 247, 252, 261n3, 266n75
Hoi An, 226
Hok Heng Keng shrine, 343
Hokkaido, 51
Hokkien Association (Bangkok), 342
Hokkien community in Bangkok, 339–44
Hokkien Shrine Association, 343
Hok Lian Keng shrine, 339, 343
Ho-ling, 112
Holle, Karl Frederik, 91
Hoogervorst, Tom, 110
Hornay, António, 229, 231, 232
Hornay, Francisco, 229, 233
Hornay, Gonsalvo de, 229
Hornay, Jan de, 229
Hornell, James, 114
Horridge, Adrian, 103, 104
Huai-sheng-si mosque, 128
Huang Chao, 127
Hundred Years War, 57

Hung Yen province, 253
Huntingdon, Samuel, 49
Hurles, M.E., 107
Husayn, Sultan, 135

I

Ibn Battuta, 130–31, 132, 140n24, 142n39
Ibn Khurdadhbih, 126
Ibn Lakis, 110
Idenburg, Alexander Willem Frederik (Governor-General), 315
Al-Idrisi, 111, 115, 127
Iioka Naoko, 247
Ilocos, 193
Iloilo, 187
al-Imam (journal), 285, 309, 310
Imperial Alchemy, 13, 271
India, 37, 39, 59–60, 61, 87–88, 130
Indian Ocean, 190
Indische Gids, De, 305
Indische Partij (IP), 310, 315
Indochina Resource Centre, 19n37
Indonesia
  attitudes to the past in, 31–35, 95–96
  under Dutch colonialism, 86, 278, 288n11, 305
  Islam and nationalism in, 303–22
  New Order, 33, 38–39, 40
  1965 coup, 8, 18n30, 31
  Palawan Nasional, 284
  Pancasila, 38–39
  as part of Southeast Asia, 101–2
  peace agreement with Aceh, 12
  shipbuilding traditions, 108–10, 146–76
Indonesia Merdeka (journal), 319
Indonesian Communist Party (PKI), 31–32, 319
Indonesian National Revolution, 35
Institute of Southeast Asian Studies, 10, 13
International Centre for Aceh and Indian Ocean Studies, 13

Index

Iranun, 200, 201
Irenaeus, Saint, 95
al-Irshad education movement, 286, 307
Isfahan, 7, 131
Isfahan rebellion, 132, 134
Iskandar Muda, Sultan, 165, 166
Iskandar Thani, Sultan, 275
Islam
   calendar, 87–89
   Hanafi school, 137
   Indonesian nationalism and, 303–22
   in the Malay world, 74, 76, 87
   Paji group and, 229
   Reid's studies of, 125
   Shafii school, 130, 273
   spread in Southeast Asia, 125–38
   Sunni vs. Shia, 132
al-Islam (journal), 311
al-Islamiyah Association, 311

J
Jakarta, 4
Jambi, 274, 284, 295n101
Jam'iat al-Khayr, 285, 286, 307
Japan
   historical integration, 50–54, 55–56, 58
   impact of European arrivals, 75
   Mongol attack on, 73
   present-day, 77
   silver trade and, 183, 247, 261n6
   trade with Southeast Asia, 74, 249, 260
   victory over Russia, 310
   volunteer force in Ayutthaya, 241
   Yayoi period, 105–6
Japanese language, 105
Java
   Aji Saka myth, 97n2
   Arab migration to, 224
   in Hadhrami trade networks, 278, 280, 283
   in *Hikayat Hang Tuah*, 92
   Hindu-Buddhist monuments, 87
   influences on Japan, 105–6
   Islam in, 131, 132, 137, 139n9, 305
   literature, 155, 158–62, 172n25
   maps, 91, 96
   Ming voyages and, 136–37
   in regional trade patterns, 74, 112
   shipbuilding traditions, 109, 148
   use of *primbon* almanacs and *candrasangkala*, 88, 98n15
   wet rice cultivation method, 105, 108
Java in a Time of Revolution, 1944–46, 34
Javanese language, 105, 114, 171n13, 172n25
Jayadiningrat, Achmad, 312
Jaya Simhavarman II, King of Champa, 140n21
Jeddah, 164
Jeffrey, Robin, 9, 19n39
Jepara, 155, 162
Jerome, Saint, 95
Jesus Maria (ship), 193
Jin Ji, 132
Jiu Tang shu, 138n4
João IV, King of Portugal, 229
Johns, A.H., 274
Johore, 87, 162
Jomon culture, 105–6
Jones, A.M., 111
jong, 158
Joratan, 137
Joyoboyo, King, 99n19
al-Jufri, Sayyid Idrus, 295n101
al-Jufri clan, 276, 278, 295n101
al-Junayd, Sayyid Umar b. Ali, 283
al-Junayd clan, 279, 283
jung ships, 109

K
Kadt, Jacques de, 34
al-Kaf clan, 279

Kalimantan, 277
Kalus, Ludvik, 140n23
Kartini, Raden Ajeng, 312
Kasim, Tengku, 279
Kathiris, 295n98
Kathirithamby-Wells, Jeyamalar, 7, 17n21
Ke Cho, 252–53
Kedukan Bukit inscription, 149
kelulus, 155–58
Kern, R.A., 135
Khatib, Ahmad, 307
Khoo Kay Kim, 7, 17n23
Khun Sawatdiphokhakon, 339
Kian An Keng shrine, 339, 343
Kidung Sunda, 155, 173n26
Kiev, 51
Kingdom of Siam, The, 242
King's Crown, The, 89
Kinh Bac province, 254, 261
Kipling, Rudyard, 101
Kirch, Patrick, 103
KITLV Press, 10
Klaung Garai, 131, 140n21
Koninklijke Paketvaart Maatschappij (KPM), 282
Korawasrama, 93
Korea, 74
Kota Kapur, 149
Krakatoa, 96
Krom Tha Sai, 339, 344
Kuan Im Teng shrine, 339
Kubu, 275
al-Kudsi, Sayyid Muhammad Zain, 280
Kusumasumantri, Iwa, 320
Kwan Oo shrine, 346, 349

L
Laffan, Michael Francis, 304, 309, 310, 320
Lamaholot region, 229, 231

Lamreh, 129
lancang, 149, 152f, 171n13
lancaran, 150–55, 158, 171n13
Langdon, Robert, 205n54
Laos, 87
Lasem, 137
Last Stand, The, 10
Latin, 53
Latrobe University, 19n39
Laws of the Three Seals, 242
Lee, James, 49
Lee Kuan Yew, 39
Lepanto, Battle of, 146
Le Quy Don, 252
Le Roy Ladurie, Emmanuel, 10, 20n50
Le Thanh Ton, 248
Le-Trinh dynasty, 248–49, 252–53, 259
Leur, J.C. van, 35, 36, 38
Lewis, Martin, 116, 117n9
Lieu Hanh cult, 256–57
Lifao, 230, 232
Limbong, Drahman, 284
Lim Seng Kit, 339
Lingga, 151
Li Tana, 22n61, 129
literacy, 55
Little Ice Age, 57
Lodewijcksz, G.M.A. Willem, 165
Lombard, Denys, 14, 37, 69
Lombok, 279
London School of Economics, 15n5
Loubère, Simon de la, 242
Louis IX, King of France, 130
Louis XIV, King of France, 53
Loukin, 126
Luang Phakdiphatthrakon, 344
Lukacs, John, 32
Luwu, 279
Luzon, 137, 200
Lyon, Eugene, 202n5

Index

M
Ma'abar, 129
Maanyan language and people, 107, 113, 114–15
Mac family, 248–49
Madagascar, 106–15
Madiun Revolt, 31, 32
Madrasah al-Saqqaf, 280
Madura, 162, 165, 274
Magellan, Ferdinand, 163, 184
Mahan, Alfred, 112
Mahathir bin Mohamad, 39
Mahayana Buddhism, 87
Mahmud, Malik, 13
Ma Hong Fu, Haji, 133
Ma Huan, 133–34
Majapahit, 74, 87, 132–33, 134, 137, 314
Majlis al-Nur, 286
Majumdar, R.C., 37, 38, 242
Makassar, 36–37, 87, 90, 167, 184, 272
Maktab Daimi, 288n13
Malabar Coast, 130
Malacca
  consolidation, 74, 87, 184
  in Hadhrami trade networks, 278
  Islam in, 87, 137
  mixed race families in, 224, 225
  origins of the *orang kaya*, 272
  Portuguese capture of, 86, 146–47, 162, 225
  Tamil Hindus in, 224
  wars, 92, 151, 153f, 155
Malacca Strait, 113
Malagasy language, 106–7, 110, 113–14
Malang, Regent of, 311
Malay Annals, 134
Malay Concordance Project (MCP), 168n5
Malaysia, 8, 18n31, 71

Malay texts
  "Annals of Semarang and Cirebon," 133, 137
  Hikayat Hang Tuah, 91–92, 148, 150, 163, 164, 166, 169n5
  influence of Islam on, 87, 89–90
  nautical terminology in, 149–50, 155, 163–64, 167, 169n5
  Sejarah Melayu, 134, 150, 163, 164, 169n5, 171n13
Malay world
  Austronesian origins, 102–4
  commerce and migration in, 74
  concept of, 71
  Islamization, 74
  languages, 102, 106–7, 110, 113–14, 117n23
  mixed marriages in, 222
  ships of, 145–76
Al-Malik al-Zahir, Sultans (Samudera), 129–30, 135
Al-Malik al-Zahir Rukn al-Din Baybars al-Bundukdari, Sultan (Mamluk dynasty), 129–30
Mallari, Francisco, 194
Mamluk dynasty, 129
Manado, 282
al-Manar (journal), 285, 309
Manchuria, 61
Mangkupraja, Gatot, 320
Mangunkusumo, Cipto, 306, 308, 311, 313, 314, 319–20
Mangunkusumo, Gunawan, 314
Manikmaya, 93
Manila, 183, 184–89
Manila galleon trade, 183–220
Mansur Shah, Sultan, 150
Marcos, Ferdinand E., 102
Mariana Islands, 190, 191, 193, 197, 198, 201
Mariano, Luis, 106
Marinduque, 187

Marquesas Islands, 103
Marr, David G., 919n37
Marre, Aristide, 113
Marsden, William, 106, 222
Marvels of India, 110
Maryanov, Gerald Seymour, 7, 18n27
Masbate, 187
Al-Mas'udi, 138n6
Mataram, 112
Mathers, William, 205n53
Mathewson, Duncan, 205n46
Mauny, Raymond, 110, 115
Ma Yong-long (Ma Yong-liang), 137
McGee, Terry, 15n4
Medieval Climate Anomaly, 56–57
Medina, Juan, 194
Mediterranean and the Mediterranean World in the Age of Philip II, The, 9, 37
Melaka. *See* Malacca
Mempawah, 276, 277
Menanbun, Daeng, 275
Mendes Pinto, Fernão, 164
Merewa, Daeng, 275
Merina kingdom, 114
Mexico, 183, 186, 188
Minangkabau, 272, 278, 307, 308, 310
Mindoro, 187
Ming dynasty
  Javanese polities and, 133
  overthrow, 200
  Tongking and, 249, 254, 257, 264n57
  trans-Pacific trade and, 185–86
  voyages, 73, 133, 135–38
Ming shi-lu, 137
Minye Tujuh, 135
Misbach, Haji, 319
Moluccas, 113
Mongolia, 61
Mongols, 57–58, 60–61, 62, 73, 86, 129, 130

Mozambique, 110
Muara Kaman, 113
Muara Tebu, 274
al-Mu'ayyad (journal), 285
Mughal empire, 59, 60, 61, 62
Muhammad Ali, Raja, 278
Muhammad b. Aquil, Sayyid, 285
Muhammad b. Aquil b. Yahaya, 280
Muhammad b. Hamid, 275
Muhammad b. Hashim, Sayyid, 285
Muhammadiyah movement, 307–8, 313, 318, 319
Muhammad Shah (ruler of Lambri), 135
Muis, Abdul, 316
al-Munir (journal), 310, 311
al-Munir, Jamal al-Alam Badr, 274

N
Nahdlatul Ulama (NU), 318
Nalanda-Sriwijaya Centre, 13
Nam Đinh area, 252
"Nanhai," 69–79
Naning War, 274
National University of Singapore (NUS), 12
Na-wu-na, 131, 132
Negapatam, 92
Neolithic Revolution, 103
Netherlands. *See* Dutch colonial power
Netherlands Indies. *See* Indonesia
New Cambridge History of Islam, 13
New Guinea, 11
New Zealand, 3, 4, 11, 104, 117n9
Ngampel, Sunan, 137
Ngo Lenh Cong (General), 258
Nguyen Duc Nghinh, 254
Nguyen dynasty, 248
Nguyen Thái Duong, 258
Nieuhof, Johan, 227
Ningbo, 260
Ninh Thuan Province, 140n21
Nino de Tavora, Juan, 197

Njai Gede Pinatih, 137
Noer, Deliar, 308
Noor, Habib, 274
North Atlantic Ocean, 190
Novel of Iskandar, 92
Nuestra Señora de Concepcion (ship), 197–98, 199, 205n53
Nuestra Señora de la Encarnacion (ship), 195
Nuestra Señora de los Remedios (ship), 199

O

Old Javanese-English Dictionary, 172n25
orang kaya class, 272–86, 287n8
Orford, Joseph Robinson, 16n12
Orford studentships, 5, 16n12
Orientalism, 48
Ottoman empire, 146, 163, 164, 283, 295n97
Owen, Norman G., 102
Oxford University, 15n10
Oxford University Press, 19n40

P

Pacific Ocean, 184, 189, 190, 191, 193, 202n5
Padang, 310
Pagan, 51, 86
Pahang, 151, 280, 284
Paji, 229
Paku Alam, 315
Palembang, 92, 137, 149, 276, 278, 282, 285
Pali, 53
al-Palimbani b. Abd al-Rahman al-Jawi, Sayyid Abd al-Samad, 275, 290n35
Palmer, John, 277, 279, 281
Paluh, Sayyid, 274, 284
Pare-Pare, 279
Parker, Noel Geoffrey, 10, 20n51

Parlindungan, Mangaraja Onggang, 133, 137–38, 141n28
Partai Sarekat Islam (PSI), 317–22
Pasai, 151
Patani, 158
Patapahan, 278
Patih Unus, 109, 155, 162
Pegu, 87, 109
Pekalongan, 278
Penang, 223, 274, 277, 279, 281
Penfui, Battle of, 233
Pengkhianatan G/30/S-PKI (film), 33
penjajap, 158, 173n28
Perak, 273
peranakan, 222
Peranakan chronicles, 133, 137–38, 141n28
Perani, Daeng, 275
Perceptions of the Past in Southeast Asia, 9
Pereira, Nicolau, S.J., 151
Peru, 186
Pham Thi Thuy Vinh, 254, 258
Phan Đài Doãn, 260
Phan Huy Chú, 262n8
Philipe, Andres, 194
Philip II, King of Spain, 184, 196
Philippines, 102, 183–202
Pho Hien, 253
Phraya Chodukratchasetthi, 339–44
Phuai Eng School, 344
Pigafetta, Antonio, 163
Pigeaud, Theodore G. Th., 134, 143n51
Pires, Tomé, 155
PKI (Partai Komunis Indonesia), 31–32, 319
Pliny the Elder, 112
Pluvier, Jan M., 7, 17n20
Poem on the Ship, 89
Poensen, C., 306
Poerbatjaraka, 172n26
Polo, Marco, 61, 129

Polynesian cultures, 38
Pontianak, 273, 274, 275–76, 277, 279, 281
Portugal
  arrival in Southeast Asia, 86, 147
  capture of Malacca, 146, 155
  historical sources on Southeast Asia, 91, 109, 155, 162, 164, 167, 244
  mixed-race marriages and, 224–26, 227–28, 231–34
  overseas Chinese and, 347
  push out of the Mediterranean, 75, 76–77
  ships and nautical terminology, 148–51, 155, 158, 163–66, 185
  silver trade and, 247
Potosi, 200
PPPKI (Permufakatan Perhimpunan Politik Kebangsaan Indonesia), 320
Priangan, 280
primbon, 88, 93
Protected Malay States, 1874–95, 15n3
"protected rimlands" concept, 50, 59
Proudfoot, Ian, 168n5
Pu Ha-ting, 139n14
Pu Kai-zong, 128
Pu Luo-e, 128
Pun Thao Ma shrine, 339, 342, 343
Purcell, Victor, 5–6, 11, 16n13
Pu Shou-geng, 128, 131, 132

Q
al-Qadri, Habib Husayn b. Ahmad, 277
al-Qadri, Sayyid Abd al-Rahman, 274, 275, 282al-Qadri, Sayyid Abdul al-Rahman, 275, 281
al-Qadri, Sultan Kasim b. Abdul Rahman, 277–78, 279, 281
al-Qadri clan, 276

Qin dynasty, 70
Qing dynasty, 59–61, 62–63, 73, 75
Quanzhou, 126, 127–28, 130–32, 139n7
Quilon, 130

R
Rahmat, Raden, 133
Rajiman, 313
Rama I, King of Siam, 245n7
al-Ram-Hormozi, Bozorg ibn Shahriyar, 110
ar-Raniri, Nuruddin, 90, 275
Rasul, Haji, 308
Rasulid dynasty, 127
Ratu-Langie, Gerungan S.S.J., 312
Reagan, Ronald, 39
Red River Delta, 251
Reid, Anthony
  academic career, 7–14, 71–72
  doctoral students and advisees, 22n71
  doctoral thesis, 5–6
  early life, 3–6
  influence, 35–41, 221, 246, 271, 303
  on interracial unions, 256
  on Tongking, 249, 259
Reid, Helen (née Gray), 4, 6
Reid, John Stanhope, 4, 14nn1–2
Rembang, 109
Research School of Pacific and Asian Studies (RSPAS), 8, 9, 10, 14, 18n33, 19(nn37, 39)
Reynolds, Craig J., 11, 21n60
Rhodes, Alexander de, 252, 253–54, 256
Rhodes, Cecil, 15n10
Rhodes Scholarships, 15n10
Riau, 276
rice cultivation, 105, 108, 114
Ricklefs, Merle C., 141n30, 305, 313
Rida, Muhammad Rashid, 307, 309

Ripangi, Ahmad, 309
Rivai, Abdul, 315
Rodrigues, Francisco, 91
Roff, William R., 7, 15n4, 17n24
Rojo y Vieyra, Manuel Antonio de (Archbishop), 192
Rong Lek shrine, 346
Ronkel, Ph. S. van, 306
Royal Historical Society, 13
Russia, 50, 52, 54, 56–57, 60, 62, 63, 66n24
Russian Orthodoxy, 55
Ryukyu, 51

S
sada (*sayyid*s), 272–86
Sadka, Emily, 4, 14n3
Safiuddin, Sultan Taha, 274, 284, 295n101
Sagap, Sayyid, 284
Sai-fu-ding, 131–32
Saipan, 197
Saleh, Abdul Rahman, 31
al-Salih, Sultan Malik, 129
al-Shihab, Sayyid Ali, 278
al-Shihab dynasty, 275, 276, 278–79
Salim, Haji Agus, 313, 316, 317, 320, 321
Salim, Sayyid Ali b. Abu Bakr b. al-Shaykh Abu b. Bakr, 282
Salim b. Muhammad, Sayyid, 279
Samar, 184, 187, 195
Sambas, 137
sampan, 149, 170n12
Samudera, 129, 130, 135
San Antonio (ship), 193, 199
San Bernadino Strait, 191, 192, 195
San Chao Kao shrine, 344
Sanggau, 276
Sang Hyang Kamahayanikan, 93
San Lucas (ship), 202n5
San Luis (ship), 194
San Pablo (ship), 202n5

Sanskrit, 53, 113–14
Santisima Trinidad (ship), 201
Santo Cristo de Burgos (ship), 194
al-Saqqaf, Sayyid Alwi Shaykh, 282
al-Saqqaf, Sayyid Muhammad, 283
al-Saqqaf, Sayyid Muhammad Ba Husayn, 278
al-Saqqaf, Sayyid Muhammad b. Ahmad, 280, 295n97
al-Saqqaf, Umar b. Muhamad, 281, 282
al-Saqqaf clan, 278, 279, 283, 295n97
Sarekat Islam (SI), 311, 315–22, 330n149
Sayyid, Dol, 274
School of Oriental and African Studies (SOAS), 6, 15n4, 16n15
Schurz, William Lytle, 199, 219n42
Scott, Edmund, 98n9
Scott, James C., 39, 55
Sejarah Melayu, 134, 150, 163, 164, 169n5, 171n13
Selga, Miguel, 193, 220n64
Semarang, 133, 137, 278
Senapelan, 278
Señora del Pilar de Zaragosa y Santiago, 195, 205n46
Sharp, Andrew, 103
ships and shipbuilding, 108–10, 146–76, 187
shipwrecks, 126, 189–202, 205(nn46, 53), 209–17
Short, Anthony, 7, 17n25
SI (Sarekat Islam), 311, 315–22, 330n149
Siak, 275, 276, 277, 278
Siam. *See also* Ayutthaya
  in Hadhrami trading networks, 279
  in *Hikayat Hang Tuah*, 92
  integration, 47, 50, 51, 54, 59, 62
  naval fleets, 167
  Theravada Buddhism in, 87
silk trade, 249–51, 266n75

silver trade, 58, 186, 200, 247, 258–59, 260n6, 262n8
Simmonds, Stuart, 16n15
Singapore
  fall, 3
  founding of, 150
  in Hadhrami network, 274, 278, 279, 280, 281, 283
  Islamic journals, 285, 309
  naval battle near, 151, 154f
Singer, Steve, 218n29, 220n64
Sin Heng Keng shrine, 339
al-Sjafi, Sayyid Ali b. Muhammad, 279
Slametmuljana, 142n40
Smail, John, 35
Smith, Daniel (Captain), 281
Snouck Hurgronje, Christian, 306, 309, 311, 312, 317
Social Science Research Training Centre, 19n41
Soerabajasch Handelsblad, 305
Solor archipelago, 228–29, 233
Song dynasty, 59, 62, 128, 129
Son Nam province, 266n75
Son Tay province, 266n75
Sorsogon, Gulf of, 187, 195
South China Sea, 193, 241
Southeast Asia
  Austronesian identity, 38, 86, 102–4
  as a category, 101–2
  concepts of space and time in, 85–97
  disproving European exceptionalism, 47–63
  the Mediterranean analogy and, 9–10, 37, 69–79
  Reid's conceptualization of, 36–41
  terms for, 37, 71
Southeast Asia in the Age of Commerce, 36, 48, 72, 125, 221, 271
Southeast Asia in the Early Modern Era, 167n1

Souza, George, 247
Soviet Union, 76
Spain, 76, 146, 162, 183–220
Sri Lanka, 148
Sri Tribuana, 150
Srivijaya, 74, 112, 148, 149
SS Vidar, 278
Stutterheim, Willem F., 172n26
Sucesos de las Filipinas, 197
Sudirohusodo, Wahidin, 313
Suharto, 34, 38, 102
Sukarno, 33, 38, 95, 96, 304, 319, 320
Sulawesi, 9, 74, 117n23, 279
Suleiman, 126
Sultans' Garden, 90
Sulu, 201
Sumatra, 74, 96, 113–14, 127, 135
Sumbawa, 90
Sun Heng Keng shrine, 339, 343
Surabaya, 133, 134, 278, 279, 282
Surakarta, 279
Suriokusumo, R.M.S., 314
al-Surkatti, Ahmad, 285
Suryaningrat, Suwardi, 315, 316
Suryopranoto, Sidoardjo, 329n121
Suryoputro, 312
Sutherland, Heather, 69, 271
Sutomo, 313
Sweden, 13, 16n17
Syaifuuddin, Sultan, 279
Syair Perahu, 89
Syair Sultan Maulana, 167
Syiah Kuala University, 13
Syria, 130

T
Tabriz, 131, 132
Tagalogs, 187
Taiwan, 38, 103
Tajuddin, Sultan Ahmad, 276
Taj us-salatin, 89
Tamils, 224

Index   399

Tamnaeng Na Thahan Hua Müang,
    242, 245n6
Tanganyika, 110
Tang dynasty, 70, 73, 86, 127, 138n4
Tan Malaka, 34
Tatsuro, Yamamoto, 131
Tawalisi, 131
Tebing Tinggi, 279
Teochiu community in Bangkok,
    344–45
Terengganu, 92, 135, 274, 275, 276,
    284
Ternate, 225, 282
Thai-Yunnan Project, 9
Thang Long, 251, 256
Thanom Kittikachorn, 102
"The meaning of the sacred numbers,"
    95–96
Theosophical Society, 313
Theravada Buddhism, 55, 87
Tibet, 61
Tieo Seng Ke, 339
Tilley, Charles, 10, 20n52, 50
Timor, 221–34
Tirtoadisuryo, 33
Tirtokusumo, R.A., 313
Toán Thu, 264n58
Toer, Pramoedya Ananta, 32–33
Tongking, 246–61
Topasses, 227–34, 236n30
Torajas, 279
Toyota Foundation, 10
Traidos Prabandh, Prince of Siam,
    347, 348, 349
Tran dynasty, 257, 260
Tran Quoc Vuong, 248
Trayala grave, 132–33
Trinh dynasty, 248, 251, 258
Trowulan grave, 132–33, 141n28
Truong Tho Kien, 258
tsunami of 2004, 12, 40
Tuan Guru, 274
Tuanku Rao, 141n28

Tuban, 134, 137
Tu Xuong, 256
typhoons, 190–202

U
Uganda, 108
Uighurs, 141n32
Ujung Pandang, 19n41
United Nations, 14n2, 16n13
United States, 75, 78
University of Amsterdam, 17n20
University of Auckland, 15n5
University of British Columbia, 15n4
University of California Los Angeles
    (UCLA), 12
University of Hull, 17n22
University of London, 15n4, 16n19,
    17n21
University of Malaya, 7, 16(nn15, 19),
    17n23, 18n26, 71
Uphairatchabamrung Temple, 341,
    342, 343
Urdaneta, Andrés, 162, 184, 189,
    202n5
Uthman, Sayyid, 275

V
van der Parra, Petrus, 225
Varthema, Ludovico de, 91
Victoria (ship), 184
Victoria University of Wellington, 4,
    5, 13, 14n3, 15nn4–5, 17n24
Vietnam
    in the age of commerce, 246–61
    in ancient trading system, 112, 126
    destruction of Champa, 244
    integration, 47, 50, 54, 59
    present-day, 263n34
    Samuel Baron's account of, 226
    textual sources on naval warfare,
        148
Vietnam Today, 19n37
Vijayanagara dynasty, 130

Visayas, 200
VOC (Dutch East India Company)
　exports of silk, 262n18, 263n33
　impact on naval warfare, 167
　relations with local polities, 74, 229
　silver trade, 247, 249, 258–59, 262n8
　struggle against Portuguese, 231
　use of Portuguese language, 225–26
Vries, Jan de, 56

W

Wachirawut, King of Thailand, 337, 338
Wallerstein, Immanuel, 112–13
Wang Dahai, 224
Wang Gungwu, 7, 8, 12, 16n19, 18n33
Waqwaq people, 110–11
Washington, DC, 4
weapons, 58, 90, 157f, 158, 159f, 162
Westerling, Raymond "the Turk," 32
Western Malayo-Polynesian, 102
Wijeyewardene, Gehan, 9, 19n43
Wink, André, 138n6
Wiryosanjoyo, Satiman, 314
Wisseman Christie, Jan, 111–12

women, 39
Workers' Educational Association, 15n5
World Health Organization, 14n2
World War II, 3
Wyatt, David, 7, 18n26

X

Xian-he mosque, 139n14
Xie Qing'gao, 223
Xinjiang, 61
Xi-yang fan-guo-zhi, 137

Y

Yale University, 15n4
Yangzhou, 126, 129, 139n14
Yemen, 127, 130
Ying-yai sheng-lan, 133
Yongle emperor, 73, 135, 142n41
Yuan dynasty, 128–29, 131. *See also* Mongols
Yuanshi (History of Yuan), 131–32

Z

Zaid, Abu, 127
Zhao Rugua, 148
Zheng He, 73, 133, 135–38
Zoetmulder, Petrus Josephus, 172n25

Titles in the Nalanda-Sriwijaya Studies Centre Series

General Editors: Tansen Sen and Geoff Wade

1. *Nagapattinam to Suvarnadwipa: Reflections on the Chola Naval Expeditions to Southeast Asia*, edited by Hermann Kulke, K. Kesavapany and Vijay Sakhuja
2. *Early Interactions between South and Southeast Asia: Reflections on Cross-Cultural Exchange*, edited by Pierre-Yves Manguin, A. Mani and Geoff Wade
3. *Anthony Reid and the Study of the Southeast Asian Past*, edited by Geoff Wade and Li Tana
4. *Hardships and Downfall of Buddhism in India*, by Giovanni Verardi